RESEARCH NOW

VISUAL MEDIA
SCIENCE
LIFE ONLINE
POP CULTURE

RESEARCH NOW

CONTEMPORARY WRITING IN THE DISCIPLINES

EDITED BY DANIEL BURGOYNE AND RICHARD GOODING

SOCIAL MEDIA
GLOBAL CITIZEN
SOCIETY
ENVIRONMENT
DEMOCRACY
POSTHUMAN

broadview press

BROADVIEW PRESS – www.broadviewpress.com
Peterborough, Ontario, Canada

Founded in 1985, Broadview Press remains a wholly independent publishing house. Broadview's focus is on academic publishing; our titles are accessible to university and college students as well as scholars and general readers. With over 600 titles in print, Broadview has become a leading international publisher in the humanities, with world-wide distribution. Broadview is committed to environmentally responsible publishing and fair business practices.

The interior of this book is printed on 100% recycled paper.

© 2018 Daniel Burgoyne and Richard Gooding

Library and Archives Canada Cataloguing in Publication

Research now : contemporary writing in the disciplines / edited by Daniel Burgoyne and Richard Gooding.

Includes bibliographical references.
ISBN 978-1-55481-329-2 (softcover)

1. Report writing. 2. Academic writing. 3. Research. I. Gooding, Richard, 1960-, editor II. Burgoyne, Daniel, 1966-, editor

LB2369.R47 2018   808.02   C2018-901382-6

Broadview Press handles its own distribution in North America:
PO Box 1243, Peterborough, Ontario K9J 7H5, Canada
555 Riverwalk Parkway, Tonawanda, NY 14150, USA
Tel: (705) 743-8990; Fax: (705) 743-8353
email: customerservice@broadviewpress.com

Distribution is handled by Eurospan Group in the UK, Europe, Central Asia, Middle East, Africa, India, Southeast Asia, Central America, South America, and the Caribbean. Distribution is handled by Footprint Books in Australia and New Zealand.

Broadview Press acknowledges the financial support of the Government of Canada through the Canada Book Fund for our publishing activities.

Copy-edited by Michel Pharand

Book design by Chris Rowat Design

PRINTED IN CANADA

CONTENTS

Introduction 9

ONE **POPULAR CULTURE AND VISUAL MEDIA** 21

Introduction 21

A "Educating The Simpsons: Teaching Queer Representations in Contemporary Visual Media," Gilad Padva 23

B "Cripples, Bastards and Broken Things: Disability in *Game of Thrones*," Katie M. Ellis 38

C "Images of Women in General Interest and Fashion Magazine Advertisements from 1955 to 2002," Katharina Lindner 52

D "Avenger, Mutant, or Allah: A Short Evolution of the Depiction of Muslims in Marvel Comics," Nicholaus Pumphrey 70

E "Frozen Jet Set: Refrigerators, Media Technology, and Postwar Transportation," Paul Gansky 87

TWO **SOCIAL MEDIA AND LIFE ONLINE** 103

Introduction 103

A "Fantasy Facebook: An Exploration of Students' Cultural Sources," Amber E. Ward 105

B "Fraping, Social Norms and Online Representations of Self," Wendy Moncur, Kathryn M. Orzech, and Fergus G. Neville 117

C "The Role of Narcissism in Self-Promotion on Instagram," Jang Ho Moon, Eunji Lee, Jung-Ah Lee, Tae Rang Choi, and Yongjun Sung 136

D "Exploring Rape Culture in Social Media Forums," Kristen L. Zaleski, Kristin K. Gundersen, Jessica Baes, Ely Estupinian, and Alyssa Vergara 145

E "Blogging a Research Paper? Researched Blogs as New Models of Public Discourse," Lisa A. Costello 161

THREE **ENVIRONMENT AND SOCIETY** 179

Introduction 179

A "Continent-wide Analysis of How Urbanization Affects Bird-Window Collision Mortality in North America," Stephen B. Hager et al. 181

B "Green Screen or Smokescreen? Hollywood's Messages about Nature and the Environment," Ellen Elizabeth Moore 197

C "The Enrollment of Nature in Tourist Information: Framing Urban Nature as 'the Other,'" Ylva Uggla and Ulrika Olausson 216

D "Green Infrastructure as Life Support: Urban Nature and Climate Change," Sheryn D. Pitman, Christopher B. Daniels, and Martin E. Ely 234

E "Environmental Science and Public Policy in Executive Government: Insights from Australia and Canada," Briony M. Lalor and Gordon M. Hickey 256

FOUR **DEMOCRACY AND THE GLOBAL CITIZEN** 279

Introduction 279

A "The Networked Young Citizen: Social Media, Political Participation and Civic Engagement," Brian D. Loader, Ariadne Vromen, and Michael A. Xenos 281

B "Democracy is Democracy is Democracy? Changes in Evaluations of International Institutions in Academic Textbooks, 1970–2010," Klaus Dingwerth, Ina Lehmann, Ellen Reichel, and Tobias Weise 292

C "Social Media, Public Discourse, and Governance," Maria Consuelo C. Ortuoste 317

D "Politics and Patriotism in Education," Joel Westheimer 325

E "Using Social Media Dialogically: Public Relations Role in Reviving Democracy," Michael L. Kent 340

FIVE **SCIENCE AND PUBLIC DISCOURSE** 357

Introduction 357

A "Our Year on Twitter: Science in #SocialMedia," Louise J. McHeyzer-Williams and Michael G. McHeyzer-Williams 360

B "How to Be Cautious but Open to Learning: Time to Update Biotechnology and GMO Legislation," Sven Ove Hansson 370

C "Vaccination, Fear, and Historical Relevance," Rob Boddice 378

D "Olfactory Identification Decline as a Preclinical Biomarker for Alzheimer's Disease," Jamie Knight 391

E "Foreshadowing Alzheimer's: Variability and Coupling of Olfaction and Cognition," Jamie E. Knight and Andrea M. Piccinin, University of Victoria, BC, Canada 403

F "Olfactory Impairment in Presymptomatic Alzheimer's Disease," Robert S. Wilson, Steven E. Arnold, Julie A. Schneider, Patricia A. Boyle, Aron S. Buchman, and David A. Bennett 409

SIX **HUMAN AND POSTHUMAN** 421

Introduction 421

A "The Cyborg Revolution," Kevin Warwick 423

B "In Defence of Posthuman Dignity," Nick Bostrom 441

C "Posthuman," Nicholas Gane 453

D "The Final Frontier? Religion and Posthumanism in Film and Television," Elaine Graham 459

A Note on Statistics by James Johnson 471

Glossary 475

Permissions Acknowledgements 481

INTRODUCTION

WELCOME TO THE BOOK

As you begin your university education, you will encounter researchers who speak, write, and even seem to think in unfamiliar ways. For example, what you think of simply as "posing" and "self-promotion" in selfies posted on social media might be referred to as "self-disclosure" and "impression management" by researchers. "Global warming" might give way to "anthropogenic climate change," which is explained using technical terms such as "radiative forcing" or "the clathrate gun hypothesis." As time goes by, you will begin to acquire researchers' ways of thinking, speaking, and writing. As you immerse yourself more deeply in your major—whether that's economics or philosophy or microbiology—you'll find yourself speaking and writing in ways that would have confused your younger self.

This collection has been assembled to help you make that transition. Here you will find a variety of work written by scholars engaged with topics that attract intense public interest—visual and social media, the environment, and global citizenship, among others. Most of the publications reprinted here are articles that first appeared in academic journals aimed at specialists, but there are other forms of research writing too, including a book chapter by a senior scholar and a proposal by a graduate student. These studies were written by researchers from around the world working in the sciences, social sciences, and humanities. At the time of publication, most held academic positions in universities, but some contributors were graduate students, post-doctoral fellows, civil servants, and even people working for non-governmental organizations (or NGOs). Some studies were written by individuals, others by groups that collaborated—one lists 56 contributors from three countries. What they have in common, despite differences in subject matter and academic approach, is that all are examples of research, a term we'll define for the moment as "the creation of knowledge" before we explore it further in the next two sections.

In selecting publications for this reader we have been guided by a number of considerations. We began with six topics that have attracted the attention of scholars and the public alike: popular visual media such as advertisements and movies, on-line conduct, the interplay of environmental concerns and public policy, democracy and global citizenship, public engagement with scientific research, and a cluster of concerns (including cyborgs and human medical enhancement) that we place under the umbrella term "the posthuman." We wanted to include only complete studies that had been published within the last decade and that were representative of a variety of academic disciplines but were accessible to interested non-specialists like ourselves (two instructors in English departments) and, we hope, you. In practical terms, this meant fudging (but only a little) on two counts. First, the articles you read here occupy the shorter end of the range of academic studies, most running from 3,000 to 8,000 words. Second, we have avoided including research that is so heavily dominated by statistics and other mathematical treatments that even the discussion sections and conclusions would be incomprehensible to the non-specialist reader. That said, we have included some studies that have stretches of statistics you'll find difficult, even incomprehensible at times (we certainly did). Don't worry, though: in the headnotes to those articles we give you some guidance and have included a brief appendix on what statistics do and how non-statisticians can navigate them.

The statistics are the most obvious obstacle to the non-specialist, but there are other challenges for the newcomer to research writing—or even seasoned readers who are venturing outside their discipline. Fortunately, with a little guidance on our part and a little effort on yours, these challenges are manageable. Here, and in the introductions, headnotes, and Glossary terms that precede the essays, as well as the discussion questions that follow them, we aim to help orient you to research that we hope will be as enjoyable as it is challenging.

GENRE THEORY AND RESEARCH WRITING

It's likely—in fact, almost certain—that in high school you were given rules for writing. Some of these are perfectly good general principles: sentences begin with capital letters and end with full stops; *its* is possessive, while *it's* is a contraction for *it is*; *I* is the subject of a verb, *me* is the object; and so on. Other rules don't serve nearly as well as general writing principles. You may have been trained to write five-paragraph essays that rely on a three-part thesis statement appearing at the end of the first paragraph. But you won't find a single five-paragraph essay in this reader, because the form functions best as a tool for overworked teachers to assess writing quickly, and in any case becomes unworkable once an essay exceeds about a thousand words. Or you may have been told not to use passive constructions. If that was the case, you may be struck by the frequency with which the writers of the articles in this reader do exactly that, particularly when they describe their research methods.

You may even have been quietly disapproving of the contractions in the paragraph above. Stop it. We know what we're doing.

Clearly, then, the question of rules needs some rethinking. An alternative to the idea that good writing is governed by inflexible rules is to think of it as *situated*—that is, embedded in particular contexts. These contexts encourage some practices while discouraging others. If you were told in high school to avoid using first-person pronouns, that may be because your teachers wanted you to direct your attention towards the evidence you were using and away from your personal opinions on the subject at hand. The research articles that follow could hardly be characterized as expressing personal opinions, yet first-person pronouns abound. There must, then, be something about the situation that encourages researchers to ignore the rules you broke at your own peril in high school. A closer examination reveals that *I* and *we* are words usually reserved for verbs related to the impersonal activities of reasoning—acts that would remain the same no matter who was conducting the study. For example, the study by Wendy Moncur et al. (*et al.*, from a Latin term meaning "and others," indicates that Moncur wrote the article with at least two other authors) of the practice of online "fraping" in the section "Living Online" applies the pronoun "we" to the verbs "consider," "suggest," "contend," "present," and "hypothesize," among many others. In these uses, there's nothing at all personal about how the pronoun is used.

Many scholars who study writing (and language uses more generally) examine how particular contexts give rise to distinct forms of expression. The complicated interplay between language users (writers and readers, speakers and listeners), social context, and language forms is the subject matter of *genre theory*, the critical approach that guides our selection and handling of texts here. For these scholars, language is fundamentally a social practice, a set of tools used by definable communities to achieve shared goals—math teachers aiming to improve numeracy in students, mountain bikers and ballet dancers trying to improve a set of physical skills, and researchers engaged in producing knowledge. In your own classes, if you listen carefully, you may catch your instructors using expressions like *discourse community* or *situated practices*, terms familiar to academics working in writing studies; or perhaps you will hear less specialized language that nonetheless points to what we might call a *genre-theoretical* orientation to writing—attention to writers, readers, contexts, and forms of expression.

When most of us think of genres, we think first of forms (the fourteen-line sonnet, the syncopated rhythms in jazz) but it's not difficult to see that the rules and patterns of a given genre are connected to specific social situations. That is, genres aren't independent of the people and circumstances who create and consume them. Sometimes we can even hear the social situation in the genre, as is the case with "country" music. More often, we can trace the genre back: for example, science fiction became popular during a time when science and technology were profoundly impacting society; hip hop first developed in the inner cities of the United States. If we look closely at most genres, we eventually see that what makes them formally distinct is a product of the social situation where they emerge or where they are used. Take the job application letter. We all know the elements, and we know the situation that gives rise to the form—the individual with a set of skills seeking formal employment from an individual or company—encourages some choices and discourages others. Word processed applications in some fonts (but not others) are good; handwritten applications are not. "Dear Ms. ——" is an acceptable form of address; "Hey Cindy" is not. "Yours sincerely, Sandra Lee" is an appropriate sign-off; "love, Mike 'the Terminator' Jones" would be disastrous. This exercise can be applied to virtually any kind of communication—written or oral—that you can imagine: marriage proposals, tenancy agreements, Facebook posts, conversations with the police officer who pulls you over for speeding.

Thinking about the publications included in this reader, we can say that the defining feature of the situation that gave rise to them is *research*. This is hardly surprising, since all were written, in part or whole, by scholars working in universities, institutions whose main mandate, along with education, is research. We've already defined research as the creation of knowledge, but we can go further. Research presents an addition or correction to what is known among specialists working in a particular field (for instance, the discovery of a new exoplanet [an addition] or, a few years ago, the reclassification of Pluto as a dwarf planet [a correction]). In cases where a consensus hasn't yet been reached, research may lend support to one of the positions currently held in the scholarly community (for example, new evidence on the question of whether Vitamin E supplements are likely to improve or damage one's health).

Broadly speaking, research may be empirical, interpretive, or applied. Empirical research proceeds through observation and experimentation. Its concern is real-world phenomena, and it is typically concerned with accumulating and analyzing *data*. We usually associate empirical research with the sciences, but researchers working in social sciences like sociology or economics also deal in part with empirical research. By contrast, interpretive research, which characterizes fields like literary studies or philosophy, addresses human concerns that can't be counted or otherwise measured—the nature and limits of animal rights, for instance. A third approach, applied research, finds real-world uses for empirical or interpretive research: think of the engineer who uses findings on the tensile strength of new building materials to design cables for suspension bridges, or the clinician who turns research on how patients talk about their illness into new protocols for assessing hospital admissions.

Another useful distinction is between academic *disciplines*, the various fields of academic inquiry. It should be no surprise that a Professor of Cybernetics (such as Kevin Warwick, whose work appears in the section "Human and Posthuman") would ask very different kinds of questions than a Professor of Philosophy (Nick

Bostrom in the same section), even though both are examining the general issue of human enhancement. We can call this attention to the demands of one's own intellectual field *disciplinarity*, and recognize that it, too, results in different forms of writing arising from the specifics of the research situation. At the same time, it's worth recognizing that many research publications draw upon multiple academic disciplines: the study by Stephen B. Hager et al. on bird-window collisions in the section "Environment and Society" includes contributions by biologists, engineers, and mathematicians; Elaine Graham, whose work on religion and posthumanism rounds out the section "Human and Posthuman," is writing as both a theologian and a specialist in media studies. We can call such research *interdisciplinary*.

KNOWLEDGE-MAKING: TRADITIONS OF INQUIRY, QUANTITATIVE AND QUALITATIVE METHODS, AND THE PATH TO PUBLICATION

No matter what discipline produces research (or for that matter whether the research is empirical, interpretive, or applied), scholars rarely work in a vacuum, independent of previous studies on a subject. Adding to or correcting what other researchers have already established assumes familiarity with prior research—what's widely called the *state of knowledge*. For that reason, you'll find that the beginnings of research papers typically refer to past research to construct an overview of the state of knowledge before the scholars identify some gap or error that the new study will address. Interestingly, most published studies conclude by formulating a new state of knowledge that takes into account the newly produced knowledge while recognizing shortcomings that still need to be addressed. We can call instances of this general orientation towards knowledge-making—citing past research, establishing and then amending the state of knowledge, and then passing along a new state of knowledge to future researchers—*traditions of inquiry*.

The question of how knowledge is produced by individual studies is a defining feature of each research situation. The broadest distinction we can formulate about knowledge-making practices is between quantitative and qualitative methods. As the term suggests, quantitative methods are concerned with counting and measuring real-world phenomena. Quantitative methods are associated mainly with the sciences and social sciences, but sometimes make their way into the humanities as well. Scholars conducting quantitative research typically devote much attention to the methods used to gather and analyze data, including experimental design, so that other researchers can evaluate their knowledge-making practices and replicate their work. Reflecting the specific research situations that apply to quantitative research, published studies often adopt a predictable reporting structure, the IMRD (Introduction, Methods, Results, Discussion) format. Qualitative research, by contrast, examines matters that aren't open to counting and measurement. Most commonly arising out of disciplines housed in faculties like Arts, Fine Arts, and Law, qualitative research bears the traces of quite different research situations. While Kate Ellis's discussion of representations of disability in *Game of Thrones* (Section 1, "Popular Culture and Visual Media") doesn't follow the IMRD structure favoured by Jang Ho Moon et al. in their quantitative analysis of narcissism and self-promotion on Instagram (Section 2, "Social Media and Life Online"), it reveals its qualitative orientation by articulating a theoretical framework (critical disability theory) and taking care to define complex terms (like disability and ableism) in ways that are useful for the particular study. Amber Ward's study of her middle-school students' cultural sources (Section 2, "Social Media and Life Online") presents a more obvious example of qualitative method. She analyzes the self-portrait sculptures of a small number of her students, carefully emphasizing her own *subject position* (as a teacher). Clearly the number of students isn't meaningful from a quantitative perspective. Also, her role as the designer of the assignment and her relationship with the students as their teacher means that her research is far from objective. Ward directly discusses scholarship that informs her qualitative approach and her emphasis on *praxis*, or extending theory to practice. For Ward, research isn't just about creating knowledge of the world; it is about changing the world.

Whether a research study employs quantitative or qualitative methods, or (as often happens in the social sciences) some combination of the two, its path to establishing its position in a tradition of inquiry almost always runs through the process of *peer review*. This is equally true of articles appearing in academic journals and books published by university and scholarly presses. Peer review, also known as *refereeing*, entails careful scrutiny of an unpublished study by other researchers who have standing in the field. In the case of quantitative research, peer reviewers typically ensure that the study under review has taken into account relevant prior research, applied sound methodology (including statistics and other math), interpreted results effectively, and contributed to the state of knowledge. Peer reviewers assessing qualitative research perform a similar role, though they may be more concerned with assessing the theoretical framework and the quality of the interpretive analysis rather than questions of experimental design or statistical methodology. In each case, peer review may involve as few as one and as many as half a dozen referees. The referees may know who wrote the prospective article, or they may not (in which case, the peer review is *blind*). It should also be noted that the peer review system means that publication isn't guaranteed, and researchers may need to submit their research to several journals or academic presses before it is accepted. Not surprisingly, the more prestigious and influential the journal, the lower its acceptance rate. The scientific journal *Nature* publishes less than 8% of the manuscripts it receives; the literary journal *PMLA* (Publications of the Modern Language Association) accepts about 9%.

FORMS AND GENRES

Because different approaches towards knowledge-making, not to mention different disciplines, entail different research situations, research writing displays a wide range of organizational patterns, vocabularies, and even conventions of citing and documenting sources. As you read the articles collected in this book, you'll acquire a sense of that diversity. For the moment, however, we can describe some of the distinct forms you'll encounter.

If we work our way through the research process, from inception to published study, we can begin with the *research proposal*, exemplified in Section 5 ("Science and Public Discourse") by Jamie Knight's Master of Science thesis proposal on olfaction as an early indicator of Alzheimer's disease. As the word "proposal" suggests, proposals are written early in the research process, after the researcher has thought of some way to advance the state of knowledge but before the research has been undertaken (or at least before it has proceeded very far). Proposals are extremely common, but they're rarely published. They're written by undergraduate students undertaking term projects, graduate students embarking on a thesis or dissertation, and established academics hoping to present conference papers, win grant competitions, or acquire book contracts. In fact, there's a good chance that you'll write a proposal before you complete the writing class you're taking now, and you'll probably write several before you finish your degree. In each case, the proposal is designed to be evaluated by someone else, in a process that approximates peer review. Proposals typically begin by establishing the state of knowledge through a *literature review* (i.e., a survey of relevant research publications), before identifying some inadequacy in the state of knowledge (a gap or error) and proposing a *research question*. Research proposals typically outline a method for answering the research question (in the sciences and social sciences) or articulate a theoretical framework for proceeding (in the humanities).

A step closer to academic publication is the *research poster*, a genre that typically represents research in progress but not yet completed. Our example, appearing in "Science and Public Discourse," is also by Jamie Knight, along with Andrea Piccinin, her supervisor. Research posters and oral presentations are staples of academic conferences, most of which bring together researchers from a single discipline (e.g., immunology) or multiple disciplines at work in the same field (such as Medieval studies, which may include papers by linguists, historians, literature specialists, and even archaeologists). Most research posters include both textual and visual elements (such as maps, diagrams, or data tables) and may represent an intermediate stage between the completion of the research activity (e.g., an experiment or survey) and publication in a peer-reviewed journal. Perhaps because they are well-suited to presenting data visually and less well suited to representing complex arguments or textual analysis, research posters are common in the sciences and social sciences, disciplines that rely on quantitative research, but rare in the humanities.

The most common form of academic publication is the peer-reviewed journal article, a genre exemplified by the majority of the studies reprinted in this reader. The journal article is a vastly diverse genre, but most begin with an *abstract*, a paragraph-length summary of the study designed, in part, to allow readers to make a quick decision about whether the study is worth closer attention. After that, it becomes difficult to make sound generalizations about journal articles, since they typically bear numerous marks of their individual disciplines. We've already mentioned the tendency of quantitative disciplines to use the IMRD structure, and of qualitative research to devote attention to questions of definition and theory. You'll find numerous examples of both orientations in the sections that follow. You may also notice that journal articles are often heavily marked by discipline-specific vocabulary. The list of keywords following the abstract in Hager et al.'s study of bird-window collisions (Section 3, "Environment and Society") includes terms familiar to biologists, such as "anthropogenic mortality" and "behavioural divergence," while the keywords from Padva's article on *The Simpsons* include "gay subjectivities" and "queer representation," everyday terms in LGBTQ studies.

TIPS FOR READING THE ARTICLES

One of our goals is to help you improve your ability to read scholarly articles. To this end, we have created a sort of framework to help you with each reading: 1) a headnote that introduces the piece; 2) a list of terms that you can look up in the Glossary at the back of the book; 3) a biographical note about the authors; and 4) discussion questions.

The headnotes begin by identifying two important details: when and where the article was originally published. The date can give you a sense of currency and help you relate the article to other research. The title of the academic journal or book the study appeared in provides a glimpse of the larger conversation being joined: for example, Ward's "Fantasy Facebook" was published in the journal *Art Education*. Paul Gansky's "Frozen Jet Set: Refrigerators, Media Technology, and Postwar Transportation" was published in *The Journal of Popular Culture*. The headnote will then say something about the article as an example of writing in the research genres: in the case of Ward, we emphasize the use of qualitative method. Finally, the headnote will direct you to think about something while reading. Often, scholarly articles make many different, complex moves. Their arguments are often more nuanced and variable than essays written by students, and so a little guidance can be helpful.

The list of "Glossary terms" that immediately follows the headnote directs you to the Glossary at the end of the book, where you will find short definitions and notes. In choosing these terms, we've selected what might be called "discourse" terms:

words that refer to knowledge-making conventions. These include terms that refer to the situation of research (e.g., "peer review" or "disability studies"), specific genres (e.g., "research proposal," "poster"), and the form of research genres (e.g., aspects of method such as "coding/regression analysis"; or component parts, such as "methods" and "discussion" sections). In short, these terms will provide a sense of the background moves and the frameworks within which the researchers are working, and they will help orient you on the organization of the article and what is important.

As you read the articles, you will find many other specialized terms that we haven't glossed. Whether these words reflect the large vocabularies of highly educated writers, or whether they reveal the assumed background knowledge of the intended audience (i.e., it is specialized language used within the discipline or tradition of inquiry that the article is joining), these terms pose a challenge and an opportunity to you as a beginning scholar. The challenge, of course, is that you may not understand the word. The opportunity is to empower yourself by developing a practice of looking words up in a dictionary. A standard dictionary or "academic dictionary" app will be helpful with unfamiliar words. Some of the more specialized disciplinary terms may be defined in the study itself (sometimes briefly in parentheses and sometimes at greater length), but in the case of those that aren't, you can reference specialized online dictionaries through your university library: just identify the discipline (e.g., sociology) and search for "dictionary of sociology." We suggest that you keep a log of these terms and record their basic meaning. Doing so will help you grow your vocabulary and will also help orient you in navigating the important specialized terms in a given discipline or area of research. You will also see that the discussion questions often ask you to investigate specific terms.

You'll find a biographical note about the author(s) in a footnote immediately following each article. We've kept these notes as short as possible, with just enough information to give you a sense of what the authors do and what they study. If you are especially interested in a given article, consider looking the author up on a search engine such as Google or in your library's databases to see if you can find more detailed explanations of research areas or other publications. If you look up the article using a specialized search engine such as Google Scholar, you will be able to see roughly how often it has been cited by other researchers. If you have a pressing question for the authors, look up their contact information and send them a query by email (or tweet, as the case may be).

Following each article, you will find discussion questions. You'll find that they isolate key issues and provide approaches to critically think about the research. Consider, for instance, question one following Katie Ellis's article on disability in *Game of Thrones*: "How familiar are you with the idea of ableism? Have you considered how disability is portrayed in television and film?" (p. 51). If you've watched it, the HBO show *Game of Thrones* may be of considerable interest to you, and Ellis's analysis is quite enlightening, but the article also works as an introduction to the idea of ableism and the area of disability studies. You can take these ideas and examine many other aspects of society and culture. Even if you aren't assigned to do these questions, we suggest that you give them a quick read.

Finally, some advice on reading scholarly articles is in order. If you have a writing handbook, it likely has a section with some useful tips. Take them seriously. Reading scholarly articles takes practice and it benefits from an active approach. Here are our five tips:

1. Try to grasp the "big picture." Immediately following many of the headnotes, you will find an abstract. The abstract isn't the beginning of the article; rather, it is a summary of the article that is usually written by the author. As such, it is an overview. Like the headnote we provide, the abstract will provide a sense of the big picture of the article. Read it carefully. Also, you will usually find a list of "key terms" provided by the author at the end of the abstract. These will likely be quite different from the Glossary words that we provide, cueing you to the specialized vocabulary being used in the article and also indicating terms that you can use if you want to search for similar research.

   After the abstract, read the introduction and the conclusion. Note that the introduction may cover several paragraphs and in the IMRD model is often explicitly labelled. Often, you'll recognize the end of the introduction because there will be a heading for a new section. Read both the introduction and the conclusion carefully using tip number two below. This isn't a novel where spoilers are off limits. It's okay to read the conclusion before the middle of the article. You will find that the introduction and conclusion provide two very different glimpses of the big picture. Whereas the introduction introduces the research project and relates it to the state of knowledge, the conclusion discusses the project and the findings in a more comprehensive manner. Often, you may find that the conclusion is where the overall argument or its implications are most clearly stated. The sooner you can grasp the big picture, the more you will be able to orient yourself on the more complex details.

2. Orient yourself on the organization of the article. If it has a standard format, such as IMRD (Introduction, Methods, Results, Discussion), you will be able to better understand what is going on within each section. You'll know that the Methods section is going to explain how the researcher tried to answer the research question. For instance, in the study of bird-window collisions, Hager et al. explain their quantitative approach: they selected 281 buildings from 40 university campuses; they surveyed bird carcasses at particular times of day during the autumn migratory season; they engaged in statistical analysis, and so on. By being clear about the purpose and function of different sections, you will be able to move around the article

and make more meaningful connections. Other articles have different headings, but sometimes these heading also signal generic purposes. For instance, in Ellen Moore's "Green Screen or Smokescreen," there is a "Literature Review" section, in which Moore reports key findings from a few earlier studies. This section establishes the state of knowledge for the rest of her article. Other articles will have headings that are entirely unique, but which nevertheless help clarify the purpose of their respective sections. Consider Ellis's headings. After two paragraphs that introduce the article, Ellis has four section headings: "Disability and TV," "*Game of Thrones* Disability and Blogger Insights," "Are People with Disability Valued as Legitimate Television Audiences?," and "Conclusion." If they are present, use the section headings to guide your understanding of the organization of the article.

3. Be an active reader. On a paragraph-by-paragraph basis, perhaps in the margin or in a notebook, try to capture what you think are the most important points and isolate specialized terms and key abstractions (the terms that come up over and over again). Don't copy these points (or just highlight them); rather, use short words and phrases to put them into your own words. (At certain points, you might want the break out and write a short summary, but on an ongoing basis just actively note what you think is important.) This will require that you make choices and even lose some of the nuance of what is being said. That's okay. What is important is that you actively decide what is important and create short expressions of it that you can review at a glance. This approach will slow you down—you may have to reread as you go—but it will significantly increase your comprehension.

4. Read through the whole article and be patient when you don't understand. Reading academic research is hard work, and you may have to read the study more than once. There will be points where you get lost or confused. Perhaps some background knowledge is assumed (didn't you read such and such a book?) or there is a statistical equation that you don't understand. In these moments, don't panic and don't flee. It is important to work through the difficult material and keep going. Don't skip it, because then you will start skimming and you will become even more lost. Perhaps looking carefully is a more apt approach than reading. Read through the difficult section and keep going. Place a question mark in the margin or pose a specific question to raise with your class or to look up (even a small question, such as "What is a 'political economy'?"). By working through difficult material and setting small comprehension goals, you will be better able to integrate the article into your overall understanding later. By reading the whole article, you will get to know the lay of the land, as it were.

5. Write your own brief summary in your own words. Using the author's words leads to passive engagement. When you complete a section or come to the end of the article, write a short summary that captures your sense of both the big picture and what is most important. This doesn't need to be polished; but if you write a complete summary, you will find it helpful later when you need to discuss or write about the article. It will reduce the need to reread. Actively putting your understanding into your own words will improve your comprehension.

That's it! We hope you enjoy the readings.

Daniel and Rick

ACKNOWLEDGEMENTS

We want to acknowledge the help of Lindsay Church, Ashley Thorup, and Tyeson Davies Barton. Lindsay helped prepare the articles and write the headnotes and discussion questions. Ashley helped find articles. Tyeson helped write glossary entries.

POPULAR CULTURE AND VISUAL MEDIA

INTRODUCTION

Popular culture encompasses many aspects of our lives in the twenty-first century. It shapes how we dress, much of what we do, and even how we think of ourselves. One of the most obvious forms of popular culture is visual media, such as television and advertisements. Not only are visual media examples of popular culture, they also help us glimpse how popular culture shapes our lives.

Visual media are an ancient part of human culture. Think about cave paintings. And visual media aren't confined to popular culture: consider the graphs and the research poster that you'll encounter later in this reader, or forensic photographs presented at trials. That said, the convergence of visual media and popular culture in the twentieth century provided a spectacular vehicle for shared experience and ideas among billions of people. Not only do movies, television, and comics make a lot of money, they are also promotional tools for a wide range of products and consumption practices driven by global capitalism. In short, there is a lot at stake in the study of popular culture and visual media.

It isn't easy to critically evaluate the visual media in our lives, in part because they are so embedded in our daily experience and in part because they evolve so rapidly and place such extraordinary demands on us. Consider, for instance, the HBO series *Game of Thrones* (discussed in Ellis's essay), which has changed the form and content of television and been surrounded by perpetual controversy. For these reasons, visual popular culture has long drawn the attention of researchers.

Researchers in a variety of disciplines study popular media in order to understand how they are constructed, how they reflect and promote social and political values, and much else. Early research was often quite pessimistic, seeing popular visual media such as television and Hollywood cinema as "dumbing down" art and creating passive consumers incapable of critically evaluating what they were watching (or buying, or identifying with). These concerns persist: Lindner's "Images of Women in General Interest and Fashion Magazine Advertisements," included in this section, is a good example. While Lindner's findings suggest a persistent problem, namely sexism in advertisements, that is consistent with the view that popular culture shapes us in negative ways, Gansky finds something more hopeful. In his study of advertisements for refrigerators in the early 1960s, Gansky shows how advertisements don't always succeed. Sometimes consumers resist the powerful claims placed upon them by mass media. Both Lindner and Gansky show something else as well. As you read these articles, consider how popular culture connects different parts of our lives. For Lindner, advertisements in magazines connect to the conventional social roles of men and women. Gansky shows how the advent of television changed how fridges were imagined. Sometimes popular culture shapes the simplest things in our lives.

Some recent research has shifted to a more optimistic focus, often inspecting emerging progressive approaches to social issues in popular visual media. So, in this section, you will find articles attending to changing representations of marginalized groups, including gay characters in *The Simpsons*, persons with disabilities in *Game of Thrones*, and Muslims in Marvel comic books.

The research represented in this section takes place in the Social Sciences and Humanities. The prominence of visual media in popular culture has reshaped some areas of the university: for example, while much of the initial study of popular culture originated in sociology, recently departments of media and culture studies have been appearing. And other departments, such as English, now routinely include the study of film and television. One thing that distinguishes this research from, say, the research you'll find in the sections on the environment or democracy, is that both professors and students often describe it as fun. Padva writes about using *The Simpsons* in the classroom. Ellis focuses on characters such as Tyrion Lannister, beloved by millions of fans. Pumphrey researches superheroes in Marvel Comics. And yet they all tackle difficult topics, such as sexual orientation and ableism, which tells us something about the directions research is taking in the present-day university.

As you read these articles, reflect on the different types of visual media in your life. In what ways does media affect you? Do you like or even identify with stories or characters in certain media, such as television, comics, or magazines? How critical are you of the visual media in your life?

A. "EDUCATING THE SIMPSONS: TEACHING QUEER REPRESENTATIONS IN CONTEMPORARY VISUAL MEDIA," GILAD PADVA

Gilad Padva's* 2008 article "Educating The Simpsons" first appeared in Journal of LGBT Youth. *In it Padva discusses "Homer's Phobia," an award-winning episode of* The Simpsons *that aired in 1997. He begins by referring to the increased public visibility of gays and lesbians in the period following the notorious 1969 police raid on the Stonewall Inn, a gay bar in Manhattan, before discussing media representations of LGBT characters. Padva's close attention to a single episode of* The Simpsons *is a good example of qualitative analysis conducted in media studies. The study concludes with advice for educators committed to using* The Simpsons *to encourage "greater tolerance for social, ethnic, religious or sexual minorities" (p. 33).*

Glossary terms: qualitative research, media studies, scholarship of application

Abstract
This article analyzes queer representation in contemporary visual media and examines how the episode "Homer's Phobia" from Matt Groening's animation series *The Simpsons* can be used to deconstruct hetero- and homosexual codes of behavior, socialization, articulation, representation and visibility. The analysis is contextualized in the interaction between mainstream and independent cinemas, and particularly, the rise of the New Queer Cinema and Television in the 1990s and the representation/exploitation of queer subjectivities in TV sitcoms of that period.

Keywords: camp, curriculum, film, gay subjectivities, queer representation, The Simpsons, TV, visual media

The visual media, mainly popular films and TV programs, offer an excellent tool for high school and university educators to encourage sexual tolerance, and in particular to promote a supportive attitude towards queer students. Through analysis of queer representations in contemporary visual media, the teacher can relate to

* Gilad Padva works in the Department of Film and TV at Tel Aviv University and the Department of Photographic Communication at Hadassah College Jerusalem, Israel. His research centres on cinema and television studies, gender and queer theory, media aesthetics, popular communications, camp subculture, and popular music.

the position and contribution of the queer subjectivity to the narrative framework, from the exposition through the climax and resolution; to the visibility of the queer protagonist (physique, clothing, make-up, hairstyle, accessories, etc.); to the (non) conventional and (un)acceptable acts of the queer character; and, of course, to the sexual language in the dialogue.

Most of the images that we encounter in popular communications reflect the experiences and interests of the majority groups in our society—whom producers wish to "sell" to advertisers (Gross, 1998). Elihu Katz and Paul Lazarsfeld (1955, cited in Gross, 1998) analyzed the patterns of media images of majority and minority groups and found: (1) a vast preponderance of majority images, produced by and for majority groups; (2) a much smaller proportion of programming that includes or focuses on minorities, also produced by and largely for majority group members; and (3) the smallest portion of media content about, by and for minorities.

Until the mid-1990s, lesbians and gay men were ignored in most films and TV programs. When they did appear, it was in negatively stereotyped roles that emphasized their departure from the "natural" order. They were the group whose opponents are least inhibited by the consensus that protects other minorities from the more public displays of bigotry.

This article provides a pedagogic framework for analyzing queer representations in contemporary visual media. In particular, it examines how the episode "Homer's Phobia" from Matt Groening's animation series *The Simpsons* can be used to (humorously) deconstruct hetero- and homosexual codes of behavior, socialization, articulation, representation and visibility.[1] Such an analysis, however, should be contextualized in the dynamic interaction between mainstream and independent cinemas, and, particularly, the rise of the New Queer Cinema and Television in the 1990s and the representation/exploitation of queer subjectivities in TV sitcoms of that period.

The Simpsons, a gay-friendly animated sitcom, focuses on a yellow family that comprises Homer, a useless father and husband who works at the local nuclear plant; Marge, his wife, a caring housewife and mother, characterized by her good temper and blue, beehive hairstyle; Bart, their son, an impudent prankster and mischievous child; Lisa, his intelligent, aware, and sensitive sister; and Maggie, their crawling baby sister. This series began as short cartoons on the Tracy Ullman Show in the late 1980s (Doty, 2006). From its inception in 1989, the stand-alone show quickly became one of the Fox Network's highest-rated and critically-acclaimed programs despite its often-scathing critique of dominant American institutions (Tingleff, 1998).

I have selected "Homer's Phobia" as a case study here because of the significant popularity of this Emmy Award-winning 15th episode of *The Simpsons*' 8th season, aired on February 16, 1997. First, I offer a scholarly counter-cultural analysis of this episode in regard to its politics of sexuality and gay-straight alliance, and to its visualized socio-linguistic strategies of subverting homophobia and sissy-phobia. Then I offer a set of recommendations for the classroom educator, organized as a 10-step plan for teaching *The Simpsons* to adolescents.

Queering the Simpsons

With the increased visibility of gay men and lesbians in the post-Stonewall era, gay-themed episodes, some with recurring or regular gay and lesbian characters, have challenged negative, preconceived ideas about homosexuality by putting a comical spin on the questions 'Who is gay?' and 'Who isn't gay?' The answers are intended to surprise the audience. Consequently, the issue of identity plays a central role in the majority of gay-themed sitcom plots, which typically involve someone coming out of the closet, someone being mistaken as gay or straight, or a heterosexual pretending to be gay for fun or profit (Tropiano 2002).

The popular subgenre of *animated* TV sitcoms in the late 1990s and 2000s, however, integrates semi-anarchistic humor and spectacular imagery that often challenge conventional ethnic, social, gender and sexual patterns of representation. This subgenre includes, for example, *Beavis & Butthead*, *King of the Hill*, *Daria*, *Family Guy*, *The Kid*, and *The Simpsons*. *The Simpsons*, in particular, is one of the world's most successful American television exports, syndicated in over 60 countries since 1991 (Chocano, 2001). In its imaginative, disruptive, and even surrealistic way, this subgenre often criticizes conservatism, bigotry, and prejudice with humor.

Mainstream Hollywood has historically reinforced the hegemonic sexual order (Russo, 1981; Johnson & Keith, 2001; Keller, 2002). Until the late 1980s, moviegoers seeking gay or lesbian fare had limited options, mostly avant-garde and experimental film. Emanuel Levy (1999) notes that that dynamic changed in the early 1990s, when an independent film movement, New Queer Cinema, began to coalesce. Gradually, several animated sitcoms in the 1990s and early 2000s included gay-identified characters, e.g., Greg Corbin, the local News anchor in *American Dad!*; the intellectual dog Brian's gay cousin in *Family Guy*; Dale Gribble's father and one of Bill Dauterive's relatives at the Château d'Haute in *King of the Hill*; Simon the villain who often dresses up in women's clothing in *Trollz*; and Mr. Burns' assistant Waylon Smithers, Homer's male secretary Karl, the kitsch antique store owner John, Marge's cynical older sister Patty Bouvier, and the characters of Elton John and Ian McKellen in *The Simpsons*.

Jonathan Gray (2003) suggests that *The Simpsons* has turned on its family sitcom brethren, situating its action within an anti-suburb that is depicted as xenophobic, provincial, and narrow-minded. Brilliantly parodying the traditional family sitcom neighborhood, *The Simpsons'* town of Springfield satirizes and challenges rather than extols the American Dream. This series criticizes the hypocrisy within the American educational system, religious, political, and even economic systems

(Tingleff, 1998). Notably—through Bart, Homer, and Grandpa—*The Simpsons* even challenges categories of male sexuality. Sam Tingleff notes that the relationship between the vicious, albeit decrepit, Mr. Burns, who owns the local nuclear plant, and his younger assistant Smithers, is a consistent attack on male sexual norms. Smithers' loyalty comes not from monetary desires, but his quasi-sexual attraction towards Mr. Burns. Furthermore, the males of *The Simpsons* challenge categories of male sexuality and demonstrate its flexibility. For instance, Homer shaves his "bikinizone" for a presumed swimsuit competition; he kisses his secretary Carl (voice of the gay icon Harvey Fierstein) on the lips, and later mistakenly calls his wife "Carl" in bed; his favorite song is "It's Raining Men"; and he says Oliver North was "just poured into that uniform." And in one episode, when Grandpa Simpson can't take his pills, the elder turns into a woman, later accepting flowers and a date from a male suitor (Tingleff, 1998). Moreover, when Lenny, Homer's co-worker, is dying, he sees a heaven full of Carls. On the other hand, Homer suggests that Lisa could win a class election over Nelson by starting a rumor that he's gay. And when a Gay Pride parade passes the Simpsons' house, Homer disapproves of his dog's attempt to hook up with an effeminate, leather-clad dog.

In the gay classic episode "Homer's Phobia" (written by Ron Hauge and directed by Mike B. Anderson, 1997), the Simpsons befriend "John," a mustachioed kitsch trader (resembling and voiced by the cult filmmaker and gay icon John Waters). The fact that he is gay makes Homer fear his potential effect on Bart. After a series of ridiculous attempts to turn Bart into a "real man" (and consequent arguments with his wife Marge), Homer assures his son that his love for him is unconditional, whether he is straight or gay.

The anti-homophobic contribution of this episode to the empowerment of GLBT young viewers is based on its three political premises: celebrating queer counter-culture, embracing straight-gay alliance, and promoting diversity and multiculturalism.

Celebrating Queer Counter-Culture

The Simpsons' friendship with John starts during their visit to the latter's "Cocka-mamie's" antique store. Marge tries to sell Grandma's Civil War doll to John in order to pay an exorbitant Springfield Gas Company bill. John tells her that the doll is nothing but a Johnny Reb bottle from the early 1970s. Homer counters that it's still better than the junk that John is selling, and he wonders how a grown man can love a nostalgic box or a toy. John replies: "It's camp! The tragically ludicrous? The ludicrously tragic?" Eventually, Homer invites John over to see their home, which is "full of valuable worthless crap." John is delighted.

Camp is defined in the *Oxford Dictionary* (1996) as "Affected, theatrically exaggerated; effeminate; homosexual." Susan Sontag (1999 [1964]) categorically defined camp as a vision of the world in terms of a particular kind of style:

It is the love of the exaggerated, the 'off,' of things-being-what they-are-not…The androgyne is certainly one of the great images of Camp sensibility…What is most beautiful in virile men is something feminine; what is most beautiful in feminine women is something masculine. (p. 56)

Jack Babuscio identified camp with queer subculture based on "gay sensibility" as a creative energy reflecting a consciousness that is different from the mainstream; a heightened awareness of certain human complications of feeling that spring from the fact of social oppression (1999 [1978], pp. 117–18).

Sontag did not see camp as political resistance or queer alternative. Rather, she insisted that camp is a certain mode of aestheticism, centered, not on beauty, but on artifice and stylization. She insisted

Even though homosexuals have been its vanguard, Camp taste is much more than homosexual taste. Obviously, its metaphor of life as theater is peculiarly suited as a justification and protection of a certain aspect of the situation of homosexuals. (The Camp insistence on how not to be 'serious,' on playing, also connects with the homosexual's desire to remain youthful.) (pp. 54–56)

The camp performance, however, is primarily a materialization and practice of queer fantasies based on communicated queer imageries. The camp performance is political, "as it challenges straight mechanisms of discipline and control, and provokes hetero-fantasies produced by those mechanisms that aimed to shape straight (self) image and queer image, as inferior and abused subjectivity" (Padva, 2000, p. 224).

The Simpsons episode's visual vocabulary is dominated by camp. For instance, John wears flamboyant, striped shirts from the 1970s and his store contains many telling artifacts: Godzilla toy, piggy bank, pink flamingo (echoing John Water's eponymous cult film), a statue of an Easter Island native head, cola bottle, floral wall decoration, etc. All these items are highly camp, as they are related to kitsch, extravagance, "good" bad taste, artificiality, style, and retrostyle, and also to feminine or "girly" behavior, demonstrated in John's clothing choices and his coy intonation and gestures.

Ironically, John finds the Simpsons extremely camp. He is thrilled by the corn-printed curtain in their kitchen, the color scheme, the rabbit ears antenna, the Hi-C soft drink and Lisa's necklace ("Pearls on a little girl! It's a fairy tale!"). Homer asks him if his records have camp value, and John flatters him: "You yourself are worth a bundle, Homer! Why, I could wrap a bow around you and slap on a price tag." Homer laughs and starts dancing with John to an Alicia Bridges disco record ("I Love the Nightlife"). Marge comments that Homer has "certainly taken a shine to him."

The next morning, Homer decides to invite John and his wife over for drinks. But Marge does not think John is married. In fact, she tells Homer that "John is a ho-mo-sexual" (adopting the apparently scientific/medical definition). In response, Homer shouts hysterically.

Soon afterwards, Homer sees Bart wearing a Hawaiian shirt, choosing a pink cake over a brown one, and dancing to Cher's "Shoop Shoop Song (It's In His Kiss)," wearing a large black wig with a pink bow. Bart's drag show is traumatic for his father. No confusion is allowed over his child's sexual identity and orientation (two concepts Homer repeatedly mixes up). Homer suspects that his son is gay, not because Bart is attracted to boys, but because he does not behave manly enough. Homer sees Bart's dance, not as innocent child's play, but as a camp performance, identified (even in Homer's presumably straight mind) with "transvestite" gay identity, and therefore, as extremely "problematic." He consequently resolves to "normalize" his son. Homer's endeavors might be explained by Foucault's (1990–1992 [1976]) theorizing of the pedagogization of children's sex as a double assertion: that all children indulge or are prone to indulge in sexual activity; and that, being unwarranted, simultaneously "natural" and "contrary to nature," this sexual activity poses a physical and moral, individual, and collective danger. Parents, families, educators, doctors, and psychologists have to take steps—especially against masturbation and other "problematic" praxes of sexuality. If Bart had demonstrated involvement in straight activity, on the other hand, Homer might regard it as desired confirmation of his child's (hetero)normality.

As Marjorie Garber (1992) points out, in mainstream culture it appears just as unlikely that a gay man will be pictured in nontransvestite terms as it is that a transvestite man will be pictured in nongay terms. "It is as though the hegemonic cultural imaginary is saying to itself: if there is a difference (between gay and straight), we want to be able to see it," she adds:

and if we see a difference (a man in woman's clothes), we want to be able to interpret it. In both cases, the conflation is fueled by a desire to tell the difference, to guard against a difference that might otherwise put the identity of one's own position in question (p. 130).

While Homer is threatened by John's (homo)sexuality and its "effeminizing" influence on Bart, the female protagonists—wife Marge, their individualistic preadolescent daughter Lisa, and baby Maggie—sympathize with their new friend. Marge, in particular, likes gossiping with John, who demonstrates his impressive knowledge of celebrities' secret lives, and she adores him for his sense of humor, creativity, friendship, stylishness, and delicacy. These qualities are contrasted to her husband's stupidity, egocentricity, misbehavior, clumsiness, and machismo. It is no wonder that Marge immediately becomes John's best (female) friend, his devoted "fag hag."

Embracing Straight-Gay Alliance

The term "fag hag" dates back to the United States in the late 1960s, dismissively directed at women who were considered not attractive enough to socialize with "real men." But like so many derogatory terms, it was reclaimed in the 1990s as a stereotypic term to be worn with pride. In the ideal, gay men introduced their female friends into a world free from sexual harassment, where the emphasis was on fun and where, more often than not, they would find themselves the center of flattering and unthreatening attention. Hence, "[F]ag haggery was in fashion" (Button, 2000, p. 46). Further, Simon Button notes that a frisson of sexual flirtation, or some kind of sexual dynamics, does in fact often occur between gay men and straight women when they first meet. As Stephen Maddison (2000) points out:

> If hags and fags are 'sisters,' then we are indeed queer ones. The sistership we have the potential to share by virtue of our mutual oppression within hetero-patriarchal regimes, is 'queered' as a function of the way our identities are circumscribed by the homosocial narratives that uphold those regimes. (p. 194)

Marge's "sistership" with John is a bonding between a straight woman and a gay man who enjoys his own stylishness, neatness and effeminacy. In contrast to many straight men *and* some sissy-phobic gay men, John celebrates rather than mocks male femininity, sissiness and stylishness. He and Marge share "feminine" insights and feelings in a friendship that signifies an alternative, equal, and respectful relationship between a man and a woman in conservative small Springfield.

After Bart points a giant, phallic and colorful plastic pistol at him, Homer's worry becomes stronger. He suspects that his wife is ignoring John's malicious homosexualization of Bart, and he makes foolish attempts to save his son from gayness. For instance, he forces his Bart to look at a huge sexist advertising billboard, showing two female models in bathing suits smoking cigarettes; after a long look at the models, Bart only (homo)erotically wishes for "anything slim."

Homer decides that if he is to turn the boy into a man, Bart will need manhood and virility in his environment. During their visit to the local steel mill, Roscoe, the muscular and mustachioed manager, asks the ultravirile, muscular workers to say 'hello' to the Simpsons. In response, they wave effeminately, "Hello-o." Homer wonders if the whole world has gone insane, watching a slender worker running-in-place while his mate theatrically slaps his back: "Stand still, there's a spark in your hair!" and the worker replies: "Get it! Get it!" Then a tanned bodybuilder in hotpants walks past Homer holding a vat of hot steel and announcing "Hot stuff, comin' through!"—a phrase that echoes gay pornography. Roscoe states, "We work hard. We play hard," and pulls a chain. Surprisingly, a high-tech disco ball descends and the entire mill turns into a nightclub called "The Anvil," with flickering spotlights, smoke effects, dance floors, mustachioed bodybuilders, and muscular young men at work, proudly exposing their torsos. All the workers dance to "Everybody Dance Now," except Homer, who is in shock and leaves this male-only enclave, shading Bart's eyes.

Edmund White (2000 [1980]), in his discussion of the political vocabulary of homosexuality, notes that in the past, feminization, at least to a small and symbolic degree, seemed a necessary initiation into gay life. Today, almost the opposite seems to be true. Many gay men sport beards, army fatigues, work boots, etc. They build up their bodies or are "busy arraying themselves in these castoffs and becoming cowboys, truckers, telephone line-men, football players (in appearance and some-times also in reality)" (p. 192). In this way, the ultra-virile spectacle at the gay steel mill can be perceived as a high-camp drag show. Drag, according to Judith Butler (1993), is first and foremost an ironic exercise that liberates the dominant gendered perceptions of reality and expectations of others. What is "performed" in drag, But-ler adds, is the sign of gender, a sign that is not the same as the body that it figures, but that cannot be read without it. The sign, understood as a gender imperative— "girl!"—reads less as an assignment than as a command and, as such, produces its own insubordinations (p. 237).

Earl Jackson (1995) suggests that a truly subversive gay representational practice must contest not only the gay subject's experience of heterosexist persecution, but also his experience of patriarchal privilege. He notes that certain gay male cultural practices that transvalue deviance as a positive mode of self-identification contain at least an implicit critique of the normative male ideal (and the dominant heterosexual sex/gender system) from which the gay male deviates. Sam Fussell (1999 [1994]) contends that even apparently straight male bodybuilding signs a reversal of sex roles, with the bodybuilder taking a traditionally female role: body as object. Further, Fussell observes, "whether it be beefcake or cheesecake, it's still cake…" (p. 46).

David Halperin (1995) contends that gay muscles, in particular, deliberately flaunt the visual norms of straight masculinity, which impose discretion on masculine self-display and require that straight male beauty exhibit itself only casually or inad-vertently. Brian Pronger (2000) also contends that gay muscles, commercialized as they are, have at least one significant character of drag performances: they are ironic. "Musculature," he notes, "within a gay ironic sensibility signifies the subversion of patriarchal power by acting as homoerotic enticements to other men" (pp. 689–90). Homer is not only surprised by the muscular men's queerness. He is also astonished by their proud cultural identity: their dress (and undress), language ('Hot stuff, comin' through!'), behavior (dancing and having fun), and mood (happy), which contradict his image of gays as low-life, dubious and miserable people. This lively discotheque is a demonstration of power, as it presents an alternative culture, part of an alternative camp lifestyle. Homer feels threatened by the spectacular: "This is a nightmare! You're all sick!" He pathologizes gayness as deviation from the "natural" order. Camp, as a queer counter-cultural political praxis, uses its innovative and inspirational deviancy to contest the oppressive social order. This deviation is also political because camp reflects an aesthetic and ethical refusal to be visually hetero-normalized or silenced by dominance (Meyer, 1994; Padva, 2000).

Promoting Diversity and Multiculturalism

Homer's phobia primarily derived from ignorance. His negative reaction towards the gay workers/clubbers is caused by guilt for what he considers his son's deviancy. Pointedly, Homer is not demonized. From this perspective, not only gays but also straight Homer are victims of the same oppressive "natural" sexual order that stig-matizes and discriminates against sexual minorities and imposes restricting hetero-masculine codes of visibility, behavior, and sexual expression on men. Although he does not recognize it, Homer too transgresses the (hetero)sexual representational regime, by wearing Hawaiian shirts, dancing with another man, etc.

Homer wonders how it could be possible that a gay son has developed in a straight family. As Eve Kosofsky Sedgwick pointed out (1990), the double-edged potential for injury in the scene of gay coming out results partly from the fact that the erotic identity of the person who receives the disclosure is also apt to be implicated in, and hence perturbed, by it.

In an earlier scene, Homer blames Marge for being "too feminine around the boy" and she replies that if there is actually a problem with Bart worth worrying over, it must be that he's not spending time with his dad. But Homer's own transgressive masculinity might be implicated in his son's suspected homosexuality.

Michael Kimmel (2001) contends that homophobia is a central organizing prin-ciple of our cultural definition of manhood. He suggests that homophobia is more than the irrational fear of gay men, more than the fear that straights might be per-ceived as gay men. David Leverentz (1986) points out that the word "faggot" has nothing to do with homosexual experience or even with fear of homosexuals. Rather, it arises from the depths of manhood: a label of ultimate contempt for anyone who seems sissy, untough, uncool.

Homer, horrified by the gay steel mill/dance club, decides to socialize his son into the hetero-masculine world through a male brotherhood that putatively includes him-self, the paranoid local bar-owner Moe, and the town's notorious drunk Bernie—three unappealing male role models. When Bart hears about his dad's plan to go hunting with him and his friends, he whispers: "Something about a bunch of guys alone together in the woods...seems kinda gay." The three (straight and narrow) losers get drunk and fall asleep near the bonfire. Homer is shown gently and compassion-ately holding his sleeping son. Desperate to provide Bart with an animal to kill, the hunting group breaks into a reindeer pen. Homer orders him to shoot a reindeer after Bernie has assured him (ironically) that shooting a reindeer is like killing a beautiful man. Suddenly, the deer attack the unwelcome guests, who are rescued at the last moment by John's Japanese Santa Claus robot.

John has earned Homer's gratitude: "Hey, we owe this guy, and I don't want you calling him a sissy. This guy's a fruit, and a...no, wait, wait, wait: queer, queer, queer! That's what you like to be called, right?" and John wittily replies, "Well, that or John." Lisa remarks that this is about as tolerant as her dad gets, so John should be flattered. Here, language demonstrates the change that has occurred in Homer's thinking when he agrees to use the other's terminology as a sign of respect.

The word "queer," as Cherry Smith (1996) points out, defines a strategy, an attitude, a reference to other identities, and a new self-understanding. "Both in culture and politics," Smith notes, "queer articulates a radical questioning of social and cultural norms, notions of gender, reproductive sexuality and the family" (p. 280).

Embracing the idea of unconditional love, Homer tells Bart in the final scene that he loves him because he is his son, gay or not. Bart looks quite surprised to be identified by his parent as gay, before he has recognized himself to be gay. This presents the whole identification process as questionable and contradicts Homer's (and some of the viewers') fixation over gender roles and sexual identities.

The hit song "Everybody Dance Now" (associated with the disco in the steel mill) forms the soundtrack for the final scene, as John's car drives off and Bart's face is shown in increasing close-ups matching the rhythm and lyrics, "I've got the power." The makers of the "Homer's Phobia" episode dedicated it to the steelworkers of America and, winking, exhorted them to "Keep reaching for that rainbow," metaphorically liberating their hyper-masculine territory from its monologic perception.

This episode's multicultural perspective, embracing diversity and open-mindedness, is based on universal ideas of freedom, liberty, equality, justice, tolerance, solidarity, and compassion. The outwardly naïve medium of animation here mediates sexual pluralism through (unexpected) comic situations that parody homophobia rather than homosexuals. The creators have knowingly encoded many gay expressions (e.g., "Dad, you are the living end!"), erotic innuendos (e.g., the gay steel workers' dance club is called "The Anvil"), intertextual hints (e.g., Homer recalls the hit song "It's Raining Men"; and John's car beeper plays Judy Garland's "Somewhere Over the Rainbow"). Although straight audiences too enjoy this episode, its hyperbolic scenes particularly empower gay viewers, who likely identify the linguistic maneuvers and decode the queer meanings. In "Homer's Phobia's" utopian vision, homophobia is just a phase; the hysterical drama queens are primarily Homer and his bigoted straight friends; and an amplified machismo is as theatrical as a flamboyant drag show. Although an analysis of this TV program episode in the classroom is not going to change homophobic attitudes overnight, it can promote a better understanding of gender hierarchies, erotic identifications, passion, pride, and prejudice in our society.

Educating the Simpsons and Their Viewers in 10 Steps

The following plan for discussing *The Simpsons* episode in class, based on the above analysis, focuses on 10 major subjects organized chronologically according to the development of the plot. This plan, which is intended for all students, contextualizes sexual oppression and liberation, and the rejection and acceptance of "the Other." Its goal is greater tolerance for social, ethnic, religious or sexual minorities.

Stereotypes. Prior to the screening of "Homer's Phobia" in class, the class should discuss the powerful politics of stereotyping in popular culture, focusing on the stereotypes' semiotic power as an instrument for identifying and stigmatizing people (Misson, 2005). The teacher can start this discussion with prevailing articulations of ethnic, religious and socioeconomic minorities in mass media. Then the class should study sexism by examining discrimination and objectification of women in advertising. Finally, the class should address the misrepresentation of sexual minorities in popular communications (Gross, 1998). Such a measured sequential discussion can create a more tolerant atmosphere.

Identification with the Other. Following the screening, the teacher can ask the students if they sympathize with John, the kitsch trader, and how this episode promotes identification with him. For example, are the viewers supposed to adopt John's perspective on Homer's phobia?

Effeminacy. The class can analyze the politics of effeminacy in regard to John's portrayal as a stylish, sissy drama queen (Bristow, 2000; Letts, 2005). The main question is, whether this sort of articulation reconfirms the immediate association of homosexuality and effeminacy, or, rather, whether it celebrates effeminacy as a legitimate variation of contemporary masculinity, particularly in gay camp subculture (Padva, 2000).

Homophobia. Homer's hostility towards John should be analyzed in regard to his immediate association of manhood and heterosexuality, derived from his premise of what is "usual" and what is "unusual," and his suspicions regarding John's influence on Bart's sexuality. The class might discuss the absurdity of Homer's rebuke of Marge and Lisa (after they have spent a delightful day with John): "He didn't make you gay, did he?!" The class might also discuss why boys are generally considered more at risk from gay influence than girls are.

Gay-Straight Alliance. The friendship between John and Marge provides an opportunity to discuss gay-straight alliance and potential solidarity between different disempowered (in this case, women and gay men). The students should also consider the obstacles, especially the risk to their power position, encountered by straight males who want to be gay allies.

Family. When same-sex-attracted or transgender young people are "coming out," their parents often undergo a process of "coming in." They come in to the reality of their child's sexuality or gender expression, and any homophobic/gender dualist assumptions and prejudices they may hold (Pallotta-Chirolli, 2005). Marge and Homer's discussion regarding Bart's apparent homosexuality, in which the father blames the mother for their child's transgression, can be analyzed here in light of the idea of unconditional love between parents and offspring (Sedgwick, 1990).

Masculinities. "Homer's Phobia" not only criticizes the sexual regime but also the prevalent, dominant gender definitions of masculinity. It explores a range of masculinities—from Homer's male performance (both his traditional conscious machismo and his bouts of unconscious nonconformity), to his bigoted friends from the local bar, to John's neatness and stylishness. These representations invite the question: what makes a man a man? Is it male genitalia? How can one create his own definition of manhood and reconsider stereotypical straight male attributes (e.g., aggressiveness, brutality, insistence, objectifying women, and homophobia?). And what does the scene in the steel mill teach us about pride and prejudice?

Naming the Other. After Homer and the others are rescued from the rampaging deer, Homer thanks John and tries not to call him a sissy but, rather, "queer" or simply "John." This scene relates to the power of who gets to name the minority. A teacher can emphasize the importance of naming, by referring to contemporary self-identifications and the changing labels acceptable to different minority groups (e.g., negro vs. black, Indian vs. Native American).

(Mis)identification. At the end of the episode, Homer tells Bart that he loves him because he is his son—gay or not. Bart of course is baffled. Homer's supposition can stimulate a discussion about our daily evaluation of different sorts of people according to biased perspectives, stereotypes, and false criteria.

Different Readings, Different Perspectives. Finally, the teacher can relate to the polysemic character of this episode that enables different audiences to enjoy it from their varying perspectives. The students can suggest some possible alternative interpretations of different groups: straight adolescents, queer adolescents, parents of straight children, parents of queer children, open queers, closeted queers, and Afro Americans (who are conspicuously ignored in this episode).

Note

[1] *The Simpsons'* "Homer's Phobia," recognized and appreciated by most of our students, demonstrates the power of the comic medium, both to question sexual axioms and to mock common phobias.

References

Babuscio, J. (1978). The cinema of camp (Aka Camp and the gay sensibility). *Gay Sunshine Journal*, 35; reprinted in Cleto, F. (Ed.). (1999). *Camp: Queer aesthetics and the performing subject* (pp. 117–35). Edinburgh: Edinburgh UP.

Bristow, J. (2000). Effeminacy. In Haggerty, G.E. (Ed.), *Gay histories and cultures: An encyclopedia* (pp. 268–70). New York: Garland.

Butler, J. (1993). *Bodies that matter: On the discursive limits of "sex."* New York and London: Routledge. Button, S. (2000). Best friends. *Attitude* 75 (July 2000), 46–48.

Chocano, C. (2001). Matt Groening. *Salon*. Retrieved April 2, 2005. www.salon.com/people/bc/2001/01/30/groening/print.html.

Cover, R. (2000). First contact: Queer theory, sexual identity, and "mainstream" film. *International Journal of Sexuality and Gender Studies*, 5(1), 71–89.

Doty, A. (2006). The Simpsons: TV program. In Gerstner, D.A. (Ed.), *Routledge international encyclopedia of queer culture* (p. 522). London and New York: Routledge.

Downey, J. (1994). Sexual orientation issues in adolescent girls. *Women's Health Issues*, 4, 117–21.

Edwards, W. (1996). A sociological analysis of an in/visible minority group: Male adolescent homosexuals. *Youth & Society*, 27(3), 334–55.

Foucault, M. (1990–1992 [1976]). *The history of sexuality.* Vol. I: An introduction. Translated by R. Hurley. Harmondsworth, Middlesex: Penguin Books.

Fussell, S. (1994). Body builder americanus. In Goldstein, L. (Ed.), (1999). *The Male body: Features, destinies, exposures* (pp. 43–60). Ann Arbor: U of Michigan P.

Garber, M. (1992). Vested interest: Cross-dressing and cultural anxiety. London and New York: Routledge.

Gibson, P. (1989). Gay male and lesbian youth suicide. In Feinlein, M.R. *Prevention and intervention in youth suicide: Report to the Secretary's Task Force on Youth Suicide*, 3 (pp. 110–42). Washington, DC: U.S. Department of Health and Human Services.

Gove, B. (1996). Framing gay youth. *Screen*, 37(2), 174–92.

Gray, J. (2003). Imagining America: The Simpsons and the anti-suburb go global. Paper presented at Communication in *Borderlands: The 53rd Annual Conference of the International Communication Association*, San Diego, California, USA. May 23–27.

Gross, L. (1998). Minorities, majorities and the media. In Liebes, T., Curran, J., and Katz, E. (Eds.), *Media, ritual and identity* (pp. 87–102). London and New York: Routledge.

Halperin, D. (1995). *Saint Foucault: Towards a gay hagiography.* New York: Oxford UP.

Jackson, E., Jr. (1995). *Strategies of deviance: Studies in gay male representation.* Bloomington: Indiana UP.

Johnson, P. & Keith, M. (2001). *Queer air waves: The story of gay and lesbian broadcasting.* Armonk, NY: M.E. Sharpe.

Katz, E. & Lazarsfeld, P. (1955). *Personal influence: The part played by people in the flow of mass communications.* New York: Free P.

Keller, J. (2002). *Queer (Un)friendly Film and Television*. Jefferson, NC: McFarland.

Kimmel, M. (2001). Masculinity as homophobia: Fear, shame, and silence in the construction of gender identity. In Whitehead, S.M. & Barrett, F.J. (Eds.), *The masculinities reader* (pp. 266–87). Cambridge, Oxford, and Malden, MA: Polity.

Letts, W. (2005). Sissy boy. In Sears, J. (Ed.), *Youth, education, and sexualities*. Vol. 2 (pp. 795–99). Westport, CT, and London: Greenwood P.

Leverentz, D. (1986). Manhood, humiliation and public life: Some stories. *Southwest Review*, 71.

Levy, E. (1999). The new gay and lesbian cinema. In *Cinema of outsiders: The rise of American independent film* (pp. 442–93). New York and London: New York UP.

Maddison, S. (2000). *Fags, hags and queer sisters: Gender dissent and heterosocial bonds in gay culture*. Houndmills and London: Macmillan P.

Meyer, M. (1994). Introduction: Reclaiming the discourse of camp. In *The politics and poetics of camp* (pp. 1–23). London and New York: Routledge.

Misson, R. (2005). Stereotypes. In Sears, J. (Ed.), *Youth, education, and sexualities*. Vol. 2 (pp. 836–39). Westport, CT, and London: Greenwood P.

The Oxford Dictionary. (1996). Oxford and New York: Oxford UP.

Padva, G. (2000). Priscilla fights back: The politicization of camp subculture. *Journal of Communication Inquiry*, 24(2), 216–43.

Padva, G. (2004). Edge of seventeen: Melodramatic coming-out in new queer adolescence films. *Communication and Critical/Cultural Studies*, 1(4), 355–72.

Pallotta-Chiarolli, M. (2005). Parents, responses to homosexuality. In Sears, J. (Ed.), *Youth, education, and sexualities*. Vol. 2 (pp. 605–08). Westport, CT, and London: Greenwood P.

Pronger, B. (2000). Physical culture. In Haggerty, G. (Ed.), *Gay histories and cultures: An encyclopedia* (pp. 688–90). New York: Garland.

Russo, V. (1981). *The celluloid closet: Homosexuality in the movies*. New York: Harper & Row.

Sedgwick, E.K. (1990). *Epistemology of the closet*. Berkeley and Los Angeles: U of California P.

The Simpsons (1997). Homer's Phobia. Created by M. Groening; episode written by R. Hauge; directed by M. Anderson. Distributed by Gracie Films in association with 20th Century Fox Television. Retrieved June 22, 2008. www.snpp.com/epidoses/4F11.html

Smith, C. (1996). What is this thing called queer? In Morton, D. (Ed.), *The material queer: A lesbigay cultural studies reader* (pp. 227–85). Boulder, CO, and Oxford: Westview P.

Sontag, S. (1964). Notes on camp. *Partisan Review*, 31(4), 515–30; reprinted in Cleto, F. (Ed.), *Camp: Queer aesthetics and the performing subject* (pp. 53–65). Edinburgh: Edinburgh UP.

Szalacha, L. (2004). Educating teachers on lgbtq issues: A review of research and program evaluations. *Journal of Gay & Lesbian Issues in Education*, 1(4), 67–79.

Tingleff, S. (1998). "I will not expose the ignorance of the faculty": The Simpsons as a critique of consumer culture. *The Simpsons Archive*. Retrieved April 2, 2005. www.snpp.com/other/papers/st.paper.html.

Tropiano, S. (2002). *The prime time closet: A history of gays and lesbians on TV.* New York: Applause.

White, E. (1980). The political vocabulary of homosexuality. In Michaels, L. & Ricks, C. (Eds.), *The state of the language* (pp. 235–46). Berkeley and Los Angeles: U of California P; reprinted in Burke, L. Crowley, T. & Girvin, A. (Eds.), *The Routledge language and cultural theory reader* (pp. 189–96). London and New York: Routledge.

DISCUSSION QUESTIONS

1. What does the research Padva cites at the beginning of the article suggest about why lesbian and gay characters were largely ignored by mainstream film and TV until the mid-1990s? When such characters did appear, how were they represented? Why?

2. Padva discusses the increased representation of gay characters in "the post-Stonewall era" (p. 25). What distinguishes animated sitcoms from the live-action sitcoms that preceded them? In Padva's view, what distinguishes *The Simpsons* from other animated sitcoms?

3. Padva's article proceeds through detailed analysis of a single *Simpsons* episode. What do you see as the advantages and disadvantages of this approach compared with discussing the representation of the same concerns over a wider range of episodes?

4. This study frequently scrutinizes and develops complex definitions of familiar terms (e.g., "queer," "fag hag," "homophobia"). For example, at one point Padva quotes the *Oxford Dictionary*'s definition of "camp" before developing the term by using the work of Susan Sontag. What working definition of "camp" does Padva ultimately arrive at? Why is the term important in Padva's discussion of the "Homer's Phobia" episode?

5. The last section of Padva's article turns from media studies to "a set of recommendations for the classroom educator" (p. 25), a strategy sometimes called "the scholarship of application." Assess this sudden shift. How well has Padva prepared the reader for this moment? Does Padva's strategy add something important to the discussion? Or would the article have achieved as much if it had ended before the section "Educating the Simpsons and Their Viewers in 10 Steps" (p. 33)?

B. "CRIPPLES, BASTARDS AND BROKEN THINGS: DISABILITY IN *GAME OF THRONES*," KATIE M. ELLIS

This 2014 article, published in a special issue of M/C Journal: A Journal of Media and Culture, *examines the HBO television series* Game of Thrones *from the vantage of disability studies. Ellis* draws on the reception of the show, especially by disabled bloggers, in order to show how its many disabled characters counter ableism, specifically the ways that disability is "socially constructed as an illegitimate identity and positioned as outside of boundaries of normality" (p. 39). As you read this article, pay attention to how it challenges your ideas about disability and society. How do other visual media you are familiar with represent disability (if at all)?*

Glossary terms: ableism, disability studies

Games of Thrones was awarded a Media Access Award in 2013 in recognition of its efforts in "promoting awareness of the disability experience, accessibility for people with disabilities, and the accurate depiction of characters with disabilities" (Winter Is Coming). In addition to this award, the individual character Tyrion Lannister has amassed somewhat of a cult following for his depiction of disability. As Sparky, a blogger for *Fangs for the Fantasy* comments:

> Normally when disabled characters are included they are shunted to the side and most certainly not central to the story line. From the moment Tyrion is introduced having sex with multiple women, it was clear that his role would be far different from the norm. Disabled people are very seldom seen as sexual beings. Tyrion is not only sexual, it would be fair to describe him as hypersexual. For Tyrion, expressing his sexuality is part of how he declares his manhood, in a world that simply seeks to dismiss him because of his size.

According to Dan Harvey and Drew Nelles, *Game of Thrones* is "fundamentally, a show about power: who has it, who doesn't, the fickleness and impermanence of its favour" (Harvey and Nelles). They argue that following the murders of Ned, Robb, and Catelyn Stark, the show embraced more ambiguous heroes such as Tyrion and

---

* Katie Ellis is a senior research fellow in the department of Internet Studies at Curtin University. Her research focuses on disability and digital and networked media.

indicated who the audience should identify with by turning them into misfits—
cripples, bastards and broken things. While the call for papers for this special issue
identifies Jon Snow's illegitimacy as potentially allowing him to redeem a "society
that has become morally, if not openly, itself illegitimate," several characters with
disabilities occupy the same illegitimate status as Jon Snow. *Game of Thrones* includes
a number of characters with disability, both lifelong impairments (Hodor, Tyrion,
Shireen, Lysa, Seylse) and those acquired through injury, illness, or misfortune
(Bran, Jamie, the Hound, Theon/Reek, Aemon, Beric, Illyn Payne, Khal Drago).
Some of these characters, particularly Tyrion, demonstrate the same potential to
reject "political corruption and violence" while also critiquing broader practices of
social disablement.

Isaac Stein argues that notions of legitimacy and illegitimacy impact on the social
experience of disability. For Stein, impairments such as a broken thumb are socially
legitimate and acceptable to acknowledge and compensate for, while long-term or
permanent impairments (or disabilities) are feared and result in "confusion, uncertainty and social awkwardness" when encountered in an ableist society. Critical
disability theorist Tobin Siebers describes this as the ideology of ability. He explains
that a pervasive but contradictory ideology revolves around human ability, which
has resulted in people with disability being marginalised as less than human and
excluded from society and indeed critical theory. Disability is socially constructed
as an illegitimate identity and positioned as outside of boundaries of normality. As
transgressive figures who exist outside socially created boundaries of normality and
humanness, people with disabilities shore up these boundaries (see Davis; Garland-
Thomson; Hall; McRuer; Kumari Campbell; Siebers; Mitchell and Snyder). Siebers
calls for disability studies to investigate the "social meanings, symbols and stigmas
attached to disability identity" as part of a broader questioning of "enforced systems
of exclusion and oppression" (Siebers 3). Tyrion Lannister enacts the same critique
throughout *Game of Thrones* when he identifies as "bastard in [his] father's eyes"
and later claims to have been "on trial" his whole life "for being a dwarf." *Game of
Thrones* introduces a number of important disability critiques around the social
meanings and stigmas that surround disability. Indeed, characters with disability
hold central narrative positions, occupy the screen in close ups and are given a significant amount of on screen time. Critiques such as adapting the environment to
suit an impaired body rather than attempting to cure or exclude that body occur
often in *Game of Thrones* (notably through Bran and Jamie). These critiques have not
gone unnoticed by disabled bloggers. This paper draws on these disability critiques
within the *Game of Thrones* television text itself and amongst disability bloggers to
approach the intersection between disability and illegitimacy from a critical disability and television studies perspective.

Disability and TV

Game of Thrones, the television adaptation of George R.R. Martin's fantasy novels *The Song of Ice and Fire*, is set on the fictional continents of Essos and Westeros with the majority of action taking place on Westeros. As the seven kingdoms of Westeros engage in civil war for the iron throne, the exiled last lineal descendant of the overthrown dynasty amasses an enormous army of freed slaves in the hopes of reclaiming the throne. At the same time, following a decade of summer, an impending winter looms dangerously, along with mythical threats from the north. Adapted for television by HBO, it is a much-lauded example of what Thomas Doherty describes as "arc TV" (Doherty) and what Dean DeFino refers to as the "HBO effect" (DeFino).

"Arc TV" is a new form of television which rejects old conventions such as narrative resolution and static characters. Shows such as *Game of Thrones* instead prefer "long arcs of character and plot development filmed in big-ticket productions" (anonymous). Similarly, the "HBO effect" refers to the rejection of formulaic, safe television content designed to appeal to a mass market and the impact of this rejection on popular culture generally. Greg Metcalf (2) also recognises the impacts of this rejection in his book *The DVD Novel*. He argues that prior to the 1970s television characters were not permitted to evolve because

> You could not rely on viewers to watch every episode or to remember information from week to week, so storylines had to conclude in a single viewing. Everything had to be tied up and put back in the box. This created a dramatic limitation on writing. The main characters had to remain the same from episode to episode...so viewers saw familiar people acting the same whenever they came back.

Theorists such as Doherty, DeFino, and Metcalf argue that changes in the way we access television has fundamentally changed television (see also Sepinwall; Ellis and Goggin; Napoli; Gray). Digital modes of access such as DVRs, DVDs, tablet TVs, and high-quality cable have given greater cultural legitimacy to television. The ability to binge-watch television and access comprehensive behind-the-scenes commentaries, as well as the views of other fans through online wikis and forums, has seen characters evolve and change in unprecedented ways. As Metcalf explains, television is no longer ephemeral; producers can expect audiences to build up extensive knowledge bases regarding narratives and individual characters and indeed watch an entire season within a short period of time. The success of television is no longer reliant on reinforcing the beliefs of a mass audience through the regurgitation of familiar characters behaving the same way week to week. This holds significant potential for the inclusion of characters with disability who are now able to venture outside discourses of tragedy and inspiration. Consider, for example, Jamie Lannister, who began *Game of Thrones* a heartless character willing to murder a child to keep his sexual relationship with his sister secret. Once losing his hand, he rescues Brienne of Tarth, an outsider character by virtue of her height and androgynous appearance, from a brutal gang rape. Similarly, the more screen time afforded to The Hound, the more sympathetic he becomes as we gradually learn the origins of his scars and fear of fire (Harvey and Nelles). Doherty also draws on examples of characters with disabilities, such as *Breaking Bad*'s Walter White and *Homeland*'s Carrie Mathison, in his explanation of arc TV, which he likens to novels, serious plays, and films in their embrace of back story and evolution. As Ellis and Goggin argue, these depictions hold great potential for a complex representation in which disability is explored in terms of both adjustment and as an ordinary part of life.

Traditionally, critiques of disability on television have concentrated on under-representation, negative stereotypes, and inaccurate portrayals of normalisation (Müller, Klijn and Van Zoonen). Stereotypes have been of particular concern with theorists identifying both damaging stereotypes and so-called more legitimate ways of depicting disability (see Longmore; Barnes; Cumberbatch and Negrine; Darke; Harnett). For example, in his seminal book *The Politics of Disablement*, Michael Oliver argued that people with disability were never presented as ordinary people with ordinary problems; they were always super-heroes, villains, or tragic individuals. Applying this framework to *Game of Thrones* suggests an entirely negative representation. For example, when Bran acquires a spinal injury he also becomes a telepathic super-hero. Jamie Lannister, who threw Bran from a castle in an attempt to protect his incestuous secrets, is later punished with his own impairment when enemies amputate his hand. Tyrion himself subscribes to three stereotypes Longmore argues are fundamentally negative—criminality, adjustment and sexuality.

While these disabled characters in *Game of Thrones* may be super-heroes, villains, or tragic individuals, the narrative frequently speaks to the broader notion of social disablement:

> Since its earliest episodes, [*Game of Thrones*] has introduced us to a paralyzed boy with a supernatural gift, has endeared us to a Little Person defined not by his height but by his wit, and has regularly mined the lives of "cripples, bastards, and broken things" to celebrate their strengths and complexities. In fact, it is a fantastic credit...that Game of Thrones is not commonly thought of as a show that "deals with" disability—it is something even better: a show that embraces the reality that no one is easily definable. (David Radcliff cited in Winter Is Coming)

In Rebecca Mallet's view, disability studies' focus on stereotypes as opposed to how we read disability has seen research into disability and television stagnate. Alison Wilde suggests a framework for a more comprehensive analysis of depictions of disability that takes into account the potential for diversity:

rather than focussing upon stereotypes…the central question about better portrayals and the social engagement with disability issues, is about how to achieve cultural recognition on equal terms, to work towards cultural images where being depicted as good, evil, wise, ordinary, extra-ordinary or change-able, is as possible for people with impairments as it is for other people.

In addition to these academic theorists, TV reviewers such as Alan Sepinwall note a shift in television production. Sepinwall identifies a number of television shows, including, among others, *The Sopranos*, *Lost*, *Friday Night Lights*, and *Breaking Bad*, as "game changers" in the television landscape because they targeted smaller and more diverse audiences. They took risks to challenge cultural assumptions about how we establish borders of normality and define ourselves. *The Sopranos*, which challenged the notion of having a moral and likeable leading character, is a case in point. Disability occurs frequently throughout *The Sopranos* as "just another fact of life" (LeBesco 55). According to LeBesco, *The Sopranos* reversed the ideology of ability by making disability more comforting and familiar (55) by making it legiti-mate. *Game of Thrones*, which has "the most disabled characters of any television drama today—perhaps ever" (Harvey and Nelles), performs a similar function, as evidenced by important discussions occurring in online blogs and forums dedicated to both the show itself and the experience of disability.

Game of Thrones Disability and Blogger Insights
Sarah, a blogger with Crohn's Disease, argues that the representation of disabilities in *Game of Thrones* doesn't "get talked about enough." She offers a complex defini-tion of disability which recognises its dependence on the way we construct the world through the built environment and prejudicial attitudes which result in inflexible procedures, practices, and people. She identifies the ways disability is central to the narrative through characters such as Shireen, Hodor, Bran, and Tyrion. Focusing in particular on Tyrion she describes three features of his characterisation which have important implications for disability on television,

> It's not often you get 1) a story about a disabled person, 2) that isn't a cheesy, "uplifting" story meant to motivate able-bodied people into appreciating their own lives, who 3) gets to consistently point out how terribly society treats people like him.

Sarah's critique illustrates Mallett and Wilde's suggestions to "pay attention to the transgression of established boundaries" (Mallett 9) rather than listing negative stereotypes. Tyrion regularly transgresses established boundaries of existing cultural images of people of restricted growth (see Gerber), as That Stark boy comments:

> I began to love the series because of Tyrion, I was just fucking tired of seeing
> dwarves as clowns in every goddamned show I watched—and hear everyone
> around me applauding—and when I saw that dwarf that was just as complex
> as any other character I knew this show was just as badass as they said. (That
> Stark boy comment on Winter Is Coming)

Tyrion who describes having a "tender spot in [his] heart for cripples and bastards
and broken things," faces prejudice from the society in which he lives. He is constantly devalued by his father, Tywin, who resents him for his disability and his
mother's death in childbirth. Tywin describes wanting to carry Tyrion into the sea
and "let the waves wash [him] away," variously calling him a "stunted fool" and
"an ill-made, spiteful little creature full of envy, lust, and low cunning." Although
Tywin constantly reminds Tyrion of his socially devalued qualities, Tyrion displays
intellect, compassion, loyalty, bravery, and wit. Significantly, his compassion extends
to the rival family, the Starks.

When Bran loses the use of his legs, Tyrion evokes a social model argument, that
with the right environmental modifications and adaptive technology, people with
disabilities should be able to participate equally: "With the right horse and saddle,
even a cripple can ride." Although Bran does not want to identify as a cripple, Tyrion's
adapted saddle allows him to ride a horse. As Sparky argues,

> the disabled would navigate the world with much greater ease and far less
> limits if the world weren't so completely designed around the needs of able
> bodied people with so little consideration for what the disabled need.

Aside from the bastard Jon Snow, who also occupies a liminal position, Tyrion is the
only character who discusses Bran's future in relation to what he can still do, while
others, including Arya, Catelyn, Robb, and Ned, focus on what he can't, with Cersei
and Jamie suggesting it is cruel to even keep him alive (Sparky).

Bran's impairment and the reactions of those around him offer a window into
important philosophical matters, such as mortality and personhood, the good life,
and the choices we make (Tedesco 2012). As he lies comatose, Jamie encourages
Bran's father Ned Stark to end the boy's suffering with a quick and merciful death
rather than allow him to live on as a "cripple." As viewers, we know Jamie's motivations are not entirely related to ending Bran's "torment," but are more concerned
with keeping Jamie's own secret—that he pushed Bran from the castle to prevent him
from revealing Jamie and Cersei's incestuous relationship and possible illegitimate
children. For Tedesco, Bran's impairment does not warrant euthanasia because it
would not prevent him from living a good life and having meaningful relationships,
though it would end his favourite hobby—climbing.

However, it is not uncommon for the news media in particular to perpetuate a view that you are better dead than disabled (Haller). Consider Jamie's position on killing Bran in light of his future disablement. When Jamie loses his hand he is no longer able to wield a sword and thus loses his job, social standing, and the thing he most loves to do. With neither Bran or Jamie subject to the mercy deaths Jamie advocates, they offer illustrations that question the popular refrain that you are better dead than disabled.

However, another *Game of Thrones* character Khal Drago's mercy killing at the hands of his wife Daenerys Stormborn is potentially warranted for Tedesco on the basis of a difference between humanness and personhood. Australian philosopher Peter Singer rose to notoriety for advocating the death of disabled infants in his 1985 publication *Should the Baby Live?* He argued that parents be permitted to euthanize disabled babies up to 28 days after their birth (Kuhse 195). Singer justified his argument on a separation of humans and persons. Tedesco uses the medical crises of Bran and Drago respectively to illustrate the difference between humanness and personhood. Whereas Bran would recover and go on to lead a good life, albeit with restrictions, is both human and person, Drago who has become uncommunicative with a blank stare has according to Tedesco and Singer's arguments, lost the qualities that make him a person, although he remains biologically human. Comparing the plights of Bran and Drago raises a number of tricky questions regarding humanity, legitimacy, and the social context of disablement.

A number of disability advocates, notably Harriett McBryde Johnson, took issue with Singer's argument and challenged his assumptions around killing disabled infants, suggesting instead that social disablement should be addressed: "We shouldn't offer assistance with suicide until we all have the assistance we need to get out of bed in the morning and live a good life" (Johnson). To return to Tywin's social exclusion of Tyrion, it began in his infancy, when Tywin would have preferred to kill Tyrion at birth as Singer recommends. However, disability activists caution against advocating to end the lives of people with impairments socially designated as illegitimate, such as Drago's, asking who will be next (Drake).

Tyrion's advice to Jon Snow about living with the stigma of illegitimacy and how to deal with other people's prejudice is a clear statement about disability rights and inclusion that, although set in another time and place, has resonance today. He says: "Let me give you some advice, bastard: Never forget what you are. The rest of the world will not. Wear it like armour, and it can never be used to hurt you." Tyrion identifies with Jon Snow because "all dwarves are bastards in their father's eyes."

Bloggers identify other aspects of Tyrion's characterisation that subvert the typical representations of disability. In contrast to Longmore's argument that all representations of disability are fundamentally negative stereotypes of criminality, adjustment, and sexuality, disabled blogger Andrew Pulrang observes more progressive elements:

Tyrion's main attributes are his sense of humor, in contrast to everyone else's deadly seriousness, his sexual appetites, his love of drink, and, increasingly, his knowledge and knack for strategy. The interesting thing about his sexual exploits is that in the context of this fantasy world, he's not depicted as a pervert or predator, as people with disabilities sometimes are in fiction, but as a more or less straightforwardly hard-partying dude. People joke about it, but no differently than they would any other randy young man in Westeros. There's a kind of equality here, but when he actually starts to fall in love, we see Tyrion again slow to accept that love and real attachment can happen for him.

Tyrion's (and by extension Peter Dinklage's) status as the star of *Game of Thrones* was solidified in Season 4 when on trial for Joffrey's murder, which he did not commit. He in essence accused the world of perpetuating prejudice against people with disabilities.

I wish to confess. I wish to confess! I saved you…I saved this city…all your worthless lives. I should've let Stannis kill you all. I'm guilty…guilty…is that what you want to hear? [Tywin: "You admit you poisoned the king?"] No. Of that I'm innocent. I'm guilty of a far more monstrous crime. I'm guilty of being a dwarf. [Tywin: "You are not on trial for being a dwarf."] Oh, yes, I am. I've been on trial my entire life. [Tywin: "Have you nothing to say in your defense?"] Nothing but this: I did not do it. I did not kill Joffrey but I wish that I had! Watching your vicious bastard die gave me more relief than a thousand lying whores! I wish I was the monster you think I am! I wish I had enough poison for the whole pack of you! I would gladly give my life to watch you all swallow it! I will not give my life for Joffrey's murder, and I will get no justice here.

Tyrion "claims" disability in this scene. He claims both his impairment (that of being a "dwarf") and further, the social disablement he is constantly subjected to. Such an act, according to Siebers as cited in Stein, "marks one as a target [and] exposes and resists the prejudices of society." Tyrion embraces this identity to become an ambiguous hero within *Game of Thrones* and among its audiences. The impassioned monologue prompted an equally impassioned Twitter response through #FreeTyrion (Steiner). Significantly, this Twitter discussion was located in the broader online discussion of *Game of Thrones* and not disability-specific blogging sites. It is unusual for characters with disabilities to hold leading roles on television (Cumberbatch and Negrine) and even more unusual for audiences to identify with disabled characters (Rodan, Ellis, and Lebeck). Even disabled audiences will identify with non-disabled television characters rather than their onscreen disabled counterparts (Wilde). Disability critiques are introduced in *Game of Thrones* through Tyrion, who embraces his socially created illegitimacy in order to expose the way people in a position of difference are constantly judged and treated in discriminatory ways in spite of any contribution they make to their communities and society.

Are People with Disability Valued as Legitimate Television Audiences?
While Tyrion exposes the ways people with disabilities are marked as illegitimate members of the community and treated in discriminatory ways, the airing of *Game of Thrones* on Foxtel in Australia reveals the way people with disabilities, particularly people with hearing impairments who require closed captions, are not valued as audience members. For example, following the screening of the first episode of Season 3, a Foxtel viewer posted to the Foxtel Facebook fanpage:

> HEY FOXTEL WHY ARENT YOU BROADCASTING SUBTITLES WITH GAME OF THRONES FIRST SCREENING??? IT HAS THEM ON SUBSEQUENT SCREENINGS (SOMETIMES) please please please SCREEN THEM FOR PEOPLE WHO STRUGGLE TO HEAR (Miles)

A Foxtel representative responded that they were unable to provide captions on the fast-tracked screenings because "we do not have the time to be able to add these captions or the Digital Dolby surround sound into this screening. The following screening on at 8:30 pm, which is only 7 hours after the screening in the US, will have both the closed captions and surround sound included" (Foxtel comment on Miles).

Television accessibility is emerging alongside representations of disability as a site of social disablement (Jaeger; Goggin and Newell; Ellis and Kent; Ellcessor). To draw again on the notion of illegitimacy as the process of social exclusion (see Grytten and Maseide), the lack of captioning on first run programming is an example of the ways people with disability are not regarded as an important audience (Ellcessor).

While critics of Foxtel's business model argue that viewers are forced to subscribe to packages when they only wish to watch one show (LeMay), audiences with disabilities frustrated by the lack of accessibility are also taking issue with Foxtel's claim that they are providing express services, when the service is in fact useless to them. To return to Miles, "I pay huge $ for my Foxtel subscription and I expect better service, as do the thousands of other subscribers who rely on subtitles to enjoy tv" (Miles).

In Australia, the provision of captions is mandated by the *Broadcasting Services* Act (1992) and the *Disability Discrimination* Act (1992). Recent changes to the BSA mandate that captioning must be available on 100% broadcast content between 6 am and midnight on free-to-air television. However, subscription television, such as Foxtel, is subject to a more complicated set of rules, with quotas relating to the genre of programming (see Media Access Australia). *Game of Thrones* is celebrated as a leading example of the new, cleverly scripted televisual environment illustrative of the culture formerly ascribed to cinema (Weissmann; Ellis and Goggin). Another disappointed fan attempted to neutralise the ideology of ability by suggesting viewers without hearing impairments, just trying to keep up with all the names and locations, would also benefit from the provision of captions:

> For hearing impaired people, a series like Game of Thrones is almost unwatchable without the captions. I know people with full hearing that still turn the captions on because there are so many people and names. (Stombat)

Conclusion

Disability is a value judgement based on whose bodies are considered legitimate in particular spaces. Tyrion Lannister occupies a body that is marginalised in both the fictional fantasy realm in which he exists and today's society. Yet both disabled and nondisabled bloggers recognise him as a compelling character who is changing the nature of disability representation.

Game of Thrones is an example of the recent diversification of television content. This diversification has pioneered a new type of storytelling and led to an environment where television could be taken seriously (Sepinwall). Like a number of programmes featured in this new televisual arena, *Game of Thrones* features characters with disability and develops them as complex people with strengths *and* weaknesses. As evidenced through discussion occurring on disability blogs considered throughout this article, audiences identify with Tyrion in particular, not despite his liminal or illegitimate status but because of it.

While characters with disabilities hold central narrative positions and enact disability critiques by claiming their illegitimate status in *Game of Thrones*, audience members with disabilities are still subject to "enforced systems of exclusion and oppression" (Siebers 3) via inaccessibility, such as a lack of captions. This social exclusion again positions people with disabilities as illegitimate.

References

Anonymous. "Television's New Golden Age." *Wilson Quarterly*, 37.1 (2013): 110–11.

Barnes, Colin. "Disabling Imagery and the Media: An Exploration of the Principles for Media Representations of Disabled People." *Disability Archive*, 1992. 15 Sep. 2014. www.leeds.ac.uk/disability-studies/archiveuk/Barnes/disabling%20imagery.pdf.

Cumberbatch, Guy, and Ralph Negrine. *Images of Disability on Television.* London: Routledge, 1992.

Darke, Paul. "The Changing Face of Representations of Disability in the Media." *Disabling Barriers—Enabling Environments.* Ed. John Swain *et al.* Los Angeles: Sage, 2004. 100–05.

Davis, Lennard. *Enforcing Normalcy: Disability, Deafness, and the Body.* London: Verso, 1995.

DeFino, Dean. *The HBO Effect.* New York: Bloomsbury, 2013.

Doherty, Thomas. "Storied TV: Cable Is the New Novel." *The Chronicle of Higher Education*, 17 Sep. 2012. 2 Sep. 2014. http://chronicle.com/article/Cable-Is-the-New-Novel/134420/.

Drake, Stephen. "Disabled Are Fearful: Who Will Be Next?" *LA Times*, 29 Oct. 2003.

Ellcessor, Elizabeth. "Captions On, Off on TV, Online: Accessibility and Search Engine Optimization in Online Closed Captioning." *Television & New Media* 2011. http://tvn.sagepub.com/content/early/2011/10/24/1527476411425251.abstract?patientinform-links=yes&legid=sptvn;51vl.

Ellis, Katie, and Gerard Goggin. *Disability and the Media*. New York: Palgrave Macmillan, 2015.

Ellis, Katie, and Mike Kent. *Disability and New Media*. Routledge Studies in New Media and Cyberculture. New York: Routledge, 2011.

Finkelstein, Victor. "Representing Disability." *Disabling Barriers—Enabling Environments*. Ed. John Swain *et al*. London: Sage, 2004. 13–20.

Garland-Thomson, Rosemarie. "Integrating Disability: Transforming Feminist Theory." *Gendering Disability*. Ed. Bonnie G. Smith and Beth Hutchison. New Brunswick, NJ: Rutgers UP, 2004. 73–103.

Gerber, David. "The 'Careers' of People Exhibited in Freak Shows: The Problem of Volition and Valorization." *Freakery: The Cultural Spectacles of the Extraordinary Body*. Ed. Rosemarie Garland-Thomson. New York: New York UP, 1996. 38–54.

Goggin, Gerard, and Christopher Newell. *Digital Disability: The Social Construction of Disability in New Media*. Lanham: Rowman and Littlefield, 2003.

Gray, Jonathan. *Television Entertainment*. Communication and Society. Ed. James Curran. New York: Routledge, 2008.

Grytten, Nina, and Per Maseide. "What Is Expressed Is Not Always What Is Felt: Coping with Stigma and the Embodiment of Perceived Illegitimacy of Multiple Sclerosis." *Chronic Illness*, 1 (2005): 231–43.

Hall, Kim Q. *Feminist Disability Studies*. Bloomington, IN: Indiana UP, 2011.

Haller, Beth. "The New Phase of Disability Humor on TV." *Representing Disability in an Ableist World*. Louisville: Avacado P, 2010. 153–74.

Harnett, Alison. "Escaping the 'Evil Avenger' and the 'Supercrip': Images of Disability in Popular Television." *Irish Communications Review*, 8 (2000): 21–29.

Harvey, Dan, and Drew Nelles. "Cripples, Bastards, and Broken Things: Disability in Game of Thrones." *Hazlift*, 10 June 2014. 3 Sep. 2014. www.randomhouse.ca/hazlitt/feature/cripples-bastards-and-broken-things-disability-game-thrones.

Jaeger, Paul. *Disability and the Internet: Confronting a Digital Divide*. Disability in Society. Ed. Ronald Berger. Boulder, CO, and London: Lynne Rienner, 2012.

Jenkins, Henry. *Convergence Culture: Where Old and New Media Collide*. New York: New York UP, 2006.

Johnson, Harriet McBryde. "Unspeakable Conversations." *New York Times* 16 Feb. 2003. 10 Oct. 2014. www.nytimes.com/2003/02/16/magazine/unspeakable-conversations.html.

Kumari Campbell, Fiona. *Contours of Ableism: The Production of Disability and Abledness*. New York: Palgrave Macmillan, 2009.

Kuhse, Helga. *Should the Baby Live? The Problem of Handicapped Infants / Helga Kuhse and Peter Singer*. Ed. Peter Singer. Oxford: Oxford UP, 1985.

LeBesco, Kathleen. "Disability, Gender and Difference on The Sopranos." *Women's Studies in Communication*, 29.1 (2006): 39–59.

LeMay, Renai. "Screw You, Australia: Game of Thrones Goes Foxtel-Only." *Delimiter*, 3 Feb. 2013. 9 Oct. 2014. http://delimiter.com.au/2014/02/03/screw-australia-game-thrones-goes-foxtel/.

Longmore, Paul. "Screening Stereotypes: Images of Disabled People in Television and Motion Pictures." *Images of the Disabled, Disabling Images*. Ed. Alan Gartner and Tom Joe. New York: Praeger, 1987. 65–78.

Mallett, Rebecca. "Choosing 'Stereotypes': Debating the Efficacy of (British) Disability-Criticism." *Journal of Research in Special Educational Needs*, 9.1 (2009): 4–11.

McRuer, Robert. *Crip Theory: Cultural Signs of Queerness and Disability*. Cultural Front. Ed. Michael Berube. New York and London: New York UP, 2006.

Media Access Australia. "How You Can Repeal Red Tape and Improve Captioning." *Media Access Australia*, 2014.

Metcalf, Greg. *The DVD Novel: How the Way We Watch Television Changed the Television We Watch*. California: Praeger, 2012.

Miles, Christine. "Facebook Post." *Facebook*, 22 May 2013. 8 Oct. 2014. www.facebook.com/FOXTEL/posts/10152863155815074.

Mitchell, David, and Sharon Snyder. *Narrative Prosthesis: Disability and the Dependencies of Discourse*. Ann Arbor: U of Michigan P, 2000.

Müller, Floris, Marlies Klijn, and Liesbet van Zoonen. "Disability, Prejudice and Reality TV: Challenging Disablism through Media Representations." *Telecommunications Journal of Australia*, 62.2 (2012): 28.1–28.13.

Napoli, Philip M. *Audience Evolution: New Technologies and the Transformation of Media Audiences*. New York: Columbia UP, 2011.

Nelson, Jack. "The Media Role in Building the Disability Community." *Journal of Mass Media Ethics*, 15.3 (2000): 180–93.

Oliver, Mike. *The Politics of Disablement*. Basingstoke, England: Macmillan Education, 1990.

———. *Understanding Disability: From Theory to Practice*. Houndmills, England: Macmillan, 1996.

Pulrang, Andrew. "Pop Culture Review: Tyrion Lannister, 'Game of Thrones.'" *Disability Thinking*, 1 May 2013. 3 Sep. 2014. http://disabilitythinking.blogspot.com.au/2013/05/pop-culture-review-tyrion-lannister.html.

Rodan, Debbie, Katie Ellis, and Pia Lebeck. *Disability, Obesity and Ageing: Popular Media Identifications*. Surrey: Ashgate, 2014.

Ross, Karen. "But Where's Me in It?: Disability, Broadcasting and the Media." *Media, Culture & Society*, 19 (1997): 669–77.

Sarah. "Cripples, Bastards, and Broken Things: Disability in Game of Thrones." *Skept-ability*, 6 June 2014. 3 Sep. 2014. http://skeptability.com/2014/06/06/cripples-bastards-and-broken-things-disability-in-game-of-thrones/.

Sepinwall, Alan. *The Revolution Was Televised: The Cops, Crooks, Slingers and Slayers Who Changed TV Drama Forever*. Austin, Texas: Touchstone, 2012.

Siebers, Tobin. *Disability Theory*. Ann Arbor: U of Michigan, 2008.

Sparky. "The Disabled Can Play the Game of Thrones." *Fangs for the Fantasy*, 30 Mar. 2012. 4 Sep. 2014. www.fangsforthefantasy.com/2012/03/disabled-can-play-game-of-thrones.html.

Stein, Isaac. "Breaking a Disabled Limb: Social and Medical Construction of 'Legiti-mate' and 'Illegitimate' Impairments." *Disability Studies Quarterly*, 30.3/4 (2010). 18 Sep. 2014. http://dsq-sds.org/article/view/1294/330.

Steiner, Amanda. "'Game of Thrones' Fans Call to #Freetyrion after Fiery Speech." *Hol-lywood Life*, 12 May 2014. 4 Sep. 2014. http://hollywoodlife.com/2014/05/12/free-tyrion-game-of-thrones-twitter-fans-react-speech-laws-of-gods-and-men/#.

Stombat. "No Closed Captions on New Programs." Telstra, 16 Apr. 2013. 9 Oct. 2014. http://crowdsupport.telstra.com.au/t5/Foxtel/No-closed-captions-on-new-programs/td-p/148074.

Tedesco, Matthew. "Life or Death in Westeros and beyond the Narrow Sea." *Game of Thrones and Philosophy: Logic Cuts Deeper than Swords*. Ed. Henry Jacoby. New Jersey: Blackwell Wiley, 2012.

Weissmann, Elke. *Transnational Television Drama: Special Relations and Mutual Influence between the US and UK*. Basingstoke: Palgrave Macmillan, 2012.

Wendell, Susan. *The Rejected Body: Feminist Philosophical Reflections on Disability*. London & New York: Routledge, 1996.

Wilde, Alison. "Are You Sitting Comfortably? Soap Operas, Disability and Audi-ence." *Dis: cover!* 2 (2004). 18 June 2013. http://disability-studies.leeds.ac.uk/files/library/wilde-Alison-Wilde-Dis-cover-2-Adapted-Paper.pdf.

Williams, Bronwyn T. *Shimmering Literacies: Popular Culture & Reading & Writing Online*. New York: Peter Lang, 2009.

Winter Is Coming. "Game of Thrones Wins Award Honoring Disability Aware-ness." *Winter Is Coming*, 22 Oct. 2013. 6 Apr. 2014. http://winteriscoming.net/2013/10/game-of-thrones-wins-award-honoring-disability-awareness/.

DISCUSSION QUESTIONS

1. How familiar are you with the idea of ableism? Have you considered how disability is portrayed in television and film?

2. Discuss Ellis's claim that disability "is socially constructed as an illegitimate identity and positioned as outside of [the] boundaries of normality" (p. 39). Consider this claim in relation to the presence or absence of disabled characters in mainstream television or film.

3. Inspect Ellis's list of references. What types of sources is she using? Which ones are scholarly, and what is their main focus? Which ones are non-scholarly, and how does she make use of these sources in her essay?

4. Assuming you are somewhat familiar with this television show, how does Ellis's focus on disability affect your sense of it? Does it confirm something you already recognized? Or does it introduce something new? Do you agree with Ellis's analysis?

5. Undertake a brief analysis of a film or television program that features a character with a disability. Does the film or movie you've chosen represent disability more or less effectively than Ellis argues *Game of Thrones* does? Why?

C. "IMAGES OF WOMEN IN GENERAL INTEREST AND FASHION MAGAZINE ADVERTISEMENTS FROM 1955 TO 2002," KATHARINA LINDNER

This article, published in 2004 in the journal Sex Roles, *examines how women are represented in magazine advertisements. Drawing on extensive past analysis of magazine advertisements and women, Katharina Lindner* adopts a longitudinal approach to analyzing how women were portrayed between 1955 and 2002 in the general interest magazine* Time, *and in* Vogue, *which is geared toward a female readership. In what she calls "a disturbing result," Lindner finds that the way women are depicted has changed very little: "stereotypical images of women are found quite frequently" (p. 65). These results are "disturbing," Lindner argues, because "[e]xposure to gender role stereotyping in advertisements is related to negative attitude toward women and stereotypical ideas about how they are supposed to behave and the roles they are supposed to occupy within society" (p. 64). As you read this article, you may find some of its findings obvious, but consider nonetheless how it challenges assumptions you may have about how women's role in society has changed from the 1950s to the early twenty-first century.*

Glossary terms: gender roles, longitudinal study, coding, feminism, intercorrelation, quantitative research, data reduction

Abstract

This study was designed to examine the portrayal of women in advertisements in a general interest magazine (*Time*) and a women's fashion magazine (*Vogue*) over the last 50 years. The coding scheme used for this analysis was based on the one developed by sociologist Erving Goffman in the 1970s, which focuses primarily on the subtle and underlying clues in the picture content of advertisements that contain messages in terms of (stereotypical) gender roles. The results of this study show that, overall, advertisements in *Vogue*, a magazine geared toward a female audience, depict women more stereotypically than do those in *Time*, a magazine

---

* Katharina Lindner is a Lecturer in the Division of Communication, Media & Culture and a member of the Centre for Gender & Feminist Studies at the University of Stirling in the United Kingdom. Her research is interdisciplinary, intersecting film and media, gender, and sport studies, with a focus on gender and queer theory, film, media sport, and affect.

with the general public as a target audience. In addition, only a slight decrease in the stereotypical depiction of women was found over time, despite the influence of the Women's Movement.

Keywords: gender roles, gender stereotypes, advertising, magazines, content analysis

Every day people are bombarded by visual advertisements that encourage them to buy particular products or services. However, these images also act as socializing agents that influence our attitudes, values, beliefs, and behaviors (Kang, 1997). Advertisements contain messages about gender roles in terms of appropriate behavior and appearance for both men and women. They shape our ideas of what it means to be male or female in this society. One of the most influential and most often-cited scholars on the media, especially print advertising and its impact on gender relations in society, is Erving Goffman (1979). He emphasized that advertisements often contain very subtle clues about gender roles and may operate as socializing agents on several levels. Because advertisements are publicly broadcast, the men and women portrayed are often perceived to represent the whole population, and men and women in the advertisements seem to accept these portrayed behaviors, thereby validating the stereotyped roles.

Research suggests that exposure to gender role stereotypes in advertising often influences gender-stereotyped attitudes (Signorielli, 1989). Results of a study by Kilbourne (1990) revealed that people, after being exposed to advertisements that depict women in stereotypical roles, showed significantly more negative attitudes toward women, especially concerning their managerial skills, than after being exposed to advertisements that depict women in professional roles that require such skills. These results suggest that there is indeed a relationship between the way women are portrayed in advertising and people's ideas about how women are supposed to behave and the roles they are supposed to occupy within society.

Lanis and Covell (1995) conducted a study on images of women in advertising and their effects on beliefs about sexual aggression. Analysis of the data revealed that sexually explicit images of women, as opposed to "non-traditional role-reversed portrayals of women performing a variety of competent social functions" (p. 643), resulted in increased gender role stereotyping and acceptance of interpersonal aggression and violence against women among the male participants. These results were replicated in a study by McKay and Covell (1997), which showed that after being exposed to sexually explicit advertisements, both men and women showed greater gender role stereotyping, rape myth acceptance, and acceptance of sexual aggression against women. Results also showed that both men and women were less supportive of feminism and the Women's Movement after being exposed to sexually explicit advertisements.

Evidence suggests that gender stereotypes in advertisements also have an effect on people's psychological well-being (Jones, 1991). For example, according to a study

(Posavac, Posavac, & Posavac, 1998) on the effects of exposure to pictures of fashion models from popular women's magazines on young women's concerns with body weight, even passive exposure to such images resulted in negative body image and increased weight concern. Negative body image is often the result of a social comparison process, in which discrepancies are perceived between the cultural ideal of attractiveness, usually characterized in the media by a particular emphasis on thinness, and women's views of their own bodies. Negative body image is particularly problematic because it is positively correlated with eating disorders.

Given these associations between the portrayal of women in advertisements and gender-stereotyped beliefs about women as well as women's psychological well-being, longitudinal studies have been conducted to examine exactly how women have been depicted in print advertisements. What roles do they occupy? What activities do they engage in and what kinds of behavior do they display? In what environments are they shown? How are they depicted in relation to men? And how have these images changed over time?

The earliest studies were inspired by the Women's Movement in the early 1970s; this research consistently showed that advertisements confined women primarily to traditional mother, home, or beauty/sex-oriented roles, which were not representative of women's diverse roles in society. In a comparative study of the roles portrayed by women in print advertisements in 1958, 1970, and 1972, Belkaoui and Belkaoui (1976) analyzed the contents of eight general interest magazines (i.e., *Life, Look, Newsweek, The New Yorker, Time, Saturday Review, U.S. News and World Report,* and *Reader's Digest*). They found that advertisements in 1958 showed women mostly as housewives in decorative roles and idle situations or as low-income earners with limited purchasing power.

That study, in addition to two others of the portrayal of women in the same general interest magazines in 1970 (Courtney & Lockeretz, 1971) and in 1972 (Wagner & Banos, 1973), showed that despite the influence of the Women's Movement, women continued to be portrayed in stereotypical roles. Courtney and Lockeretz (1971) and Wagner and Banos (1973) found that women were hardly ever shown in out-of-home working roles, especially as professionals, and they were never depicted as venturing far away from home by themselves or with other women. Rather, they were represented as dependent on men's protection. Men were often shown as regarding women as sex objects or as domestic adjuncts. In addition, women were primarily found in advertisements for cleaning products, drugs, clothing, and home appliances, whereas men were shown in advertisements for cars, travel, alcoholic beverages, cigarettes, and banks.

A follow-up of these studies was conducted by Sullivan and O'Connor (1988), who compared print advertisements of 1983 to advertisements of the 1950s and 1970s. Their sample of advertisements was drawn from *People, Saturday Evening Post, Life, Newsweek, The New Yorker, Reader's Digest, Time,* and *U.S. News and*

World Report. These magazines were chosen because of their broad appeal and their likelihood of depicting women in a wide variety of roles. They found that the 1983 advertisements more accurately reflected the true diversity of women's social and occupational roles than did those of earlier decades. There was an increase in women shown as employed and a higher percentage of women in positions that require meaningful decision-making (in the workplace as well as in everyday situations). Women were more often shown as independent of men and as occupying equal social roles. However, the trend toward gender equality (i.e., men and women engaging in more similar activities and behaviors) was counteracted by an increase in women portrayed in purely decorative and sexualized roles. In other words, progress in one area seemed to be counterbalanced by setbacks in another (Faludi, 1991). A backlash seemed to have occurred in response to women gaining power and being portrayed in more influential positions, which was perceived as a threat to male dominance in society. An increase in sexualized, as well as degrading, submissive, and objectified, images of women reestablished the power imbalance between the sexes.

The previously mentioned studies focused primarily on the manifest content of the advertisements. Goffman (1979) developed a technique, referred to as frame analysis, which focuses on the more subtle clues that provide important messages about gender relations. His coding system concentrates on hands, eyes, knees, facial expressions, head posture, relative sizes, positioning and placing, head-eye aversion, and finger-biting and -sucking. Goffman found that gender stereotyping in advertisements occurred primarily in ways that can be captured by the following categories: *relative size, function ranking, feminine touch, ritualization of subordination,* and *licensed withdrawal.* He argued that these categories are indicative of gender differences in "social weight," that is social power, influence, and authority.

In terms of *relative size,* men are often taller and take up more space than women do in advertisements, which could be a way of suggesting men's superiority over women. *Function ranking* refers to advertisements in which women are shown in less prestigious occupations than men or as controlled by men, whereas men control the actions of others. When depicted together, men are likely to perform executive roles and control the whole situation. *Feminine touch* refers to women touching themselves in unnatural ways or caressing and cradling other objects, whereas men use their hands to manipulate things. Women are also often shown in contexts that suggest the *ritualization of subordination,* meaning that women adopt postures that indicate submission to control by others. They lower themselves physically, lie down at inappropriate times, or are embraced by a man. Correspondingly, men often adopt an erect position, with their heads held up high, which is usually a sign of superiority and power. *Licensed withdrawal* refers to women being depicted as removing themselves psychologically from the social situation. Their attention often drifts away, they gaze into the distance as if they were not part of the scene, and they appear to be disoriented. This leaves women dependent on the protection of others, whereas men stay alert and ready for potential threats to their control of the situation.

In his book *Gender Advertisements*, Goffman (1979) presented many examples of magazine advertisements that showed women in previously-mentioned ways. However, Goffman's methodology, especially his sampling technique, has been criticized. He drew biased samples, deliberately choosing advertisements from newspapers and magazines that showed gender differences that represented his preconceptions, instead of randomly selecting advertisements to analyze. He argued that the purpose of his study was the *discovery* and *presentation* of the various ways in which gender stereotyping occurs. Thus, conclusions about gender portrayal in the population of print advertisements cannot be drawn on the basis of this sample.

To examine the generalizability of Goffman's claims, a number of studies have been conducted using his coding scheme and more representative samples. Despite some shifts in the portrayal of women since the early 1970s, there seems to be no serious trend toward less gender stereotyping. Kang (1997), for example, conducted a study in which she used Goffman's five coding categories and added two new categories—*body display* (i.e., degree of nudity, body-revealing clothes) and *independence/self-assertiveness* (i.e., women's overall image in terms of independence and self-assurance)—in order to examine any changes in the way women have been portrayed in magazine advertising since the late 1970s. The results of her study of advertisements in *Vogue, Mademoiselle,* and *McCall's* from 1979 and 1991 reveal that very few changes have occurred in the stereotypical portrayal of women. The findings indicate, however, that the types of stereotyping have changed; advertisements show more stereotypical depictions in the categories of licensed withdrawal and body display and less stereotyping in the categories of relative size and function ranking. Kang (1997) concluded that even though some advertisers have begun to feature more powerful and independent women, "only superficial cultural alterations are transferred to advertisements, while the underlying ideological foundation remains untouched" (p. 994). Thus, even though women are not exclusively portrayed in the stereotypical mother and housewife roles anymore, other, more subtle ways have been used to portray women as inferior to men. Women might be portrayed more often as professionals, for example, but at the same time there is also a remarkable increase in sexualized images of women or images that show them as mentally removed from the situation at large.

In another study, Goffman's coding scheme was used to analyze the advertisements in the 1985 issues of *Good Housekeeping, Sports Illustrated,* and *Time* ("traditional" magazines) as well as *Ms., Gentlemen's Quarterly,* and *Rolling Stone* ("modern" magazines; Belknap & Leonard, 1991). Overall, feminine touch, ritualization of subordination, and to some extent licensed withdrawal, were discovered frequently. Contrary to the authors' hypothesis, no differences were found in the stereotypical portrayal of women in the more "traditional" magazines and the more "modern" ones.

In another study concerning the depiction of women in magazine advertisements, the categories introduced by Goffman were used, and *location* (i.e., domestic versus public settings), *movement* (i.e., ability to move fast and far), and *risk-taking* (i.e., involvement in high-risk activities), were used as additional coding categories (Umiker-Sebeok, 1996). The researcher argued that control over space, the ability to move freely, and the ability to block and control others' movements are associated with social power and control. The results of the analysis of the advertisements in 38 different magazines published in 1993 and 1994, randomly selected from a municipal recycling bin, revealed that some shift in the portrayal of women had taken place. However, the changes have been superficial and occurred more in terms of the type of stereotyping than in the amount of stereotyping. There were fewer depictions of women in the traditional housewife and mother roles, for example. However, this shift seems of minor importance compared to the relatively stable ways of portraying women as unable to exhibit the same amount of control over their environment as men do (or can).

Specifically, it was found that in terms of relative size, women tended to take up more space than men, and had a thin or ectomorphic body type, whereas men were large and muscular. In addition, men tended to be taller than women and they tended to be shown looking down at women. Men also displayed postures that increased their body size, whereas women were shown in postures that reduced the space their bodies occupied; for example, women were more often shown lying down and men more often standing up. Psychological withdrawal was observed in women more than in men; women were shown as uninvolved or withdrawn from the social situation by covering their faces or mouths or gazing at some unidentified object outside the picture frame. All of these behaviors signal vulnerability and need for protection. In terms of function ranking, men were likely to take control over women's bodies, by lifting them up, containing their space by encircling their bodies, by blocking access to the woman's body, or by putting their arms around women's shoulders. Women, on the other hand, were usually more likely to hold on to a man's arm or to rest their own weight on a man's body. Also, in terms of location, women were more likely than men to be decontexualized; that is, women were more often shown in unidentified environments. They were also more often shown in the bathroom or bedroom, often in some form of self-absorbed grooming or not engaged in any activity at all. Men, on the other hand, were more frequently depicted in nondomestic settings and in the workplace. There were also differences in how men and women were portrayed manipulating the environment. Men were more often shown using tools to control or manipulate their environment, whereas women were shown using the so-called "feminine touch," caressing an object, or tracing its contours. In the category of movement, the Umiker-Sebeok (1996) study showed that men were represented with the ability to move faster than women and to control larger amounts of space. Men were also shown as involved in high-risk physical activities more often than women; high-risk activities were associated with higher chances of breaking down obstacles and achieving power. As did previous researchers, Umiker-Sebeok concluded that there has been some shift in terms of gender codes in print advertising, mainly in the type of stereotyping that occurs, but that these changes have been superficial, and the underlying messages have remained largely unchanged.

This seems to be the overall conclusion that can be drawn when comparing the results of the previously discussed analyses of images of women based on Goffman's categories. A shift has occurred from portraying women as socially inferior and subordinate to men in very blunt and obviously stereotypical ways (e.g., by showing them in domestic settings) to images of women that contain rather subtle messages about gender roles and about women's place in the social power hierarchy.

Rationale and Hypotheses

Because advertising is such a crucial factor in forming our perceptions of gender roles, systematic analyses of print advertisements are necessary to gain better understanding of the way women are portrayed. The previously mentioned studies show that some shifts in the depiction of women in print advertising occurred between the 1950s and the early 1990s, such that women were portrayed less often in the traditional housewife or mother roles and more often in professional roles. There seemed to be a tendency countering this progress, however, in that women were more frequently depicted in other ways that suggest stereotypical gender roles. Women have been increasingly shown in highly sexualized ways, for example, or as adopting body postures that suggest a need for protection and control.

To get a better understanding of the kind and extent of the changes that have occurred over a longer period of time than the time spans covered in previous studies, magazine advertisements from 1955 to 2002 were examined. In addition, to determine whether changes in the portrayal of women over time are different in women's fashion magazines than in general interest magazines, advertisements from both *Vogue* and *Time* were analyzed. The reasons for choosing advertisements from these particular magazines in the sample is that both *Vogue* and *Time* have published for the entire time period included in this study. Thus, there were two independent variables, namely publication year and magazine type. The dependent variables were based on a combination of parts of Goffman's scheme (i.e., relative size, function ranking, feminine touch, ritualization of subordination, and licensed withdrawal). The coding categories were added by Kang (1997; i.e., body display) and Umiker-Sebeok (1996; i.e., movement and location), and a new category developed for this study (i.e., objectification). "Objectification" refers to portrayals of women that suggest that their major function or purpose in the advertisement is to be looked at.

As Kang (1997) and Umiker-Sebeok (1996) pointed out, only superficial changes in the images of women have occurred over time, such as a decrease in the obvious portrayal of women as smaller ("relative size") or inferior to men ("function ranking"). The underlying messages about appropriate gender roles, however, have remained largely unchanged, with an increase in the more subtle ways of stereotyping, such as "feminine touch," "ritualization of subordination," and "licensed withdrawal." Therefore, it was hypothesized that changes over time would be found for the different coding categories. More specifically, stereotyping in terms of "feminine touch," "ritualization of subordination," "licensed withdrawal," "body display," and "objectification" was expected to increase over time. These categories are associated with sexualized images of women and more subtle ways of stereotyping. Stereotyping in terms of "relative size," "function ranking," "movement," and "location," on the other hand, was expected to decrease over time, because these categories are associated with a more "traditional" way of stereotyping by showing women in positions of inferiority.

With regard to magazine type, it was hypothesized that advertisements in *Vogue* would portray women more stereotypically than would advertisements in *Time*. *Time*, a general interest magazine geared to a broader audience that covers a broad range of topics, was expected to portray women in a greater variety of roles that are more realistic in terms of the roles women actually occupy in society. In addition, the majority of the coding categories were associated with sexualized images of women, which were, again, expected to be found more frequently in *Vogue* with its focus on beauty and fashion, than in *Time*, with its more serious and sophisticated content that includes political and economic issues.

Method

In this study, a longitudinal approach was taken to analyze the portrayal of women in a general interest magazine and a women's fashion magazine from 1955 to 2002. The sample consisted of the issues of *Time* in the first 4 weeks of January and June in the years 1955, 1965, 1975, 1985, 1995, and 2002, as well as the January and June issues of *Vogue* in the same years. The months of January and June were selected to avoid a bias in the sample based on the time of the year the advertisements were published. (It could be expected, for example, that advertisements in magazine issues of the summer months include more instances of "body display.") By including summer as well as winter issues, the sample was expected to reveal greater insight regarding the overall picture of the way women are portrayed. Exceptions due to unavailability of certain magazines had to be made for the 1985 issues of *Vogue* (the October and December issues were coded) as well as the 2002 issues of *Time* (the first four issues of both October and December were coded instead). Some pages were missing in some of the magazines, so there is a possibility that not all of the advertisements were included in the analysis.

Only advertisements that showed one or more women, either in the presence or absence of one or more men, were coded in this study. The coding categories were conceptually defined as follows:

(1) *Relative size.* When both men and women are present, the man is taller and/or bigger than the women and takes up more space in the picture.

(2) *Function ranking.* When both men and women are present, the man serves as the instructor or performs an executive role.

(3) *Feminine touch.* The woman touches herself (e.g., hair, face, lips) or her clothes in an unnatural way or uses her fingers and hands to trace the outline of an object, cradle it, or caress its surface. This type of touching is to be distinguished from the utilitarian kind, which involves grasping, manipulating, or holding objects.

(4) *Ritualization of subordination.* The woman lowers herself physically in some form or other of prostration; canting postures are associated with acceptance of subordination. This includes lying or sitting on the ground, bed, or sofa—whether in the presence of another person or not, canting of the head or entire body. Also included in this category is a woman being embraced by a man who inhibits her movement, or a woman leaning against a man's shoulder or holding on to his arm for support, dependent on, and subordinate to the man present.

(5) *Licensed withdrawal.* The woman removes herself psychologically from the situation at large or is shown mentally drifting from the physical scene, leaving her disoriented and dependent on the protectiveness of others. This is indicated by an expansive smile or laughter, covering the face or mouth, or withdrawing her gaze from the scene at large. Being involved in a phone conversation also falls into this category.

(6) *Body display.* The woman is shown wearing revealing, hardly any, or no clothes at all, which is often associated with sexualized images of women.

(7) *Movement.* The woman is inhibited in her movement, by being wrapped in a blanket for example, which limits the amount of control she can exert on the environment.

(8) *Location.* The woman is shown in a domestic environment, such as the kitchen, bedroom, or bathroom. This also includes depicting the woman in a decontexualized, that is, unidentifiable, environment that does not allow for any purposeful activities.

(9) *Objectification.* The woman is portrayed in such a way as to suggest that being looked at is her major purpose or function in the advertisement.

Each advertisement was coded on a yes-or-no basis according to whether it contained a stereotypical depiction of women in the different categories. Advertisements with one or more women (either in the presence or absence of one or more men) were coded using all of the categories. Advertisements that contained only women (one or more) were not coded for relative size and function ranking. Advertisements that contained only men were not included in this study.

A research assistant was trained to use the coding scheme without revealing to her the exact purpose or hypotheses of the study. The issues of both *Vogue* and *Time* used in the process of reaching consensus and testing for interrater reliability were randomly selected. The first 20 advertisements from the June 1965 issue of *Vogue* and the first 20 advertisements from *Time* in the 1st week of January 1975 were coded by the researcher and the assistant together in order for the assistant to gain practice with the coding process and in order to reach consensus about how the coding scheme would be used. Then, two issues of both *Vogue* and *Time* were randomly selected, and a total of 70 advertisements, 40 from *Vogue* (the first 20 advertisements each from both the January 1965 issue and the January 2002 issue), as well as 30 from *Time* (the 17 advertisements in the January 1985 issues and the 13 advertisements in the January 1995 issues) were coded by the researcher and the assistant separately. Their codes were then compared to test for interrater reliability. The percent agreements for the different coding categories ranged from 86 to 97% (M = 91.7; relative size: 96%, function ranking: 96%, feminine touch: 86%, ritualization of subordination: 89%, licensed withdrawal: 90%, body display: 94%, movement: 97%, location: 91%, objectification: 87%); mean = 91.7%. Once interrater reliability was established, the author coded the remaining advertisements.

Results: Descriptive Statistics

A total of 1,374 advertisements were coded for this study. Table I shows the number of advertisements coded for each magazine in each month. Percentages of the total number of advertisements that met the criteria of each of the coding categories are shown in Table II. Overall, 78% of all advertisements contained stereotypical images of women in at least one of the categories. Women were often depicted as mentally drifting from the scene and thus being unprepared and vulnerable to potential threats in their environment ("licensed withdrawal": 31.9% of all advertisements), as lowering themselves physically and adopting postures that indicate submission to control by others ("ritualization of subordination": 33.0%), and as being mere objects whose only function was to be looked at ("objectification": 40.0%). Stereo-typing in terms of "movement," on the other hand, that is, the portrayal of women as inhibited in their ability to control space, was relatively low; only 2.5% of all advertisements met the criteria for this category.

Table I. Number of Advertisements in *Vogue* and *Time* Coded Each Year

	1955			1965			1975			1985			1995			2002		
	Jan.	June	Total	Jan.	June	Total	Jan.	June	Total	Jan.	June	Total	Oct.	Dec.	Total	Jan.	June	Total
Vogue	72	36	108	58	102	160	41	33	74	79	126	205	107	64	171	55	64	119
																Oct.	Dec.	Total
Time	49	107	156	36	62	98	33	39	72	34	39	73	21	26	47	40	51	91

Note. $N = 1,374$.

Table II. Overall Stereotyping in Each Coding Category

	% of advertisements falling into the category
Relative size	11.1
Function ranking	7.3
Feminine touch	21.1
Ritualization of subordination	33.0
Licensed withdrawal	31.9
Body display	11.0
Movement	2.5
Location	24.2
Objectification	40.0

Table III. Average Percentages of Stereotyping For Each Coding Category

	M	SD	Range
Relative size	13.13	12.18	0.0–36.4
Function ranking	12.62	16.84	0.0–65.4
Feminine touch	18.72	13.58	0.0–47.2
Ritualization of subordination	31.58	10.38	7.7–51.5
Licensed withdrawal	29.07	16.79	5.0–65.5
Body display	10.61	6.79	1.6–24.2
Movement	1.98	3.19	0.0–13.1
Location	22.27	14.48	4.8–55.2
Objectification	33.69	27.23	0.9–74.1

Data Reduction

To calculate percentages for each coding category separately for each magazine in each month, the number of advertisements that depicted women stereotypically in each category in a particular issue was divided by the total number of advertisements in that issue. This yielded 24 percentages for each category (i.e., *Vogue* January 1955, *Vogue* June 1955… *Vogue* January 2002, *Vogue* June 2002; *Time* January 1955, *Time* June 1955… *Time* October 2002, *Time* December 2002). Shown in Table III are the means, standard deviations, and ranges of these 24 percentages for each category.

Intercorrelations

An analysis of how the different coding categories were intercorrelated (see Table IV) showed very strong negative correlations between "objectification" and both "relative size" and "function ranking," which suggests that magazines that show women as mere objects to be looked at were less likely to depict women as smaller than men and in an inferior role. There were, however, very strong positive correlations between "objectification" and all the other categories (with the exception of "movement," where no significant correlation was found), which indicates that in magazines in which women were objectified, they were also very likely to be shown using the feminine touch, subordinating themselves, being mentally withdrawn from the scene, wearing revealing or hardly any clothes, or in domestic or decontextualized settings. In addition, "relative size" was negatively correlated with "feminine touch," "ritualization of subordination," and "licensed withdrawal." These results suggest that in magazines that portrayed women stereotypically in terms of "relative size," that is, as smaller and as taking up less space in the picture than men, women were less likely to be portrayed in other stereotypical ways.

Effects of Magazine Type and Publication Year

A two-way analysis of variance (ANOVA) was conducted to test for main effects of the two independent variables—magazine type (*Vogue* vs. *Time*) and publication year (1955–75 versus 1985–2002)—and for interaction effects between the

Table IV. Intercorrelations Between the Different Coding Categories

	Relative size	Function ranking	Feminine touch	Ritualization of Subordination	Licensed Withdrawal	Body display	Movement	Location	Objectification
Relative size	—								
Function ranking	.29	—							
Feminine touch	−.74***	−.46*	—						
Subordination	−.62**	−.27	.67**	—					
Withdrawal	−.70***	−.42*	.73**	.57**	—				
Body display	−.49*	−.47*	.54**	.51*	.32	—			
Movement	.15	.09	.17	.01	−.04	−.22	—		
Location	−.46*	−.15	.59**	.48*	.74**	.21	.17	—	
Objectification	−.76***	−.63**	.78***	.61**	.78***	.52**	−.10	.55**	—

$*p < .05. **p < .01. ***p < .001.$

Table V. Percentages of Stereotyping for Each Coding Category by Magazine Type and Publication Year

	Magazine type			Publication year		
	Vogue	*Time*	$F(1, 20)$	1955–75	1985–2002	$F(1,20)$
Relative size	3.5	22.8	41.8***	14.5	11.8	0.79
Function ranking	2.7	22.6	12.18**	10.8	14.5	0.42
Feminine touch	29.9	7.5	76.96***	22.7	14.7	9.87**
Subordination	38.2	25.0	19.33***	35.1	28.1	5.30*
Withdrawal	41.48	16.66	26.90***	29.8	28.4	0.09
Body display	14.4	6.8	10.29**	11.5	9.7	0.60
Movement	1.7	2.2	0.20	3.8	0.2	9.93**
Location	30.0	14.5	9.06**	24.5	20.0	0.76
Objectification	59.2	8.2	248.72**	32.5	34.9	0.59

$*p < .05. **p < .01. ***p < .001.$

two for the different coding categories. Publication years were combined into two groups to increase the number of data points in each group. Table V shows the mean and significance tests. There were no significant interactions for any of the coding categories.

For "relative size," there was a main effect for magazine type, as this kind of stereotyping occurred more frequently in *Time* ($M = 22.8\%$) than in *Vogue* ($M = 3.5\%$). No main effect for publication year was found.

A similar magazine main effect was found for "function ranking," as more of this type of stereotyping occurred in *Time* ($M = 22.6\%$) than in *Vogue* ($M = 2.7\%$). Again, results did not reveal a significant main effect for publication year.

For "feminine touch," significant main effects were detected for both independent variables. This stereotypical behavior among women was more often shown in Vogue ($M = 29.9\%$) than in Time ($M = 7.5\%$) and more often in earlier years (1955–75, $M = 22.7\%$) than in more recent years (1985–2002, $M = 14.7\%$).

Main effects for both independent variables were also found for "ritualization of subordination," as women were more often depicted as adopting postures that indicate submission to control by others in *Vogue* ($M = 38.2\%$) than in *Time*

($M = 25.0\%$), and more frequently between 1955 and 1975 ($M = 35.1\%$) than between 1985 and 2002 ($M = 28.1\%$).

There was a main effect for magazine type for "licensed withdrawal," as women were shown as mentally drifting from the scene at large with much greater frequency in *Vogue* ($M = 41.5\%$) than in *Time* ($M = 16.7\%$). However, no main effect for publication year was detected.

"Body display" as a means of stereotyping, that is, women wearing revealing or hardly any clothes, was found significantly more often in *Vogue* ($M = 14.4\%$) than in *Time* ($M = 6.8\%$). Again, there was no main effect for publication year.

No main effect for magazine type was found for "movement." However, there was a main effect for publication year, as issues in earlier years ($M = 3.8\%$) showed women inhibited in their ability to move more frequently than did those in more recent years ($M = 0.2\%$).

In terms of "location," a significant main effect for magazine type was detected. Women were shown in domestic settings or in decontextualized environments much more frequently in *Vogue* ($M = 30.0\%$) than in *Time* ($M = 14.5\%$). There was no main effect for publication year.

A similar main effect was found for "objectification," as *Vogue* ($M = 59.2\%$) featured significantly more advertisements that showed women as objects to be looked at than did *Time* ($M = 8.2\%$). There was, again, no main effect for publication year.

In summary, there were main effects for magazine type: advertisements in *Time* were more stereotypical than in *Vogue* for "relative size" and "function ranking." In all other categories, with the exception of "movement," for which no main effect for magazine type was found, advertisements in *Vogue* portrayed women more stereotypically than did those in *Time*. Main effects for publication year were found for "feminine touch," "ritualization of subordination," and "movement," as stereotyping occurred more frequently in earlier years (between 1955 and 1975) than in later years (between 1985 and 2002) for all three categories.

Discussion

The messages conveyed in advertisements shape our ideas about appropriate gender roles as well as our attitudes toward and expectations of men and women (Signorelli, 1989). Exposure to gender role stereotyping in advertisements is related to negative attitude toward women and stereotypical ideas about how they are supposed to behave and the roles they are supposed to occupy within society (Kilbourne, 1990). In addition, it is related to more accepting beliefs of sexual aggression against women (Lanis & Covell, 1995), to rape myth acceptance, and to negative attitudes toward feminism and the Women's Movement (McKay & Covell, 1997). Finally, it is related to negative body image in women, to an increase in weight concern, and to the development of eating disorders (Posavac et al., 1998). In other words, these images are associated with the way women are treated, looked upon, and feel about themselves, with the kind of behavior and appearance that is expected from them, and, even more generally, with our ideas of what constitutes masculinity and femininity in our culture.

Overall, the results of this study show that stereotypical images of women are found quite frequently; 78% of the magazine advertisements portrayed women stereotypically with regard to at least one of the coding categories. This is a disturbing result considering the impact advertisements have on our values and beliefs about women and the roles they are supposed to play within society. Stereotyping occurred frequently with regard to objectifying women ("objectification"), showing women as subordinate to men ("ritualization of subordination"), or depicting women as mentally withdrawn from the larger scene ("licensed withdrawal"). The existing imbalance in terms of social power between men and women is reinforced through these images, as the stereotyping of women in these categories is associated with lower degrees of social power and control.

In addition, few significant changes over time were found in the images of women in magazine advertisements, except for decreases in "feminine touch," "ritualization of subordination," and "movement." The results for all other categories revealed that the extent to which women were shown in stereotypical roles has remained fairly constant throughout the years. This is a rather surprising finding considering the changes in the actual roles women occupy in real life that have occurred since the Women's Movement and the subsequent trends toward equality, especially with regard to the business world. Women's progress in gaining social power is thus counteracted by disempowering women in visually subtle ways.

Significant differences in the portrayal of women were found in terms of magazine type. With the exception of "relative size," "function ranking," and "movement," stereotyping in *Vogue* was considerably higher than in *Time*. Although no significant difference was found for "movement," advertisements in *Time* portrayed women more stereotypically than advertisements in *Vogue* in terms of "relative size" and "function ranking"—the only two categories for which the role of a woman in relation to a man was coded. These results show that advertisements in *Time*, the general interest magazine, reinforce stereotypical gender roles that showed women as smaller, weaker, inferior, or as dependent on a man. Advertisements in *Vogue*, on the other hand, rarely showed this kind of stereotyping, but do reinforce an inferior and weak image of women by showing them in the following ways: as tracing the outline of an object or caressing its surface instead of using their hands to manipulate their environment ("feminine touch"); as lowering themselves physically, sitting or lying on the ground, and being embraced or holding on to a man's body in search of protection ("ritualization of subordination"); as mentally drifting from the situation or as withdrawing their gaze from the scene, leaving them unprotected and unprepared for potential threats in their environment ("licensed withdrawal"); as wearing revealing, hardly any, or no clothes at all ("body display"); as occupying

domestic settings such as the kitchen, bedroom, or bathroom, where their activities are restricted to housework, grooming, and preparation for potential sexual
activities, or in a decontextualized environment in which no purposeful activity is
possible ("location"); and as objectified, where their only purpose was to be looked
at ("objectification").

These differences between magazine types are remarkable, considering that the
women's fashion magazine (*Vogue*) is geared to a female audience; yet its advertisements portrayed women more stereotypically than did advertisements in the
general interest magazine (*Time*). The fact that advertisements in *Time* portrayed
women stereotypically primarily in terms of "relative size" and "function ranking"
might be due to the readership toward whom *Time* as a general interest magazine is
geared. Most other ways of stereotyping, such as "feminine touch," "body display,"
or "licensed withdrawal," are usually associated with sexualized images of women,
which might be considered inappropriate to be shown in a magazine such as *Time* that
has a more serious target audience and that covers a broader range of more serious
and significant issues than *Vogue* does. In other words, stereotyping in *Time* occurs
without the use of sexualized images of women, whereas in *Vogue*, these sexualized
images are the primary way of portraying women in positions of inferiority and low
social power. This portrayal of women as inferior and "flawed" is a necessity for the
existence of a women's fashion magazine such as *Vogue*, which is primarily a means for
advertising and selling products that are suggested to be a "cure" for women's feelings
of inferiority and inappropriateness. The illusion is created that purchasing and using
these products will make women sexy and beautiful, and thus happy and successful.

The lack of an interaction between publication year and magazine type suggests
that, between 1955 and 2002, the images of women in *Vogue* have been consistently
more stereotypical than those in *Time*. This also supports the aforementioned notion
of women's feelings of inferiority being a necessity for the existence of a women's
fashion magazine such as *Vogue*.

There are some aspects of this study that could be improved in future research.
One possibility is to use a more detailed coding system to detect the more subtle
stereotypical ways in which women are portrayed. Especially in terms of "location,"
a coding scheme that differentiates between the portrayal of women in a traditional
domestic setting, that is in the kitchen, bedroom, or bathroom, and in a decontextualized environment would have been more useful with regard to detecting changes
in the *type* of stereotypical locations in which women are shown. In both of these
settings, women are restricted in their range of possible activities, but in a decontextualized environment this restriction is not as obvious and the message about appropriate gender roles might be more subtle. Similarly, other categories such as "function
ranking," "ritualization of subordination," "licensed withdrawal," and "movement"
could be more sensitive to these subtle differences in stereotyping. There are many
different ways of showing women in inferior roles, as adopting postures that indi-

cate submission to control by others, as mentally drifting from the larger scene, or as inhibited in their ability to move and to control space. A coding system sensitive enough to detect those subtle differences would reveal more information in terms of changes that have occurred over time within the different categories.

For the future, it would be interesting to investigate the images of men in magazine advertisements and how these images have changed over time. Especially in terms of body image and male beauty, there seems to be a trend toward showing men in equally unrealistic ways, as overly muscular and athletic, for example. Considering the negative effects the portrayal of beauty can have on women's health (e.g., eating disorders), further investigation of men's portrayal in magazine advertisements will give more insight regarding the connection between these images and increased body image concerns in men.

Another idea for possible future research is to examine the relationship between gender portrayal in advertisements and the gender of those responsible for deciding what types of advertisements are actually published in a magazine. Do the differences in the way men and women are depicted in magazine advertisements depend on the gender of the editors? Is stereotyping in women's images higher or lower in magazines with male editors?

Finally, further research is needed on the effect that advertisements in general, and their gender-role portrayal specifically, have on those who are exposed to them. Some existing research suggests that the exposure to stereotypical gender roles can have an influence on people's attitudes and behavior (Kilbourne, 1986; Lanis & Covell, 1995; McKay & Covell, 1997; Signorelli, 1989), but not enough knowledge exists about the exact mechanism behind this association. How do we get from being exposed to stereotypical gender roles to having gender-stereotypical attitudes and behaving in gender-stereotypical ways?

There are many unanswered questions with regard to the role that images in print advertisements and in the media in general play in terms of the actually existing gender roles in our society. Are these images a mere reflection of the real world and the roles men and women play in it? Or are these roles created and then reinforced through the images we see repeatedly? The ability to understand the role these images play regarding our attitudes and behavior is increasingly important because of their omnipresence in today's media-saturated environment. They contain subtle yet powerful messages about what it means to be a man or a woman in our society, and about the appropriate and socially accepted behaviors associated with either gender.

Acknowledgments
I thank Dr Katherine Black (Department of Psychology at the University of Hartford) for her support and supervision of the study on which this article is based. I also thank Hege Lauvik for volunteering as a research assistant.

References

Belkaoui, A., & Belkaoui, L.M. (1976). A comparative analysis of the roles portrayed by women in print advertisements. *Journal of Marketing Research, 8*, 168–172.

Belknap, P., & Leonard, W.M. (1991). A conceptual replication and extension of Erving Goffman's study on gender advertisements. *Sex Roles, 25*, 103–118.

Courtney, A., & Lockeretz, S. (1971). A woman's place: An analysis of the roles portrayed by women in magazine advertisements. *Journal of Marketing Research, 8*, 92–95.

Faludi, S. (1991). Backlash: The undeclared war against American women. New York: Crown.

Goffman, E. (1979). *Gender advertisements*. New York: Harper and Row.

Jones, M. (1991). Gender stereotyping in advertisements. *Teaching Psychology, 18*, 231–34.

Kang, M.-E. (1997). The portrayal of women's images in magazine advertisements: Goffman's gender analysis revisited. *Sex Roles, 37*, 979–97.

Kilbourne, W.E. (1990). Female stereotyping in advertising: An experiment on male-female perceptions of leadership. *Journalism Quarterly, 67*, 25–31.

Lanis, K., & Covell, K. (1995). Images of women in advertisements: Effects on attitudes related to sexual aggression. *Sex Roles, 32*, 639–49.

McKay, N.J., & Covell, K. (1997). The impact of women in advertisements on attitudes toward women. *Sex Roles, 36*, 573–83.

Posavac, H.D., Posavac, S.S., & Posavac, E.J. (1998). Exposure to media images of female attractiveness and concerns with body weight among young women. *Sex Roles, 38*, 187–201.

Signorielli, N. (1989). Television and conceptions about sex roles: Maintaining conventionality and the status quo. *Sex Roles, 21*, 341–60.

Sullivan, G.L., & O'Connor, P.J. (1988). Women's role portrayal in magazine advertising: 1958–83. *Sex Roles, 18*, 181–88.

Umiker-Sebeok, J. (1996). Power and construction of gendered spaces. *International Review of Sociology, 6*, 389–404.

Wagner, L.C., & Banos, J.B. (1973). A woman's place: A follow-up analysis of the roles portrayed by women in magazine advertisements. *Journal of Marketing Research, 10*, 213–14.

DISCUSSION QUESTIONS

1. In the first few pages of the article, Lindner spends considerable time recreating how previous researchers have analyzed the portrayal of women in advertising. Why does she do this? How does her research contribute to this tradition of inquiry?

2. Adapting the coding schemes of Erving Goffman and later researchers, Lindner uses nine coding categories in her analysis of *Time* and *Vogue*. Inspect the advertisements in one present-day general interest and one women's magazine using these nine categories. (Make sure to use actual magazines rather than searching online for sexist advertisements, which will result in a biased sample.) Can you find instances of each category? Prepare an analysis of several ads to demonstrate how the categories work.

3. Some of Lindner's coding categories may seem more important to you than others. For instance, is it especially surprising that the relative size of male models is larger than that of female models? Which categories are the most significant?

4. Lindner notes that Goffman was criticized for being too selective in choosing his sample advertisements. Discuss the strengths and weaknesses of Lindner's approach to analyzing samples.

5. In her conclusion, Lindner identifies a number of paths for future research. How could you adapt one of these paths to propose a new research question, perhaps for a study of your own?

D. "AVENGER, MUTANT, OR ALLAH: A SHORT EVOLUTION OF THE DEPICTION OF MUSLIMS IN MARVEL COMICS," NICHOLAUS PUMPHREY

This article, which appeared in 2016 in The Muslim World, *an academic journal specializing in Islamic Studies, applies canonical theory to trace changes in the representation of Muslim characters in Marvel comics in the years surrounding the 9/11 terrorist attacks. As you read Nicholaus Pumphrey's* account of how the pre-9/11 "orientalist stereotype" of Muslims (p. 74) was ultimately replaced by the figure of the "hero who happens to be Muslim" (p. 71), try to identify intermediate stages that Pumphrey identifies and the historical reasons for those changes.*

Glossary terms: canonical criticism, Orientalism, Islamic Studies

Marvel Comics is known for being edgy and controversial, always pushing the mold. In the 1960s, the X-Men seemingly symbolized the civil rights movement. The X-Men are a team of mutants, a new species that are born with special powers, making them feared and hated by humans. They are led by Professor X to bring about peace between humans and mutants, but the villain Magneto believes in fighting for dominance over humans.[1] In 1966, Marvel introduced the first black superhero, the Black Panther, who rules his own African country, which is far more advanced than America.[2] In 1973, Marvel did the unthinkable and killed a major character in its main series, *Spider-Man*. The teenage Peter Parker, who was given powers when bitten by a radioactive spider, could not save his girlfriend Gwen Stacy, and she died in such an ambiguous way that the reader thought: "Spider-Man killed Gwen Stacy."[3] In 1992, Marvel character Northstar came out as the first openly gay mutant, who would later have the first gay wedding ceremony in comics.[4] It should be no surprise that Marvel introduced Muslim superheroes.

Before 9/11, Muslims were figures of orientalist imagination: always characterized as Arabs and depicted in stereotypical dress and manner, with dark skin, turbans, large moustaches, and often riding carpets or camels. After 9/11, Marvel perpetuated the stereotypical portrayal of "terrorists" in many of their comics; most visible was the retcon story arc of Iron Man called *Extremis*. However, comics are

---

* Nicholaus Pumphrey is an Assistant Professor in the Department of History, Culture, and Society at Baker University in Baldwin City, Kansas. His research specialties include pop culture, archaeology, and Islamic studies.

not written from one ideology and there are a plethora of writers and artists with diverse political and religious affiliations that will work on a single series over time. A single issue alone will have many different authors and artists, who sometimes have not even met each other.[5] Authors like the Scotland-born Grant Morrison did not trust the rampant American patriotism of post-9/11 comics and created Soorya Qadir, an Afghani mutant with the ability to control sand. As a fully veiled Muslim, she is a direct response to the Muslim paranoia of this time period but still based on stereotypes of Muslim women. In more recent years, many Muslim artists and writers have emerged to develop their own American-Muslim, heroic narratives. In 2014, a Pakistani-American teenage girl named Kamala Khan debuted as the new Ms. Marvel, the first Muslim superhero to carry her own book.

My understanding of how readers make meaning from comics is based on issues of context and canon, coming directly from literary exegetical methods of biblical and Qur'anic studies, especially Canonical Criticism. Dominant trends in American media and culture often determine the authoritative narrative within comics that is reinforced by the canonization of story arcs and biographies of characters. However, Marvel's narratives have evolved drastically from the stereotypical Muslim terrorist to the portrayal of a female hero who happens to be Muslim. There is an obvious linear line in the way Muslims are drawn in comics before 9/11 to the present. It is evident that American Muslims, like any minority, deal with dangerous stereotyping, but as Marvel further develops its characters, many have shifted to a more complex Muslim hero. This progression culminates in Ms. Marvel, with Marvel mainstreaming Muslim-Americans and diversifying their heroes to represent a multi-cultural America.

Critical Comic and Canonical Theory

The entire story arc or biography of a character is determined by a long list of events and books called a canon, literally meaning 'measuring stick' in Greek. Canonical Theory developed from the "assumption that biblical texts were generated, transmitted, reworked, and preserved in communities for which they were authoritative."[6] It also explores "the process of adaptation by which the community signified earlier traditions to function authoritatively."[7] Communities are not static and frequently change, and with them so do their opinions on canon. In comics, the construction of canon is the acceptance or dismissal of certain texts or story arcs of a comic book or a specific character. Two elements of the comic canon are "continuity (the literal narrative elements of a character's story) and tradition (the more general conventions of the superhero genre, so tight and narrow as to come close to another level of continuity)."[8] Like biblical texts, the authority of comic canons is also controlled by lived communities and the traditions built around them, and much like clergy, the writers, artists, and editors attempt to direct, alter, or modernize the canon while not straying from the continuity.

A particular story or text can become canonical for one community and be considered non-authoritative to another. In the Gospel of Thomas, Jesus fashions birds out of clay and makes them come to life; however, this is considered a non-canonical text to most Christians and thus is not included in the biography of Jesus. However, in the Qur'an (5:110), Jesus also fashions birds out of clay, making it integral to the canonical biography of Jesus in Islam. There are several comics that create alternate stories that are considered extra-canonical. Usually these narratives are considered outside of the accepted canon. For example, the comic entitled "What If Spider-Man had Rescued Gwen Stacy?" reversed her death from the 1973 Spider-Man issue.[9] Today, canon debates in comics typically involve the argument that comic book movies do not belong in the biography of a character, although the movie often informs what happens in the current books, mostly to attract more readers and sell more comics. However, an event like the creation of kryptonite on the radio show *Adventures of Superman* became so popular that it actually became part of the accepted canon of the comic books.[10]

Like any literary work, comic books are driven by the context in which they were conceived. Joseph Darowski edits a collection in which contributing authors argue that current events influence the writing of a comic, such as the AIDS crisis and Marvel developing the Legacy virus that kills only mutants.[11] Darowski's dissertation examined the history of the X-Men, who are known for being the most progressive and liberal team, and he charted issues of race, ethnicity, and gender.[12] He shows that political and religious beliefs of "mainstream" America were reflected in the characters. For the first time in the series' history, the X-Men were mainly an all-female team in the 1990s. However, when the terrorist attacks occurred on 9/11, the team went back to a predominantly white male team. Whether these are conscious decisions made by the authors or editors typically cannot be determined. Stan Lee, the creator of X-Men (among other classic superheroes) and former president of Marvel Comics, often said he would write anything to make money and wrote what the readers would buy.[13]

To accept an origin story of a certain comic book character often means *not* acknowledging the historical context in which that narrative was written. This is very similar to theological readings of the Qur'an or Bible, where a community rereads the text in light of a contemporary situation, ignoring the cultural context in which it was written, commonly leading historical-critical scholars to argue against those readings. If the apostle Paul argues against non-normative sexualities in the New Testament book Corinthians, it is a result of the context of Corinth at this time and its history of prostitution. However, this text is often read as what is appropriate or not appropriate sexuality in contemporary communities. Much of Amina Wadud's work on the Qur'anic view of women has been to emphasize that the text "represents the social, cultural, and historical context in which that individual woman lived," and too often people make "universal" claims out of that context.[14]

The other consequence of the canon is the smoothening of multiple authors. Historically, the disagreeing timelines and two separate creation stories of Genesis 1 and 2 have created theological issues that result in an attempt to unify the multiple authors and narratives into a singular story with only one author. When creating the canon of a character, the multiplicity of authorship is removed and only one authentic story is created. Regardless of the concerns of the historical-critical scholar, this is what communities do. They define and redefine canons and scriptures in order to have an authentic model to represent their lived experience, with the text and their lived realities often mutually defining one another. Thus, it is easy to imagine that before and after 9/11, comics were very much different texts, with the depiction of Muslims fluctuating with popular American opinion.[15]

Pre-9/11

Within most comics, stereotypes and superhuman powers frequently go hand in hand. For example, *Giant Size X-Men* #1 introduced the most popular X-Men team, with mutants like Colossus (a large Russian mutant from the Cold War who transforms into steel), Wolverine (a short, hairy Canadian mountain-man who walks the line between human and animal), and Storm (an African girl who could control the weather).[16] All the names and backstories of each character are based on stereotypes. Before 9/11, Marvel Comics followed the same logic and based most Muslim characters on orientalist stereotypes that would be recognizable and supported by the American audience, creating a canonical depiction.[17]

There were figures such as Sinbad, the typical orientalist pirate with which most Americans are familiar. He often wore a turban, pointy shoes, and rescued damsels, dressed like belly dancers, from monsters and jinn.[18] Another was the Arabian Knight, Abdul Qamar, who also wore a turban, Turkish styled trousers, and pointy shoes. He was bearded, flew a magic carpet, brandished a large scimitar, and was meant to be the Arab version of Nick Fury, America's greatest spy.[19] Lastly, Egyptian Amahl Farouk, the Shadowking, is a villainous telepath whose power rivals that of the X-Men's leader, Professor X. He has a history of enslaving mutants and humans to do his bidding. Although he wore a fez, that was the extent of his stereotypical dress, and he is often depicted not as a human but as a blue monster of pure psychic energy. Americans primarily thought only of Muslims as foreigners from the "Orient." As a result, heroes and villains were stereotyped and from the Middle East or North Africa.

Monet St. Croix, codename M., is an interesting exception to the stereotype, considering she is from Algeria, a Muslim-majority country, but does not openly discuss her religion in the narrative. However, in a 2011 issue of *X-Factor*, M. explains that she is Muslim.[20] Davis and Westerfelhaus feel that "fans were surprised" because never has her "Muslimah identity played much of a role in defining her character."[21] But they also allude to the fact that since she does not dress in a stereotypical Muslimah fashion, instead wearing provocative clothing, fans were clueless.[22] Based on this understanding, readers could not process her Muslim heritage because she did not exhibit any stereotypical signs, and as a result, the part of her canon that originally expressed that she could have a Muslim background is ignored. Instead, the accepted Muslim characters for Marvel readers before 9/11 were orientalist stereotypes.

9/11 and Post 9/11

It would be an understatement to say that 9/11 changed America and American media. With the propagation of the Muslim terrorist stereotype in the media, all facets of American popular culture reaffirmed extremist portrayals of Muslims and, as a result, hate crimes against Muslims reached an all-time high.[23] Suddenly the stereotypical Muslim terrorist was everywhere throughout Marvel, as well as the rest of the comic industry. An Islamic terrorist was an easy villain in which a narrative could be constructed without having to explain the backstory. As Jehanzeb Dar notes:

> We have seen the Muslim terrorist as an incredibly one-dimensional villain. Whether he is trying to nuke Israel, hijack planes and aircraft carriers or is disguised as an ancient pre-Islamic Persian, the Muslim terrorist is no one to sympathize or empathize with. He has no story, no family, and no other purpose but to cause war and destruction against the West. When nothing appreciative is learned about Muslim and Arab characters, the stereotypes blur the distinction between real-life extremists and the overwhelming majority of Muslims and Arabs, who are peaceful and multi-dimensional human beings like everyone else.[24]

The terrorist character was not a new one. In fact, Jack Shaheen noted in his 1991 study that out of 149 instances of "evil" Arabs in comics, 50 of those were labeled terrorists.[25] After 9/11, the Muslim terrorist stereotype became even more prominent in comics.

Mark Diapolo remarked that superhero comics sell the most when there is conflict in society, and this is true regarding 9/11.[26] Most critics assume the movie industry is what pulled the comics industry out of the 1990s lull, but quite possibly it was propagated by 9/11 and the ultra-American patriotism. Given that Marvel Comics is centered in New York, they pulled their heroes out of the Marvel Universe and placed them in the real world and placed both heroes and villains standing at Ground Zero together. According to Grant Morrison:

> They were compelled to acknowledge the event as if it had occurred in their own simulated universe ... If al-Qaeda could do to Marvel Universe New York what Doctor Doom, Magneto, and Kang the Conqueror had failed to do, surely that meant that Marvel heroes were ineffectual. September 11 was the biggest challenge yet to the relevance of superhero comics.[27]

Amazing Spider-Man #36 was released with an all-black cover as a symbol of mourning.

The last scene of *Amazing Spider-Man* #36 portrays Dr. Doom crying. Victor von Doom was the arch-nemesis of the Fantastic Four and one of Marvel's first supervillains.[28] He has attempted to rule the Marvel multi-verse and even sent children to Hell.[29] The narrator states, "Even those we thought our enemies are here because some things surpass rivalries and borders. Because the story of humanity is written not in towers but in tears. In the common coin of Blood and Bone. In the voice that speaks within even the worst of us, and says **this is not right**. Because even the worst of us, however scarred, are still human. Still feel. Still mourn the random death of innocents."[30]

Grant Morrison upholds Doom's tears in *Amazing Spider-Man* #36 as significant and describes the scene as follows: "This was the 'World's Greatest Super-Villain' who had himself attacked New York on numerous occasions... but here he was sobbing with the best of them, as representative not of evil but of Marvel Comics' collective shock, struck dumb and moved to hand-drawn tears by the thought that anyone could hate America and its people enough to do this."[31] However, the event did not just represent the shock of Marvel comics, but also helped reinforce the Muslim terrorist stereotype. This poignant scene confirms for readers that within the canon of Marvel's evil villains Muslim terrorists are worse.

Marvel even joined the "War on Terror" by releasing a new Avengers team called the Ultimates, which included some of the most popular heroes like Iron Man (billionaire Tony Stark who wears a weaponized suit of armor) and Captain America (Steve Rodgers who was transformed into a super soldier during World War II).[32] In *The Ultimates 2*, Marvel rehashed one of Captain America's old villains called the Red Guardian, originally a Soviet equivalent to Captain America created during the Cold War; however, in this series, he is the Azerbaijani Colonel named Abdul al-Rahman. A young Muslim, al-Rahman volunteered to become a super soldier after watching Captain America lead the invasion into Iraq.[33] Morrison states:

> Marvel stepped into the post-9/11 breach with global-political thrillers that acknowledged contemporary events without dwelling on them. *The Ultimates*, re-created with Mark Millar's gleefully right-leaning heroes, gave a voice to Bush's America's posturing, superheroic fantasies of global law enforcement in a posttraumatic world. It was both a glorification and a satire of those attitudes.[34]

However, not all fans give authenticity to satire and instead uplift the glorification.

More directly in conversation with Islam was the "Extremis" story line in *Iron Man* volume 4.[35] The traditional backstory of Iron Man describes him as a rich arms dealer who is crippled by his own weapons and is forced to live in a suit of iron.

A satire against the arms race, he is someone using technology to fight his own weapons. In the 1960s and 1970s, Iron Man had to combat the communist powers that America was currently fighting: the Soviet Union, China, and Vietnam. In 2005, Marvel decided to update the origin story with Warren Ellis at the helm, with the war on terror replacing the war on communism.[36] The accepted canon for the hero is changed to suit the particular conflict of the time so that the reader would be able to personally understand the comic better, and as a result, purchase more comics. The problem with Iron Man is that the average reader misunderstands the satire and instead sees a billionaire playboy with fast cars.

In the new biography, Iron Man sells arms to al-Qaeda, which in turn uses the weapons against him, resulting in a piece of shrapnel in his chest. They lock him in a cave and order him to build weapons for them. Instead, he builds the Iron Man suit to keep the shrapnel from piercing his heart and allow him to escape. In Issue 5, Tony escapes the cave yelling, "Say hello to the Iron Man, you terrorist scum."[37] Instead of fighting communists, Iron Man now fights Muslim terrorists. This story gained major attention when it was used as the source material that spawned three "blockbuster" *Iron Man* films, and two *Avenger* films.[38] Morrison states, "As a result, more and more Marvel comics, including some of my own, had scenes set in the Middle East or on board hijacked aircraft."[39] These were an attempt to show the realism of the 9/11 context in comics, but frequently the scenes were, as Morrison puts it, "wrapped in the flag of shameless patriotism."[40] Jon Favreau, who directed the first two Iron Man films, believes the popularity of the genre is a result of 9/11, but as escapism that does not require any responsibility to directly address reality. Instead of fighting the "terrorists," Iron Man could do it for them.[41] As a result, writers recapitulated dangerous stereotypes of Muslims in order to sell comics and movie tickets. The movie received scrutiny for its portrayal of "Muslim terrorists" in the most oriental fashion.[42]

In *New X-Men*, Grant Morrison creates a new scenario of outcast mutants based on the original plot of X-Men. However, now mutants are bullying mutants, who eventually align themselves with Magneto in disguise. Paralleling the events of 9/11, Magneto takes New York City hostage and bends it to his will. Whether metaphorically referencing African Americans or Jews, the X-Men were always an analogy for minorities, but in Morrison's *New X-Men*, he "pulls from and sheds a light on the political climate of post-9/11 America, particularly the cultural cost of the War on Terror."[43] Morrison states, "Over its forty-issue run, *New X-Men* turned into a diary of my own growing distrust of a post-9/11 conformity culture that appeared to be in the process of greedily consuming the unusual and different."[44] Quickly, the outcasts go from being responsible for the paranoia to becoming victims of it.

Among the outcast mutants is a Muslim teen named Sooraya Qadir, codename Dust.[45] According to Eric Garneau and Maura Foley, Morrison created Dust in order to reject the post-9/11 fear. He used the stereotypes in order to mock this world and have people see a misunderstood hero.[46] Morrison provides that Dust is a mutant refugee from Afghanistan, who is fleeing the Taliban. However, it is hard to determine if readers understand the satire or have their myths confirmed, especially since she is a stereotypical Muslim woman wearing a *niqab* and *abaya*. In *New X-Men* vol. 2, issue 2, Dust, now written by Nunzio DeFilippis and Christina Weir, tells her roommate that it is not right to show her body to men and boys, a stereotypical response written by outsiders of Islam.[47] Her powers range from controlling sand to becoming a sand storm, ironic since she is from Afghanistan instead of North Africa. When she is introduced, she can only speak one word, *turaab*, meaning 'dust'. Stereotypically, she speaks Arabic instead of Pashto or Dari.

As a result of characters like Dust, post-9/11 Muslims are portrayed in a complex way that is both damaging and uplifting. Nolwenn Mingant states, "In fact, the 9/11 events seem to have had the paradoxical effect of leading Hollywood to become more sophisticated in the way it depicts Arabs and Muslims. Far from being radicalized, the representation became 'more nuanced' and 'more balanced.'"[48] She asserts that complexity gives Muslims a type of power and a voice that they did not have before. Although Dust is meant to empower Muslim women, she also reemphasizes the stereotypical view of Muslim women wearing *burqas*. Davis and Westerfelhaus believe Dust is placed in the right position to disrupt the narrative:

> By situating Dust within the monomyth metanarrative informing the superhero genre, she is afforded a liminal license that permits her entry into American mainstream culture, even though some of her beliefs and practices are perceived by some to be at variance with the culture's core values…In introducing Dust, Marvel managed to make a place within its universe for a Muslimah superheroine, but that place is a small one, far removed from its narrative center.[49]

This may be true for the informed reader, and the creators attempted to push the canon in this direction; however, with both Dust and Iron Man "Extremis" emphasizing the stereotypical portrayals of post-9/11 Muslims, it only reaffirms American perceptions of Muslims.

Contemporary Comics: Ms. Marvel
Twelve years after the debut of Dust, Marvel relaunched *Ms. Marvel* with a Muslim protagonist. Ms. Marvel, as a character, is meant to be the epitome of the female superhero and the face of Marvel. When Marvel's version of Superman, Captain Marvel, died, they decided that Carol Danvers should take his powers in 1977 and become the first Ms. Marvel.[50] The biography at the beginning of the new Carol Danvers comic states that, "When former U.S. Air Force pilot Carol Danvers was caught in the explosion of an alien device…she was transformed into one of the

world's most powerful super-beings. She now uses her abilities to protect her planet and fight for justice as an Avenger. She is Earth's Mightiest Hero…she is…Captain Marvel."[51] The current Ms. Marvel is a Pakistani-American girl named Kamala Khan created by Sana Amanat, G. Willow Wilson, and artist Adrian Alphona. Amanat, an editor at Marvel, is known for creating Miles Morales, the first African American-Latino Spider-Man. G. Willow Wilson, journalist and Muslim convert, writes several comics and graphic novels, such as *Cairo* and *Air*, which expresses her idea that to be Muslim is to be American, a main point in *Ms. Marvel*.

Kamala Khan is a teen who idolizes Carol Danvers. She deals with strict, traditional parents and a religious brother who is constantly praying and wears a *thobe* and a *taqiyah*. Kamala also goes to a *masjid*, where the boys and girls are separated. In the very first page of *Ms. Marvel*, we see Kamala's friend Nakia in a *hijab*; however, our hero has her face pressed next to a BLT trying to smell bacon, which she calls delicious infidel meat.[52] Wilson and Amanat create the same situation as Spider-Man, a young kid trying to deal with strict parents, being bullied at school, and being different. The major difference with Spider-Man and Ms. Marvel is that Kamala's parents are strict because they are Pakistani immigrants, and her friends are constantly bullied because of their religion.

Nakia is told by a girl named Zoe, in *Ms. Marvel* #1, "Your headscarf is so pretty…But I mean nobody **pressured** you to start wearing it, right? Your father or somebody? Nobody's going to, like, **honor kill** you? I'm just **concerned**." Nakia responds, "Actually, my dad wants me to take it off. He thinks it's a **phase**."[53] Zoe responds, "Really? Wow, cultures are so **interesting**." Kamala does not know how to deal with the situation, much like the bacon; she really does not understand if she wants to be a part of white American culture. She even states about Zoe, "she's so nice."[54] In Ms. Marvel #14, her brother explains to Bruno, the white guy who likes her, "My parents expect Kamala to marry someone like us. Because they don't want our heritage to die out. They want their grandkids to feel connected to their religion, their language…They want their daughter to be **proud** of who she is, and to pass that pride down to the next generation."[55]

When she gains her powers, Kamala is surrounded by mist and sees Iron Man, Captain America, and Ms. Marvel, who tell her that she will be given powers. She assumes that this must be the work of Allah, but states to Ms. Marvel that she doesn't know who she is supposed to be.[56] This is a common theme in Wilson's works, which attempts to show that one does not need to fulfill cultural stereotypes or to conform to societal norms. Instead, people should just be themselves. Sana Amanat stated, "It was really not about a Muslim character for the sake of her being Muslim, but trying to find that sort of larger universal connectivity that she can have as a character…And that's really when we knew we had a great story, because it very much had a universal struggle, something that I think people of all ages can still connect to it—about sort of the idea of trying to be yourself and people telling you that you can't be."[57]

The comic sold out as soon as it was released, even reaching the *New York Times* bestsellers list for graphic novels, and it won the 2015 Hugo Award for graphic work. In many issues of *Ms. Marvel*, the fan mail expressed how diverse peoples could relate to Kamala, whether they are immigrants, Muslims, people of color, or none of the above; regardless, it was evident that people had been longing for this comic. This outcry was a response to the prevalent authority and canon being supported by authors. G. Willow Wilson herself states, "And the fan response was phenomenal, above and beyond anything that we had ever expected for this character and this book."[58] *Ms. Marvel* #1 depicted Kamala with the top of the comic being just above her nose, not showing the entirety of her face. Her fans immediately took to the Internet and took photos holding the issue to their face.[59] By doing this, Marvel and the fans expressed that Kamala represented more than just a Muslim girl from Jersey, but instead she was a hero that was relatable to everyone. She is her fans. This act not only humanized Muslims but superhumanized them, making a Muslim teen a mainstream hero.

Wrapped in this discussion are issues of race, gender, and privilege. The stereotypical comic reader is white, male, and ranging in age from 25 to 40.[60] When DC Comics re-released their major comic series, such as *Superman* and *Batman*, they reported that 93% percent of their readers were male and only 2% were younger than 18.[61] With explicit diversity and gender representation in comic characters, authors, and artists, *Ms. Marvel* represents a more progressive, interconnected work that a new generation of fans can relate to. As a result, when comics shift to a more diverse audience, they usually receive a push from the average reader. When Donald Glover tweeted that he might audition for Spider-Man, he was surprised when he received such a negative response based on his race.[62] Most of the detractors couched their racism in issues of canon, and said that to change the ethnicity of the character was to not accurately portray the character, showing what was authentic for them. As a result, Amanat created Miles Morales. These issues were also brought to the forefront by the casting of Michael B. Jordan as an African American Human Torch, one of the Fantastic Four who has pyro-kinesis, and even when *Ms. Marvel* won the Hugo Award, fans cried out that the attempt to be politically correct was discriminating against the white-male majority.[63]

Ms. Marvel, Miles Morales, and the current Thor (who is a woman) allow the minority reader to access power and authority and subvert the stereotype of the young white-male-only reader. These characters provide readers with a more nuanced and diverse concept of hero. Since the release of these characters, female readership has grown with some stats reporting 46% female readers.[64] Kamala has now become a symbol to fight against bigotry. In the spring of 2015 in San Francisco, Pamela Gellar, president of the American Freedom Defense Initiative and host of the "Draw the Prophet" cartoon contest, paid for anti-Muslim ads to be placed on city buses and trains, showing Hitler shaking hands with Muslim leaders. In response someone covered the ads with Ms. Marvel (Fig. 1).[65]

Fig. 1. Ms. Marvel covering anti-Muslim ads, nbcnews.com.

Both being female and Muslim, Sana Amanat and G. Willow Wilson are a driving force for the inclusion of a more informed depiction of diverse characters, especially Muslims. It is their insider perspective that is attractive to a new diverse readership and shifts the dominant portrayal of Muslims that was previously authorized, leading to Ms. Marvel being a new American superhero.

Conclusion

With the popularity and length of tradition, these texts have been uplifted to scriptural status, complete with canons. Understanding the production of the character portrayals in response to context and adherents is similar to the study of theological communities and their sacred texts. Fans of comics often argue continuity, canon, and which tradition is better (or who is the best artist or author). Recently, these arguments have been directed to the "proper" race or religion of a character depicted in films, as if a character is so 'sacred' that she should not be changed. Now, fans and creators are pushing for Muslim heroes that are more than just orientalist depictions and negative stereotypes. Signifying that in 14 years after 9/11, comics have either progressed with a more informed reader, or Muslim authors and artists have been given a voice to express their identity. Examining the scope of comics indicates major trends of how Muslims are portrayed and the pervasiveness of stereotypical representations of Muslims. Scholars of Islam who are unaware of these trends are ignoring a large facet of Islam in America, one that permeates American popular culture and media.

Comic creators and readers mutually define and dictate the directions of a story through their own personal contexts. Fans reading during the Cold War readily accepted villains from the Soviet Union. If the dominant media presentation of Muslims is orientalist, then comic writers and artists will portray them as such, without complaint from the readers. When the paradigm shifted during 9/11, comic canons and origins were rewritten in order to modernize the narratives. This modernization allowed for the stereotypical illustration of Muslim terrorists, with the overall theme of a jingoist narrative creating a clear dichotomy between good and evil, American and Muslim. Marvel attempted to add complexities, such as Scottish author Grant Morrison who created Dust in order to counter the 9/11 paranoia, although it is difficult to determine if this portrayal uplifted Muslim heroes, reinforced stereotypes, or perhaps both simultaneously.

Nearly fourteen years after 9/11, Marvel developed a more complex Muslim hero who does not necessarily fit a stereotypical mold. When Kamala first becomes Ms. Marvel, she actually becomes a tall, blonde Carol Danvers. Sana Amanat states, "It was about identity. It was about the concept of being given all these labels from a very very young age and trying to sort of create your own...your own definition of them."[66] Soon after this first transformation, she realizes she needs to be Kamala and not Carol Danvers. This was a fulfillment of Wilson's question, "Who am I supposed to be?" This is the new spokesperson for Marvel, the hero that takes her name from the company. A high school Muslim girl of Pakistani descent who is all hero and all-American.

Notes

[1] J.J. Darowski, "Reading the Uncanny X-Men: Gender, Race, and the Mutant Metaphor in a Popular Narrative" (PhD Diss., Michigan State University, 2011).

[2] S. Lee (w) and J. Kirby (a). "The Black Panther," *Fantastic Four* 1/52 (July, 1966).

[3] G. Conway (w) and G. Kane (a). "The Night Gwen Stacy Died," *The Amazing Spider-Man* 1/121 (June, 1973).

[4] Lobdell (w) and M. Pacella (a). "The Walking Wounded," *Alpha Flight* 1/106 (March, 1992) and M. Liu (w) and M. Perkins (a). *Astonishing X-Men* 3/51 (June, 2012).

[5] Ande Parks (comic artist and author) in discussion with the author, October 2015.

[6] M.C. Callaway, "Canonical Criticism," in *To Each Its Own Meaning: An Introduction to Biblical Criticisms and Their Application*, eds. S.L. McKenzie and S.R. Haynes (Louisville: Westminster John Knox P, 1999), 142.

[7] M.C. Callaway, "Canonical Criticism," in *To Each Its Own Meaning: An Introduction to Biblical Criticisms and Their Application*, eds. S.L. McKenzie and S.R. Haynes (Louisville: Westminster John Knox P, 1999), 143.

[8] Geoff Klock, *How to Read Superhero Comics and Why* (New York: Continuum International Publishing Group, 2002), 4.

[9] T. Isabella (w) and G. Kane (a), "What if Gwen Stacy Had Lived?" *What if?* 1/24 (Dec., 1980). The cover actually reads, "Whatever you do Spider-Man...Don't Save Her!" as if the break in continuity would cause a catastrophic destruction of the current timeline.

[10] George Ludlam, "The Meteor from Krypton," *The Adventures of Superman* (June 1943).

[11] Found in his edited collection, J.J. Darowski (ed.), *The Ages of the X-Men: Essays on the Children of the Atom in Changing Times* (Jefferson, North Carolina: McFarland & Company, Inc., 2014).

[12] J.J. Darowski, "Reading the Uncanny X-Men: Gender, Race, and the Mutant Metaphor in a Popular Narrative" (PhD Diss., Michigan State University, 2011).

[13] See J. McLaughlin (ed.), *Stan Lee: Conversations* (Oxford: UP of Mississippi, 2007).

[14] Amina Wadud, *Qur'an and Woman: Rereading the Sacred Text from a Woman's Perspective* (Oxford: Oxford UP, 1999), 29.

[15] The best example of how this affects our texts is that the *New X-Men* written by Grant Morrison, where he creates Dust, was not accepted wholly into the canon of X-Men canon by Marvel, and various aspects of the story line were written out.

[16] L. Wein (w) and D. Cockrum (a), "Deadly Genesis," *Giant Size X-Men* 1/1 (May, 1975).

[17] I only note those major characters who lasted longer than a few issues. They do not include the countless "Arab Terrorists" found throughout comics. For more about this, see J. Shaheen, "The Comic Book Arab," *The Link*, 24/5 (1991), 1–11.

[18] Sinbad first appeared in Marvel Comics in 1974: L. Wein (a) and G. Tuska, "The Golden Voyage of Sinbad!" *Worlds Unknown* 1/7 (June, 1974).

[19] Arabian Knight's first appearance is in *Incredible Hulk* #250: B. Mantlo (w) and S. Buscema (a), "Monster!" *Incredible Hulk* 1/250, (August, 1980).

[20] P. David (w) and E. Lupacchino (a), *X-Factor* 1/217 (March, 2011).

[21] J. Davis and R. Westerfelhaus, "Finding a Place for a Muslimah Heroine in the Post-9/11 Marvel Universe: New X-Men's Dust," *Feminist Media Studies*, 13/5, (2013), 800–09: 802–03.

[22] J. Davis and R. Westerfelhaus, "Finding a Place for a Muslimah Heroine in the Post-9/11 Marvel Universe: New X-Men's Dust," *Feminist Media Studies*, 13/5, (2013), 800–09: 802.

[23] Christopher Ingraham, "Anti-Muslim Hate Crimes are Still Five Times More Common Today than before 9/11," *Washington Post* (February 11, 2015). https://www.washingtonpost.com/news/wonk/wp/2015/02/11/anti-muslim-hate-crimes-are-still-five-times-more-common-today-than-before-911/.

[24] J. Dar, "Holy Islamophobia, Batman! Demonization of Muslims and Arabs in Mainstream American Comic Books," in *Teaching Against Islamophobia*, eds. J. L. Kincheloe, S.R. Steinberg, and C.D. Stonebanks (New York: Peter Lang, 2010), 99–110: 105.

[25] J. Shaheen, "The Comic Book Arab," *Link* 24/5 (1991): 1–11, 10.

[26] M. Diapolo, *War, Politics, and Superheroes: Ethics and Propaganda in Comics and Film* (Jefferson, North Carolina and London: McFarland & Company Inc., 2011), 1–3.

[27] G. Morrison, *Supergods: What Masked Vigilantes, Miraculous Mutants, and a Sun God from Smallville Can Teach Us About Being Human* (New York: Spiegel & Grau, 2011), 346–47.

28 S. Lee (w) and J. Kirby (a). "Prisoners of Doctor Doom!" *Fantastic Four* 1/5 (July, 1962).

29 J. Hickman (w) and E. Ribic (a), "Doom Messiah," *Secret Wars* 1/2 (July, 2015) and M. Waid (w) and M. Wieringo (a), "Unthinkable," *Fantastic Four* 3/68 (June, 2003).

30 J.M. Straczynski (w) and J. Romita, Jr. (a). "Stand Tall," *Amazing Spider-Man* 2/36 (Dec., 2001).

31 G. Morrison, *Supergods: What Masked Vigilantes, Miraculous Mutants, and a Sun God from Smallville Can Teach Us About Being Human* (New York: Spiegel & Grau, 2011), 347.

32 M. Millar (w) and B. Hitch (a), "Super-Human," *Ultimates* 1/1 (March, 2002).

33 M. Millar (w) and B. Hitch (a), "Wolf in the Fold," *Ultimates* 2 1/7 (Sept., 2007).

34 G. Morrison, *Supergods: What Masked Vigilantes, Miraculous Mutants, and a Sun God from Smallville Can Teach Us About Being Human* (New York: Spiegel & Grau, 2011), 348.

35 This is not Iron Man's first battle with Muslim extremists. Just two years earlier he fights against a rogue Iraqi sub that plans on bringing nuclear war to the United States. However significant, this pales in comparison with the retcon that directs Tony's entire backstory to blame Muslims for his "condition." For more analysis, see J. Kahan and S. Stewart, *Caped Crusaders 101: Composition Through Comic Books*, 2nd ed. (Jefferson, NC: McFarland, 2010).

36 W. Ellis (w) and A. Granov (a). "Extremis Part I," *Iron Man* 4/1 (Jan., 2005).

37 W. Ellis (w) and A. Granov (a). "Extremis Part V," *Iron Man* 4/5 (March, 2006).

38 *Iron Man* was released in 2008 and grossed $318,298,180. *Iron Man 2* was released on 7 May 2010 and grossed $312,057,433, and *Iron Man 3* was released on May 3, 2013 and grossed $408,992,272. The *Avengers* was released on May 4, 2012 and grossed $623,279,547 and *Avengers: Age of Ultron* was released on 1 May 2015 and grossed $458,991,559. All figures are found at http://www.imdb.com/.

39 G. Morrison, *Supergods: What Masked Vigilantes, Miraculous Mutants, and a Sun God from Smallville Can Teach Us About Being Human* (New York: Spiegel & Grau, 2011), 355.

40 G. Morrison, *Supergods: What Masked Vigilantes, Miraculous Mutants, and a Sun God from Smallville Can Teach Us About Being Human* (New York: Spiegel & Grau, 2011), 355.

41 J. Favreau, interview by *Superherohype*, http://www.superherohype.com/features/97449-jon-favreau-on-the-iron-man-franchise, September 12, 2008.

42 L. Jackson, *Muslims and Islam in U.S. Education: Reconsidering Multiculturalism* (London: Routledge, 2014).

43 E. Garneau and M. Foley, "Grant Morrison's Mutants and the Post-9/11 Culture of Fear," in *The Ages of the X-Men: Essays on the Children of the Atom in Changing Times* (ed.) Joseph J. Darowski (Jefferson, North Carolina: McFarland & Company, Inc., 2014), 178–88: 179.

[44] G. Morrison, *Supergods: What Masked Vigilantes, Miraculous Mutants, and a Sun God from Smallville Can Teach Us About Being Human* (New York: Spiegel & Grau, 2011), 356.

[45] G. Morrison (w) and E. van Sciver (a). "Dust," *New X-Men* 1/133 (Dec., 2002).

[46] E. Garneau and M. Foley, "Grant Morrison's Mutants and the Post-9/11 Culture of Fear," in *The Ages of the X-Men: Essays on the Children of the Atom in Changing Times* (ed.) Joseph J. Darowski (Jefferson, North Carolina: McFarland & Company, Inc., 2014), 178–88: 182–83.

[47] N. DeFilippis (w), C. Weir (w), and R. Green (a). "Choosing Sides 2 of 6: Assembly," *New X-Men* 2/2 (August 2004).

[48] N. Mingant, "Beyond Muezzins and Mujahideen: Middle-Eastern Voices in Post-9/11 Hollywood Movies," in *Muslims and American Popular Culture* vol. 1 (eds.), I. Omidvar and A.R. Richards (Santa Barbara: Praeger, 2014), 167–94: 168.

[49] J. Davis and R. Westerfelhaus, "Finding a Place for a Muslimah Heroine in the Post-9/11 Marvel Universe: New X-Men's Dust," *Feminist Media Studies*, 13/5, (2013), 800–09: 807.

[50] G. Conway (w) and J. Buscema (a), "This Woman, This Warrior!" *Ms. Marvel* 1/1 (Jan., 1977).

[51] K.S. DeConnick (w) and D. Lopez (a), "A Christmas Carol: Part One of Two," *Captain Marvel* 8/10 (Feb., 2015).

[52] G.W. Wilson (w) and A. Alphona (a), "Meta Morphosis," *Ms. Marvel* 3/1 (April, 2014).

[53] G.W. Wilson (w) and A. Alphona (a), "Meta Morphosis," *Ms. Marvel* 3/1 (April, 2014).

[54] G.W. Wilson (w) and A. Alphona (a), "Meta Morphosis," *Ms. Marvel* 3/1 (April, 2014).

[55] G.W. Wilson (w) and T. Miyazawa (a), "Crushed: Part Two of Three," *Ms. Marvel* 3/14 (April, 2015).

[56] G.W. Wilson (w) and A. Alphona (a), "Meta Morphosis," *Ms. Marvel* 3/1 (April, 2014).

[57] K. Couric, "The Rise of the Female Superhero," *Yahoo*, (August 12, 2015), https://www.yahoo.com/katiecouric/rise-of-the-female-superhero-ever-since-superman-126459307033.html.

[58] K. Couric, "The Rise of the Female Superhero," *Yahoo*, (August 12, 2015), https://www.yahoo.com/katiecouric/rise-of-the-female-superhero-ever-since-superman-126459307033.html.

[59] A good example is from Barbara Holm's review of the first issue: Barbara Holm, "Ms. Marvel #1 Review," *Huffington Post* (February 19, 2014), http://www.huffingtonpost.com/barbara-holm/ms-marvel-1-review_b_4816852.html.

[60] Neil Shyminsky, 2006. "Mutant Readers, Reading Mutants: Appropriation, Assimilation, and the X-Men," *International Journal of Comic Art*, Fall, 8, no. 2: 387–405 (2006), 389.

[61] Lana Hudson, "DC Comics Survey Reports 'New 52' Readership 93% Male, Only 5% New Readers [Updated]," *Comics Alliance* (February 10, 2012), http://comics alliance.com/dc-comics-readers-survey-reports-new-52-readership-93-male/.

[62] E. Dodds, "There are so Many Reasons Donald Glover Should be the Next Spider-Man," *Time*, http://time.com/3703175/donald-glover-next-spider-man/. This issue is also evident in the response to Idris Elba being cast as Heimdall in "Thor" or even the rumor that he will be the next James Bond.

[63] Josh Rottenberg, "'Fantastic Four's' Message for Comic Fans Who Hate New Cast," *La Times* (June 3, 2015), http://www.latimes.com/entertainment/herocomplex/la-et-hc-josh-trank-simon-kinberg-fantastic-four-casting-controversy-story.html and Andrew Wheeler, "'Ms. Marvel' Wins at Hugo Award Dogged by Political Manipulations," *Comics Alliance* (August 24, 2015), http://comics alliance.com/hugo-awards-2015-ms-marvel/.

[64] Noah Berlatsky, "The Female Thor and the Female Comic-Book Reader," *The Atlantic* (July 21, 2014), http://www.theatlantic.com/entertainment/archive/2014/07/just-how-many-women-read-comic-books/374736/.

[65] F. Kai-Hwa Wang, "Comic Heroine Ms. Marvel Saves San Francisco From Anti-Islam Ads," *NBC News*, (January 27, 2015). http://www.nbcnews.com/news/asian-america/comic-heroine-ms-marvel-saves-san-francisco-anti-islam-ads-n294751.

[66] Sana Amanat, interview by Ta-Nehisi Coates, "What if Captain America were Muslim and Female/New York Ideas 2015," *AtlanticLive* (May 21, 2015), https://www.youtube.com/watch?v=2Y1ihwPplL4.

DISCUSSION QUESTIONS

1. Pumphrey devotes a section to identifying the central concerns of canonical theory. According to Pumphrey, what is a canon, who defines it, and what are the main factors in how canons are determined?

2. Pumphrey notes that a superhero's backstory (or "retcon") is often changed in response to important historical events, offering Iron Man as an example. How did Iron Man's backstory change after 9/11? Do you see any downside to changing the details of a superhero's background?

3. List some of the ways in which representations of Muslim women (Muslimahs) in the years immediately following 9/11 both perpetuated Islamophobic stereotypes and challenged them.

4. Pumphrey suggests that the inclusion of characters such as Kamala Kahn, the most recent incarnation of Ms. Marvel, has been instrumental in both reshaping the demographics of comic-book readers and the response to post-9/11 Islamophobia. What kinds of evidence does he offer?

5. Pumphrey begins his conclusion by remarking, "With the popularity and length of tradition, these texts [comics featuring superheroes] have been uplifted to scriptural status, complete with canons" (p. 80). What do you think he means? Does the claim seem justified by the argument Pumphrey presents?

E. "FROZEN JET SET: REFRIGERATORS, MEDIA TECHNOLOGY, AND POSTWAR TRANSPORTATION," PAUL GANSKY

This 2015 article from The Journal of Popular Culture *illustrates how daily objects and practices are part of popular culture. Focusing on the marketing of refrigerators following World War II, Paul Gansky* takes on a central debate in the study of pop culture: to what extent the meaning and value of pop culture is controlled by advertisers and manufacturers rather than consumers. Gansky argues "that the power to define a technology is much more contested" than is often thought (p. 88). As you read this article, consider how Gansky's research challenges assumptions that you might have about household appliances and pop culture.*

Marketed to consumers since the late 1910s, and technologically established by the 1930s, it seems unlikely that the refrigerator's cultural meanings would undergo any substantial alterations in the post-World War II period. Despite the Great Depression, refrigerators were installed in 50% of American households by 1940 (Friedberg 44–45). World War II rationing of the devices did not stop nearly 85% of homes from gaining a unit by 1944 (Covert 315–42), with another 20 million refrigerators sold by 1949 (May 166). Throughout these periods, research on the appliance has argued that strategies for inserting the refrigerator into domestic life were largely unvaried. In print advertisements and sponsored articles, the appliance served as an emancipator of housewives from the drudgery of preserving and preparing food (Cowan 119, 128; Friedberg 18–49; Nickles 583–84). On the television program *Queen for a Day* (1956–1964), suburban mothers competed for refrigerators stocked with a month's worth of meals by divulging their emotional and financial woes. Accordingly, in his 1959 Kitchen Debate with Soviet Premier Nikita Khrushchev, Vice President Richard Nixon argued that the fridge, part of a technologically superior American lifestyle, would stimulate gender equality worldwide by freeing women from the kitchen (May 16–20). Garlanded in labor-saving rhetoric, the refrigerator on a practical level nonetheless guaranteed women's continued involvement with household duties. Its ubiquitous presence in kitchens also ensured that their work was rendered invisible (Oldenziel and Zachmann 6).

---

* Paul Gansky is a PhD candidate at the University of Texas, Austin. He investigates health, hygiene, and postwar American domesticity.

In the postwar era, until sales plateaued around 1970, the appliance's cultural values underwent significant changes, however, with ramifications that have remained unexplored. Refrigerators were constructed in explicit relation to television, an emergent medium sold in this era as collapsing time and distance, turning viewers into globetrotters. Print advertisements, the General Motors promotional film *Out of This World* (1964), and Disney's film *A Tour of the West* (1955) similarly framed refrigerators as televisual vessels to distant and unexplored geographies. Wondrous enclosures that turned female consumers into passive sightseers, refrigerators also implicitly affirmed that women would be monitored by domestic technology. Materially, refrigerators took on the physical characteristics of television, with portable units designed like TVs—presaging contemporary forays into amalgamating media and appliances (Spigel, "Designing" 404–05).

Looking into the appliance's postwar tenure as an entertainment medium allows for an unprecedented glance into how advertisers and manufacturers competed with consumers over the refrigerator's position in domesticity. I argue that, as TV reinforced "media" as synonymous with pleasure, leisure and social progress, and profoundly restructured definitions of household spaces and activities, manufacturers seized the chance to sever the refrigerator from its former connections to labor. Its identity newly flexible, the appliance now generated its own visual space onto which women's desires could be projected and fulfilled. The device's detour into televisuality consequently suggests that cultural research into the evolution of technologies must consider objects as interrelated, their meanings fluidly shared and overlapping. Concentrating upon the postwar refrigerator particularly reveals how a budding form like television can generate innovation around a preexisting, discursively stable, and ostensibly unrelated object.

This study is further unlike previous appliance scholarship, in which advertising and corporate-level decisions are seen as effectively establishing and rearticulating the devices in popular culture (Grahame 285–89). I argue that the power to define a technology is much more contested. The postwar refrigerator provides a perspective into how fantastical directions in marketing and engineering did not succeed in delineating the appliance as something other than a kitchen aid. Newspaper reports and government hearings in the 1950s and 1960s about consumer interactions with the refrigerator provided a different take on its actual daily use. Influencing the Sears and Roebuck training film *Freeze-In* (1969), the device was literally considered a coffin due to design flaws, as well as pervasive disparities in the gendered division of domestic labor. In this case, acknowledging failures is integral to understanding how cultural discourses around a popular object's identity are bounded, controlled, and ultimately reinforced.

A Household of New Boundaries

Seeds for the refrigerator's relationship with television have their roots in marketing rhetoric from the final years of World War II. Appliance production resumed after federal rationing ceased over the materials necessary to make refrigerators (Cohen 136–37). Accordingly, an increased amount of advertising transmogrified the device into an entity that made the suburban household its own world. In their 1944–1945 layouts inside the covers of *Life* and *The Saturday Evening Post*, the Nash-Kelvinator Corporation termed its refrigerators "magic compartments." These units carried with them an expanded cultural geography expressed in edible terms. Overflowing with steaks, pheasant, and "all the green things our garden will grow," fridges and freezers also promised "luxurious things like ice cream, asparagus, and brook trout" ("Sunday"). There was so much food of such a variety, the ads suggested, that a family would never need to leave their picket-fenced "kingdom" ("We'll Live"). Every personally-owned appliance was a ceaseless well of vitality, making the entire house a self-sustaining familial and technological node.

Interestingly enough, such refrigerator advertisements coincided with early marketing for the television set. During this period, the spaces exhibited in an unbroken procession on television were defined as containing the exterior world within the private interiors of the home (Sconce 127–29). In the process, advertisers, social commentators, and TV industry leaders opined that viewers, sitting in the discrete intimacy of their living rooms and dens, would be privy to a flowing, hyper-real world of global imagery (Spigel, *Make Room* 14–15). As TV moved into the American household, it produced its own living room where it operated as the new focal point. As this space became a site of viewership rather than conversation or creation, TV edged out or subsumed items that previously took up space and attention in the family room, such as the fireplace, the grand piano, or the radio (Spigel, *Make Room* 38–39). Images abounded of an entranced family gathered around their new electronic guest, implying television's ability to bring the nuclear unit closer together.

In the kitchen, similar imagery had circulated around the refrigerator since at least the early 1920s, suggesting the appliance's potential influence upon television. As Roland Marchand states, a repeated visual trope featured a wife, her children, and less frequently her husband, encircling a brand new refrigerator. This near-religious "icon" elicited reverence for its size, design, and technological capability to preserve perishable food (269–71). While variations on this imagery continued into the 1950s, Sandy Isenstadt argues that a majority of magazine advertisements moved away from touting the fridge's mechanical engineering (311). Instead, they approximated architectural discourses for continuous living spaces and dissolved boundaries between inside and outside. Refrigerator design in the postwar era was therefore no longer self-referential, building only upon the styles of previous models (Nickles 599, 609; Smith 380, 379).

Advertisers now classified refrigerators as an immersive window that brought foods from around the world into a single, controllable place within the house. For instance, in 1953, the fridge manufacturer Bendix championed their design, "The Refrigerator Door Built Like a Big Bay Window," with a wide rather than shallow design that allowed owners to "put more foods in sight" (Isenstadt 318). Slightly less frequently, advertisements actually fused the appliance to human sight. The Philco Corporation, manufacturer of radio and television sets, and sponsor of the distinguished live anthology drama television series, *The Philco Playhouse* (1948–1955), tried such a combination in their 1950 *Good Housekeeping* ad, "All the things a woman has always wanted." The layout partially superimposes a refrigerator over a housewife's elated face. Its "11 cubic feet" of interior space and open door approximate the "super size" scope of her gaze, not so subtly making the housewife half of a mechanical, readymade servant (179).

As a result, the fridge resembled a primarily visual innovation, holding a landscape that could be reached instantly. In fact, as Philco and Bendix's ad copy exemplifies, postwar consumers were encouraged to think of the appliance as fully encompassing nature. By discursively collapsing the refrigerator into something as thin, clear, and apparently simple as a window, this imaginative rearticulation of the American "cold chain" rendered invisible the human and mechanical labor that harvested, prepared, and shipped refrigerated foods. It also denied the time and energy housewives spent making this panoply of chilled ingredients into meals. In their place, visions of an instantaneous "garden in the machine" bloomed, where food seemed to sprout from the inside of the appliance (Isenstadt 319).

Refrigerator ad campaigns not only participated in an architectural climate that called for sheets of glass and fewer walls, as Isenstadt believes. Defining the appliance as a window also bore a strong resemblance to TV rhetoric. Spigel notes that television sets in women's home magazines appeared near "panoramic window views." Or they projected and were framed by natural or urban vistas. Analogous to the sights seen through the refrigerator, the landscapes suggested the clarity and scope that TV could offer (*Make Room* 102–07). The symbolism, akin to the bay window refrigerator, neatly elided television's black box complexity. It domesticated the device, which, like refrigerators and many other household innovations in the postwar era, straddled the line between ease of use and mechanical incomprehensibility (Parks 259–61).

Given these discursive similarities between technologies, the arrival of TV offered a fresh way for the fridge to be sold as a pleasurable rather than functional object. Harnessing the exterior world for private domestic benefit, and visually streaming discrete units of food in advertisements, the appliance became a screen, and its users became viewers.[1] Turned into a site of projection as well as consumption by marketing, the device literalized the sense of spatial collapse and immediacy associated with TV. Citizens actually consumed the landscapes contained within the appliance, rather than simply seeing them by way of TV's electronic window. As a result, the refrigerator evidences the extent to which postwar advertisers and manufacturers of domesticity were invested in mediatizing the household, testing the viability of turning unlikely objects like the fridge into sites of spectatorship. Most major refrigerator outfits such as Nash-Kelvinator, Bendix, Philco, and General Motors were also television manufacturers or sponsors. Constructed similarities between technologies thereby suggest that companies were interested in converging the experience of using these devices in consumers' minds, profitably housing both the kitchen and the living room under the same corporate stamp.

From America to the Universe

Honing its connotations with sight to a greater degree, media beyond print publications concentrated on defining the refrigerator as a televisual outlet for travel. Nowhere were these sentiments more apparent than in General Motors' promotional film *Out of This World* (1964), produced for its hugely popular Futurama ride at the 1964 New York World's Fair. Parent company of Frigidaire, and largest TV sponsor in 1950, GM used refrigerators in the ride and the movie to illustrate their global dominance technologically, creating a better way of life for viewers (Boddy 262). The film presented Futurama exhibits where lasers mowed down forests, and satellites and submarine trains combed outer space and ocean depths for resources, highlighting improvements in transportation. Yet the civilizing genius of General Motors and Frigidaire was couched in products that roughly twenty-nine million visitors could conceivably buy after seeing the film or riding Futurama. So the company's loftier advancements were channeled into appliances in GM's "Kitchen of the Future," particularly the company's refrigerators, seen as vessels to exotic new landscapes. The fridge consequently ensured consumers' visual participation in postwar modernity. A voyage would take place whenever they opened the appliance, which the film suggested was akin to witnessing world events through television. Previous emphasis on viewing a natural landscape through a refrigerated window was replaced by a theme of mediated, global interaction.

GM's film and its appliance therefore placed American domesticity at the heart of geographic, technological, and economic control. The corporation's movie evoked the centralization of viewers performed by television. TV was defined as a shared activity of gazing upon the world that nonetheless addressed and entertained each viewer individually (Spigel, *Make Room* 22). *Out of This World* correspondingly begins by encouraging audiences, "Forget the world around you. Forget the *people* around you. You are entering Futurama, alone with your own thoughts." Onscreen, a blond middle-class housewife, serving as a proxy for GM's valuable female customer base, reclines in one of Futurama's seats on the ride's moving tram. Framing the ride as the realm of her thoughts, the film suggests that GM can foresee, satisfy, and supervise any woman's individual dreams.

Out of This World's personalized form of address is also suggestive of the tremendous isolation of suburban women (May 186). Stationed aside from relatives and friends in sprawling new housing developments, and working largely within the house, wives relied tenuously upon their husbands and children for emotional and moral support, as well as "fun, excitement, and diversion" (184). Within this prevailing dominion of domestic containment, GM's film ameliorated alienation in a novel way. Their appliances do not simply provide a respite from a family's needs, ease women's workload, or engender togetherness. They satisfy dreams of personal getaways. Throughout the film there is not a single mention of labor or family occurring around the fridge. Onscreen the appliance is always already stocked with prepared food in the background, seen as an afterthought to the refrigerator's new identity as a woman's own vehicle.

To prove to housewives that refrigerators specifically resemble televisions as conduits for journeying internationally, GM first frames its appliances in *Out of This World* as moveable. Early in the film, *Out of This World* presents a refrigerated cart to the housewife for "wheeling into a game room, or out onto a patio, perfect for keeping foods and drinks cool for informal entertaining." The new portability of this fridge, available in any room of the house, materially reflects the era's preoccupation with the televisual privileges of an immediate, interconnected world, the household a zone of electronic movement between sites of leisure. Fortifying the relationship between technologies onscreen, the fridge is wheeled right next to a television set, their dimensions and boxy shape the same, while the voiceover intones that the cart is a new site around which entertainment is built.

The cart prepares audiences for the refrigerator's ability to do more than create enjoyable diversions throughout the home. *Out of This World* suggests that American women can fluidly inhabit a variety of cultures through Frigidaires. Whenever the housewife gazes across the interior expanse of a fridge, the filmmakers fade to kitchens in Italy, the "exotic" East, the "Orient," and Spain. As the cart's door swings wide, for example, the homemaker's face superimposes over its interior. She is replaced by a shot of the Italian kitchen, incorporating owner, commodity, and foreign nation in a seemingly unbroken sweep. Each fade happens in time to the opening of the refrigerator door, giving it a unique agency over the visuals. Blurring the distinction between the film's construction and the appliance's hardware, *Out of This World* suggests that it is the device putting users across disparate spaces and timeframes. The ease with which the refrigerator literally carries the housewife through the world is remarkably evocative of the visual suturing of disparate spaces made by television.

Using the appliance to teleport effortlessly between distant locations presages an early broadcast, *Our World* (1967), designed to showcase TV as a medium of transportation. The show employed the "electronic wizardry" of satellite television to present what Lisa Parks calls a sanguine "Western fantasy" of "global presence"

("Our World" 74–75). Viewers were explicitly told that they would be turned into omniscient travelers, participating in onscreen worlds rather than viewing them. Airing across twenty-four nations and including scenes from fourteen participating countries, the satellite broadcast beamed images of landlines, microwave links, studios, ground stations, control rooms and especially video cameras. These shots acquainted viewers with the awesome apparatus underwriting the show's imagery, and interconnecting nations to place viewers in spaces beyond the living room (78, 82–84). At the same time, these shots were unaccompanied by explanation, presenting television as a technology that could not be parsed, but only experienced.

In *Out of This World*, the recondite refrigerator takes on the role of the television system. In this way, the filmmakers imbue the kitchen appliance with a transcendent mediated aura. Part of the Kitchen of the Future, it is framed as a terrifically advanced piece of technology. Sharing space with fictitious vehicles like submarine trains, the film also suggests that the appliance is beyond the comprehension of many postwar citizens, women especially. Repeatedly surprising her, the Frigidaire teleports the housewife between locations before she is even fully aware of a shift. "Oh! It happened again!" she exclaims upon arriving in the Asian-themed kitchen, her face a mixture of curiosity and startled admiration as she steps away to reconsider the refrigerator she just touched. Consequently, the supernatural appliance evokes the power of the corporate media conglomerates like GM to materially achieve popular American daydreams of travel and global connection. Women's capacity to actualize their own longings, or even direct their basic movements, is disavowed.

Despite the fridge's ability to leapfrog nations and cultures, its transfer of users is constructed as gently unmooring. It integrates different dimensions and cultures only up to a point. *Out of This World* again echoes *Our World* in this regard, which Parks remarks operated "not as a sphere of cultural exchange but rather as a return to the Western self" (77). Spearheaded by the BBC in London, *Our World* used its electronic architecture and the images it gathered as evidence of Western intellectual, industrial dominance. Segments involving The Beatles recording "All You Need Is Love," for instance, filled the vacuum of an unseen, undeveloped Third World (76, 78–79, 81).

Similarly, no matter where *Out of This World* lands via the refrigerator, natives of Spain, Italy, or the Far East remain invisible. Potentially disruptive interactions are avoided. A humble blonde housewife has the kitchen and the whole world to herself. Viewers are encouraged to attribute her privilege to the enduring authority of GM. For instance, the sophisticated mechanization of the corporation's refrigerators is highlighted in comparison to each foreign culture's retrograde traditionalism— marked by a golden statue of Buddha, adobe walls, and palm fronds. Despite the dizzying ethnic environments onscreen, the film therefore assures its presumably white viewers that touring a new congregation of nationalities will not erase their identities. As long as they buy the corporation's appliances, American citizenry will remain easily demarcated and clearly in control.

The refrigerator consequently operates similar to the media infrastructure of *Our World*, fixing the US as the axis of modernity, and the embodiment of women's fantasies. In the Oriental kitchen segment, for example, the housewife pantomimes bowing to a painstakingly trimmed Japanese bonsai, yet her awe remains reserved for the Frigidaire, at dead center in the film's frame. "Oh, now *there's* something I like!" she exclaims, dashing over to open and admire the unit's recessed storage capabilities, as well as its decidedly stars-and-stripes bill of fare: canned hot dogs, pickles, and soda. As the housewife enthuses, the fridge is a private space apart, a traveling enclosure where the nation and its form of domesticity is nonetheless always available—even if the appliance is located overseas. So although GM's film initially suggests that the refrigerator can take its female users to any culture, it also implies American culture and especially American domesticity are ultimately the spheres housewives desire to dwell within.

Constructing the appliance as a televisual vessel therefore allowed General Motors, and refrigerator manufacturers in general, a new latitude to address female domestic isolation and to prescriptively solve it through the purchase of their Frigidaires. The refrigerated cart notwithstanding, overtures toward actually making the appliance a vehicle largely remained discursive, however. This is not to say that fabricating a relationship with television should simply be treated as an imaginative flourish on the part of GM. Supporting an illusion of women escaping the house, *Out of This World*'s trope of a televised refrigerator allowed the corporation to apply an entertaining patina to an implicit, conservative wish to surveil female consumers anywhere. Combining their refrigerators with a visual media technology lauded for its eye onto the world (Sconce 128), and a popular related theme of travel, GM moved to normalize itself and its products as a pervasive presence outside the household.

Cinema, Refrigerators, and Travel

Advances in television, perhaps more than any other media technology, provoked the discursive reinvention of refrigerators during the postwar period. Its identity was particularly malleable in this era; however, the appliance was open to fertilization with other technologies. New film innovations were also occasionally joined to the kitchen device under a banner of expanded transportation, though with a markedly diminished emphasis on female consumers. In collaboration with Walt Disney, the refrigerator manufacturer Kelvinator sold its product as a suggestively cinematic vehicle for encountering the marvels of American landscapes. The opening of Disneyland in July 1955 featured a novel panoramic screen projection system called Circarama, sponsored by the American Motors Corporation, parent company of Kelvinator refrigerators. Inside the theater's entrance, visitors traversed an immense circular foyer showcasing AMC's newest automobiles. The cars were matched by the Foodarama, Kelvinator's model fridge. Defined by placards as a gargantuan collection of seven climates, the appliance was designed to accommodate everything from beef to unchilled bananas (Sampson).

Foodarama's expanded, delicately calibrated, inner space was considered coterminous by Kelvinator and Disney with the broadened horizons available to the nation's moviegoers, courtesy of the entertainment empire's striking evolutions in cinematic technology. The arrangement of the Circarama theater's screens in a circle mirrored the round foyer viewers had just walked through—an attempt to make Disney's film indistinguishable from the palpable world and the products therein (Sampson). To make the connection even more overt in visitor's minds, Circarama's main feature, *A Tour of the West*, began with Kodachrome slides of Foodarama units and sedans that flashed in increments across the theater's eleven screens, blurring appliances with vehicles. The products' movement toward the edges of the display tutored viewers' sight in the incredibly widescreen range of vision offered within Disney's setup.

This also meant that the refrigerator, like the automobile, was enlarged beyond its actual size and literally overlaid onto vast panoramic shots of the American West. The space filled onscreen by the banana bin or meat compartment would gradually be given over to an image of a mythic "last frontier" like the Grand Canyon, Monument Valley, or modern-day Los Angeles. Circarama viewers were sensitized to the appliance's ability to contain landscapes and be a vessel through those scenes. The fridge visually stood in for the image-capturing power of Disney's unseen multi-camera, multiprojector arrangement. Like a wardrobe or a desk, the Foodarama, with its bananas neatly separated from its steaks in customized drawers, was also a space of classification and categorization. By superimposing a personal portal for consumption, such as the fridge over sublimely untamed landmarks, Circarama's visitors were encouraged to see the appliance as ordering United States geography. In Disneyland, then, the refrigerator as an object and a cinematic image became synonymous with the way Americans would visualize, travel, and ultimately claim a postwar nation as it unfurled around them.

Lost in the Refrigerator

Given the high-profile stature of GM and Disney's films, and the related, pervasive print advertising in the postwar era, it seems odd that conceptions of the refrigerator as an entertainment medium did not take hold. Why? Though Peter Grahame states that semiotic and symbolic changes in advertising largely dictate the terms upon which the refrigerator is defined (291), I argue that constructing any pop cultural object's identity is a process that needs discursive changes to be made materially manifest, thus altering its potential uses. Redefinition also requires consumer participation. In this case, as the refrigerator was interpolated as a televisual vehicle, its new distinctiveness was matched by a brief but widespread national hysteria. This revealed the appliance not as a zone of spatiotemporal simultaneity, or a window onto another landscape, but as a cavity that "does not allow enough aid to enter to support life," an inescapable coffin (*Hearing* 27).

Although there had been sporadic reports of suffocation inside wooden iceboxes occurring during the 1920s and 1930s, in the late 1940s through the 1960s, new media began actively charting the "fridge scare." It coalesced around the deaths of some 309 children, usually three to five years old, within home refrigerators and freezers ("No-Latch"). Stories of mortality ranged across rural, suburban, and urban locations, from Crawfordville, Arkansas to Queens, New York, a bleak reminder that nearly 95 percent of homes were outfitted with these cold white cubes ("Nine Children"; "Queens Boy"). The furor quickly led to three Congressional hearings from 1954 to 1956, spawning the creation of a bill requiring "Safety Devices on Household Refrigerators."

As statements during a 1954 Senate hearing before a subcommittee on Interstate and Foreign Commerce emphasized, deaths were usually attributed to abandoned iceboxes, freezers, and refrigerators, left in vacant apartments, yards, and cellars, places considered attractive to children for hiding or playing (35). These appliances, equipped with latching mechanisms that sealed the door tightly to pressurize and efficiently cool air, could not be opened from the inside.[2] At the same time, as "Hidden Danger!" a National Safety Council poster warned, the highly insulated construction of the appliance kept victims from being heard or seen, a reminder that refrigerators were not actually transparent screens (35). In the poster's striking image, a boy, a girl, and their dog peer inquisitively into a decrepit unit, its door hanging slightly ajar, tempting the youngsters to investigate. "Hidden Danger!" warps the alluring presentations seen in *Out of This World*, at Circarama, or common advertising imagery which portrayed children gazing into the wide-open, fully-stocked window of a refrigerator, such as the 1955 layout in *Home and Garden* for Kelvinator's Foodarama (12). The National Safety Council poster grimly revealed that the same technology that helped to feed and even entertain the family could also destroy it, and illustrated that not all refrigerators were benignly under the command of housewives.

Perilous opportunities to explore the insides of a fridge were plentiful. As Paul B. Reed, director of Education for the Refrigeration Service Engineers Society (RSES), stated in the 1954 hearing, of the 50 million refrigerated appliances in use in the US, nearly 3 million per year were discarded (35). As a result, the nation's media networks were marshaled to broadcast a significant amount of public service announcements created by the National Safety Council and the National Electrical Manufacturers Association. In 1953 and 1954 alone, the government warned citizens via radio and television spots, layouts in 2,000 different newspapers and magazines, publicity on retail floors, 400,000 safety stickers, and some 26,000 posters hung up in schools, grocery stores, and other public sites (55). RSES also composed an educational film entitled *Don't Leave a Deathtrap*, shown to fire and police departments and parent teacher organizations, which reiterated the soundproof, airless danger refrigerators posed (27). In light of these campaigns, at least a few of the viewers of *Out of This World* in 1964 must have regarded GM's time-and-space traveling Frigidaire with a shade of skepticism.

Certain deaths did escape comment during the Congressional hearings and public exposure of the fridge scare. In 1954, for example, *The Washington Post* reported that a 59-year-old farmwife, Mrs. Clyde Phetteplace, committed suicide by climbing into a refrigerator, a move her husband could apparently not explain (5). While similar acts were not common, or at least frequently accounted for, they did suggest a deep dissatisfaction with postwar existence on the part of many housewives. Their ennui was refracted onto the items in their tailored "dream kitchens" where they were to happily work as "skillful domestic servants" (Hayden 17). Many of them refused to negotiate their repressive surroundings by demanding an extravagant design for their appliances, as Shelley Nickles argues (587), or happily accept these devices as proof of their husbands' financial strength and stability (May 166–67). Rather, women such as filmmaker Gunvor Nelson in the film *Schmeerguntz* (1965) graphically illustrated the disgusting, monotonous drudgery that actually took place around the appliances designed to elevate her life. Additionally, in 1963, as two major texts, Betty Friedan's *The Feminine Mystique* and Mary McCarthy's *The Group*, brought exponentially greater scrutiny toward gender inequality within the home, prominent poet Sylvia Plath committed suicide in her London apartment. Sealing her kitchen with wet clothes and towels, she turned on the gas, and placed her head in the oven—a stark emblem of the suffocation of female identity and intelligence in the confines of the kitchen (Kirk 104).

Housewives like Phetteplace or Plath were not alone in sensing that refrigerators, among other household appliances, did not create a global community of leisure and travel, but quite literally led owners nowhere, severed from friends, family, and their own identities. By the late 1960s, manufacturers and department stores were, according to their private media records, willing to agree. A mere five years after *Out of This World*, the "internal training" film, *Freeze-In* (1969), depicts a dead young woman carried along by pallbearers atop a freezer serving as her casket. Briefly coming to life, she cries bitterly about her freezer, "It's just a cold, dark hole! Inconvenient and nothing but a coffin!" In its ensuing runtime, this film illustrates the combined efforts of Coldspot, maker of refrigerators and freezers, and Sears Roebuck and Co. to combat any detrimental connotations their products have to oblivion, death, or female alienation.

Produced by the Calvin Corporation for Sears and Coldspot, *Freeze-In* tapped Arte Johnson, Judy Carne, and Gary Owens, three stars from *Rowan and Martin's Laugh-In* (1968–1973), a highly popular, sexually and politically edgy variety TV show, to teach salesmen how these appliances could be peddled to female consumers. Coldspot products were given a makeover, blasted with red paint and chrome, emphasizing design rather than comparisons to media technologies as a locus for consumer satisfaction. Replete with a throbbing psychedelic soundtrack and plenty of go-go dancing, the training film suggested that Coldspots could strike a libidinal spark. Hearing moaning and squealing coming from a Coldspot "Time-Bank," Carne opens its lid to find Johnson covered in lipstick kisses, glasses askew. His blissful excuse: "You gotta keep moving in here to keep warm." Rather than a death trap, or a site of delirious private tourism, the freezer and refrigerator registered as loveseats, perfect for a burgeoning set of consumers more likely to "swing" than wear sober skirts and gray flannel suits.

The training film significantly denies that the refrigerator might also serve as a site for female sexuality to be explored. Carne's character is framed as a chaste waif looking for a mechanical aid to keep her hungry husband fed; she is a mini-skirted update on the ideal housewife whose personal fantasies rotate solely around self-less service. Her spouse, on the other hand, finds a hidden, bikini-clad nymphet whenever he opens the fridge, a clear reversal of his entombed wife. The gimmick illustrates that even though appliances may be implicated in the work women do for their husbands, the refrigerator, a device of disillusionment, can still serve as a space for wishful projection and instant gratification for other family members. Unlike advertisements such as *Out of This World*, which targeted women, this film appeals to its intended audience of male retailers to sell Coldspots to maintain a certain set of subservient gender roles in the home.

Further attempting to revise gloomy conceptions of refrigerators, without actually changing the division of labor around the device, *Freeze-In* refrained from describing a televisual vehicle that female customers could travel through. The Coldspot Time-Bank is classified for housewives as a personal "filing system," its insides ruled by "findability, accessibility, flexibility, and visibility." These four tenets mean that women will always know where things, are since they can adjust shelves to see and retrieve everything in the Time-Bank easily. "Visibility" in this film operated quite unlike the sense of sight defined by the "bay window" advertisements like those of Bendix, opening onto pastoral vistas. Nor was the fridge cast as an entertainment center. *Freeze-In* used vision to simply underline the ease of navigability within a Coldspot. As a result, the film implied that this company's models could not possibly overwhelm or dismay housewives.

In spite of the pervasive free-love innuendos, and the construction of spatially regimented interiors, Coldspot, Sears, and *Laugh-In* were ultimately unable to overcome a sense of fridges and freezers as yawning voids that entrapped and oppressed consumers. *Freeze-In* is the rare kind of advertising instance that fails to answer its own revelation of product drawbacks. A sketch near the end of the film, involving Johnson and Carne as husband and wife, subversively suggests that they are engulfed in a limitless abyss populated by subpar food and tense relationships. The scenario presents them at a kitchen table, crouched behind newspapers. Carne whispers to the audience that her husband is "going to be so proud of me when he finds I've stored a year's supply of salami sandwiches in my new Time-Bank." Cut to Johnson, who sneers, "If she serves me another salami sandwich today, I'll...(he growls)...and maybe something else too." Johnson's reaction reveals that the organization and efficiency of refrigerated food does not ensure quality or satisfaction. In fact, the Time-Bank represents the sinister outcome of technological convenience, birthing a domestic existence bereft of any freshness or variety. Perhaps even more alarming, *Freeze-In* suggests that such lack of diversity might instigate not only detachment and aloofness in couples, but abuse, an insinuation the film never counters.

Conclusion

Sears' and Coldspot's strained effort with *Laugh-In* to rescue the identities of their kitchen appliance serves as an important marker. From the final stages of World War II in 1945 to *Freeze-In*'s release in 1969, popular media conceptions of the refrigerator's role in Americans' lives changed drastically. For advertisers and manufacturers, generating comparisons to the new, culturally disruptive television placed the refrigerator in a position to profitably become a part of a household now defined by media technology and consumption. The refrigerator as a screen also suggested the extent to which postwar technological modernity as a whole rotated on a thesis of increased visuality. In this way, it is of paramount importance that future cultural research, working with popular media representations, treat objects like the fridge as part of a permeable, mutually influential, technological ecology. Speaking to the very real proximity of these devices, this approach acknowledges the strategies of many companies to sell not a single item, but an entire space and way of life.

It is additionally necessary for such scholarship, especially scholarship about domestic devices and the postwar period, to expand its scope far beyond the realms of advertising. Although actual responses from consumers and users remain largely undocumented, even a brief consideration of newspaper and government publications suggests that refrigerators were met in the 1950s and '60s with apprehension and outright despair rather than enthusiasm. Such sentiments counter common definitions of corporations as virtually omniscient about their products or their production of consumers. Beyond the control of those that built them or bought them, refrigerators were in fact profoundly troubling, particularly for the housewives who opened their doors on a daily basis and clearly understood that the refrigerator did not connect them to a global community. Nor did the refrigerators offer personal consolation for the acute detachment consumers felt from friends and family. Refrigerators were no mere part of an amorphous, intangible "problem that has no name," as Betty Friedan once famously defined the postwar female experience. They were its material embodiment.

Notes

[1] The language of "discrete units" arranged in uninterrupted series or "sequences" comes from Raymond Williams, credited with coining the theory of TV "flow," where an uninterrupted stream of information is beamed directly into the home and at viewers. See Williams 86–95.

[2] Under the Refrigerator Safety Act of 1956, discussed in the 1954 Senate hearing, the industry eventually settled on a magnetic seal around the door for all units made after October 1958, which allowed a refrigerator to remain airtight while also opening from inside under fifteen pounds of pressure (48).

Works Cited

"All the Things a Woman Has Always Wanted." *Good Housekeeping* (Spring 1950): 179. Print.

Boddy, William. "The Studios Move into Prime Time: Hollywood and the Television Industry in the 1950s." *Hollywood: Critical Concepts in Media and Cultural Studies*. Vol. 1. Ed. Thomas Schatz. London: Routledge, 2004. Print.

Cohen, Lizabeth. *A Consumers' Republic: The Politics of Mass Consumption in Postwar America*. New York: Vintage, 2003. Print.

Covert, Tawnya Adkins. "Consumption and Citizenship During the Second World War." *Journal of Consumer Culture* 3.3 (2003): 315–42. Print.

Cowan, Ruth Schwartz. *More Work for Mother: The Ironies of Household Technology from the Open Hearth to the Microwave*. New York: Basic Books, 1985. Print.

"Farmwife Ends Life Crawling into Icebox," *Washington Post*, 23 July 1954: 5. Print.

Friedberg, Susanne. *Fresh: A Perishable History*. Cambridge, MA: Belknap P, 2009. Print.

Grahame, Peter R. "The Refrigerator in Consumer Discourses between the Wars." *The Socialness of Things: Essays on the Social-Semiotics of Objects*. Ed. Stephen Harold Riggins. New York: Mouton de Gruyter, 1994. 285–309. Print.

Hayden, Dolores. *Redesigning the American Dream: The Future of Housing, Work and Family Life*. New York: Norton, 1984. Print.

Isenstadt, Sandy. "Visions of Plenty: Refrigerators in America around 1950." *Journal of Design History* 11.4 (1998): 311–21. Print.

Kirk, Connie Ann. *Sylvia Plath: A Biography*. Santa Barbara, CA: Greenwood P, 2004. Print.

Marchand, Roland. *Advertising the American Dream: Making Way for Modernity, 1920–1940*. Berkeley: U of California P, 1985. Print.

May, Elaine Tyler. *Homeward Bound: American Families in the Cold War Era*. New York: Basic Books, 1988. Print.

Nickles, Shelley. "More Is Better: Mass Consumption, Gender, and Class Identity in Postwar America." *American Quarterly* 54.4 (2002): 581–622. Print.

"Nine Children Killed in Two Icebox Traps." *New York Times*, 14 Aug. 1953. Print.

"No-Latch Iceboxes Scored on Safety." The Refrigeration Service Engineers Society of Chicago. 1966. Print.

Oldenziel, Ruth, and Karin Zachmann. *Cold War Kitchen: Americanization, Technology, and European Users.* Ed. Ruth Oldenziel and Karin Zachmann. Cambridge, MA: MIT P, 2009. Print.

Parks, Lisa. "Cracking Open the Set: Television Repair and Tinkering with Gender 1949–1955." *Television and New Media* 1.3 (2001): 257–77. Print.

———. "Our World, Satellite Televisuality, and the Fantasy of Global Presence." *Planet TV: A Global Television Reader.* Ed. Lisa Parks and Shanti Kumar. New York: New York UP, 2003. 74–93. Print.

"Queens Boy Found Dead in Icebox." *New York Herald Tribune*, 17 May 1956. Print.

Sampson, Wade. "A Tour of the West: Circarama 1955 and American Motors." *Mouse Planet.* 29 July 2009. Web.

Sconce, Jeffrey. *Haunted Media: Electronic Presence from Telegraphy to Television.* Durham and London: Duke UP, 2000. Print.

Spigel, Lynn. "Designing the Smart House: Posthuman Domesticity and Conspicuous Production." *European Journal of Cultural Studies* 8.4 (2005): 403–26. Print.

———. "Installing the Television Set: Popular Discourses on Television and Domestic Space, 1948–1955." *Private Screenings: Television and the Female Consumer.* Eds Lynn Spigel, Denise Mann. Minneapolis: U of Minnesota P, 1992. Print.

———. *Make Room for TV: Television and the Family Ideal in Postwar America.* Chicago and London: U of Chicago P, 1992. Print.

"Sunday...Some Day" by Nash-Kelvinator. Advertisement. *Life*, 9 Oct. 1944: Inside front cover. Print.

"This Is How a Woman Fights" by Nash-Kelvinator. *Good Housekeeping* (March 1943): 42. Print.

US House of Representatives Committee on Interstate and Foreign Commerce. Hearing on S. 2876 and S. 2891, *A Bill to Require Inside Latches on the Doors of Household Refrigerators Shipped in the Interstate Commerce*, 83rd Cong., 2nd sess., 1954. Print.

US House of Representatives Committee on Interstate and Foreign Commerce. Hearing on H.R. 2181, *A Bill to Require Safety-closing Devices on the Doors of Household Refrigerators Shipped in Interstate Commerce*, 84th Cong., 1st sess., 1955. Print.

"We'll Live in a Kingdom All of Our Own" by Nash-Kelvinator. Advertisement. *Life*, 25 Jan. 1945: Inside Front Cover. Print.

Williams, Raymond. "Programming: Distribution and Flow." *Television: Technology and Cultural Form.* New York: Schocken Books, 1974. Print.

DISCUSSION QUESTIONS

1. Because the American kitchen in the 1950s and 1960s was largely a gendered space, Gansky's analysis of fridges repeatedly intersects with the discussion of gender. Prepare a summary of the article that elucidates the importance of gender to the refrigerator in the postwar period.

2. Compare Gansky's findings about the refrigerator with what you know about another appliance or common mass-manufactured object found in households, perhaps one that is associated with men.

3. Choose one of Gansky's sources and locate it in your library. How does Gansky use the source? How does inspecting the source directly affect your sense of how he uses it?

4. Gansky traces a tension between the portrayal of the refrigerator as a means to a "global community of leisure and travel" (p. 97) and the counter possibility of gendered alienation in the postwar kitchen. What explains this tension? How does Gansky account for it?

5. Gansky describes the refrigerator as a "televisual vessel" (p. 94). What does he mean by this? Can you identify and analyze another televisual vessel? This will require you to define "televisual vessel" and to explain why your choice is televisual.

SOCIAL MEDIA AND LIFE ONLINE

INTRODUCTION

Something that likely separates your life experiences from those of your professors is familiarity from a young age with social media. Moreover, like the research subjects of the studies in the next section, you may live large parts of your life online. But what are social media, and what does it mean to live online? We might think of social media as the most widespread expression of Web 2.0, a term first used in 1999 that has come to refer to a vast array of interactive technologies and services that allow users to create and post content that includes text, photos, and videos; interact with other users and respond to material posted by them; participate in virtual communities and social networks; and, perhaps most importantly, create, manage, and perform social identity. As for the question of what it means to live online, that's the central concern of the studies that follow.

While social media may seem to have been around forever, it's worth remembering that Facebook made its appearance not that long ago, on February 4, 2004, as a site for Harvard students. Other popular social media are even more recent: today, the top 15 include YouTube (2005), Twitter (2006), Tumblr (2007), Instagram (2010), and Snapchat (2010). To be sure, some social media predate Facebook—notably Linkedin (2002), which has survived and adapted, as well as the now defunct Friendster (2002) and the little-used Myspace (2003).

Given this timeline, users' involvement with social media is by definition a recent phenomenon, albeit one that has attracted vast interest from the general public and academic researchers alike. A Google Ngram search—a rough way of visualizing how frequently a term appears in books—shows a sharp spike in the term around the year 2000 (Google Ngrams don't currently return results after 2008):

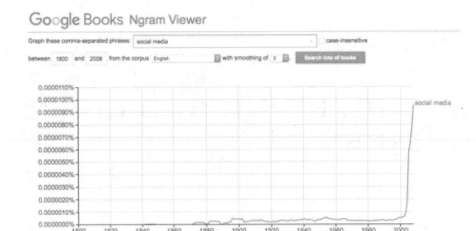

A Google Scholar search of the term "social media" turns up more than 2 million results. Closer attention reveals that the phenomenon has attracted the research attention of numerous academics, including social psychologists, economists, sociologists, researchers in business and media studies, and even linguists and musicologists.

The following selection of articles offers a brief introduction to recent research on the experiences of those who use social media. The studies represent both qualitative (e.g., Ward, Moncur et al., and Costello) and quantitative research (Moon et al., and Zaleski et al.), and emerge from a variety of academic disciplines, including psychology (Moon et al.), education (Ward), and sociology (Moncur et al.). Most are organized according to standard IMRD format, but the article on blogging (Costello) has a somewhat less formal, almost reflective organization. As you read these studies, try to keep in mind how researchers construct knowledge for other specialists in the field (and in at least one case for non-specialists) and how you may be implicated in the systems and practices the researchers describe.

A. "FANTASY FACEBOOK: AN EXPLORATION OF STUDENTS' CULTURAL SOURCES," AMBER E. WARD

This article, published in Art Education, *represents an unusual approach to research insofar as it utilizes qualitative method and emphasizes the subject position of the researcher (as teacher). Qualitative method is often used in educational research. Amber Ward* recreates a middle-school art project involving self-portrait sculpture based on Fantasy Facebook friendship. As you read this article, pay attention to how Ward positions herself and makes direct observations of her students and their work. Also notice how she summons scholarship on qualitative research, art education, semiotics (the study of signs), and popular culture to explain her approach and contextualize her inferences. The italicized prelude establishes the site of qualitative research.*

Glossary terms: qualitative research, subject position, semiotics

Shortly after the tardy bell rang, I asked my middle school art students to come to the front of the room and to gather around me in a semi-circle. Commotion accompanied this shuffle, but the students quieted once seated. I climbed onto the demonstration table and sat with my legs crossed just a few feet away from the onlookers.

I began speaking softly: "Late Sunday night I was surfing the Internet and discovered a new website called Fantasy Facebook. While on this site, I realized that I had the opportunity to potentially friend anyone, from the past to the present." I then passed around some of my favorite Grateful Dead 'bootleg' cassettes and tattered ticket stubs. I showed my art students a few 8" x 10" photographs of lead guitarist and singer, Jerry Garcia. The Grateful Dead paraphernalia smelled like Nag Champa incense and reminded me of my college years.

In a whisper, I continued speaking to an attentive class, "I was able to search for and to locate the late Jerry Garcia on Fantasy Facebook. After posting a very unique image and description of myself, I asked Jerry to be my friend. He accepted." By that point, the students realized I had made up the story, and smiled.

"Each of you will create your own unique image by constructing a self-portrait sculpture, which will serve as your profile picture on an imaginary website called Fantasy Facebook." Finally, I asked individual students, "Who would you like to friend on Fantasy Facebook?"

---

* Amber E. Ward is a Middle School Art Educator for Shawnee Mission School District, Shawnee, Kansas. She conducted this research in partial fulfillment of degree requirements for the MA in Art Education at Maryland Institute College of Art.

During the last two years, I have been reconnecting with friends and acquaintances from my recent, and not so recent, past on Facebook. Fond memories have filled my head while perusing familiar photographs from as far back as the 1980s. I have also experienced a hint of anxiety when reminded of that tumultuous and unsettling developmental stage we know as adolescence. Influenced by the cultural standards of my middle-class upbringing, I first conformed with, and then later rebelled against, the status quo. Thinking back, I wish I had been given the freedom and opportunity to really explore my values and beliefs during adolescence.

When examining my middle school art students, I questioned the ways in which cultural sources might have impacted their aesthetic choices with regard to personal appearance. I also wondered how these cultural sources might have inspired students' aesthetic choices when constructing art. Specifically, I asked: What kinds of cultural sources influence the aesthetic choices middle school art students make when constructing a self-portrait sculpture to communicate self-identity to a chosen *friend*? I consider *cultural sources* to be information "framed by established systems of shared meanings, beliefs, values, and understanding" (Anderson & Milbrandt, 2005, p. 48) developed through social groups or establishments like family and friends, academic institutions, and the popular media of entertainment and marketing (Banks, 1993). In short, social groups and their transmitted messages inform a culture's values and beliefs. Second, *aesthetic choices* are "the conscious arrangement of selected sensory elements that communicate an intended meaning" (S. Johnson, personal communication, 19 December 2009). Third, to *communicate* means the way middle school art students transmit messages or exchange information in order to feel connected. Lerner, Freund, De Stefanis, and Habermas (2001) define *self-identity* as "a psycho-social construct that represents the meshing, or integration, of personality and the contemporaneous (situational) and historical context" (p. 34). Self-identity relates to the way middle school art students want to be perceived by someone they value (S. Johnson, personal communication, 28 March 2009). A *chosen friend* is an individual viewer from Fantasy Facebook whom the middle school art student values and would like to befriend. This *friend* could be real or imagined; from the past, present, or future; and famous or unknown.

I have been deeply committed to shaping an art curriculum that offers students a more meaningful and authentic experience. In addition, I have been interested in the notion of students as victims of their popular culture pronounced by many contemporary art education scholars. Young people seem much more complex than this. I tested these assumptions by carefully considering the artmaking processes and final artwork of my middle school art students. The Fantasy Facebook: Self-Portrait Sculpture instructional unit served as the case for an investigation of the kinds of cultural sources that influence students' aesthetic choices. Seventh- and eighth-grade 3-D Art students worked on this unit each day for eight weeks and seemed to love every moment of it. Learning outcomes emphasized: (1) designing preliminary sketches and interpreting plan worksheets to develop ideas for artwork; (2) drawing from observation and applying this knowledge to new applications (i.e., sculpting); (3) synthesizing and analyzing media, techniques, and processes to create a unique and expressive self-portrait sculpture; and (4) formulating responses to artwork from thoughtful, empathetic, and analytical points of view.

Authentic assessment is identified as a meaningful, collaborative process whereby students and teachers work together to evaluate student performance and knowledge gained during and after the artmaking process (Anderson & Milbrandt, 2005).

The Big Idea

At the beginning of the instructional unit, I asked individual students, "Who would you like to *friend* on Fantasy Facebook?" In doing this, I exposed students to the *big idea* of fantasy. This gave them an opportunity to communicate self-identity to a chosen *friend*. When communicating self-identity, students also revealed influential cultural sources. According to Walker (2001), "Big ideas—broad, important human issues—are characterized by complexity, ambiguity, contradiction, and multiplicity" (p. 1). She continues, "Because they provide artmaking with significance, big ideas are important to the work of professional artists—and of students if student artmaking is to be a meaning-making endeavor" (p. 1).

During eight years as a middle school art educator, I have realized that art students are thirsty for meaning and substance. They crave and deserve more than:

- media-specific instruction and production;
- technical, skills-based instruction and production;
- and/or prescriptive and formulaic "how-to" instruction and production.

Please do not misunderstand. Art students should obtain knowledge and understanding of media, techniques, and processes. When introducing big ideas, students *want* to learn these processes so that their artwork accurately and successfully delivers an intended message. Instead of structuring a unit around linocuts or line, for example, art educators may want to consider promoting big ideas and artmaking experiences that allow students to communicate their values, beliefs, and self-identity. In the next section, I will outline two opposing theories within our field: formalism and pragmatism. In addition, I will present a historical perspective on aesthetics while revealing my aesthetic philosophy through the Fantasy Facebook instructional unit. I will then introduce three of my middle school art students and images of their artwork created as part of the instructional unit.

A Tale of Two Theories

Formalism

Many art educators realize that students' artwork often informs how outsiders (i.e., parents, faculty, administration) view the success of our programs. Desai and Chalmers (2007) state, "Formalist notions of art that still emphasize conformity and obedience largely govern the kinds of art projects assigned in school today" (p. 7). I consider this and wonder: Do our instructional approaches continue to hearken back to the eighteenth-century origins of art education? Stankiewicz (2001) states, "One motivation for art education became the desire to emulate one's betters by cultivating and demonstrating good taste, aesthetic sensitivity, and artistic skills" (p. 3). During the eighteenth century, for example, upper-class North Americans "aspired to emulate European aristocracy by creating and living in a world of beauty and refinement" (Stankiewicz, 2001, p. 3). In turn, the middle class studied and imitated the upper class. Throughout art education history, formalist ideals have molded and influenced aesthetics, while neglecting to acknowledge visual art as a means of communication, expression, and/or social change. However, noteworthy art educators have attempted to resolve this disconnect by examining the context surrounding artmaking and artwork. In the following section, I will discuss these art educators and introduce the study of art and context.

Pragmatism
During the late nineteenth and early twentieth centuries, John Dewey's pragmatic theory established a connection between aesthetics and context. Dewey believed that aesthetics were communicated, understood, and examined by using knowledge gathered from relationships and environments (Efland, 1990; Freedman, 2003). It is within this social context that viewers assign meaning and value to a work of art. According to Anderson and Milbrandt (2005), pragmatism "focuses on the context in which a work is made, seen, or used. An extensive examination of context is the most important factor in determining the nature and value of a work" (p. 84). In other words, pragmatism supports the notion that aesthetics exist socially and subjectively, as values are transmitted through viewers' unique experiences and interpretations.

Beginning in the 1960s, pragmatic ideology was again emphasized when Vincent Lanier, Corita Kent, and June King McFee combined visual arts with the sociology of art and popular culture (Chalmers, 2005). These progressive leaders changed the course of art education by introducing everyday objects as topics for discussion and by re-introducing art as a form of meaning-making and communication. At that time, scholars also began to debate the aesthetic qualities of both the popular and fine arts. Conversations surrounding context fueled such debates.

As we moved into the twenty-first century, Dewey's views of aesthetics and context have continued in visual culture art education (VCAE). VCAE is the study of attitudes, beliefs, and values from visual artifacts and performances found in popular culture and across other disciplines (Duncum, 2001; Tavin, 2003, 2005). When examining such attitudes, beliefs, and values, the viewer gains access to the social meaning as part of the artifact and/or performance. Here again, aesthetics exist within a social and subjective context. Formalists, on the other hand, believe that the value of an artwork depends upon its ability to successfully utilize various elements and principles of design. From this perspective, aesthetics become objective and emphasize power and beauty.

Distinguished from formalism, VCAE promotes empowerment, as students examine meanings associated with their influential cultural sources (Anderson & Milbrandt, 2005). Under the realm of VCAE, I introduced students to the big idea of fantasy (Facebook), which allowed me to explore students' influential cultural sources. During the instructional unit, the students and I investigated concepts that were personally significant and relevant through dialogue. Through artmaking, the students engaged in risk-taking by solving open-ended art problems without predetermined solutions or outcomes. In what follows, I introduce three of my students and their artwork.

Mary, Almanzo, and Nellie

During the Fantasy Facebook instructional unit, I closely studied three 3-D Art students (via interviews, observations, and written responses), their artmaking processes, and final artwork. After presenting each of the three students, I identify the influential cultural sources discovered during the instructional unit. Using purposeful "maximum variation sampling" (Merriam, 1998, p. 62), I chose Mary, Almanzo, and Nellie (pseudonyms) with the following criteria in mind: (1) gender diversity, (2) economic diversity, (3) ethnic diversity, and (4) levels of class participation.[1] Such diversity would allow for possible differences in artmaking processes occurring in the students' artwork during the Fantasy Facebook instructional unit.

MARY. Mary's (see Figure 1) classmates thought she was an excellent artist; certainly, the number of drawings in her sketchbook demonstrated hours of practice. These sketches tended to be very colorful, wild, and expressive. Mary chose to befriend Albert Einstein on Fantasy Facebook. Her self-portrait sculpture reflected this choice (see Figure 2). *Mary valued originality, which she learned through conversations held and visual media seen within her academic and creative culture.*

Figure 1. Mary

Figure 2. Mary's Self-Portrait

ALMANZO. This hardworking, conscientious, and kind seventh-grade boy aimed to please. Almanzo (see Figure 3) had fluffy blonde hair, bright blue eyes, and a big smile. He wanted to befriend football legend Jerry Rice on Fantasy Facebook. Almanzo's self-portrait sculpture reflected this decision (see Figure 4). *Almanzo valued both athletics and the relationship with his father. He learned these values through conversations held and visual media seen within personal and popular culture.*

Figure 3. Almanzo   **Figure 4.** Almanzo's Self-Portrait

NELLIE. Nellie (see Figure 5) was a bright and confident seventh-grader. She participated in the middle school's selective and competitive gifted education program. Nellie hoped to befriend Barack Obama on Fantasy Facebook. Her self-portrait sculpture reflected this selection (see Figure 6). *Nellie valued both her ethnicity and conventional (social) beauty. She learned these values through conversations held and visual media seen within personal and popular culture.*

Figure 5. Nellie

Figure 6. Nellie's Self-Portrait

Through the Fantasy Facebook instructional unit, I was interested in revealing my students' voices as they expressed the social values that influenced their everyday lives. Anderson and Milbrandt (2005) state that, "from a postmodern perspective, any given meaning exists only in a socially constructed web of other meanings. These meanings are constructed in a group context, through dialogue" (p. 6). While observing the three students, I overheard several comments and questions, such as: "No offense, but your skin color is really dark"; "Can I make [my sculpture] skinnier than I actually am?"; and "Why do you want to meet Albert Einstein?"

Contemporary art educators like Paul Duncum (1999, 2001) and Kerry Freedman (1994, 2000, 2003) continue to argue that the popular and visual culture pervading advertising and entertainment media have been increasingly important in shaping students' personal aesthetics. However, it is reasonable to question whether popular culture has created defenseless victims, or subjects of its bombardment of messages (Eisenhauer, 2006). By studying the students and their artwork during the Fantasy Facebook instructional unit, I investigated concerns similar to those raised by these scholars. I also gained greater clarity regarding the kinds of cultural sources that influenced the aesthetic choices middle school students made when communicating self-identity in an artwork. When comparing and contrasting Mary's, Almanzo's, and Nellie's influential cultural sources, two over-arching—yet disparate—themes emerged: (1) visual media from popular culture and (2) verbal language from personal culture. In the remainder of this article, I examine these themes more closely by providing examples.

Visual Media from Popular Culture

Visual media from popular culture influenced the aesthetic choices middle school art students make when constructing a self-portrait sculpture to communicate self-identity to a chosen *friend*. Almanzo and Nellie used visual media from popular culture as a form of visual communication by consciously arranging their physical features and by selecting their media. Through this communication, these two hoped to be understood by and to be attractive to their Fantasy Facebook *friends*.

Almanzo valued socio-cultural symbols that emphasized an athletic physical appearance when attempting to attract Rice's attention. The life-sized bust (see Figure 4) had a serious and focused gaze and expressionless body language like a trading card image. Notably, Almanzo and his father traded football cards as a favorite pastime. In addition, Almanzo's sculpture's hair was tousled, as if just finishing a workout or game. The sculpture wore one of Almanzo's tee shirts and a purchased football jersey, which he embellished with "80" and "Rice." Trading cards also reveal a player's team number and last name. In contrast, Nellie's feminine sculpture (see Figure 6) stood 13" tall. Her sculpture's physical characteristics, body posture, and youthful clothing appeared to be aligned with qualities common to Barbie dolls. During 3-D Art class—and as part of a teacher-directed Response—Nellie wrote, "I want [Obama] to be attracted to me for all of my beautiful reasons." Nellie seemed to believe that Obama would find conventional (social) beauty valuable and attractive. Seemingly, Almanzo and Nellie abandoned their real self-identities in favor of creating what they believed to be more attractive selves.

According to Rolling (2004) and Smith-Shank (2004), self-identities are ever changing signs "constructed from personal experience, from interpsychological detritus, from cultural debris, [and] from popular residue" (Rolling, 2004, p. 72). With this in mind, adolescents' self-identities are often entirely subjective and in a constant state of flux. These changes occur as they construct new knowledge about their social groups and institutions. Arguably, the act of visual communication and attraction through self-portraiture may be interpreted as an exercise in self-identity exploration and not abandonment. Almanzo and Nellie represented themselves through an evolutionary process that combined ideas from experiences and interactions with objects from personal and popular culture.

I also discovered that all three students became personally empowered through the identification process with their chosen *friends*. During an interview, I questioned Mary about her sculpture's posture. She replied, "I'm pointing at [the whiteboard] harshly, like...I stand up for what I believe." Through the Fantasy Facebook unit, I learned that Mary valued originality and imagination. Almanzo stated, "Whenever I wear a jersey, it makes me feel that I've encouraged myself to keep on moving and try my best." Also, during an interview, Nellie said, "I want to meet Barack Obama. He is the first African American president. He is very inspiring because he beat some pretty steep odds." She continued, "Besides [having similar] skin color, we have a lot of the same views." When sculpting their artwork, Mary, Almanzo, and Nellie all added garments or clothing remnants from home, including a shirt, a blouse, and blue jeans. To summarize, by analyzing interviews and final artwork, I learned that my three students became personally empowered when constructing a self-portrait sculpture to communicate self-identity to a chosen *friend*.

Verbal Language from Personal Culture

Verbal (in contrast with visual or written) language from personal culture was the second overarching theme from this instructional unit. With help from Bal-lengee-Morris and Stuhr (2001), I define verbal language from personal culture as conversations and interactions within one's family, friends, and peers that help define gender, religion, ethnicity, and economic class. Verbal language from personal culture influenced the aesthetic choices middle school art students make, but not as prevalently as the previous theme: visual media from popular culture. Interestingly, it seems that verbal language from personal culture influenced students' aesthetic choices more profoundly, especially when choosing a *friend* on Fantasy Facebook.

All three students admired, respected, and honored their Fantasy Facebook *friends* (i.e., Einstein, Rice, and Obama). Both Almanzo and Nellie discovered their *friends* through dialogue with their parents, while Mary learned about Einstein from her third-grade science teacher. Almanzo wanted to befriend the legendary football star Jerry Rice on Fantasy Facebook. He learned about Rice as a young boy through conversations with his father. Early in the unit I discovered that Almanzo and his father had a very close relationship and enjoyed spending time together. This relationship inspired Almanzo to value Rice and to choose him as a *friend*. Nellie hoped to befriend Barack Obama. Similarly, Nellie learned about her friend from her family. During an interview Nellie stated, "[The Obamas] focus a lot on the family, which is really good. They have a lot of family values in common with [my family]." Like Obama, Nellie is biracial. I also learned that the communication within Nellie's family fueled her ethnic pride. This pride appeared to influence Nellie's aesthetic choices not only when constructing a self-portrait sculpture to communicate self-identity, but also when choosing Obama as a *friend*. In summary, verbal language from personal culture deeply influenced students' aesthetic choices and choice of *friends*.

According to Eaton (1988), "Our languages and what we value are tightly interwoven. As we learn to use words, we also learn what our culture considers worth talking about. Thus aesthetic values are transmitted through language" (pp. 143–44). As I have demonstrated, language influenced Mary, Almanzo, and Nellie's aesthetic values. Eaton (1988) has defined aesthetic value as "the value a thing or event has due to its capacity to evoke pleasure that is recognized as arising from features in the object traditionally considered worthy of attention and reflection" (p. 143). In other words, socio/cultural values and language aid in determining the aesthetic value of a thing or event.

To summarize, popular culture influenced students' personal aesthetics. In this case, students used visual media from popular culture to attract the attention of an individual that they truly admired, respected, and honored. Through the identification process, students became personally empowered. While influential, I do not believe that visual media from popular culture creates defenseless victims, or subjects of its bombardment of messages (Eisenhauer, 2006). When sculpting, Mary, Almanzo, and Nellie seemed to *consciously* arrange their physical features and select their media in order to transmit messages. Therefore, the students seemed to understand visual media from popular culture as a universal language communicated within and by specific social groups or establishments. Deacon (2006) states, "One of the key elements...that distinguishes art from mere adornment is the enigmatic tendency to communicate a significance or meaning" (p. 29). Because these students' aesthetic choices led to an exhibition of cultural signs that visually attracted and communicated, I have concluded that aesthetics can become socially functional.

Conclusion

Some contemporary art educators have used pragmatic theory as a platform to suggest that students' personal aesthetics are primarily assembled and understood through the visual media of popular culture. However, I argue that there is a more significant, authentic, and balanced understanding of the complex relationship between a variety of cultural influences and the role of aesthetics in students' lives. Ideally, I would like to find more VCAE literature addressing this intricate relationship.

Through the Fantasy Facebook instructional unit, I studied Mary, Almanzo, and Nellie, their artmaking processes, and final artwork. This experience has improved my instructional approaches and has the potential to improve other teaching practices within the field of art education. By striving to translate theory into practice and by suggesting that art educators introduce students to the big ideas that explore values, beliefs, and self-identity, I have advocated for instruction that offers students a more meaningful and authentic experience. Such art instruction may offer art educators new ways to engage students through deeper learning, thus informing and transforming the way visual art is currently taught in schools.

Note

[1] In addition to receiving written permission from the school's Principal and from the school district's Associate Superintendent Educational Services, I gathered student and parent signatures on formal consent forms for participation in the study.

References

Anderson, T., & Milbrandt, M. (2005). *Art for life: Authentic instruction in art*. New York: McGraw-Hill.

Ballengee-Morris, C., & Stuhr, P.L. (2001). Multicultural art and visual cultural education in a changing world. *Art Education*, 54(4), 6–13.

Banks, J.A. (1993). The canon debate, knowledge construction, and multicultural education. *Educational Researcher*, 22(5), 4–14.

Chalmers, G. (2005). Visual culture education in the 1960s. *Art Education*, 58(6), 6–11.

Deacon, T. (2006). The aesthetic faculty. In Mark Turner (Ed.), *The artful mind* (pp. 21–53). Oxford, England: Oxford UP.

Desai, D., & Chalmers, G. (2007). Notes for a dialogue on art education. *Art Education*, 60(5), 6–12.

Duncum, P. (1999). A case for an art education of everyday aesthetic experience. *Studies in Art Education*, 40(4), 295–311.

———. (2001). Visual culture: Developments, definitions, and directions for art education. *Studies in Art Education*, 42(2), 101–12.

Eaton, M.M. (1988). *Basic issues in aesthetics*. Belmont, CA: Wadsworth.

Efland, A.D. (1990). *A history of art education: Intellectual and social currents in teaching the visual arts*. New York: Teachers College P.

Eisenhauer, J.E. (2006). Beyond bombardment: Subjectivity, visual culture, and art education. *Studies in Art Education, 47*(2), 155–70.

Freedman, K. (1994). Interpreting gender and visual culture in art classrooms. *Studies in Art Education, 35*(3), 157–70.

———. (2000). Social perspectives on art education in the US: Teaching visual culture in a democracy. *Studies in Art Education, 41*(4), 314–29.

———. (2003). *Teaching visual culture: Curriculum, aesthetics, and the social life of art*. New York: Teachers College P.

Lerner, R.M., Freund, A.M., De Stefanis, I., & Habermas, T. (2001). Understanding developmental regulation in adolescence: The use of the selection, optimization, and compensation model. *Human Development, 44*, 29–50.

Merriam, S.B. (1998). *Qualitative research and case study applications in education: Revised and expanded from case study research in education*. San Francisco: Jossey-Bass.

Rolling, J.H., Jr. (2004). Text, image, and bodily semiotics: Repositioning African American identity. In D.L. Smith-Shank (Ed.), *Semiotics and visual culture: Sights, signs, and significance* (pp. 72–79). Reston, VA: National Art Education Association.

Smith-Shank, D.L. (2004). What's your sign? Searching for the semiotic self. In D.L. Smith-Shank (Ed.), *Semiotics and visual culture: Sights, signs, and significance* (pp. 1–4). Reston, VA: National Art Education Association.

Stankiewicz, M.A. (2001). *Roots of art education practice: Art education in practice series* (M.G. Stewart). Worcester, MA: Davis.

Tavin, K. (2003). Wrestling with angels, searching for ghosts: Toward a critical pedagogy of visual culture. *Studies in Art Education, 44*(3), 197–213.

———. (2005). Opening re-marks: Critical antecedents of visual culture in art education. *Studies in Art Education, 47*(1), 5–22.

Walker, S.R. (2001). *Teaching meaning in artmaking: Art education in practice series* (M.G. Stewart). Worcester, MA: Davis.

DISCUSSION QUESTIONS

1. Ward italicizes words to create emphasis. How effective do you think this technique is? Why?

2. Early in the article (second body paragraph), Ward defines "cultural sources," "aesthetic choices," "communicate," "self-identity," and "chosen friend." Examine how she defines these terms. How do these definitions compare with your own sense of these terms?

3. In the section "A Tale of Two Theories," Ward introduces formalism and pragmatism. Why does she privilege and apply the second theory? Identify specific findings in the "Mary, Almanzo, and Nellie" section that help illustrate pragmatism.

4. Unlike many scholarly articles, Ward's subject position is explicitly present in this article. What do we learn about Ward? Why does she foreground these aspects of herself?

5. Discuss the value of qualitative work such as this. In her conclusion, Ward states that she strives "to translate theory into practice" (p. 114). Does her work succeed in this regard?

B. "FRAPING, SOCIAL NORMS AND ONLINE REPRESENTATIONS OF SELF," WENDY MONCUR, KATHRYN M. ORZECH, AND FERGUS G. NEVILLE

This media studies article, published in Computers in Human Behavior *in 2016, is an example of qualitative research that builds on previous scholarship to develop a definition of a significant phenomenon. Using the common IMRD format, Moncur et al.* discuss 'fraping,' which the abstract refers to as "the unauthorised alteration of content on a person's social networking site (SNS) profile" (p. 117). As you read the study, notice how the researchers develop this initial definition to present fraping as a specific kind of "unauthorised alteration" (p. 128) accepted by some social groups (and frowned upon by others) in specific contexts for very particular reasons.*

Glossary terms: IMRD, qualitative research, semi-structured interview, grounded theory, coding

Abstract

This paper reports on qualitative insights generated from 46 semi-structured interviews with adults ranging in age from 18 to 70. It focuses on an online social behaviour, "fraping," which involves the unauthorised alteration of content on a person's social networking site (SNS) profile by a third party. Our exploratory research elucidates what constitutes a frape, who is involved in it, and what the social norms surrounding the activity are. We provide insights into how frape contributes to online sociality and the co-construction of online identity, and identify opportunities for further work in understanding the interplay between online social identities, social groups and social norms.

1. Introduction

In this paper, we consider fraping, an activity that involves the unauthorised alteration of information on an individual's (the victim's) online social network site (SNS) profile by a third party (the "frapist"). This alteration of information happens in an

---

* Wendy Moncur is the Interdisciplinary Chair of Digital Living at Duncan of Jordanstone College of Art and Design, University of Dundee, where she leads the Digital Living Research Group.

Kathryn M. Orzech is a postdoctoral researcher at the University of Dundee, where she works on the Charting the Digital Lifespan project.

Fergus G. Neville is a Research Fellow at the School of Psychology and Neuroscience at the University of St. Andrews in St. Andrews, Scotland.

offline context, when the victim leaves their phone or computer unlocked and the frapist uses the device to make changes to the victim's profile without their knowledge. It can be understood as a performative social activity within a technologically mediated society, involving the presentation of selected facets of an individual's identity for a chosen audience.

Our analysis of fraping emerged out of an exploratory, qualitative program of research, Charting the Digital Lifespan, which examined how participants live out their lives in online contexts. Data from interviews with participants ranging in age from eighteen to seventy gave us insights into what fraping is, who is involved in it, the implicit social norms that govern fraping, and the sanctions that are applied when these norms are violated. We situate these findings in the context of existing research in social identity, online representations of self, and social norms.

The paper therefore contributes a definition of fraping that is grounded in our qualitative data, plus insights into social norms and the role that fraping plays in online sociality and the co-construction of online identity.

2. Background
2.1. Social Identity and Representations of Self
The social identity approach to group behaviour specifies that one may have multiple social identities with associated social norms that become salient in different social contexts (Taifel & Turner, 1979; Turner, Hogg, Oakes, Reicher, & Wetherell, 1987). Goffman argues that the representations of these social identities are achieved through performances that involve the construction of an edited, perhaps inaccurate, version of self that is crafted with an audience in mind (1959). He also identifies the involvement of a co-operative team of actors in co-constructing and presenting this crafted impression to an audience in any given social context. This team of actors share a sense of familiarity and solidarity, and keeps each others' secrets from the audience when such action is deemed appropriate.

The Internet offers multiple social environments in which to perform representations of social identity. Social media tools facilitate these performances, both extending offline sociality (DiMaggio, Hargittai, Neuman, & Robinson, 2001) and also providing opportunities to represent oneself and interact in ways that are uniquely digital. For adolescents in particular, such tools can boost or diminish their interpersonal and intrapersonal experiences (Davis, 2013). Online representations of self are increasingly kaleidoscopic. Individuals construct different versions of themselves depending on "the function of each online space; the social norms governing interaction within that space; and the perceived audience that one may encounter" (Emanuel & Stanton Fraser, 2014, p. 147). These representations may be co-constructed, with the very social nature of many digital involvements lending themselves to "a coherent sense of aggregate self with friends" (Belk, 2013, p. 487). The information disclosed online varies across these representations of self, influenced by the goals of the discrete context of the online space. For example, Emanuel et al. found that individuals disclosed more conservative and factual personal information on job-seeking websites, and more personal attitudes, preferences, and subjective qualities on dating websites (2014). Positive audience responses to online representations of self can boost social self-esteem and well-being, as shown by Valkenburg et al. in their study of adolescents (2006). Performative representations of self are not necessarily truthful. Page (2014) describes multiple instances of hoax online identities that are used in performances of self, including hoax blogs by (purportedly) a teenage US leukaemia sufferer and a lesbian girl in Syria.

2.2. Online Social Norms and Sanctions

The construction and deployment of online representations of self in online enactments of sociality is accompanied by an emergence of social norms and sanctions that govern the content and use of these representations (McLaughlin & Vitak, 2012).

Social norms are shared beliefs within a social group regarding the appropriate ways to feel, think and behave (Reynolds, Subaši, & Tindall, 2015; Turner, 1991). While social norms can operate at an individual level, they are more commonly social rules that function in relation to shared group identities (Neville, 2015). For example, one might have various social identities (e.g., parent, academic, football supporter) that are salient in different social contexts (home, office, stadium), and each has different social norms governing how one is expected and ought to behave in each setting (being caring, objective or partisan) (Turner et al., 1987). Moreover, social norms are the mechanism by which social groups can influence their members' behaviour (Cialdini, Reno, & Kallgren, 1990). First, where the correct behavioural choice is potentially ambiguous, behaviour can be shaped by perceptions of how fellow group members feel and act. This is because members of one's social group are seen as credible guides to the appropriate (i.e., normative) way to act in a group-relevant situation. Second, groups can exert social control upon their members by threatening exclusion or sanction if group norms are violated (Turner et al., 1987).

Social norms vary between social groups, including online groups (Emanuel et al., 2014; Neville, 2015). Individuals develop their understanding of acceptable norms through the groups that they belong to, are familiar with, or aspire to join, and different norms apply for different groups. For example, gossip, joking and arguing online are framed as normative, gendered activities under a banner of 'drama' by teenage group members, yet these same activities can easily be perceived as 'bullying' by non-group members (Marwick & Boyd, 2011). Normative online behaviours can also be observed amongst parents, where gender affects the number of photos that they post on Facebook of their baby after the birth—with fathers usually posting far fewer images than mothers (Bartholomew, Schoppe-Sullivan, Glassman, Kamp Dush, & Sullivan, 2012). As children grow up, parents usually adopt further norms around (e.g.) how many photos they post on social media of their children, and the nature of the photos, with fathers particularly concerned about posting photos that showed signs of physical maturation in their young daughters (Ammari, Kumar, Lampe, & Schoenebeck, 2015). As children mature and move towards adulthood, their views of normative representation of self online may be at odds with those of their parents (Yardi & Bruckman, 2011). People's choices in how they represent themselves online are affected by age, and also by their motivation for having an online presence. They may be motivated, for example, by a desire to belong to a (virtual) community and to have a sense of companionship, or to maintain pre-existing relationships (Hollenbaugh & Ferris, 2015). Whilst there are many differences in online behaviours across groups and individuals, there are also commonalities across the lifespan. Young and old (even the oldest old) hope that their posts will be met with responses from the target audience (Lenhart, Purcell, Smith, & Zickuhr, 2010). There are also common concerns over trade-offs between privacy and sociability (Brandtzæg, Lüders, & Skjetne, 2010) and the value placed on privacy (Christofides, Muise, & Desmarais, 2012).

Many of these social norms are not articulated as official 'rules.' Instead, they are understood by individuals either through observing the actions of others online and their consequences, or by carrying out actions online and experiencing the consequences directly (Burke, Marlow, & Lento, 2009). Positive feedback is seen as a motivating factor (ibid). We suggest that an example here is the 'Like' button on Facebook, which gives useful feedback to Facebook users (both those who post content, and observers) over what content is appreciated by members of their social network on Facebook. A large number of 'Likes' for a post may serve to encourage posts of a similar nature. An absence of 'Likes'—or a flurry of negative comments—may discourage creation of posts that are less popular, reinforcing tacit norms over the kind of content that the social network appreciates.

2.3. Fraping

Against this background of how individuals represent themselves socially online, and the accompanying social norms, this paper considers the phenomenon of fraping, which has only gained currency very recently (Graham & Mathis, 2013). In the limited existing scholarly literature on fraping, Lumsden and Morgan (2012) associate the phenomenon with antisocial activities of cyber bullying and trolling.[1] Outside of academia, politicians and the judiciary have also interpreted fraping as deeply antisocial (McInerney, 2013). At least one judge has found a defendant guilty of criminal damage for fraping an ex-girlfriend's Facebook page, after charges were brought by police (Barrett & Mishkin, 2014). The tabloid press has focussed attention on humiliating frapes involving spurned lovers, e.g. (Curtis, 2016). Even the numerous contemporary definitions offered by the Urban Dictionary conflict (Graham & Mathis, 2013): 'frape' is defined both as a "combination of the words 'Facebook' and 'Rape' ..." (which sounds extremely negative) and as a (rather more innocuous) activity whereby "Profile pictures, sexuality and interests are commonly changed; however, fraping can include the poking or messaging of strangers from someone else's Facebook account."[2] There is confusion over what fraping actually is.

We contend that fraping may be seen as a modern form of practical joke or prank. Some scholars argue that such jokes and pranks can play important social roles. For example, Kuipers (2015) suggests that jokes and pranks can bring groups together by emphasising shared world views, while Smith (2009) contends that they demonstrate the strength of social relationships by testing them. Moreover, ridicule may be a universal phenomenon across cultures, which can uphold shared social norms by mocking those who violate them (or are seen to do so) (Billig, 2005).

A central contribution of this paper, therefore, is to define the term "fraping": what it is, who is involved in it, the implicit social norms that govern fraping, and the sanctions that are applied when these norms are violated.

3. Method

Our study was carried out as part of a larger program of research (Durrant, Moncur, Kirk, Trujillo-Pisanty, & Orzech, in press; Moncur, Durrant, & Martindale, 2014), in which we engaged with participants who had recently undergone a life transition, and explored how their online expressions of self had changed across this transition. Such life transitions are characterised by change, as the central actor typically makes major adjustments, learning to cope with new experiences and developing new skills (Hulme, 2014), including online ones (Anderson & Tracey, 2001). Our overarching goal was to understand how online representations of self change across the human lifespan.

We carried out individual,[3] semi-structured interviews with 46 research participants across three transition points in the human lifespan—leaving secondary school, becoming a parent, and retiring from work. We refer to these participants respectively as young adults, new parents and retirees throughout the paper. The University of Dundee granted ethical approval for this project. Research participants were (i) 15 young adults (ii) 16 new parents, and (iii) 15 recent retirees. Two of the new parents were in the same age group as the young adults (<23 years old), but had undergone the additional transition to becoming parents—with its associated demands for maturity—and are reported on as being part of the new parent group. The sample size was informed by Guest et al.'s guidance on estimating where saturation is likely to occur (2006). We took a nonprobabilistic, purposive sampling approach, with participants selected to maximize diversity within the three groups (e.g., young adults in work and at University, new parents and retirees of varying ages with a variety of occupations), rather than for any special affinity to technology or social media. Demographic data about study participants are shown in Table 1. We recruited participants through several different community organizations, including a community choir and a playgroup for pre-school children, and through the authors' personal connections in their community. In identifying participants in the text below, we have used pseudonyms followed by the participant group (YA 1/4 young adult; NP 1/4 new parent; R 1/4 retiree) and actual age—e.g., Mary-R65. Chosen pseudonyms were informed by the most popular names for the relevant age group and gender, within the region where our study was conducted (National Records of Scotland Web Team, 2013). Interviews all took place in the same mid-sized city (~150,000 residents) in the UK between December 2013 and December 2014.

Table 1
Participant demographics.

Group	Gender (count)		Age (years)		Years between transition & interview		Career area
	Female	Male	Mean	Range	Mean	Range	
Young adults	7	8	19.7	18–23	2.6	0.7–5.6[a]	Direct to work (4) Direct to University (4) Work & attending University (7)
New parents	10	6	33.3	17–50	1.3	0.1–2.5	Administration (2) Business management (1) Customer Service (2) Education (2) Information Technology (2) Public Utility (1) Research (3) Social Media/Marketing (2) Social work (1)
Retirees	7	8	64.8	59–70	3.6	1–10	Health care (3) Social work (3) Education (2) Civil Engineering (2) Customer Service (2) Law/Property Management (2)[b] Publishing (1)

[a] In the UK, students may choose to leave school at any time after they are 16, or remain in school for one or two more years to undertake further study that prepares them for University or employment.
[b] Frequently seen together in the UK; the participants were a solicitor and a chartered surveyor.

Interviews typically ran for 1 1/2–2 h. The same interview topics were used regardless of participant age, with broad and open questions asked about participants' behaviour on social media. We captured "thick descriptions" of participants' experiences, focussing on "detail, context, emotion, and the webs of social relationships that join persons to one another" (Denzin, 2001, p. 206) by asking about the ways in which people presented themselves and communicated with one another using digital technology. Interviews were recorded and transcribed in full. The interview data was analysed using a Grounded Theory approach. (Strauss & Corbin, 1998) In line with this approach, the themes that emerged were generated inductively. Our interview questions did not ask explicitly about fraping: however, we did ask, "Have you ever pretended to be someone else online?" At the level of open coding, fraping was mentioned as a form of pretending; axial coding explored causes and consequences of this phenomenon, as detailed below. Using selective coding across the totality of our data, fraping was not a core code; instead, "pretending and posing" crossed ages and social groups in a way that fraping did not, as explained in this paper's discussion. Although it was not universal, fraping was still common enough in our interviews to allow for fruitful exploration around definitions, methods, and social norms of fraping.

4. Results

13 participants mentioned fraping explicitly during interviews: 9 young adults (2 female, 7 male), 4 new parents (2 male, 2 female). Retirees did not mention it explicitly. Herein we present insights generated into what constitutes a frape, the actors involved, the implicit social norms attached to frapes, and the sanctions imposed when these norms are violated.

4.1. What Is a 'Frape'?

Participants identified a 'frape' as involving a change to an individual's social networking account, carried out opportunistically by another person without the account owner's knowledge or consent. Common fraping activities included changing the account owner's profile page or photo: "...just the casual Facebook profile change" (Jack-YA18). Young adults usually saw frapes as practical jokes: "such a terrible form of humour" (Andrew-YA21). They identified that a crucial part of a contemporary frape was that it should stand out in some way as being inconsistent with the victim's normal posting behaviour and online identity. There should be a clue to enable the victim to know that they had been fraped. This was illustrated by Jack-YA18, who immediately noticed that someone else had changed his profile picture without his consent, when he showed the interviewer his Facebook page. Frapes happened when a victim left a device unlocked or signed on using someone else's device, and a perpetrator took the opportunity presented to frape:

> "I keep leaving my phone unlocked. So they keep going in and messing (with my phone)...That was the first time it's happened to me in a while. So my guard was down." —Jack-YA18

> "...it would have been somebody on my Facebook that wasn't supposed to be on my Facebook, taking the fun out of me." —Callum-YA18

Steps taken to avoid being fraped included only signing in at home, on one's own devices: "I don't...sign into Facebook in other people's houses or anything very much." —Andrew-YA21.

The majority of young adults who described fraping saw it as an opportunistic and sometimes subversive act carried out amongst friends. The central aim of a frape was usually to amuse an audience comprised of either the victim and/or members of their social network. The joke could take the form of puzzling the victim, for example by changing their birthday on Facebook. This kind of change involved a temporal aspect to the joke, as the victim might not realize that they had been fraped for quite some time:

"…it was…my birthday a couple of weeks ago, and no Happy Birthdays on my Facebook. And I was thinking, 'What is this?' Turns out, one of the frapes that somebody had done to me was to change my birthday. So it wasn't actually coming up on Facebook…. It was funny." —Callum-YA18

Frapes could also be intended to tease the account owner, and to amuse those who knew their personal tastes: "…we go into my friend['s account], who is…really neurotic about things…. we all post lyrics to songs that he really hates, but…make some of them the wrong word, because that bugs him so much." —Andrew-YA21. Some were simply playful: "Sports. Someone added that when they were on my page without me knowing. I don't do any sports. I keep that, just because it's hilarious." —Rebecca-YA21.

The mischievous motivation behind fraping predates Facebook—illustrated by Cameron-YA18's reminiscences about use of MSN Messenger when he was still at primary[4] school: "If you were at somebody else's house, you would grab it [someone else's MSN account on their home computer] and see what you could get away with saying, without someone noticing that it wasn't them. But that was when we were just getting computers, so we were just starting to learn how to cause mischief on them."

4.2. Who Is Involved?

Most young adults admitted to both perpetrating and being the victims of frapes. New parents were aware of what fraping was, but did not admit to doing it—although one couple did admit to acting as bystanders in the same room when someone else was fraping. Neil-NP36 saw fraping as something that "university students and the young people in work" did. Retirees were largely unaware of what fraping was, and none of them admitted to fraping. Amongst young adults, fraping was often carried out between flatmates and friends. Spending a lot of time together in the same shared space afforded plentiful opportunities to access each other's devices whilst they were unlocked:

"Yeah, I've been fraped…At least every week, because with…the shared flat, I mean, it's just no privacy." —Callum-YA18

"…one of my flatmates is so bad, leaves Facebook open and I just can't not [frape]. But it is never anything shocking." —Kirsty-YA18

However, not all young adults engaged in fraping. Some viewed fraping negatively, as a waste of time: "I see that, and just think 'Oh my gosh!' I think that's so weird, I just wouldn't have time to do that" (Lauren-YA19). Other young adults were deterred from fraping through a perceived lack of the skills needed to carry it off successfully. These participants also recognised fraping as a time-consuming activity, but viewed it more positively, identifying required skills including subtlety, thinking on the spot, and cleverness: "...I try to [frape], but I'm not very subtle about it, the way some other people are. I'm not very...good at thinking on the spot, whenever a computer is open and somebody is logged in. So I tend not to bother." —Callum-YA18. Perpetrators of frapes could have a distinctive style that acted as a signature despite the ostensible anonymity of the act: "I think with fraping though...you always know that it is somebody else. I think with frapes, you can guess who it is that's fraped you." —Gavin-YA21

4.3. Implicit Social Norms
4.3.1. variation across groups

Feelings aroused by frape varied across groups. They included amusement, bemusement, defensiveness, disinterest and dislike, and mapped on to age.

Young adults often found fraping funny, even when they were the victim—as long as the frape was considered to be well judged and amusing. Describing a frape that detailed what she had said on a drunken night out, Rebecca-YA21 told us: "I just left it there. It was on my page. I could have said, 'Oh, take that down,' but it was quite funny." Describing another fraping incident, the same participant highlighted the acceptability of frapes that contained an element of playful irony as a clue:

> "Someone's posted, 'I've just realised that Harry Potter is a waste of time. What have I been doing with my life?' And it got loads of likes and people going, '[Rebecca-YA21], I can't believe that' and I'm thinking, 'It wasn't me, it was someone else!'" —Rebecca-YA21

As she was a well-known 'Harry Potter' fan, Rebecca-YA21's Facebook friends acknowledged the frape and showed their appreciation for its ironic nature through comments and use of Facebook's 'Like' button. Despite the acknowledged association with humour, young adults could also be defensive about frapes. They were reluctant to admit to doing anything that could be seen as unpleasant: "Maybe only ever [fraping] as a joke or something, but not [pretending to be someone else]...properly" (Ryan-YA20).

In contrast, new parents felt that fraping was an unpleasant thing to perpetrate or experience: "I haven't even done that (fraping). I just feel bad (for the victim). I've certainly been in the room for it." —Claire-NP33. It may be that they found it immature, as implied by Fiona-NP30: "No, I hate that idea. I really don't like practical jokes and stuff like that. I absolutely hate that idea." Both young adults and new parents expressed a sense that a frape victim was partly to blame themselves, through being careless or naïve enough to leave their device unlocked: "Folk have *actually* [their emphasis] left themselves logged in." —Neil-NP36.

Some retirees expressed disinterest in pranks carried out via social media in general (although they did not name fraping explicitly): "...for Facebook...people put stupid jokes and things and I don't really [do that], I can't be bothered." —Anne-R70. Moira-R63 was sufficiently irritated that she took action against members of her online social network who "…write a lot of rubbish, you know they put on stupid jokes and videos and YouTube and things that I'm not really interested in, so I have hidden them in the past."

4.3.2. when is fraping off-limits?
Young adults identified that it was unacceptable to frape someone that they did not know:

"It's more like friends playing jokes, like using your pictures to make funny images, like pranks, not really anything else…I guess when you look at it seriously, it could be considered invasion of privacy [but] because it was a friend [it was OK]…If it was a random person that had done that [fraped] it would be a huge deal." —James-YA19

Where individuals entrusted account and password details to someone else—for example, a partner or family member—there was a tacit expectation that fraping should not occur, and was off limits. It did not even occur to young adults to frape their parents, if they had their login details:

"I see my father's Facebook account and my mum's, because they don't really use it, they aren't really into Facebook. So it was me and my sister who created their Facebook account for them, so we know the passwords and…my mum sometimes just gives me pictures and says 'Upload this to my Facebook,' and then I have to get into her Facebook and upload it from her Facebook." —James-YA19

Couples in a relationship often shared login details with their partner, too. Again, it did not occur to them to frape each other:

"Steven has access to all my information, and vice versa, so I can get logged in to all his stuff and he get logged into my stuff."

(Interviewer: But you have no reason to…do silly things on his account?) "No." —Neil-NP36

4.4. Sanctions
Whilst the victim often left content changes on their Facebook page that had been made via a frape, not all frapes were welcome. Embarrassing material could be removed by the victim: "It could be 50/50, I usually have to take it down, 'cause

they're either stupid or...embarrassing." —Callum-YA18. Obscene content and unflattering photos could also be taken down: "If they posted something rude then I would get rid of it...And if there was a photo that I really, really didn't like, where I thought, 'Oh, God, I look awful, that's just not acceptable, I don't want that in the world,' I would ask the person to get rid of it." —Rebecca-YA21.

Social norms of deletion were also based upon the acceptability of the behaviour being depicted within the social group. Rebecca-YA21 found it acceptable for frapes to depict inebriation, but not being sick as a result of inebriation: "If...you're [depicted] in...a gutter being sick or something,...it would be like, 'Take that down, that's not great.' If I had a picture of one of my friends throwing up somewhere, I'd be like, 'Okay, I'll get rid of that.' But if it's just them rambling or being entertaining, then that's fine, I would say." —Rebecca-YA21.

When implicit rules regarding embarrassing, unflattering and obscene content were broken, the frapist expected the content that they posted on a victim's social media site to be removed. Kirsty-YA18 admitted to fraping flatmates and friends "quite a lot," but identified the content as unacceptable herself and acknowledged that her subjects deleted it. She added content that was "...not...that awful but...things that would make them look daft if they kept it up. I would delete it, if someone put that stuff on ..." —Kirsty-YA18.

4.5. A Definition of Fraping

In summary, we found that a 'frape' involves a change to an individual's social networking account, carried out opportunistically by another person without the account owner's knowledge or consent. It is performative, enacted for a mediated audience, with the intention of anonymously disrupting an individual's online representation of self. It is an accepted activity for some young adults, if contained within a peer group of young adults who know each other. Frapes that are embarrassing or obscene are likely to be deleted by the victim once they are spotted, but frapes that are amusing or playful are likely to be left visible on the victim's profile page. Fraping is not an accepted activity for older adults, nor is it acceptable amongst social groups with mixed membership in terms of age, even when such a group includes young adults.

5. Discussion

5.1. Social Norms of Fraping

Analysis of our qualitative data revealed that fraping is usually an opportunistic activity intended to amuse others, carried out within a group of young people who are friends offline (where the frapist gains access to the victim's device) and online (where the frape is enacted). Implicit social norms dictate who may be the victim of a frape, the content, and whether the victim leaves the frape up on their social network page or takes it down once discovered.

There were clear differences in the acceptability of fraping among the three groups of participants. Young adults admitted to having perpetrated frapes, and regarded them as benign rather than malign when carried out amongst friends and flatmates. For young adults, successful fraping involved a change to a friend or flatmate's status or profile photo, carried out without their permission when they left their device or social media site unlocked. If a friend or flatmate did leave their device or social media site unlocked, they were seen as 'fair game,' but fraping someone who had shared their password with you was not acceptable. Our young adult participants performed and realised playful social interactions when they participated in fraping. Valued frape content was amusing, subtle, took a while to spot, or made a joke about some facet of personality or behaviour that clearly identified it as a frape to the victim's friends—the chosen audience. This playful quality distinguishes frapes from hacks, which involve manipulating a computer program skilfully to gain unauthorised access to another computer system, and from trolling, where the intent is somewhat malign and the trolls do not (usually) know their victim (Hardaker, 2010). It also distinguishes it from cyberbullying, where perpetrators may use jokes on their victims to deliberately harmful and distressing effect (Huang & Chou, 2010). Embarrassing, unflattering, and obscene frape content was likely to be deleted, representing the same exertion of social control through sanctions previously observed offline in social groups (Turner et al., 1987). Further, frapes were not carried out in other social groups that young adults belonged to—for example, their family.

In contrast to young adults, participants from the new parents' and retirees' groups did not report having committed frapes, and regarded them as unpleasant or pointless. The relevance of social groups to fraping was made clear by Neil-NP36, who described it as an activity for 'young people' and 'university students.' A frape with explicit content may therefore have been perceived as acceptable and humorous within a young adult friendship group, but offensive when appraised by others outwith that group.

Although retirees professed to be mystified by why anyone would bother with fraping (and were unfamiliar with the term), they did use social media in a playful manner (Stenros, Paavilainen, & Kinnunen, 2011)—for example, through subversive representations of self. For example, Ian-R60 maintained four distinct false identities online through Facebook, Twitter, Flickr, and email, using witty 'spoof' names. These online identities all linked to some aspect of his real life—zeal for a certain television series, a passion for listening to certain radio programs, a desire to participate in contests and quizzes, and an interest in certain sports activities.

5.2. Online Sociality and Disrupted Representations of Self

The social interactions realised through fraping involve multiple actors (frapist, victim, audience). The frapist and victim know each other offline, and the activity is rooted in offline physical proximity, relying on the victim's profile being accessed by the frapist via the victim's unlocked device. Online, the frapist interacts with the victim's audience indirectly through the victim's profile, disrupting the victim's self-representation through the illicit addition of content. This kind of disruption has previously been observed offline by Goffman, who found that adding unsolicited material to an individual's representation of self created for them an "appreciable chance of being slightly embarrassed or a slight chance of being deeply humiliated" (1959, p. 156)—reminiscent of the frapes that our participants told us about. Through the frape, the victim's profile becomes a shared and co-constructed performance space containing the victim's self-representation, the frapist's disruption of it, and (arguably) an element of the frapist's self if they are identifiable. The audience for these performances is comprised of the victim and the victim's online social network group on Facebook.

The victim may respond to the fraped content by displaying a willingness to participate in the joke, or by deeming it unacceptably embarrassing or humiliating, and deleting it.

Use of the victim's profile by the frapist adds a further layer of nuance to existing understandings of the co-constructed nature of online identity. In the context of Facebook, individuals typically construct their own profiles and control the material that appears on their timeline. They can also control whether they are 'tagged' in images and comments posted on others' social media pages. However, they cannot control whether material that references them on another's pages is posted or not. Thus control of one's online representation(s) of self is not total: the boundaries are porous. Fraped content is a part of this, within the context of Facebook use, contributing to "the expressive Internet,...the practice and performance of technologically mediated society" (Tufekci, 2008, p. 547). These porous boundaries present a risk—termed a "face threat" by Wohn and Spottswood—to an individual's desired online identity, as content added by others (whether on the individual's social media pages or elsewhere online) can undermine and challenge that desired identity (Wohn & Spottswood, 2016).

5.3. Limitations and Future Work

We recognise that the study represents attitudes in a small sample of participants (46), in one geographic location in the UK. We have compared the views and behaviours of three groups: young adults, new parents, and recent retirees around fraping. We have not explored the views and behaviours of (e.g.) young adults in different contexts. The social identity literature suggests that an individual can perceive the acceptability of the same attitudes and behaviours in different ways at different times, depending on which of their social identities—with corresponding norms—are salient to them (Turner et al., 1987). Testing this hypothesis for the online behaviour described in this paper (i.e., fraping) by comparing, for example, young adults' norm perceptions when in a friendship group and a working environment, presents a next step for future research.

Further work is also needed to understand whether fraping occurs beyond Facebook, as our participants' experiences centre on this one platform. Only one instance of similar activities on another platform (MSN Messenger) was given, and this activity predated Facebook. Trends amongst young adults change very quickly. We anticipate that fraping via Facebook is likely to fall out of fashion quickly, but that indirect, playful, and subversive interactions that affect representations of self and expressions of sociality may shift to other social media platforms—for example, Snapchat, Tumblr, Instagram. These interactions may be realised in quite different ways due to the technical affordances associated with each of the platforms, yet retain the social function of jokes and pranks previously described by scholars such as Kuipers (2015), Billig (2005), and Smith (2009).

Further, we hypothesise that such jokes and pranks will be seen as unacceptable, and perceived as face threats (Wohn & Spottswood, 2016), on sites where self-presentation has a professional context (e.g., LinkedIn), regardless of age. There may be consequences for a frapist's group membership if their apparent online behaviour is seen to have violated a group norm. This may lead to disapproval from ingroup members (Chekroun, 2008) and in extreme cases even exclusion from the group (Turner et al., 1987).

Finally, this study took place at a point in time. We do not know whether young adults will continue to enact playful, disruptive, indirect social interactions through activities such as frapes as they grow older, or whether they will view them as unpleasant (as new parents did), or irrelevant (as some retirees did). We will have to wait to find out, as the Internet and the young adults who have grown up with it both mature.

Acknowledgements
We thank the participants who we interviewed for this research. Charting the Digital Lifespan research project was funded by EPSRC Grant Reference No EP/L00383X/1.

Notes

[1] Trolling is "the practice of behaving in a deceptive, destructive, or disruptive manner in a social setting on the Internet...to make users appear overly emotional or foolish in some manner" (Buckels, Trapnell, & Paulhus, 2014).
[2] http://www.urbandictionary.com/define.php?term1/4Frape.
[3] With the exception of Michael and Claire, a couple who were interviewed together.
[4] Primary school 5–11 years old.

References
Ammari, T., Kumar, P., Lampe, C., & Schoenebeck, S. (2015). Managing children's online identities: how parents decide what to disclose about their children online. In Proc. CHI' 15 (pp. 1895–1904). New York, NY, USA: ACM. http://dx.doi.org/10.1145/2702123.2702325.

Anderson, B., & Tracey, K. (2001). Digital living: the impact (or otherwise) of the Internet on everyday life. American Behavioral Scientist, 45(3), 456–75. http://dx.doi.org/10.1177/00027640121957295.

Barrett, C., & Mishkin, S. (2014, February 7). Ex-boyfriend fined €2,000 for Facebook "frape" [News]. Retrieved May 6, 2016, from www.ft.com/cms/s/0/186f95d6-01d4-11e4-bb71-00144feab7de.html?siteedition1/4uk#axzz36IKyYLBF.

Bartholomew, M., Schoppe-Sullivan, S., Glassman, M., Kamp Dush, C., & Sullivan, J. (2012). New parents' Facebook use at the transition to parenthood. Family Relations, 61(3), 455–69.

Belk, R.W. (2013). Extended self in a digital world. Journal of Consumer Research, 40(3), 477–500. http://dx.doi.org/10.1086/671052.

Billig, M. (2005). Laughter and ridicule. SAGE Publications Ltd. Retrieved from https://uk.sagepub.com/en-gb/eur/laughter-and-ridicule/book226971.

Brandtzæg, P.B., Lüders, M., & Skjetne, J.H. (2010). Too many Facebook "Friends"? content sharing and sociability versus the need for privacy in Social Network Sites. International Journal of Human-Computer Interaction, 26(11e12), 1006e1030. http://dx.doi.org/10.1080/10447318.2010.516719.

Buckels, E.E., Trapnell, P.D., & Paulhus, D.L. (2014). Trolls just want to have fun. Personality and Individual Differences, 67, 97–102. http://dx.doi.org/10.1016/j.paid.2014.01.016.

Burke, M., Marlow, C., & Lento, T. (2009). Feed me: motivating newcomer contribution in social network sites. In Proceedings of the SIGCHI conference on human factors in computing systems (pp. 945–54). New York, NY, USA: ACM. http://dx.doi.org/10.1145/1518701.1518847.

Chekroun, P. (2008). Social control behavior: the effects of social situations and personal implication on informal social sanctions. Social and Personality Psychology Compass, 2(6), 2141–58. http://dx.doi.org/10.1111/j.17519004.2008.00141.x.

Christofides, E., Muise, A., & Desmarais, S. (2012). Hey mom, what's on your Facebook? comparing Facebook disclosure and privacy in adolescents and adults. Social Psychological and Personality Science, 3(1), 48–54. http://dx.doi.org/10.1177/1948550611408619.

Cialdini, R.B., Reno, R.R., & Kallgren, C.A. (1990). A focus theory of normative conduct: recycling the concept of norms to reduce littering in public places. Journal of Personality and Social Psychology, 58(6), 1015–26. http://dx.doi.org/10.1037/0022-3514.58.6.1015.

Curtis. (2016, May 2). Ulster student who sneaked away from one-night stand is humiliated on his Facebook [News]. Retrieved May 6, 2016, from www.dailymail.co.uk/news/article-3433217/Student-sneaked-away-one-night-stand-humiliated-woman-posted-performance-Facebook-left-phone-behind.html.

Davis, K. (2013). Young people's digital lives: the impact of interpersonal relationships and digital media use on adolescents' sense of identity. Computers in Human Behavior, 29(6), 2281–93. http://dx.doi.org/10.1016/j.chb.2013.05.022.

Denzin, N.K. (2001). Interpretive interactionism (2nd ed.). SAGE Publications.

DiMaggio, P., Hargittai, E., Neuman, W.R., & Robinson, J.P. (2001). Social implications of the Internet. Annual Review of Sociology, 27, 307–36.

Durrant, A., Moncur, W., Kirk, D.S., Trujillo-Pisanty, D., & Orzech, K.M. (2016). On presenting a rich picture for stakeholder dialogue. Brighton, UK: Design Research Society (in press).

Emanuel, L., Neil, G.J., Bevan, C., Fraser, D.S., Stevenage, S.V., Whitty, M.T., et al. (2014). Who am I? Representing the self offline and in different online contexts. Computers in Human Behavior, 41, 146–52. http://dx.doi.org/10.1016/j.chb.2014.09.018.

Emanuel, L., & Stanton Fraser, D. (2014). Exploring physical and digital identity with a teenage cohort. In Proceedings of the 2014 conference on interaction design and children (pp. 67–76). New York, NY, USA: ACM. http://dx.doi.org/10.1145/2593968.2593984.

Goffman, E. (1959). The presentation of self in everyday life. Garden City, NY, USA: Doubleday.

Graham, C., & Mathis, K. (2013). Frape, Stalking and Whores: semantics and social narrative on Facebook. In Crossing channels, crossing realms: Immersive worlds and transmedia narratives. Inter-Disciplinary Press. Retrieved from www.inter-disciplinary.net/publishing/product/crossing-channels-crossing-realms-immersive-worlds-and-transmedia-narratives/.

Guest, G., Bunce, A., & Johnson, L. (2006). How many interviews are enough? an experiment with data saturation and variability. Field Methods, 18(1), 59–82. http://dx.doi.org/10.1177/1525822X05279903.

Hardaker, C. (2010). Trolling in asynchronous computer-mediated communication: from user discussions to academic definitions. Journal of Politeness Research, 6(2), 215–42. http://dx.doi.org/10.1515/jplr.2010.011.

Hollenbaugh, E.E., & Ferris, A.L. (2015). Predictors of honesty, intent, and valence of Facebook self-disclosure. Computers in Human Behavior, 50, 456–64. http://dx.doi.org/10.1016/j.chb.2015.04.030.

Huang, Y., & Chou, C. (2010). An analysis of multiple factors of cyberbullying among junior high school students in Taiwan. Computers in Human Behavior, 26(6), 1581–90. http://dx.doi.org/10.1016/j.chb.2010.06.005.

Hulme, A. (2014). Next steps: Life transitions and retirement in the 21st century. Calouste Gulbenkian Foundation. Retrieved from http://gulbenkian.org.uk/files/01-07-12-Next%20steps%20-%20Life%20transitions%20and%20retirement%20in%20the%2021st%20century.pdf.

Kuipers, G. (2015). Good humor, bad taste: a sociology of the joke. Berlin, Germany: Walter de Gruyter GmbH & Co.

Lenhart, A., Purcell, K., Smith, A., & Zickuhr, K. (2010). Social media & mobile Internet use among teens and young adults. Millennials. Pew Internet & American Life Project. Retrieved from http://eric.ed.gov/?id1/4ED525056.

Lumsden, K., & Morgan, K.M. (2012). 'Fraping', 'Sexting', 'Trolling' and 'Rinsing': Social Networking, Feminist Thought and the Construction of Young Women as Victims or Villains. In Proceedings of forthcoming feminisms: Gender activism, politics and theory (BSA Gender Study Group Conference) (pp. 1–17). Leeds, UK. Retrieved from https://dspace.lboro.ac.uk/2134/15756.

Marwick, A.E., & Boyd, D. (2011). The Drama! Teen conflict, gossip, and bullying in networked publics (SSRN Scholarly Paper No. ID 1926349). Rochester, NY: Social Science Research Network. Retrieved from http://papers.ssrn.com/abstract1/41926349.

McInerney, L. (2013, March 11). Senator's "frape" gaffe signals that panic—not reason—rules social media debate. Retrieved June 18, 2015, from www.the42.ie/readme/lisa-mcinerney-senators-frape-gaffe-signals-that-panic-not-reason-rules-social-media-debate-823980-Mar2013/.

McLaughlin, C., & Vitak, J. (2012). Norm evolution and violation on Facebook. New Media & Society, 14(2), 299–315. http://doi.org/10.1177/1461444811412712.

Moncur, W., Durrant, A., & Martindale, S. (2014). An Introduction to Charting the Digital Lifespan. In CHI 2014 Workshop on Designing Technology for Major Life Events. Toronto, Canada.

National Records of Scotland Web Team. (2013). The top ten names: Every fifth year from 1975 [Document]. Retrieved July 31, 2015, from www.nrscotland.gov.uk/statistics-and-data/statistics/statistics-by-theme/vital-events/names/babies-first-names/how-the-top-names-have-changed/the-top-ten-names-every-fifth-year-from-1975.

Neville, F. (2015). Preventing violence through changing social norms. In Oxford textbook of violence prevention: Epidemiology, evidence, and policy (pp. 239–44). Oxford UP.

Page, R. (2014). Hoaxes, hacking and humour: analysing impersonated identity on social network sites. In P. Seargeant, & C. Tagg (Eds.), The language of social media (pp. 46–64). Palgrave Macmillan UK. Retrieved from http://link.springer.com/chapter/10.1057/9781137029317_3.

Reynolds, K.J., Subasi, E., & Tindall, K. (2015). The problem of behaviour change: from social norms to an ingroup focus. Social and Personality Psychology Compass, 9(1), 45–56. http://doi.org/10.1111/spc3.12155.

Smith, M. (2009). Humor, unlaughter, and boundary maintenance. Journal of American Folklore, 122(484), 148–71. http://doi.org/10.1353/jaf.0.0080.

Stenros, J., Paavilainen, J., & Kinnunen, J. (2011). Giving good "face": playful per-
    formances of self in Facebook. In Proceedings of the 15th international academic
    MindTrek conference: Envisioning future media environments (pp. 153–60).
    New York, NY, USA: ACM. http://doi.org/10.1145/2181037.2181062.
Strauss, A., & Corbin, J.M. (1998). Basics of qualitative research: Techniques and
    procedures for developing grounded theory. SAGE.
Taifel, H., & Turner, J.C. (1979). An integrative theory of intergroup conflict. In The
    social psychology of intergroup relations (pp. 33–47). Monterey: Brooks-Cole.
Tufekci, Z. (2008). Grooming, Gossip, Facebook and Myspace. Information, Com-
    munication & Society, 11(4), 544–64. http://doi.org/10.1080/13691180801999050.
Turner, J.C. (1991). Social influence (Vol. xvi). Belmont, CA, USA: Thomson Brooks/
    Cole Publishing Co.
Turner, J.C., Hogg, M.A., Oakes, P.J., Reicher, S.D., & Wetherell, M.S. (1987). Redis-
    covering the social group: a self-categorization theory (Vol. X). Cambridge, MA,
    USA: Basil Blackwell.
Valkenburg, P.M., Peter, J., & Schouten, A.P. (2006). Friend networking sites and
    their relationship to adolescents' well-being and social self-esteem. Cyber Psychol-
    ogy & Behavior, 9(5), 584–90. http://doi.org/10.1089/cpb.2006.9.584.
Wohn, D.Y., & Spottswood, E.L. (2016). Reactions to other-generated face threats
    on Facebook and their relational consequences. Computers in Human Behavior,
    57, 187–94. http://doi.org/10.1016/j.chb.2015.12.021.
Yardi, S., & Bruckman, A. (2011). Social and technical challenges in parenting teens'
    social media use. In Proceedings of the SIGCHI conference on human factors
    in computing systems (pp. 3237–46). New York, NY, USA: ACM. http://doi.
    org/10.1145/1978942.1979422.

DISCUSSION QUESTIONS

1. In Section 2 (Background), Moncur et al. report research into both how people perform their social identity for different audiences and the role of social norms in regulating online behaviour. Why is this background important to their discussion of fraping?

2. The slang term "fraping"—a combination of "Facebook" and "raping"—has negative connotations and may strike you as offensive, yet Moncur et al. note that the practice may be seen positively among some social groups. Among these groups, in what ways does fraping entail an element of consent that other online intrusions, for instance hacking and cyber-bullying, do not?

3. Although Moncur et al. interview 46 participants, they refer to their research as qualitative. Given the fairly large number of participants, what are some of the reasons why "qualitative" may be a better descriptor than "quantitative"?

4. Briefly summarize the main differences in attitudes toward fraping among young adults, new parents, and the recently retired—the three groups Moncur et al. study.

5. Moncur et al.'s discussion concentrates on Facebook and notes that "control of one's online representation(s) of self is not total" (p. 129). In what other ways does Facebook entail surrendering one's representation of oneself to others?

C. "THE ROLE OF NARCISSISM IN SELF-PROMOTION ON INSTAGRAM," JANG HO MOON, EUNJI LEE, JUNG-AH LEE, TAE RANG CHOI, AND YONGJUN SUNG

This 2016 psychology article, which appeared in the journal Personality and Individual Differences, *uses quantitative analysis to examine the relationship between narcissism and self-promoting behaviour (e.g., posting selfies and frequently updating profile pictures) in a study of more than 200 Instagram users in Korea. As you read the article, note how carefully Moon et al.* define narcissism and then use statistical analysis to identify connections between specific aspects of narcissism and particular patterns of Instagram use. If you don't have a background in statistics, you may find parts of the Results section difficult—even impossible—to understand. Don't worry: the "Discussion" section will clarify matters.*

Glossary terms: Likert scale, psychology, quantitative research, regression analysis

Abstract

Instagram, the rising photo-sharing social networking site, has gained an enormous amount of global popularity. This study examined the relationship between narcissism and Instagram users' self-promoting behavior. A total of 212 active Instagram users in Korea completed an online survey. The results showed that individuals higher in narcissism tended to post selfies and self-presented photos, update their profile picture more often, and spend more time on Instagram, as compared to their counterparts. They also rated their Instagram profile pictures as more physically attractive. Additionally, the results showed that Grandiose Exhibitionism positively predicted and Leadership/Authority negatively predicted the frequency of selfie postings and profile picture updates, as well as profile picture evaluations. However, Entitlement/Exploitativeness exhibited no effect on any of the self-promotion behaviors on Instagram.

---

* Jang Ho Moon is an Associate Professor in the Department of Public Relations and Advertising at Sookmyung Women's University in Seoul, South Korea.

Eunji Lee, Jung-Ah Lee, and Yonjun Sun hold positions in the Department of Psychology, Korea University, Seoul, South Korea.

At the time this article was published, Tae Rang Choi Stan was a PhD candidate at the Richards School of Advertising and Public Relations, University of Texas at Austin.

Introduction

Social networking sites (hereafter SNSs), such as Facebook, Twitter, and Instagram, provide a new venue for individuals to present themselves and manage their social relationships online. With the emergence of social technologies available to Internet and smartphone users, SNS-based communication provides novel venues for self-disclosure, self-presentation, and impression management (Rui & Stefanone, 2013). In particular, Instagram, a mobile photo-sharing application, has attracted SNS users to present themselves via a variety of photographs and short videos by making the process easier than ever. A recent study indicated that two key motivations for using Instagram are self-expression and social interaction, suggesting that Instagram users utilize pictures of all sorts of things to present their actual and ideal selves, as well as to maintain social relationships (Lee, Lee, Moon, & Sung, 2015).

A growing body of personality research suggests that narcissism is one of the most powerful predictors of self-promotional content via social media (Carpenter, 2012). Narcissism refers to "a personality trait reflecting a grandiose and inflated self-concept" and is characterized by an unrealistic positive self-view (Buffardi & Campbell, 2008), especially of traits, such as status, physical appearance, social popularity, and intelligence (Campbell, Rudich, & Sedikides, 2002). The most widely used Narcissistic Personality Inventory (NPI) has been analyzed repeatedly by psychologists to delineate its multidimensional construct (Emmons, 1984; Raskin & Terry, 1988). Ackerman et al. (2011) identified a three-factor model, in which they proposed Leadership/Authority (LA), Grandiose/Exhibitionism (GE), and Entitlement/Exploitativeness (EE) as the three key factors of narcissism. The three factors differ in terms of being either adaptive or maladaptive forms of narcissism. Specifically, the LA factor (e.g., "I like having authority over people") is regarded as an adaptive type of narcissism, marked by social boldness, optimism, and a focus on interpersonal relations with others (Brown, Budzek, & Tamborski, 2009; Emmons, 1984; Hickman, Watson, & Morris, 1996). Comparatively, maladaptive forms of narcissism, including the GE factor (e.g., I like to look at myself in the mirror) and the EE factor (e.g., I find it easy to manipulate people), are characterized by an intrapersonal focus on the self, neuroticism, and a willingness to exploit others (Ackerman et al., 2011; Brown et al., 2009).

The rise in levels of narcissism among millennials (Twenge, Konrath, Foster, Campbell, & Bushman, 2008), in addition to the development of a variety of SNSs, warrants more academic research regarding the relationship between narcissism and SNS usage. Empirically, individuals high in narcissism are very active on SNSs (Ong et al., 2011), and more likely than their counterparts to display self-promotional content on their static profiles (Mehdizadeh, 2010). Nevertheless, to the authors' best knowledge, no studies have investigated the relationship between narcissism and users' self-promoting behaviors on Instagram. Thus, the current study focused on the relationship between narcissism and users' self-promoting behaviors on Instagram, profile picture-related behaviors, and general Instagram usage. Research shows that nearly half of the photos posted and shared on Instagram are categorized as "selfies" (24.2%) or self-presented photos with friends (22.4%) (Hu, Manikonda, & Kambhampati, 2014). In line with prior literature on this topic, the current study hypothesized that narcissism would be positively associated with the frequency of selfie postings (H1-a), the proportion of selfies (i.e., a self-portrait photograph that one has taken of oneself; only one human face is present in the photo) in a photo collection (H1-b), and the proportion of self-presented photos (i.e., a photograph that one has taken with others; at least two human faces are in the photo) in a photo collection (H1-c). With regard to profile pictures, it was hypothesized that individuals higher in narcissism would update their profile picture more frequently (H2-a) and evaluate their physical attractiveness in the current profile picture more positively than those lower in narcissism (H2-b). Further, it was hypothesized that narcissism scores would positively correlate with the time spent per day (H3-a), the number of photos posted (H3-b), the number of followers (H3-c), and the number of followings (H3-d) on Instagram. Finally, this study examined the relative effects of the three key components of the NPI (LA, GE, and EE) on self-promoting behaviors on Instagram.

Method

Participants

An online consumer survey was conducted during a 3-week period from November to December 2014 in Korea. The sample for this study was recruited by a major research firm in Asia (Macromill Embrain) with an office in Seoul, Korea. Potential survey respondents, who were members of a virtual research panel managed by the research company, were randomly selected and notified by e-mail of the opportunity to take part in this study. All participants who completed the survey received virtual currency incentives from the research firm.

The initial sample consisted of 239 Instagram users aged 20–39 years. The final sample size (N = 212; 110 females) reflects a reduction in the initial number of participants who were eliminated due to incomplete surveys. The average age of respondents was 28.8 years (SD = 5.28).

Measures

Narcissism was assessed using a translated version of the 13-item Narcissism Personality Inventory (NPI-13) (Gentile et al., 2013). Respondents rate how much they agree with the items' descriptions of themselves on a 7-point Likert scale. The NPI-13 yields a total score and three subscale scores: LA (4 items, α = 0.89), GE (5 items, α = 0.85), and EE (4 items, α = 0.84). In the present study, the total NPI-13 score, ranging from 13 to 89 (α = 0.95), was used to test the three proposed hypotheses. Higher scores indicate higher levels of narcissism. In addition, the three separate subscale scores were employed to examine the relative effects of each factor of narcissism on self-promoting behavior.

With regard to user behavior, measures were derived from prior SNS studies (Carpenter, 2012; Moore & McElroy, 2012; Ong et al., 2011). Participants were requested to estimate their frequency of selfie postings, and the percentage of selfies and self-presented photos in their Instagram accounts. They were asked to report the frequency of profile picture updates and rate their physical appearance in their current profile picture on three adjectives (attractive, fashionable, and cool) using a 7-point Likert scale. In this study, all respondents reported being in their current profile picture. A profile picture rating score was obtained by summing these three self-ratings; Cronbach's alpha was high (0.85). Finally, the participants were requested to report the amount of time spent on Instagram per day, the number of all photos posted, the number of followers, and the number of followings.

Table 1
Partial correlations among the variables and their means and standard deviations.

Measure	1	2	3	4	5	6	7	8	9	10	M	SD
1. NPI-13	—	0.30**	0.17*	0.14*	0.31**	0.49**	0.15*	0.12	0.11	0.08	49.22	14.56
2. Frequency of selfie postings		—	0.65**	0.48**	0.64**	0.33**	0.27**	0.15*	0.15*	0.08	3.07	1.63
3. Proportion of selfies			—	0.62**	0.46**	0.25**	0.24**	0.09	0.10	0.05	19.25	24.31
4. Proportion of self-presented photos				—	0.37**	0.25**	0.19*	0.07	0.13	0.14*	32.08	30.70
5. Frequency of profile picture updates					—	0.30**	0.23**	0.23*	0.15*	0.12	3.14	1.55
6. Self-evaluation of profile picture						—	0.22**	0.12	0.19*	0.20*	4.35	1.17
7. Time spent per day on Instagram							—	0.27**	0.37**	0.25**	30.07	27.51
8. Number of all photos posted								—	0.52**	0.39**	61.06	109.92
9. Number of followers									—	0.82**	59	85.73
10. Number of followings										—	69	96.25

Notes: Control variables: age, gender. M = mean; SD = standard deviation.
** $p < 0.01$.
* $p < 0.05$.

Results

Hypotheses Tests

To control for the effects of age and gender, partial correlations among the variables of interest were calculated. As shown in Table 1, higher scores on the NPI-13 were positively correlated with the frequency of selfie postings ($pr = 0.30$, p b 0.001), the proportion of selfies ($pr = 0.17$, p b 0.05), and the proportion of self-presented photos ($pr = 0.14$, p b 0.05), supporting H1-a, b, and c. The correlations between narcissism and participants' frequency of profile picture updates ($pr = 0.31$, p b 0.001), and self-evaluation of their profile picture ($pr = 0.49$, p b 0.001) were statistically significant, thereby supporting H2-a and b (see Table 1).

In addition, we observed significant positive correlations between narcissism and the amount of time spent per day on Instagram ($pr = 0.15$, p b 0.05), supporting H3-a. However, narcissism was not significantly related to the number of all photos posted (H3-b; $pr = 0.12$, $p = 0.08$), the number of followers (H3-c; $pr = 0.11$, $p = 0.11$), or the number of followings (H3-d; $pr = 0.08$, $p = 0.25$).

Furthermore, a series of regression analyses were performed to examine the relative effects of the three factors of narcissism on self-promoting behaviors on Instagram. The proportion of selfies, frequency of selfie postings, frequency of profile picture updates, and self-evaluations of profile pictures were regressed, respectively, on the average ratings of the three factors of narcissism (see Table 2).

Proportion and Frequency of Selfie Postings

The overall regression model was significant, $R2 = 0.07$, $F(3, 208) = 5.10$, p b 0.01. The result of the regression analysis indicated that both GE ($\beta = 0.35$, p b 0.001) and LA ($\beta = -0.35$, p b 0.05) were significant predictors of the proportion of selfies in their Instagram account. However, EE was not a significant predictor ($\beta = 0.18$, p = 0.31). In the analysis of the frequency of selfie postings, the regression model was also significant, $R2 = 0.15$, $F(3, 208) = 13.78$, p b 0.001, and both GE ($\beta = 0.55$, p b 0.001) and LA ($\beta = -0.40$, p b 0.01) were found to be significant predictors. Yet, EE ($\beta = 0.16$, p = 0.33) was not a significant predictor of selfie-posting frequency.

Table 2
Results of the multiple regression analyses.

Item	GE				LA				EE			
	B	SE	β	t	B	SE	β	t	B	SE	β	t
Proportion of selfie postings	7.55	2.84	0.35	2.65**	−6.78	3.04	−0.35	−2.22*	3.71	3.63	0.18	1.02
Frequency of selfie postings	0.80	0.18	0.55	4.45*	−0.51	0.19	−0.40	−2.27**	0.23	0.23	0.16	0.98
Frequency of profile picture updates	0.52	0.17	0.38	2.97**	−0.38	0.19	−0.31	−2.05*	0.35	0.22	0.26	1.54
Self-evaluation of profile picture	0.62	0.12	0.59	5.17***	−0.26	0.13	−0.27	−2.00*	0.21	0.15	0.20	1.35

Note: β is the standardized regression coefficient.
*** $p < 0.001$.
** $p < 0.01$.
* $p < 0.05$.

Profile Picture Update and Evaluation

Both GE ($\beta = 0.38$, pb < 0.01) and LA ($\beta = -0.31$, pb < 0.05) were found to be significant predictors of profile picture updates ($R2 = 0.13$, $F(3, 208) = 10.64$, p b 0.001). Finally, similar results were found for the profile picture evaluation. That is, both GE ($\beta = 0.59$, p b 0.001) and LA ($\beta = -0.27$, p b 0.05) were significant predictors ($R2 = 0.30$, $F(3, 208) = 29.93$, p b 0.001). However, EE was not a significant predictor of profile picture updates or evaluation (p N 0.10).

Discussion

This study examined the relationships among narcissism and self-promoting behaviors on Instagram. Our study confirmed that more narcissistic individuals tend to post selfies and self-presented photos and update their profile picture more often as compared to less narcissistic individuals (Fox & Rooney, 2015). In addition, more narcissistic individuals rated their Instagram profile pictures as more physically attractive, lending some support to the notion that more narcissistic people are concerned about their physical appearance (Vazire, Naumann, Rentfrow, & Gosling, 2008). Finally, users with higher levels of narcissism tend to spend more time on Instagram, supporting the current understanding of the relationship between narcissism and SNS behavior (Mehdizadeh, 2010). Notably, narcissism was not associated with the total number of photos posted. These results are consistent with those of Ong et al. (2011), whereas they contradict those of Buffardi and Campbell (2008), thereby calling for additional research.

More importantly, our regression analyses showed that regardless of the dependent variables, the results were consistent. That is, GE was significant in predicting the proportion of selfies, frequency of selfie postings, frequency of profile picture updates, and profile picture evaluations in Instagram. Our findings are consistent with those of prior research (Ackerman et al., 2011; Carpenter, 2012), suggesting that individuals high in GE tend to have a more inflated self-view and are more likely to express a somewhat distorted self-concept via a variety of SNSs. Wright (2012) suggested that, unlike those high in LA, narcissists with high GE try to compensate for low self-esteem through self-promoting behaviors online, especially via selfies on SNSs.

Further, the LA factor was a significant but negative predictor of all the self-promoting variables. As discussed, LA is regarded as an adaptive type of narcissism, marked by social boldness, optimism, and a focus on interpersonal relatedness to others, suggesting that individuals high in LA value social relationships. Thus, they are less likely to promote themselves using pictures and SNSs than are those high in GE. As they have relatively higher levels of self-esteem, they do not see a strong need for online self-promotion, especially on Instagram (Sedikides, Rudich, Gregg, Kumashiro, & Rusbult, 2004). Thus, additional research with the LA subscale of the NPI is needed for a more comprehensive understanding of the links between narcissism and self-promoting behaviors online.

Finally, the EE factor was not a significant predictor of any of the dependent variables. As a form of maladaptive narcissism, those high in EE tend to underevaluate others to increase their low self-esteem (Ackerman et al., 2011). Thus, future research should examine the relationship between EE and Instagram users' evaluations and reactions to others' selfies and self-promoting behavior online. For example, follow-up research might empirically examine whether individuals who are high in EE read, comment, or "like" others' posts (including varied self-promotional content, such as selfies).

It is worth noting that the current study is limited by the use of the shorter measure of trait narcissism, the NPI-13. Future research employing the longer (40-item) version of the NPI is needed. Another limitation is the use of self-reported data for measuring participants' self-promoting behaviors on Instagram. Further investigations with actual measures of self-promoting behaviors on social media are necessary.

Despite these limitations, the current study provided evidence that personality, and narcissism in particular, might account for various self-promoting behaviors on Instagram. In addition, the findings of this study call for additional studies examining the relative impact of the three sub-components of narcissism. Such findings should help researchers and practitioners alike further appreciate the important concept of narcissism as an individual difference factor as well as its impact on self-promoting behaviors on social media.

References

Ackerman, R.A., Witt, E.A., Donnellan, M.B., Trzesniewski, K.H., Robins, R.W., & Kashy, D.A. (2011). What does the narcissistic personality inventory really measure? Assessment, 18(1), 67–87. http://dx.doi.org/10.1177/1073191110382845.

Brown, R.P., Budzek, K., & Tamborski, M. (2009). On the meaning and measure of narcissism. Personality and Social Psychology Bulletin, 35(7), 951–64. http://dx.doi.org/10.1177/0146167209335461.

Buffardi, L.E., & Campbell, W.K. (2008). Narcissism and social networking web sites. Personality and Social Psychology Bulletin, 34(10), 1303–14. http://dx.doi.org/10.1177/0146167208320061.

Campbell, W.K., Rudich, E.A., & Sedikides, C. (2002). Narcissism, self-esteem, and the positivity of self-views: Two portraits of self-love. Personality and Social Psychology Bulletin, 28(3), 358–68. http://dx.doi.org/10.1177/0146167202286007.

Carpenter, C.J. (2012). Narcissism on Facebook: Self-promotional and anti-social behavior. Personality and Individual Differences, 52(4), 482–86. http://dx.doi.org/10.1016/j.paid.2011.11.011.

Emmons, R.A. (1984). Factor analysis and construct validity of the narcissistic personality inventory. Journal of Personality Assessment, 48(3), 291–300.

Fox, J., & Rooney, M.C. (2015). The dark triad and trait self-objectification as predictors of men's use and self-presentation behaviors on social networking sites. Personality and Individual Differences, 76, 161–65. http://dx.doi.org/10.1016/j.paid.2014.12.017.

Gentile, B., Miller, J.D., Hoffman, B.J., Reidy, D.E., Zeichner, A., & Campbell, W.K. (2013). A test of two brief measures of grandiose narcissism: The narcissistic personality inventory-13 and the narcissistic personality inventory-16. Psychological Assessment, 25(4), 1120–36. http://dx.doi.org/10.1037/a0033192.

Hickman, S.E., Watson, P.J., & Morris, R.J. (1996). Optimism, pessimism, and the complexity of narcissism. Personality and Individual Differences, 20(4), 521–25. http://dx.doi.org/10.1016/0191-8869(95)00223-5.

Hu, Y., Manikonda, L., & Kambhampati, S. (2014). What we Instagram: A first analysis of Instagram photo content and user types. AAAI: Proceedings of ICWSM.

Lee, E., Lee, J.-A., Moon, J.H., & Sung, Y. (2015). Pictures speak louder than words: Motivations for using Instagram. Cyberpsychology, Behavior and Social Networking, 18(9), 552–56. http://dx.doi.org/10.1089/cyber.2015.0157.

Mehdizadeh, S. (2010). Self-presentation 2.0: Narcissism and self-esteem on Facebook. Cyberpsychology, Behavior and Social Networking, 13(4), 357–64. http://dx.doi.org/10.1089/cyber.2009.0257.

Moore, K., & McElroy, J.C. (2012). The influence of personality on Facebook usage, wall postings, and regret. Computers in Human Behavior, 28(1), 267–74. http://dx.doi.org/10.1016/j.jchb.2011.09.009.

Ong, E.Y., Ang, R.P., Ho, J.C., Lim, J.C., Goh, D.H., Lee, C.S., & Chua, A.Y. (2011). Narcissism, extraversion and adolescents' self-presentation on Facebook. Personality and Individual Differences, 50(2), 180–85. http://dx.doi.org/10.1016/j.paid.2010.09.022.

Raskin, R., & Terry, H. (1988). A principal-components analysis of the narcissistic personality inventory and further evidence of its construct validity. Journal of Personality and Social Psychology, 54(5), 890–902.

Rui, J., & Stefanone, M.A. (2013). Strategic self-presentation online: A cross-cultural study. Computers in Human Behavior, 29(1), 110–18. http://dx.doi.org/10.1016/j.chb.2012.07.022.

Sedikides, C., Rudich, E.A., Gregg, A.P., Kumashiro, M., & Rusbult, C. (2004). Are normal narcissists psychologically healthy?: Self-esteem matters. Journal of Personality and Social Psychology, 87(3), 400–16.

Twenge, J.M., Konrath, S., Foster, J.D., Campbell, W.K., & Bushman, B.J. (2008). Egos inflating over time: A cross-temporal meta-analysis of the narcissistic personality inventory. Journal of Personality, 76(4), 875–902. http://dx.doi.org/10.1111/j.1467-6494.2008.00507.

Vazire, S., Naumann, L.P., Rentfrow, P.J., & Gosling, S.D. (2008). Portrait of a narcissist: Manifestations of narcissism in physical appearance. Journal of Research in Personality, 42(6), 1439–47. http://dx.doi.org/10.1016/j.jrp.2008.06.007.

Wright, K.B. (2012). Emotional support and perceived stress among college students using Facebook.com: An exploration of the relationship between source perceptions and emotional support. Communication Research Reports, 29(3), 175–84. http://dx.doi.org/10.1080/08824096.2012.695957.

DISCUSSION QUESTIONS

1. Early in their study, Moon et al. offer a general definition of narcissism, followed by a model that identifies three factors. What are these factors, and why do Moon et al. further characterize them as "adaptive" and "maladaptive"?

2. Why, specifically, do Moon et al. choose to study Instagram rather than some other social media platform, such as Facebook or Twitter?

3. In the "Introduction," Moon et al. make a number of statements followed by an abbreviation that they don't explicitly define (i.e., H1-a, H1-b, etc.). Given the context, what do you think these abbreviations mean? Why do they abbreviate them here?

4. This paper uses a technique called regression analysis, which is a way of estimating the relationship between multiple variables. What variables do Moon et
   al. examine, and what conclusions does regression analysis allow them to reach?

5. Like many research papers, this study draws attention to its own limitations.
   What are these? Can you identify others that Moon et al. don't mention?

D. "EXPLORING RAPE CULTURE IN SOCIAL MEDIA FORUMS," KRISTEN L. ZALESKI, KRISTIN K. GUNDERSEN, JESSICA BAES, ELY ESTUPINIAN, AND ALYSSA VERGARA

This 2016 article from Computers in Human Behaviour *examines rape culture in social media. Kristen Zaleski, Kristin Gundersen, Jessica Baes, Ely Estupinian, and Alyssa Vergara* analyzed various newspapers in order to "explor[e] how social media comment threads following newspaper articles shape discourse on attitudes and viewpoints about rape and sexual assault" (pp. 147–48). Zaleski et al. focused their research on the unbiased collection and surveillance of data in order to gather the most accurate results, and sorted these results into themes and sub-themes. As you read the article, consider what the findings say about rape culture as a whole and try to answer the research question proposed by the above authors, that is, how comment threads "shape discourse on attitudes and viewpoints about rape" (pp. 147–48).*

Glossary terms: data analysis software, ethics, gender studies, naturalistic observation

Abstract

Current research has yet to examine the phenomenon of rape culture, particularly within social media forums. The present study investigated the attitudes about rape, rapists, and gender-based violence within the comments section of newspaper articles reporting about rape and sexual assault. Naturalistic observation was used in order to gather statements within the comment sections following newspaper articles posted on either the periodical website or the periodical's Facebook page. Four themes and various sub-themes emerged from the data. The major themes include Victim Blaming and Questioning, Survivor Support, Perpetrator Support, and Trolling Statements about Law and Society. Notable findings were found in the amount of victim-blaming statements made in the comments responding to articles

---

* Kristen L. Zaleski is a Clinical Associate Professor at the University of Southern California. She has a dual specialty in civilian and military sexual trauma.

    Kristin K. Gundersen is a Research Program Manager at the University of Southern California.

    Jessica Baes is a Social Service Practitioner in California.

    Ely Estupinian was a Research Assistant at the University of Southern California at the time this article was written.

    Alyssa Vergara is a Clinical Social Worker.

(25.8 per cent) and perpetrator-support comments were found responding to every article collected, except for one. The authors discuss the implications of rape culture within and outside social media and suggest future research to be conducted to further understand the impacts of rape culture within the online sphere.

Keywords: gender, social media, discrimination, rape culture, sexual assault

1. Introduction

Digital media consumption in contemporary society has become a standard of how many people acquire their news and viewpoints on cultural issues. For instance, the American Press Institute survey found that 69 percent of respondents accessed news information from their laptops and computers within the last week (American Press Institute, 2014). Recently, the Media Insight Project surveyed 1,046 Millennials and found that 85 percent polled say, "keeping up with the news is somewhat important" and 69 percent of these individuals read news daily (Media Insight Project, 2015). Most interesting, 86 percent of Millennials report seeing "diverse" opinions in social media on news topics and 40 percent of them pay for a news-specific service, application, or digital subscription (Media Insight Project, 2015). The digital communication through websites and news reports being posted by individuals on those websites contributes to an intersection of cultural discourse about news related events. Thus, leading some sociologists to name the phenomenon as the "digitalization of everyday life" (Lövheim, Jansson, Paasonen, Sumiala, & Teologiska, 2013). This digitalization of everyday life both obscures and reminds us of that fact that identity, agency, and power cannot be attributed to the individual or the machine alone: rather they are the outcome of interactions and negotiations within a network of actors (p. 26).

Social science researchers and feminist research have both started to focus on how women, people of color, and sexual identities take shape through words on a webpage. For instance, a recent study by Moss-Racusin, Molenda, and Cramer (2015) analyzed over 831 online comments responding to journalistic articles discussing scientific evidence of gender bias in STEM fields, most notably amongst STEM faculty members. Using thematic analyses, researchers found that although most comments acknowledged that a gender bias exists, and some even called for social change, there was still a sizable amount of denial and justifications of gender bias.

Stavrositu and Kim (2015) examined how blogs and the resulting comments sections influence opinions and intentions of the writers making the comments. It was found that user-generated comments could interfere with the message given by the blog itself. Interestingly, when commenters shared optimistic narratives, it could influence the person reading the comment to agree with them. Conversely, if the person commented pessimistically about a risk (in this study, the risk was skin cancer), the responder would not see themselves exposed to the same risk, but rather different from the other commenter.

Similarly, pessimistic discourse in a comment thread has also been shown to shape public commentary on social media. Anderson, Brossard, Scheufele, Xenos, and Ladwig (2014) found that both positive and negative discourse can be helpful in shaping and molding public opinion, however the amount of negative discourse can also have a negative impact on healthy dialogue. They state:

> Much in the same way that watching uncivil politicians argue on television causes polarization among individuals, impolite and incensed blog comments can polarize online users based on value predispositions utilized as heuristics when processing the blog's information (Anderson et al., 2014, p. 383).

This article will study the digital discourse of rape culture within comment threads that follow a sexual assault news story. The cultural phenomenon of 'rape culture' has been defined by Herman (1984) to be created in society because "it fosters and encourages rape by teaching males and females that it is natural and normal for sexual relations to involve aggressive behavior on the part of males" (p. 52). Recently, *Time* contributor Zerlina Maxwell described rape culture as "a culture in which sexual violence is the norm and victims are blamed for their own assaults" (Maxwell, 2014). Furthermore, Suran (2014) declared that rape culture was no longer a subculture of feminism, but a systematic and collective problem. Suran asserts that rape culture shows that the "cultural or societal explanation of rape [has] moved causation from a micro to a macro level" and is due to "the prevailing heterosexual power hierarchy to which we have all been inured" (2014, p. 277–78).

Grubb and Turner (2012) reviewed rape myths, gender roles, and substance-use on victim blaming. In this analysis, men demonstrated a higher rape myth acceptance than women, a finding also supported by Suarez and Gadalla (2010). Furthermore, men also blame women more often than women blame women for an alleged rape. Of particular relevance to the present study, Grubb and Turner (2012) discovered that the literature states that women who consume alcohol prior to being raped had higher rates of victim blaming by both sexes, as compared to women who were assaulted while sober.

Most recently, Boux and Daum (2015) examined how technology and social media is used in the investigation of rape and sexual assaults when perpetrators and their peers document the incident. The researchers asserted that technology creates new avenues for victim blaming in regard to rape cases and society, overall. Consequently, it was found that social media challenges, as well as reinforces, rape culture within society by adding rape myth commentary to the discussion. The present researchers seek to expand on this innovative research by exploring rape culture within social media.

Moreover, the present researchers are interested in exploring how social media comment threads following newspaper articles shape discourse on attitudes and viewpoints about rape and sexual assault. Specifically, if rape cultural beliefs are observed to be a part of comment threads. As the incidence of sexual assault rises among men and women in the United States, and the media reports on it, the researchers seek to explore how viewpoints on the crime of sexual assault are discussed in social media comment threads. That is, is there a discourse of rape culture within the thread of comments under newspaper articles reporting about rape?

2. Methods

2.1. Publications

The researchers reviewed newspaper periodicals in order to assess for evidence of rape culture. According to documentation by the Alliance for Audited Media (2013), the researchers gathered the top four newspapers in the United States, as determined by average circulation of the top twenty-five U.S. newspapers. This list included digital editions, comprising those accessible on computers, smartphones, tablets, restricted websites, as well as branded applications.

The periodicals chosen for the present study included the *Wall Street Journal, New York Times, USA Today,* and *Los Angeles Times.* As of 2013, the total average circulation for the periodicals were 2,378,827 for *Wall Street Journal,* 1,865,318 for *New York Times,* 1,674,306 for *USA Today,* and 653,868 for *Los Angeles Times.* These four periodicals were chosen based on their rank of being the most popular in the United States.

2.2. Comments Section

The present study used naturalistic observation of the comments section that followed a newspaper article posted on either the periodical website or the periodical's official Facebook page. The researchers collected the string of comments from each comment thread under an article, de-identified each comment, and uploaded the data into QSR NVivo 10 (2015) Qualitative Analysis Software. The comments were de-identified in order to keep the anonymity of the commenters, as this study did not gather consent from commenters. Due to the anonymous nature of this study, it is probable that one person (commenter) may have posted multiple comments within one comment thread. Thus, the study did not focus on the specific commenters themselves, but rather coded each comment as separate—even if the same commenter generated these comments. Therefore, the units of analysis for this study were comments within the comment thread, not the person making the comment. The researchers determined that by coding comments separately from the commenter, the study would be able to capture the complexities of rape culture.

2.3. Procedure

Data collection was completed between December 2014 and March 2015. To control for subjective selection bias of articles by the researchers—as well as to control for any news-cycle patterns—the researchers established parameters on data collection. Comment threads were collected only from articles that included the words "Rape" or "Sexual Assault" in the newspaper title. Additionally, the researchers alternated the location of where the data was collected, two months from Facebook posts and two months directly from the periodical website. This was an attempt to collect comments from differing audiences. One audience, the population that reads newspaper articles directly from a website and must pay a monthly subscription fee to comment in threads. The second audience, the population that reads and comments on an article as it appears in their Facebook feed and does not pay a fee to provide feedback. This was in order for the analysis to include two possibly different populations. One population that reads a newspaper regularly and has disposable income and time to subscribe to a newspaper website and another population that is more casual in how they consume the news. It is noted that it is likely that there may be overlap between these two populations.

The data collection process controlled for researcher selection bias and news media cycle bias by only selecting articles posted in the first seven days of each month—rather than self-selecting articles—to observe rape culture as it occurs in a week's time. The researchers collected the comment threads on average three days after the article was posted online to allow the dialogue to commence within the comment threads. Therefore, it is possible that more comments were posted after the data was already collected.

In total, the researchers collected 4,239 comments between December 2014 and March 2015 from 52 newspaper articles (19 articles in December 2014, 5 articles in January 2015, 5 articles in February 2015, and 23 articles in March 2015).

2.4. Media Climate during Data Collection

For context of the commentary occurring within the present data collection, it is important to note the headlines that were reported during this particular news cycle. Many of the articles collected had discourse on Bill Cosby's accusations of sexual assault, *Rolling Stone*'s article on a campus sexual assault, and a documentary about an Indian gang rape. By the end of the data collection—March 2015—Bill Cosby had been accused of sexual misconduct by 35 women, 17 of whom came forward during the data collection. Further, *Rolling Stone* had reported an article titled "A Rape on Campus" that reported the rape of Jackie, a student, while at a fraternity party at the University of Virginia. The story was later discredited and retracted by the publisher. Lastly, the documentary titled, "India's Daughter" was released towards the end of data collection that spurred a great deal of conversation on the 2012 gang rape of a 23-year-old medical student in India. However, these reports were only half of the collected sample. The rest varied in reporting from high-profile athletes to small-town, non-celebrity sexual assault crimes.

2.5. Data Analysis

Once de-identified, each article's comment thread was placed in a Word document and uploaded separately into NVivo. Data analysis was conducted using QSR NVivo 10 (2015) Qualitative Analysis Software and qualitative content analysis was the mode in which data was seen. As discussed by Babbie (1999), the research team sought to achieve "enhanced accountability" (p. 423). In order to control for inter-rater reliability all researchers independently coded December 2014 articles and then met regularly to ensure agreement between observed themes. For the remaining three months, the principal investigator coded each article along with at least one researcher. If a discrepancy was found in the coding between two researchers, the team of five researchers discussed and agreed on the correct analyses.

Initially the coding began identifying labels of victim blaming and survivor support, yet soon expanded into 28 identified labels, most which were labeled from a direct quote of the comments being analyzed. Once all the data was saturated, the team created four major themes that represented at least 50 percent (n = 26) of the total articles. Accordingly, there may be other themes within the data that were not as frequent and thus not identified by the researchers.

3. Results

The major themes that emerged from the qualitative content analysis include, Victim Blaming and Questioning, Survivor Support, Perpetrator Support, and Statements about Law and Society. For more information on thematic findings, refer to Table 1, which summarizes all major themes and sub-themes coded in data analysis. These themes, along with various sub-themes, will be discussed in detail below, along with quotations from the data to exemplify the themes. All quotations are direct quotes, which the researchers did not edit nor correct grammar, language, or use of capital letters.

Table 1.
Qualitative Content Analysis of Rape Culture in Social Media Forums

Themes	Sub-themes
Victim Blaming and Questioning	Giving instructions to rape survivors The survivor's story is too unbelievable to be real A hidden agenda was prominent as the reason to 'make up' a rape story The passage of time made the story unbelievable False accusations (aka 'using the rape card' as a defense) Alcohol and drugs (victim consented when drinking)
Survivor Support	Confession made to support the survivor in the story Information giving in support of the survivor
Perpetrator Support	Humor and ridicule Double standards
Trolling Statements about Law and Society	Media reporting bias Discrediting rape culture Racial and cultural statements about rape Gender differences

3.1. Theme 1: Victim Blaming and Questioning

Within the Victim Blaming and Questioning theme, the discussions centered around how believable the survivors' reports were and the circumstances surrounding the alleged assault that would make the survivor an unbelievable story-teller. Often, these comments took the form of sarcasm and implicit blame within the statement. Overall, the researchers coded 1,097 comments, or 25.8 percent of the total comments, thus making this the largest coded theme. In fact, this theme was present in every article examined except for one. The one article it was not included in was the only article collected that had no comments. Examples of discourse within this major theme included:

"Can someone please explain to me how a boy is raped??? If he's not willing, there's nothing going on downstairs."

"15 and 16 year old girls have been having sex WITH CELEBRITIES and then claiming rape to get money for decades. This is blackmail pure and simple."

"How do you 'take advantage' of young girls partying at a sex palace?"

The researchers divided the Victim Blaming and Questioning theme into six thematic areas, where blaming and questioning were most prominent. These six sub-themes and examples of the discourse include:

Sub-theme 1: Giving instructions to rape survivors. "I respectfully suggest to women who have been raped, a horrible and dehumanizing crime. Go to the police immediately or as soon as possible. Forget about the University administration. They aren't trained and they seek to protect their own interests not yours."

Sub-theme 2: The survivor's story is too unbelievable to be real. "Since I write fiction, it was easy to spot the [Rolling Stone] story of Jackie as a pathetically weak attempt by modern J- School grad to 'punch up' some classic 'rape' archetypes. I loudly call out fake, fraud and BS."

Sub-theme 3: A hidden agenda was prominent as the reason to 'make up' a rape story. "Anyone who doesn't recognize the political agenda behind these attacks on Cosby hasn't been paying attention."

Sub-theme 4: The passage of time made the story unbelievable. "40 years later, she's a middle-age washed-up never-was actress and she needs money. What can she do for quick cash?"

Sub-theme 5: False accusations (aka 'the rape card' as a defense). "Like the race card, the rape card is easily played, because there's no good defense against it even when it's played badly. I'm betting that even the truth won't stop the protesters in the Times photo, because it COULD HAVE BEEN TRUE—right?"

Sub-theme 6: Alcohol and drugs (victim consented when drinking). "There needs to be a law to protect men and teenage boys from charges made against them for rape or sexual misconduct by women and girls who are stupid enough to get drunk and allow this to happen then turn around and blame the male. If you are dumb enough to get drunk and put yourself in this position then too bad for you it's your own stupidity."

3.2. Theme 2: Survivor Support

Within the Survivor Support theme, comments were coded that reflected a genuine support for the survivor's reports and actions. Comments often included personal stories or statistics to defend the survivor from other comments that led to blame. Of the total comments collected, these comments totaled 694, or 16.3 percent of total comments. Interestingly, in the sub-theme 'Confession' the research team found it notable that 14 comments out of 694 comments discussed personal stories about rape and sexual assault. Overall, the comments were evenly spread between providing education, personal disclosures, anecdotal stories, and a stance that rape is not rare. Examples of discourse within this major theme included:

> *"As a former UVA fraternity brother, I do not doubt one detail of the events described in The Rolling Stone article, with all the excesses, abuses and absurdities. Unless you've witnessed one, it's hard to fathom the drunken, chaotic, and lawless abandon of a Virginia frat party, or the 'elite' entitlement."*

> *"As to the people here saying go to the court system, please… Who wants to be victimized twice."*

The researchers divided the Survivor Support theme into two thematic areas. These two sub-themes and examples of the discourse include:

Sub-theme 1: Confession made to support the survivor in the story. "This is the first time I am speaking about my rape when I was 14 by a counselor at camp who was also a coach and I hear he is still in the school system. I wish there was no statute of limitations (like in other countries) and I wish also the courts changed to be a friendlier place for victims. I am gaining the courage to say something the impact on my life (to me, maybe not to others) has been enormous."

Sub-theme 2: Information giving in support of the survivor. "Sexual assault does not happen by accident. The predator targets an individual, has a well-thought out strategy, and commits rape. This happens on campus, in corporate settings, and in the military. The rapist usually is older and has more social standing or power than the victim. The rapist also leaves her with a threat that 'no one will believe you' and, sadly, most victims believe it."

3.3. Theme 3: Perpetrator Support

The Perpetrator Support theme was rife with sarcasm, personal stories to endorse accused-perpetrators, and double standards revolving around gender. At times, comments exhibited banter back and forth with demeaning sexualized comments about the rape survivors and the suffering of falsely accused men. Though the comments totaled only 253, or 6 percent of total comments, these comments were found in every article collected except for one. Examples of discourse within this major theme included:

"A 30 year old woman 'raped' me at age 14 and continued to 'rape' me until age 21. I would have faced a firing squad before accusing her of anything."

"LOL. That's the only reason I got laid so much in college."

The researchers divided the Perpetrator Support theme into two thematic areas. These two sub-themes and examples of the discourse include:

Sub-theme 1: Humor and ridicule. "Somewhere and at sometime, a sexual assault occurred at a fraternity. Therefore any accusation about a sexual assault at a fraternity is true, because it is a fraternity. If you disagree, than you support sexual assault."

Sub-theme 2: Double standards. "Ask any guy, it is impossible for any man, especially a teenager, to be 'raped' by an NFL cheerleader!"

3.4. Theme 4: Trolling Statements about Law and Society

The Trolling Statements about the Law and Society theme were not a direct attack on the survivor or perpetrator referenced within the article, but rather a voice inciting hate or ridicule of an entire group of individuals that often was specific to race or culture. As described by Williams (2012), people who troll online are not insulting a specific person, but would prefer to create a wider disagreement that extends to broader subject matter and will incite a larger dialogue. The comments in this theme revealed blatant racism and sexism, and made negative, degrading, controversial statements that involved the greater legal society, political climates, and cultural norms. These comments totaled 982 comments, or 23.1 percent of total comments, which is the second largest coded theme. Examples of discourse within this major theme included:

"What we can expect from that poor country where cows life's better than people's?"

"This is an issue with the undocumented."

The researchers divided the Trolling Statements about the Law and Society theme into four thematic areas. These four sub-themes and examples of the discourse include:

Sub-theme 1: Media reporting bias. "My point is, if the alleged rapists had been black, Fox News would not need a Police report or forensic evidence to begin 24 h worth of programing to the effect that the rape was all the fault of Obama's America. But because the players don't fit the narrative—silence."

Sub-theme 2: Discrediting rape culture. "Twisted statistics to inflate the so-called rape hysteria program initiated by feminists is tantamount to misandry. Where the roles reversed I'm quite sure the feminists would blame this on the patriarchal society. Same animal, different name."

Sub-theme 3: Racial and cultural statements about rape. "Politicians call it 'blowing the dog whistle.' Ferguson was winding down, time to start up another distraction."

Sub-theme 4: Gender differences. "'Protecting' boys from having sex with older women they find attractive is a waste of taxpayer dollars that could be better spent protecting the group that needs more protecting—girls. The attempt to make the law gender-blind here is misguided."

4. Discussion

The present study sought to examine how prominent rape culture is within online social media forums following news articles reporting about rape and sexual assault. The results show that rape culture is prominent within online social media comment threads and victim blaming is the prevailing attitude in which it is expressed. Even though there are many factors, it appears victim blaming and questioning may be the driving force of rape culture in social media, as it creates hostility and discourse within the comment threads, leading to more commentary. As discussed by Franiuk, Seefelt, Cepress, and Vandello (2008), victim blaming permeates social media as well as popular culture. Thus, these attitudes seep into the collective thought of society and impact how society views rape and sexual assault. Instead of seeing the issue of sexual assault as an epidemic, this victim blaming and questioning attitude clouds one's judgment to believe rape is merely an individual issue and the survivor's fault.

Beyond the research question, the qualitative analysis exposed two notable findings, including the topic of survivor disclosure and differences in comments made based on whether the accused rapist was a celebrity or within pop-culture. The first notable finding of survivor disclosure suggests that some survivors "fight" the victim-blaming attitudes in social media threads by bringing a personal narrative into the discussion. Suran (2014) asserts that survivors who tell their story are breaking down rape culture. That is, when survivors feel marginalized by the process of reporting, they turn to social media to regain their voice. By posting to social media, the general public is able to view these stories and have an active voice in rape culture by "liking," "commenting," and "retweeting" the articles about the survivors' stories (p. 302), in turn, creating a collective call to action. Thus, social media seems to have changed the way in which society talks about sexual assault and rape. This is an area of future research that could be valuable in exploring.

The second notable finding included how celebrity status played into the comments about guilt versus innocence. This was especially true in the articles that centered on celebrities, such as Bill Cosby and Dustin Penner, as well as the University of Virginia rape scandal in *Rolling Stone*. Within those comment threads, there was more victim blaming and less perpetrator support as when compared to the comment threads centered on non-celebrity people. See Figs. 1 and 2 for displays on findings regarding popular culture. These findings support prior research conducted by Knight, Giuliano, and Sanchez-Ross (2001) that found perceptions about rape were influenced by the race and celebrity status of a defendant. This research supports their hypothesis that being a celebrity gives one the benefit of the doubt in the public's eye and that race or culture plays a role in the perceptions about rape. See Figs. 3 and 4 for displays of these particular findings.

Article Topic Includes Popular Culture

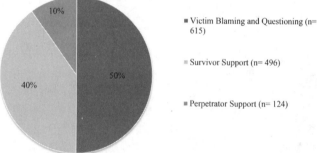

- Victim Blaming and Questioning (n= 615)

- Survivor Support (n= 496)

- Perpetrator Support (n= 124)

Fig. 1. Showcasing themes within comments under an article with the topic of popular culture.

Article Topic Does Not Include Popular Culture

- Survivor Support (n= 66)

- Perpetrator Support (n= 31)

- Victim Blaming and Questioning (n= 28)

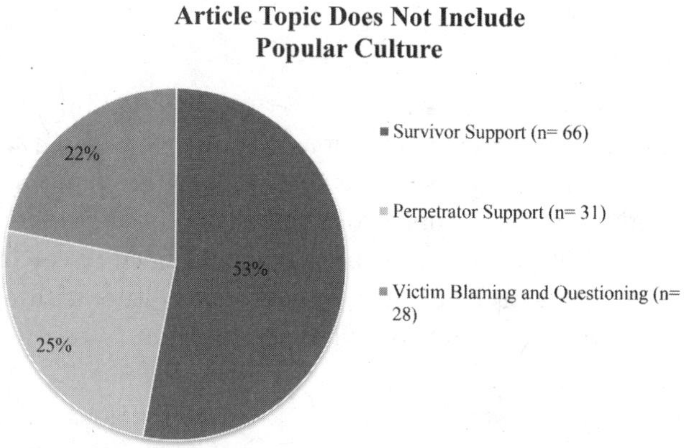

Fig. 2. Showcasing themes within comments under an article that does not include the topic of popular culture.

Accused Rapist in Article was American

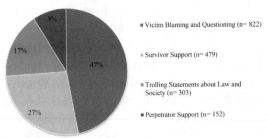

Fig. 3. Showcasing themes and sub-themes within comments under an article where the accused rapist was American.

Accused Rapist in Article was Not American

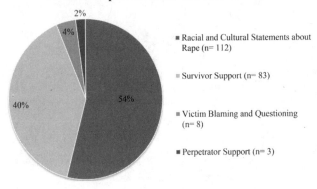

Fig. 4. Showcasing themes and sub-themes within comments under an article where the accused rapist was not American.

Given that the present study was the first of its kind, it is suggested that further research be conducted. With further research, studies may be designed to analyze a wider segment of comment threads online, as well as media reporting trends. It would be interesting to monitor active accounts' commentary and track if these comments influence and shape public opinion over time. This continued research would provide a deeper understanding of the phenomenon of rape culture within social media comment threads and the Internet, as a whole.

5. Limitations
Despite the authors' efforts to select articles in a systematic method, there are limitations to this study that prevent further conclusions from being drawn. First, during

the data collection period, the media climate was rampant with articles about rape and sexual assault, particularly on high profile cases. Bill Cosby is a revered celebrity who is loved by many, which may have influenced the audiences' views toward Mr. Cosby and the accusations against him may have prompted his fans to automatically jump to his defense, thereby increasing perpetrator support. Moreover, the *Rolling Stone* article was retracted not long after its publication, which caused an outcry of "sensationalizing rape" by painting the accused rapist in a sympathetic light and possibly increasing victim blaming in online forums.

Second, it is noted that utilizing the two groups of study, the periodical website and the periodical's official Facebook page may be limiting. That is, these two forums generally require an individual to use their true identity such as name and gender. Thus, the comments analyzed may not reflect how the commenter truly felt in fear of having their identity and comment be connected. Even though individuals may use pseudonyms for their paid subscription accounts, the account is also linked to a credit card, which may cause some hesitation on the part of the commenter. Also, those commenting on Facebook may not post genuine beliefs about rape and sexual assault in fear of family and friends seeing the comment threads on their news feed. Despite this, the researchers observed open and comprehensive commentary in the content analyzed.

Third, given the data was de-identified for privacy, the researchers only coded comments without a connection to the commenter. Thus, it is possible that a particular individual in a minority set of beliefs may dominate a thread of a particular theme. Also, due to de-identification, it is not possible to determine if gender had any influence on a commenter's perception. Even if the researchers maintained the identification of the commenters, it is common for individuals to use screen names, aliases, and gender-neutral names on social media forums, prohibiting the researchers from gathering data on the commenters' gender. A study by McAndrew and Jeong (2012) found that females engaged Facebook more often than males and sought out "gossip seeking behavior" more often than males (p. 2364). Examining the gender differences among the commenters could bring valuable information into who is writing perpetrator-supporting comments versus who is writing survivor-supporting comments. Additional information beyond gender, such as trauma history, education, nationality, and cultural identity may also illuminate which commenters have more victim blaming attitudes than others, as well as racial and gender-based discriminatory comments.

Another consideration is the relationship and personality traits of those that spend time commenting on newspaper articles online. That is, it would be interesting to note the correlation between relationship status and personality traits with how a person comments online. In a 2012 article, McAndrew and Jeong found that men in relationships spent less time on Facebook than those who were single. Similarly, Skues, Williams, and Wise (2012) found that individuals with more Facebook 'friends' and expressing a personality trait of "openness" were the highest Facebook users. The study defined "openness" as "having a wider range of interests and are more prepared to pursue those interests" (p. 2417). Interestingly, this study also found that Facebook users who were found to have a significant effect for "loneliness" had the most Facebook 'friends.' The postulation made by the authors was that lonely people engage more often on Facebook as an effort to acquire more friends. Thus, it can be ascertained that those same individuals spent time commenting on various threads on Facebook, including newspaper articles.

References

Alliance for Audited Media. (2013, April 1). *Top 25 U.S. Newspapers for March 2013*. Retrieved from http://auditedmedia.com/news/research-and-data/top-25-us-newspapers-for-march-2013.aspx.

American Press Institute. (2014, March 17). *How Americans get their news*. Retrieved from www.americanpressinstitute.org/publications/reports/survey-research/how-americans-get-news/.

Anderson, A.A., Brossard, D., Scheufele, D.A., Xenos, M.A., & Ladwig, P. (2014). The "nasty effect": online incivility and risk perceptions of emerging technologies. *Journal of Computer-Mediated Communication, 19*(3), 373–87. http://dx.doi.org/10.1111/jcc4.12009.

Boux, H.J., & Daum, C.W. (2015). At the Intersection of Social Media and Rape Culture: How Facebook postings, texting and other personal communications challenge the "real" rape myth in the criminal justice system. *Journal of Law, Technology, and Policy, 1*, 149–86.

Franiuk, R., Seefelt, J.L., Cepress, S.L., & Vandello, J.A. (2008). Prevalence and effects of rape myths in print journalism—The Kobe Bryant case. *Violence Against Women, 14*(3), 287–309.

Grubb, A., & Turner, E. (2012). Attribution of blame in rape cases: A review of the impact of rape myth acceptance, gender role conformity and substance use on victim blaming. *Aggression and Violent Behavior, 17*(5), 443–52.

Herman, D. (1984). The rape culture. In J. Freeman (Ed.), *Women: A feminist perspective*. Mountain View, CA: Mayfield.

Knight, J.L., Giuliano, T.A., & Sanchez-Ross, M.G. (2001). Famous or infamous? the influence of celebrity status and race on perceptions of responsibility for rape. *Basic and Applied Social Psychology, 23*(3), 183–90.

Lövheim, M., Jansson, A., Paasonen, S., Sumiala, J., Teologiska fakulteten, Humanistisk-samhällsvetenskapliga vetenskapsområdet. Religionsbeteendevetenskap. (2013). Social media: Implications for everyday life, politics and human agency. *Approaching Religion, 3*(2), 26.

Maxwell, Z. (2014, March 27). *Rape culture is real*. Retrieved from http://time.com/40110/rape-culture-is-real/.

McAndrew, F.T., & Jeong, H.S. (2012). Who does what on Facebook? Age, sex, and relationship status as predictors of Facebook use. *Computers in Human Behavior, 28*, 2359–65.

Media Insight Project. (2015, March 16). *How Millennials Get News: Inside the habits of America's first digital generation.* Retrieved from http://www.american pressinstitute.org/publications/reports/survey-research/millennials-methodology/.

Moss-Racusin, C.A., Molenda, A.K., & Cramer, C.R. (2015). Can evidence impact attitudes? Public reactions to evidence of gender bias in STEM fields. *Psychology of Women Quarterly*, 1–16. http://dx.doi.org/10.1177/0361684314565777.

NVivo Qualitative Data Analysis Software (2015). QSR International Pty Ltd. Version 10.

Skues, J.L., Williams, B., & Wise, L. (2012). The effects of personality traits, self-esteem, loneliness, and narcissism on Facebook use among university students. *Computers in Human Behavior, 28*, 2414–19.

Stavrositu, C.D., & Kim, J. (2015). All Blogs are not Created Equal: The role of narrative formats and user-generated comments in health prevention. *Health Communication, 30*(5), 485–95.

Suarez, E., & Gadalla, T.M. (2010). Stop blaming the victim: A meta-analysis on rape myths. *Journal of Interpersonal Violence, 25*(11), 2010–35. http://dx.doi.org/10.1177/0886260509354503.

Suran, E. (2014). Title IX and social media: Going beyond the law. *Michigan Journal of Gender and Law, 21*, 273–311.

Williams, Z. (2012). *The guardian.* www.theguardian.com/technology/2012/jun/12/what-is-an-internet-troll.

DISCUSSION QUESTIONS

1. Zaleski et al. explain that "blogs and the resulting comments sections influence opinions and intentions of the writers making the comments. It was found that user-generated comments could interfere with the message given by the blog itself" (p. 146). Discuss why you think this is, including any personal examples you have seen in your own online experience.

2. The authors chose "the top four newspapers in the United States" (p. 148) for their study. Choose a recently published article that discusses rape or sexual assault from a different news website than those used in the article and examine the 'comments' section. Compare your own findings to those of your classmates and of the article. How would you account for any differences between your findings and Zaleski et al.'s? When discussing, ensure you do not use the commenters' names.

3. In section 2.4, "Media climate during data collection," Zaleski et al. explain how they collected data during a time when there was a lot of media coverage of Bill Cosby's rape allegations, and in section 5, "Limitations," they acknowledge that his status as a "revered celebrity...may have influenced the audiences' views toward Mr. Cosby and the accusations against him" (p. 157). If we accept the claim that the support for Cosby did "increas[e] perpetrator support" (p. 157) overall, does this still add to the dialogue of how society views rape and rape culture in general? How so?

4. The largest coded theme in the study's findings is section 3.1, "Theme 1: Victim Blaming and Questioning." Looking at the six sub-themes present in this section, discuss why you think this category resulted in the most comments. How does victim blaming and questioning fit into our larger problem of rape culture? If possible, come up with some ideas that might help shift the conversations online from blaming and questioning to understanding and survivor support.

5. Figures 1 and 2 show the differences in victim blaming, perpetrator support, and survivor support when the topic included figures from popular culture and when they did not. What are the results of figures 1 and 2? The authors also give a reason for these results, stating that "being a celebrity gives one the benefit of the doubt in the public's eye" (p. 155). Why do you think this is? Can you think of other examples from recent history that further support this hypothesis?

E. "BLOGGING A RESEARCH PAPER? RESEARCHED BLOGS AS NEW MODELS OF PUBLIC DISCOURSE," LISA A. COSTELLO

In this 2015 article published by Teaching English in the Two-Year College, *author Lisa Costello* discusses her creation of a hybrid research assignment for her university students that integrates the academic writing of a research paper with the personal blog. Costello argues that "[b]y combining the strengths of an old format with the strengths of a new format" (p. 173), students can begin to understand the "changing milieu of public discourse into which they can and should enter as informed participants" (p. 162). As you read this article, consider whether you agree with Costello's hypothesis that this hybrid form of research writing prepares students to "becom[e] participants instead of spectators" (p. 174) in public discourse.*

Glossary terms: composition studies, case study

Abstract
A hybrid assignment, a research-based academic essay paired with a research-based weblog, incorporates elements from both personal and academic writing to challenge students to critically think about how and why they write privately and publicly. Students writing into this new model of public discourse can experiment with stance and tone across genres to exercise their abilities as responsible and flexible writers.

In her 2009 NCTE report, "Writing in the 21st Century," Kathleen Blake Yancey calls on the composition field to find *"new models of writing"* to address rapidly changing writing forms and environments, both in print and online (1). She notes that digital writing is "everywhere," in text messages, blogs, and chat rooms, and it is writing that "belongs to the writer, not an institution," and thus writers "want to compose and do—on the page and on the screen and on the network—*to each other.*" Writers share and dialogue in these new forms, "but mostly," she argues, they want "to participate," and so it is crucial for writing teachers to create methods and assignments that employ new forms to help our students "compose often and compose well" (4–5).

---

* Lisa A. Costello teaches composition and other writing courses at Georgia Southern University. She does interdisciplinary research in first-year writing, gender studies, and Holocaust studies, focusing on new media and rhetorical processes.

Notable in her list of new forms of literacies is the mention of blogs. This format has become common in composition classrooms as more studies indicate its efficacy in helping students gain control of their material and their voices. This essay does not intend simply to advocate for the use of the blog in the classroom, but rather to build on its use with a hybridized assignment that attempts to capture the positive attributes of both traditional research essay assignments and those of the modern blog. As Sullivan and Longnecker point out, blogs can be problematic in student achievement of writing skills because they often result in a "stream of consciousness style of writing" and "can become a soapbox" where opinion is not necessarily adequately substantiated. In contrast, the traditional research essay, while useful in teaching research skills and the structures of genres, has been regarded as frequently stifling to student interest, ownership, and expertise of knowledge in a topic. My assignment answers Yancey's call for new models of writing and addresses writers' desire to participate by blending an "old" form (research essay) with a "new" one (blog) that seeks the goals that blogs claim: interactivity, ownership, collaboration, and active learning (Seitzinger; Sullivan and Longnecker; Williams and Jacobs); but the assignment also teaches traditional research and argument structure and addresses the new roles of writers and audiences. Juxtaposing the two forms together creates a new model of composing that can help students see how each format informs the other, and perhaps how we might "retrofit" earlier models for new contexts (Yancey 6). In using these new models, students also need to attend to their "role of writing for the public," for this *is* the changing milieu of public discourse into which they can and should enter as informed participants.

Informed public discourse requires informed citizens, and indeed the strength of blogs for a classroom full of eager learners resides in their social and public aspect. Kenneth Bruffee has argued "for students to go public with their writing to receive feedback, on the grounds that public writing in classrooms deemphasizes teacher authority and promotes student-writers' ability to see themselves as responsible writers and to view writing as a social activity" (Lowe and Williams xii). In this social exchange, students learn that with new forms, "the biggest change is the role of audience: writers are everywhere, yes, but so too are audiences" (Yancey 5). My hybrid assignment blends the traditional research essay with a blog in an attempt to help students create a bridge between the writing they "want to do" with writing they "have to do" by framing that writing as personal and a part of public discourse; it is writing that has real consequences.

Why the Blog?

My years teaching first-year composition have made me realize that often students were not only writing mostly to me, regardless of the assigned audience, but also were either too afraid to voice their opinions or so unafraid as to blurt out overly opinionated statements devoid of evidentiary justification. Nancy Burkhalter agrees that for her students, sometimes "the most frightening aspect of the [argument] task stems from having to express their opinion" (30). For me, assigning more research did not seem to help, and having open classroom discussions sometimes made it worse. I started to think about ways I could creatively experiment with students to help them build their opinion on issues as well as let them experiment with style and tone. Because my institution stresses the sequence of genres as a way to build writing skills, experimenting with genre seemed a logical step. But I also felt that *caring* about topics was a key element that students were missing, because caring about something makes people want to participate; I wanted them to participate through writing. I let students pick their own topics, which seemed useful until I discovered how many students have been taught to write to the prompt. I tried service learning, but while it can be empowering, I found it to be an enormous burden on students (especially nontraditional students such as veterans, first-generation students who help support their families, and those in caregiver roles—large populations at my institute). Service has always been a way for students to show they cared about their community; I wondered if there might be a way to play with aspects of writing into a "public" without actually spending time in that "public." Could an online format be a way for students to nuance their opinions for real people as a way to step, just a little, into a public space?

My hypothesis with this assignment was that as students moved from a private audience to a public audience and from more academic to more personal writing, their stake in the topic would change because they could write in their own voice as "experts" and because they were aware of that unlimited audience. I was hoping to see more commitment to their topics and to the writing process in general. Students need to be encouraged to find nuances in their stances not only through "sides of the argument presented," which is a cognitive challenge for students that Burkhalter also notes (30). The crucial "turn" here is to develop the stance and research base first in a traditional essay, and then to rewrite that same material for a public audience in a blog so that students can focus on the changes in audience/tone and form. Using a personal stance born from strong emotion *and* informed opinion, students create a moderate form of public discourse, a kind of moderation of opinion that they may not see often modeled in the media (e.g., CNN or Fox News). "Going public" with those stances can create students who are better prepared, and perhaps even more willing, to participate in public discourse because they understand the real consequences of writing (Williams and Jacobs 240).

There are numerous online formats that are available, such as blogs, Facebook (FB), and Twitter (Instagram and Snapchat were not yet widely used when I worked with these students), and most do not require a great deal of technological expertise. I also had the option of using a course management blog/forum type format for students to voice opinions and keep writing in a constantly open revision loop. In looking at the research available on blogs (it is now much more extensive), I discovered

Ferdig and Trammell's four pedagogical benefits of using blogs in the classroom: "(1) encourages students to develop expertise in their subject matter, (2) stimulates student interest and ownership of the topic, (3) creates a community of learners and practice and (4) exposes students to diverse perspectives" (Williams and Jacobs 390). My reasons for choosing the blog overlap these and expand them. Students need to "own" their topic, and in order to do this they have to own the writing space into which they write. Sites like FB and Blackboard do not allow much personal design input. Although blogs have templates, they can be personalized with colors and pictures, and students find them more "intuitive" to use (Sullivan and Longnecker 390). One student, Megan, described the design of her blog as follows: "The layout of my blog, including: color, font, images, videos, and design, were constantly changing. Eventually, I settled on a format where I felt my blog represented me."

My second reason overlaps with expertise and diverse perspectives. Student expertise can help build opinions, and audience awareness includes diverse perspectives. Jane Danielewicz highlights the need for writing to become effectively interactive with its audiences. "True participation," she insists, "is marked by language inflected with the distinctiveness of an individual's identity and voice" (425). I want students to model this kind of nuanced opinion by thinking about how to present a position in light of real audiences and diverse perspectives. Another student, Heidi, found a humorous video she thought was insulting to the special needs populations in her topic, "but after watching it and finding out that the Special Olympics endorsed it, I found that I can use it to help illustrate the need to break stereotypes and advocate reform." She discovered the source, assessed it, researched what others thought of it, and figured out where it fit into her argument.

Lastly, I thought about student participation in public discourse, which is not a pedagogical outcome in the above but has since become one of the most important aspects of writing in new models, according to Yancey. The blog can effectively allow students to share their opinions as public discourse. A Chinese artist and dissident, recently interviewed for Index on Censorship, stated: "I do my blog because this is the only possible channel through which a person can express a personal opinion in China" (WeiWei 2). Simmons and Grabhill insist there is increasing interest "in how people can write to change communities" (419), and because writing can change communities, it is important to foster students' sense of the *necessity* of participating in those public spaces. The idea of participation as a social activity—citizens participate in public discourse by interacting with it—because it occurs increasingly in online spaces—should be expanded to include not only reading or analyzing new media in the classroom, but also having students develop and support their stance on issues as they create and participate in that digital discourse. These are the advantages of the blog over other online formats, but the key is combining the strengths of the "new form" blog with the "old form" research essay in several specific ways to improve students' abilities to write nuanced opinions.

The Writing Assignment

Technology in the composition classroom has been discussed since the late 1980s (Stefanac; also Brooks, Nichols, and Priebe; Carlson; Lindgren; Rodzvilla). Digital and multimodal composing practices have been the focus of textbooks, national conferences (CCCC: "Computers and Writing"), journals (*Computers and Composition*), and pedagogy programs such as Ohio State's Digital Media and Composition Workshop. Blogs have already been used successfully in the classroom as journals, as collaborative writing tools, and as research and revision exercises to show how writers write for a public audience (Costello; Goodwin-Jones; Lowe and Williams; McCorkle; Tougaw).

This hybrid assignment, however, uses not just the blog but also the research essay to create a new model that explores how the formats can function in concert. Part 1 requires an academic research paper, in which students present a cultural issue as a problem and provide several solutions that have been applied or theorized. Students are asked to research this issue extensively and complete prewriting assignments that focus on finding and organizing research (such as annotated bibliographies). The academic research essay is written with a private and closed audience and purpose in mind. Part 2 of this assignment requires students to re-present the problem and solutions they researched in part 1 in a blog format and to decide on the solution they think will be most feasible, effective, far-reaching, or practical, providing additional research on this specific solution. In part 2 students are allowed informal and personal language. Linked media images and research are required as they build the blog site. Students are asked to consider their research for new audiences and purposes in a public realm. Each student writes a rationale essay that explains his or her choices in the blog in design, research, organization, and text. Part 2 is listed on the syllabus simply as the fourth writing assignment: "a blog." At the outset of the course, students know only that they will be writing a research paper and a blog linked by the same subject matter; they do not know they will rewrite the same material in different genres.

While it is true that entries into public discourse could be achieved through a class chapbook of writing produced for their campus or by producing a brochure for a local charity, these options are also more expensive and less accessible than an open source program online. Though a chapbook or brochure has real audiences and effects, students' personal "stepping out into" public discourse is less tangible because their opinion is not the focus or the goal of the project, nor do they necessarily "see" a real audience in their minds. Students take an especially productive risk in putting their opinion out into the public sphere on the blog and supporting it with their strong research base (developed in part 1), because the blog audience is a special "public"—both broad in scope and potentially large in number.

The research paper builds students' confidence in their research choices, organization, and position, and the blog builds students' confidence and ability to "participate" in dialogues about that position because it is immediate and interconnected. It is immediate when students have the *potential* of receiving instant response and engaging in a dialogue (though in most cases it is not yet realized). It is interconnected when students engage with the research conversation about a topic through embedded links, comments, and imagined audiences. They link to research as they write, and knowing that their audience can link there as well increases their responsibility to those sources. Embedded links then connect to other related sources, extending the dialogue into the larger, interconnected cyberspace, something that cannot be achieved with a different format. One student, Emily, wrote: "During the first paper I was writing for one person, but the audience was unlimited in my blog, this was very hopeful for me." Potentially reaching an "unlimited" audience is not something that can be achieved with a project in print distributed locally, and taking a stand in front of that large audience encourages students to practice, especially since many have never even "been asked to give their view on anything, let alone persuade someone to agree with them in writing" (Burkhalter 30). Many examples they may see online include strong opinions but not much evidentiary support.

Students regularly see these kinds of undeveloped opinions in online spaces where writers are often unapologetic about their one-sided opinions. One online diarist called "Johnny Reb" explains that his identity as a Civil War aficionado allows him the freedom to speak uncensored about topics of race and politics. "This stance," Laurie McNeill states, "serves as a reminder of both the online diarist's freedom from the external censorship inherent in the traditional publishing process and the implications of that freedom for online readers and writers" (31), but it can also be inflammatory, narrow-minded, and misinformed. In both academic writing and social media spaces, students tend to take on single perspectives as writers and write to one person.

We know students are already writing profusely on social media, phones, and email, and they find online forms like wikis and blogs easy to use (Avci and Askar 202). They participate in media production, broadcasting, and revising their own autobiographies in online spaces, many on a daily or hourly basis. They have identities and voices that are malleable depending on the pictures or links they may post that day, and yet these stances and opinions are often so abbreviated that students take them on and off, like exchanging dirty clothes for clean ones, without thinking about why or how their thinking has changed. Such stances, though mutable, remain rather narrow and undeveloped.

In her oft-visited blog "Baghdad Burning," Iraqi Riverbend blogs sympathetically to both Iraqi and American audiences with nuanced perspectives about the American occupation. Tess Pierce sees blogs like Riverbend's as examples of how writers can take on multiple identities in order to address different perspectives on one issue (202). These perspectives are similar to discursive code-switching, and part of the exercise of this assignment is to have students move back and forth between levels of authority in voice and tone—using one topic in a research essay and then adding more research to it in a blog. How they build and *re-present* this opinionated position then depends on the changing genre and audience they discover in the blog. This rewriting could be achieved by writing an essay and then rewriting that material into an op-ed or a poem, but the multimodal design of the blog—and its public nature—make this re-presentation for an audience more radical and conscious. Students have to critically think about their argument in a different way, and they have the freedom to add linked research, videos, images, and gadgets like polls and games for audience interaction, which are not options in most other forms.

Data Collection and Method
The data come from a first-year student population at a regional college in the Southeast. I collected IRB-approved student writing samples from ENGL 1102 students over the course of a year in several sections that I taught. Student comments were culled from ungraded reflective letters about the assignments (submitted after all other grades were already recorded), rationale essays, and formal, anonymous evaluations. I was hoping that asking them to highlight their opinions and support them in two different settings might help students understand that they had an opinion worth sharing. The blogs did show a greater stake in how they presented and supported their opinions for this larger, public audience.[1] The unanticipated result was that many students were still afraid to share their opinions. Taking a stand for their peers or me could result in a poor grade and was inhibiting, but the possibility of a public audience disagreeing with them inhibited them even more. One student, Frances, was so aware of potential response that she said, "I was also scared because I have seen sites where there are hostile audiences bashing people['s] thoughts, and my topic was very controversial."

Writing to Participate
The hybrid assignment aims to strengthen students' sense of tone and audience as they write and support their opinions in private and public contexts. The blog specifically gives them a space in which they want to participate. Blogs "help students develop the ability to adapt suitable voices for various contexts" (Tougaw 252), but to assume these varied stances based in research takes practice. As W. Michele Simmons and Jeffrey T. Grabhill suggest, the "problem of knowledge and . . . of performance" that beginning writers face may prevent "'nonexpert' participants from entering 'public deliberations'"; that is, newer writers with little experience are reluctant to assume a strong opinion in writing because they don't feel like experts (421). By writing a traditional essay first, students gain research knowledge and argument organization expertise so they can enter into those "public deliberations" with more confidence.

By adding the blog, I ask students to aggregate sources as a way to make their opinion the centerpiece—to nuance that strong opinion with source material as a dialogic exercise. I want them to *have a stake* in that public discourse and enter into a responsible dialogue connected with others online. One student, Christine, stated: "My research changed a little because I had to make sure that if anyone came to my site and I was talking about something they could go to the link and immediately see what I was talking about, where[as] in the paper I just told you." The implications of that larger audience checking her sources puts her out "in public" much more than with just me or peers as readers. Megan S. also felt the public nature of the blog space: "This project gave me the opportunity to connect with people who had the same concerns as I did."

It might seem that connected, online communities might be more ephemeral and remote than a real community service project would be, or that an online audience is not enough of an incentive for students to want to participate. Students building expertise around something they care about and then writing in forms in which they want to participate is a huge first step; as Howard Rheingold notes, however, "speaking your mind is necessary to be hearable, but doesn't guarantee that you will be heard" (99). Thus, students inserting their opinion into a public space with an unlimited audience is an important second step, because having audiences "who can respond to bloggers is as important as introducing people to blogs as vehicles of potential public influence" (Rheingold 99). It is important to keep in mind that since "public voice can be characterized not just as active, but as generative—a public is brought into being in a sense by the *act of addressing* some text in some medium to it" (102; emphasis added), a real "public" in this assignment does not require a responding audience to be present at this stage. Student writers perceive the existence of that public audience into which they project a stance, and projecting that position for public review is a risk that raises the stakes of that stance.

The first "public" for students is their classroom peers for essays and in-class peer review, an audience of which they are hyperaware. The public online, "unidentified" and somewhat amorphous, is by nature larger and broader; social media constantly reminds them they are being watched and, even more importantly, "liked" on a twenty-four-hour basis. Because they cannot make assumptions about an online audience, who may hold radically alternate perspectives on topics due to age, ethnic, or regional influences, I have found that students have a greater personal stake and sense of value with those other audiences in mind. Other formats outside the classroom in which students might publish their works, such as a campus chapbook or brochure, will not have the same audience reach, even though it is a "real" audience. One student, Casey, wrote in her evaluation: "I do feel successful that my topic is out there to be read," but she adds her doubt: "if readers come." But would she know or be sure about the readers of a campus publication in print either? A community audience is just as likely to ignore print material or throw it away as they are not to click on a blog. But when the blog could reach thousands around the world instead of hundreds in halls across the quad, the numerical odds are greater in students' minds that a public might or could be reached (Lowe and Williams; Sullivan and Longnecker).

Another student, Sammy, writing about animal rights, talked about how sharing the information changed her approach to her writing. Writing and rewriting for Sammy were the "easy" parts: "However, sharing all that information and opinions made it more real. People could read what I wrote and know my stance on the issue. So it was kind of like I had to be committed to my topic because I was proposing a solution to it." To consider that "people could read" what Sammy wrote begins the "act of addressing" that Rheingold suggests is crucial to considering public audiences.

Many students considered the larger audience as they wrote, knowing that anyone could read their work, though most discovered that their blogs did not receive public comments. One student did receive a comment that critiqued his use of a research quote on economics. He asked me what he should say, not yet realizing that this continuing dialogue in the public realm was now up to him. In future iterations of this assignment, I would like to work with students on creating tags for their blogs and using other methods that might help those blogs appear in Internet searches. But the lack of "public" commentary from anonymous readers did not prevent students from performing for a "public." Sharing opinions and creating writing and design for review increased the performance and commitment of my students in their writing.

Student Writing Samples: The Essay and the Blog

In the following paragraphs, I include writing samples from two students, with samples from both their essays and their blogs, to show in detail how their position and tone changed across the two forms. In her problem essay, Brooke chose to address the lack of reconstruction efforts in New Orleans post-Hurricane Katrina:

> There are in fact some causes that could have been dealt with long before this life changing incident. One of the causes is that the governor of New Orleans knew that his city was at risk and did not act upon it. In agreement with Kates, a writer for the National Academy of Science, "For three centuries, New Orleans sought to lessen the impacts of its recurrent floods and hurricanes by providing marginal increases in safety. However for doing so they laid the groundwork for the next catastrophic failure" (1). New Orleans was also constructed with levees that were rebuilt and raised. It was estimated that the population before Katrina was 437,186 and they lived halfway below sea level. A few years before the hurricane hit scientist had warned the governor that the big one was coming and no one proceeded to take caution. One of the largest effects of the levee ignorance is Hurricane Katrina herself. Another effect is the loss of thousands of lives and homes.

In Brooke's discussion of some of the causes of Hurricane Katrina in the essay, she explains the mayor's stance (inaccurately calling him governor) without providing a source. Though the research is good, her attribution to Kates is a little awkward. She has a strong topic sentence but does not follow through, as she begins with causes but ends with effects.

This is Brooke's blog entry on the same aspect of the topic (you can find Brooke's blog at http://br00k1e7.blogspot.com):

Every Problem Can Be Prevented
Oh k so for like over 60 years scientists have been telling the politicians and governors that the levees are not very strong and with a really bad hurricane they wont hold it. The federal government needed to take steps to increase local government commitment to planning and hazard mitigation by making relatively small adjustments to the Disaster Mitigation Act of 2000 and the Flood Insurance Act. For three centuries, New Orleans sought to lessen the impacts of its recurrent floods and hurricanes by providing marginal increases in safety. However for doing so they laid the groundwork for the next catastrophic failure. One effect of the levees not being maintained and rebuilt was Hurricane Katrina doing damage, and another were the thousands of lives taken just from people being lazy. Although the levees broke 3 and a half years ago, there are houses still right around them that are still messed up and no one lives in them. [Brooke posted her own photograph on the blog in this entry from an alternative Spring Break trip.]

In the blog entry, she is dealing with the same information. She begins the paragraph (or entry) with an assertive title: "Every Problem Can Be Prevented." Compare the first two sentences of each. In the essay she writes, "There are in fact some causes that could have been dealt with long before this life changing incident," and in the blog she writes, "Oh k so for like over 60 years scientists have been telling the politicians and governors that the levees are not very strong and with a really bad hurricane they wont hold it." The second example, with the entry title concisely labeling this section as being about "causes," shows a stronger personal stance on the topic by using detail and getting right to the point that scientists have been saying for years: the levees are not strong enough. The second sentence too reveals a stronger stance about the topic. In the essay, she makes a claim without evidence. In the blog entry, she makes the causes less about the mayor and more about government systems failing in general, which shows how she critically analyzed the new knowledge she found; she understands more perspectives than just the "easy" one that blames the local mayor. She then cites a linked article about the Flood Insurance Act. The use of the research link has not weakened her research—she does not let that link speak for itself—but has made the research more direct and focused, so that she can also mention the Disaster Mitigation Act. Although she still discusses effects in this paragraph, her ability to see the situation from several perspectives is evident. She uses the same basic research, but it now presents a more complex issue with a stronger personal stance and more clarity and depth.

Casey's problem essay was about the lack of recycling in Chatham County, Georgia. The essay sample is from her final paragraph, in which she mentions mandatory recycling or expansion as one of the possible solutions:

> The City of Savannah has created the beginning of what could be a great recycling program with a high impact on the environmental crisis. But that is the problem, it is just the beginning and so much more could be done with the recycling program to make it as effective as it should be. The city's single-stream recycling program is a major positive for residents. More residents recycle in the city than on Tybee Island because of the single-stream program; the program makes it more convenient to recycle. The problem is not many residents are recycling within the program, so nothing is really being done. The city and county could institute a mandatory program or a pay-as-you-throw program, where residents are charged for the amount of trash they throw away. Savannah and Chatham County in its whole could make a major impact and be a role model for the rest of Costal Georgia if they changed their program. Ultimately, the whole of Chatham County, from the city limits to Tybee Island, needs to be included within the new recycling program. The only way the city is going to make any impact on the recycling problem is if it expands its program to more residents.

In the essay sample, there is good information, but she does not cite any sources, nor does she develop any of these items. In the last sentence, even though it implies a "should," it is not very forceful in its assertion.

Here is the sample writing from the blog on the same aspect of the topic of recycling (you can find Casey's blog at http://recyclesav.blogspot.com):

Maybe one day.
Mandatory recycling for Chatham County, not just the city of Savannah, could help the Coastal Georgia region in so many ways. All the facts add up; it makes sense to recycle and even saves cents! We could make a huge impact on the environmental crisis at hand if we just recycled.

The irony of this whole situation is that Chatham County residents want to recycle! They want to be included in the program. Chatham County residents created a proposal for the unincorporated portions of the county, but were shot down by commissioners. The commissioners stated that the program was too expensive, especially with the economy at the moment. But that did not stop them. Residents have created a petition to keep their effort alive. The petition needs 17,000 signatures in order to amend the [commissioners'] decision.

Like Brooke, Casey begins with a creative title, "Maybe one day," that suggests what this section is about. Her topic sentence asserts a solution that could work really well, but in the essay this information is buried in the middle of the paragraph. With the use of "we" in the blog entry, Casey's stance on this topic comes through strongly, as does her consideration of a larger audience. She is clearly a resident of Chatham County, a fact that increases her ethos as a writer tremendously, but that was totally absent in the essay. In addition, in comparison to the last paragraph of the essay, the blog entry talks specifically about a problem and solution process in action, the counterargument by the commission, and then the extended action by the public—the petition, and she links it to the blog entry. She has creatively presented a fuller scenario, not just to explain what the city did, but to suggest her participation in that public—the "all of us"; in other words, there were multiple perspectives in this evolving issue that we did not see before. Although the linked petition is the only research she links in this paragraph, this lack is mediated in my mind by the greater sense of personal stance and audience awareness she reveals in the blog. This entry underscores not only that the audience is present, but that she is a part of that public that can effect change. In response to a "public," Casey's opinions became stronger because she perceived an audience who listened.

Limitations and Recommendations

Though most of the students in this sample enjoyed preparing a blog, the assignment has limitations. Using sites such as Blogger.com or WordPress was easy and free, but occasionally the computer lab access to these free programs was patchy. Blogger.com has frozen some students out of their accounts for unexplained reasons. But there are now many more platforms from which to choose if you want to try this in your classroom. Joyce Seitzinger has an outstanding breakdown of the sites and clear steps for creating blogs with your students (8). I have described how the technological framework works for students, but for a few it was the format itself that proved the biggest obstacle to writing and thinking. Autumn wrote: "Blogging was very unfamiliar to me. I don't feel that I was as concise with what I wanted to communicate. I'm more comfortable with formal papers; therefore taking on an informal tone was difficult for me. I felt like the broken-up style of the blog messed with my thought process a little." This presents an argument against my hypothesis that the online format might be an easier way for some students to write, but it is also an argument about how changing and blending formats helps students reflect on how they think and, consequently, how they write.

Other students found the public audience a disadvantage rather than an advantage, especially as they were asked to take a stand in front of that audience. Megan S. said: "Now my ideas were out in the open for everyone to see; I felt vulnerable." Jessica found the personal writing intimidating: "I also didn't really like trying to be more casual with it. I knew I would not get much support for my topic, so speaking from a personal tone or sounding too opinionated might turn readers off." I am still encouraged, however, that though students like Megan and Jessica felt vulnerable or afraid that they would deter readers with their personal opinion, putting that opinion out into a public got them thinking about the implications of taking that stand—a good learning outcome in terms of audience awareness.

The data sample in this study is limited, and the conclusions, therefore, are preliminary. I have used blogs as revision tools with success, and I have used blogs as research logs with much less success. The use of the blog itself does not automatically guarantee positive learning outcomes or student engagement. In putting together the hybrid assignment, I hoped to have students consider writing in two contexts and forms of writing to increase their topic expertise and to consider audience in a very real way as a "public" who listens. The effect of the "social presence" on learning should not be underestimated. In one study where students used blogs, a student described how it felt to write for the closed audience and the open audience. The student described feeling "odd writing unpublished in Word: 'It was like—like talking to someone who was not listening'" (Seitzinger 7). Increased interest and engagement for students was a positive result of this combined assignment. The use of the two forms together could become a new model of composing to help students see how each format informs the other, or even how earlier models might be "retrofit[ted]" for new contexts (Yancey 6). I am hoping to further this study with more samples to test the efficacy of the blog as a companion to a research essay and to test the continued interest level of students in that juxtaposition.

Results and Conclusions

Rhetoricians have called "publics" emergent, as well as "multiple and changing" (Hauser xi), evolving *through* discourse and constituted *by* discourse. Part of the exercise of this assignment is to have students move back and forth between levels of authority in voice and tone. The mutability of the audience and form directs how they *re-present* their position and build their research. By combining the strengths of an old format with the strengths of a new format, students could see how the forms worked in concert as a newly created hybrid, maybe even a new model for public discourse. Students increased the complexity and depth of their topics, as they also strengthened their confidence in their research choices, organizations, and position on that topic.

Performing in public as "authorities" increased their commitment to their topics, as I had hypothesized. Brooke said: "I did feel more committed because I actually wanted to write my blog because I knew other people would be looking at it. I also felt committed to it because I got to pick it and it was something that was really important to me." Casey agreed: "As a result of the blog, I feel motivated that maybe something can be done soon about my problem because I spent so much time and focus on the problem and all the information is there." Teaching students to care enough to take an enthusiastic position on a topic in writing matters because our society, though based on the participation of its citizens, requires less and less of an active role. It is important to me to see that students are beginning to think through those public roles in the world around them, both active and passive, to consider becoming participants instead of spectators.

Rheingold has argued, "knowing how to take a tool into one's hand is no guarantee that anyone will do anything productive, but without such knowledge about how to use and how to 'repurpose,' productive use is less likely—and hegemonic control becomes more likely by those who do know exactly how to exercise the power of the new media" (103–04). With the data I have presented here, I suggest that using a traditional research essay and transforming that material into public blog-writing can create "productive use" and give students the experience of presenting their opinions to a wide public. Though researchers such as Ferdig and Trammel have claimed lofty pedagogical goals for blogs, and many students in this data sample did become more committed to problems occurring in their worlds, not all students will. Students who have practice stating and backing up their opinions, in private and in public, however, *may be* more likely to become active participants in their worlds. This assignment explores the changing contexts of both private and public writing, which might help students see that FYC is not the last writing class they will ever take, but is, rather, their first *opportunity* in college to acquire the writing skills they will need to succeed in whatever career paths they may choose.[2]

Notes

[1] With FERPA (Family Educational Rights and Privacy Act) in place, instructors should present privacy issues to students. Blogs have the option of remaining in draft form without having any entry posted to the Internet. Not one student has yet exercised this option in my classroom.

[2] I would like to thank the anonymous readers at TETYC for their reviews of this manuscript. Thanks also to R, D, L, and J for their comments.

References

Avci, U., and P. Askar. "The Comparison of the Opinions of University Students on the Usage of Blog and Wiki for Their Courses." *Educational Technology & Society* 15.2 (2012): 194–205. *Academic Search Premier*. Web. 15 Apr. 2015.

Brooks, Kevin, Cindy Nichols, and Sybil Priebe. "Remediation, Genre, and Motivation: Key Concepts for Teaching with Weblogs." *Into the Blogosphere*. Ed. Laura

Gurak, et al. U of Minnesota, 2004. Web. 10 Oct. 2012.

Burkhalter, Nancy. "To the Moon!—A Launch Pad for Encouraging Students to Express Their Opinions." *English Teaching Forum* 4 (2011): 30–35. Print.

Carlson, Scott. "Weblogs Come to the Classroom." *Chronicle of Higher Education* 28 Nov. 2003: A33–34. Print.

Conference on College Composition and Communication. Committee on Computers in Composition and Communication. "Computers and Writing Conference: Call for Proposals." CCCC, 2015. Web. 21 Apr. 2015.

Costello, Lisa. "The New Art of Revision? Research Papers, Blogs, and the First-Year Writing Classroom." *Teaching English in the Two-Year College* 39.2 (2011): 151–67. Print.

Danielewicz, Jane. "Personal Genres, Public Voices." *College Composition and Communication* 59.3 (2008): 420–50. Print.

Goodwin-Jones, Bob. "Blogs and Wikis: Environments for On-line Collaboration." *Language Learning and Technology* 7.2 (2003): 12–16. *Project Muse.* Web. 30 Aug. 2010.

Hauser, Gerard A. Foreword. *The Public Work of Rhetoric: Citizen-Scholars and Civic Engagement.* Ed. John M. Ackerman and David J. Coogan. Columbia: U of South Carolina P, 2010. ix–xii. Print.

Lindgren, Tim. "Blogging Places: Locating Pedagogy in the Whereness of Weblogs." *Kairos: A Journal of Rhetoric, Technology and Culture* 10.1 (2005). Web. 9 June 2011.

Lowe, Charles, and Terra Williams. "Moving to the Public: Weblogs in the Writing Classroom." *Into the Blogosphere.* Ed. Laura Gurak et al. University of Minnesota, 2004. Web. 15 Sept. 2014.

McCorkle, Ben. "English 109-02: Intensive Reading and Writing II: Reading, Writing, Blogging." *Composition Studies* 38.1 (2010): 109–19. Project Muse. Web. 29 July 2010.

McNeill, Laurie. "Teaching an Old Genre New Tricks: The Diary on the Internet." *Biography* 26.1 (Winter 2003): 24–47. *Project Muse.* Web. 01 July 2013.

Pierce, Tess. "Singing at the Digital Well: Blogs as CyberFeminist Sites of Resistance." *Feminist Formations* 22.3 (2010): 196–209. *Project Muse.* Web. 15 July 2013.

Rheingold, Howard. "Using Participatory Media and Public Voice to Encourage Civic Engagement." *Civic Life Online: Learning How Digital Media Can Engage Youth.* Ed. W. Lance Bennett. Cambridge: MIT P, 2008. 97–118. Print.

Riverbend. Baghdad Burning. N.d. Web.

Rodzvilla, John, ed. *We've Got Blog: How Weblogs Are Changing Our Culture.* Cambridge: Perseus, 2002. Print.

Seitzinger, Joyce. "Be Constructive: Blogs, Podcasts, and Wikis as Constructivist Learning Tools." *The E-Learning Guild's Learning Solutions: Practical Applications of Technology for Learning.* 31 July 2006. Web. 1 Apr. 2015.

Simmons, W. Michele, and Jeffrey T. Grabhill. "Toward a Civic Rhetoric for Tech-
    nologically and Scientifically Complex Places: Invention, Performance, and Par-
    ticipation." *College Composition and Communication* 58.3 (2007): 419–48. Print.

Stefanac, Stephanie. *Dispatches from Blogistan: A Travel Guide for the Modern Blogger.*
    Berkeley: New Riders, 2007. Print.

Sullivan, M., and N. Longnecker. "Class Blogs as a Teaching Tool to Promote Writ-
    ing and Student Interaction." *Australasian Journal of Educational Technology* 30.4
    (2014): 390–401. Web. 15 Feb. 2014.

Tougaw, Jason. "Dream Bloggers Invent the University." *Computers and Composition*
    26.4 (2009): 251–68. *Elsevier.* Web. 10 Dec. 2011.

Weiwei, Ai. "Truth, No Matter the Power: Controversial Chinese Artist and Dis-
    sident Ai Weiwei's Only Fear Is Silence." Interview by Simon Kirby from *Index
    Censorship.* Reprinted in *Utne Reader* May–June 2009. Web. 15 June 2011.

Williams, Jeremy B., and Joanne Jacobs. "Exploring the Use of Blogs as Learning
    Spaces in Higher Education Sector." *Australasian Journal of Educational Technol-
    ogy* 20.2 (2004): 232–47. Web. 1 Jan. 2009.

Yancey, Kathleen Blake. "Writing in the 21st Century." *National Council of Teachers
    of English.* Feb. 2009. Web. 2 Feb. 2015.

DISCUSSION QUESTIONS

1. Costello provides links to two of her students' blogs (http://recyclesav.blogspot.
   com and http://br00k1e7.blogspot.ca/). Take a look at their blog entries to get
   a feel for how they chose to write about their respective topics. Discuss your
   findings (for example, do you think the entries are as research-heavy as Costello
   describes them?).

2. The article stresses the fact that online forms of discourse are quick to change
   and adapt. Looking at how Costello frames the blogging part of her assignment,
   and keeping in mind the overall goal (to create students who are comfortable
   engaging in public discourse), can you identify two or three ways that this project could be adapted to fit within the context of social media today?

3. Costello suggests that "the use of the two forms together [blogging and research
   papers] could become a new model of composing to help students see how each
   format informs the other" (p. 162). Explain how Costello envisions this happening. Do you agree with Costello? Why or why not?

4. Costello writes about how the assignment was created in part to help students
   become more comfortable writing for both public and private audiences. How
   does the article describe the difference between those two audiences, and what

were some of the fears that Costello's students described in regards to writing in each capacity? As academics yourselves, do you face any similar fears with your own writing?

5. At the beginning of "Results and Conclusions," Costello observes that "[r]hetoricians have called 'publics' emergent, as well as 'multiple and changing' (Hauser xi), evolving *through* discourse and constituted *by* discourse" (p. 173, original emphasis). How are "publics" emergent? Keeping in mind the assignment described in this article, discuss specific examples of how the "public" is "constituted by discourse." What does it mean to say that discourse constitutes the public?

ENVIRONMENT AND SOCIETY

INTRODUCTION

A selection of readings on the environment might come from disciplines as diverse as ecology, climatology, soil science, and oceanology. Indeed, whole university departments and faculties—Forestry, Science, Earth and Ocean Sciences—devote considerable resources to studying the environment. Expand the term into 'the environment and society' and it takes only a moment to imagine relevant research being conducted in the faculties of Medicine, Arts and Social Sciences, and Engineering. At this point, excluding academic disciplines conducting pertinent research may seem a greater challenge than including them.

When you think about the environment, your first thoughts may well turn to ecology: you might think of ecosystems—arctic or arboreal biomes—made up of plant and animal producers, consumers, and decomposers, and of the physical systems that support them. But chances are that your thoughts eventually will turn to the sometimes strained relationship between humans and those systems. In Europe, legislation relating to the environment dates back at least to the Middle Ages, with laws regulating the burning of wood and coal, not out of concern for the environment but to protect the health of humans, a concern that became more pressing with the onset of the Industrial Revolution in the eighteenth and nineteenth centuries.

In the West, the idea that the environment is not simply a set of resources to be exploited but something that needs protection from human activity is relatively recent, becoming prevalent only during the Romantic era (you may remember vivid representations of nature from your high-school readings of Wordsworth). The beginning of the modern environmentalist movement is much later, and is frequently attributed to Rachel Carson's 1962 book, *Silent Spring*, which drew public attention to the damaging effects of pesticides on the environment.

Current debates on the environment often take the form of a contest between two opposing models: the environment as something to be exploited economically vs. the environment as something to be protected against economic exploitation. Should the goal of limiting climate change by reducing CO_2 emissions be pursued at the expense of economic growth? Should pipelines be constructed through biologically sensitive ecosystems? Should sensitive ecological areas be protected from mining or petroleum extraction? Although such questions are often addressed from the perspectives of competing social values, responsible discussion is informed by research emerging from a wide range of academic disciplines, some of which are represented in the studies that follow. To be sure, research is indispensable to informed discussion.

Each of the research articles in this section examines some point where human and environmental concerns intersect. For example, Hager et al. examine the effects of urbanization on fatal bird-window collisions. In keeping with the issue of how cities interact with the natural environment, Pitman et al. discuss the uses of green infrastructure in mitigating the effects of climate change. The articles in this section also consider the environment from a variety of perspectives, including its physical features (in the case of the two studies just mentioned), how it is represented in different media (Uggla and Olausson's study of tourism websites and Moore's analysis of popular cinema), and the processes by which governments arrive at environmental policy (Lalor and Hickey's discussion of environmental policy-making).

As you read these studies, try to keep in mind the broader social goals the research points to. Keep in mind also how these articles challenge your own assumptions and values. Does Moore's analysis of Hollywood movies have implications for your own assessment of mass media representations of climate change or other environmental issues? What price seems reasonable to pay to construct cities that cause fewer disruptions to migratory birds or to reduce the effects of climate change in urban settings? How should politicians striving to develop responsible environmental policy balance the advice of experts with that of the general public? This research does, after all, have significant real-world implications.

A. "CONTINENT-WIDE ANALYSIS OF HOW URBANIZATION AFFECTS BIRD-WINDOW COLLISION MORTALITY IN NORTH AMERICA," STEPHEN B. HAGER ET AL.

In this study, which appeared in 2017 in the journal Biological Conservation, *a team of nearly sixty researchers* examines the effects of urbanization on bird-window collisions, a phenomenon that kills nearly a billion birds a year in North America. The researchers point out that although much is known about the effects of building types and immediate surroundings on bird-window collisions, much less is known about the subject of their study: the interaction of these factors and "urbanization at large spatial scales" (p. 181). As you read this article you will come across statistical terms—e.g., eigenvalues, Poisson distribution—that you couldn't possibly be expected to understand. Don't worry about these: they're aimed at specialists whose interest lies in evaluating or replicating the study's methods. Your own identity as a reader is probably closer to that of the urban planner who is interested in the practical applications of the study.*

Glossary terms: Pearson's r, principal component analysis

Abstract

Characteristics of buildings and land cover surrounding buildings influence the number of bird-window collisions, yet little is known about whether bird-window collisions are associated with urbanization at large spatial scales. We initiated a

---

* Stephen B. Hager, Bradley J. Cosentino, Miguel A. Aguilar-Gómez, Michelle L. Anderson, Marja Bakermans, Than J. Boves, David Brandes, Michael W. Butler, Eric M. Butler, Nicolette L. Cagle, Rafael Calderón-Parra, Angelo P. Capparella, Anqi Chen, Kendra Cipollini, April A.T. Conkey, Thomas A. Contreras, Rebecca I. Cooper, Clay E. Corbin, Robert L. Curry, Jerald J. Dosch, Martina G. Drew, Karen Dyson, Carolyn Foster, Clinton D. Francis, Erin Fraser, Ross Furbush, Natasha D.G. Hagemeyer, Kristine N. Hopfensperger, Daniel Klem Jr., Elizabeth Lago, Ally Lahey, Kevin Lamp, Greg Lewis, Scott R. Loss, Craig S. Machtans, Jessa Madosky, Terri J. Maness, Kelly J. McKay, Sean B. Menke, Katherine E. Muma, Natalia Ocampo-Peñuela, Timothy J. O'Connell, Rubén Ortega-Álvarez, Amber L. Pitt, Aura L. Puga-Caballero, John E. Quinn, Claire W. Varian-Ramos, Corey S. Riding, Amber M. Roth, Peter G. Saenger, Ryan T. Schmitz, Jaclyn Schnurr, Matthew Simmons, Alexis D. Smith, Devin R. Sokoloski, Jesse Vigliotti, Eric L. Walters, Lindsey A. Walters, J.T. Weir, Kathy Winnett-Murray, John C. Withey, Iriana Zuria. The original article identifies a wide variety of academic and government affiliations across Canada, Mexico, and the United States. We have not included those details here.

continent-wide study in North America to assess how bird-window collision mortality is influenced by building characteristics, landscaping around buildings, and regional urbanization. In autumn 2014, researchers at 40 sites (N = 281 buildings) used standardized protocols to document collision mortality of birds, evaluate building characteristics, and measure local land cover and regional urbanization. Overall, 324 bird carcasses were observed (range=0–34 per site) representing 71 species. Consistent with previous studies, we found that building size had a strong positive effect on bird-window collision mortality, but the strength of the effect on mortality depended on regional urbanization. The positive relationship between collision mortality and building size was greatest at large buildings in regions of low urbanization, locally extensive lawns, and low-density structures. Collision mortality was consistently low for small buildings, regardless of large-scale urbanization. The mechanisms shaping broad-scale variation in collision mortality during seasonal migration may be related to habitat selection at a hierarchy of scales and behavioral divergence between urban and rural bird populations. These results suggest that collision prevention measures should be prioritized at large buildings in regions of low urbanization throughout North America.

Keywords: bird-window collisions, anthropogenic mortality, lights out program, bird migration, habitat selection, behavioral divergence

1. Introduction

Annual avian mortality resulting from collisions with buildings is estimated at nearly 1 billion birds in North America (Klem, 1990; Machtans et al., 2013; Loss et al., 2014). Numerous bird species are affected by bird-building collisions, including species of conservation concern (Machtans et al., 2013; Loss et al., 2014). Nocturnally migrating birds are known to strike the windows of buildings in large cities after becoming attracted to and disoriented by artificial lighting or when low cloud cover forces individuals to fly at altitudes below the top of many sky scrapers (Longcore and Rich, 2004). During the daytime hours, birds may strike windows after mistaking the reflected environment in sheet glass for habitat and open flight space (Klem, 1989; Martin, 2011). Window collision risk is primarily related to structural features of buildings and land cover features immediately surrounding buildings. For example, mortality is highest at large buildings with many windows and lowest at small structures with proportionately fewer windows (O'Connell, 2001; Hager et al., 2008, 2013; Klem et al., 2009; Machtans et al., 2013; Loss et al., 2014; Kahle et al., 2016; Ocampo-Peñuela et al., 2016). Moreover, bird-window collisions are more frequent at buildings surrounded by low levels of impervious surfaces (e.g., paved roadways, sidewalks, and parking lots) and structures (e.g., buildings) (Hager et al., 2013; Cusa et al., 2015). Differences in building size and the patchy nature of development in cities and towns create strong spatial variation in the number of birds that collide with glass (Bayne et al., 2012; Hager et al., 2013; Machtans et al., 2013; Loss et al., 2014).

Although building characteristics and local land cover are important drivers of bird-window collisions, we do not understand how urbanization at large spatial scales affects collision mortality. Regional urbanization may influence mortality by mediating bird community structure and abundance (e.g., Blair, 1996; Pennington et al., 2008), particularly if there is covariation between species distributions and susceptibility of species to collisions. Urbanization may also affect bird-window collisions by shaping intraspecific variation in behavioral traits associated with collision risk, such as flight behavior. For example, behavioral divergence is commonly found between urban and non-urban bird populations due to phenotypic plasticity or adaptation (Sol et al., 2013). The degree of broad-scale urbanization may work with local-scale factors to affect collision risk in an additive fashion. Alternatively, associations between urbanization and either community structure or behavioral traits may lead to variation in the effects of building features and landscaping on collision risk between urban and rural areas.

Our objective was to examine how local factors (i.e., building structural features and land cover) and large-scale urbanization together affect continent-wide variation in bird-window collision mortality. We monitored buildings that varied in size and land cover types for collision mortality at 40 locations across North America during the autumn migratory season, and then examined the relative effects of building size, local land cover, and regional urbanization on collisions. We included models with interaction terms to determine if the effects of building size and local land cover on collision mortality depended on broad-scale urbanization. Knowledge of local and regional-scale drivers of bird-window collisions would assist in prioritizing mitigation measures aimed at reducing collision mortality at the riskiest structures and landscapes in North America.

2. Materials and Methods

2.1. Study Buildings

We surveyed 281 buildings for bird carcasses across 40 college and university campuses in North America with varying degrees of urbanization (Fig. 1). Stratified sampling was used to identify a target of six building strata composed of building size (small, medium, large) and nearby landscaping (high vs. low vegetation cover). The following guidelines informed our building selection: small buildings: 1–2 story single-family residences (< 186 m^2); medium buildings: 2–4 story office buildings (186–4181 m^2); and, large buildings ≥ 5 stories in height (> 4181 m^2). We used Google Earth imagery to visually estimate the percent vegetation surrounding candidate study buildings within 50 m. Buildings at each site were separated by at least 100 m to reduce spatial dependence of land cover features. The median number of study buildings at each site was 6 (range: 4–21).

2.2. Carcass Surveys

Carcass surveys were completed in the autumn migratory season (late August through late October) in 2014. We chose the autumn season because the incidence of collision mortality across North America is consistently highest in the autumn compared to other seasons (e.g., Klem, 1989). Surveys were conducted daily between 1400 and 1600 h, as mortality predominantly occurs between sunrise and early afternoon (Hager and Craig, 2014; Kahle et al., 2016) and scavengers are most likely to remove carcasses between sunset and sunrise (Klem, 1989; Hager et al., 2012; Hager and Craig, 2014; Kahle et al., 2016). Conducting surveys between the time of peak mortality and peak scavenging should minimize detection bias associated with scavengers (following Hager and Cosentino, 2014). Surveys were occasionally completed in the morning if inclement weather was expected in the afternoon, and all surveys at one site (Oklahoma State University) were conducted in the morning due to evidence of significant collision mortality during the pre-dawn hours and some scavenging during the morning and afternoon (T. O'Connell, S. Loss, and C. Riding, unpublished data).

We conducted a 'clean up' survey one day prior to the start of official carcass surveys. During clean-up surveys, all bird carcasses that may have accumulated in the time before the study period were removed. Failing to remove carcasses in this manner would likely have led to positive bias in estimates of bird mortality (Hager et al., 2013).

Buildings were surveyed for a median of 21 consecutive days (range: 5–60), not including the 'clean-up' survey. Daily surveys consisted of observers making two complete passes, one clockwise and one counterclockwise, around the perimeter of each building (Hager and Cosentino, 2014). One or two observers conducted each survey. When surveyed by a single observer, the observer walked the perimeter in one direction, and the second pass was made in the opposite direction. All bird carcasses noted in single-observer surveys were documented and collected immediately upon finding a carcass. When surveyed by two observers, each observer walked the building perimeter once in opposite directions. Carcasses located by each observer during surveys were not immediately collected. Instead, observers quickly noted the general location of a carcass on the data sheet. After observers finished surveys, they compared notes on carcasses observed and then returned to those sites for carcass documentation and collection. Multiple passes should result in greater cumulative detection probability compared to a single pass. Overall, the survey protocol minimized bias associated with imperfect detection of bird carcasses resulting from window collisions by (a) surveying between known times of peak bird mortality and removal of carcasses by scavengers, and (b) maintaining high cumulative detection probability of carcasses by field observers (Hager et al., 2012, 2013; Hager and Cosentino, 2014; Kahle et al., 2016).

Observers searched for bird carcasses in areas clear of vegetation, on the top, inside, and ground around all shrubs, in thick ground cover (e.g., ivy, Hedera sp.), and around and under objects such as trashcans. Carcasses were counted if they were located under a building window within 2 m of the edge of the building (Hager and Craig, 2014). Observers recorded the location of carcasses seen during each pass. When two observers surveyed buildings, observers were instructed to not share information about their survey with each other until after surveys were completed.

We identified bird carcasses to species either during carcass surveys or in the laboratory following collection (following Hager and Cosentino, 2014). Bird carcasses that lacked species-specific anatomic features were classified as 'unidentified.' All carcasses were deposited in museums and teaching collections or were disposed of according to animal welfare guidelines (see Document S1 for details [not included here]).

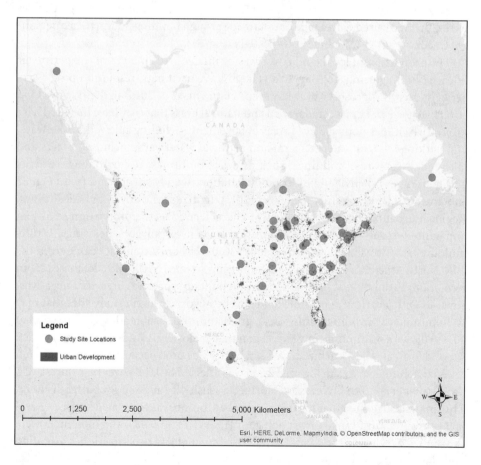

Fig. 1. Map depicting urban development and locations of study sites (N = 40) that conducted bird-window collision monitoring to assess the building structural, local land cover, and regional urbanization affecting bird-window collision mortality in North America in autumn 2014.

2.3. Building Structural and Land Cover Covariates

Three metrics of building size were quantified for each building: window area, number of stories above ground, and floor space area (i.e., summed area of each floor of a building). A tape measure was used to quantify window area by measuring all accessible exposed sheet glass (including clear, tinted, and reflective windows) on all sides of each building. Window area for out-of-reach exposed sheet glass was measured from digital photographs in ImageJ (Abràmoff et al., 2004). We excluded window measurements for windows behind screening material (which we assumed reduces the collision effect by covering sheet glass) and for windows above portions of a building's perimeter that could not be surveyed for bird carcasses (e.g., ledges and roof tops). The median window area for study buildings was 156m^2 (range = 0.05–2879) (Fig. S1 [not included here]). We counted the number of stories or floors above ground level (median = 2 stories, range = 1–14), and floor space area estimates were either measured with a tape or obtained through building maintenance personnel (median = 2183 m^2, range = 18–33,031) (Fig. S1).

The proportion of local land cover was estimated within 50 m of the perimeter of each building using ArcMap 10.3 (Fig. S1). We used high-resolution Bing Maps aerial imagery (Microsoft® BingTM Maps Platform APIs, 2016) to digitize five land cover categories: a) grass (landscaped and natural grass that may have included bare ground), b) impervious surface (areas of pavement, including sidewalks, roadways, and parking lots), c) water (natural and artificial waterways, including ponds and lakes), d) structures (buildings, such as office buildings, residential apartments and houses, and sheds), and e) woody vegetation (woody shrubs and trees; Fig. S2 [not included here]). A single observer (SBH) digitized land cover for all buildings. Regional urbanization for each site was characterized as the proportion of 'urban and built up space' within 5 km of a minimum convex polygon enclosing all study buildings at a site (Fig. S2; Latifovic et al., 2010). Urbanization data came from the 2010 North American Land Change Monitoring System (NALCMS) database (250m resolution; Latifovic et al., 2010). 'Urban and built up space' was used, as it negatively covaries with a variety of possible land cover categories among study sites that may be important to birds, including forest, grassland, and scrubland. We used ArcMap 10.3 to derive a minimum convex polygon that enclosed all study buildings for each site and to create the 5 km buffer. A 5 km buffer was used because previous research found that bird density during migration was affected by land cover (e.g., forest) at 5 km (Bonter et al., 2009). We also performed a sensitivity analysis for buffer distance. This analysis suggested that the degree of urbanization was correlated between 3 and 50 km around minimum convex polygons (Pearson's r > 0.48), and inferences were the same regardless of the spatial extent used to quantify urbanization (Cosentino and Hager, unpublished data).

2.4. Statistical Analysis

We used principal components analysis (PCA) to identify latent variables that summarized covariation among building size, local land cover around buildings, and regional urbanization. The specific metrics assessed included window area; floor space area; number of stories; proportions of woody vegetation, grass, impervious surface, and structures within 50 m; and urbanization within 5 km. Proportion of water within 50 m was zero for almost all sites, so we excluded it from the analysis. In order to help meet the assumption of multivariate normality for PCA (McGarigal et al., 2000), we applied log transformations to window area, floor space, and number of stories, and logit transformations were applied to all land cover variables (Warton and Hui, 2011). The PCA was computed on the correlation matrix, and all principal components with eigenvalues ≥1 were retained.

We used generalized linear mixed models to examine the relationship of PCA-derived variables of building size, local land cover, and regional urbanization with the number of bird carcasses. The response variable was the number of carcasses found at each building across all surveys. We specified the log-transformed number of surveys at each building as an offset variable to account for varying effort. We used a Poisson distribution and log link as the error distribution for number of carcasses. Site was included as a random effect to account for non-independence in mortality among buildings at the same site.

We analyzed 14 models with different combinations of the explanatory variables. Models included a null model (intercept only), additive combinations of the explanatory variables, and models with a single interaction effect and up to one additional explanatory variable. Interaction effects were examined between each possible pair of the three explanatory variables. We compared the relative support of models with Akaike's Information Criterion (AIC), and models were considered to have competitive support when the difference between AIC of each model and the most-supported model was ≤2 (Burnham and Anderson, 2002).

3. Results

We documented 324 bird carcasses at 40 sites across North America in autumn 2014 (mean = 8.1 carcasses per site, range = 0–34) (Table S1 [not included here]). Of these, 275 carcasses (84.9%) were identified to species. Mortality in several species was relatively widespread across sites, such as Common Yellowthroat, *Geothlypis trichas* (13 sites), Ovenbird, *Seiurus aurocapilla* (11 sites), and Ruby-throated Hummingbird, *Archilochus colubris* (8 sites). Moreover, mortality was highest in migrants (91%) compared to residents (9%), and nearly all carcasses observed (99%) were passerine and near-passerine species (e.g., doves, hummingbirds, cuckoos, and woodpeckers) (Table S1 [not included here]).We retained three principal components with eigenvalues ≥1 that described covariation in building size, landscaping around buildings, and regional urbanization. The three components collectively accounted for 70% of the variance (Table 1). The first axis (PC1) explained 29% of the variance and had high positive loadings for window area, floor space area, and number of stories; therefore, we interpreted PC1 as an index of building size. The second axis (PC2) explained 21% of the variance and had a strong negative loading for woody vegetation and a strong positive loading for impervious surfaces within 50 m of buildings. We therefore interpreted PC2 as an index of landscaping around buildings that was independent of regional urbanization. The third axis (PC3) explained 20% of the variance and had a negative loading for grass within 50 m and positive loadings for structures within 50 m of buildings and urbanization within 5 km of study sites. We therefore interpreted PC3 as an index of regional urbanization, which influences variation in coverage by grass and structures in the immediate vicinity around study buildings.

Bird-window collision mortality was strongly associated with an interaction effect between building size (PC1) and regional urbanization (PC3), which was included in the only two models with competitive support (Table 2). Collision mortality was positively related to building size, but the positive effect of building size on mortality was strongest in areas with low levels of regional urbanization and weak to nonexistent in regions with high levels of urbanization (Fig. 2, Fig. S3 [not included here]). Collision mortality was consistently low for small buildings, regardless of large-scale urbanization (Fig. 2). Landscaping around buildings was included in the second-best supported model, but was not an important driver of collision mortality compared to building size and regional urbanization (Table 2).

4. Discussion

We found that building size had a strong positive effect on bird-window collision mortality during autumn migration, but the strength of this effect depended on the degree of urbanization at the regional scale. The positive relationship between collision mortality and building size was greatest in regions of low urbanization containing locally extensive landscaped grass and few structures (i.e., 'rural' landscapes with low values of PC3). Collision mortality was low to nonexistent in regions that were highly urbanized. The mechanisms shaping broad-scale variation in bird-building collision mortality during autumn migration may be related to habitat selection and habitat use at a hierarchy of scales and behavioral divergence among urban and rural populations.

Habitat selection and habitat use in migratory birds occurs at a hierarchy of spatial scales that would ultimately place birds in close proximity to buildings and at risk of fatal collisions with windows (Johnson, 1980; Hutto, 1985; Jones, 2001). At large scales, migrating birds select among numerous widely spaced habitat types using geophysical (rivers, mountains, celestial, and magnetic), meteorological (weather), and social (intraspecific vocalizations) cues and experience (Berthold, 2001). For example, forest-adapted birds often select rural habitats (e.g., open and low-intensity

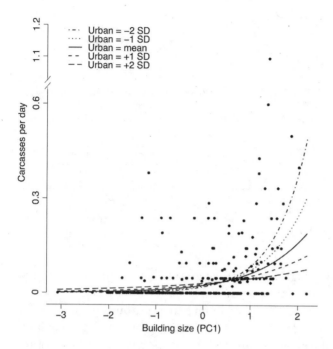

Fig. 2. Interaction effect between building size and regional urbanization on number of bird carcasses. Number of bird carcasses is expressed as the number of carcasses collected per day. Best-fit lines represent model-averaged predictions across all models in Table 1 when urbanization is held at low (−2 SD, −1 SD), average, and high (+1 SD, +2 SD) values. Landscaping and number of surveys were held constant at their means. Building size, local landscaping, and regional urbanization are latent variables from a principal component analysis (Table 1). Note the break point on the y-axis.

Variable	Factor loadings		
	PC1	PC2	PC3
Window area	0.92	0.12	0.03
Floor space	0.94	0.10	− 0.05
Stories	0.78	− 0.01	0.27
Wooded (50 m)	− 0.07	− 0.92	0.24
Grass (50 m)	− 0.09	0.12	− 0.78
Impervious (50 m)	0.11	0.87	0.26
Structures (50 m)	0.02	0.10	0.55
Developed (5 km)	0.07	0.00	0.70
Eigenvalue	2.60	1.66	1.35
Proportion of variance explained	0.29	0.21	0.20

Table 1. Principal component analysis (PCA) of building size (PC1), landscaping within 50 m of buildings (PC2), and urbanization within 5 km of sites (PC3).

Model	ΔAIC	ω_i	L	K	b_B (SE)	b_L (SE)	b_U (SE)	b_{INT} (SE)
B + U + B*U	0.00	0.61	−420.10	5	0.94 (0.08)	–	0.12 (0.10)	−0.28 (0.08)
B + U + B*U + L	1.12	0.35	−419.66	6	0.94 (0.08)	0.07 (0.07)	0.11 (0.10)	−0.27 (0.08)
B	7.67	0.01	−425.94	3	0.84 (0.07)	–	–	–
B + L	8.12	0.01	−425.16	4	0.84 (0.07)	0.09 (0.07)	–	
B + L + B*L	8.45	0.01	−424.33	5	0.86 (0.08)	0.13 (0.08)	–	−0.11 (0.08)
B + U	9.67	0.00	−425.93	4	0.84 (0.07)	–	0.00 (0.09)	–
B + L + U	10.11	0.00	−425.16	5	0.84 (0.07)	0.09 (0.07)	0.00 (0.09)	–
B + L + B*L + U	10.45	0.00	−424.33	6	0.86 (0.08)	0.13 (0.08)	0.00 (0.09)	−0.11 (0.08)
B + L + U + L*U	12.05	0.00	−425.13	6	0.84 (0.07)	0.09 (0.07)	−0.01 (0.09)	0.02 (0.07)
Intercept	161.65	0.00	−503.92	2	–	–	–	–
L	162.30	0.00	−503.25	3	–	0.07 (0.06)	–	–
U	163.64	0.00	−503.92	3	–	–	0.01 (0.08)	–
L + U	164.27	0.00	−503.24	4	–	0.08 (0.06)	−0.02 (0.08)	–
L + U + L*U	165.50	0.00	−502.85	5	–	0.08 (0.06)	0.01 (0.09)	−0.06 (0.06)

Table 2. Model selection statistics and beta coefficients (b) for associations between number of bird carcasses and building size (B; PC1), landscaping around buildings (L; PC2), and urbanization (U; PC3) (note that building size, landscaping, and urbanization are latent variables from a principal component analysis [Table 1]). AIC is the difference between AIC of each model and the most-supported model, i is the Akaike weight of model i, L is the log-likelihood, and K is the number of parameters.

developed spaces containing high levels of lawn grasses, some structures, and low levels of impervious surfaces) over other available habitats, such as areas of high urbanization (Zuckerberg et al., 2016). In addition to the cues birds use in selecting rural areas during migration, data from RADAR studies suggest migrating birds are negatively influenced during nighttime by broad-scale city glow wherein birds become entrapped by artificial light (Buler and Dawson, 2014). Regional lighting patterns should be associated with urbanization, and light radiating from low-rise and large buildings in small cities within rural areas may be more of an attractant compared to similar sized buildings in a highly urbanized landscape. If so, a large-scale beacon effect would cause birds and collisions to be more diluted among large buildings in urban areas (resulting in less of an effect of building size) than in rural areas (resulting in more of an effect of building size).

Once settled in rural areas, collision risk would be influenced at the local scale by the manner in which birds use habitats. In contrast to the generalized cues associated with broad-scale habitat selection, birds engage in relatively short-distance exploratory forays in search of food and shelter (Hutto, 1985; Cohen et al., 2014; Slager et al., 2015). 'Morning flight' is one such foray during migration that occurs within 2 h after sunrise wherein migrants move throughout the landscape above tree height in search of preferred or higher-quality habitats (Wiedner et al., 1992; Van Doren et al., 2015). As morning gives way to afternoon, birds settle in habitats, with movements becoming localized and restricted to short-distance foraging bouts (e.g., Hutto, 1985; Paxton and O'Brien, 2008). Thus, window collision risk would be relatively high for birds flying above tree height during morning flight since they would be exposed to windows at this height in low-rise and tall buildings, and collision risk should be magnified in rural areas containing proportionately more migrants than in urban areas. Fewer birds flying below tree height during morning flight would result in lower collision risk at windows close to ground level, such as those in houses (1–3 stories in height), regardless of the degree of urbanization.

An alternative (though not necessarily mutually exclusive) explanation for the influence of regional urbanization on collision mortality is behavioral divergence between urban and rural populations of birds. Behavioral divergence along urbanization gradients may occur due to phenotypic or behavioral plasticity, e.g., learning from non-fatal strikes based on previous experience and gaining new anti-collision behaviors as novel solutions to the problems posed by sheet glass in buildings (Dukas, 1998, 2004; Sol et al., 2013). For example, the number of structures is associated with degree of urbanization (e.g., PC3), and thus birds in urban areas would experience more opportunities for bird-building collisions and subsequent learning from those strikes than rural populations. There is evidence that the relatively large brain size in birds makes them primed for behavioral plasticity, and especially learning (Lefebvre and Sol, 2008; Møller and Erritzøe, 2017). Learning to avoid windows may be further influenced by variation between urban and rural populations in boldness or rates of activity, motivational states, and strategies related to life history traits, such as migration, that would affect the value of learning (Dukas, 1998). Moreover, individuals in urban populations may simply move less frequently or for shorter distances across the environment due to highly localized and abundant food sources (i.e., fruiting trees, feeders). If urban individuals move less, the probability of striking windows may be reduced. Juveniles (hatch-year birds) are reported to suffer higher rates of collision mortality than adults (Hager et al., 2013; Kahle et al., 2016). For those urban-dwelling juveniles that do not die, learning may occur early in development, which could alter nervous system functioning that controls motor responses to avoid windows later in life (Sol et al., 2013).

Aside from phenotypically plastic behaviors, evolutionary processes may underpin differential behavioral adjustments for urban and rural bird populations that lead to variation in collision mortality (Brown and Brown, 2013; Sol et al., 2013). For example, variation in the ability of migratory birds to see and avoid windows may exist between populations. This variation would be expected to result in proportionately lower collision mortality in urban birds en-route to areas of winter residency (during autumn migration) and summer breeding (during spring migration). Over time, this same variation could be adjusted by natural selection to bring urban populations to a new adaptive landscape (Dingemanse and Wolf, 2013). Such a scenario would assume that the relative strength of selection to perceive windows as barriers to flight in urban areas is high and population size is large (Sol et al., 2013).

Overall, birds have adapted to urban environments in the evolutionary history of their migratory behavior (Sol and Lefebvre, 2006; Marzluff, 2014), and behavioral divergence may be important in generating differences in collision mortality between rural and urban populations.

4.1. Conservation Implications

The results of this research allow for a better appreciation of the spatial context for why up to 1 billion birds die annually throughout much of North America after hitting windows in buildings (Klem, 1990; Machtans et al., 2013; Loss et al., 2014). At broad-scales, the beacon effect we hypothesize in rural landscapes suggests the potential benefit of implementing lights-out programs (e.g., visit www.audubon.org/conservation/project/lights-out) in cities and towns of all sizes, not just in large cities characterized by dense urbanization. At local scales, collision mortality can be reduced or eliminated with effective prevention measures that account for variation in (a) window size, tinting, and surface treatments and (b) visual systems in birds vulnerable to striking windows (Martin, 2011). For example, collision risk may be reduced by constructing buildings with a small amount of sheet glass, and retrofitting windows in existing buildings with frit patterns on glass surfaces (Barton et al., 2017). Indeed, effective prevention measures would be further informed by understanding how bird-window collisions are influenced by the degree of urbanization (a) at sites other than college campuses, and (b) in building types that were not well-sampled in our study, e.g., convention centers, stadiums, extremely tall and abnormally-shaped buildings with exterior walls composed almost entirely of sheet glass.

The spatial complexities of this issue become amplified as one also considers the temporal scale of bird-window collisions. The driving factors of collision mortality reported here for autumn migration may be the same factors influencing collision mortality during spring migration. However, the intrinsic (e.g., hormonal) and extrinsic (e.g., geographic cues) biologic features that influence bird migratory behavior differ between spring and autumn migration, leading to variation in habitat selection, habitat use, and behavioral divergence between the seasons. Relatively little is known about bird-window collisions outside of migration periods, and therefore about the structural-environmental and behavioral-ecological drivers of mortality during the winter and summer (Hager and Craig, 2014; Kummer et al., 2016).

Many of the studies on habitat selection of birds during migration cite the importance of rural landscapes for conservation and management. Annual estimates of avian survival suggest that mortality is highest during migration (Sillett and Holmes, 2002), and conserving rural landscapes may positively affect survival. The tradeoff with this conservation approach is the inherent threats to survival that rural landscapes pose to birds, such as predation by domestic and feral cats and collisions with communication towers, automobiles, and buildings (Drewitt and Langston, 2006; Longcore et al., 2013; Loss et al., 2013, 2014). Hierarchical and full life-cycle population models that include anthropogenic sources of mortality, such as bird-window collisions, should be used to assess the population dynamics of vulnerable species (Hostetler et al., 2015).

Supplementary data to this article can be found online at http://dx.doi.org/10.1016/j.biocon.2017.06.014.

Acknowledgements

The Ecological Research as Education Network (http://erenweb.org) kindly provided support for the organization and management of this collaborative project. All co-authors followed the project's protocol on animal welfare policy, appropriate local, state, and federal permitting, and IACUC (Document S1 [not included here]). We would like to thank the general participants (N = 143; see Table S2 [not included here] for a list of participant names) involved in the project that contributed data according to the project's protocols and guidelines and submitted data in time for analysis, and for the assistance of numerous undergraduate and graduate students. The editor and two anonymous reviewers offered useful comments on a prior draft of this paper.

References

Abràmoff, M.D., Magalhães, P.J., Ram, S.J., 2004. Image processing with ImageJ. Biophoton. Int. 11 (7), 36–42.

Barton, C.M., Riding, C.S., Loss, S.R., 2017. Magnitude and correlates of bird collisions at glass bus shelters in an urban landscape. PLoS One 12 (6), e0178667.

Bayne, E.M., Scobie, C.A., Rawson-Clark, M., 2012. Factors influencing the annual risk of bird–window collisions at residential structures in Alberta, Canada. Wildl. Res. 39 (7), 583–92.

Berthold, P., 2001. Bird Migration: A General Survey. Oxford University Press on Demand.

Blair, R.B., 1996. Land use and avian species diversity along an urban gradient. Ecol. Appl. 6 (2), 506–19.

Bonter, D.N., Gauthreaux Jr., S.A., Donovan, T.M., 2009. Characteristics of important stopover locations for migrating birds: remote sensing with radar in the Great Lakes basin. Conserv. Biol. 23 (2), 440–48.

Brown, C.R., Brown, M.B., 2013. Where has all the road kill gone? Curr. Biol. 23 (6), R233–R234.

Buler, J.J., Dawson, D.K., 2014. Radar analysis of fall bird migration stopover sites in the northeastern US. Condor 116 (3), 357–70.

Burnham, K.P., Anderson, D.R., 2002. Information and likelihood theory: a basis for model selection and inference. In: Model Selection and Multimodel Inference: A Practical Information-theoretic Approach. 2. pp. 49–97.

Cohen, E.B., Moore, F.R., Fischer, R.A., 2014. Fuel stores, time of spring, and movement behavior influence stopover duration of Red-eyed Vireo Vireo olivaceus. J. Ornithol. 155 (3), 785–92.

Cusa, M., Jackson, D.A., Mesure, M., 2015. Window collisions by migratory bird species: urban geographical patterns and habitat associations. Urban Ecosyst. 18 (4), 1427–46.

Dingemanse, N.J., Wolf, M., 2013. Between-individual differences in behavioural plasticity within populations: causes and consequences. Anim. Behav. 85 (5), 1031–39.

Drewitt, A.L., Langston, R.H., 2006. Assessing the impacts of wind farms on birds. Ibis 148 (s1), 29–42.

Dukas, R., 1998. Cognitive Ecology: The Evolutionary Ecology of Information Processing and Decision Making. University of Chicago Press.

Dukas, R., 2004. Evolutionary biology of animal cognition. Annu. Rev. Ecol. Evol. Syst. 35, 347–74.

Hager, S.B., Cosentino, B.J., 2014. Surveying for Bird Carcasses Resulting From Window Collisions: A Standardized Protocol (No. e406v1). PeerJ PrePrints.

Hager, S.B., Craig, M.E., 2014. Bird-window collisions in the summer breeding season. PeerJ 2, e460.

Hager, S.B., Trudell, H., McKay, K.J., Crandall, S.M., Mayer, L., 2008. Bird density and mortality at windows. Wilson J. Ornithol. 120 (3), 550–64.

Hager, S.B., Cosentino, B.J., McKay, K.J., 2012. Scavenging affects persistence of avian carcasses resulting from window collisions in an urban landscape. J. Field Ornithol. 83 (2), 203–11.

Hager, S.B., Cosentino, B.J., McKay, K.J., Monson, C., Zuurdeeg, W., Blevins, B., 2013. Window area and development drive spatial variation in bird-window collisions in an urban landscape. PLoS One 8 (1), e53371.

Hostetler, J.A., Sillett, T.S., Marra, P.P., 2015. Full-annual-cycle population models for migratory birds. Auk 132 (2), 433–49.

Hutto, R.L., 1985. Habitat selection by nonbreeding, migratory land. In: Habitat Selection in Birds, 455.

Johnson, D.H., 1980. The comparison of usage and availability measurements for evaluating resource preference. Ecology 61 (1), 65–71.

Jones, J., 2001. Habitat selection studies in avian ecology: a critical review. Auk 118 (2), 557–62.

Kahle, L.Q., Flannery, M.E., Dumbacher, J.P., 2016. Bird-window collisions at a west-coast urban park museum: analyses of bird biology and window attributes from Golden Gate Park, San Francisco. PLoS One 11 (1), e0144600.

Klem Jr., D., 1989. Bird-window collisions. Wilson Bull. 606–20.

Klem Jr., D., 1990. Collisions between birds and windows: mortality and prevention (Colisiones de pájaros con ventanas: mortalidad y prevención). J. Field Ornithol. 120–28.

Klem Jr., D., Farmer, C.J., Delacretaz, N., Gelb, Y., Saenger, P.G., 2009. Architectural and landscape risk factors associated with bird–glass collisions in an urban environment. Wilson J. Ornithol. 121 (1), 126–34.

Kummer, J.A., Bayne, E.M., Machtans, C.S., 2016. Use of citizen science to identify factors affecting bird–window collision risk at houses. Condor 118 (3), 624–39.

Latifovic, R., Homer, C., Ressl, R., Pouliot, D., Hossain, S.N., Colditz, R.R., Olthof, I., Giri, C., Victoria, A., 2010. North American Land Change Monitoring System (NALCMS). Remote Sensing of Land Use and Land Cover: Principles and Applications. CRC Press, Boca Raton.

Lefebvre, L., Sol, D., 2008. Brains, lifestyles and cognition: are there general trends? Brain Behav. Evol. 72 (2), 135–44.

Longcore, T., Rich, C., 2004. Ecological light pollution. Front. Ecol. Environ. 2 (4), 191–98.

Longcore, T., Rich, C., Mineau, P., MacDonald, B., Bert, D.G., Sullivan, L.M., Mutrie, E., Gauthreaux, S.A., Avery, M.L., Crawford, R.L., Manville, A.M., 2013. Avian mortality at communication towers in the United States and Canada: which species, how many, and where? Biol. Conserv. 158, 410–19.

Loss, S.R., Will, T., Marra, P.P., 2013. The impact of free-ranging domestic cats on wildlife of the United States. Nat. Commun. 4, 1396.

Loss, S.R., Will, T., Loss, S.S., Marra, P.P., 2014. Bird–building collisions in the United States: estimates of annual mortality and species vulnerability. Condor 116 (1), 8–23.

Machtans, C., Wedeles, C., Bayne, E., 2013. A first estimate for Canada of the number of birds killed by colliding with building windows. Avian Conserv. Ecol. 8 (2).

Martin, G.R., 2011. Understanding bird collisions with man-made objects: a sensory ecology approach. Ibis 153 (2), 239–54.

Marzluff, J.M., 2014. Welcome to Suburbia: Sharing Our Neighborhoods With Wrens, Robins, Woodpeckers, and Other Wildlife. Yale UP.

McGarigal, K., Cushman, S., Stafford, S.G., 2000. Multivariate Statistics for Wildlife and Ecology Research. vol. 279 Springer, New York.

Microsoft® BingTM Maps Platform APIs, 2016. Retrieved from: www.microsoft.com/maps/product/print-rights.html.

Møller, A.P., Erritzøe, J., 2017. Brain size in birds is related to traffic accidents. Royal Soc. Open Sci. 4 (3), 161040.

Ocampo-Peñuela, N., Winton, R.S., Wu, C.J., Zambello, E., Wittig, T.W., Cagle, N.L., 2016. Patterns of bird-window collisions inform mitigation on a university campus. PeerJ 4, e1652.

O'Connell, T.J., 2001. Avian window strike mortality at a suburban office park. Raven 72 (2), 141–49.

Paxton, K.L., O'Brien, C., 2008. Movement patterns and stopover ecology of Wilson's Warblers during spring migration on the lower Colorado River in southwestern Arizona. Condor 110 (4), 672–81.

Pennington, D.N., Hansel, J., Blair, R.B., 2008. The conservation value of urban riparian areas for landbirds during spring migration: land cover, scale, and vegetation effects. Biol. Conserv. 141 (5), 1235–48.

Sillett, T.S., Holmes, R.T., 2002. Variation in survivorship of a migratory songbird throughout its annual cycle. J. Anim. Ecol. 71 (2), 296–308.

Slager, D.L., Rodewald, P.G., Heglund, P.J., 2015. Experimental effects of habitat type on the movement ecology and stopover duration of spring migrant Northern Waterthrushes (Parkesia noveboracensis). Behav. Ecol. Sociobiol. 69 (11), 1809–19.

Sol, D., Lefebvre, L., 2006. Behavioral flexibility and response in birds to changes in the environment. In: Journal of Ornithology (vol. 147, no. 5, pp. 34–34). Springer, 233 Spring Street, New York, NY 10013 USA (August).

Sol, D., Lapiedra, O., González-Lagos, C., 2013. Behavioural adjustments for a life in the city. Anim. Behav. 85 (5), 1101–12.

Van Doren, B.M., Sheldon, D., Geevarghese, J., Hochachka, W.M., Farnsworth, A., 2015. Autumn morning flights of migrant songbirds in the northeastern United States are linked to nocturnal migration and winds aloft. Auk 132 (1), 105–18.

Warton, D.I., Hui, F.K., 2011. The arcsine is asinine: the analysis of proportions in ecology. Ecology 92 (1), 3–10.

Wiedner, D.S., Kerlinger, P., Sibley, D.A., Holt, P., Hough, J., Crossley, R., 1992. Visible morning flight of Neotropical landbird migrants at Cape May, New Jersey. Auk 500–10.

Zuckerberg, B., Fink, D., La Sorte, F.A., Hochachka, W.M., Kelling, S., 2016. Novel seasonal land cover associations for eastern North American forest birds identified through dynamic species distribution modelling. Divers. Distrib. 22 (6), 717–30.

DISCUSSION QUESTIONS

1. This paper is unusual in that it has more than fifty authors. Setting aside the obvious reason—that people were needed to note and collect specimens in many locations across North America—why do you think so many authors were necessary? What does the high number of authors suggest about the nature of scientific inquiry?

2. Hager et al. carefully chose the time of year (autumn migration) and day (mid-afternoon) to perform their carcass surveys. What advantages and limitations do they see in this approach?

3. The statistical analysis is admittedly very difficult. What measures do Hager et al. take to help out the reader who isn't a statistician?

4. Applying the insights of the end of the Results and beginning of the Discussion section, keeping in mind the interplay of "building size, local land cover around buildings, and regional urbanization" within 5 km (p. 183), offer a brief account of the relative risks of a fatal bird-window collision in your home vs. the building you take this class in.

5. Imagine you are a planner for a city located on an important migratory route. Based on the research you've just read, what advice would you give developers to minimize bird-window collisions?

B. "GREEN SCREEN OR SMOKESCREEN? HOLLYWOOD'S MESSAGES ABOUT NATURE AND THE ENVIRONMENT," ELLEN ELIZABETH MOORE

Published in Environmental Communication, *this 2016 article inspects recent Hollywood films aimed at younger viewers in terms of how they represent nature and the environment in the broader context of climate change and other environmental issues. Ellen Moore* adapts an established method of analysis of images and films called symptomatic reading, which identifies ideological messages by paying attention to what a text (in this case a film) presupposes about certain topics (in this case, the environment). These messages can take the form of answers to unstated questions, silences, things that can't be said, and contradictions. Moore finds a range of conflicted messages about the environment and consumerism. As you read this article, reflect on your own experience of watching these films. To what extent do films such as these encourage consumerism or otherwise contribute to environmental problems even while they seem to present positive environmental messages?*

Glossary terms: culture industry, ideology, symptomatic reading

Abstract

This paper examines ideologies about nature and the environment in popular, animated Hollywood films—including *The Lorax, Wall-E,* and *Ice Age 2*—through a symptomatic reading. The primary goal of the analysis is to elucidate key omissions in these texts through an assessment of the problematic—defined in this research as an a priori answer to perceived audience concerns regarding the role of consumerism and corporate culture in environmental problems. Silences in the films revolve around: how environmental problems are defined; what the consequences are; who the responsible parties are; and what potential solutions exist to mitigate them. The significance of the research is underscored by the formation of an increasingly intimate relationship between children, consumer culture, and commercial media in the USA, as well as the increasingly dire information emerging about global environmental issues. This analysis reveals the dual, often conflicting, messages

* Ellen Moore is Senior Lecturer of Culture, Arts and Communication at the University of Washington, Tacoma. Her research in critical media studies focuses on representations of the environment and ethnicity.

that commercial film provides for its young audiences about pivotal environmental problems and their potential resolution.

Keywords: hypercommercialism, political economy, film, mass media, environment

In 2012, Universal Pictures released *The Lorax*, a film based on Dr Seuss' children's book of the same name published 30 years earlier. The book addressed the environmental harm caused by overconsumption, and Universal claimed the movie contained the same message; however, it also included embedded advertisements and numerous product tie-ins (Hetter, 2012). Product placement and the flood of marketing that accompanied the film drew criticism that the studio was corrupting Seuss' original environmental message by replacing it with one of consumption.

Drawing from the controversy surrounding *The Lorax*, this paper seeks to identify messages regarding environmental problems and their solutions as presented in popular Hollywood movies for children—including *Ice Age 2: The Meltdown* (Fox Pictures, 2006), *Wall-E* (Disney, 2008) and *The Lorax* (Universal, 2012)—through the *symptomatic reading* defined by Althusser and Balibar (2009). The analysis provides the basis for a critique of American hypercommercialism and consumer culture as contextualized within a political economy framework, placing the focus on concentrated media ownership and the concomitant drive for profit as a way to understand how messages about the environment are distorted by the culture industry for young audiences.

The significance of the research is underscored by the formation of an increasingly intimate relationship between children, consumer culture, and commercial media in the USA. According to McDonagh and Brereton (2010), "film has a profound influence in framing how we conceptualize and address ourselves and lifestyles, and by inference our global problems" (p. 134). *Green Screen*—the opening title for this work—is a media industry term used to describe a technique where a green or blue screen is used to combine two images to create an illusion. This research demonstrates how the term becomes an appropriate metaphor for the conflicting, dual messages that the culture industry provides for its audiences about important environmental problems and their potential resolution.

Literature Review

As Kellner notes, dominant ideologies "must be understood within the context of the political economy and system of production of culture" (1995, p. 37). Currently there is a small number of Hollywood "majors" owned by the well-known roster of conglomerates—including Universal Pictures (Comcast), Columbia (Sony), Paramount (Viacom), Warner Bros (Time Warner), 21st Century Fox, and Walt Disney/Buena Vista pictures (Disney). While there are some "breakthrough" studios (like independently operated Lionsgate, which produced the surprise blockbuster series *Twilight* and, more recently, the *Hunger Games* franchise), movies from the six "majors" dominate the American movie landscape, accounting for 76% of films released in 2012 (Nash Information Services, 2013). The fact that a small number of players owns an increasingly large amount of the US media landscape is well documented in academic literature (Andersen & Gray, 2007; Bagdikian, 2004; McChesney, 2008, 2004; Miller, 2002), and likely comes as no surprise to US media scholars. As a result, this paper outlines existing political economy discussions as they relate directly to mediated representations of the environment. While broader trends are considered, special attention is paid to recent changes in children's consumer culture and the focus on the child audience in Hollywood's treatment of environmental issues.

The Media Are Hypercommercial

The trend of media deregulation and resulting waves of conglomeration that started in earnest in the 1980s and have continued to the present day is well documented in political economy scholarship, leaving few to question that the US media system is both hypercommercial and highly concentrated. In his discussion of hypercommercialism, McChesney contends that American culture is subject to incessant commercial "carpet bombing" (2004, p. 146) that leaves no space untouched. The trend of hypercommercialism in the USA is in perfect step with the exponential growth of consumer culture there, with numerous scholars noting that consumption has become the foundation of the US cultural system (McAllister, 2006; McDonald & Wearing, 2013; Schor, 2009; Steinberg, 2011; Turow & McAllister, 2009).

Most germane to the current project is the recognition of a relatively new focus on children by American corporations. In the corporate system, children are not excluded from consumer culture but instead are highlighted in it. Schor (2004) notes that marketing to the child audience became a multi-billion dollar industry when companies realized the increased spending power of children. The primary consequence of this recognition is that children are being incorporated into the marketplace as part of a broader trend in American capitalism, where "life stages" translate into different types of potential markets (Langer, 2004, p. 254). Steinberg (2011) terms this new marketing focus on children as "kinderculture," a type of hypercommercialism aimed directly at children. The three key implications of a new children's consumer culture is that children, now considered a highly lucrative market, are targeted as a key demographic (McAllister, 2006; Schor, 2004); invited into consumerist identities at increasingly young ages (Hill, 2011; Jennings, 2006); and offered very few non-commercial opportunities in American media culture (Schor, 2004).

The Culture Industry in a Hypercommercial Society

The hypercommercial milieu in which Hollywood operates has a well-documented impact on all aspects of the industry—from origination to content and marketing. While the increase of product placement in movies has been well documented

(Andersen & Gray, 2007; McChesney, 2008; Miller, 2002; Wasko, 2003), commercially driven, non-media entities—like toymaker Hasbro—are going a step farther by partnering with studios to produce blockbusters like *GI Joe: Retaliation* (2013), *Battleship* (2011), and *Transformers* (2009).[1] The reason toymakers have entered into the movie-making business is clear: the potential to create highly lucrative ancillary markets using product tie-ins, resulting in an "unprecedented synergy" between movie producers and merchandisers (Townsend, 2011, p. 56). As a result, many contemporary "blockbuster" films are criticized for simply being vehicles to sell products to young audiences (Barnes, 2010; Townsend, 2011; Wasko, 2003), prompting Andersen and Gray (2007) to suggest that "films are no longer singular narratives, rather, they are iterations of entertainment supertexts, multimedia forms that can be expanded and resold almost ad infinitum" (p. 176).

Representations of Environmental Problems in Hollywood

In a hypercommercial society, how does a highly concentrated culture industry represent a subject like the environment? Kellner (1995) notes that the general rule is to appeal to the lowest (and largest) "common denominator" by avoiding topics that are too controversial while choosing issues that resonate with a broad audience (pp. 16–17), creating what Barnes (2010) terms "tent-pole productions" that draw in as many viewers as possible. The fact that a large majority (90%) of Americans worry about the quality of the environment[2] (Gallup, 2014), to the point where they prioritize environmental health over economic growth (Swift, 2014), means that an increasing number of studios have incorporated environmental themes into many of their recent productions.[3] Once studios focus on the environment, however, they must make delicate decisions regarding *how* to portray it, for its representation invites consideration of the role of human activity—including consumption—in the formation and continuance of environmental problems. For an industry engaged primarily with the act of *selling*, the environment thus becomes both an alluring yet precarious topic to cover.

Ingram (2004) observes that one way studios can address environmental problems *and* cater to corporate ownership is to approach the subject from a mainstream environmental perspective, which places "environmental concerns within the needs of a capitalist economy to sustain commodity consumption, profit maximization and economic growth" (p. 13). *The Happening* (20th Century Fox, 2008) provides an instantiation: although the plot focused on trees killing humans to stop their mindless consumption, Apple products featured throughout the film contradict the anti-consumption message. In their "eco-critical" reading of the *Fast and Furious* film franchise (from the 1950s original to the more contemporary remakes), Murray and Heumann (2009b) observe that although more information has become available in the last few decades about the global scale of environmental degradation, the films continue to "advocate a heightened abuse of nature and ecosystems" that work within central themes of consumption (p. 144). These examples are not isolated: McDonagh and Brereton (2010) note that "filmic representations of nature, while multifarious, have a tendency to present nature as the resource for business and the market to engage in economic progress" (p. 133). Thus, representation of the environment in Hollywood is subject to what Beder (1998) refers to as "economic framing," where the environment is defined only through its relevance to the capitalist system.

Although the movie industry is the focus of this research, there are clear parallels to other sectors of the media industry due to conglomerations' cross ownership of both news and entertainment industries. Similar to the movie industry, environmental problems in commercial news are: ignored or marginalized (Beder, 1998; Heinz, 2005); presented as dramatized, episodic events with clear "good" and "bad" guys (Anderson, 1997; Boykoff & Boykoff, 2007); solved through technology (Schor, 2009); provided with little or no context to help the reader understand the complexity of the issue (Beder, 1998; Corbett & Durfee, 2004); and subordinated to competing commercial interests (Beder, 1998; Hansen, 2010). The similarities between the news and entertainment industries reveal that the way Hollywood treats a subject like the environment is not an exception to the rule; instead, the consistent subjugation of environmental concerns is part of a broader capitalist logic in a concentrated market.

Ideological Implications of Representations of the Environment

Hansen (2010) contends that "The artifacts of media culture are...not innocent entertainment but are thoroughly ideological artifacts bound up with political rhetoric, struggles, agendas, and policies" (p. 8). Mediated representations of the environment are important to study when it comes to youth because, although children learn about the world around them from myriad sources—including family, community leaders, school, and peers—they are developing increasingly intimate relationships with technology and mediated content due to media proliferation. Animated films provide "intricate teachings" that are reinforced by other sources in childhood (Lugo-Lugo & Bloodsworth-Lugo, 2009, p. 167), and encourage specific understandings about individuals' place in society (Giroux and Pollock, 2010, p. 84), which is relevant when considering how children consider their role in environmental problems faced on a global scale. For this reason, Mayumi, Solomon, and Chang (2005) argue that popular films need to address environmental issues because of their educational role and potential to reach a broad audience. The clear educational potential of film invites discussion as to what sorts of lessons about the environment are given to children by a hypercommercial, concentrated culture industry.

Theoretical and Interpretive Frameworks

In order to understand the messages about the environment sent to young media audiences, this research analyzes *Ice Age 2*, *Wall-E*, and *The Lorax*. The films were chosen based on two criteria: (1) the environment had to be a central narrative in each film, and (2) each film had to be produced by a Hollywood "major."

In their critical work on Marx's *Das Capital*, Althusser and Balibar (2009) broadly define *symptomatic reading* as a "dual reading" (p. 32) that consists of an initial interpretation of a text focusing on manifest details (in this case, the narrative and characters), followed by a "second," deeper reading designed to reveal ideological messages through identification of key "lacunae," or silences in the text (p. 86). The central purpose of a symptomatic reading is to elucidate the problematic, which Althusser and Balibar describe as "an answer given to its absent question" (p. 32). Storey (2012) provides a clear demonstration of the utility of identifying "silences" about the environment through the problematic, noting that the common depiction of automobiles as isolated in natural settings is a way to counteract potential questions about cars' contribution to both pollution and road congestion:

> showing cars in both nature (unpolluted) and space (uncongested) confronts the claims…In this way, the criticisms are answered without the questions themselves having been formally posed. The emphasis placed on nature and space is, therefore, a response to the twin questions (which remains unasked in the advertisement itself—in the text's 'problematic'). (pp. 75–76)

Here, Storey reveals the a-priori "answer" provided by advertisers to perceived concerns about environmental impact. It is this advance answer to as-yet unarticulated concerns that creates key *lacunae* within a text, for the problematic often serves to silence future questions by making them appear irrelevant. In symptomatic interpretation, then, the first reading examines the manifest text and progresses to identify the "lapses, distortions, silences and absences" characteristic of the latent text and its ideological foundations (Storey, 2012, p. 244). In permitting a focus on silences, the key reason for using this interpretive framework is able to highlight what media producers may want to ignore—or actively deflect attention away from.

Applied to this research, there are several potential "silences" regarding environmental problems that can be examined in the films including: (1) what problems exist; (2) how they are defined; (3) what their causes are; (4) who is responsible; (5) the potential impacts and consequences; and (6) what solutions are available. As Entman (1993) notes, "omissions of potential problem definitions, explanations, evaluations, and recommendations may be as critical as the inclusions in guiding the audience" (p. 54). The assessment of silences reveals the problematic embedded in the texts as well as the films' subjectivity—how they invite their young audiences into certain identities. This type of interpretation coheres with Althusser's critical praxis, where ideology is defined by a relationship between the producer of a text and the subject, including how the subject is positioned by the text (Althusser, 2008).

Analysis

Manifest Reading

Ice Age 2: The Meltdown. Fox Searchlight Pictures released this film as the second sequel in the Ice Age franchise that focuses on the adventures of a small pack of ice-age mammals: "Sid" the sloth; "Diego" the saber-toothed tiger; and "Manny" the woolly mammoth. The Environmental Media Association, which works with Hollywood studios on their environmental rhetoric, gave it their highest award in 2007. The film begins with a vignette of "Scrat," a squirrel who gives perpetual chase for an elusive acorn. He finds it, but in the process pokes holes in a giant ice wall that begins to spout water. In this way, the film introduces the concept of climate change and attendant melting ice in a comical fashion as Scrat attempts to stop the flow of water with various body parts. Once the central part of the film begins, it is clear that "global warming" (identified by that name in several scenes) is impending. At first no one believes the claims, but most animals become alarmed once the veracity of the warming is established, and a character named "Fast Tony" benefits from the confusion by selling useless "survival" items. The animals travel together in a group to a "boat" (made out of a gargantuan piece of curved wood) to escape the flood and the carnivorous monsters freed by the melting ice. Eventually, a portion of the ice wall holding back the water breaks and the flood occurs, appearing as gigantic waves cresting mountaintops that thunder toward the animals. It looks as though all animals will perish until Scrat reappears: prized acorn in paw, he punctures a second set of holes in the wall, creating a fissure through which all the water can escape. Once the waters recede, the consequences of the melting ice are revealed: areas once covered in ice are replaced with green pastures; Sid capitalizes on the remaining water to start a swim school; Manny finds the rest of his herd and realizes his species is not extinct. The film ends on a positive note for all animals except one: a turtle that was killed by the monsters.

Wall-E. This film was the brainchild of Pixar executives operating under Disney after its acquisition in 2006. In addition to winning numerous awards and nominations for cinematic quality,[4] Keim (2008) in *Wired Magazine* described it as "the decade's most powerful environmental film." *Wall-E* opens on a somber note with a slow aerial pan of a large American city at dusk with large skyscrapers below. More detail is provided until it is gradually revealed that the majority of the "buildings" are actually thousands of stacked trash cubes.

From this point, the film quickly introduces the audience to the significant environmental problems on earth: mountains of trash that seem to have no end; massive dust storms; and no vegetation or humans anywhere, since earth can no longer support life. The role of large corporations in this environmental apocalypse is made clear through the vestiges of "Buy N Large" (BNL): old billboards for the corporation clutter the skyline; "dollar" bills littering the ground are actually BNL currency;

and a "public service announcement" reveals that the last American president was the CEO of BNL.

Few creatures survive in this desolate landscape: one is "Wall-E," a solar-powered, rusty, dirty, slightly crazy, but likeable robot whose task is to clean up the world while the humans live on a large spaceship. The only other organism that has survived is a cockroach that Wall-E keeps as a pet. In his loneliness he has become an obsessive collector of trash, saving jewelry boxes, lighters, car keys, an iPod that plays "Hello Dolly," and Apple "mice" that scurry across the floor when he comes home.

The film then introduces the audience to the superficial lives of humans on the spaceship who are: overweight due to lack of physical activity and continuous involvement with computer screens; controlled by BNL; and obsessed with consumption. The catalyst for positive change comes not from the humans but in the form of a new robot called Eve-A. Luminously white, sleek, powerful, and weightless (unlike Wall-E, she never touches the ground and can fly), she is the one who proves that earth is habitable again, fights off the bad guys (BNL robots), and helps to bring a potentially enlightened group of humans back to earth who have learned important lessons.

The Lorax. This Universal Pictures film won several awards, including Teen Choice and Kids Choice. The film is based on Dr Seuss' book of the same name that is widely considered an unequivocal critique of American consumer culture and a chronicle of "the human race's ecological crimes" (Little, 2012). Similar to the first two films, *The Lorax* focuses on a specific environmental problem—in this case, the loss of indigenous forests and wildlife. The narrative focuses on Ted, a young boy who lives in an artificial landscape devoid of natural vegetation. The suburb in which he lives contains semblances of plant life—colorful plastic trees and flowers—but they are entirely manufactured. Due to the lack of trees, as well as the nearby factories, the air quality is so low that one company—run by the uniformly charmless and single-minded businessman Mr. O'Hare—sells bottled air to those who can afford it. Ted, like most of the town's younger inhabitants, is not concerned about the loss of living trees because he does not know that real ones ever existed. He plays with his remote-controlled airplane, rides his sleek razor-type scooter around town, and shyly chases after his female neighbor. Once he hears about the existence of trees, however, he goes in search of a knowledgeable yet elderly recluse named "The Oncler" who holds the key to the mystery of their disappearance: all the trees were destroyed, he explains, through the production of "thneeds," odd-looking items that serve only an ornamental purpose. In his desire for profit, the Oncler did not listen to a small creature called the "Lorax" who lived in the forest and tried to stop its destruction. The Lorax provides the moral compass in the film: he knows that needless consumption is wrong and that trees are needed for a healthy environment. Ted's ultimate attempt to reintroduce a tree into the environment is thwarted by O'Hare, who thinks enlightenment of the population will hurt his business. Through

Ted, O'Hare is defeated and the people in the town realize the importance of trees for environmental health. In the end, wisdom about the connection between over-consumption and environmental degradation resonates across generations, enabling the natural environment to thrive.

Symptomatic Reading
The films described above have clear commonalities and differences. The films are distinct in the type of environmental issue addressed and overall narrative and char-acters. The similarities, however, are more numerous, and involve broader themes of consumption through key omissions. The following section includes the results of the "second" Althusser and Balibar (2009) reading to identify crucial silences and examine what they reveal about Hollywood's treatment of environmental issues for young audiences.

Ice Age 2: The Meltdown. At a superficial level, Fox Searchlight's *Ice Age* sequel can be seen as an environmental film in that it provides an introduction to—and encour-ages awareness of—"global warming" by making the issue central to the narrative and by speaking directly to the child audience about environmental degradation. In addition, the film presents it as an authentic and considerable threat: the ani-mals' terror of both the approaching mountainous waves and the sea monsters they bring provide clear cues that climate change brings significant danger and requires attention for its resolution. In this sense, the film introduces a sense of *realism* as described by Ingram (2004) and Whitley (2008), where texts make a claim to events in the outside world. Ties to the real world, however, dissolve when one considers omissions in the text.

One of the first silences in the film is there is no clear definition of "global warm-ing": it is presented only as a warming trend that results in melting ice and floods, which is reinforced by the continuous use of the outdated and misleading phrase for climate change. Also absent is any clear cause of the warming: it cannot be due to human activity, as there are no humans in the film, which is a significant absence given that the vast majority of scientific data reveals that human activity is at the very least partly responsible for these changes (Nuccitelli, 2013). Instead, the film hints that "Scrat" the squirrel has precipitated the disaster through his comical hunt for a nut. The text contains the same silence regarding possible resolutions: the animals are doomed to drown in the flood until Scrat once again intervenes and the flood waters recede. Perhaps the most important lacuna exists in the lack of consequences: after the flood, almost every animal has a better life in a warmer, greener environment.

The numerous silences in the film—regarding the definition, causes, conse-quences, and solutions for climate change—fulfill the function of the problematic to preclude additional questions and ward off critique by presenting "global warm-ing" as a simple phenomenon with an unknown etiology that can be resolved quickly and simply to the benefit of living creatures. This representation serves to alleviate concerns over a very serious and complex issue by hinting that climate change, far from being a threat to life, actually benefits it.

Wall-E. Unlike *Ice Age 2*, *Wall-E* defines its environmental problem and attendant consequences very clearly: overconsumption, operating within a powerful consumer culture driven by large corporations, is devastating the planet. The film makes clear which parties are responsible for the degradation: equal blame is assigned to both the large corporation "Buy N Large" as well as the humans who have let this happen. The text invites audiences to be horrified by overconsumption's catastrophic effect on the environment, including the devastated natural landscape, but also the deteriorated human mind and body, providing an "overt" critique of consumerism, as Murray and Heumann (2009a) note. In so doing, the film "risks engagement with controversial elements of the environmentalist agenda in more overt ways than any previous animation" (Whitley, 2008, p. 141) and appears to be an example of the "radical" environmentalism defined by Ingram (2004) that operates outside the typical consumerist milieu. However, like *Ice Age 2*, there are significant silences that become apparent in the latter half of the film with the comparison of Wall-E to Eve.

Wall-E, with his rusty, aging body that functions as a trash compactor, represents humans' past sins of overconsumption and willful ignorance. Firmly rooted to the ground, he is cumbersome and dirty, representing the trash he is trying to organize. By stark contrast, Eve's weightlessness and luminosity hint that she has no negative impact on the earth: she's a different breed of technology that represents a clean, enlightened future. Significantly absent from her presentation is an explanation of her actual role in a clean environment. Does she represent a break from older patterns of wasteful manufacture, overconsumption, and environmental degradation? Eve's physical form itself presents the *problematic*, for her spotless body seems associated with no waste at all, and thus can allay the potential concerns of young audiences watching the film regarding her role in earth's future.

The silences surrounding Eve's production invite additional exploration of this unusual heroine into a film critiquing consumption. The first important clue about Eve comes from Disney's acquisition of Pixar two years prior to the creation of *Wall-E* that enabled Steve Jobs, founder of Pixar and Apple, to become a board member and largest shareholder at Disney (La Monica, 2006). It was Jobs' influence at the three companies involved—Pixar, Disney, and Apple—that shaped the creation of both Wall-E and Eve. According to Stanton, *Wall-E*'s director (in Siklos, 2008):

> I wanted Eve to be high-end technology—no expense spared—and I wanted it to be seamless and for the technology to be sort of hidden and subcutaneous. The more I started describing it, the more I realized I was pretty much describing the Apple playbook for design.

The way in which Eve was designed (through meetings with Stanton and creative designers at Apple) prompted Siklos (2008) to note, "It may be the first time a character was based on a true corporate sibling." The collaboration between the corporations explains the product placements in the film, including the Apple "mice" in Wall-E's home, Wall-E's classic Apple start-up "chime" when he reboots, and Disney's *Hello Dolly* shown on an iPod. It is important to note, however, that *Wall-E* represents a new trend in Hollywood away from mere product placement:

> People talk about how products and brands will sponsor movies...that's what's going to happen. But Apple has already done that here without being directly involved...I would call it product *homage*. And that is way more valuable than product placement. It doesn't just reinforce a single Apple product it reinforces Apple's *entire design approach* from MacBook to iPod to iPhone. (McQuivey, in Bulik, 2008, emphasis added)

Returning to the problematic, *Wall-E* provides assurance that, while humans have made mistakes, the environment will be protected in the future with a combination of enlightenment and cleaner technology. But it is important to note that it is not just any technology—or any corporation—that can provide a sustainable future. "Buy N Large," a thinly veiled reference to giant discount retailers like Wal-Mart, is a hazard for the environment, as is older technology and overweight individuals, whose "middle America" obesity stands in for the gluttony and selfishness associated with mindless consumption. Thus, while the film purports to criticize environmental degradation due to overconsumption, it really functions as a critique of the working and middle classes, for it is only the wrong type of consumption (say, buying in bulk at discount prices) that leads to catastrophe.

Ultimately, there appear to be three messages contained in the film. In the first half, young audiences receive the messages that humans live on a finite planet with limited natural resources and that overconsumption is harmful for the environment. The message delivered in the second half of the film, which completely contradicts and disarms the power of the first two messages, is that the purchase of Apple products is good for the planet. Children are invited to see Eve—and associated Apple products—as part of the solution to environmental problems rather than an integral part of the old, destructive consumption pattern. Thus, although there is initially an "ecologically attuned version of environmental attentiveness" that Whitley (2008, p. 150) recognizes, the message is completely undercut by the fact that Apple products provide the starring roles.

The Lorax. Universal Picture's *The Lorax* contains an environmental message that can be distilled into one clear point: mindless consumption of useless "thneeds" unequivocally causes environmental destruction. The film defines deforestation and loss of wildlife habitat clearly, as it does the consequences: the forests are not able to grow fast enough to sustain high demand for products, and the loss of native forest precipitously decreases biodiversity and harms humans. The film also identifies the cause of environmental damage clearly, placing responsibility for the destruction on both the corporations that mass produce "thneeds" as well as the people that engage in overconsumption. The film (like the book) parodies the "fads" prevalent in consumer culture where useless items are collected and highly prized for a short time, providing a powerful critique of American hypercommercialism.

The film falters slightly by individualizing the problem in the form of both the young boy Ted and the evil Mr. O'Hare. Ingram (2004) notes that Hollywood often avoids a strong critique of consumer culture through *individualization*, where blame for environmental problems is placed on one bad person or corporation: by this logic, once that person or organization is stopped, an entire environmental issue is resolved. In *The Lorax*, Ted is seen as the solution to the problem of deforestation: he alone can bring a healthy environment back. Conversely, Mr. O'Hare provides the one impediment to Ted's endeavors: Ted must defeat him before the environment can thrive. The film thus presents a simplistic solution to a very complex problem and ignores the deep structural realities and complexities of environmental degradation.

On the whole, however, *The Lorax* avoids the central silences observed in the first two films regarding environmental problems. For the most part, it also avoids the rampant product placement seen in *Wall-E*.[5] The one true lacuna is closely tied to the film's marketing. The fact that the film had over seventy product tie ins (Hetter, 2012), including products like Hewlett Packard printers (using "green" packaging) and a new Mazda Hybrid SUV, prompted *New York Times* critic A.O. Scott (2012) to note that "The movie is a noisy, useless piece of junk, reverse-engineered into something resembling popular art in accordance with the reigning imperatives of marketing and brand extension."

The silence regarding real solutions to environmental problems, paired with the mass marketing that accompanied the film, points to the problematic: the problem with consumption of "thneeds," according to the movie, is that they are not green enough. What is needed is not less consumption, but more "sustainable" consumption. The film thus accomplishes an elegant sleight of hand: while the movie itself provides a compelling critique of consumption, the child-focused marketing surrounding the film reassures young audiences that they will not hurt the environment if they simply consume the "right" way. The incorporation of this problematic precludes discussion of environmentally friendly alternatives like reducing consumption and *reusing* existing goods.

Ideological Implications of the Symptomatic Reading
Analysis reveals that there are common ideological threads woven through the films. All three movies present real environmental issues as urgent and worthy of attention. This type of portrayal has the potential to underscore the serious nature of environ-

mental degradation for young audiences and provide a call to change, as Mayumi et al. (2005) note. Unfortunately, while the problems presented in the films are "real" in the sense that they correlate to ongoing environmental concerns, significant silences about viable solutions serve to undercut any serious message about environmental protection. Specifically, the films studiously avoid identifying individual sacrifice and change as the answer: in *Wall-E* the environment was saved by enlightened Apple products; in *The Lorax* people just needed to plant one tree after deposing an evil CEO; and in *Ice Age 2* all the animals needed to do to survive the effects of climate change was to move to a different neighborhood.

Accompanying key omissions is individualization: as Ingram (2004) notes, the consequences of individualization are two-fold: it both obscures the complexity of environmental problems and reduces them to a simple cause-and-effect set of circumstances. The films attempt to reassure children that their role in environmental problems is negligible, that one person or entity will fix it for them, and that the American consumerist lifestyle is not only acceptable but needed for a healthy environment. In sum, while all three films appear to adopt what Ingram (2004) terms radical environmentalism, their "environmental" messages are entrenched within a capitalist framework, reinforcing a mainstream, consumerist mindset.

The finding that these environmental films "reproduce capitalist ideologies" (Ingram, 2004, p. 14) is perhaps no surprise: as Whitley argues, sustainability rhetoric in the "West" is "designed to accommodate relatively minor changes in outlook and lifestyle to the underlying norms of economic growth and productivity" (2008, p. 2). However, the consequences of doing so is striking: Hollywood takes an issue that has the potential to provide a serious critique of existing consumer culture and effectively removes the critique through commodification, turning the environment into simply another product in the concentrated media marketplace.

The subordination of environmental concerns to what McAllister (2006, p. 273) calls the "economic imperative" results in a paradox: commercial media, playing an increasingly central role in children's lives, are the very source that will not provide children with accurate and useful information about the environment that is crucial to their futures. The American media oligarchy effectively removes "alternative viewpoints" and enables "corporate media to promote dominant ideas and frame public discussion and debate" (Andersen & Gray, 2007, p. 97). The lack of critical perspective about environmental issues is undergirded by an absence of discussion about how we have reached this point. McChesney (2004) argues that "as marketers intrude deeper into our children's lives…hypercommercialization goes mostly unmentioned in the media or political culture" (p. 165). As a result, the general public is not often allowed "behind the curtain" to observe how the media industry works.

Different generations learn different behaviors and perspectives: "At base, generational differences are cultural differences: as cultures change, their youngest members are socialized with new and different values" (Twenge, Campbell, & Freeman, 2012,

p. 1045). The Althusserian perspective that ideology is related to the construction of the audience as a particular subject provides one clue as to how this socialization occurs in the current hypercommercial media landscape: while these Hollywood films give superficial attention to the need for community and care for the environment, they "hail" their young audiences solely as consumers and not citizens, leaving little room for the construction of other potential subjectivities or identities. As Giroux and Pollock (2010) note, media monopolies like Disney transform "kids' culture [into] not merely a new market for the accumulation of capital but a petri dish for producing new commodified subjects" (p. 3). Through "environmental" films like those analyzed in this research, young people are invited to approach the environment as self-interested consumers, a vantage point that fundamentally limits which solutions to environmental problems are considered viable.

Conclusion

Similar to major environmental problems like climate change, deforestation, and pollution, US media formations underscore their importance by ignoring international borders. Although the subject matter of this research is Hollywood film—and, by inference, US audiences—it is clear that the reach of the American culture industry goes well beyond the borders of the USA. Disney's most recent blockbuster *Frozen* provides an excellent example of US media's global influence: grossing close to $1.2 billion from worldwide box offices (Lynskey, 2014), it was released in 41 different countries worldwide (National Public Radio, 2014) and was number one at the box office in Japan for almost three months (Sim, 2015). Miller, Govil, and McMurria (2004) describe Hollywood as a global industry that dominates not only the cultural landscape of the USA but also the media culture of other countries, making a clear case for cultural imperialism. As awareness of the urgency of international environmental problems continues to rise, the culture industry continues to make the environment a central focus; at the same time, however, it does a serious disservice to young audiences by undercutting any meaningful messages about sustainable change and deflecting attention away from personal responsibility and toward increased consumption. It is this "dual message" of environmentalism framed by consumerist pursuits that provides the "green screen" metaphor in the title of this research. As Giroux and Pollock (2010) argue, it is essential to secure:

> young people's right to learn and think deeply about the effects of their actions within the complex network of human and animal life on this planet...A critical education that explores the complexity of self and society...is the only way to equip youth with compelling reasons for why they should choose not to taint their innocence by inadvertently colluding in processes that further...the world's problems. (p. 88)

McChesney (2008) observes that, "If we learn nothing else from the political economy of media it is that commercialism comes at a very high price and with massive externalities" (p. 20). The externalities, in this case, relate to massive environmental damage as the cost of doing business with the global child audience. Although there is existing scholarly work recognizing a potentially symbiotic relationship between capitalism and care for the environmental (see Arsel & Buscher, 2012 on neoliberal markets and Brockington, Duffy, & Igoe, 2008 on capitalism and conservation), this research contends that increasing levels of consumption and trends of hypercommercialism on a global scale are pushing the world toward an ecological tipping point (Schor, 2009). As powerful conglomerates continue to expand their influence in an international marketplace, we need a greater diversity to repeatedly confront the flood of commercial messages and consumerist ideologies from the culture industry.

Notes

1 Bell (2012) notes that Hasbro is planning at least five more movies based on its games, including *Candy Land*, *Ouija*, and *Monopoly*.

2 This number is an aggregate of different categories for concern over the environment, including "a great deal" (31%); "a fair amount" (35%); and "only a little" (25%) about environmental health.

3 Examples include *Erin Brokovich*; *A Civil Suit*; *The Day After Tomorrow*; *The Constant Gardener*; *The Happening*; *Promised Land*; *Fern Gully*; *Ice Age 2*; *Happy Feet*; *Wall-E*; and *The Lorax*.

4 Best Original Screenplay (Academy Awards) and Best Film (American Film Institute), among others.

5 In the opening scene, Ted kneels down to play with his toy aircraft. What becomes visible at this angle is Ted's shoes: white high tops with a black circle near the ankle that resemble Converse All Stars. During the film release, the Converse website and other stores displayed shoes featuring *The Lorax* characters.

References

Althusser, L. (2008). Ideology and ideological state apparatuses. In J. Storey (Ed.), *Cultural theory and popular culture: A reader* (pp. 303–12). London: Routledge.

Althusser, L., & Balibar, E. (2009). *Reading capital*. New York, NY: Verso.

Andersen, R., & Gray, J. (2007). *Battleground: The media*. Boston, MA: Greenwood.

Anderson, A. (1997). *Media, culture and the environment*. New York, NY: Routledge.

Arsel, M., & Buscher, B. (2012). Nature™ Inc.: Changes and continuities in neoliberal conservation and market based environmental policy. *Development and Change*, 43, 53–78. doi:10.1111/j.1467-7660.2012.01752.x.

Bagdikian, B. (2004). *The new media monopoly*. Boston, MA: Beacon.

Barnes, B. (2010, July 26). Marketing 'Tron: Legacy' bring the hardest sell yet. *New York Times*. Retrieved from www.nytimes.com/2010/07/26/business/media/26tron.html.

Beder, S. (1998). *Global spin: The corporate assault on environmentalism.* Vermont: Chelsea Green.

Bell, C. (2012, April 13). Battleship and 5 other movie game projects in the works. *Huffington Post.* Retrieved from www.huffingtonpost.com/2012/04/13/battleship-board-game-movies-candy-landmonopoly_n_1423194.html.

Boykoff, M.T., & Boykoff, J.M. (2007). Climate change and journalistic norms: A case-study of US mass-media coverage. *Geoforum*, 38, 1190–1204. doi:10.1016/j.geoforum.2007.01.008.

Brockington, D., Duffy, R., & Igoe, J. (2008). *Nature unbound: Conservation, capitalism and the future of protected areas.* Oxford: Earthscan.

Bulik, S. (2008, July 17). 'Wall-E' gives glimpse of product placement's future. *Advertising Age.* Retrieved from http://adage.com/article/madisonvine-news/wall-e-glimpse-product-place-ment-s-future/129715/.

Corbett, J.B., & Durfee, J.L. (2004). Testing public (un)certainty of science: Media representations of global warming. *Science Communication*, 26(2), 129–51. doi:10.1177/1075547004270234.

Entman, R. (1993). Framing: Toward clarification of a fractured paradigm. *Journal of Communication*, 43(4), 51–58. doi:10.1111/j.1460-2466.1993.tb01304.x.

Gallup. (2014). Climate change: Environment. *Gallup Poll.* Retrieved from www.gallup.com/poll/1615/environment.aspx.

Giroux, H., & Pollock, G. (2010). *The mouse that roared: Disney and the age of innocence.* New York. NY: Rowman & Littlefield.

Hansen, A. (2010). *Environment, media, and communication.* New York, NY: Routledge.

Heinz, T. (2005). From civil rights to environmental rights. *Journal of Communication Inquiry*, 29(1), 47–65. doi: 10.1177/0196859904269996.

Hetter, K. (2012, March 13). Is the Lorax message what people need? *Cable News Network.* Retrieved from www.cnn.com/2012/03/13/living/lorax-movie/index.html.

Hill, J. (2011). Endangered childhoods: How consumerism is impacting child and youth. *Media Culture & Society*, 33, 347–62. doi:10.1177/0163443710393387.

Ingram, D. (2004). *Green screen: Environmentalism and Hollywood cinema.* Exeter: University of Exeter.

Jennings, N. (2006). Advertising and consumer development. In S. Mazzarella (Ed.), *20 questions about youth and media* (pp. 103–16). New York, NY: Peter Lang.

Keim, B. (2008, July 11). The environmentalism of Wall-E. *Wired.* Retrieved from www.wired.com/2008/07/the-environment/.

Kellner, D. (1995). *Media culture.* New York, NY: Routledge.

La Monica, P. (2006, January 25). Disney buys Pixar. *Cable News Network.* Retrieved from http://money.cnn.com/2006/01/24/news/companies/disney_pixar_deal/.

Langer, B. (2004). The business of branded enchantment. *Journal of Consumer Culture*, 4, 251–77. doi:10.1177/1469540504043685.

Little, A. (2012, November 9). Stealing the sunlight. *New York Times.* Retrieved from www.nytimes.com/2012/11/11/books/review/the-story-of-the-blue-planet-by-andri-snaer-magnason.html?_r=0.

Lugo-Lugo, C.R., & Bloodsworth-Lugo, M.K. (2009). "Look out New World, here we come"? Race, racialization, and sexuality in four children's animated films. *Cultural Studies, Critical Methodologies*, 9, 166–78. doi:10.1177/1532708608325937.

Lynskey, D. (2014, May 13). Frozen-mania: How Elsa, Anna and Olaf conquered the world. *The Guardian*. Retrieved from www.theguardian.comfilm/2014/may/13/frozen-mania-elsa-anna-olaf-disney-emo-princess-let-it-go.

Mayumi, K., Solomon, B.D., & Chang, J. (2005). The ecology and consumption themes of the films of Hayao Miyazaki. *Ecological Economics*, 54(1), 1–7. doi:10.1016/j.ecolecon.2005.03.012.

McAllister, M. (2006). Just how commercialized is children's culture? In S. Mazzarella (Ed.), *20 questions about youth and media* (pp. 267–80). New York, NY: Peter Lang.

McChesney, R. (2004). *The problem of the media*. New York, NY: Monthly Review P.

McChesney, R. (2008). *Political economy of the media*. New York, NY: Monthly Review P.

McDonagh, P., & Brereton, P. (2010). Screening not greening: An ecological reading of the greatest business movies. *Journal of Macromarketing*, 30(2), 133–46. doi:10.1177/0276146710361921.

McDonald, M., & Wearing, S. (2013). *Social psychology and theories of consumer culture*. New York, NY: Routledge.

Miller, C.M. (2002, January 7). What's wrong with this picture? *The Nation*, pp. 18–22.

Miller, T., Govil, N., & McMurria, J. (2004). *Global Hollywood: No. 2*. London: British Film Institute.

Murray, R.L., & Heumann, J.K. (2009a). WALL-E: From environmental adaptation to sentimental nostalgia. *Jump Cut: A Review of Contemporary Media*, 51. Retrieved from http://ejumpcut.org/archive/jc51.2009/WallE/text.html.

Murray, R.L., & Heumann, J.K. (2009b). Car culture and the transformation of the American landscape in *The Fast and the Furious*. In R.L. Murray & J.K. Heumann (Eds.), *Ecology and popular film: Cinema on the edge* (pp. 143–64). Albany: State U of New York P.

Nash Information Services. (2013). *2012 Domestic grosses*. Retrieved from www.boxoffice-mojo.com/yearly/chart/?view2=worldwide&yr=2012.

National Public Radio. (2014, February 24). 'Let it go': A global hit in any language. Retrieved from www.npr.org/2014/02/24/282081061/let-it-go-a-global-hit-in-any-language.

Nuccitelli, D. (2013, May 16). Survey finds 97% of climate science papers agree warming is man-made. *The Guardian*. Retrieved from www.theguardian.com/environment/climate-consensus-97percent/2013/may/16/climate-change-scienceofclimatechange.

Schor, J. (2004). *Born to buy*. New York, NY: Scribner.

Schor, J. (2009). *Plenitude*. New York, NY: Penguin P.

Scott, A.O. (2012, March 1). How the Grinch stole the Lorax. *New York Times*. Retrieved from www.nytimes.com/2012/03/02/movies/dr-seuss-the-lorax-with-ed-helms-and-danny-devito.html.

Siklos. (2008, May 12). Apple and Eve revealed. *Fortune*. Retrieved from http://archive.fortune.com/2008/05/09/technology/siklos_walle.fortune/index.htm?source=yahoo_quote.

Sim, S. (2015, January 28). Disney's 'Frozen' helps Japan box office reach record sales once again. *International Business Times*. Retrieved from www.ibtimes.com/disneys-frozen-helps-japan-box-office-reach-record-sales-again-1798156.

Steinberg, S. (2011). *Kinderculture: The corporate construction of childhood*. Boulder, CO: Westview P.

Storey, J. (2012). *Cultural theory and popular culture: An introduction*. Athens: U of Georgia P.

Swift, A. (2014). Americans again pick environment over economic growth. *Gallup poll*. Retrieved from www.gallup.com/poll/168017/americans-again-pick-environment-economic-growth.aspx?utmsource=ENVIRONMENT&utm_medium=topic&utm_campaign=tiles.

Townsend, A. (2011, July 11). State of play: Toy companies have become Hollywood's new auteurs. *Time*. Retrieved from http://content.time.com/time/magazine/article/0,9171,2080765,00.html.

Turow, J., & McAllister, M. (2009). *The advertising and consumer culture reader*. New York, NY: Routledge.

Twenge, J.M., Campbell, W.K., & Freeman, E.C. (2012). Generational differences in young adults' life goals. *Journal of Personality and Social Psychology*, 102, 1045–62. doi:10.1037/a0027408.

Wasko, J. (2003). *How Hollywood works*. London: Sage.

Whitley, D. (2008). *The idea of nature in Disney animation*. Aldershot: Ashgate.

DISCUSSION QUESTIONS

1. Are you familiar with the films that Moore discusses? If so, how do you respond to her analysis of these films? What elements of her discussion did you recognize? What is new? Is Moore ignoring key details in the films?

2. Moore provides "manifest" and "symptomatic" readings of these films. What does each way of reading involve? Most importantly, what is symptomatic reading? Choose a film that Moore doesn't discuss and create manifest and symptomatic readings of it to share with the class.

3. Ideology involves the beliefs and ideas that are shared by society or a group within that society. In Marxist theory, ideology is seen as key to how the dominant classes maintain power. Ideology often involves false consciousness, a masking of contradictions that allows the exploited classes to accept exploitation or simply to perpetuate power on the part of the dominant classes. Moore is drawing on the Marxist Althusser's ideas about ideology, which she defines as follows: "The Althusserian perspective that ideology is related to the construction of the audience as a particular subject provides one clue as to how this socialization occurs in the current hypercommercial media landscape: while these Hollywood films give superficial attention to the need for community and care for the environment, they 'hail' their young audiences solely as consumers and not citizens, leaving little room for the construction of other potential subjectivities or identities" (p. 210). Take some time, perhaps working with a partner, to work through this definition carefully and explain it in your own words, giving original examples that Moore doesn't discuss.

4. In the conclusion, Moore notes research that "contends that increasing levels of consumption and trends of hypercommercialism on a global scale are pushing the world toward an ecological tipping point" (p. 211). Discuss this possibility with reference to your own consumption practices.

C. "THE ENROLLMENT OF NATURE IN TOURIST INFORMATION: FRAMING URBAN NATURE AS 'THE OTHER,'" YLVA UGGLA AND ULRIKA OLAUSSON

This 2012 article from Environmental Communication *examines the relationship between nature and culture in tourist information. It focuses on the construction of nature in tourist marketing as the "other." Using the tourist information website for Stockholm as an example, Ylva Uggla and Ulrika Olausson* examine how advertisers turn nature into a commodity for tourist consumption. The authors argue that "[t]he enrollment of nature in city marketing... contributes to concealing the environmental consequences of increased urban density" (pp. 230–31). As you read this article, consider the consequences of commodifying nature and viewing it as something completely removed, or "othered," from humanity.*

Glossary terms: ecocriticism, empiricism, epistemology, framing theory, qualitative research, semiotics

Abstract

This article is based on the assumption that nature inevitably plays a role in urban place-making. Today, cities worldwide are engaged in place promotion in which nature is constructed as a commodity to consume. This article explores the enrollment of nature in tourist information with a specific analytical focus on the relationship between nature and culture. Guided by framing theory and citing the case of tourist information in Stockholm, the article empirically demonstrates how nature is enrolled in tourist information and turned into a commodity through three distinct but related frames that, in various ways, construct nature as "other": nature as the familiar other, nature as the exotic other, and pristine nature. The article concludes that the enrollment of nature in city marketing reproduces the modern nature-culture divide, which enables the commodification of nature and helps conceal the environmental consequences of increased urban density.

---

* Ylva Uggla is Professor in the School for Humanities, Education and Social Science at Örebro University in Sweden. Her research interests include the regulation and management of environmental risks.

Ulrika Olausson is Professor of Media and Communications Studies at Jönköping University in Sweden. Her research interests include journalism and global environmental risks.

Keywords: Construction of Place, Place Promotion, City Marketing, Tourist Information, Urban Nature, Framing Theory, Frame Analysis

Discussion of the meaning and implications of urban form is not new. Planning history manifests ongoing polarized debate between centrists, favoring the compact city, and decentrists, pleading for urban decentralization. In contemporary debate, the problems of urbanization and industrialization have been reformulated in terms of sustainable development. In European urban planning, the reaction to urban sprawl has been a trend toward concentration and an emphasis on the "compact city." The goal is to achieve sustainability and to promote urban qualities, such as high density, diversity, and vitality (Salingaros, 2006).

Urbanization reshapes the landscape and "produces new kinds of nature" (Asikainen & Jokinen, 2009, p. 351), implying that nature inevitably plays a role in urban place-making. The various images of the ideal city that appear, for example, in planning and place promotion, evince modernity's "double scripting" of both nature and the city (Kaika, 2005; see also Cronon, 1996). Applied here, this concept describes how nature represents both the sacred and the uncivilized, while the city represents both human distortion and the high point of civilization.

The construction of place encompasses both material production and symbolic order; hence, an important aspect of the construction of place is how places are imbued with meaning. To become meaningful, places must be verbalized and narrated, and various means of communication must contribute stories and images that advance the construction of place and foster understandings of what is fair, reasonable, and desirable (Lichrou, O'Malley, & Patterson, 2008; Stokowski, 2002). The discursive construction of the city as a place can be analyzed from various perspectives, drawing, for example, on urban policy, planning documents, and debates; architectural or urban movement journals or websites; city marketing; media coverage; and everyday interaction.

Planning and city marketing are two pivotal and interrelated aspects of the politics of urban development, which is increasingly characterized by entrepreneurialism. Today, cities all over the world are engaged in place promotion and the creation of city brands in a competition to attract investment capital and visitors. In this endeavor to "sell the city," leisure activities are subjected to market logic and nature is transformed into a commodity. This commodification of nature and the use of nature in place promotion imply new consumption opportunities (Corbett, 2006). Research into contemporary planning discourse reveals a trend toward concentration and a specific vision of what represents a desirable presence of nature in the city. This primarily means natural settings with certain urban features and can be defined as safe, well-arranged areas, mainly parks that contribute to the city's beauty and attractiveness and to citizens' well-being, and small green spaces such as "pocket parks" (Nordh, Hartig, Hagerhall, & Fry, 2009; Tunström, 2007; Uggla,

2012). The construction of nature in city marketing is less researched, however. Given the aforementioned subjection of leisure activities to market logic and the commodification of nature in place promotion, tourist information provides a critical case for empirically examining how, more precisely, the commodification of nature in place promotion is constituted.

This article explores how nature is enrolled in tourist information, with a specific analytical focus on the relationship between nature and culture, which is a relevant object of study considering the ambiguous character of the modern understanding of this relationship (Kaika, 2005). Accounts of the links between humans and nature, as they appear in the history of ideas, convey messages that identify humankind as both a destroyer and a rescuer, and wilderness or "natural nature" as both a threat and a refuge (Merchant, 2003; Nash, 2001; Oelschlaeger, 1991). The current, more or less hegemonic discourse of sustainable development unites a number of such diverse elements, and is firmly based on the modern concept of the nature-culture divide (Uggla, 2010). The main argument of the present article is that nature is enrolled in tourist information and turned into a commodity through three distinct, but related, frames that in various ways construct nature as "other."

The analysis is based on a case study of Stockholm, focusing on its official tourist information as displayed on the Internet-based Stockholm Official Visitors Guide (2011). Many cities draw on the interplay between the city and nature, or on the attractiveness of nearby nature reserves or National Parks, for example. Compared to other capitals, however, Stockholm stands out through the prominence it accords to nature when enrolling it in city marketing activities, situating "wild nature" in the midst of the city. Likewise, the use of the keyword "nature" in the Official Visitors Guide distinguishes this website from others of a similar kind, and thereby enables analysis of how nature is framed in this particular context. Since nature is an elusive concept, this website, by presenting its own version of what represents urban nature, serves as suitable material for this kind of analysis. The case of Stockholm thus provides an example that can elucidate the phenomenon of enrollment of nature in urban place-making (Cronon, 1996; Walton, 1992).

The City as Place, Product, and Commodity

Modernity is characterized by mobility, and modern cities are ever-changing places of discontinuity and frequent unintended encounters (Franklin, 2010, p. 4). As Doreen Massey (2005, p. 140) puts it: "What is special about a place is precisely that thrown togetherness, the unavoidable challenge of negotiating a here-and-now." Yet people tend to experience and perceive a place as a whole, with the built-up and natural settings together making up a qualitative total phenomenon (Bott, Cantrill, & Myers, 2003).

Places are embedded in particular social and cultural contexts and constructed "through a variety of social, cultural and semiotic processes" (Sampson & Goodrich,

2009, p. 903). Communication of place includes the cultivating of a sense of place, as well as the naturalizing of particular ways of being or living. Using nature as a universal concept in communication of place implies a moral imperative of this nature, naturalizing certain ways of thinking and acting (Cronon, 1996, p. 35). As aforementioned, however, nature comes in a wide variety of guises. The process that assigns meaning to a place always involves a particular understanding of nature and society, and specific choices that affect people's lives and the environment (Lichrou et al., 2008, p. 35; Stokowski, 2002, p. 374). In this sense, "environmental communication is the ever-present and multifaceted shadow of—natural and cultural—place in human symbolic action" (Carbaugh, 1996, p. 41). Thus, in the communication of places—for instance, in planning documents and tourist information—social relationships, relationships between humans and nonhumans, and relationships between the city and nature are continuously negotiated.

To be effective, tourist information has to make the destination consumable for the tourist (Corbett, 2006). In the endeavor to attract people and capital, cities strive to create place identity and present themselves as unique. However, the bulk of their marketing activities, especially tourist information, draws on almost identical notions of consumption that stress design, culture, and spectacular or iconic buildings. In this sense, cities become "clone cities" devoid of local identity (Dahles, 1998, p. 64; Harvey, 1989, p. 12). This is a paradox of tourist information, since tourism is based on the idea of "otherness," experiences that are out of the ordinary, and on authenticity.

Tourism is a leisure activity based on the value of mobility and distinct from the activities of everyday life. In seeking the authentic other, whether it be nature or another culture, the tourist also seeks her authentic self, a self detached from ordinary routines and free from stress (Corbett, 2006). Accordingly, tourist information presents the destination as thoroughly wonderful and amazing. The tourist destination, in most cases, becomes a place where the tourist goes to meet the authentic other, but which she never truly comes close to. The tourist "gaze" consumes landscapes and townscapes, and to meet this gaze, places are constructed as products or commodities without annoying elements (Urry & Larsen, 2011, p. 4ff; Corbett, 2006). Hence, tourist information fixes the city in time and space, and provides narrow snapshots of the dynamic processes involved in place-making (Lichrou et al., 2008, p. 32).

The marketing of clone cities mainly describes them as metropolitan commercial centers, but other characteristics may also be featured in tourist information, such as a good environment, cleanliness and "greenness," and proximity to nature. Considering the commercial rationale of tourist information, this is an area of importance for further study.

Analytical Framework and Materials

Framing theory is the analytical framework used in this article to capture how nature is enrolled in tourist information. Goffman (1974) was one of the first scholars to use the concept in its current sense: as an interpretative framework for attaching meaning to events, processes, and phenomena, that is, as an "implicit organizing idea" (Gamson, 1992, p. 3) that provides meaning or, put differently, a "cognitive window" (Pan & Kosicki, 1993, p. 59) through which the world is seen to be meaningful. Both the production as well as the reception of frames may occur consciously, though they may well be unconscious, shaped by culture and socialization.

It is impossible to avoid framing, because reality is always mediated through epistemology; the only question concerns the kind of frames being (re)produced (or possibly transformed) in text and talk (Lakoff, 2010). The selection of a worldview through framing processes is well-described by Entman in his frequently cited statement: "To frame is to *select some aspects of a perceived reality and make them more salient in a communicating text*" (Entman, 1993, p. 52, italics in original). Framing is, thus, largely about salience, which entails highlighting pieces of information to make them more meaningful and memorable. The process of making information salient also includes omitting other types of information, that is, diverting attention away from certain aspects of what is being communicated in favor of others (Entman, 1993).

In media studies, applying framing theory to the study of news media has become markedly popular over the years—especially in connection with quantitative methodologies such as content analysis. However, there is reason to reclaim the concept and employ it in studies of mediated communication in general, since frame analysis draws on literature from a range of disciplines, including sociology, communications, linguistics, and psychology (Scheufele & Tewksbury, 2007). In the present study of tourist information, framing theory has been chosen as the analytical framework because, as argued by Pan (2011), the mediatization processes of advertising include and highlight certain aspects of reality and exclude others, thereby "direct(ing) the tourist's gaze" (Santos, 2004, p. 122). These mediated messages are of particular importance when people have limited experience of a place; and because the media framing usually predates the physical experience, people already have a dominant frame on which to rely when they actually experience the destination (Santos, 2004). Some scholars (e.g., Papadopoulos, 1993) even claim that frames are more important than the "real" experience of a place, since people might discard the facts rather than choose to reject the frames. The framing mechanisms in tourism advertising give people valuable clues about how to relate new information about a place to existing frames.

When conducting frame analysis, it is important not to reduce the analysis to mere topics or themes (Olausson, 2009; Reese, 2007). The topic of a text is only one of various elements constituting the frame as a whole; one particular frame could easily apply to several topics, and one single topic can be the product of more than one frame (Carragee & Roefs, 2004). As aptly put by Reese (2007, p. 151), "if they [i.e., researchers] cannot show how the frame does more 'organizing' and 'structuring' work, I prefer they not use the label." This stresses the necessity of capturing how frames intersect and interrelate with various communicating texts, rather than regarding them as contained within individual text items.

Materials and Method for Data Analysis
In 2003, Stockholm Business Region, a company owned by the city of Stockholm, engaged a branding agency to develop a new brand for Stockholm, which resulted in the Stockholm Official Visitors Guide (2011; www.visitstockholm.com/en). This website is the official portal for Stockholm's tourist information.

The empirical material consists of the website's main welcome page (referred to in the following as the home page) and 37 additional pages located by searching on the site with the keyword "nature." Apart from the home page, the pages are formatted like online news items. At the head of each page is the brand logo and a search field. The eye-catcher, with few exceptions, is a photographic image. Below the image is a headline followed by a brief introduction and the main text (see Appendix 1 [not included here]). The home page includes a slide show with photographic images and captions, as well as "Editor's tips," "What's on," and "Popular on visitstockholm.com." In addition, 20 keywords, including "nature," are presented on the home page as a "cloud." The entire cloud, presented on a separate page, includes approximately 480 keywords. Searching for the keyword "nature" yielded 43 hits (November 7, 2011). Six of these pages were excluded because they either dealt with other issues (such as "Adventures for children" or "The Stockholm card") or contained the word "natural" in a different sense (e.g., "In a city built on the water, there are naturally many spa opportunities"), which left 37 web pages (see Appendix 2 [not included here]).

The present study is qualitative, differing both in terms of amount of material and methodology of data analysis from the quantitative approaches often used in frame analysis. As noted elsewhere (Olausson, 2009), framing theory offers little guidance when it comes to specific data analysis methods, especially qualitative ones. When selecting a method for qualitative analysis there are several established options, including socio-semiotics (e.g., Gottdiener, 1995) and critical discourse analysis (e.g., Olausson, 2009). However, in order to thoroughly operationalize the framing perspective in the analysis and avoid any "conceptual fuzziness" (Borah, 2011, p. 256), we have created an analytical "toolbox" for identifying the frame-shaping elements of the texts. This toolbox is based on the three discursive strategies (intentional or unintentional) identified by Entman (1993, p. 53) as commonly used by communicators to make information salient. The identification of salient information also enables the analysis of that which is *not* made salient. This aspect will primarily be addressed in the concluding section of the paper.

Analytical Tools

- *Placement of information in the structure of the text.* Which themes and topics—e.g., statements, arguments—are granted prominence (in a hierarchal order) and thereby made salient? Special attention is paid to headlines and captions.
- *Repetition of information.* In what ways are certain items of information repeated and thus made salient?
- *Association of information with culturally familiar symbols.* In what ways are certain items of information anchored in a familiar interpretative framework and thus made salient?

In addition, the following commonly studied "framing devices" and their relationships have been used in the analysis (Borah, 2011, p. 249; cf. Entman, 1993; Lakoff, 2010):

- *Metaphors.* In what ways are metaphors used to make information salient?
- *Catchphrases.* In what ways are phrases designed to capture attention used to make information salient?
- *Visual images.* In what ways are visual images used to make information salient?
- *Distinctions and contrasts.* In what ways are distinctions and contrasts used to make information salient?

The aforementioned analytical tools have been systematically applied to each item in the selection and constitute the foundation of the analysis. In order to ensure the reliability and systematics of the analysis, the analytical operation of these tools is visible in the analysis of the nature frames presented in the following section. The quotations from the web pages are intended to increase the transparency of the connection between the empirical material and the argumentation. They serve an illustrative function and are typical examples drawn from a larger body of empirical material.

As for the generalizability of the results, the study does not claim to contribute knowledge in the general statistical sense; that is, the results are not directly transferrable to every existing case of tourist information. Instead, the case of tourist information in Stockholm should be regarded as an *exemplar* (Flyvbjerg, 2006), that is, a critical case which illustrates the more general problem of how nature is enrolled in urban place-making (cf. Höijer, 2008). As noted by Flyvbjerg (2006, p. 219), drawing on Kuhn, "a scientific discipline without a large number of thoroughly executed case studies is a discipline without systematic production of exemplars, and a discipline without exemplars is an ineffective one."

Framing Nature as "the Other" in Marketing Stockholm
The results will be reported below under three thematic headings corresponding to the main frames identified in the analysis: *nature as the familiar other*, which constructs the city and nature as different but complementary; *nature as the exotic other*, which concerns the qualitative difference between the city and nature, and between humans and nature; and *pristine nature*, which constructs nature as untouched by humans. The concepts of the familiar and the exotic other are inspired by Papadopoulos's (2002) discussion of the construction of the self in relation to "the other." We realize that the concepts of familiar and exotic are context dependent. Familiarity and recognition of cultural signs may also differ between various social groups. Likewise, signs of exotic and distant places or phenomena may be well-known cultural symbols which can be used in communication. Nevertheless, we found these concepts helpful in distinguishing between various ways of framing the otherness of nature.

Nature as the Familiar Other
The photograph, heading, and caption of the green and blue city from the slide show on the home page illustrate the interplay between the city and nature, which is a recurrent theme in the empirical material. The slide show has a salient position on the page, and one of its images, which was repeated for most of 2011, is a view of the inner parts of Stockholm featuring two green islands (Skeppsholmen and Kastellholmen) in the foreground. In the spring, summer, and part of autumn, this photo was the first thing that met the visitor's eye on the website. Under the heading "The green and blue city" the caption of this photo runs:

> Greenery and water extend far in among the government buildings, teeming streets and distinguished old residential blocks. Here you will also find the Royal National City Park, consisting of a chain of parks from Ulriksdal in the north to Fjäderholmarna in the south. (16)

This image and its heading and caption celebrate Stockholm as a city endowed with greenery and water, natural features that exist side by side with the features of a big city, implied by mentioning the government buildings and teeming streets. This framing of nature as complementing the city plays on contrast, yet implies harmony and peaceful coexistence. The tourist information depicts Stockholm as a city where one can "combine natural and cultural experiences" (11), see animals and observe rare species (37), and swim or paddle in the city center. The following quotation further illustrates the notion of an uncomplicated interplay between the city and nature:

> You can paddle between all the city's islands, going ashore for a meal or a coffee, and then why not head out into the archipelago. (23)

This catchphrase indicating harmonious coexistence between nature and the city is supported by a photographic image of a woman in a kayak on sunny water silhouetted against some of the inner parts of Stockholm. This view of nature and the city as being in full harmony presents the destination city as a complete product (Corbett, 2006).

Like the woman in the kayak, other outdoor activities such as cycling, swimming, skiing, and ice-skating represent experiences outside the ordinary routines of everyday life. In the Nordic context, such leisure activities are usually associated with health, wholesomeness, and experiencing nature in the outdoors. As conveyed in the quotation above, experiences of nature are associated with a situation free from stress and obligations. Similarly, the following caption presents natural settings that are waiting to meet human desires in an atmosphere of freedom:

> Along the wooded bays of Lake Mälaren, [you can take] a dip when the spirit moves you. (18)

Here, nature provides a setting where you can obey the promptings of the spirit. The photographic images on these web pages support the message in the texts by showing active and healthy people in peaceful and beautiful surroundings.

A similar message, associating nature with peace and beauty, is repeated in statements presenting natural settings within the city. For example, starting with the catchphrase "[Rosendal's Garden] is one of Stockholm's true gems," the text on this page presents the garden as a setting for recreation:

> The garden café is located in a fantastic setting...Many Stockholmers make the pilgrimage to Rosendal on sunny days, but there's room for numerous guests. In the summer, you can sit in the apple orchard. (24)

In this statement, nature represents an attractive space in which to seek rest. Implicit in this way of framing nature is the idea of "hybrid consumption" (Corbett, 2006, p. 23). Here, like on the kayaking page cited above, and on a number of other pages in the empirical material, nature provides beautiful locations and scenery to be consumed by the tourist, at the same time as it is used to promote other consumption opportunities, for example, cafes and restaurants.

The themes of outdoor activity and of nature as a setting for recreation indicate a complementary and uncomplicated relationship between the city and nature. Through the enrollment of nature in tourist information, the city is constructed as a place that offers the possibility of wholesome activities and recreation in beautiful settings. However, the statements and images work together to underscore the idea of the city and nature as different, though this is done implicitly within the frame of nature as the familiar other. Only occasionally is this difference between the city and nature explicitly mentioned in the empirical material. One example is when Stockholm is presented as a city full of contrasts, as in the caption below:

> Stockholm is full of contrasts, from historic to trendy, from bright summers to dark winters, and from bustling city life to natural oases. (11)

Here, the city is associated with bustle and depicted as full of life, whereas nature is depicted as offering refuge. Apart from a few such examples, the empirical material focuses on the good things nature contributes. Accordingly, in the tourist information, the urban characteristics of the city are tacitly indicated by drawing on contrasts between nature and the city, and by associating nature and experiences of it with peacefulness, beauty, and freedom from the stress of everyday life. At the same time, through the uncomplicated and harmonious interplay between nature and city within this frame, the city is also to some extent ascribed the same characteristics as nature.

The framing of nature as the familiar other is based on the idea of contrast and difference between the city and nature, but without any tension or antagonism between them. Admittedly, within this frame, the city is constructed as a metropolis, yet characteristics commonly associated with big cities, such as crowding, traffic jams, pollution, and noise, are almost completely absent. Instead, in this framing the characteristics associated with nature apply to the city as well. By framing nature as the familiar other, Stockholm is constructed as a beautiful, peaceful, and wholesome metropolis characterized by a harmonious relationship between nature and culture. This also turns nature into an artifact, resulting in hybrid consumption, the fusion of consumption items; as a tourist, you consume both material products and nature as setting. Likewise, nature as setting and natural scenery is enrolled to promote the consumption of other products.

Nature as the Exotic Other

Framing nature as the exotic other is another way of "othering" nature. This frame is composed of statements, catchphrases, and images that imply a *qualitative* difference between the city and nature. This frame includes tensions and potential opposition between the city and nature to a greater extent than the frame of nature as the familiar other.

The depiction of nature as qualitatively different from the city is constructed by, for example, photographic images of extensive natural landscapes. When humans are present in the scenery they are there for a specific purpose, for example, to hike, skate, or go backpacking. One photo shows a couple with backpacks standing at the top of a steep cliff, making them seem small in relation to the vast landscape (29). One prominent theme in the tourist information is the adventure that nature has in store for those inclined toward outdoor experiences. Here nature stands for exciting activities that are out of the ordinary. Such experiences of nature are invigorating and rewarding, but also taxing and sometimes even dangerous. The following catchphrase indicates that outdoor adventures usually include an element of struggle and discomfort:

> For those who like adventures and nature but prefer to eat and sleep comfortably, Stockholm Adventures offers packages with [sailing, kayaking, and hiking]. (29)

The Stockholm Adventures concept promises to smooth over the inconveniences normally associated with outdoor adventures. By doing so, experiences of nature are packaged and offered as ready-made products, which in turn implies two things. First, experiences of nature are presented as qualitatively different from city life. Speaking with Corbett (2006), we could say that the tourist information holds out the expectation that you can encounter the authentic other—"nature"—without the usual discomfort and annoyances. Second, nature is offered in adventure packages available for tourist consumption. The tourist information also advertises various guided tours led by "knowledgeable guides" (28) and "nature guides [who] are highly educated" (30), constructing nature as something which inexperienced people need help to enter and appreciate. Another topic that illustrates this kind of tension is skating on natural ice, an activity representing nature as something extraordinary and invigorating but at the same time requiring guidance and safety equipment to be experienced pleasantly—and safely. Under an eye-catching photographic image of skaters in a vast landscape, the catchphrase on the web page points out that "skating on natural ice is an exhilarating experience" (17). The accompanying text elaborates on the necessity of taking certain precautionary measures to ensure a safe encounter with nature.

Although never explicitly stated in the tourist information, this framing of nature and leisure activities invokes the idea of free time as another consumption opportunity. It is not only the nature experience itself that is there to be consumed. Outdoor activities, as depicted here, require specific equipment or guides, which indicates a certain kind of hybrid consumption. Here, nature is not an artifact used in the promotion of products, but a product itself that requires other products to be attainable.

Within the theme of outdoor nature experiences, the framing of nature as the exotic other is reinforced by an eye-catching photographic image that plays with the categories of familiarity and exoticism. It can be found on the web page of STHLM Outback, a company offering guided tours, and shows a group of people with binoculars standing in a field against a broad horizon, evoking associations with African animal-watching safaris (28). This image uses a familiar cultural symbol of distant places to exoticize homegrown nature, highlighting the qualitative difference between the city and nature.

The photographic image mentioned above contributes to another prominent theme in the frame of nature as the exotic other, that is, the consuming gaze. This theme depicts humans as observers who experience fulfillment by watching the strange and mysterious other. The museum could be seen as an emblematic site for the consuming gaze, where nature is bluntly transformed into a commodity. Here, nature is represented by a variety of nonhuman species, often from distant times and destinations, which tourists can experience. The text on the web page of the Swedish Museum of Natural History tells about the Swedish natural environment and its diversity, yet the photographic image, prominently positioned on the page, shows animals from far away in time and space, in this case, an elephant and a mammoth (32). Other examples of this kind of othering are found on the web pages of the Aquaria Water Museum, Skansen's Aquarium, the Bergius Botanic Garden and Park, and the Butterfly House. On these web pages, photographic images show uncommon or wild species, often from remote places. These images are supported by texts that repeatedly advertise these kinds of uncommon species, for example, "saki monkeys, giant iguanas and yellowbeaked toucans in the misty rain forests" (26), "living Amazon rainforest with giant catfish, stingrays and piranhas" (2), "the world's largest water lily" (34), and "exotic butterflies [that] inhabit this lush, tropical environment" (35). These exotic animals are there for humans to watch and be amazed by. At the same time as they represent the wilderness and the other of human society and culture, these animals live in captivity in the city, to be consumed by the tourist gaze. In this way, the tourist information stereotypes nature, transforming it into a "spectacle" (cf. Hall, 1997).

The frame of nature as the exotic other constructs the city and nature as qualitatively different, implying a potential opposition between them. In this frame, nature possesses partly conflicting characteristics, since it represents both the desirable and the strange. Nature is implicitly constructed as different from the city and human culture, which come to represent comfort and convenience in contrast to the challenges of outdoor adventures. Furthermore, this frame also constructs nature as the other versus humans. The concepts of the wild, the unusual, and the distant in time and space, together with the suggestion of potential dangers that build up this frame, alienate humans from nature and nonhuman species. By framing nature as the exotic other, city-marketing enrolls nature by making salient its fundamentally different, but intriguing, character. Within this frame, the tourist is offered outdoor adventures, including the natural landscape and natural scenery, as products. In this sense, nature can be exploited both as product to be bought from a company and as product to be consumed by the tourist gaze.

Pristine Nature

Similar to the frame of nature as the exotic other, the frame of pristine nature constructs a qualitative difference between the city and nature, and between humans and nature. The frame of pristine nature in the empirical material is based on the notion of wilderness and natural nature, that is, nature untouched by humans, as being both possible and actual. Thereby, this frame constructs a spatial separation of nature from both humans and the city. Humans can visit and experience pristine nature, but cannot be an integral part of it. In this frame, nature is metaphorically depicted as "wild" and "virgin" (25), alluding to the idea of a nature free from human intrusion.

In the tourist information, pristine nature is mainly situated near yet outside the city, offering, for example, the possibility to experience "wild animals in natural settings" just outside the city center (25) or in nature and bird preserves in the archipelago. The following catchphrase states that you can find this kind of untouched nature in Stockholm and its surroundings:

> Stockholm and the surrounding area have many good hiking trails through untouched nature with spectacular views and historic settings. (14)

The photographic image that is the eye-catcher on this page shows wooded scenery pierced by sunbeams and a fallen tree over the trail. Although a footbridge provides a human trace, the fallen tree implies that this is a natural or primordial landscape. Similar depictions of untouched nature are found in photographic images on other pages that show natural scenes with no or only a few human traces. For example, the page for Stockholm's nature guides (30) that has a photo of a glade with a reflection in the mirror-still water, and the page for Bullerö (6) that has a photo of cliffs and the horizon with just two anchored sailboats, indicating that humans are only there as temporary visitors. In the frame of pristine nature, the tourist is offered an opportunity to escape dreary everyday life and experience sublime nature. By enrolling nature, the tourist information affords a "paradise contrived" (Corbett, 2006, p. 137) to be consumed both as setting and by the tourist gaze.

Interestingly, the tourist information also holds out the possibility to experience "wild nature" in the middle of the city (38). One of the pages, advertising the National City Park, an emblematic site of urban nature in Stockholm, offers encounters with "deer and hares, even foxes and elks, and [the opportunity] to see rare birds and insects, right inside the city" (37). This theme is repeated, for example, under the heading "Urban wilderness" on one of the pages (38), and on another page that advertises the National City Park, pointing out that virgin, untouched nature can be a reality even in the city. At the same time, by making salient the unlikelihood of this experience, the following description, accompanied by a photo of natural scenery devoid of humans, implies the inherent tension in the concept of pristine nature in the city:

> ...secluded swimming spots, rocky hilltops and areas with wild, virgin nature where you will have difficulty imagining you're in the middle of the big city. (25)

The text indicates that wild, virgin nature is uncommon in the city, though it can occasionally be found in certain areas. This kind of nature is desirable, but is an anomaly in a big city. The frame of pristine nature constructs nature as unspoiled and free from human intrusion. However, by repeatedly advertising pristine nature in the tourist information, this kind of nature is also turned into a commodity. First, pristine nature is enrolled to "sell the city" as a tourist destination. Second, pristine nature is an asset to be consumed both as a setting and by the tourist gaze.

Like the frame of nature as the exotic other, the frame of pristine nature imbues nature with extraordinary qualities. In this frame, nature represents the wild, engendering extraordinary experiences and offering spectacular views. Both frames are based on the concept of a qualitative difference between nature and the city and between humans and nature. Likewise, both frames are largely based on the concept of experiences of nature, where nature is turned into a product to be consumed by the tourist. However, the two frames differ in essential ways. Nature as the exotic other can be met in the form of captive animals at museums or zoos; however, these display creatures, while representing wild nature, live in confinement and are completely dependent on humans. The frame of pristine nature, on the other hand, constructs nature as "virgin," "natural," and "untouched." To experience this kind of nature, one must go there as a temporary visitor, that is, find secluded spots within the city or leave the city altogether. The frame of pristine nature in tourist information is thus ambiguous, since it constructs nature simultaneously as unspoiled and an asset to be consumed.

Conclusions

Promoting a certain place as unique entails the construction of place, to differentiate it from other comparable destinations. In the tourist information, where nature is used to define what is special about the city, nature is framed. Framing implies the selection of certain aspects that are made salient at the expense of others, which are inevitably downplayed or disregarded in the communication. In the course of doing so, a particular sense of place and a particular understanding of nature are cultivated, "naturalizing" both the city and nature in different ways. This article empirically shows how the different frames of nature are co-present and intersect each other in tourist information.

The analysis in this paper evinces three frames of nature—the familiar other, the exotic other, and pristine nature—in which the meaning of nature is negotiated in relation to its supposed counterpart: human culture and society. These three frames build on and contribute to our understanding of the city and nature and of humans and nature as being different from each other. We would argue that it is precisely this discursive divide between nature and culture that enables the commodification of nature.

In modern society, free time is "yet another consumption opportunity and recreation just another market" (Corbett, 2006, p. 111). When tourist information, as demonstrated in the present study, frames nature as something distinct from culture, the salient purpose of which is to contribute to the city's attractiveness, the tourist's gaze is directed toward experiences of consumption. As shown, nature can be turned into an object of consumption in various ways. For example, outdoor experiences may be packaged as ready-made products. Nature can be exhibited by placing stuffed animals in museums or captive animals in zoos. Nature can also be turned into an artifact in the promotion of other products or of the city itself. Nature and culture are tied to each other but the relationship is asymmetrical: it is hardly nature that capitalizes on culture but rather the reverse.

One important consequence of framing nature as "the other," in our case, is the lack of acknowledgment of the potential inconsistency between Stockholm as a metropolis and environmental preservation. Often, when humans' relationship with or assumed superiority to nature has been problematized, human culture and urbanization have been criticized. For example, in nineteenth-century Romanticism, urban life, the city, and civilization were viewed as a distortion, whereas natural nature was idealized and praised for its beauty and splendor (Hay, 2002, p. 5ff.). The frame of pristine nature constructs nature in a similar way, though without criticizing the city and urban life. Since the nineteenth century, the environmental movement has taken various guises, ranging from the conservation movement to eco-feminism. During this time, urbanization and industrialization have frequently met with criticism implying that modern humans are the root cause of environmental degradation. None of this criticism is salient in the framings of nature. The frame of nature as the familiar other fosters an understanding of an uncomplicated interplay between the city and nature. In the frames of nature as the exotic other and as pristine nature, the potential inconsistency between the city and nature remains implicit.

Considering the character of the empirical material, these results are admittedly neither surprising nor spectacular. What else could be expected of tourist information? We would argue, however, that it is precisely these kinds of culturally deeply rooted, naturalized, and taken-for-granted frames that exert the most influence on our values, norms, and behaviors (Carbaugh, 1996; Carragee & Roefs, 2004); it is their apparent triviality that makes them effective (Moscovici, 2000). Considering the rapidly growing tourism industry, it is necessary to highlight the possible negative effects on environmental consciousness of framing nature as "the other" in city marketing, regardless of how "natural" these framings may seem.

Although the enrollment of nature in the construction of the city as a place is based on conceiving both nature and a clean environment as essential assets, the tourist information studied does not acknowledge any of the environmentally harmful features commonly associated with big cities when framing nature. Nor does it offer any alternative to the dominant modern understanding of the relationship between humans and nature. The enrollment of nature in city marketing thereby contributes to concealing the environmental consequences of increased urban density, and lends legitimacy to the exploitation and commodification of nature for the purpose of urban development.

References

Asikainen, E., & Jokinen, A. (2009). Future natures in the making: Implementing biodiversity in suburban land-use planning. *Planning Theory & Practice, 10,* 351–68.

Borah, P. (2011). Conceptual issues in framing theory: A systematic examination of a decade's literature. *Journal of Communication, 61,* 246–63.

Bott, S., Cantrill, J.G., & Myers, O.E., Jr. (2003). Place and the promise of conservation psychology. *Research in Human Ecology, 10,* 100–12.

Carbaugh, D. (1996). Naturalizing communication and culture. In J.G. Cantrill & C.L. Oravec (Eds.), *The symbolic earth: Discourse and our creation of the environment* (pp. 38–57). Lexington: The U of Kentucky P.

Carragee, K., & Roefs, W. (2004). The neglect of power in recent framing research. *Journal of Communication, 54*(2), 214–33.

Corbett, J.B. (2006). *Communicating nature: How we create and understand environmental messages.* Washington, DC: Island P.

Cronon, W. (1996). Introduction: In search of Nature. In W. Cronon (Ed.), *Rethinking the human place in nature* (pp. 23–56). New York, NY: W.W. Norton.

Dahles, H. (1998). Redefining Amsterdam as a tourist destination. *Annals of Tourism Research, 25,* 55–69.

Entman, R. (1993). Framing: Toward clarification of a fractured paradigm. *Journal of Communication, 43,* 52–58.

Flyvbjerg, B. (2006). Five misunderstandings about case-study research. *Qualitative Inquiry, 12*(2), 219–45.

Franklin, A. (2010). *City life.* London: SAGE.

Gamson, W. (1992). *Talking politics.* Cambridge: Cambridge UP.

Goffman, E. (1974). *Frame analysis: An essay on the organization of experience.* New York, NY: Harper & Row.

Gottdiener, M. (1995). *Postmodern semiotics: Material culture and the forms of postmodern life.* Oxford: Blackwell.

Hall, S. (1997). The spectacle of the other. In S. Hall (Ed.), *Representation: Cultural representations and signifying practices* (pp. 225–79). London: SAGE.

Harvey, D. (1989). From managerialism to entrepreneurialism: The transformation in urban governance in late capitalism. Geografiska Annaler. *Series B, Human Geography, 71,* 3–17.

Hay, P. (2002). *Main currents in western environmental thought.* Bloomington: Indiana UP.

Höijer, B. (2008). Ontological assumptions and generalizations in qualitative (audience) research. *European Journal of Communication, 23*(3), 275–94.

Kaika, M. (2005). *City of flows. Modernity, nature, and the city.* New York, NY: Routledge.

Lakoff, G. (2010). Why it matters how we frame the environment. *Environmental Communication, 4*, 70–81.

Lichrou, M., O'Malley, L., & Patterson, M. (2008). Place-product or place narrative(s)? Perspectives in the marketing of tourism destinations. *Journal of Strategic Marketing, 16*, 27–39.

Massey, D. (2005). *For space.* London: SAGE.

Merchant, C. (2003). *Reinventing Eden: The fate of nature in western culture.* London: Routledge.

Moscovici, S. (2000). *Social representations: Explorations in social psychology.* Cambridge: Polity P.

Nash, R. (2001). *Wilderness and the American mind.* New Haven, CT: Yale UP.

Nordh, H., Hartig, T., Hagerhall, C.M., & Fry, G. (2009). Components of small urban parks that predict the possibility for restoration. *Urban Forestry & Urban Greening, 8*, 225–35.

Oelschlaeger, M. (1991). *The idea of wilderness.* New Haven, CT: Yale UP.

Olausson, U. (2009). Global warming—global responsibility? Media frames of collective action and scientific certainty. *Public Understanding of Science, 18*, 421–36.

Pan, S. (2011). The role of TV commercial visuals in forming memorable and impressive destination images. *Journal of Travel Research, 50*, 171–85.

Pan, Z., & Kosicki, G.M. (1993). Framing analysis: An approach to news discourse. *Political Communication, 10*, 55–75.

Papadopoulos, N.G. (1993). What product and country images are and are not. In N.G. Papadopoulos & L.A. Heslop (Eds.), *Product-country images: Impact and role in international marketing* (pp. 3–38). New York, NY: International Business P.

Papadopoulos, R.K. (2002). The other other: When the exotic other subjugates the familiar other. *Journal of Analytical Psychology, 47*, 163–88.

Reese, S.D. (2007). The framing project: A bridging model for media research revisited. *Journal of Communication, 57*, 148–54.

Salingaros, N.A. (2006). Compact city replaces sprawl. In A. Graafland & L. Kavanaugh (Eds.), *Crossover: Architecture, urbanism, technology* (pp. 100–15). Rotterdam: 010 Publishers.

Sampson, K., & Goodrich, C. (2009). Making place: Identity construction and community formation through ""sense of place"" in Westland, New Zealand. *Society and Natural Resources, 22*, 901–15.

Santos, C.A. (2004). Framing Portugal: Representational dynamics. *Annals of Tourism Research, 51*, 122–58.

Scheufele, D.A., & Tewksbury, D. (2007). Framing, agenda setting, and priming:

The evolution of three media effects models. *Journal of Communication, 21,* 5–31.

Stockholm Official Visitors Guide. Stockholm. The Capital of Scandinavia (2011). Retrieved from www.visitstockholm.com/en/.

Stokowski, P.A. (2002). Languages of place and discourses of power: Constructing new senses of place. *Journal of Leisure Research, 34*(4), 368–82.

Tunström, M. (2007). The vital city: Constructions and meanings in the contemporary Swedish planning discourse. *Town Planning Review, 78,* 681–98.

Uggla, Y. (2010). What is this thing called "natural"? The nature-culture divide in climate change and biodiversity policy. *Journal of Political Ecology, 17,* 79–91.

Uggla, Y. (2012). Construction of "nature" in urban planning: A case study of Stockholm. Town Planning Review, 83, 69–85.

Urry, J., & Larsen, J. (2011). *The tourist gaze 3.0.* London: SAGE.

Walton, J. (1992). Making the theoretical case. In C. Ragin & H. Becker (Eds.), *What is a Case?* (pp. 121–37). Cambridge: Cambridge UP.

DISCUSSION QUESTIONS

1. Uggla and Olausson use framing theory "to capture how nature is enrolled in tourist information" (p. 220). What is framing theory as it is defined in the article? How do the authors explain the use of framing theory in relation to tourist information?

2. The article explains that in some cases "frames are more important than the 'real' experience of a place, since people might discard the facts rather than choose to reject the frames" (p. 220). Why do you think this is? Come up with an example of a place that you think would support this argument (for example, New York City). Be prepared to explain your choice of place.

3. Within the context of framing nature as "other," the authors touch on the idea of "hybrid consumption." What is hybrid consumption, and what examples are given that represent this type of consumption?

4. Identify and define the three ways that nature is described as "other" in the article. Then go to the tourism website of your own city (or a city of your choice) and determine whether it also uses any of these "othering" techniques in its own marketing of nature. Be prepared to explain your findings.

5. In the conclusion of the article, Uggla and Olausson make note of "the possible negative effects on environmental consciousness of framing nature as 'the other' in city marketing, regardless of how 'natural' these framings may seem" (p. 230). Write a paragraph that explains your understanding of and offers your opinion on the consequences of 'othering' nature from humanity.

D. "GREEN INFRASTRUCTURE AS LIFE SUPPORT: URBAN NATURE AND CLIMATE CHANGE," SHERYN D. PITMAN, CHRISTOPHER B. DANIELS, AND MARTIN E. ELY

Pitman et al.'s* work, published in 2015 in Transactions of the Royal Society of South Australia, *is a good example of a review article. In it, the writers summarize recent research on the benefits of green infrastructure for urban environments before recommending concrete measures that urban planners can take to mitigate the effects of climate change. As you read the article, note how most sections begin with a description of an environmental problem before providing an account of what recent research indicates about the role of green infrastructure in reducing the problem.*

Glossary terms: review article

Abstract

Green Infrastructure is the network of green spaces and water systems that delivers multiple environmental, social and economic values and services to urban communities. This living network strengthens the resilience of urban environments to respond to the major current and future challenges of climate change, growth, health, and biodiversity loss, as well as water, energy, and food security. With the rapid expansion of towns and cities around the world, the far-reaching value of Green Infrastructure is increasingly recognised by scientific, planning, and design communities. A key strategy area of the South Australian Green Infrastructure Project has been the development of a sound and credible evidence base to demonstrate the multiple benefits of and make the case for investment in Green Infrastructure. A review of local and global literature, with an emphasis on the most recent peer-reviewed research, was carried out between 2012 and 2014. The body of evidence

---

* Sheryn D. Pitman is an Adjunct Research Fellow at the school of School of Pharmacy and Medical Sciences at the University of South Australia in Adelaide.

Christopher B. Daniels is a professor at the School of Natural and Built Environments at the University of South Australia.

Martin E. Ely holds a PhD from the School of Architecture, Landscape Architecture and Urban Design at Adelaide University. He is a member of the Australian Institute of Landscape Architects.

firmly establishes the many and diverse benefits of Green Infrastructure. These include modification of temperatures and climatic conditions, improved human health and well-being, enhanced community liveability, more effective water management, increased economic prosperity, greater opportunity for biodiversity conservation, and more extensive urban food production. The primary focus of this paper is the contribution of Green Infrastructure to climate adaptation and protection.

Keywords: green infrastructure, urban nature, urban climate, urban biodiversity

Introduction

In a global context, towns and cities have become the predominant human habitats. In 2010 cities were home to 3.5 billion people, equating to 50.5% of the world's population. Net population growth is now occurring almost entirely within towns and cities and by 2050 urban environments will need to accommodate an additional 2.6 billion people, including 86% of the industrialised world and 64% of the developing world (Potter, 2013). Contained within the rapid expansion of towns and cities, however, is the real risk of creating unliveable and unhealthy environments (McMichael, 2000). The provision of essential services to these ever-increasing populations is critical to preventing them from becoming slums (Potter, 2013). A substantial body of research into what delivers many of these essential services and makes urban environments liveable, safe, healthy, and prosperous provides guidance and direction for the challenges of the future (Ely & Pitman, 2014).

Green Infrastructure is increasingly recognised by scientific, health, planning and design professionals and practitioners as playing an essential role in strengthening the resilience of urban environments and communities as they respond to major current and future challenges of growth, health, climate change, and biodiversity loss, as well as water, energy, and food security. In recognition of the potential for Green Infrastructure to improve urban environments in South Australia, the Green Infrastructure partnership project was formed between the Botanic Gardens of South Australia, Renewal SA, Adelaide and Mount Lofty Ranges Natural Resources, and the Department of Planning, Transport and Infrastructure. A key undertaking of this project has been the development of a sound and credible evidence base to clarify and confirm the value of Green Infrastructure and to make the case for both public and private investment in Green Infrastructure (Ely & Pitman, 2014). Carried out between 2012 and 2014, the study methodology comprised a systematic and comprehensive review of literature on the benefits of Green Infrastructure. Key informants in academic and government organisations in all Australian states were initially contacted to identify the most recent literature in different fields of research. In deciding which studies to review, preference was given to peer-reviewed and published literature, and to evidence from other reputable sources, (such as reports conducted or commissioned by government bodies or non-government agencies). The most recent (post-2000) evidence was preferred, although older studies considered to be seminal in nature, or where more recent research was limited, were included. Studies from across the world were reviewed; however, local Australian studies were accessed where possible to reflect local climatic and other conditions.

Green Infrastructure has been variously defined, with the three most common approaches focusing on the role of ecosystem services (de Groot et al., 2012), green engineering (Margolis & Robinson, 2007), and linked green spaces (Benedict & McMahon, 2002). The most valuable definition, however, is considered to be a synthesis of all three (Foster, Lowe, & Winkelman, 2011). The Green Infrastructure project has described Green Infrastructure as the network of green spaces and water systems that delivers multiple environmental, social and economic values and services to urban communities (Ely & Pitman, 2014). This network includes parks and reserves, gardens and backyards, waterways and wetlands, streets and transport corridors, pathways and greenways, farms and orchards, buffers and windbreaks, squares and plazas, roof gardens and living walls, sports fields and even cemeteries. This Green Infrastructure network is underpinned by the services provided by healthy ecosystems. Such services include provisioning (such as food, water, fibre, and fuel), supporting (such as soil formation and nutrient cycling), regulating (such as climate, flood and disease regulation, and water purification) and cultural services (such as aesthetic, spiritual, symbolic, educational, and recreational) (Millennium Ecosystem Assessment, 2003). Ecosystem services apply at a range of scales, from the global to the local, and the links between ecosystems and human health, prosperity, security, and identity are firmly established (Mainka, McNeely, & Jackson, 2008; Millennium Ecosystem Assessment, 2005).

Both plants and water are fundamental and central elements of Green Infrastructure. Vegetation provides a multitude of services such as shade and cooling, water cleansing and management, noise abatement, light diffusion, wind protection, air filtering, soil conditioning, and habitat for wildlife. Water in urban environments is equally important and manifests in many forms. More than just groundwater, surface water and atmospheric water, urban water also includes stormwater, recycled water, and desalinated water. The way in which these water sources are combined and utilised in urban environments can vary considerably. Animals also contribute to these environmental services through decomposition of waste, nutrient cycling in soils, pollination, and seed dispersal (Daniels & Roetman, 2014). Many animals also support Green Infrastructure by removing pollution and wastes and controlling the spread of disease-carrying organisms. Biological diversity, including plants, animals, and micro-organisms, plays an essential role in the health and resilience of natural systems and their ability to recover from disturbances such as disease, drought, fire, and flood (Daniels & Roetman, 2014).

In addition, two key features of Green Infrastructure are multi-functionality (Sandström, 2002) and connectivity (Benedict & McMahon, 2002). Green Infrastructure delivers multiple benefits from and to the urban space it occupies and, by linking plant and water assets or features, it provides a system of connected spaces and services that create value for both people and the local underpinning ecosystems. Achievement of successful Green Infrastructure in towns and cities requires working with natural systems to create landscapes that are healthy and functional (Benedict & McMahon, 2002), thereby diminishing the undesirable impacts often generated within both traditional and contemporary urban environments (Grinde & Patil, 2009).

A substantial body of evidence (Ely & Pitman, 2014) has firmly established the many and diverse functions and benefits of Green Infrastructure and supports a Green Infrastructure approach to urban planning, design, and development. To facilitate access, this literature has been grouped into seven themes relevant to contemporary perspectives and discussions. There are, however, numerous areas of intersection and overlap between these seven areas, and each is simply a starting point for exploration of the subject matter. These include human health and well-being, community liveability, climate adaptation and modification, water management, economic prosperity, biodiversity conservation, and urban food production. The primary focus of this paper, however, is the contribution of Green Infrastructure to climate adaptation and climate protection, with brief references to other benefits.

Green Infrastructure and Climate Adaptation

Green Infrastructure is, in itself, a way of helping urban environments adapt to changing climates. As a change adaptation measure, it has two key areas of benefit in particular. First, it builds the resilience of urban human communities to protect against likely warmer temperatures, stronger winds, increased flooding, and changed rainfall patterns. Through temperature reduction, wind speed modification, more efficient water management, and protection from extreme weather events, Green Infrastructure delivers direct services and benefits to urban communities and can do so within short time frames as well as for the longer term. Secondly, by creating habitat and supplying essential resources, Green Infrastructure can assist plants and animals to survive both the relentless, anthropogenic modification of the natural environment and climate change. While adaptation has become a core element of climate policy and research (Ford, Berrang-Ford, Lesnikowski, Barrera, & Heymann, 2013), Green Infrastructure itself has not been widely recognised as an adaptation measure. Few measurement indicators are in place by which to judge how effective a Green Infrastructure approach may be (Bowler, Buyung-Ali, Knight, & Pullin, 2010). Many elements of Green Infrastructure, however, are measurable (Natural England, 2013) and have been found to make significant differences to urban climates and to the well-being of urban communities.

Temperature Reduction

The urban heat island (UHI) effect, where the air and surface temperatures of cities are typically much higher than surrounding landscapes (Bornstein, 1968; McPherson, 1994; Rosenfeld, Akbari, Romm, & Pomerantz, 1998), is recognised as a significant contributor to health risks in large cities including increased distress and mortality rates in extreme weather events such as 'heat waves,' especially among the elderly (Loughnan, Coutts, Tapper, & Beringer, 2012; Loughnan, Nicholls, & Tapper, 2010; Tapper, 2010). The UHI can also affect economic vitality by making places uncomfortable and unattractive. Described as an unintended consequence of urbanisation (Harlan et al., 2007), the UHI is exacerbated by a number of factors: the predominance of artificial surfaces which modify energy flows (Quattrochi & Ridd, 1994), creating higher surface temperatures and reduced soil evaporation that would otherwise cool surfaces (Miller, 1980); lack of vegetation and reduced tree cover leading to reduced shading of surfaces and transpiration cooling by tree canopies (Federer, 1976; Miller, 1980); and reduced humidity due to increased heat loads and transfer of rainfall into stormwater drainage systems (Miller, 1980).

Health implications of the UHI are well-documented. The relationship between heat and mortality has long been acknowledged (Haines, Kovats, Campbell-Lendrum, & Corvalán, 2006). Reports from the USA and Australia indicate that, during last century, excessive heat exposure contributed to more deaths than occurred as a result of natural disasters such as hurricanes, lightning, tornadoes, floods, and earthquakes combined (McKeon, 2006; U.S. EPA, 2011). In Victoria it was found that the heat wave preceding the Black Saturday bushfires in 2009 contributed to 374 excess deaths above what would normally be expected for that period in inner Melbourne, a figure more than double the number of people who died in the fires. This also represented a 62% increase in total mortality and an eight-fold increase in direct heat-related presentations to emergency departments (Department of Human Services [DHS], 2009). The potential for urban heat accumulation also increases with global warming. Climate change predictions for Australia, for example, indicate an increase in the number of warm nights and heat waves which may pose significant threats to human health (Alexander & Arblaster, 2009).

Recent evidence also points to the fact that nothing ameliorates the heat island effect as well as plants. In Sydney in 2010 a pilot research program used thermal imagery to examine the degree to which different components of the urban environment and associated landscapes contribute waste heat to the urban climate (City Futures Research Centre, 2010). The findings were used to develop a Thermal Performance Index representing the transience contributions of elements, ranked from hottest to coolest (radiators to coolers). Indications were that albedo reflects heat, light-coloured elements contribute less heat than dark-coloured elements, and water bodies store heat. It was also found, however, that unless the thermal energy was transformed by living vegetation, the problem of excess heat in the urban environment persisted. Trees providing shade in a grassy park had a three to four degree transient contribution over the diurnal cycle and a seven to eight degree transience when shading pale-coloured paving. Unshaded grass in a park had a 12 degree transience and vegetated swales had a six to nine degree transience (City Futures Research Centre, 2010).

The modification of urban climates, especially through temperature reduction, is one of the outstanding benefits of Green Infrastructure. A large body of recent research has shown that trees and other vegetation can help reduce the UHI effect through two major natural mechanisms: these include temperature reduction through shading of urban surfaces from solar radiation; and evapotranspiration, which has a cooling and humidifying effect on the air (Akbari et al., 2001; Georgi & Zafiriadis, 2006; McPherson, 1994; McPherson, Herrington, & Heisler, 1988; Moore, 2012; Pokorny, 2001). Urban trees are considered to operate effectively as natural 'air conditioners' (Pokorný, 2001).

Shading
The surfaces of pavements and buildings can reach very high temperatures unless shaded (Kjelgren & Montague, 1998). By shading ground surfaces, trees reduce the amount of radiation reaching, being absorbed by, and then being re-radiated from paved surfaces (Roberts, Jackson, & Smith, 2006). Trees can intercept most of the sun's energy, and while some is reflected, most is absorbed and used in photosynthesis. Research shows that tree canopies are able to reduce the temperatures of the surfaces they shade by as much as 25°C (Akbari, Kurn, Bretz, & Hanford, 1997; Livesley, 2010). It is also known that shading by trees is more effective in reducing surface temperatures than shading by non-natural materials (Georgi & Dimitriou, 2010). Shading effects of different tree species have been found to vary according to their Leaf Area Index (LAI), a ratio of leaf area per unit of ground surface area. Research in the USA has demonstrated that increasing the amount of leaf area in urban or suburban areas can have a substantial effect on surface temperatures (Hardin & Jensen, 2007). The value of the shading and cooling effect of trees has been further demonstrated by research showing that people in buildings with little or no surrounding vegetation are at higher risk of heat-related morbidity (Loughnan et al., 2010).

Evapotranspiration
Transpiration is the process by which water is taken up from the soil by roots, and released into the atmosphere through the stomata in leaves. Most of the water taken up by a tree is used for transpiration, which has the important function of cooling the leaves during evaporation (Gates, 1968). The conversion of water from liquid to gas during evaporation requires energy which removes heat from the leaves, cooling the leaves and surrounding air. Evapotranspiration refers to the combined effects of transpiration from plant leaves and evaporation from exposed soil surfaces. Plants

require water for transpiration, highlighting the need to maintain soil moisture in urban environments in order to maximise the temperature reduction effects of evapotranspiration (Dimoudi & Nikolopoulou, 2003; Tapper, 2010).

Water Management

Water is an integral element of Green Infrastructure, whether it is rainwater, groundwater, stormwater, recycled water, desalinated water, or water in creeks, rivers, wetlands, lakes, and reservoirs. Clean fresh water is not only essential for the survival of the human inhabitants of a city; water supports vegetation and wildlife while providing significant climatic benefits in its own right. Despite the fact that in many cities water is largely hidden from view, and the natural water cycle is severely modified or replaced by an artificial urban water cycle that operates differently (Thompson & Sorvig, 2007; Wong, 2006), water continues to connect places, ecosystems, and people in diverse and fundamental ways. Effective Green Infrastructure is intimately linked with effective water management. Safe and affordable water supplies, green landscapes that help combat UHI effects and enhance urban amenity, healthy urban waterways and fauna habitat, and protection from flooding are just some of the ways in which efficient water management contributes to the liveability of towns and cities (Wong, 2011). Urban water bodies such as reservoirs, lakes, rivers, and wetlands, also help to cool the urban environment (Maunsell, 2009; Rinner & Hussain, 2011; Saaroni & Ziv, 2003; Sun & Chen, 2012; Wong, Tan, Nindyani, Jusuf, & Tan, 2012) with the concept of an 'urban cooling island' (UCI) making its way into the literature. Recent research has shown that the shape and location of a UCI can influence the extent of the cooling effect (Sun, Chen, Chen, & Lü, 2012).

Water Sensitive Urban Design

Water Sensitive Urban Design (WSUD) practices, such as bio-filtration systems, stormwater harvesting, passive landscape irrigation, and use of porous surfaces, contribute to Green Infrastructure by providing harvested stormwater and vegetated stormwater management systems (Wong, 2011). WSUD is both a mitigative and adaptive response to urban climate management and supports the green spaces that provide shade, cooling and clean air to towns and cities (Coutts, Tapper, Beringer, Loughnan, & Demuzere, 2013). In addition to supporting vegetation, WSUD helps retain water in the urban landscape and returns moisture to urban soils. This is in stark contrast to the traditional approach to water infrastructure which either allows stormwater to drain away from the urban environment or deliberately removes it as a waste product. It makes great sense to link the various forms of Green Infrastructure to stormwater harvesting practices in order to utilise large volumes of stormwater run-off. With a considerable amount of research pointing to the value of trees and other vegetation in urban environments, it is logical to make the most efficient use of water to support this vegetation, particularly in places where water is scarce or unreliable.

Flooding and Storm Protection

The need for greater resilience in the face of not only higher temperatures, but more extreme weather events such as storms and floods, challenges the traditional ways of planning and designing towns and cities. Urban flooding has long been a problem faced by many cities around the world (Mark, Weesakul, Apirumanekul, Aroonnet, & Djordjevic, 2004). Green Infrastructure refers to a practical approach to designing for greater resilience, and practices such as WSUD, including stormwater harvesting and re-use, are some of the most effective climate change adaptation responses, reducing the likelihood and consequences of a number of risks (Maunsell, 2009). Well-vegetated areas with porous surfaces, as well as the capacity to capture, retain and reuse water, facilitate better adaptation to storms and flooding. Urban trees help control runoff through canopy interception and increased soil infiltration (Fazio, 2010) as well as through soil stabilisation (Cullington & Gye, 2010). WSUD strategies are increasingly being used to address issues of urban flooding (Veerbeek, Ashley, Zevenbergen, Rijke, & Gersonius, 2012) and improve the health of urban waterways.

Flooding poses a particular problem for low-lying coastal settlements that are also impacted by rising sea levels and storm surges of varying intensities. The importance of coastal wetlands in providing storm protection has been demonstrated around the world and is well-documented. A 2005 assessment of the Rekawa mangrove ecosystem in Sri Lanka calculated its economic value to be about US$217,000 per year, of which US $60,000 was directly attributed to erosion control and protection from storm damage (Ramsar Convention on Wetlands, nd). The estimated value of mangroves in Thailand for protection against coastal disasters such as wind storms and floods has been calculated at US$5,850ha, while storm protection provided by coastal wetlands in the United States was estimated to be US$23 billion per year (Costanza et al., 2008). Costanza and colleagues suggest that, should the frequency and intensity of storms increase as predicted, the protection value of coastal wetlands will also increase. Coastal wetlands provide one example of the immense value of natural ecosystems, which both underpin and are a part of Green Infrastructure in urban environments. The ecosystem services provided by healthy ecosystems clearly extend beyond the confines of human settlements themselves and provide protection in ways that have not often been evaluated or even acknowledged. The extent to which ecosystem services are protected and extended underlies the capacity of a city for resilience in the face of extreme weather events (Watson & Adams, 2010).

Air Quality

Air quality is of particular concern in urban environments. According to Harlan and Ruddell (2011, p. 126), 'the interactions of global climate change, urban heat islands, and air pollution are predicted to place increasing health burdens on cities.' As cities grow in size and density, increased levels of pollutants such as particulate matter, smoke from wildfires and pollens are expected to result in deteriorating urban air quality with harmful impacts on human health. Air pollutants contribute to both respiratory and cardiovascular illnesses as well as allergies (Harlan & Ruddell, 2011). Elevated temperatures in urban heat islands accelerate the formation of urban smog and, by reducing urban temperatures, smog levels are also reduced (Akbari et al., 2001). Green Infrastructure, the connected network of plants and water systems, contributes to improved air quality through carbon sequestration, shading, and temperature reduction, reduced emissions through energy conservation, capturing of particulate matter by vegetation, wind protection, improved water management, and healthy ecosystems. An increase in aeroallergens such as pollens has also been associated with increased levels of CO_2 concentrations and higher temperature (Beggs, 2004). Changes to the length and timing of pollen seasons, as well as to pollen distributions, have been recorded, and while the impact of climate change on aeroallergens requires further research, careful consideration of plant species to be used in urban environments is warranted (Beggs, 2004).

Wind Speed Modification

Wind in urban environments is complex and dependent on a number of factors, including street and building design and orientation. Tall buildings can create pathways of high wind velocity, known as wind tunnels. Wind can benefit urban areas by transporting air pollutants away from the city and decreasing temperatures, but can also raise the wind-chill factor, carry dust and smoke, and compromise comfort and safety (Hang, Sandberg, & Li, 2009; Memon, Leung, & Liu, 2010). Vegetation can contribute to modification of wind patterns by obstructing, guiding, deflecting, and filtering the movement of air (Miller, 2007). Planting trees to buffer against and reduce wind speeds has long been a practice in many parts of the world, especially the planting of semi-porous windbreaks in rural settings. A barrier of approximately 35% wind-permeable material, for example, can create a long, calm zone that can extend up to 30 times the windbreak height (Caborn, 1965). Management of wind speeds has the potential to benefit towns and cities by improving human health and safety, mobility, and generally making urban environments more liveable. Another advantage of the wind-shielding effect of trees can be the improved heating (in winter) and cooling (in summer) performances of buildings where high wind speeds are decreased, with studies indicating substantial savings in the costs of energy use through air conditioning (Akbari & Taha, 1992; Heisler, 1989).

Protecting Biodiversity against Climate Change

The importance of cities in biodiversity conservation grows with increasing urbanisation (Goddard, Dougill, & Benton, 2010; Kowarik, 2011). Biodiversity conservation has the potential to be a major benefit and function of Green Infrastructure, with effective networks of green spaces and water systems known to reduce habitat fragmentation and contribute to species diversity and health (Angold et al., 2006;

Benedict & McMahon, 2002; Tzoulas et al., 2007). There is growing recognition that a city with abundant green and blue spaces harbors a healthy biodiversity, although an emphasis on the importance of connectivity is manifest (Goddard et al., 2010; Heller & Zavaleta, 2009). Often both the species richness and the animal and plant biomass in a well-vegetated city exceed that of the surrounding area (Blair, 1996; Fontana, Sattler, Bontadina, & Moretti, 2011; Goddard et al., 2010; Marzluff, 2001), although it can be the case that the modified city environment contains less native than exotic species (Blair, 1996; McKinney, 2002). Cities have often been developed on biodiversity hotspots, areas with abundant or reliable water supplies and fertile soils (Cincotta, Wisnewski, & Engelman, 2000), while peri-urban environments are likely to be substantially modified for agricultural or industrial uses. An appropriate and connected combination of plentiful food resources, nesting locations, and permanent water supplies in urban environments has the potential to ensure that, for many native and local species, towns and cities can become safe havens (Andersson et al., 2014; Daniels & Roetman, 2008; Goddard et al., 2010). With climate change increasingly challenging mobile native animal species, causing population shifts and migrations, cities also become home to waves of animal refugees. For example, pale-headed flying foxes have taken up residence in cities along Australia's eastern and southern coast because they have been forced southward by complex climate-change-mediated events, and cities supply the best remaining habitats for them.

While cities have the potential to provide good habitat and refuge for many species, the converse can also be true (Goddard et al., 2010). Changes to urban climates, atmosphere, hydrology, soil chemistry and biology, vegetation and animal populations and distributions, can all contribute to a diminished functioning of ecological systems (Zipperer & Pickett, 2012). In addition, urbanisation can promote transmission of wildlife diseases and provides harbours for a major wildlife predator, the domestic cat (Goddard et al., 2010). Some of these changes and challenges may be exacerbated in a changing climate, as altered weather patterns affect not only the abundance and distribution of water and vegetation but also the animals that depend on them (Daniels & Roetman, 2014). With climate modelling for many cities suggesting that temperatures will increase further and that rainfall patterns will change, the effective management of urban climate and water systems will be just as critical for other species and for healthy ecosystems as for humanity.

Other Benefits of Green Infrastructure
Green Infrastructure produces a number of other climate-related benefits, including reduced energy use for air-conditioning (Coutts, Beringer, & Tapper, 2007; Donovan & Butry, 2009; Laband & Sophocleus, 2009; Sawka, Millward, Mckay, & Sarkovich, 2013), decreased temperatures of vehicles and parking spaces (Scott, Simpson, & McPherson, 1999), protection from UV radiation and associated health problems

(Grant, Heisler, & Gao, 2002), and extended life of various materials and surfaces (McPherson & Muchnick, 2005).

Green Infrastructure also contributes to the physical, psychological, and social health of human communities (Abraham, Sommerhalder, & Abel, 2010; Grinde & Patil, 2009; Pretty, 2004), impacts positively on the economic vitality of neighbourhoods and centres (Donovan & Butry, 2010; Laverne & Winson-Geideman, 2003; Plant, 2006; Sander, Polasky, & Haight, 2010; Wachter & Gillen, 2006; Wolf, 2004, 2005), improves air quality (Nowak, 1995; Nowak, Hoehn, & Crane, 2007; Escobedo et al., 2008; Rogers, Jarratt, & Hansford, 2011), buffers against noise (Fang & Ling, 2003, 2005; Van Renterghem et al., 2013), makes neighbourhoods safer (Kuo & Sullivan, 2001) and contributes to attractiveness, comfort, sense of place, and enjoyment of urban environments (Dwyer, Schroeder, & Gobster, 1994; Gehl & Gemzøe, 2001; Moore, 2000; Moore & Mitchell, 1993; Swanwick, 2009).

Edward O. Wilson's 'biophilia hypothesis' emphasises the innate connection humans have with nature (Kellert & Wilson, 1995), and Richard Louv's now well-known term 'nature-deficit disorder' describes the adverse effects on children of alienation from nature (Louv, 2006). Another interesting finding concerns perceptions of large trees. In a rapidly changing world, the enduring nature of large trees provides a sense of permanence and stability that is otherwise increasingly absent, and this has been found to be of great importance to many people (Dwyer et al., 2003). Green Infrastructure connects individuals and communities with nature. It is well recognised that urban nature is vital to creating a sense of place and, therefore, improved social cohesion (Armstrong, 2000; Daniels & Roetman, 2014; Leyden, 2003; Swanwick, 2009). Through well-planned and designed Green Infrastructure, urban places can deliver natural elements and networks, and the benefits of nature in urban environments cannot be underestimated.

Practical Strategies for Improving the Climate Adaptation Effects of Green Infrastructure

A number of studies, including some using thermal imaging, have contributed to Green-Infrastructure-related strategies for reducing climate and UHI effects. Within the Evidence Base, a range of specific strategies have been identified, such as:

- Use vegetation cover to shade thermally massive ground surfaces and increase evapotranspiration (Akbari et al., 2001; Georgi & Zafiriadis, 2006; McPherson, 1994; McPherson et al., 1988; Pokorný, 2001)
- Plant trees with a Leaf Index Area of 5.3 (similar to a deciduous temperate forest) to achieve a greater than 30% canopy cover over ground (Hardin & Jensen, 2007)
- Match water management systems to vegetation for optimal evapotranspiration effects (Tapper, 2010)

- Use permeable surfaces to encourage water infiltration and subsequent evapo-transpiration; these should be as large as possible and no less than 30% of the available site area (Beecham, 2012)
- Use stormwater harvesting and Water Sensitive Urban Design for passive irrigation of street trees and other vegetated areas (Wong, 2011)
- Use recycled water systems for irrigating parks, gardens, and other vegetated areas (Living Victoria Ministerial Advisory Council, 2011)
- Encourage appropriate micro-level wind management to maximise cooling effects (Heisler, 2010)
- Utilise active adiabatic cooling systems such as water bodies and pools, which have a cooling influence through evaporation (Monteith, 1981; Schmidt, 2003).
- Use high-albedo materials on major urban surfaces such as rooftops, streets, and pavements, as light surfaces retain and re-radiate less heat.
- Replace dark asphalt surfaces with surfaces of albedo greater than 0.4. Ensure pavements have an albedo value greater than 0.5. (Akbari et al., 2001)
- Use green roofs and living walls to cool buildings through evapotranspiration and reduce energy demands and carbon dioxide emissions (Alexandri & Jones, 2008; Skinner, 2006)
- Protect, restore, and rehabilitate wetlands, both inland and coastal (Ramsar Convention on Wetlands, 2012)

Conclusion

This review of research and literature has found that the modification of urban climates, especially through temperature reductions, is one of the outstanding benefits of Green Infrastructure, both for human welfare and for the wildlife with whom we share the city. Plants and water systems are shown to be highly effective in cooling and regulating urban climates, and represent a significant adaptive capacity. Shading, evapotranspiration, wind speed modification, protection during extreme weather events, reduced water runoff and flooding, and improved air quality are some of the ways in which Green Infrastructure can assist in urban climate adaptation. In the case of green roofs and walls, an added advantage is achieved in reduced energy consumption for heating and cooling of buildings through the thermal mass of soil and plants. Global climate changes in general and recent droughts in many parts of the world have highlighted the need to make better use of Green Infrastructure in the public realm.

A growing recognition of the relationship between Green Infrastructure and urban ecology signifies maturation of the Green Infrastructure concept. The notion of cities providing protection for wildlife in a highly urbanised and warmer world, rather than being 'dead zones' (Daniels & Roetman, 2014), is gathering momentum, and studies are now examining how cities might be better planned and designed to accommodate various animal species (Fontana et al., 2011; Mayer, 2010; Shochat,

Lerman, & Fernández-Juricic, 2010). Urban environments with clean and permanent water, suitable food plants, shade and shelter, healthy soil and reduced risk of hazards such as high winds, floods and bushfires have considerable potential to contribute to the conservation of many vulnerable animal populations. The role of Green Infrastructure in protecting and conserving both flora and fauna in cities is largely unexplored, and presents possibilities for biodiversity conservation that may also lead to improved ecosystem health and function.

Changing the way we plan, design, and build is the next important step. Achievement of successful Green Infrastructure necessitates a new way of thinking about urban environments that requires an integrated approach and a thorough understanding of its multiple benefits. Green Infrastructure is embedded in the interconnectedness of natural systems and their interface with human systems. Towns and cities have evolved into large-scale human habitats that aim to provide a multitude of services and benefits for their inhabitants. Irrespective of climate change, with increasing populations, density, and congestion, these same environments could well become increasingly unhealthy and uncomfortable places with high health and economic costs. In the face of a changing climate, it is anticipated that such effects will be intensified. On the positive side, there is a compelling body of evidence that effective Green Infrastructure can provide significant life-support and make a vital contribution to creating cooler, healthier, more bio-diverse and more liveable towns and cities both in Australia and throughout the world.

References

Abraham, A., Sommerhalder, K., & Abel, T. (2010). Landscape and well-being: A scoping study on the health-promoting impact of outdoor environments. *International Journal of Public Health, 55*(1), 59–69. doi:10.1007/s00038-009-0069-z.

Akbari, H., Kurn, D.M., Bretz, S.E., & Hanford, J.W. (1997). Peak power and cooling energy savings of shade trees. *Energy and Buildings, 25*(2), 139–48. doi:10.1016/S0378-7788(96)01003-1.

Akbari, H., Pomerantz, M., & Taha, H. (2001). Cool surfaces and shade trees to reduce energy use and improve air quality in urban areas. *Solar Energy, 70*(3), 295–310. doi:10.1016/S0038-092X(00)00089-X.

Akbari, H., & Taha, H. (1992). The impact of trees and white surfaces on residential heating and cooling energy use in four Canadian cities. *Energy, the International Journal, 17*(2), 141–49. doi:10.1016/0360-5442(92)90063-6.

Alexander, L.V., & Arblaster, J.M. (2009). Assessing trends in observed and modelled climate extremes over Australia in relation to future projections. *International Journal of Climatology, 29*(3), 417–35. doi:10.1002/joc.v29:3.

Alexandri, E., & Jones, P. (2008). Temperature decreases in an urban canyon due to green walls and green roofs in diverse climates. *Building and Environment, 43*(4), 480–93. doi:10.1016/j.buildenv.2006.10.055.

Andersson, E., Barthel, S., Borgström, S., Colding, J., Elmqvist, T., Folke, C., & Gren, Å. (2014). Reconnecting cities to the biosphere: Stewardship of green infrastructure and urban ecosystem services. *Ambio, 43*(4), 445–53. doi:10.1007/s13280-014-0506-y.

Angold, P.G., Sadler, J.P., Hill, M.O., Pullin, A., Rushton, S., Austin, K. . . . Thompson, K. (2006). Biodiversity in urban habitat patches. *Science of the Total Environment, 360*(1–3), 196–204. doi:10.1016/j.scitotenv.2005.08.035.

Armstrong, D. (2000). A survey of community gardens in upstate New York: Implications for health promotion and community development. *Health & Place, 6*(4), 319–27. doi:10.1016/S1353-8292(00)00013-7.

Beecham, S. (2012). Trees as essential infrastructure: Engineering and design considerations. In TREENET Proceedings of the 13th National Street Tree Symposium 2012. Adelaide, South Australia.

Beggs, P.J. (2004). Impacts of climate change on aeroallergens: Past and future. *Clinical & Experimental Allergy, 34*(10), 1507–13. doi:10.1111/j.1365-2222.2004.02061.x.

Benedict, M.A., & McMahon, E.T. (2002). Green infrastructure: Smart conservation for the 21st century. *Renewable Resources Journal, 20*(3), 12–17.

Blair, R.B. (1996). Land use and avian species diversity along an urban gradient. *Ecological Applications, 6*(2), 506–19.

Bornstein, R.D. (1968). Observations of the urban heat island effect in New York city. *Journal of Applied Meteorology, 7*(4), 575–82. doi:10.1175/1520-0450(1968)007<0575:OOTUHI>2.0.CO;2.

Bowler, D.E., Buyung-Ali, L., Knight, T.M., & Pullin, A.S. (2010). Urban greening to cool towns and cities: A systematic review of the empirical evidence. *Landscape and Urban Planning, 97*(3), 147–55. doi:10.1016/j.landurbplan.2010.05.006.

Caborn, J.M. (1965). *Shelterbelts and windbreaks.* London: Faber and Faber.

Cincotta, R.P., Wisnewski, J., & Engelman, R. (2000). Human population in the biodiversity hotspots. *Nature, 404* (6781), 990–92. doi:10.1038/35010105.

City Futures Research Centre. (2010). *Final report: Micro-urban-climatic thermal emissions: In a medium-density residential precinct.* City Futures Research Centre, FBE/UNSW, Hassell. Sydney, Australia. Retrieved from www.be.unsw.edu.au/sites/default/files/upload/pdf/cf/research/cityfuturesprojects/heatisland/Final_Report_ Hassell.pdf.

Costanza, R., Pérez-Maqueo, O., Martinez, M.L., Sutton, P., Anderson, S.J., & Mulder, K. (2008). The value of coastal wetlands for hurricane protection. *AMBIO: A Journal of the Human Environment, 37*(4), 241–48. doi:10.1579/0044-7447(2008)37[241:TVOCWF]2.0.CO;2.

Coutts, A.M., Beringer, J., & Tapper, N.J. (2007). Impact of increasing urban density on local climate: Spatial and temporal variations in the surface energy balance in Melbourne, Australia. *Journal of Applied Meteorology and Climatology, 46*(4), 477–93. doi:10.1175/JAM2462.1.

Coutts, A.M., Tapper, N.J., Beringer, J., Loughnan, M., & Demuzere, M. (2013). Watering our cities: The capacity for water-sensitive urban design to support urban cooling and improve human thermal comfort in the Australian context. *Progress in Physical Geography, 37*(1), 2–28. doi:10.1177/0309133312461032.

Cullington, J., & Gye, J. (2010). Urban forests: A climate adaptation guide. In *Part of the British Columbia Regional Adaptation Collaborative (RAC)*. British Columbia, Canada: Ministry of Community, Sport and Cultural Development. Retrieved from www.retooling.ca/_Library/docs/Urban_forests_Guide.pdf.

Daniels, C.B., & Roetman, P. (2008). *Including biodiversity as a component of sustainability as Australian cities grow: Why and how?* In TREENET Proceedings of the 9th National Street Tree Symposium 2008. Adelaide, South Australia.

Daniels, C.B., & Roetman, P.E. (2014). Urban wildlife. In J. Byrne, N. Sipe, & J. Dodson (Eds.), *Australian environmental planning: Current problems and future prospects* (pp. 118–29). London: Routledge.

de Groot, R., Brander, L., van der Ploeg, S., Costanza, R., Bernard, F., Braat, L....van Beukering, P. (2012). Global estimates of the value of ecosystems and their services in monetary units. *Ecosystem Services, 1*(1), 50–61. doi:10.1016/j.ecoser.2012.07.005.

Department of Human Services. (2009). *January 2009 Heatwave in Victoria: An assessment of health impacts.* Victorian Government Department of Human Services, Melbourne. Retrieved from http://docs.health.vic.gov.au/docs/doc/January-2009-Heatwave-in-Victoria:-an-Assessment-of-Health-Impacts.

Dimoudi, A., & Nikolopoulou, M. (2003). Vegetation in the urban environment: Microclimatic analysis and benefits. *Energy and Buildings, 35*(1), 69–76. doi:10.1016/S0378-7788(02)00081-6.

Donovan, G.H., & Butry, D.T. (2009). The value of shade: Estimating the effect of urban trees on summertime electricity use. *Energy and Buildings, 41*(6), 662–68. doi:10.1016/j.enbuild.2009.01.002.

Donovan, G.H., & Butry, D.T. (2010). Trees in the city: Valuing street trees in Portland, Oregon. *Landscape and Urban Planning, 94*(2), 77–83. doi:10.1016/j.landurbplan.2009.07.019.

Dwyer, J.F., Nowak, D.J., & Noble, M.H. (2003). Sustaining urban forests. *Journal of Arboriculture, 29*(1), 49–55.

Dwyer, J.F., Schroeder, H.W., & Gobster, P.H. (1994). The deep significance of urban trees and forests. In R. Platt, R. Rowntree, & P. Muick (Eds.), *The ecological city: Preserving and restoring urban biodiversity* (pp. 137–50). Amherst, MA: U of Massachusetts P.

Ely, M., & Pitman, S. (2014). *Green infrastructure: Life support for human habitats,* Botanic Gardens of South Australia. Green Infrastructure, Botanic Gardens of South Australia. Retrieved from www.environment.sa.gov.au/botanicgardens/Learn/Green_Infrastructure.

Escobedo, F.J., Wagner, J.E., Nowak, D.J., De la Maza, C.L., Rodriguez, M., & Crane, D.E. (2008). Analyzing the cost effectiveness of Santiago, Chile's policy of using urban forests to improve air quality. *Journal of Environmental Management, 86*(1), 148–57. doi:10.1016/j.jenvman.2006.11.029.

Fang, C.-F., & Ling, D.-L. (2003). Investigation of the noise reduction provided by tree belts. *Landscape and Urban Planning, 63*(4), 187–95. doi:10.1016/S0169-2046(02)00190-1.

Fang, C.-F., & Ling, D.-L. (2005). Guidance for noise reduction provided by tree belts. *Landscape and Urban Planning, 71*(1), 29–34. doi:10.1016/j.landurbplan.2004.01.005.

Fazio, J.R. (2010). *How trees can retain stormwater runoff.* Tree City USA Bulletin No. 55. Arbor Day Foundation, Nebraska City, NE.

Federer, C.A. (1976). Trees modify the urban microclimate. *Journal of Arboriculture, 2*(7), 121–27.

Fontana, S., Sattler, T., Bontadina, F., & Moretti, M. (2011). How to manage the urban green to improve bird diversity and community structure. *Landscape and Urban Planning, 101*(3), 278–85. doi:10.1016/j.landurbplan.2011.02.033.

Ford, J.D., Berrang-Ford, L., Lesnikowski, A., Barrera, M., & Heymann, S.J. (2013). How to track adaptation to climate change: A typology of approaches for national-level application. *Ecology and Society, 18*(3), 40. doi:10.5751/ES-05732-180340.

Foster, J., Lowe, A., & Winkelman, S. (2011). *The value of green infrastructure for urban climate adaptation.* Report by the Centre for Clean Air Policy. Retrieved from http://dev.cakex.org/sites/default/files Green_Infrastructure_FINAL.pdf.

Gates, D.M. (1968). Transpiration and leaf temperature. *Annual Review of Plant Physiology, 19*(1), 211–38. doi:10.1146/annurev.pp.19.060168.001235.

Gehl, J., & Gemzøe, L. (2001). *New city spaces.* Copenhagen: The Danish Architectural Press.

Georgi, J.N., & Dimitriou, D. (2010). The contribution of urban green spaces to the improvement of environment in cities: Case study of Chania, Greece. *Building and Environment, 45*(6), 1401–14. doi:10.1016/j.buildenv.2009.12.003.

Georgi, N.J., & Zafiriadis, K. (2006). The impact of park trees on microclimate in urban areas. *Urban Ecosystems, 9*(3), 195–209. doi:10.1007/s11252-006-8590-9.

Goddard, M.A., Dougill, A.J., & Benton, T.G. (2010). Scaling up from gardens: Biodiversity conservation in urban environments. *Trends in Ecology & Evolution, 25*(2), 90–98. doi:10.1016/j.tree.2009.07.016.

Grant, R.H., Heisler, G.M., & Gao, W. (2002). Estimation of pedestrian level UV exposure under trees. *Photochemistry and Photobiology, 75*(4), 369–76.

Grinde, B., & Patil, G.G. (2009). Biophilia: Does visual contact with nature impact on health and well-being? *International Journal of Environmental Research and Public Health, 6*(9), 2332–43. doi:10.3390/ijerph6092332.

Haines, A., Kovats, R.S., Campbell-Lendrum, D., & Corvalán, C. (2006). Climate change and human health: Impacts, vulnerability and public health. *Public Health, 120*(7), 585–96. doi:10.1016/j.puhe.2006.01.002.

Hang, J., Sandberg, M., & Li, Y. (2009). Effect of urban morphology on wind condition in idealized city models. *Atmospheric Environment, 43*(4), 869–78. doi:10.1016/j.atmosenv.2008.10.040.

Hardin, P.J., & Jensen, R.R. (2007). The effect of urban leaf area on summertime urban surface kinetic temperatures: A Terre Haute case study. *Urban Forestry & Urban Greening, 6*(2), 63–72. doi:10.1016/j.ufug.2007.01.005.

Harlan, S.L., Brazel, A.J., Jenerette, G.D., Jones, N.S., Larsen, L., Prashad, L., & Stefanov, W.L. (2007). In the shade of affluence: The inequitable distribution of the urban heat island. *Research in Social Problems and Public Policy, 15*, 173–202.

Harlan, S.L., & Ruddell, D.M. (2011). Climate change and health in cities: Impacts of heat and air pollution and potential co-benefits from mitigation and adaptation. *Current Opinion in Environmental Sustainability, 3*(3), 126–34. doi:10.1016/j.cosust.2011.01.001.

Heisler, G.M. (1989). *Effects of trees on wind and solar radiation in residential neighborhoods.* Northeastern Forest Experiment Station, USDA Forest Service, Northeastern Research Station, Forest Resources Laboratory. ANL No. 058719, Argonne National Laboratory, Argonne, IL.

Heisler, G.M. (2010). Energy savings with trees. *Journal of Aboriculture, 12*(5): 113–25.

Heller, N.E., & Zavaleta, E.S. (2009). Biodiversity management in the face of climate change: A review of 22 years of recommendations. *Biological Conservation, 142*(1), 14–32. doi:10.1016/j.biocon.2008.10.006.

Kellert, S.R., & Wilson, E.O. (Eds.). (1995). *The biophilia hypothesis.* Washington, DC: Island P.

Kjelgren, R., & Montague, T. (1998). Urban tree transpiration over turf and asphalt surfaces. *Atmospheric Environment, 32*(1), 35–41. doi:10.1016/S1352-2310(97)00177-5.

Kowarik, I. (2011). Novel urban ecosystems, biodiversity, and conservation. *Environmental Pollution, 159*(8–9), 1974–1983. doi:10.1016/j.envpol.2011.02.022.

Kuo, F.E., & Sullivan, W.C. (2001). Environment and crime in the inner city: Does vegetation reduce crime? *Environment & Behavior, 33*(3), 343–67. doi:10.1177/00139160121973025.

Laband, D.N., & Sophocleus, J.P. (2009). An experimental analysis of the impact of tree shade on electricity consumption. *Arboriculture & Urban Forestry, 35*(4), 197–202.

Laverne, R.J., & Winson-Geideman, K. (2003). The influence of trees and landscaping on rental rates at office buildings. *Journal of Arboriculture, 29*(5), 281–90.

Leyden, K.M. (2003). Social capital and the built environment: The importance of walkable neighborhoods. *American Journal of Public Health, 93*(9), 1546–51. doi:10.2105/AJPH.93.9.1546.

Livesley, S. (2010). *Energy saving benefits of shade trees in relation to water use.* In TREENET Proceedings of the 10th National Street Tree Symposium. Adelaide, South Australia.

Living Victoria Ministerial Advisory Council. (2011). *Living Melbourne living Victoria road map.* Melbourne: Victorian Government Department of Sustainability and Environment.

Loughnan, M., Coutts, A., Tapper, N., & Beringer, J. (2012). *Identifying summer temperature ranges for human thermal comfort in two Australian cities.* In WSUD 2012: Water sensitive urban design; Building the water sensitive community; 7th international conference on water sensitive urban design, 21–23 February 2012, Melbourne Cricket Ground (p. 525). Engineers Australia.

Loughnan, M., Nicholls, N., & Tapper, N. (2010). When the heat is on: Threshold temperatures for AMI admissions to hospital in Melbourne Australia. *Applied Geography, 30*(1), 63–69. doi:10.1016/j.apgeog.2009.08.003.

Louv, R. (2006). *Last child in the woods: Saving our children from nature-deficit disorder.* Chapel Hill, NC: Algonquin Books of Chapel Hill.

Mainka, S.A., McNeely, J.A., & Jackson, W.J. (2008). Depending on nature: Ecosystem services for human livelihoods. *Environment: Science and Policy for Sustainable Development, 50*(2), 42–55. doi:10.3200/ENVT.50.2.42-55.

Margolis, L., & Robinson, A. (2007). *Living systems: Innovative materials and technologies for landscape architecture.* Berlin, Germany: Walter de Gruyter.

Mark, O., Weesakul, S., Apirumanekul, C., Aroonnet, S.B., & Djordjevic, S. (2004). Potential and limitations of 1D modelling of urban flooding. *Journal of Hydrology, 299*(3–4), 284–99. doi:10.1016/j.jhydrol.2004.08.014.

Marzluff, J.M. (2001). Worldwide urbanization and its effects on birds. In J. Marzluff, R. Bowman, & R. Donnelly (Eds.), *Avian ecology and conservation in an urbanizing world* (pp. 19–47). Norwell, MA: Kluwer Academic Publishers.

Maunsell. (2009). *City of Melbourne climate change adaptation strategy, June 2009.* Melbourne, Australia: Maunsell Australia Pty Ltd.

Mayer, P. (2010). Urban ecosystems research joins mainstream ecology. *Nature, 467*(7312), 153–53. doi:10.1038/467153b.

McKeon, G. (2006). Living in a variable climate. Article prepared for the 2006 Australia State of the Environment Committee, Department of Environment and Heritage, Canberra.

McKinney, M.L. (2002). Urbanization, biodiversity, and conservation: The impacts of urbanization on native species are poorly studied, but educating a highly urbanized human population about these impacts can greatly improve species conservation in all ecosystems. *BioScience, 52*(10), 883–90.

McMichael, A.J. (2000). The urban environment and health in a world of increasing globalization: Issues for developing countries. *Bulletin of the World Health Organization, 78*(9), 1117–26.

McPherson, E.G. (1994). Cooling urban heat islands with sustainable landscapes. In R. Platt, R. Rowntree, & P. Muick (Eds.), *The ecological city: Preserving and restoring urban biodiversity* (pp. 151–71). Amherst: U of Massachusetts P.

McPherson, E.G., Herrington, L.P., & Heisler, G.M. (1988). Impacts of vegetation on residential heating and cooling. *Energy and Buildings, 12*(1), 41–51. doi:10.1016/0378-7788(88)90054-0.

McPherson, E.G., & Muchnick, J. (2005). Effect of street tree shade on asphalt concrete pavement performance. *Journal of Arboriculture, 31*(6), 303.

Memon, R.A., Leung, D.Y., & Liu, C.-H. (2010). Effects of building aspect ratio and wind speed on air temperatures in urban-like street canyons. *Building and Environment, 45*(1), 176–88. doi:10.1016/j.buildenv.2009.05.015.

Millennium Ecosystem Assessment. (2003). *Ecosystems and human well-being: A framework for assessment.* Washington, DC: Island P.

Millennium Ecosystem Assessment. (2005). *Millennium ecosystem assessment synthesis report.* Washington, DC: Island P.

Miller, D.R. (1980). The two-dimensional energy budget of a forest edge with field measurements at a forest parking lot interface. *Agricultural Meteorology, 22*(1), 53–78. doi:10.1016/0002-1571(80)90028-X.

Miller, R.W. (2007). *Urban forestry: Planning and managing urban greenspaces.* Long Grove, IL: Waveland P.

Monteith, J.L. (1981). Evaporation and surface temperature. *Quarterly Journal of the Royal Meteorological Society, 107*(451), 1–27. doi:10.1002/qj.49710745102.

Moore, C.W., & Mitchell, W.J. (1993). *The poetics of gardens.* Cambridge, MA: MIT P.

Moore, G.M. (2000). *Treenet: A management system and choices for Australia.* In TREENET Proceedings of the Inaugural Street Tree Symposium, 2000, Adelaide, South Australia.

Moore, G.M. (2012). The importance and value of urban forests as climate changes. *The Victorian Naturalist, 129*(5), 167.

Natural England. (2013). *Green infrastructure: Valuation tools assessment.* Natural England Commissioned Report NECR126. Retrieved from http://publications.naturalengland.org.uk/publication/6264318517575680.

Nowak, D.J. (1995). *Trees pollute? A "TREE" explains it all.* In Proceedings of the 7th National Urban Forestry Conference. Washington, DC: American Forests (pp. 28–30).

Nowak, D.J., Hoehn, R., & Crane, D.E. (2007). Oxygen production by urban trees in the United States. *Arboriculture and Urban Forestry, 33*(3), 220.

Plant, L. (2006). *Brisbane: 'Beautiful one day, perfect the next'—is there room for improvement.* In TREENET Proceedings of 7th National Street Tree Symposium. Adelaide, South Australia

Pokorný, J. (2001). Dissipation of solar energy in landscape—Controlled by management of water and vegetation. *Renewable Energy, 24*(3–4), 641–45. doi:10.1016/S0960-1481(01)00050-7.

Potter, G. (2013). Urbanizing the developing world. In L. Starke (Ed.), *Worldwatch Institute Vital Signs, Vol. 20* (pp. 113–16). Washington, DC: Island P.

Pretty, J. (2004). How nature contributes to mental and physical health. *Spirituality and Health International, 5*(2), 68–78. doi:10.1002/(ISSN)1557-0665.

Quattrochi, D.A., & Ridd, M.K. (1994). Measurement and analysis of thermal energy responses from discrete urban surfaces using remote sensing data. *International Journal of Remote Sensing, 15*(10), 1991–2022. doi:10.1080/01431169408954224.

Ramsar Convention on Wetlands. (2012). *The benefits of wetland restoration.* Briefing Note, Number 4, May 2012. Retrieved from http://www.ramsar.org/bn/bn4.pdf.

Ramsar Convention on Wetlands. (n.d.). *Shoreline stabilisation and storm protection.* Wetland Ecosystem Services, Factsheet 3. Retrieved from www.ramsar.org/pdf/info/services_03_e.pdf.

Rinner, C., & Hussain, M. (2011). Toronto's urban heat island—Exploring the relationship between land use and surface temperature. *Remote Sensing, 3*(12), 1251–65. doi:10.3390/rs3061251.

Roberts, J., Jackson, N., & Smith, M. (2006). *Tree roots in the built environment* (No. 8). London: Research for Amenity Trees, The Stationary Office Limited.

Rogers, K., Jarratt, T., & Hansford, D. (2011). Torbay's Urban Forest: Assessing urban forest effects and values: A report on the findings from the UK i-Tree Eco pilot project. *Treeconomics,* Exeter.

Rosenfeld, A.H., Akbari, H., Romm, J.J., & Pomerantz, M. (1998). Cool communities: Strategies for heat island mitigation and smog reduction. *Energy and Buildings, 28*(1), 51–62. doi:10.1016/S0378-7788(97)00063-7.

Saaroni, H., & Ziv, B. (2003). The impact of a small lake on heat stress in a Mediterranean urban park: The case of Tel Aviv, Israel. *International Journal of Biometeorology, 47*(3), 156–65.

Sander, H., Polasky, S., & Haight, R.G. (2010). The value of urban tree cover: A hedonic property price model in Ramsey and Dakota Counties, Minnesota, USA. *Ecological Economics, 69*(8), 1646–56. doi:10.1016/j.ecolecon.2010.03.011.

Sandström, U.G. (2002). Green infrastructure planning in urban Sweden. *Planning Practice and Research, 17*(4), 373–85. doi:10.1080/02697450216356.

Sawka, M., Millward, A.A., Mckay, J., & Sarkovich, M. (2013). Growing summer energy conservation through residential tree planting. *Landscape and Urban Planning, 113,* 1–9. doi:10.1016/j.landurbplan.2013.01.006.

Schmidt, M. (2003). Energy-saving strategies through the greening of buildings; the example of the institute of physics of the Humbolt University in Berlin, Adlershof, Germany. Rio3—World Climate and Energy Event, Rio de Janeiro, Brazil.

Scott, K.I., Simpson, J.R., & McPherson, E.G. (1999). Effects of tree cover on parking lot microclimate and vehicle emissions. *Journal of Arboriculture, 25*(3), 129–42.

Shochat, E., Lerman, S., & Fernández-Juricic, E. (2010). Birds in urban ecosystems: Population dynamics, community structure, biodiversity, and conservation. In

J. Aitkenhead-Peterson, & A. Volder (Eds.), *Urban ecosystem ecology* (pp. 75–86). Madison, WI: American Society of Agronomy, Crop Science Society of America, Soil Science Society of America.

Skinner, C.J. (2006). Urban density, meteorology and rooftops. *Urban Policy and Research, 24*(3), 355–67. doi:10.1080/08111140600876976.

Sun, R., & Chen, L. (2012). How can urban water bodies be designed for climate adaptation? *Landscape and Urban Planning, 105*(1–2), 27–33. doi:10.1016/j.landurbplan.2011.11.018.

Sun, R., Chen, A., Chen, L., & Lü, Y. (2012). Cooling effects of wetlands in an urban region: The case of Beijing. *Ecological Indicators, 20,* 57–64. doi:10.1016/j.ecolind.2012.02.006.

Swanwick, C. (2009). Society's attitudes to and preferences for land and landscape. *Land Use Policy, 26,* S62–S75. doi:10.1016/j.landusepol.2009.08.025.

Tapper, N. (2010). How trees save lives: The role of a well-watered landscape in liveable cities. In D. Lawry, & B. Merrett (Eds.), *TREENET Proceedings of the Eleventh National Street Tree Symposium* (pp. 25–33).

Thompson, J.W., & Sorvig, K. (2007). *Sustainable landscape construction: A guide to green building outdoors.* Washington, DC: Island P.

Tzoulas, K., Korpela, K., Venn, S., Yli-Pelkonen, V., Kaz mierczak, A., Niemela, J., & James, P. (2007). Promoting ecosystem and human health in urban areas using Green Infrastructure: A literature review. *Landscape and Urban Planning, 81*(3), 167–78. doi:10.1016/j.landurbplan.2007.02.001.

US EPA. (2011). *Heat island impacts.* Retrieved from www.epa.gov/heatisland/impacts/index.htm.

Van Renterghem, T., Hornikx, M., Forssen, J., & Botteldooren, D. (2013). The potential of building envelope greening to achieve quietness. *Building and Environment, 61,* 34–44. doi:10.1016/j.buildenv.2012.12.001.

Veerbeek, W., Ashley, R.M., Zevenbergen, C., Rijke, J., & Gersonius, B. (2012). *Building adaptive capacity for flood proofing in urban areas through synergistic interventions.* In WSUD 2012: Water-sensitive urban design; Building the water sensitive community; 7th international conference on water sensitive urban design, 21–23 February 2012, Melbourne Cricket Ground (p. 127). Engineers Australia.

Wachter, S.M., & Gillen, K.C. (2006). *Public investment strategies: How they matter for neighborhoods in Philadelphia.* The Wharton School, University of Pennsylvania, US. Retrieved May, 2007, from www.upenn.edu/penniur/pdf/Public%20Investment%20Strategies.pdf.

Watson, D., & Adams, M. (2010). *Design for flooding: Architecture, landscape, and urban design for resilience to climate change.* New Jersey: John Wiley & Sons.

Wolf, K.L. (2004). Nature in the retail environment: Comparing consumer and business response to urban forest conditions. *Landscape Journal, 23*(1), 40–51. doi:10.3368/lj.23.1.40.

Wolf, K.L. (2005). Business district streetscapes, trees, and consumer response. *Journal of Forestry, 103*(8), 396–400.

Wong, N.H., Tan, C.L., Nindyani, A.D.S., Jusuf, S.K., & Tan, E. (2012). Influence of water bodies on outdoor air temperature in hot and humid climate. In *ASCE copyright Proceedings of the 2011 International Conference on Sustainable Design and Construction| d 20120000*. Reston, VA: American Society of Civil Engineers.

Wong, T.H. (2006). An overview of water-sensitive urban design practices in Australia. *Water Practice and Technology, 1*(1), 1–8.

Wong, T.H. (2011). *Stormwater management in a water-sensitive city: Blueprint 2011*. Melbourne, Australia: The Centre for Water Sensitive Cities, Monash University.

Zipperer, W.C., & Pickett, S.T.A. (2012). Urban ecology: Patterns of population growth and ecological effects. In *Encyclopedia of life sciences* (ELS). Chichester: John Wiley & Sons Ltd. doi:10:10.1002/9780470015902.a0003246.pub2.

DISCUSSION QUESTIONS

1. Early in the Introduction, Pitman et al. offer a brief account of their methodology—how they chose which articles to review, and why. Briefly describe their selection criteria and comment on possible reasons for including such an account in their paper.

2. The abstract begins with a sentence-length definition of green infrastructure, and the introduction develops this definition considerably. Record a point-form list of the most prominent features of green infrastructure, taking care to identify its functions as well as its physical components.

3. What is the urban heat island (UHI) effect and why does it matter? What are some of the ways that green infrastructure can reduce the severity of the UHI?

4. Pitman et al. identify seven themes or prevailing concerns in the research on green infrastructure but choose to emphasize "climate adaptation and climate preservation, with brief references to other benefits" (p. 237). What are the other benefits Pitman et al. identify?

5. Imagine that you are a city planner in charge of implementing green infrastructure. Using Google Maps, print a map of an area you know (e.g., your neighbourhood, your campus, the downtown core of your city). Apply Pitman et al.'s findings to redesign the neighbourhood, identifying each design change you make on the map with a reference to Pitman et al.'s article.

E. "ENVIRONMENTAL SCIENCE AND PUBLIC POLICY IN EXECUTIVE GOVERNMENT: INSIGHTS FROM AUSTRALIA AND CANADA," BRIONY M. LALOR AND GORDON M. HICKEY

In this article, which appeared in 2013 in Science and Public Policy, *Briony M. Lalor and Gordon M. Hickey* * *conduct a qualitative study of the experiences of the cabinet ministers and senior civil servants who are responsible for environmental policy in Australia and Canada. Following conventional IMRD structure and using "grounded theory" methodology, Lalor and Hickey interviewed 36 subjects, assessing their attitudes toward the involvement of environmental scientists and the public in environmental policy issues. As you read Lalor and Hickey's work, note the researchers' careful and systematic application of commonplace terms such as "most," "usually," and "some," and try to get a sense of the kinds of changes their research subjects would like to see in the involvement of both the public and environmental scientists in environmental policy-making.*

Glossary terms: IMRD, grounded theory, semi-structured interview, coding

Abstract

This paper presents the results of an exploratory study into the science-policy experiences of former Environment Ministers (senior politicians) and Department Secretaries/Deputy Ministers (senior public servants) to better understand the role of science-based knowledge in the Executive decision-making processes of Westminster-based governments. Our participants identified a number of factors affecting the value of science-based evidence to strategic public policy processes. They described a lack of access to appropriately contextualized knowledge and a lack of accountability to demonstrate how science was considered in Cabinet decision-making. Many participants felt senior academics had an obligation to be more involved in public

---

* Briony M. Lalor wrote her PhD dissertation on soil ecology and held a postdoctoral fellowship at McGill University, Montreal, where she conducted research on "institutional challenges facing Australia, Canada and the UK as they attempt to develop truly effective, evidence-based environmental policies" (LinkedIn). She has also worked as an environmental consultant and civil servant in Australia.

Gordon M. Hickey is an Associate Professor in the Department of Natural Resource Sciences at McGill University, Montreal. According to his institutional webpage, his research program is "designed to advance the sustainable natural resource management and policy objectives of society through better understanding of the complex interactions between social and ecological systems."

policy debates, to advocate policy positions based on their research and to ask questions that could assist governments on environmental issues. Concomitant was the desire for fundamental institutional changes, including greater use of deliberative public participation tools in environmental science and policy and more networked approaches to science.

Keywords: Science-policy interface, science literacy, deliberative democracy, responsible advocacy, state/provincial government, federal government

1. Introduction

Recent science-policy debates have emphasized a growing role for science in helping to address some of society's most pressing environmental challenges (United Nations Conference on Environment and Development 1992; Scott 2007). However, improving scientific input to the development of environmental policy represents a significant and complex challenge (McNie 2007; Sarewitz and Pielke 2007; Pohl 2008; Juntti et al. 2009). Much of the recent literature on this topic suggests that, in order to better address this challenge, there is a need to identify ways to improve engagement between environmental scientists and decision-makers through communication and collaboration (Parsons 2001; MacLeod et al. 2007; McNie 2007; Foote et al. 2009; Ryder et al. 2010; Hickey et al. 2013), ultimately making science more relevant to policy-making (Gibbons et al. 2008). However, at a time when the relationship between science and society is changing (Lubchenco 1998; Gibbons 1999; Cortner 2000; Miller 2001; Schenkel 2010), neither the linear model of science (Cullen 1990; Kørnøv and Thissen 2000; Pielke 2007) nor a more complex model, where scientific, bureaucratic and political cultures clash on epistemological or value-laden grounds (Sarewitz 2004; Pielke 2004; Oreskes 2004), provides practical guidance for environmental scientists or decision-makers hoping to improve the utility of public science to public policy (Grafty 2008). Furthermore, for environmental scientists attempting to work in the science-policy nexus, effective engagement represents a long-standing and difficult challenge (Lubchenco 1998; Steel et al. 2004; Pace et al. 2010; Scott and Rachlow 2011).

Within Westminster-based systems of government (Table 1),[1] such as those used at the state/provincial and federal levels in Canada and Australia (see Fig. 1), there are a number of institutional challenges to engaging science-based knowledge in the strategic policy initiatives of government (Stewart 2004; Stevenson 2007). A key feature of the Westminster-based system is the apex policy role of the Cabinet in deciding major policy, planning, and legislative initiatives (see Fig. 2). A Cabinet is generally comprised of approximately 20 senior ministers, directed by the Prime Minister (or Premier in the case of provinces/states), who meet once a week for two to three hours in closed session (McNaughton 1999). Cabinet members are collectively responsible for public policy and function as the powerhouse of Executive government (Hennessy

1986; Palmer and Palmer 2004). While only Ministers are generally allowed to submit papers to Cabinet, most are written by public servants, relying heavily on the knowledge production, management, and communication capacity of the bureaucracy. It is then the role of the responsible Minister to present the paper and argue for a particular outcome within Cabinet—a process that is conducted in secrecy to prevent the government appearing divided and to ensure that all Ministers publicly support government policy (d'Ombrain 2004). Importantly, the precise role of Cabinet in deciding public policy will often vary between elected governments (Weller 1999).

In the context of environmental governance, a number of important challenges related to the Executive decision-making processes of the Westminster model have been emerging for government agencies in Canada and Australia. In particular, limiting the environmental impacts associated with human development activities without causing politically unpalatable economic or social impacts presents major challenges (Loucks 2007; Mercer et al. 2007; Nevill 2007; Valentine 2010). This is an area where the applied science enterprise has the potential to inform public policy options, however, little is known about the pathways through which science might best inform (and survive) Cabinet discussions on environmental issues. Importantly, Canada and Australia have broad historical, constitutional, geographic, cultural, and institutional similarities that offer the potential to learn from each other's environmental science and policy experiences. Both countries have also identified the connection between science and policy as a key issue for government (Government of Western Australia 2003; Industry Canada 2007; Australian Government 2010; Commissioner for Environmental Sustainability Victoria 2010).

Beliefs

The constitutional framework
A unitary state
No separation of powers and, therefore, no judicial review of constitution
A bicameral parliament
The doctrine of parliamentary sovereignty
Flexible constitutional conventions

The executive
A two-party system based on single member constituencies
Majority party–government control of parliament
Institutionalized opposition
Accountability through elections

The parties
The head of state and the head of government are two separate roles
Majority party control of the executive also described as the fusion of the legislature and the executive – with ministers drawn from the parliament
Concentration of executive power in prime minister and cabinet
Individual ministerial and collective cabinet responsibility to parliament
Partnership between ministers and neutral officials in which ministers have the last word

---

Table 1. The Westminster model of government: a summary statement (Rhodes and Weller 2005)

This paper presents the results of an exploratory study into the science-policy experiences of former Environment Ministers (senior politicians who sat in Cabinet) and Department Secretaries/Deputy Ministers (senior public servants) who have served in provincial/state and federal governments across Canada and Australia. Using a retrospective approach, our research sought to better understand the key pathways through which science-based knowledge can inform the Executive decision-making processes of Westminster-based government, drawing on the rich experiences and privileged insights of former apex decision-makers.

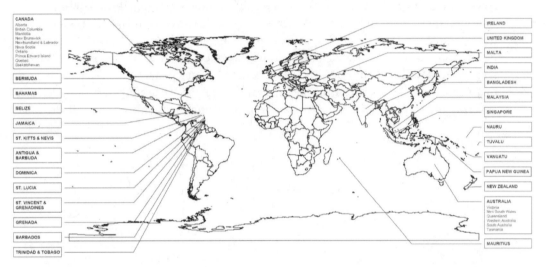

Figure 1. Jurisdictions that claim Westminster-based systems of government

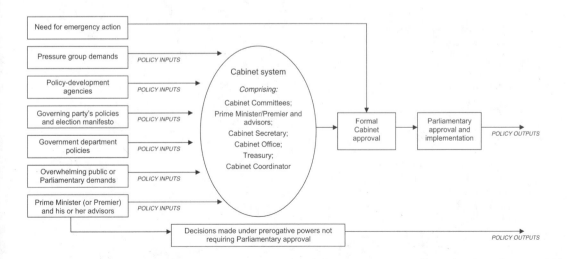

Figure 2. Prime Minister and Cabinet in the decision-making process (adapted from McNaughton 1999)

2. Methodology

This study was conducted following a grounded theory approach (Glaser and Strauss 1967; Strauss and Corbin 1997), considered particularly suitable for exploratory research into institutional behaviour (Sousa and Hendriks 2008).

2.1 Data collection

A series of one-on-one semi-structured interviews were conducted with former Ministers of the Environment (n = 20) and Department Secretaries/Deputy Ministers of Environment Departments (n=16) (or their equivalent) from the federal and state/provincial levels of government across Australia and Canada. Table 2 presents the respondent profile, including jurisdiction, average period in role, and gender information. Interviews were conducted between October 2009 and August 2010 and lasted between 1.5 and 2 hours. Semi-structured interviews were preferred so that participants could volunteer relevant (and preferred) issues but also provide coverage of key issues identified by the authors through a detailed review of the

Government	Ministers	Secretaries/Deputy Ministers
Australia		
New South Wales	1	0
Queensland	2	2
South Australia	2	1
Tasmania	0	0
Victoria	4	3
Western Australia	1	1
Federal	0	2
Total	**10**	**9**
Average term/tenure	3.7	4.5
Female participants	3	1
Canada		
British Columbia	1	2
New Brunswick	1	0
Saskatchewan	2	1
Alberta	1	1
Quebec	1	0
Manitoba	1	1
Ontario	1	0
Newfoundland and Labrador	0	1
Nova Scotia	0	0
Federal	2	2
Total	**10**	**8**
Average term/tenure	2.6	3
Female participants	2	2

Table 2. Participants by jurisdiction, average term/tenure and gender

literature. Questions were open-ended to allow participants to describe experiences in their own words (Creswell, 1994).

2.2 Data Analysis

Interview transcripts were analyzed using open and focused coding to identify key theoretical categories. The meaning and possible relationships between codes were explored recursively using memos to develop preliminary models which could then be compared to the literature to identify conceptual gaps and heighten theoretical sensitivity (Sousa and Hendriks 2008). We then assessed how well the codes of the preliminary model suited new interview data. This process resulted in the revision of some categories and the development of new categories to more accurately reflect the data. Constant comparative techniques (Boeije 2002; Strauss and Corbin 1997) were used throughout the process to assist in uncovering new properties and dimensions. In addition to memos, we also used participants' quotes to ensure that interpretations were grounded in the data. The final step involved a comparison of the emergent theoretical model with the existing literature.

2.3 Assumptions and Limitations

This study was based on the assumption that the structural and institutional impacts on the environmental science-policy interactions in Executive government could be better understood by interviewing former apex decision-makers on environmental issues in government. The results were therefore dependent on the expertise of the interviewees and subject to issues of bias, poor recall, and inaccurate articulation (Yin 1994). We minimized the impact of sampling bias by interviewing people from different jurisdictions, different political parties, and who had held the position of Minister or Department Secretary/Deputy Minister at different times in the period 1985–2007 to obtain a more complete account (Weiss 1998). To reduce the likelihood of response bias, we conducted a pre-test of our interview in August 2009 to check the questions for clarity and to avoid leading participants. Interviewer bias was checked through the transcription of each interview, while confirmation bias was minimized by using MAXQDA to analyze (code) the text (Eisenhardt 1989). Data triangulation was used to maximize construct validity and ensure the reliability and trustworthiness of our findings (Marshall and Rossman 1989; Yin 1994). The findings generated through our research are appropriate for generalization to theory rather than populations (Yin 1994), providing 'thicker' descriptions of the complexities surrounding public policy processes in Westminster-based government than a quantitative survey could offer (Dodge et al. 2005; Klenk and Hickey 2011).

3. Results

We present our results based on the responses of participants as follows: (a) the words 'generally,' 'most,' 'often,' 'the majority,' 'usually,' and 'typically' indicate the characteristic response of a majority of the relevant respondent group (50% or more); (b) the words 'some,' 'a few' and 'a number of' indicate response from 10–50% of the sample; and (c) 'all' and 'one' were also used occasionally. In order to adequately capture the rich experiences of our expert participants, we present illustrative quotes where appropriate.

Two central and pervasive themes emerged from our data. The first was the perception that Ministers had inconsistent access to appropriately 'contextualized' knowledge on environmental issues, described as being necessary to inform their decisions and those of Cabinet. When describing appropriately contextualized knowledge, our participants (both politicians and public servants) spoke to the need for credibility (scientifically robust and trusted); legitimacy (has fairly considered divergent values and beliefs of stakeholders); and salience (relevance of the information to the needs; e.g., timeliness, clarity, and brevity) (McNie 2007). The second central theme was a general lack of accountability to consider science in the Executive decision-making processes of government when dealing with environmental issues. It is interesting to note that these themes emerged despite major differences in the roles of our participants: Ministers are politicians and often somewhat transient in their service, while Department Secretaries/Deputy Ministers are often highly experienced public servants with longer terms of service. In what follows, we summarize our expert participants' recollections and perceptions on the role of science in Executive decision-making and opportunities for improving the use of science in decision-making on environmental issues.

3.1 Role of Science in Executive Decision-Making: Science Knowledge Needs

Science-based knowledge was generally described as being necessary for highlighting issues, informing decisions, and framing ideas, but it was rarely used in an 'instrumental' manner or as the basis of Ministerial/Cabinet decisions:

> ...well it's fundamental. It's necessary but not sufficient. In other words, I don't conceive how that process [forest management] could have been successfully conducted without good science, although that's only the beginning. (New South Wales, Australia, Minister)

Most Ministers described science as being instrumental when there was a relatively high degree of certainty about the social, environmental and political outcomes of the decision. For example, where there was a perceived urgent need for policy change, where science was irrefutable, when there was some degree of consensus amongst experts and where there was clear public support and/or clear political advantages.

Most Ministers and Department Secretaries/Deputy Ministers described science-based knowledge as being used in an 'elaborative' way to provide support for a particular political objective or as justification for predetermined policy objectives.

Most participants stated that only 'credible' science-based knowledge was useful to Executive decision-making. This knowledge was described as easy to understand, concise, seemingly 'undiluted' by opinions and inclusive of a range of policy options that were suitably matched to the prevailing political and socioeconomic context. Furthermore, knowledge that was made publicly available to all interested parties, rather than to 'select' groups was considered more credible. Here, participants were describing a need for access to contextualized knowledge that could assist them with balancing science-informed views with broader short- and long-term economic and social objectives in decision-making. Thorough, long-term public policy debate and significant public participation (and ultimately pressure) were described by most Ministers as being instrumental in Cabinet decisions they felt had successfully balanced environmental and societal interests. However, sustained public engagement in policy debates and processes was considered rare. Many Ministers described a lack of public engagement in policy processes as leading to the strengthening of special interest groups and opinion-based decision-making. Most Ministers also lamented the lack of accountability for government to demonstrate how policy decisions were evidence-based.

Further, most Ministers and Department Secretaries/Deputy Ministers felt that the complexity of environmental issues, combined with the increasing plurality of knowledge sources, affected the public's ability/willingness to engage in debate to influence environmental policy outcomes:

> There is a lack of life...the information is not flowing...There is not enough exchange, there is not enough forums right now, to have that exchange...we have to encourage a more public exchange between the various parties involved. (Manitoba, Canada, Minister)

This lack of public engagement was seen as being linked to *ad hoc* institutional processes for involving the public in environmental management and a systemic lack of engagement by environment-related academics in public policy debates.

The key consequence of the inherent uncertainty, lack of contextualized knowledge and accountability to use science in decision-making was delayed government action and the maintenance of the *status quo*:

> ...what I tell scientists when I talk to them about how you can influence government is that where there are disputes, government is inclined not to take action. Where there's a strong coalition of forces, government is much more inclined to take action. So, in those cases where there was some level of

scientific dispute, the natural political response is to refer it to a 'committee,' because you're not in a position to make an assessment yourself. (Victoria, Australia, Minister)

The conditions described above were seen to create a vacuum of contextualized knowledge. In this vacuum, the Ministers described their own and the Cabinet's decisions as being less likely to be based on a formal, appropriately tested or inclusive evidence and more likely to be based on their own, or their advisor's, experiences, leading to reactionary decision-making that favoured more powerful, louder, interests in society:

...we are in a real conundrum because it's now whoever shouts the loudest and gets the most sensational story [who] wins. (Ontario, Canada, Minister)

3.2 Opportunities for Improvement

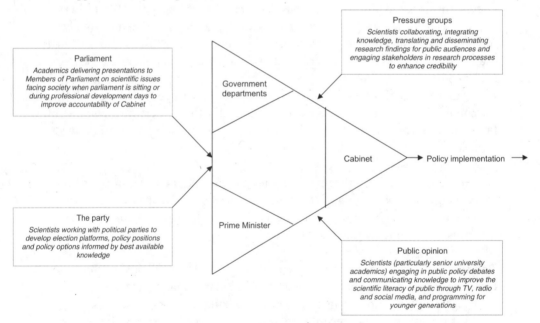

Figure 3. Participant recommendations (in italics) for improving the role of environmental science in government policy (based on McNaughton's [1999] traditional policy cycle)

Fig. 3 summarizes the opportunities identified by participants for improving the role of environmental science in Executive government. These results are further described below.

3.2.1 *environmental academics need to be more engaged*

A healthy public policy debate that included a scientifically literate public was seen as paramount to improving Ministers' access to contextualized knowledge and accountability to use science in decision-making. To achieve this, most Australian and Canadian Ministers and some senior public servants felt that environment-related academics in external organizations, such as universities (hereafter referred to as academics), had a unique moral obligation to be more engaged in policy debates to educate and ultimately improve scientific literacy amongst the public. The benefit of improving public scientific literacy was seen as a way to increase political pressure on governments to demonstrate how their decisions were based on science and to balance the impact of lobby groups. However, most Ministers and Department Secretaries/Deputy Ministers criticized what they perceived as a systemic lack of willingness of academics to enter the 'political fray,' for example:

> I think universities do not participate sufficiently in these big debates, by and large. I think they could provide a much greater leadership role with all the research they do, but they tend to want to stay pure. (Victoria, Australia, Minister)

> I want them to step up…you know, if the scientific community stepped up and said, when you make environmental policy, prove it to me. You know, 'what is your background on this?' (Ontario, Canada, Minister)

> I believe that external scientists…should be speaking out more and should at least be more accessible to the media in explaining the actualities of what is really going on…I think scientists have a social responsibility to bring their expertise into public debate where it is appropriate to do so and say, 'just a minute now, I am the person who is most knowledgeable about this in the province or in the country, and here is the latest science on this.' (Newfoundland and Labrador, Canada, Deputy Minister)

> So I think the scientific community can no longer sit in the 'Ivory Tower' and do their research, publish their papers and be above the political fray…In the next 50 years they are going to have to [engage], without in any way compromising the integrity of their research and the propositions they are putting forward based on research, but they've got to tell them, they've got to get out there. (South Australia, Australia, Minister)

Ministers generally felt the responsibility to engage in and lead public policy debates was largely that of senior academics (e.g., professors), as they were perceived to be amongst the most credible knowledge-holders in society:

...the debate over Port Philip Bay [controversial dredging project to give super-sized container ships access to Melbourne's port] should have been layered by the professor of botany or whatever it is, you know, or the professor of water resources or whatever. You know, where were they? You know they may have written stuff on I don't know, but if it's not communicated to the population then I don't know. So that's the challenge alright and to me it's unlocking a resource. You know, that's where we're wasting our detailed knowledge. (Victoria, Australia, Minister)

While one Canadian Minister felt that environmental scientists and academics could influence public policy by working within political parties, generally, Ministers felt that academics should better utilize mainstream media on a regular basis to communicate the outcomes of their research (e.g., news broadcasts) to counter populous and overly dominant tabloid news media. Furthermore, a few Ministers and Department Secretaries/Deputy Ministers in both countries highlighted the importance of providing exposure to science to younger generations to foster awareness and understanding of environmental scientific issues through programs on television, radio and social media.

While the majority of Ministers and Department Secretaries/Deputy Ministers were keen to see greater engagement of academia in public policy debates, only a few recognized the challenge this represented to individual scientists, research institutions or to the broader scientific enterprise in both countries:

... [Public outreach] is, you know, a slightly different mission and it's hard to do. You have to be tolerant and forgiving and have the time and your boss, whoever it is, the institution or the company that you're with, has to welcome it. (Victoria, Australia, Minister)

In particular, it was noted that academic credibility was influenced by the proficiency an academic had in communication and avoiding the dangers of advocacy science:

One particular tension...is when you have scientists who actually position, so they are not only providing expert opinion, but they are also jumping to a conclusion around whether or not a development should proceed...I think you see this all across the environment departments, it is a pretty common issue; they are getting too passionate and in some ways it's an occupational hazard because they are so immersed in it. (British Columbia, Canada, Deputy Minister)

A lot of scientists would fall down and they would actually, I think, undermine the credibility of their science by putting it alongside things where they didn't have such sound knowledge and information. (Victoria, Australia, Minister)

Indeed most Ministers felt that a key condition of engagement of academics in public policy debate was proficiency in communication, but this was perceived as a 'gift' few scientists had. A key consequence of this was that some Ministers would seek out knowledge from non-traditional sources, including accountancy or law firms who were perceived to have multidisciplinary teams that were more creative and adaptive than many academics:

> ...just as it's an outrage to have a surgeon who can't explain the operation they want to do to you at your bedside, it's equally outrageous to have highly skilled scientists who can't communicate with newspapers or TVs, and I just think that the game's up for that, you know, and I think what it means is that you look for your skills in spots were you shouldn't necessarily have to look for them. (Victoria, Australia, Minister)

Some Department Secretaries/Deputy Ministers thought that poor communication skills (from government and external) led to Ministers gravitating toward knowledge sources able to effectively communicate at the Ministerial level, even though they may not have been the most accurate:

> ...science's biggest fault in advising government is it tends to be prolix and technical, and governments lack patience and they turn and listen to the person who can succinctly summarize this, possibly wildly inaccurately, but they'll give greater weight to someone whose voice they can understand than someone's voice they don't understand. (Victoria, Australia, Secretary)

> It's got to be not science jargon, and wonky-wonky stuff. It has to be something the Ministers and the politicians will read and understand. And it has got to be translatable into action. (Federal Deputy Minister, Canada)

In addition, some described scientists (government and external) as being too comfortable, operating within a singular discipline model, and that the organization and establishment of interdisciplinary research to create contextualized knowledge represented an important challenge to the scientific community, requiring a cultural shift:

> ...I think it's an awkward challenge and therefore it's a good one because it is a bit counter-cultural, and it's sort of the old sciences, its science, engineering and architecture, where it's just too normal to talk to yourself. There are new disciplines where it's a prerequisite that you talk to others. I think that's what has to alter. (Victoria, Australia, Minister)

This Minister also thought that universities had an obligation to produce scientists who were comfortable communicating across disciplines, to the media, public, and to politicians. If academics were to engage, there was an expectation that they would manage their engagement in a way that did not compromise their credibility. One Canadian Minister suggested that the introduction of a mechanism to ensure academics disclose their sources of funding, and hence potential biases, when engaging in public policy debates would reduce the use of advocacy science:

> Just as the Quebec bar association made it an offense to give an appearance of lucre or mercantilist to the practice of law, I think that it goes, you know, for people who are involved in scientific publishing. (Quebec, Canada, Minister)

3.2.2 institutional changes to improve accountability and reduce political uncertainty
The desire for greater academic engagement was woven with the desire for a more robust decision-making framework that facilitated adequate public participation primarily to improve accountability but also to reduce uncertainty in decision-making and limit negative political consequences of decisions. In this regard, some Ministers and Secretaries, particularly those from the state of Victoria, Australia, advocated the use of the Green-paper/White-paper policy process as a valuable participatory decision-making tool that had positively influenced their access to contextualized knowledge and wanted to see this process used on a more regular basis. While a Canadian Minister wanted the potential value of consensus conferences, such as those used in Denmark, or environmental or citizen jury panels, to be explored:

> We have an inquest in Ontario where we have 20 citizens who sit down and they hear the evidence in terms of a criminal activity and make recommendations. I'd like the same thing with regard to environmental science. (Ontario, Canada, Minister)

In addition to their perceived obligation to educate the general public, some Ministers thought that academics and government scientists also had a responsibility to educate senior public servants, Ministers, and parliamentarians through parliamentary briefings, various parliamentary and other committees. Other educational opportunities for knowledge-sharing included the Priorities and Planning Committees of government and presentations at professional development days for parliamentarians:

> I think that's very important too, to relate the scientific material [general], which is often hidden away, to both the Department and to the Minister and to, you know, the Minister's colleagues, and I think that's something we often severely neglect. (Victoria, Australia, Minister)

Again, however, Ministers expressed concern about academic independence and credibility. As such, some Ministers thought the responsibility to organize parliamentary briefings should be left to universities or academics themselves, as opposed to the bureaucracy:

> So you've got to be careful that the MPs [Members of Parliament] getting briefed think it's a legitimate briefing and not just an expert brought in to spin the government line...and from that point of view it'd be far better if it was just the universities or the experts doing it on their own initiative. (South Australia, Australia, Minister)

4. Discussion

While it was clear that the Environment Ministers we interviewed generally believed in the value of science as a foundation for Executive decision-making, their desire for more inclusive and contextualized knowledge provides empirical support to recent discussions in the literature surrounding the changes occurring in society and science (Lubchenco 1998; Gibbons 1999; Cortner 2000; Steel et al. 2004; McNie 2007; Hessels and van Lente 2008; Hessels et al. 2009; Klenk and Hickey 2012; Hickey et al. 2013). This affects scientific activity not only at the organizational level, but also at its epistemological core (Hessels and van Lente 2008). Our research also revealed a remarkable degree of similarity in the perspectives and experiences of our elite respondents from diverse jurisdictions across Canada and Australia. This suggests that the institutional frameworks associated with Westminster-based government do influence the ways that science is perceived and utilized (or not) in strategic public policy. In particular, the responsibility for considering available evidence during strategic decision-making processes largely rests within the Executive, whose deliberations are protected by Cabinet secrecy leading to reduced transparency and public accountability for Ministers to meaningfully consider or respond to available science-based knowledge. This lack of accountability was an area that our respondents felt needed to be addressed through various pathways in order to improve the functional relationship between public science and public policy (see Fig. 3).

In 2007, the Government of Canada released a report outlining principles and guidelines for improving the use of science in decision-making in government (Industry Canada 2007). This document represented a strategy for federal government departments to improve inclusiveness and accountability to use science in internal decision-making and the briefing of their Ministers. However, the extent to which this policy document has driven improvements in the relationship between science and policy in the decision-making processes of Canada's current Executive government is not clear. According to O'Hara (2010), the relationship has broken down, with policies put in place to 'muzzle' government scientists, including restrictions on scientific knowledge dissemination to the public through media and presentation at conferences (see also *Nature* 2012). Further, significant budget cuts to 'in-house' government research (including a controversial decision to stop funding the Experimental Lakes Area in northwestern Ontario) have dramatically affected science–policy relationships and reduced environment-related science capacity at the federal level (Thompson et al. 2012; McDiarmid 2012). Conversely, in Australia, the 'Inspiring Australia' report (Australian Government 2010) outlines the need to establish a national strategy to improve science communication to the public and hence scientific literacy with the aim of improving public engagement in policy processes. As such, part of its focus is on auditing and then bolstering the support of science 'enterprises' carrying out science communication. Neither country has identified clear policies that address the desire described by our participants for institutional change to increase the use of deliberative models of public participation in environmental science and policy to improve knowledge contextualization and accountability.

The desire for institutional change described by our participants supports recent literature suggesting that while public education and information are important steps toward facilitating broader engagement in environmental decision-making, such efforts may be more effective if they are combined with a consideration of structural and institutional changes (Geczi 2007; Maibach et al. 2008; Wesselink et al. 2011). These changes should aim to give the public hope that they will influence a decision or change a situation and hence maintain a more active interest in policy-making (Parkins and Mitchell 2005). However, based on our results, it seems that efforts to embed participatory governance in bureaucratic structures may have been unsuccessful at integrating scientific input on environmental issues (Wesselink et al. 2011). Here, underlying political, economic, and institutional barriers need to be better understood (Parkins and Mitchell 2005; Geczi 2007; Newig and Fritsch 2009; Wesselink et al. 2011; Hoppe 2011). Newig and Fritsch (2009) proposed that comparison with difficult, complex, or failed cases may help. Importantly, while the Ministers and Department Secretaries/Deputy Ministers in our sample generally supported more deliberative and evidence-based models of decision-making as a response to the environmental challenges facing traditional representative democracy, these views may not be shared by all governments. Indeed, recent developments in the relationship between environmental science and public policy in Canada's Federal Government suggest a lack of political will to pursue more robust participatory and evidence-based approaches to environmental governance.[2]

Drawing on their own elite perspectives and experiences working at the apex of environmental decision-making in government, our participants felt that frequent and sustained engagement of academics in public policy debates would have significant and relatively immediate impacts on improving environmental policy outcomes while they were in office. While these viewpoints do not adequately reflect the difficulties scientists often face in attracting the attention of the mainstream media, they do support the literature arguing that academics in liberal democracies have an obligation to be involved in the policy process and to ensure that their research is socially accountable (Cohn 2006; Manning 2007; Graydon 2011; Stack 2011). Furthermore, within academia, it has been recognized that there is an urgent need to more effectively translate and communicate science to the public to help foster interest and engagement (Lubchenco 1998; Cullen 2004; Foote et al. 2009; Nelson and Vucetich 2009; Groffman et al. 2010; Pace et al. 2010; Baker et al. 2012). However, due to the complexity of environmental governance, where issues are often highly contested and politicized, much of the science can be considered to be 'in the making' (Latour 1987), with available knowledge only partially constructed and openly contested. As a result, when a scientist advocates a policy preference without outlining a transparent scientific logic, conveying contextual factors, admitting uncertainty, and reporting the potential biases, the result is considered to be 'advocacy science,' resulting in reduced credibility and the perception of an agenda (Foote et al. 2009; Nelson and Vucetich 2009; Rice 2011; Scott and Rachlow 2011). Pielke (2007) identified four potential advisory roles for scientists in public policy: pure scientist, issue advocate, science arbiter, and honest broker of policy alternatives, all of which are needed in a healthy system of scientific advice. Pielke (2007) also warns against a general push for scientists to become issue advocates, as this may undermine the authority and infrastructure of science. However, others propose that arguments against science advocacy are valuable, as they offer important insights for academics about how they should or should not advocate—not whether they should advocate (Nelson and Vucetich 2009). It is argued that such advocacy serves to maintain the social relevance and legitimacy of academia to public affairs and also provides a practical picture of science as a social process (Foote et al. 2009). Importantly, our study sought only to capture the environmental science-related viewpoints and experiences of Executive decision-makers, and necessarily simplifies the complex reality facing scientists, aspects of which may make it impossible to engage in the ways outlined in Fig. 3. Nevertheless, the general desire expressed by our participants for academics to increase their engagement in public policy debates in ways that maintain credibility supports recent dialogue promoting the need for greater reflection and deliberation on the role of academia in the public policy process and 'responsible advocacy' (Foote et al. 2009; Nelson and Vucetich 2009). This is an area that requires further research.

According to Baker et al. (2012), one of the main reasons that many environmental scientists working in academia have been reticent to engage in public debate is because there have been few incentives to do so. Hessels et al. (2009) suggested that while performance measures such as bibliometric analyses were originally introduced to enhance the societal accountability of academics, they have strengthened the 'publish or perish' norm and increased the need for peer recognition rather than a need for societal justification of academic work. Others argue that the extensive use of output indicators as measures of success results in disciplines becoming increasingly disconnected, impeding the innovations that often come from inter-disciplinary research (Osterloh and Frey 2009). Hessels et al. (2009) proposed that the social accountability of academic research could be improved if funding bodies and universities took a systemic approach to reviewing the governance of academic research to focus on the need to prove societal justification and reward academics for their engagement in public discourse. Universities are well placed to provide training opportunities for academics wanting to further develop competence and confidence in new tools to communicate what is at stake in a public policy debate and why it matters (Holland 1999; Groffman et al. 2010). However, even though better communication of scientific outputs and responsible advocacy can generally be thought of as benefiting universities, the institutional structures of many universities in Canada and Australia have not been adapted to reflect this (Foote et al. 2009; Australian Government 2010).

Despite the broad similarities between these two countries, it is the differences in the way that governments are approaching the environmental science-policy nexus that represent a significant opportunity for cross-jurisdictional learning. For example, the release of the 'Inspiring Australia' report (Australian Government 2010) opened a window of opportunity for academics in Australia to begin a discussion about how responsible advocacy should be enshrined in university policy. The outcomes of these discussions and the implementation of a national strategy in Australia to improve science communication will likely provide valuable insights for Canadian governments. Further assessment of the public debate over how institutions of science should foster knowledge creation that better matches the needs of decision-makers and delivers public value will be helpful to government agencies in both countries. A comparative review of the existing approaches to research governance in Australian and Canadian universities, including reward and incentive structures for academics, would also be beneficial, assisting institutions to create structures that better facilitate the responsible public engagement of academics (Holland 1999). Furthermore, empirical research that investigates the ideas and assumptions held by academics about their engagement in public policy debate would be valuable. In particular, a more detailed understanding of the motivation of academics to engage in public policy issues is needed.

5. Conclusions
The empirical nature of our research and the high profiles of our participants provide support for the importance of socially robust environmental science. They also provide a sense of urgency to recent dialogue concerning the need for 'responsible advocacy' within academic institutions. There was a perception that environmental academics had a moral obligation to embrace cultural change, involving greater

engagement in public policy debates and transdisciplinary research. Our findings also highlight the need for concomitant institutional changes to improve account-ability to use science in decision-making, including greater use of participatory approaches and more networked, transdisciplinary approaches to science creation and dissemination. Our results suggest that such changes could lead to more equity in environment-related decision-making processes and ultimately to decisions that have a better likelihood of balancing social, economic, and environmental con-siderations. We propose that such changes are necessary if the implementation of recent Australian and Canadian policies aiming to improve the use of science in decision-making and the communication of science are to be successful. However, environmental science and policy discussions would benefit from the identification of best-practice models in each of the two key areas seen as requiring improvement. The unique institutional similarities that exist between the states, provinces, and nations of Australia and Canada, differences in the ways the countries are approach-ing the science-policy nexus, combined with diverse social, economic, and political contexts within each setting, provide ample opportunities for greater cross-juris-dictional learning.

Notes

[1] Westminster-based parliamentary systems modeled after the United Kingdom (Rhodes and Weller 2005). It is important to note that 'Westminster-based gov-ernment' is not an uncontested term, and there are nuances in how this system is applied in different jurisdictions (Chapman 2000; Patapan and Wanna 2005).

[2] For an example, see www.deathofevidence.ca. Accessed 22 April 2013.

References

Australian Government. (2010) Inspiring Australia: A National Strategy for Engage-ment with the Sciences. A report to the Minister for Innovation, Industry, Science and Research. Canberra: Australian Government.

Baker, M.J., Williams, L.F., Lybbert, A.H. and Johnson, J.B. (2012) 'How ecological science is portrayed in mass media', *Ecosphere*, 3: 9. http://dx.doi.org/10.1890/ES11-00238.1. Accessed 23 April 2013.

Boeije, H. (2002) 'A purposeful approach to the constant comparative method in the analysis of qualitative interviews', *Quality and Quantity*, 36: 391–409.

Chapman, R. (2000) 'Accountability: Is Westminster the problem?', *Australian Jour-nal of Public Administration*, 59: 116–23.

Cohn, D. (2006) 'Jumping into the political fray: Academics and policy-making', *Institute for Research on Public Policy (IRPP) Policy Matters*, 7/3.

Commissioner for Environmental Sustainability Victoria. (2010) Science, Policy, People. State of the Environment Reporting 2013. Melbourne. Australia: State Government of Victoria.

Cortner, H.J. (2000) 'Making science relevant to environmental policy', *Environmental Science and Policy*, 3: 21–30.

Creswell, J.W. (1994) *Research Design: Qualitative and Quantitative Approaches.* Thousand Oaks, CA: Sage.

Cullen, P. (1990) 'The turbulent boundary between water science and water management', *Freshwater Biology*, 24: 201–09.

———. (2004) 'Turning the tide: How does science change public policy', World Water Day Address, given at CSIRO Land and Water Seminar, held 22 March 2004, Adelaide, Australia.

Dodge, J., Ospina, S. and Foldy, E.G. (2005) 'Integrating rigor and relevance in public administration scholarship: The contribution of narrative inquiry', *PublicAdministration Review*, 65: 286–300.

d'Ombrain, N. (2004) 'Cabinet secrecy', *Canadian Public Administration–Administration Publique Du Canada*, 47: 332–59.

Eisenhardt, K.M. (1989) 'Building theories from case study research', *Academy of Management Review*, 14: 532–50.

Foote, L., Krogman, N. and Spence, J. (2009) 'Should academics advocate on environmental issues?', *Society and Natural Resources*, 22: 579–89.

Geczi, E. (2007) 'Sustainability and public participation: Toward an inclusive model of democracy', *Administrative Theory and Praxis*, 29: 375–93.

Gibbons, M. (1999) 'Science's new social contract with society', *Nature*, 402(suppl.), C81–84.

Gibbons, P., Zammit, C., Youngentob, K., Possingham, H.P. et al. (2008) 'Some practical suggestions for improving engagement between researchers and policy-makers in natural resource management', *Ecological Management and Restoration*, 9: 182–86.

Glaser, B.G. and Strauss, A.L. (1967) *The Discovery of Grounded Theory: Strategies for Qualitative Research.* Chicago: Aldine Pub. Co.

Government of Western Australia. (2003) Hope for the Future: The Western Australian State Sustainability Strategy. Perth, Australia: Government of Western Australia.

Grafty, E.A. (2008) 'Meeting the challenges of policy-relevant science: Bridging theory and practice', *Public Administration Review*, 69: 1087–96.

Graydon, S. (2011) 'Making a case for media engagement', *Academic Matters: The Journal of Higher Education*, May 2011. www.academicmatters.ca/2011/05/making-a-case-for-media-engagement/. Accessed 22 April 2013.

Groffman, P.M., Stylinski, C., Nisbet, M.C., Duarte, C.M. et al. (2010) 'Restarting the conversation: Challenges at the interface between ecology and society', *Frontiers in Ecology and the Environment*, 8(6): 284–91.

Hennessy, P. (1986) *Cabinet.* London: Fontana.

Hessels, L.K. and van Lente, H. (2008) 'Re-thinking new knowledge production: A literature review and a research agenda', *Research Policy*, 37: 740–60.

Hessels, L.K., van Lente, H. and Smits, R. (2009) 'In search of relevance: The changing contract between science and society', *Science and Public Policy*, 36: 387–401.

Hickey, G.M., Forest, P., Sandall, J.L., Lalor, B.M. and Keenan, R.J. (2013) 'Managing the environmental science–policy nexus in government: Perspectives from public servants in Canada and Australia', *Science and Public Policy*, 40: 529–43.

Holland, B.A. (1999) 'Factors and strategies that influence faculty involvement in public service', *Journal of Public Service and Outreach*, 4: 37–43.

Hoppe, R. (2011) 'Institutional constraints and practical problems in deliberative and participatory policy making', *Policy and Politics*, 39: 163–86.

Industry Canada. (2007) A Framework for Science and Technology Advice: Principles and Guidelines for the Effective Use of Science and Technology Advice in Government Decision Making. Ottawa: Industry Canada.

Juntti, M., Russel, D. and Turnpenny, J. (2009) 'Evidence, politics and power in public policy for the environment', *Environmental Science and Policy*, 12: 207–15.

Klenk, N.L. and Hickey, G.M. (2011) 'Government science in forestry: Characteristics and policy utilization', *Forest Policy and Economics*, 13: 37–45.

———. (2012) 'Improving the social robustness of research networks for sustainable natural resource management: Results of a Delphi study in Canada', *Science and Public Policy*, 39: 357–72.

Kørnøv, L. and Thissen, W.A.H. (2000) 'Rationality in decision- and policy-making: Implications for strategic environmental assessment', *Impact Assessment and Project Appraisal*, 18: 191–200.

Latour, B. (1987) *Science in Action: How to Follow Scientists and Engineers Through Society*. Cambridge, MA: Harvard UP.

Loucks, L. (2007) 'Patterns of fisheries institutional failure and success: Experience from the Southern Gulf of St. Lawrence snow crab fishery, in Nova Scotia, Canada', *Marine Policy*, 31: 320–26.

Lubchenco, J. (1998) 'Entering the century of the environment: A new social contract for science', *Science*, 279: 491–97.

MacLeod, C.J.A., Scholefield, D. and Haygarth, P.M. (2007) 'Integration for sustainable catchment management', *Science for the Total Environment*, 373: 591–602.

McDiarmid, M. (2012) 'Budget cuts claim famed freshwater research facility', *CBC News*, 17 May 2012. www.cbc.ca/news/canada/story/2012/05/17/pol-experimental-lakes-budget-cuts.html. Accessed 23 April 2013.

Maibach, E.W., Roser-Renouf, C. and Leiserowitz, A. (2008) 'Communication and marketing as climate change intervention assets: A public health perspective', *American Journal of Preventive Medicine*, 35: 488–500.

Manning, P. (2007) 'Just how did we let this happen? We need to take science and science policy far more seriously', *Globe and Mail*, Monday, 17 December 2007.

www.theglobeandmail.com/commentary/justhow-did-we-let-this-happen/article726788/. Accessed 23 April 2013.

Marshall, C. and Rossman, G.B. (1989) *Designing Qualitative Research*. Newbury Park, CA: Sage.

McNaughton, N. (1999) *The Prime Minister and Cabinet Government*. London: Hodder and Stoughton.

McNie, E.C. (2007) 'Reconciling the supply of scientific information with user demands: An analysis of the problem and review of the literature', *Environmental Science and Policy*, 10: 17–38.

Mercer, D., Christesen, L. and Buxton, M. (2007) 'Squandering the future—Climate change, policy failure and the water crisis in Australia', *Futures*, 39: 272–87.

Miller, C. (2001) 'Hybrid management: Boundary organizations, science policy, and environmental governance in the climate 50 regime', *Science, Technology and Human Values*, 26: 478–500.

Nature. (2012) 'Editorial: The great beyond', *Nature*, 483/7387: 5–6.

Nelson, M.P. and Vucetich, J.A. (2009) 'On advocacy by environmental scientists: What, whether, why, and how', *Conservation Biology*, 23: 1090–1101.

Nevill, J. (2007) 'Policy failure: Australian freshwater protected area networks', *Australasian Journal of Environmental Management*, 14: 35–47.

Newig, J. and Fritsch, O. (2009) 'Environmental governance: Participatory, multi-level—and effective?', *Environmental Policy and Governance*, 19: 197–214.

O'Hara, K. (2010) 'Canada must free scientists to talk to journalists', *Nature*, 467: 501.

Oreskes, N. (2004) 'Science and public policy: What's proof got to do with it?', *Environmental Science and Policy*, 7: 369–83.

Osterloh, M. and Frey, B.S. (2009) 'Are more and better indicators the solution?', *Scandinavian Journal of Management*, 25/2: 225–27.

Pace, M.L., Hampton, S.E., Limburg, K.E., Bennett, E.M. et al. (2010) 'Communicating with the public: Opportunities and rewards for individual ecologists', *Frontiers in Ecology and the Environment*, 8: 292–98.

Palmer, G. and Palmer, M. (2004) 'The Prime Minister, Cabinet and Ministerial responsibility', *Bridled Power: New Zealand's Constitution and Government*, pp. 68–94. Melbourne, Australia: OUP.

Parkins, J.R. and Mitchell, R.E. (2005) 'Public participation as public debate: A deliberative turn in natural resource management', *Society and Natural Resources: An International Journal*, 18: 529–40.

Parsons, W. (2001) 'Scientists and politicians: The need to communicate', *Public Understanding of Science*, 10: 303–14.

Patapan, H. and Wanna, J. (2005) 'The Westminster legacy: Conclusion'. In: Patapan, H., Wanna, J. and Weller, P. (eds.) *Westminster Legacies: Democracy and Responsible Government in Asia and the Pacific*, pp. 242–55. Sydney, Australia: U of New South Wales P.

Pielke, R.A., Jr. (2004) 'When scientists politicize science: Making sense of controversy over The Skeptical Environmentalist', *Environmental Science & Policy*, 7/5: 405–17.

———. (2007) *The Honest Broker: Making Sense of Science in Policy and Politics.* Cambridge, UK: CUP.

Pohl, C. (2008) 'From science to policy through transdisciplinary research', *Environmental Science and Policy*, 11: 46–53.

Rhodes, R.A.W. and Weller, P. (2005) 'Westminster Transplanted and Westminster Implanted: Exploring Political Change'. In: Patapan, H., Wanna, J. and Weller, P. (eds.) *Westminster Legacies: Democracy and Responsible Government in Asia and the Pacific*, pp. 1–12. Sydney, Australia: U of New South Wales P.

Rice, J.C. (2011) 'Advocacy science and fisheries decision-making', ICES Journal of Marine Science: *Journal du Conseil*, 68: 2007–12.

Ryder, D.S., Tomlinson, M., Gawne, B. and Likens, G.E. (2010) 'Defining and using "best available science": A policy conundrum for the management of aquatic ecosystems', *Marine and Freshwater Research*, 61: 821–28.

Sarewitz, D. (2004) 'How science makes environmental controversies worse', *Environmental Science and Policy*, 7: 385–403.

Sarewitz, D. and Pielke, R. A. (2007) 'The neglected heart of science policy: Reconciling supply of and demand for science', *Environmental Science and Policy*, 10: 5–16.

Schenkel, R. (2010) 'The challenge of feeding scientific advice into policy-making', *Science*, 330: 1749–51.

Scott, A. (2007) 'Peer review and the relevance of science', *Futures*, 39: 827–45.

Scott, J.M. and Rachlow, J.L. (2011) 'Refocusing the debate about advocacy', *Conservation Biology*, 25: 1–3.

Sousa, C.A.A. and Hendriks, P.H.J. (2008) 'Connecting knowledge to management: The case of academic research', *Organization*, 15: 811–30.

Stack, M. (2011) 'Journalists and academics as public educators', *Academic Matters: The Journal of Higher Education*, May 2011.

Steel, B., List, P., Lach, D. and Shindlet, B. (2004) 'The role of scientists in the environmental policy process: A case study from the American west', *Environmental Science and Policy*, 7: 1–13.

Stevenson, T. (2007) 'Rethinking Oz: More than policy, the underlying mindset', *Futures*, 39: 200–14.

Stewart, J. (2004) 'Meaning of strategy in the public sector', *Australian Journal of Public Administration*, 63/4: 16–21.

Strauss, A.L. and Corbin, J.M. (1997) *Grounded Theory in Practice.* Thousand Oaks, CA: Sage.

Thompson, A.M., Salawitch, R.J., Hoff, R.M., Logan, J.A. and Einaudi, F. (2012) 'Environment Canada cuts threaten the future of science and international agreements', *Eos Transactions American Geophysical Union*, 93/7: 69.

United Nations Conference on Environment and Development. (1992) 'Agenda 21: Programme of Action for Sustainable Development', *United Nations Conference on Environment and Development*, held 3–14 June 1992, Rio de Janeiro, Brazil.

Valentine, S.V. (2010) 'Canada's constitutional separation of (wind) power', *Energy Policy*, 38: 1918–30.

Weiss, C.H. (1998) 'Have we learned anything new about the use of evaluation?', *American Journal of Evaluation*, 19: 21–33.

Weller, P. (1999) 'Disentangling concepts of Ministerial responsibility', *Australian Journal of Public Administration*, 58/1: 62–64.

Wesselink, A., Paavola, J., Fritsch, O. and Renn, O. (2011) 'Rationales for public participation in environmental policy and governance: Practitioners' perspectives', *Environment and Planning A*, 43: 2688–2704.

Yin, R.K. (1994) *Case Study Research: Design and Methods*. Thousand Oaks, CA: Sage.

DISCUSSION QUESTIONS

1. In their Introduction, Lalor and Hickey refer to "Westminster-based systems of government" (p. 257) and provide a brief endnote to define the term. Record a point-form list of the distinguishing characteristics of this form of government and then write a sentence or two on why the decision-making processes of Westminster-based governments might have important implications for how policies are made.

2. This study undertakes a retrospective approach—in other words, Lalor and Hickey interviewed cabinet ministers and senior civil servants *after* they had left their position. Why do you think the researchers believed this was a better approach than interviewing policy-makers who were still active? What do Lalor and Hickey identify as the possible problems with their approach?

3. The term "contextualized knowledge" occurs so frequently in Lalor and Hickey's study that it could have been included in their list of keywords. What do they mean by the term? What kind of knowledge are they referring to and what kinds of "context" are most relevant to policy-makers?

4. Write a paragraph of about 200 words in which you summarize the two major patterns of response among policy-makers that the study found.

5. What changes did Lalor and Hickey's research subjects hope to see in how researchers represented and communicated their work? What changes did they hope to see in the public's involvement in environmental policy?

DEMOCRACY AND THE GLOBAL CITIZEN

INTRODUCTION

If you grew up in a democratic state, you may think of democracy as a straightforward political model—one that is inherently good. But what is democracy? Derived from the ancient Greek words for "people" and "rule," democracy is often defined as "rule of the people." There are considerable differences between ancient and modern forms of democracy, not to mention how democracy works in different situations, but most forms share the common goal of placing more power in the hands of the people and countering abuses of power. While democracy is far from perfect, most people in western societies would agree that it is preferable to, say, monarchy or dictatorship. As Winston Churchill is said to have quipped, "Democracy is the worst form of government except all those other forms that have been tried."[1]

When inspected closely, democracy becomes complicated. As Boris DeWiel observes in *Democracy: A History of Ideas*, "True democracy will always be an ethical mess."[2] Most modern democracies go well beyond the simple idea of rule by the people—however 'the people' is defined—to include constitutional protection of human rights, including freedom of speech, limits on discrimination, and the independence of the judiciary. As the *International Encyclopedia of the Social Sciences* puts it: "Democracy is a concept that means different things to different people. For some it is a political system that ensures political equality and self-rule. To others, it is a system that allows the presence of equal opportunities and rights."[3] The exact meaning of the term (not to mention its practice) has shifted over time and often the term is cited in ways that may seem contradictory.

The articles in this section share a sense that the complications of democracy are intensifying in the context of globalization. Dingwerth et al.'s and Westheimer's articles pay attention to the global context. Dingwerth et al. focus on the changing meanings of democracy in the context of international relations. Westheimer, who is interested in patriotism and democracy in education in the USA, distinguishes between authoritarian and democratic patriotism post-9/11. Loader et al.'s research focuses on Europe, while Ortuoste looks at the Asia-Pacific.

As these articles also reveal, the Internet and emerging social media are changing how democracy works and how it is understood. In part, this is because online interactions change how people behave and how they think about political issues. The effects of these interactions transcend national borders, inviting people to see themselves as global citizens—or at least as not limited by the borders that define their national citizenship. Ortuoste's article attends to the tension between the potentially liberating uses of social media and governments' efforts to control online interactions and information sharing. Similarly, Loader et al. examine the stakes of online democracy when it crosses borders, arguing that social media is changing how younger people engage with each other and politics. Kent is concerned that technological change poses significant challenges to public relations professionals, resulting in diminished civic participation. All three of these articles recognize that online communication and nascent global citizenship are impacting democracy.

As you read these articles, consider your own experiences of using social media (or other online resources) when politics is involved. Does the Internet offer to make society more democratic? Or is it leading to increased manipulation of the "people" and increased authoritarianism? How would you define the global citizen? Are you one?

Notes

[1] Larry Diamond and Marc F. Plattner, eds., *How People View Democracy* (Baltimore: Johns Hopkins UP, 2008), p. x.

[2] Boris DeWiel, *Democracy: A History of Ideas* (Vancouver, BC: UBC P, 2014), p. 14.

[3] "Democracy," in *International Encyclopedia of the Social Sciences*, vol. 2, ed. William A. Darity, Jr. (Detroit: Macmillan Reference USA, 2008), pp. 272–76.

A. "THE NETWORKED YOUNG CITIZEN: SOCIAL MEDIA, POLITICAL PARTICIPATION AND CIVIC ENGAGEMENT," BRIAN D. LOADER, ARIADNE VROMEN, AND MICHAEL A. XENOS

This article from Information, Communication & Society *explores the influence of social media on the participatory culture of networked young citizens. Brian D. Loader, Ariadne Vromen, and Michael A. Xenos* compare the traditional modes of civil engagement that older generations practice with those of younger people whose participation is increasingly found online. Loader et al. argue that "[t]he attitudes and political values of young people . . . are regarded as important agents of social and political change" (p. 288). As you read this article, consider how the authors support this statement, if you agree or disagree with them, and why.*

Introduction

The accusations that young people are politically apathetic and somehow failing in their duty to participate in many democratic societies worldwide have been refuted by a growing number of academics in recent years (Loader, 2007; Marsh, O'Toole, & Jones, 2007). Undoubtedly many young citizens have indeed become disenchanted with mainstream political parties and with those who claim to speak on their behalf. But this should not be misinterpreted as a lack of interest on the part of youth with the political issues that influence their everyday lived experience and their normative concerns for the planet and its inhabitants. As the recent waves of protest demonstrations by young people in all their different forms and contexts testify, the suggestion that the next generation of citizens is any less politically engaged than previous ones seems at least premature. How then are we to understand the actions and political values of the future custodians of our polities and what are their implications for democratic governance?

* Brian D. Loader is Director of the School of Social and Political Sciences at York University. His research interests are in new media technologies and their socio-political diffusion.

Ariadne Vromen is Professor of Political Sociology at the University of Sydney. Her research interests include political participation, digital politics, and young people and politics.

Michael A. Xenos is Communication Arts Partners Professor as well as the Chair of the Department of Communication Arts at the University of Wisconsin-Madison. His research interest is the effects of new media on political engagement.

There can be little doubt that the institutions and practices of modern representative government have been subject to growing disillusionment from young citizens. A reluctance to vote at elections, join political parties or have a high regard for their politicians all suggest that many young people are turning away from mainstream politics in many countries (Fieldhouse, Tranmer, & Russell, 2007; Van Biezen, Mair, & Poguntke, 2012). Instead, participation in social movements, rallies, protests, and consumer boycotts all point to the possible displacement of traditional models of representative democracy as the dominant cultural form of engagement by alternative approaches increasingly characterized through networking practices. The political identity and attitudes of young citizens are thereby seen to be increasingly shaped less by their social ties to family, neighbourhood, school or work, but rather by the manner in which they participate and interact through the social networks which they themselves have had a significant part in constructing. Central to this model of 'networked individualism' (Rainie & Wellman, 2012) is the role played by the Internet and network communication technologies. Of particular relevance, and the primary focus of this edited collection, is the potential of social media platforms such as Facebook, Twitter, and YouTube for influencing the political deportment and civic engagement of what we describe as the networked young citizen.

Assembling the Networked Young Citizen

The debate on citizenship is replete with discourses that exhort young people to adopt the dutiful practices of participation that correspond to the regulatory norms established by earlier generations. Thus, active citizens should vote at elections, respect their representatives, join political groups, and engage in voluntary activities in their civic communities. It is a model of the citizen as someone who should be *seen* to support the representative system through their dutiful actions but whose voice should not be heard. Indeed, the very future prospects for democracy are seen to depend upon the support of the electorate as performed and reproduced through these acts of citizenship. Small wonder then that the political class in many democracies is so concerned about the disaffection of so many young people with these norms of participation (Putnam, 2000; Stoker, 2006).

This emergent disjuncture between conventional representative government and the everyday concerns of young people was vividly captured in a television discussion between the forthright BBC interviewer Jeremy Paxman and the charismatic and opinionated celebrity actor and comic Russell Brand in the Autumn of 2013. Brand had been invited by *The New Statesman* political magazine to be a guest editor for one of its issues and so was asked to discuss his political views on the late-night current affairs programme *Newsnight*. While a sometimes-controversial figure, this was the first time that Brand had entered the world of 'celebrity politics' (Street, 2004). Often condescending in his style of interrogation, Paxman on this occasion appeared to be genuinely engaged by Brand's arguments. What seemed to surprise

Paxman in particular was Brand's admission that he had never voted and that he extolled young people to follow his example. In this excerpt, Brand justifies his view.

> I'm not voting out of apathy, I'm not voting out of absolute indifference, and weariness and exhaustion from the lies, treachery, deceit of the political class that has been going on for generations and which has reached fever pitch where we have a disenfranchised, disillusioned, despondent underclass that are not being represented by that political system, so voting for it is tacit complicity with that system. And that is not something I'm offering up.

In many respects through this intervention in print and on television Brand is following a familiar path taken by other popular celebrities entering the political sphere. As John Street has described it, 'celebrity politics is a code for the performance of representations through the gestures and media available to those who wish to claim "representativeness"' (Street, 2004, p. 445). Thus, despite the fact that Brand does not explicitly claim to speak on behalf of younger people, his accomplished use of the media to challenge the conventional perspectives of democratic engagement can be interpreted as just such an attempt to speak more legitimately than politicians for young citizens whose voice is seldom heard (Coleman, 2002). In this sense his performance, as seen on television and more widely through YouTube, can be regarded as an act intended to disrupt the normative repetitive depictions of the dutiful citizen. Instead, when asked by Paxman to give an alternative to a model of democracy as voting, he replied with a response which foregrounds an emerging contemporary political aesthetic through which young citizens can engage.

> The time is now, change is occurring, we are at a time when communication is instantaneous and there are communities all over the world. The Occupy movement made a difference, even if only that it introduced to the popular public lexicon the idea of the 1% versus the 99%. People for the first time in a generation are aware of massive corporate and economic exploitation. These things are not nonsense and these are subjects which are not being addressed...Until they are taken seriously...why would I encourage a constituency of young people who are indifferent to vote?

The 'representativeness' of Brand is here expressed as an attempt to claim that the political class is failing to address some of the most important challenges confronting young citizens. Instead, alternative communication channels and modes of action, such as those enacted during the Arab Spring or Occupy movement, express the voice of young citizens around the world.

While less dramatic or entertaining than Brand's narrative, a groundswell of academic opinion has also suggested that the political attitudes of many young

people in many parts of the world can increasingly be characterized by a less defer-
ential and more individualized (Beck, 1992; Giddens, 1991; Inglehart, 1990), self-
actualizing (Bennett, Wells, & Rank, 2009), and critical disposition (Norris, 2002)
which marks a departure from the dutiful norms of citizenship (Dalton, 2008).
Such cultural changes to political participation are shaped of course by wider economic and social forces and they do not happen overnight. Moreover, the decline in
mainstream engagement has been ongoing for some time in many countries (Norris,
2002). Instead of regarding them as the death knell of western models of democracy
however, it may be more useful to see them as potentially heralding a recalibration
of modern political institutions and practices in ways that are more sensitive to the
dissatisfaction felt by many young people with their political systems. Young citizens
may as a consequence be finding new ways to voice their opinions and garnering new
agents of representativeness such Russell Brand to envision their views.

What then does our emerging networked young citizen look like? How can we
recognize these actors? Drawing from the literature (Bang, 2004; Beck, 1994; Bennett, Wells, & Freelon, 2011; Giddens, 1991), it is helpful to take a number of key
features to assemble what we call the *networked young citizen*. Networking young
citizens are far less likely to become members of political or civic organizations such
as parties or trade unions; they are more likely to participate in horizontal or non-
hierarchical networks; they are more project orientated; they reflexively engage in
lifestyle politics; they are not dutiful but self-actualizing; their historical reference
points are less likely to be those of modern welfare capitalism but rather global
information networked capitalism and their social relations are increasingly enacted
through a social media networked environment.

This is of course an ideal type construction and is not intended to represent all
young citizens in every respect. Its value is as a framework against which we may
assess the normative political dispositions of young people. So the networked young
citizen is not necessarily typical of all young people in every society. Our objective is
not to provide yet another generalization about all young people being characterized
as a type. Rather, we believe that it is a useful analytical device by which to assess
the evidence for cultural change. Some further clarifications need to be made to our
assemblage. First, this does not represent an all-encompassing discontinuity with
previous dutiful models. Networked young citizens may live conterminously with
other dutiful citizens and indeed share some of each other's attributes on occasion.
Second, networked citizenship can be seen as fluid and always under construction
within regulatory norms and structuring processes. A model of citizenship that is
fluid and constituent of lived experience does not suggest apathy but rather an identity whose realization has to be performed and enacted. Part of that performance
may surely include disrupting dominant discourses and repeated citations resonant
of dutiful models of citizenship (Loader, 2012). Third, networking young citizens
are shaped by different individual lived experiences that will not be the same for

everyone. Consequently, issues of inequality and power come into play. Networks and networking do not imply a power vacuum where all are equal. Instead, the benefits accrued by access to social and cultural capital through particular networks foreground the need to differentiate between social networks. Networks exhibit new regulatory norms of exclusion as well as inclusion. It also requires us to consider what kinds of capacities are required by young people for effective networked citizenship.

Are All Young Citizens Networked Equally?

The competitive advantages to be accrued through membership of the most resource-rich networks have become particularly pronounced as a consequence of the world financial crisis since 2007. While young people as a whole have been disproportionately hit harder by these events compared with other age groups, the burdens have not been evenly distributed across all young people. Educational and employment opportunities for young people have been significantly influenced by social and cultural factors such as class, ethnicity, gender, sexuality, and location.

Consequently, the economic recession has both compounded the alienation of many young citizens and threatens to produce further personal insecurity for millions of individuals as they join the ranks of the emerging *precariat* (Standing, 2011).

In Europe, for example, it is estimated that 94 million young people (15–29) face an uncertain future in the labour market and risk becoming politically and socially marginalized. A danger therefore exists of a growing mass of disenchanted young people subject to unemployment, insecure job prospects, and without voice or representation in the public domain. In August 2013, approximately one quarter of young European citizens were unemployed (Eurostat). A more accurate indicator providing figures for those 'not in employment, education or training' (NEETs) is still alarmingly high, with 14 million aged 15–29 recorded in 2011. This situation is not uniform across Member States, with NEET figures being significantly higher in the East (e.g., Romania, Bulgaria) and South (e.g., Portugal, Spain, Greece) compared with those in the North (e.g., Germany, the Netherlands, the UK, Nordic countries). In the United States, the figure for those out of work or education was almost 16% of 18–29-year-olds in October 2013. The transition from youth to adulthood in the twenty-first century is therefore beset by growing social inequality, structural unemployment, and a disaffection with politics which, when combined, are shaping the opportunities for social inclusion and security of many young citizens.

How then does the networked young citizen relate to this picture of global social and economic inequality? Recent developments suggest a strong relationship between social media use and political engagement that raises questions about the potential for social media to help stem or even reverse patterns of political inequality that have troubled scholars for years. Michael Xenos, Ariadne Vromen, and Brian D. Loader explore this contention in the second article of this special issue of *iCS* [not included here], where they articulate a model of social media and political engagement among young people, and test it using data from representative samples of young citizens in Australia, the United States, and the UK. Their results suggest a strong, positive relationship between social media use and political engagement among young people across all three countries, and provide additional insights into the role played by social media use in the processes by which young people become politically engaged. Notably, the results also provide reasons to be cautiously optimistic concerning the overall influence of this popular new form of social networking on longstanding patterns of political inequality.

For some time, a number of academics have believed that the interactive, collaborative and user-generated content capacities of social media technologies themselves offer the prospect of facilitating new modes of political communication which are more commensurate with those contemporary youth cultures associated with the networked young citizen. They point to an electoral affinity between what are perceived as the inherent democratic features of social media and their potential for enhancing the participative and deliberative skills of young citizens (Benkler, 2006; Jenkins, 2006; Leadbeater, 2008). This notion of *participatory culture* has quickly managed to gain a strong foothold in contemporary debates about social media and user engagement. The concept's primary advocate, Henry Jenkins, uses it to describe a cultural situation in which established relations between media producers and users have been disrupted to the point at which '... we might now see them as participants who interact with each other...' (Jenkins, 2006, p. 3). Hence, studies of, for instance, Facebook, blogging, and YouTube have looked into what participatory practices these environments offer and are capable of fostering. Overall, these studies have often looked for, and found, engaged online users and inspiring participatory practices—especially among young people.

But what is the impact of engagement, and participation, within participatory cultures of social media on the public orientation of young people? On this connection, the existing literature is rather unclear. The third article in this special issue [not included here], written by Mats Ekström, Tobias Olsson, and Adam Shehata, addresses this question by drawing upon longitudinal survey data from a sample of Swedish 13-to-18-year-olds. The concept of public orientation is measured by three indicators: young people's values, interests, and everyday peer talk. These indicators are analysed with reference to respondents' Internet orientations, which are conceptualized as four separate but interrelated spaces (a news space, a space for social interaction, a game space, and a creative space). The results primarily emphasize the importance of orientations towards news space and space for social interaction. Overall, the findings strongly suggest that orientations towards these spaces are related to adolescents' public orientation. The findings confirm the centrality of news and information in political socialization, but they also challenge the idea that social media platforms—such as Facebook, Twitter, and blogging—enable forms of social interaction and creative production that have an overall positive impact on young people's public orientation.

Transitions from Childhood to Adulthood

As one might expect from a period when dutiful conceptions of citizenship were de rigueur, scholars exploring how young people were socialized into their political attitudes regarded the role of parents as paramount. Values and political orientations were seen as transmitted from parent to child in a linear learning mode. The networking young citizen model, constituent of self-actualizing, reflexive, and interactive attributes, would suggest, however, a more complex and critical learning path in which the young person plays a more co-constructive role. In our next article [not included here], Emily Vraga, Leticia Bode, Jung Hwan Yang, Stephanie Edgerly, Kjerstin Thorson, Chris Wells, and Dhavan V. Shah draw upon contemporary theories of political socialization which move away from traditional transmission perspectives to consider the diverse ways in which parents and children can develop discrete political orientations. In their study during a competitive US presidential campaign, they examine various pathways through which influence occurs across generations in terms of partisanship and candidate evaluations. Their results suggest that while harmonious attitudes remain the norm, there are substantial opportunities for young citizens to demonstrate their independence, particularly when gaining different perspectives from schools and social media sources. Their findings are an important contribution to our understanding of how young networking citizens and their parents come to understand politics and the factors that shape youth socialization. Of particular influence in this new socialization perspective is the role played by social media as a means of facilitating mutual understanding between parents and young people.

How then do these social networking environments influence political talk and understanding among young citizens? Do they make it easier for young citizens to chat about the public issues which affect their lived experience? Are they more likely to share political opinions and views? Kjerstin Thorson in her contribution to this special issue [not included here] provides a microanalysis of political talk and interaction by young citizens networking on Facebook. Her investigation leads her to propose that participatory culture is shaped through social networking sites by social ambiguities that can actually increase the risk and uncertainties associated with talking politics rather than reducing them. She reports on two sets of in-depth interviews conducted to explore the ways that uncertainties about audience reception of posts on Facebook inspire strategies for 'inventing' modes of political interaction on the one hand, and, for others, to suppress opinion expression by creating the sense that talking politics on the site is a high-risk endeavour.

Alternative Networking Young Citizens?

The final article in this special issue turns to the alternative forms of political engagement as expressions of emerging political norms characteristic of the networked young citizen. James Sloam examines the role that social media has played in the development of protest movements across the continent of Europe. Networking young citizens have mobilized through mass demonstrations, such as the *indignados*, outraged against political corruption and unemployment in Spain, and the Occupy movement voicing its anger against what they see as the social inequality arising from global capitalism. Rejecting traditional political elites and organizations they have also been involved in the development of new political parties such as the German Pirate Party and the Italian Five-Star Movement. As commentators have observed, a defining characteristic of these developments has been the manner in which young people have used networks to spread and share their protests across continents and national borders (Bennett & Segerberg, 2012). Sloam seeks to demonstrate how 'digitally networked action' has enabled a 'quickening' of youth participation—an intensification of political participation among young, highly educated citizens in search of a mouthpiece for their 'indignation.'

Concluding Remarks

The engagement of each new generation of young people with the practices and institutions of democratic governance in a society is an essential means by which such a political system retains its legitimacy. Without their consent and commitment, the authority of politicians and policy-makers to represent the values and interests of future citizens is called into question. The attitudes and political values of young people are therefore often seen as foretelling the future and are regarded as important agents of social and political change. Increasingly shaped by wider forces of globalization, the digital revolution, and reflexive individualism, the concept of the networked young citizen may become a compelling one that is gaining currency through empirical investigation. It suggests an emerging generational cohort that is more sceptical of politicians and mainstream conventional political institutions. But it also raises the possibility of the networking young citizen playing a more significant role in reconfiguring our democratic practices.

Opponents of such an approach will no doubt both reject the notion of emerging political norms associated with the networked young citizen and contend that any move away from the dutiful or active citizen model will undermine liberal representative democracy. Fearful of the 'personalization' of politics as a means to undermine serious rational deliberation and even encourage populist rhetoric of the sort expressed by Russell Brand, such critics can only see these developments as evidence for the trivialization of democracy. Yet in the face of growing evidence to the contrary, these commentators seem bereft of ideas to address the growing estrangement between young citizens and mainstream political parties, politicians, and electoral engagement. The scepticism expressed by young people towards those who represent them rather than being taken as a measure of apathy could instead be seen as a perfectly legitimate democratic attitude of reflexively engaged citizens conscious of their personal circumstances.

Here the distinction between scepticism and cynicism is crucial. The former positive democratic attitude derived from a more informed population and with critical sensibilities can act to strengthen participatory models of democracy previously considered impractical due to the perceived poor quality of the electorate (Schumpeter, 1943). Through effective networking, young citizens have demonstrated a capacity to increasingly hold representatives to account and critically monitor their policies and actions. Social media combined with other networking opportunities enables the networked young citizen to reflexively consider a wider range of political discourses and share these with friends or engage in connective repertoires of political action (Bennett & Segerberg, 2012). Such processes of re-configuration do not require representative systems to disappear, but they do demand that our democratic systems need to be more culturally receptive to the lived experiences of those they serve. Coleman (2013) provides an excellent exploration of just how a central democratic act such as voting, when seen as a cultural activity, raises essential questions about its relevance to the emotional experience of those citizens expected to participate. It is an intellectual approach that is both compatible with Russell Brand's clarion call and pragmatic in its desire to reconnect voting with the electorate's everyday concerns and changing norms.

But it is also important that such reconfigurations do not disguise differential capabilities and relations of power that are also a constituent feature of networking. As Bourdieu (1984) reminds us, access to social and cultural capital is often used to ensure unequal social distinctions between citizens. In the context of growing social inequality, social networking may thus reinforce divisions that are detrimental to democracy (Schlozman, Verba, & Brady, 2012). While the present academic debate continues to be divided between those who maintain an adherence to dutiful citizenship, the contributions to this special issue have all been prepared to recognize that new forms of networked young citizenship, more compatible for the times and contemporary youth culture, may be more fruitful for both understanding contemporary developments and also for future democratic governance.

References

Bang, H.P. (2004). Culture governance: Governing self-reflexive modernity. Public Administration, 82(1), 157–90. doi:10.1111/j.0033-3298.2004.00389.x.

Beck, U. (1992). Risk society: Towards a new modernity. London: Sage.

Beck, U. (1994). The reinvention of politics: Towards a theory of reflexive modernization. In U. Beck, A. Giddens, & S. Lash (Eds.), Reflexive modernization: Politics, tradition and aesthetics in modern social order (pp. 1–55). Redwood City, CA: Stanford UP.

Benkler, Y. (2006). The wealth of networks: How social production transforms markets and freedom. New Haven: Yale UP.

Bennett, W.L., & Segerberg, A. (2012). The logic of connective action. Information, Communication & Society, 15(5), 739–68. doi:10.1080/1369118X.2012.670661.

Bennett, W.L., Wells, C., & Freelon, D. (2011). Communicating civic engagement: Contrasting models of citizenship in the youth web sphere. Journal of Communication, 61(5), 835–56. doi:10.1111/j.1460-2466.2011.01588.x.

Bennett, W.L., Wells, C., & Rank, A. (2009). Young citizens and civic learning: Two paradigms of citizenship in the digital age. Citizenship Studies, 13(2), 105–20. doi:10.1080/13621020902731116. Downloaded by [The University of British Columbia] at 09:39, 20 June 2016.

Bourdieu, P. (1984). Distinction: A social critique of the judgement of taste. London: Routledge & Kegan Paul.

Coleman, S. (2002). The people's voice. In J. Bartle (Ed.), Political communication (pp. 246–58). London: Frank Cass.

Coleman, S. (2013). How voters feel. Cambridge: Cambridge University Press.

Dalton, R.J. (2008). Citizenship norms and the expansion of political participation. Political Studies, 56(1), 76–98. Retrieved from http://doi.wiley.com/10.1111/j.1467-9248.2007.00718.x.

Fieldhouse, E., Tranmer, M., & Russell, A. (2007). Something about young people or something about elections? Electoral participation of young people in Europe: Evidence from a multilevel analysis of the European Social Survey. European Journal of Political Research, 46(6), 797–822. doi:10.1111/j.1475-6765.2007.00713.x.

Giddens, A. (1991). Modernity and self-identity. Cambridge: Polity.

Inglehart, R. (1990). Culture shift in advanced industrial society. Princeton, NJ: Princeton UP.

Jenkins, H. (2006). Convergence culture: Where old and new media collide. New York, NY: New York UP.

Leadbeater, C. (2008). We-Think: Mass innovation, not mass production. London: Profile Books.

Loader, B.D. (2007). Young citizens in the digital age: Political engagement, young people and new media. London: Routledge.

Loader, B.D. (2012). Digital democracy: Towards user-generated politics? In B. Isakhan S. Stockwell (Eds.), The Edinburgh companion to the history of democracy (pp. 479–90). Edinburgh: Edinburgh UP.

Marsh, D., O'Toole, T., & Jones, S. (2007). Young people and politics in the UK. Basingstoke: Palgrave.

Norris, P. (2002). Democratic phoenix: Reinventing democratic activism. Cambridge: Cambridge UP.

Putnam, R. (2000). Bowling alone: The collapse and revival of American community. New York, NY: Simon & Schuster.

Rainie, L., & Wellman, B. (2012). Networked: The new social operating system. Cambridge: MIT P.

Schlozman, K.L., Verba, S., & Brady, H.E. (2012). The unheavenly chorus: Unequal political voice and the broken promise of American democracy. Princeton, NJ: Princeton UP.

Schumpter, J.A. (1943). Capitalism, socialism and democracy. London: Routledge.

Standing, G. (2011). The precariat: The new dangerous class. London: Bloomsbury.

Stoker, G. (2006). Why politics matters: Making democracy work. Basingstoke: Palgrave.

Street, J. (2004). Celebrity politicians: Popular culture and political representation. The British Journal of Politics & International Relations, 6(4), 435–52. Retrieved from http://onlinelibrary.wiley.com/doi/10.1111/j.1467-856X.2004.00149.x/full.

Van Biezen, I., Mair, P., & Poguntke, T. (2012). Going, going,…gone? The decline of party membership in contemporary Europe. European Journal of Political Research, 51(1), 24–56. doi:10.1111/j.1475-6765.2011.01995.x.

DISCUSSION QUESTIONS

1. Loader et al. discuss "the potential of social media platforms such as Facebook, Twitter, and YouTube for influencing the political deportment and civic engagement of what we describe as the networked young citizen" (p. 282). Create a summary of the article that focuses on what you perceive to be the most significant points in establishing this argument.

2. The article examines how the "historical reference points" for networked young citizens "are less likely to be those of modern welfare capitalism" and more likely to be "global information networked capitalism" (p. 284). Define both 'modern welfare capitalism' and 'global information networked capitalism,' and come up with examples for both. Do young citizens relate more to the latter form of capitalism?

3. On YouTube, watch one of Russell Brand's political videos (www.youtube.com/russellbrand). Do you agree that his "performance…can be regarded as an act intended to disrupt the normative repetitive depictions of the dutiful citizen" (p. 283)? Be prepared to explain his main points in the video you chose and how they affected your pre-existing views on the subject.

4. Loader et al. suggest that the "emerging generational cohort that is more sceptical of politicians and mainstream conventional political institutions" may end up "playing a more significant role in reconfiguring our democratic practices" (p. 288). Identify a few real-world examples that indicate that this may already be happening.

5. The article notes that there are those who "contend that any move away from the dutiful or active citizen model will undermine liberal representative democracy" (p. 288). What is the dutiful or active citizen model and what are the main differences between it and the new methods employed by the networked young citizens, as described in the article? Come up with some reasons in support of both methods of participation. Do you think one or the other is inherently better, or would you advocate for some combination of the two?

B. "DEMOCRACY IS DEMOCRACY IS DEMOCRACY? CHANGES IN EVALUATIONS OF INTERNATIONAL INSTITUTIONS IN ACADEMIC TEXTBOOKS, 1970–2010,"[1] KLAUS DINGWERTH, INA LEHMANN, ELLEN REICHEL, AND TOBIAS WEISE

Published in 2015 in International Studies Perspectives, *this article is an example of research in political science. Klaus Dingwerth et al.* inspect the way "democracy" is discussed in a wide range of textbooks in the area of international relations (IR) over a period of forty years. In this sense, they engage in a longitudinal rhetorical analysis that is similar to Lindner's analysis of advertisements in section 1. While they find that the explicit mention of democracy doesn't increase over the period, they also find several significant shifts in how it is discussed, including more attention to "participation, transparency, and accountability," which "shows that democratic norms are becoming more encompassing" (p. 305). As you read this article, keep in mind how you already think about democracy. What has shaped your sense of democracy?*

Glosssary terms: international relations, longitudinal study, rhetorical analysis

Abstract

This article examines what *democracy* means when it is used in academic textbook evaluations of international institutions and how the meaning of the term "democracy" in such evaluations has changed over time. An analysis of 71 textbooks on international institutions in the policy areas of international security, environmental, and human rights politics leads us to several answers. We observe slight changes in relation to three aspects. First, the range of democracy-relevant actors expands

---

* Klaus Dingwerth is Assistant Professor in Political Theory of Global Governance at the University St. Gallen, Switzerland, and a research fellow with the Global Public Policy Institute. His research interests, described by the GPPI, "include international organizations, global environmental politics, transnational governance, international ethics, global democracy, norms in world politics and organizational studies."

Ina Lehmann is a Senior Researcher at the Sustainable Research Centre at the University of Bremen, Germany. Her research focuses on sustainable development and environmental governance.

Ellen Reichel works with UNICEF Bremen; she is a PhD student in International Relations at the University of Bremen.

Tobias Weise is a PhD student in International Relations at the University of Bremen.

over time, most notably in relation to nonstate actors as important participants in (or even subjects of) international policymaking. Second, representational concerns become more relevant in justifying demands for greater participation in international institutions. Third, international organizations are increasingly discussed not only as subjects that enhance the transparency and accountability of the policies of their member states, but also as the objects of democratic demands for transparency and accountability themselves.

Keywords: international institutions, norms, democracy, International Relations textbooks, teaching

Academic and political discourses are replete with references to fundamental change in international politics. A common narrative holds that, in response to economic globalization, states and nonstate actors have created powerful international institutions, which increasingly face demands for their democratization. From a normative point of view, many authors have argued that in the context of their enhanced authority, international institutions do not only have to fulfill their specific functions, but they need to do so in a—broadly speaking—democratic manner (Holden 2000; Anderson 2002; Zweifel 2005; Bexell, Tallberg, and Uhlin 2010). Empirically, the argument is that a variety of audiences have factually come to evaluate international institutions in the language of democracy (Zürn 2004). Their demands have been expressed, for instance, in anti-globalization protests against an undemocratic World Trade Organization or in the commitments of individual international institutions—partially in response to public demands—to become more participatory, more transparent, and more accountable (Grigorescu 2007; Tallberg, Sommerer, Squatrito, and Jönsson 2013).

In addition to such evidence for an increasing sensitivity by academics and political actors for issues of global democracy per se, some studies have also recently observed changes in political actors' understanding of democracy and key democratic values. For example, Reimann (2006) shows how, from the early 1990s onwards, the UN has steadily pointed to the democratic potential of partnerships with NGOs instead of being limited to a "one-state-one-vote" understanding of democracy. Similarly, Thérien and Dumontier (2009) find that in recent years the UN has increasingly defended a bottom-up vision of democracy that builds on the participation of private actors. In another study, Mert (2009) shows how the meaning of participation has changed from a more democratic to a more implementation-oriented understanding in Type II partnerships initiated by the 2002 World Summit on Sustainable Development.

Despite the fact that academic debates and publications seem to be more sensitive to the move toward democratic norms in evaluating international institutions than to potential changes in the meaning of (global) democracy, our argument in this article is that this seems to be reversed in conventional academic textbooks over the past four decades. While International Relations (IR) textbooks generally pay only negligible attention to democratic norms, insofar as they do at all, we can observe various changes with regard to the specific democratic norms they put forward and how they interpret these norms. Thus, our study provides two interesting results: First, in contrast to what one may have expected, textbook references to democracy do not become much more frequent over the course of the past four decades. Second, while the amount of references to democracy remains largely constant, the content of democratic norms shifts over time. When contemporary textbooks refer to democracy, they refer to it in a more diverse way than older textbooks referencing the same term.

We substantiate our claims by an examination of how the meaning of democracy has changed in 71 academic textbooks on international institutions in the areas of international security, environmental, and human rights politics from 1970 to 2010. Our study primarily tells us something about how academic thinking about the democratic legitimacy of international institutions has evolved.[2] However, by doing so, its results are relevant not only for our understanding of the discipline but also provide one avenue to getting a sense of how the mind-sets of decision-makers and public officials have changed. Textbook authors often do not only seek to give a balanced account of the state of the art (Kille 2003:426)—and possibly also the *zeitgeist*—at the time of their writing. They are also producers of such states of art. "Their texts determine how the field is defined for those who are just beginning to learn about it" (Anonymous 2003:421). Indeed, scholars have variously observed that their teaching has fundamental impacts on the perspectives adopted by their students, who, in the case of political science students, are often future decision-makers in various settings (Eriksson and Sundelius 2005:63–65). In the words of former Harvard faculty member and US Secretary of State Henry Kissinger, "the convictions that leaders have formed before reaching high office are the intellectual capital that they will consume as long as they continue in office" (quoted in Eriksson and Sundelius 2005:65). In a quantitative study, Pamela Martin and colleagues show more systematically how political science courses—though not fundamentally challenging students' general attitudes—do contribute to changing political attitudes on single issues (Martin, Tankersley, and Ye 2012:209–12). Textbooks are thus critical in shaping future knowledge and practice since they—and the value judgments they report or espouse—are part of the intellectual capital that is transmitted to the next generations of scholars and decision-makers.

Given that textbook authors should thus carefully consider what information they present and how they present it, it is astonishing how little we know about the values transmitted in IR textbooks. Those few studies that provide a systematic overview of trends in IR teaching are generally concerned with the topics, regions, theories, and methodologies being taught. Yet they pay only marginal attention to norms and values featured in the classroom (on IR teaching in general, see Jordan, Maliniak, Oakes, Peterson, and Tierney 2009; Peterson, Tierney, and Maliniak 2005; on IR textbooks in particular, see Kille 2003; Smith 2003). Thus, a central contribution of our study is to make scholars aware of how the normative side of what we teach is subject to change. We exemplify this with the help of one particular norm, namely democracy.

The outcomes of our study are that, first, a democratic yardstick is far from a dominant theme in textbook evaluations of international institutions. Second, how textbook authors understand democratic principles changes over time. Most notably, we observe an expansion of the range of legitimacy-relevant actors, a rise in representational concerns that complement functionalist justifications for participation in international institutions, and a growing relevance of international organizations as the objects of transparency and accountability demands. Third, we also find some evidence that evaluations referring to democracy vary across issue areas. They are more relevant in textbooks on international environmental politics than in textbooks on the politics of international human rights and security.

After a brief discussion of our theoretical and methodological approach, we turn to analyzing how democratic norms are referred to in different policy areas and how their meaning changes over time. This empirical analysis unfolds in three steps: We first take a closer look at all those statements in which textbook evaluations of international institutions refer either to democracy itself, or second, to particular democratic values, namely participation, and third, transparency and accountability.

Theory and Methods

At its very heart, our investigation of the use of democratic norms is concerned with the standards by which international institutions are considered legitimate. We broadly adopt Weber's (1978) notion of legitimacy as the belief in the "rightfulness" of political rule. According to this understanding, an international institution enjoys legitimacy to the extent that it is supported by a "generalized perception or assumption" among relevant communities that, in relation to the system of rule to which it belongs, the organization and its activities are "desirable, proper, or appropriate within some socially constructed system of norms, values, beliefs, and definitions" (Suchman 1995:574).

Whereas legitimacy as the belief in the rightfulness of rule is thus first of all a property ascribed to an institution, it can be employed in processes of legitimation through which actors exchange claims and counter-claims on what makes an institution desirable and whether or not it appears as legitimate. In these processes, different actors will try to argumentatively put forward their own notion of legitimacy and thereby push and pull the institutional design and actions of international institutions in one direction or another (Krebs and Jackson 2007). Our guiding questions, then, are these: For which reasons do international institutions come to be seen as acting rightfully? What are the main beliefs that textbooks transmit to those who will be either observers or participants in the process of de/legitimating international institutions—the latter either as contesters of institutions' legitimacy or as staff being responsible for the good conduct of the respective institution? This is where social norms come into play. In our conception, we follow Katzenstein's (1996:5) definition of norms as "collective expectations of proper behavior for actors with a given identity." To put it simply, we conceive of norms as the foundations on which conceptions of legitimacy rely.

Building on this perspective of norms, three theoretical assumptions underlie our argument. First, social norms are consequential. Second, they are *negotiated* and given expression in the context of social discourses. Third, academic discourse is one discursive arena in which the norms we are interested in become visible, and it is therefore interesting to examine this particular discursive arena.

The first assumption means that it makes a difference whether or not an institution is considered legitimate. On the one hand, legitimacy minimizes the need for forceful implementation of political decisions made by or within an institution since the rule addressees can generally accept the decisions (Reus-Smit 2007). On the other hand, norms can also be consequential in terms of the actors' desire to behave in socially appropriate ways and to be recognized as *good* members of a specific community. Thus, diplomats and the staff of international institutions have an interest in adhering to international norms (for empirical evidence, for example, Barnett and Finnemore 2004; Weise 2010). The second assumption, that norms are negotiated in social discourses, means that which norms matter (most) is not determined by some external standard. Rather, different social actors hold different norms. Which norms become dominant or even generally accepted is an outcome of processes in the discursive arena. In this sense, third, academic textbooks are interesting arenas since they are an important medium through which scholars present their particular views on international institutions to the younger generation and thus shape those institutions' image as being more or less legitimate among young academics.

With regard to our specific interest in democratic norms, we conceptually build on Ian Clark's notion of legitimacy norms as embodying elements of rightful membership and rightful conduct (Clark 2005). Accordingly, we analyze changes in the democratic norm from a dual perspective. On the one hand, we examine whether the norm that stipulates *who* can legitimately make international rules has changed. We ask which interests should be represented in decision-making. On the other hand, we ask whether the norm that stipulates *how* international rules ought to be made in order to count as legitimate has been amended. Here, we inquire into which democratic norms are perceived as central to the decision-making process (for example, equality, transparency, accountability).

As indicated, we focus on textbooks that discuss international institutions in the areas of international security, human rights, and environmental politics. Our study thus includes policy fields that vary at the level of institutionalization of global rule-making. While many of the most important global human rights norms were already codified by the 1970s, environmental politics was a nascent field at that time. As a result, international human rights politics has a stronger focus on the implementation of existing legal norms. In contrast, international environmental politics initially focused on the elaboration of such norms and in more recent decades has been characterized by the development of new rules as well as the implementation of existing rules. Finally, security politics was institutionalized early, but only after the end of the Cold War could a number of security institutions, most notably the United Nations, overcome constraints caused by bloc confrontation.

Within these issue areas, we base our selection of academic textbooks on a list of candidate books that we compiled with the help of academic library catalogs and web-based search tools. We narrowed down the list with the help of several criteria: How well do individual books match our definition of academic textbooks?[3] How often are they cited in other publications? In which languages were they written? Are they available?

While our corpus allows us to identify some interesting trends in the academic discourse of the 1970s to 2000s, it is not representative in a strict sense. The most important sources of potential bias are first the dominance of English language books originating from either the UK or the United States, which probably results in a tendency to report Anglo-Saxon rather than global norms.[4] Second, our preference for more widely used vs. less widely used books possibly results in a tendency to underreport discourses beyond the mainstream literatures. Keeping these limitations in mind, we believe that we can nevertheless say something about how conceptions of democracy in international institutions have changed in textbook discourses.

Methodologically, we apply an interpretative approach. We follow Robert Entman (2004) and others in the assumption that collective and individual perceptions of reality are ordered in *frames* that provide cognitive patterns to understand the world. For political issues, frames structure the perception of political problems and their possible solutions. Further, we assume that some frames also connect to norms of appropriate behavior. Thus, a typical frame we look for will provide information about norms that guide the evaluation of international institutions themselves, of their activities, and of reform proposals in relation to an institution. Thus, such an ideal-type frame would, for example, praise the United Nations as the true world parliament where all states have equal rights.

In order to identify how the meaning of democratic norms has changed over time, we first coded three kinds of legitimacy statements: (i) evaluative statements that either explicitly or implicitly include normative assessments of an international institution; (ii) proposals for new international institutions that make sufficiently clear what would be "good" about such institutions; and (iii) critiques of proposals for a new international institution. From among this corpus of statements, we only look at those evaluations that make democracy or a particular democratic value their primary standard of evaluation. These statements essentially hold that international institutions are good if they are democratic and that they ought to be reformed if they suffer from a "democratic deficit." To take into account the possibility that the coders for the different issue areas have different levels of sensitivity in either recognizing a statement as evaluative or assigning it to the democracy frame, we additionally include all those statements from the initial corpus of legitimacy statements that contain at least one term that might signal a reference to democracy or to a particular democratic value. To keep the analysis manageable, we have restricted our search to the terms democracy, participation, transparency, and accountability (as well as their respective translations for the French and German books included in our analysis).[5] This choice of terms is motivated by the idea that different conceptions of democratic governance beyond the state overlap in relation to these democratic values (Dingwerth 2007: chapter 2). Having thus identified our corpus of evaluative statements, the main thrust of our argument relies on a fine-grained, qualitative discussion of democracy-related evaluations to which we turn in the following sections.

Before we begin, however, we need to point out that evaluations of international institutions in academic textbooks rely on a plethora of normative frames—including, for example, the functional performance of international institutions, which is their capacity to solve collective problems, or the notion of sovereignty, implying that international institutions should serve as an instrument to protect national autonomy. In contrast, in all issue areas, democracy plays a rather marginal role in the evaluations by textbook authors, and this hardly changes over time. Compared to the issue areas of security and human rights politics, most references to democracy or particular democratic values occur in the issue area of environmental politics. However, even if democracy may not be invoked more frequently in textbooks, given the generally increasing academic attention to the democracy of international institutions, it is still worth looking at this particular norm in more detail, especially as the content of demands related to democracy has changed.

Empirical Analysis: Changing Notions of Democracy
Explicit References to Democracy

In our selection of books, only a few authors make explicit use of democracy as a standard to evaluate international politics. Those who do are more likely to have written their books in the 1990s and 2000s. Further, they conceive of democracy in rather diverse terms. In addition, there is neither a consensus on the notion *that* democratic norms ought to apply to international institutions, nor on *what* such a demand would essentially entail. The same applies to the domain to which democracy as a normative standard should be applied. Overall, explicit appeals to democracy come in a variety of ways. We identify two trends. First, international institutions are often ascribed an important role in national democracy promotion. Second, there is a recent demand for democratic procedures in international institutions themselves.

The first trend, the role of international institutions in promoting national democracy, is more common (see Keohane, Macedo, and Moravcsik 2009). This is primarily found in the human rights books and often applied to institutions that make democratic government a requirement for becoming a member state (such as the Council of Europe or, more recently, NATO), or to those whose activities are seen as benefiting the quality of domestic democracy (such as the MERCOSUR, OAS, OECD, OSCE, or the UN). Yet such references and statements remain rather broad and general.

The second trend, the direct application of democratic procedures to international organizations, is more nuanced. Only nine of our 71 books apply democracy to international institutions directly. Further, those nine works do not share a coherent understanding of the meaning of democracy and apply the concept to international politics in different ways. Still, we can classify the uses we identified in relation to three particular meanings of democracy: (i) democracy as *equality*, (ii) democracy as *decentralized governance*, and (iii) democracy as *empowerment*.

Democracy as Equality

First, a number of assessments of individual institutions as either democratic or undemocratic commonly refer to the formal or factual equality among participating states. For instance, a common topic of formal equality is state representation. Here, authors hold that institutions are more democratic when states have equal voting rights than when decision-making powers are based on economic power (see Buck 1998:160 on INTERSPUTNIK and INTELSAT). Similarly, the UN General Assembly is described as "the democratic assembly" in opposition to the much smaller and less representative Security Council (Weiss and Kalbacher 2008:334).

Some authors take up the issue of democracy as equality when discussing controversies in international politics. For example, they embed debates on a political post-World War II order and the creation of the UN in this understanding of democracy (see Hurd 2007: chapter 4). To illustrate, Lauren (1998:176) reports that a number of states were unhappy with the proposed UN Charter because of great-power dominance, and he reflects that "if the crusade of World War II was in the name of democratic principles, then surely the new international organization should be based on democracy."

A second controversy is associated with the creation of the Global Environment Facility (GEF) in the first half of the 1990s. The issue is discussed in environmental textbooks (see Brenton 1994; Elliott 1998; Chasek, Downie, and Brown 2006). Here, the authors frame the debates on the setup of the GEF in a democracy language when they, for example, demand "equal representation in the decision making process" (Elliott 1998:200) for developing countries. The authors also contrast the GEF to the undemocratic World Bank and thus understand it as a tool to democratize global politics.

Democracy as Decentralized Governance

The centralization and decentralization of governance is an issue that appears with some importance in the environmental politics debates. In the 1970s and 1980s, centralized global rule-making was applauded on a functional basis as a good way to solve global environmental problems (see Falk 1973:150; Kent 1979:246; Harf and Trout 1986:213–14). Yet this perception changes over time. More recent textbooks tend to see democratic potential in decentralization. For instance, Elliott (1998:118) argues that, "better governance requires... that the practice of global governance be decentralized and democratized" and that it "respond[s] more effectively to local voices and local concerns" (see also O'Neill 2009:6 for a similar argument).

Here, an international governance system is considered democratic to the extent that it does *not* have a powerful center, but is instead constituted of a plethora of competing or overlapping spheres of authority. Democratizing global governance therefore does not necessarily mean rendering international institutions more participatory, transparent, or accountable, but rather reducing institutions' central authority within the wider governance system through the creation of nontraditional authorities that develop alternative visions and provide space for the contestation of ideas and institutions.

Democracy as Empowerment

Some authors argue that international institutions are democratic when they empower their stakeholders to be active political players. For example, Hough (2008:253) criticizes international institutions for often making symbolic use of democratic ideas. They create bodies for stakeholder representation and develop special programs. Yet the elites that develop these instruments and dominate the institutions do not have sincere intentions of living up to these ideas of true stakeholder empowerment.

A similar conception of democracy as empowerment or emancipation underlies Elliott's (1998:131) discussion of the democratic potential of nonstate actors in global governance. She conceives of global civil society as an "expression of alternative visions of political practice and environmental governance" that emphasize "democratization, participation and the empowerment of marginalized voices, justice and equity and a reclaiming of the local to counter the centralizing tendencies of a reformist, institutionalist approach to global governance." Democracy, in this perspective, is equated with the "effective control of change by those most directly affected" (Elliott 1998:131, citing John Hontelez) and ultimately linked to the idea of emancipation.

Participation of Whom and for What? From Functional to Representational Arguments

Normative change becomes more visible when we move from references to democracy to references to particular democratic values such as participation, transparency, and accountability. Looking at evaluations that use participation as their normative reference point, two main observations are noteworthy. First, the range of actors that the authors see as relevant expands throughout the decades. Second, justifications for participation in international institutions become broader over time as functionality-based arguments are complemented by concerns about the representative nature of international institutions. Yet functionality-based participatory demands, which are largely unconnected to participation as a democratic value, are the ones most often used. However, over time, we witness the emergence of an understanding of participation as a means of enhancing the representation of various actors and thereby improving the democratic quality of global policymaking.

The Expansion of Relevant Actors

As discussed above, textbook authors base parts of their evaluations of international institutions on the adequacy of state participation in international decision-making. For most of them, broad participation is important because it enhances the likelihood that transboundary problems will be solved. We find this functional view of participation in many institutional contexts, such as the UN General Assembly (Flinterman 1999:146), UN conferences (Strong 1975:262; Juda 1979:91), UN operations (Papp 1984:57), and other treaty negotiations (Goetz Lall 1982:98; Desombre 2002:110). Beyond these functionalist statements, more recent textbooks also discuss the problem of North-South imbalances and their effects on developing state participation. For example, O'Neill (2009:88) discusses the "obstacles to southern participation in global environmental meetings" that result from the strained diplomatic apparatus of Southern countries.

Next to states, there has been a continuous awareness since the 1970s of the participatory demands of nonstate groups. These are individuals and the general population on the one hand and non-governmental organizations (NGOs) on the other. NGO participation in international affairs is seen as vital in a wide range of textbooks. Yet, especially in the fields of security and human rights, the authors predominantly discuss the important functions fulfilled by NGOs and demand a greater role for them in particular international regimes (Schwelb 1978:333; Forsythe 1983:218; Morgan 2006:264). In contrast, in international environmental politics (and to some extent also in the field of human rights politics), nonstate actors are also seen as central to the democratic legitimacy of international decision-making processes from the 1980s onwards. Then, the debate about who does and who should participate in global governance gained a clear focus on NGOs, and a more important role for them is demanded (for example, Elliott 1998:101). Also, particular attention is paid to NGOs from the Global South. For example, Kamminga and Rodley (1984:198) report "understandable charges that the NGO community is unrepresentative of the world as a whole" and that "wider participation by NGOs based in the Third World…is badly needed." Here, the representational function of NGOs is explicitly addressed and begins to complement the initial focus on functional benefits.

Finally, a major evolution over the past four decades is the much greater attention textbook authors pay to social groups that are traditionally marginalized in international institutions. Most notably, they comprise women's organizations, indigenous groups, and local communities. All these groups are virtually non-existent in evaluative statements drawn from the textbooks of the 1970s and 1980s, but are given a prominent role in some textbooks from the 1990s and 2000s (see, for example, Elliott 1998:147–57; Chasek et al. 2006:137; Whitworth 2008:103; Smith 2010:353).

Participation as Representation

The rise of representational ideas is most evident in relation to evaluative statements that focus on the inclusion of previously marginalized groups. As functional concerns rarely play a role in justifying demands for greater inclusion of these groups, evaluations that refer to them almost exclusively express representational concerns. In other words, they understand representation not as a means, but as a valuable end that international institutions should pursue. The general idea behind representational concerns is expressed in the notion that citizens should have "their say in international fora" (Speth and Haas 2006:136).

This idea gains larger support among textbook authors in the 1990s and 2000s. During that time, NGOs are discussed as delivering information not only to international institutions, but also to a wider public. Thereby, they make critical knowledge available and empower those participating in global governance processes (Elliott 1998:143). Second, this shift in the meaning of participation becomes visible in the increasing use of the deliberation trope in that period. The authors in the human rights and environmental politics areas describe nonstate actors as important interlocutors in international institutions. During deliberations, they make excluded voices heard. As O'Neill (2009:91) puts it, "NGOs have served as the 'conscience-keepers' of the international community" and should therefore push for "wider participation in these deliberations." Furthermore, they broaden the horizons of delegates in deliberations by providing critical perspectives, new ideas, or simply broader views on a given issue (O'Neill 2009:91–92). For instance, Speth and Haas (2006:120) argue that opening the procedures of the WTO to non-trade experts would "[give] the WTO greater legitimacy."

Finally, representational concerns are also visible when the contributions of NGOs or scientists are criticized, either in relation to elites vs. non-elites, or in relation to the representation of societal actors from the Global South. For example, Smith (2010:172) criticizes that in some human rights commissions, "only an elite inner circle of academics, activists, and politicians tends to be aware of the content." In relation to environmental science, some authors "have argued that serious inequities have existed, and often remain, in how Southern concerns and experiences are reflected on international scientific agendas" (O'Neill 2009:89). Thus, it is not only the presentation of scientific knowledge that matters, but also the representation of diverse voices in the process of knowledge creation.

The Domain of Transparency and Accountability: From States to International Organizations

We discuss demands for transparency and accountability together since textbook authors frequently use both ideas in combination and discuss them as closely linked categories. How do textbook authors evaluate international institutions with regard to these values? Two specific observations are noteworthy in this regard. First, there are larger differences between the policy fields we studied. A second observation is that, in the earlier decades, evaluations of international institutions are mainly concerned with international institutions as *providers* of (national) transparency and accountability. In recent decades, this focus is complemented by demands for the transparency and accountability of international institutions *themselves*.

First, it is striking that authors of international security textbooks do not discuss transparency as a relevant basis to evaluate the democratic performance of international institutions. Normatively speaking, security is portrayed as a "transparency-free" zone in which openness or publicity is of limited value. This is different in human rights and environmental politics textbooks. In these textbooks, we can identify a broad range of references to transparency, yet often with functional undertones. For instance, the publicity of UN regimes is applauded because it "provides for considerable transparency of the reporting system and allows for monitoring and even lobbying by non-governmental organizations" or because it "contributes to the transparency of process and helps to encourage participation" (Scheinin 1999:433; Smith 2010:170).

Here, the meaning of transparency revolves around ideas of public control, participation, and openness. Transparency is not necessarily seen as a value in itself, but serves to improve monitoring and "to publicize policy failures or successes" (O'Neill 2009:119). Transparency thereby generates information upon which those concerned can act to improve the system. Of course, the textbook corpus also holds a number of contradictory statements that are skeptical of transparency when it conflicts with demands for secrecy in state negotiations and thus reduces the chances of state compromise (for example, Luini Del Russo 1970:85). Yet those fears of waning confidentiality in international politics decline in the 1990s and later. Rather, authors now criticize the possible pitfalls of too much secrecy, like "preventing sufficient public disclosure and discussion" (Lauren 1998:265).

Our second and more important observation is that, apart from states, a number of international institutions are also subjected to demands for transparency and accountability. In contrast to our findings on democracy and participation, some IGOs—most notably the GATT/WTO, the World Bank, and the IMF—are, however, much more the focus of such demands than others. They are criticized when they do not live up to the authors' standards of transparency or accountability, but also praised for their reform efforts to improve their transparency records.

More direct references to accountability—rather than transparency or a combination of both—can be organized along two questions: Who should be accountable? To whom is accountability owed? As with participation, there is also a diversification of the actors that face demands for increased accountability. While a large number of statements—most notably in the domain of human rights—address the legal accountability of states, statements advocating the accountability of international organizations themselves have been growing stronger since the 1990s. For example, Skogly (1999:246) points out that "concern over [the] negative human rights impact of the operations of the [World Bank and IMF] themselves, and thus, their accountability in accordance with human rights law," was a relatively new phenomenon.

Concerning the actors to whom accountability is owed, there is a whole series of different actors mentioned. They range from the world community and the citizens of a state to local communities, member states of an international organization, and the stakeholders of international institutions. Interestingly, explicit references to these actors and their differentiation are made almost exclusively in statements from the 1990s. Together with the observation that the concept of liability of international organizations emerges as a theme of discussion around that time, this indicates that the notion of accountability becomes increasingly specified over our period of investigation.

The Changing Role and Meaning of Democracy in IR Textbooks: Conclusions

Our main research interest in this article was to find out what "democracy" means when it is used in textbook evaluations of international institutions and how the content of democracy-related evaluations has changed over time. An analysis of 71 academic textbooks on international security, environmental, and human rights politics leads us to several answers regarding democracy's relative importance and evolution in meaning. Also, we reflect about the meaning of such changes for IR education.

Numerically, democracy is only one normative standard among others, and it does not seem to become more central in recent decades. This may reflect both mainstream academic discourses and a conservative bias in textbook discourses. Even though, as mentioned in our introduction, a number of IR scholars now turn to analyzing the democratic credentials of international institutions (for example, Zweifel 2005; Grigorescu 2007). Frost's (1996:4) assessment almost two decades ago that IR by and large still avoids normative theorizing retains some validity. More recently, Reus-Smit and Snidal (2008), in their *Oxford Handbook of International Relations*, have called for a better integration of normative theorizing into empirical (IR) analysis (see also Deitelhoff 2010). To some extent, the lack of attention to democratic norms in textbooks that we identified may thus mirror a general reluctance of IR scholars to openly position themselves normatively.[6]

On the other hand, the more recent moves by at least some IR scholars to take normative reasoning and analysis more seriously make textbooks look like a particularly conservative genre that is relatively slow in taking up new developments within the discipline. While a survey by Peterson, Tierney, and Maliniak (2005:10–11) has shown that at least outstanding real-world events like the end of the Cold War or the 9/11 terrorist attacks directly motivate a considerable share of (US) scholars to adapt their courses, IR teaching seems to be less adaptive to theoretical developments. Although only few IR scholars still see realism as a fruitful paradigm for their own work, in their introductory courses they continue to emphasize its importance over and over again (Maliniak et al. 2007:11). The widespread neglect of underlying democratic norms and debates in IR textbooks seems thus to fit into a tradition of teaching that focuses on the long-standing canonical contents instead of cutting-edge, state-of-the-art developments.

In comparison with other discursive arenas outside academia, textbooks are characterized as having a significant time lag. For instance, a recent analysis of quality newspaper discourses on the UN, the European Union, and the G8 in four different countries claims that roughly one-third of all evaluations in this particular discursive arena relate to democratic norms (Nullmeier et al. 2010). The relevance of democratic yardsticks thus seems considerably higher in media discourses than in textbook discourses. Overall, the (numerical) lack of attention to democracy in IR textbooks calls on us as scholars not only to take the normative foundations of our discipline more seriously but also to better bring in line "what we preach (research) with what we teach (pedagogy in the classroom)" (Peterson, Tierney and Maliniak 2005:3).

Qualitatively, however, focusing exclusively on the democracy-related statements within our text corpus, we make some interesting observations with regard to discourses on the legitimation and legitimacy of international institutions. Notably, we observe normative changes in relation to three aspects that speak to both dimensions of legitimacy identified by Clark (2005), namely the dimensions of rightful actors and rightful conduct. First, in relation to Clark's first dimension, *the range of legitimacy-relevant actors expands over time*, most markedly in relation to nonstate actors and marginalized groups as legitimate participants in (or even subjects of) international policymaking. Second, and linked to notions of both rightful actors and rightful conduct, *representational concerns become more relevant* in justifying demands for greater participation in international institutions. Third, and more directly connected to ideas about rightful conduct, at least in the environmental policy and human rights fields, *international organizations increasingly become the objects of demands for transparency and accountability*, both in terms of who should be accountable and to whom accountability is owed.

More broadly, the qualitative discussion in relation to participation, transparency, and accountability shows that *democratic norms are becoming more encompassing.*

Thus, international organizations are now expected to be representative of a much greater variety of state and nonstate actors; they are expected not only to contribute to the transparency and accountability of states and interstate relations, but to also be transparent and accountable themselves. Overall, this expansion adds complexity to the normative field in which international organizations operate and increases challenges to their legitimacy.

Interestingly, despite the overall conservative bias in the form of a strong reluctance to take up normative questions in standard IR textbooks at all, it seems that when authors do take a position, they are much more sensitive to the variety of meanings that the concept of democracy can take and thereby firmly reflect current political and academic developments and discourses. The trend toward emphasizing more participation by a broader audience of stakeholders is hence very much in line with recent political and academic discourses regarding the politicization of international institutions (for example, Zürn, Binder, and Ecker-Ehrhardt 2012). Thus, to the extent that students are confronted with questions of democracy in IR textbooks, what they are taught by and large seems to be in line with the *zeitgeist*. If we assume (as we do) that norms are negotiated and that one space where they can be pushed very strongly are textbooks, as textbooks (especially for younger students) have the aura of being authoritative, then we can conclude that one message students now learn more than two or three decades ago is that democratic values apply to and can be demanded of a wide range of international actors.

Drawing on these findings, we suggest two routes for further research, the first one being more empirical and the second one more conceptual. First, so far we have taken a broad and general view on a variety of textbooks without systematically differentiating between the policy fields. However, at some points, it became clear that there might be differences in how democracy is treated in textbooks for different policy areas. For example, in contrast to environmental and human rights politics textbooks, we found that security politics textbooks hardly pay attention to transparency of international institutions. Most notably, in contrast to environmental politics books, security politics books also did not move from a functional to a representational understanding of NGO participation. To further analyze, this might provide additional relevant insights. Do students that opt for international security politics courses get another idea of global democracy than students who opt for international human rights or environmental politics?

Second, in terms of the sociology of the discipline and the teaching of IR, it would be illuminating to systematically study which criteria scholars have in mind when writing textbooks and particularly which normative orientations they want to bring across. In particular, it might be telling to reflect how IR textbook authors, on the one hand, frequently shy away from openly making democracy-related statements, but on the other hand, through the back door, their changed mind-sets in terms of which precise democratic values they endorse obviously do inform them when writing textbooks. In this sense, then, textbooks appear slightly less conservative than the mere numbers of democracy-related statements suggest, but they are instead influenced by the (normative) *zeitgeist*. Therefore, even though we find only minimal change in the overall importance of democracy in textbooks, the finding that there has been a number of changes in the perception of the democratic norm and how it is presented is highly relevant.

Notes

[1] This paper is part of the broader research project "Changing Norms of Global Governance" (www.globalnorms.uni-bremen.de) funded as a part of the Emmy Noether Program of the Deutsche Forschungsgemeinschaft (DFG, Grant No. DI1417/2-1). We gratefully acknowledge the support from the DFG. We also thank Felix Anderl, Marret Bischewski, Benjamin Brast, Nicole Gonyea, Nele Kortendiek, and Helge Staff for their excellent research assistance; Eric Duchesne, Kristina Hahn, Nina Hall, Monika Heupel, Nico Krisch, Bernd Schlipphak, the anonymous reviewers, as well as the participants in the "Institutional Dynamics in World Politics: Explaining variation in the scope, pace, and direction of international institutional change" (Wissenschaftszentrum Berlin, Germany, April 7–8, 2011), "Global Governance as Public Authority: Structures, Contestation, and Normative Change" (Hertie School of Governance, Berlin, Germany, April 15–16, 2011), and "Institutional Change in Intergovernmental Organization" (ULB-UGent, Brussels, Belgium, May 27–28, 2011) workshops for comments on earlier versions.

[2] In addition, some may argue that academic textbooks are also reflective of other discursive arenas and can therefore be treated as a shortcut to broader social discourses about international institutions. Yet this claim is more controversial, and we therefore limit our analysis to textbooks as a discursive arena that, for the reasons discussed below, is interesting in itself.

[3] According to our definition, textbooks are either explicitly labeled as such by their authors or editors, or (particularly in the 1970s and 1980s when textbooks were not yet so widespread) they should be labeled or recommended as general introductions to the respective field.

[4] The books examined include 51 books written in English, 13 in German and seven in French. Of the books written in English, two-thirds were published in the United States and the rest in the UK.

[5] Taking these search terms as a basis may lead to some overlaps, as the broader notion of democracy frequently encompasses the other notions. In the empirical analysis below, this comes to the fore when we observe that the notion of democracy as such is tied to understandings of equality or empowerment that also feature in the discussion of the notion of participation. We take this overlap as a sign that such notions gain particular relevance.

6 As outlined in the theory and methods section, the dominating orientation toward problem-solving capacity, of course, is also a reflection of underlying norms. Yet, in general, democracy seems to be perceived much more as a contested field and is often viewed as tied much more closely to personal convictions.

References

Anderson, James, Ed. (2002) *Transnational Democracy: Political Spaces and Border Crossings*. London: Routledge.

Anonymous. (2003) Editor's Note: How Do Textbooks Represent the Field of International Studies? *International Studies Review* 5 (1): 421.

Barnett, Michael, and Martha Finnemore. (2004) *Rules for the World: International Organizations in Global Politics*. Ithaca: Cornell UP.

Bexell, Magdalena, Jonas Tallberg, and Anders Uhlin. (2010) Democracy in Global Governance: The Promises and Pitfalls of Transnational Actors. *Global Governance* 16 (1): 81–101.

Brenton, Tony. (1994) *The Greening of Machiavelli: The Evolution of International Environmental Politics*. London: Royal Institute of International Affairs.

Buck, Susan J. (1998) *The Global Commons: An Introduction*. New York: Island P.

Chasek, Pamela, David L. Downie, and Janet Welsh Brown. (2006) *Global Environmental Politics*. Boulder: Westview P.

Clark, Ian. (2005) *Legitimacy in International Society*. Oxford: Oxford UP.

Deitelhoff, Nicole. (2010) Parallele Universen Oder Verschmelzung der Horizonte? *Zeitschrift für Internationale Beziehungen* 17 (2): 279–92.

Desombre, Elizabeth. (2002) *The Global Environment and World Politics*. London: Continuum.

Dingwerth, Klaus. (2007) *The New Transnationalism: Transnational Governance and Democratic Legitimacy*. Basingstoke: Palgrave Macmillan.

Elliott, Lorraine. (1998) *The Global Politics of the Environment*. Basingstoke: Macmillan.

Entman, Robert M. (2004) Projections of Power: Framing News, Public Opinion, and U.S. Foreign Policy. Chicago: U of Chicago P.

Eriksson, Johan, and Bengt Sundelius. (2005) Molding Minds That Form Policy: How to Make Research Useful. *International Studies Perspectives* 6 (1): 51–71.

Falk, Richard A. (1973) Environmental Policy as a World Order Problem. In *Environmental Policy: Concepts and International Implications*, edited by Albert Utton and Daniel H. Henning. New York: Praeger.

Flinterman, Cees. (1999) Extra-Conventional Standard-Setting and Implementation in the Field of Human Rights. In *An Introduction to the International Protection of Human Rights: A Textbook*, edited by Raja Hanski and Markku Suksi. Turku: Åbo Akademi University.

Forsythe, David. (1983) *Human Rights and World Politics*. Lincoln: U of Nebraska P.

Frost, Mervyn. (1996) *Ethics in International Affairs: A Constitutive Theory*. Cambridge: Cambridge UP.

Goetz Lall, Betty. (1982) Disarmament and International Security. In *Alternative Methods for International Security*, edited by Carolyn Stephenson. Washington, DC: UP of America.

Grigorescu, Alexandru. (2007) Transparency of Intergovernmental Organizations: The Roles of Member-States, International Bureaucracies, and Non-Governmental Organizations. *International Studies Quarterly* 51 (3): 625–48.

Harf, James, and B. Thomas Trout. (1986) *The Politics of Global Resources: Population, Food, Energy, and Environment*. Durham: Duke UP.

Holden, Barry, Ed. (2000) *Global Democracy: Key Debates*. London: Routledge.

Hough, Peter. (2008) *Understanding Global Security*. London: Routledge.

Hurd, Ian. (2007) *After Anarchy: Legitimacy and Power in the United Nations Security Council*. Princeton: Princeton UP.

Jordan, Richard, Daniel Maliniak, Amy Oakes, Susan Peterson, and Michael J. Tierney. (2009) One Discipline or Many? TRIP Survey of International Relations Faculty in Ten Countries. Teaching, Research, and International Policy (TRIP) Project, The Institute for the Theory and Practice of International Relations, The College of William and Mary. Available at www.wm.edu/offices/itpir/_documents/trip/final_trip_report_2009.pdf (Accessed June 12, 2013).

Juda, Lawrence. (1979) International Environmental Concern: Perspectives of and Implications for Developing States. In *The Global Predicament: Ecological Perspectives on World Order*, edited by David Orr and Marvin S. Soroos. Chapel Hill: U of North Carolina P.

Kamminga, Menno, and Nigel S. Rodley. (1984) Direct Intervention at the UN: NGO Participation in the Commission on Human Rights and Its Sub-Commission. In *Guide to International Human Rights Practice*, edited by Hurst Hannum. Philadelphia: U of Pennsylvania P.

Katzenstein, Peter J. (1996) Introduction: Alternative Perspectives on National Security. In *The Culture of National Security: Norms and Identity in World Politics*, edited by Peter J. Katzenstein. New York: Columbia UP.

Kent, George. (1979) Global Fisheries Management. In *The Global Predicament: Ecological Perspectives on World Order*, edited by David Orr and Marvin S. Soroos. Chapel Hill: U of North Carolina P.

Keohane, Robert O., Stephen Macedo, and Andrew Moravcsik. (2009) Democracy-Enhancing Multilateralism. *International Organization* 63 (1): 1–31.

Kille, Kent J. (2003) International Organization: What Do We Know and How Do We Pass on Our Knowledge? *International Studies Perspectives* 5 (3): 426–33.

Krebs, Ronald K., and Patrick T. Jackson. (2007) Twisting Tongues and Twisting Arms: The Power of Political Rhetoric. *European Journal of International Relations* 13 (1): 35–66.

Lauren, Paul. (1998) *The Evolution of International Human Rights: Visions Seen.* Philadelphia: U of Pennsylvania P.

Luini Del Russo, Alessandra. (1970) *International Protection of Human Rights.* Washington, DC: Lerner Law Book Co.

Maliniak, Daniel, Amy Oakes, Susan Peterson, and Michael J. Tierney. (2007) The International Relations Discipline, 1980–2006. Paper for the Annual Meeting of the American Political Science Association, Chicago, IL, August/September 2007. Available at www.wm.edu/offices/itpir/_documents/trip/the_international_relations_discipline_2007.pdf (Accessed June 12, 2013).

Martin, Pamela, Holley Tankersley, and Min Ye. (2012) Are They Living What They Learn? Assessing Knowledge and Attitude Change in Introductory Politics Courses. *Journal of Political Science Education* 8 (2): 201–23.

Mert, Ayşem. (2009) Partnerships for Sustainable Development as Discursive Practice: Shifts in Discourses of Environment and Democracy. *Forest Policy and Economics* 11: 326–39.

Morgan, Patrick M. (2006) *International Security: Problems and Solutions.* Washington, DC: CQ P.

Nullmeier, Frank, Dominika Biegon, Jennifer Gronau, Martin Nonhoff, Henning Schmidtke, and Steffen Schneider. (2010) *Prekäre Legitimitäten: Rechtfertigung von Herrschaft in der Postnationalen Konstellation.* Frankfurt: Campus.

O'Neill, Kate. (2009) *The Environment and International Relations.* Cambridge: Cambridge UP.

Papp, Daniel. (1984) *Contemporary International Relations: Frameworks for Understanding.* New York: Macmillan.

Peterson, Susan, Michael J. Tierney, and Daniel Maliniak. (2005) Teaching and Research Practices, Views on the Discipline, and Policy Attitudes of International Relations Faculty at U.S. Colleges and Universities. Teaching, Research and International Policy Project, The College of William and Mary. Available at www.wm.edu/offices/itpir/_documents/trip/trip_summary2005.pdf (Accessed June 12, 2012).

Reimann, Kim D. (2006) A View from the Top: International Politics, Norms and the Worldwide Growth of NGOs. *International Studies Quarterly* 50 (1): 45–68.

Reus-Smit, Christian. (2007) International Crises of Legitimacy. *International Politics* 44 (2): 157–74.

Reus-Smit, Christian, and Duncan Snidal, Eds. (2008) *The Oxford Handbook of International Relations.* Oxford: Oxford UP.

Scheinin, Martin. (1999) International Mechanisms and Procedures for Implementation. In *An Introduction to the International Protection of Human Rights: A Textbook*, edited by Raija Hanski and Markku Suksi. Turku: Åbo Akademi University.

Schwelb, Egon. (1978) Procédures Suivies et Mesures Prises par les Organs de L'ONU Dans le Domaine des Droits de L'homme. In *Les Dimensions Internationales des Droits de L'Homme: Manuel Destiné à L'Enseignement des Droits de L'Homme dans les Universités*, edited by Karl Vasak. Paris: UNESCO.

Skogly, Sigrun I. (1999) The Position of the World Bank and the International Monetary Fund in the Human Rights Field. In *An Introduction to the International Protection of Human Rights: A Textbook*, edited by Raija Hanskiand Markku Suksi. Turku: Åbo Akademi University.

Smith, Courtney B. (2003) Learning About International Relations in a Changing World. *International Studies Perspectives* 5 (3): 421–26.

Smith, Rhona. (2010) *Textbook on International Human Rights*. Oxford: Oxford UP.

Speth, James, and Peter Haas. (2006) *Global Environmental Governance*. New York: Island P.

Strong, Maurice. (1975) An Ecological Approach to Management. In *Politics and Environment: A Reader in Ecological Crisis*, edited by Walt Anderson. Pacific Palisades, CA: Goodyear.

Suchman, Mark C. (1995) Managing Legitimacy: Strategic and Institutional Approaches. *The Academy of Management Review* 20: 571–610.

Tallberg, Jonas, Thomas Sommerer, Theresa Squatrito, and Christer Jönsson. (2013) *The Opening Up of International Organizations: Transnational Access in Global Governance*. Cambridge: Cambridge UP.

Thérien, Jean-Philippe, and Madeleine Bélanger Dumontier. (2009) The United Nations and Global Democracy: From Discourse to Deeds. *Cooperation and Conflict* 44 (4): 355–77.

Weber, Max. (1978) *Economy and Society*. Berkeley: U of California P.

Weise, Tobias. (2010) Du Kommst Hier (Nicht) Rein! Wie Staatenvertreter als Türsteher in Fragen der Öffnung Internationaler Regierungsorganisationen mit Konkurrierenden Normen Argumentieren. M.A. dissertation, Freie Universität Berlin, Humboldt-Universität zu Berlin and Universität Potsdam.

Weiss, Thomas G., and Danielle Zach Kalbacher. (2008) The United Nations. In *Security Studies: An Introduction*, edited by Paul D. Williams. London: Routledge.

Whitworth, Sandra. (2008) Feminist Perspectives. In *Security Studies: An Introduction*, edited by Paul D. Williams. London: Routledge.

Zürn, Michael. (2004) Global Governance and Legitimacy Problems. *Government and Opposition* 39 (2): 260–87.

Zürn, Michael, Martin Binder, and Matthias Ecker-Ehrhardt. (2012) International Authority and Its Politicization. *International Theory* 4 (1): 69–106.

Zweifel, Thomas. (2005) *International Organizations and Democracy: Accountability, Politics, and Power*. New York: Lynne Rienner.

Appendix 1: List of Textbooks Included in This Study

A. *International Environmental Politics*

- Anderson, Walt. (1975) *Politics and Environment: A Reader in Ecological Crisis.* Pacific Palisades, CA: Goodyear.
- Barde, Jean-Philippe. (1992) *Economie et Politique de L'environnement.* Paris: Presses universitaires de France.
- Brenton, Tony. (1994) *The Greening of Machiavelli: The Evolution of International Environmental Politics.* London: Royal Institute of International Affairs.
- Buck, Susan J. (1998) *The Global Commons: An Introduction.* Washington, DC: Island Press.
- Caldwell, Lynton K. (1984) *International Environmental Policy. Emergence and Dimensions.* Durham, NC: Duke University Press.
- Chasek, Pamela, David L. Downie, and Janet Welsh Brown. (2006) *Global Environmental Politics.* Boulder: Westview Press.
- Dahlberg, Kenneth. (1985) *Environment and the Global Arena: Actors, Values, Policies, and Futures.* Durham, NC: Duke University Press.
- Desombre, Elizabeth. (2002) *The Global Environment and World Politics.* London: Continuum.
- Doran, Charles F., Manfred O. Hinz, and Peter C. Mayer-Tasch. (1974) *Umweltschutz, Politik des Peripheren Eingriffs: Eine Einführung in die Politische Ökologie.* Neuwied: Luchterhand.
- Dryzek, John. (1987) *Rational Ecology: Environment and Political Economy.* New York: Basil Blackwell.
- Ehrlich, Paul. (1972) *Population, Resources, Environment Issues in Human Ecology.* San Francisco: W.H. Freeman.
- Elliott, Lorraine M. (1998) *The Global Politics of the Environment.* Basingstoke: Macmillan.
- Glaeser, Bernhard. (1989) *Umweltpolitik Zwischen Reparatur und Vorbeugung: Eine Einführung am Beispiel Bundesrepublik im Internationalen Kontext.* Opladen: Westdeutscher Verlag.
- Harf, James, and B. Thomas Trout. (1986) *The Politics of Global Resources: Population, Food, Energy, and Environment.* Durham, NC: Duke University Press.
- Jänicke, Martin, and Michael Stitzel. (2003) *Lern- und Arbeitsbuch Umweltpolitik: Politik, Recht und Management des Umweltschutzes in Staat und Unternehmen.* Bonn: Verlag J.H.W. Dietz.
- Lipschutz, Ronnie. (2004) *Global Environmental Politics: Power, Perspectives, and Practice.* Washington, DC: CQ Press.
- O'Neill, Kate. (2009) *The Environment and International Relations.* Cambridge: Cambridge University Press.

- Orr, David, and Marvin S. Soroos. (1979) *The Global Predicament: Ecological Perspectives on World Order.* Chapel Hill: University of North Carolina Press.
- Park, Chris. (1986) *Environmental Policies: An International Review.* Kent: Croom Helm.
- Pirages, Dennis. (1978) *The New Context for International Relations: Global Ecopolitics.* Pacific Grove, CA: Duxbury Press.
- Porter, Gareth, and Janet Welsh Brown. (1991) *Global Environmental Politics.* Boulder: Westview Press.
- Simonis, Udo. (1996) *Weltumweltpolitik: Grundriß und Bausteine Eines Neuen Politikfeldes.* Berlin: Ed. Sigma.
- Speth, James, and Peter Haas. (2006) *Global Environmental Governance.* Washington, DC: Island Press.
- Sprout, Harold H., and Margaret T. Sprout. (1971) *Toward a Politics of the Planet Earth.* New York: Van Nostrand Reinhold Co.
- Utton, Albert, and Daniel H. Henning. (1973) *Environmental Policy. Concepts and International Implications.* New York: Praeger.
- Valantin, Jean-Michel. (2007) *Écologie et Gouvernance Mondiale.* Paris: Autrement.

B. International Human Rights Politics
- Brownlie, Ian. (1979) *Principles of Public International Law.* Oxford: Oxford University Press.
- Buergenthal, Thomas. (1995) *International Human Rights in a Nutshell.* St. Paul, MN: West Publishing.
- Claude, Richard. (1989) *Human Rights in the World Community: Issues and Action.* Philadelphia: University of Pennsylvania Press.
- Donnelly, Jack. (1993) *International Human Rights.* Boulder: Westview Press.
- Ermacora, Felix. (1974) *Menschenrechte in der sich Wandelnden Welt.* Wien: Verl. d. Österr. Akad. d. Wiss.
- Forsythe, David. (1983) *Human Rights and World Politics.* Lincoln: University of Nebraska Press.
- Forsythe, David. (2008) *Human Rights in International Relations.* Cambridge: Cambridge University Press.
- Fritzsche, Karl. (2009) *Menschenrechte Eine Einführung mit Dokumenten.* Paderborn: Schöningh.
- Hamm, Brigitte. (2003) *Menschenrechte: Ein Grundlagenbuch.* Opladen: Leske + Budrich.
- Hannum, Hurst. (1984) *Guide to International Human Rights Practice.* Philadelphia: University of Pennsylvania Press.
- Hanski, Raija, and Markku Suksi. (1999) *An Introduction to the International Protection of Human Rights: A Textbook.* Turku: Institute for Human Rights, Åbo Akademi University.

- Kimminich, Otto. (1975) *Einführung in das Völkerrecht*. Pullach: Verlag Dokumentation.
- Lauren, Paul. (1998) *The Evolution of International Human Rights: Visions Seen*. Philadelphia: University of Pennsylvania Press.
- Luini Del Russo, Alessandra. (1970) *International Protection of Human Rights*. Washington, DC: Lerner Law Book.
- Newman, Frank. (1990) *International Human Rights: Law, Policy, and Process*. Cincinnati, OH: Anderson Pub. Co.
- Robertson, Arthur Henry. (1982) *Human Rights in the World: An Introduction to the Study of the International Protection of Human Rights*. New York: St. Martin's Press.
- Schilling, Theodor. (2010) *Internationaler Menschenrechtsschutz das Recht der EMRK und des IPbpR*. Tübingen: Mohr Siebeck.
- Sieghart, Paul. (1983) *The International Law of Human Rights*. Cambridge: Clarendon Press.
- Smith, Rhona. (2010) *Textbook on International Human Rights*. Oxford: Oxford University Press.
- Vasak, Karel. (1978) *Les Dimensions Internationales des Droits de L'homme: Manuel Destiné à L'enseignement des Droits de L'homme dans les Universités*. Paris: UNESCO.

C. International Security Politics

- Chan, Steve. (1984) *International Relations in Perspective: The Pursuit of Security, Welfare, and Justice*. Basingstoke: Macmillan.
- Chauprade, Aymeric. (1999) *Dictionnaire de Géopolitique: États, Concepts, Auteurs*. Paris: Ellipses.
- Colard, Daniel. (1977) *Les Relations Internationales*. Paris: Masson.
- Colard, Daniel, and Jean-Francois Guilhaudis. (1987) *Le Droit de la Sécurité Internationale*. Paris: Masson.
- Dinstein, Yoram. (1994) *War, Aggression, and Self-Defence*. Cambridge: Grotius.
- Fierke, Karin. (2007) *Critical Approaches to International Security*. Cambridge: Polity.
- Groom, A.J.R., and Margot Ligh. (1994) *Contemporary International Relations: A Guide to Theory*. London: Pinter Publishers.
- Hopkins, Raymond F. (1973) *Structure and Process in International Politics*. New York: Harper & Row.
- Hough, Peter. (2008) *Understanding Global Security*. London: Routledge.
- Hütter, Joachim. (1976) *Einführung in die Internationale Politik*. Stuttgart: Kohlhammer.

- Knapp, Manfred, and Lothar Brock. (1990) *Einführung in die Internationale Politik: Studienbuch*. Munich: Oldenbourg.
- Krell, Gert. (2004) *Weltbilder und Weltordnung: Einführung in die Theorie der Internationalen Beziehungen*. Baden-Baden: Nomos.
- Laroche, Josepha. (1998) *Politique Internationale*. Paris: LGDJ.
- List, Martin, Maria Behrens, Wolfgang Reichardt, and Georg Simonis. (1995) *Internationale Politik: Probleme und Grundbegriffe*. Opladen: Leske + Budrich.
- Morgan, Patrick M. (2006) *International Security: Problems and Solutions*. Washington, DC: CQ Press.
- Papp, Daniel. (1984) *Contemporary International Relations: Frameworks for Understanding*. Basingstoke: Macmillan.
- Reynolds, Philip Alan. (1971) *An Introduction to International Relations*. London: Longman.
- Rourke, John. (1986) *International Politics on the World Stage*. Monterey: Brooks/Cole.
- Russett, Bruce. (1985) *World Politics: The Menu for Choice*. New York: Freeman.
- Stephenson, Carolyn. (1982) *Alternative Methods for International Security*. Washington, DC: University Press of America.
- Sullivan, Michael. (1976) *International Relations: Theories and Evidence*. Toronto: Prentice Hall.
- Tickner, J. Ann. (1992) *Gender in International Relations: Feminist Perspectives on Achieving Global Security*. New York: Columbia University Press.
- Viotti, Paul R., and Mark V. Kauppi. (1997) *International Relations and World Politics: Security, Economy, Identity*. Toronto: Prentice Hall.
- Williams, Paul D., Ed. (2008) *Security Studies: An Introduction*. London: Routledge.
- Ziegler, David. (1977) *War, Peace and International Politics*. Boston: Little, Brown and Company.

DISCUSSION QUESTIONS

1. Where do you tend to hear the word "democracy" used? What do people seem to intend when they use the term?

2. What was your understanding of democracy prior to reading this article? How does this article affect your understanding of (or thinking about) democracy? You might want to reference the section "Empirical Analysis: Changing Notions of Democracy" in order to illustrate the meanings of democracy (i.e., as equality, decentralized government, and empowerment) introduced by Dingwerth et al.

3. Review the section "Theory and Methods." Discuss the authors' method—how they set about trying to determine whether the meaning of democracy has changed over time. Why did they choose to focus on textbooks? Brainstorm another "method" for analyzing the meaning of the word democracy over this period.

4. Dingwerth et al. use the terms 'subject' and 'actor' (e.g., 'democracy-relevant actors,' 'non-state actors') in ways you might find unfamiliar. Isolate a few instances of these terms and try to define what the authors mean by them.

5. What is an NGO? Identify and look up a specific NGO and consider it as an example of what Dingwerth et al. discuss, especially in the subsection "Participation as Representation."

C. "SOCIAL MEDIA, PUBLIC DISCOURSE, AND GOVERNANCE," MARIA CONSUELO C. ORTUOSTE

This article from the Media Reviews section of Asian Politics & Policy *explores the effects of increased social media use in the Asia-Pacific. Maria Consuelo C. Ortuoste* analyzes both the positive outcomes, such as the increase in civic engagement and crowdsourced disaster relief apps, and the negative, such as enhanced government censorship and surveillance. Ortuoste argues that social media use has "intensified the battle for information sovereignty, as well as for greater democratic space for public discourse" (p. 321). While reading this article, consider how social media is used both positively and negatively, and what are the implications of these uses in your own environment.*

Glossary terms: media hegemony, review article

Social media is booming in the Asia-Pacific. Over half of the world's social media users (52.2%) and 32.8% of the world's Twitter users are located in the region, which also boasts of 426 million active users of Facebook. Social media users in the Asia-Pacific are not solely dependent on apps developed in the western hemisphere. During the third quarter of 2014, three of the 10 most popular mobile messenger apps in the region were developed in Asia (Statista, 2014, 2015a, 2015b). WeChat by Tencent is based in China, with users from China, India, Thailand, Malaysia, Taiwan, India, and Vietnam; LINE was developed in Japan and is gaining a following in Thailand, Taiwan, and Indonesia; and Kakao Talk, developed in South Korea, now has around 140 million users. Finally, social media users are not chained to their desks—97.3% access social media sites with their phones.

This convenience, accessibility, and mobility are some of the reasons why many scholars, thinkers, government leaders, advocates and activists, and non-governmental organizations (NGOs) believe that social media can promote greater participatory democracy by opening up public discourse, and can promote government accountability when people share information about alleged corruption and abuses. There are also hopes that these new tools can become the building blocks of joint or multilevel governance, as governments would, theoretically, be easier to reach and be more responsive to citizens' demands. In turn, local governments and grassroots organizations can help implement national programs.

---

* Maria Consuelo C. Ortuoste is an Associate Professor in the Department of Political Science at California State University, East Bay. Her research specialties include international security, international relations, and comparative politics of Asia.

"The Future We Want," the United Nations General Assembly's Resolution (2012), embodies these hopes. The document recognizes that information and communications technologies can promote information exchange, technical cooperation, and capacity building. To assess progress, the organization created an "e-government development index," or EGDI, which is a composite score made up of three elements: provision of online services, telecommunication connectivity, and human capacity. South Korea, Australia, and Singapore have the highest EGDIs in the world and two other Asia-Pacific countries, Japan and New Zealand, are in the top 10. Asia, as a whole, has an average EGDI of 0.4950, which is slightly above the world average of 0.4712. Not surprisingly, Northeast Asia has the highest EGDI in Asia, followed by West Asia, Central Asia, Southeast Asia, and South Asia (UNPACS, 2015).

Whether or not there is a correlation between a high EGDI and actual governance is yet to be established. All of the countries with high EGDIs were perceived as relatively corruption-free, except for South Korea. Countries with high social media penetration—China, Thailand, and the Philippines—were perceived as having serious corruption problems (Transparency International, 2014). The report from Freedom House (2015) is similarly negative—Thailand and China are rated as "not free," while Singapore and the Philippines are rated only as "partly free."

The Internet and the cell phone have definitely facilitated access to information and provided a relatively open and mobile venue for expression. And the hunger for communication and information exchange is still on the rise. Apart from WeChat, LINE, and Kakao Talk, other chat apps are being developed in Asia. These include Hike messenger, which is based in India, and Viber, which was originally run from Israel but was later bought by Japan's Rakuten. Even Alibaba, the world's largest online commercial company, has begun developing its own Internet messaging service, Laiwang (Heinrich, 2014).

A Game of Cat and Mouse

Apart from news via the established Web sites, blogs are alternative sources of information for people who live in a country with strong Internet controls. Microblogging sites, like Sina Weibo and Tencent Weibo, are very popular. According to the Chinese Academy of Social Sciences, there were 1.91 million domestic Web sites in China at the end of 2010, and microblogs increased from 17 at the beginning of 2010 to 88 by the end of the year (Epoch Times, 2011, July 15). The "2008 China Internet Public Opinion Report" discussed the growth of a "new opinion class" who are netizens, numbering up to 338 million in China in 2009, talking about their country's political and social problems. "Citizen journalists" are active content contributors, often providing information ahead of traditional and government media (Xiao, 2010). Sites such as fanfou and "jiwai.com" provided information on the 2009 Shishou riot in Hubei Province and on the "7–5" riot in Xinjiang (Feng, 2012). It was also reported that on "China's Online Public Opinion Monitoring & Measuring Department of the *People's Daily* online edition, 23 out of 77 key news stories during 2009 were broken by netizens" (Mudie, 2014, July 14).

Governments, however, have also used these technologies to strengthen their capabilities to control and monitor the Internet. During the 2009 riot in Shishou, the government shut down fanfou and iwai.com; later, Twitter and Facebook were blocked. The blogs of Liu Xiaoyuan and Teng Biao, human rights lawyers, were also closed down in 2010. In 2013, there were reports that the Chinese Communist Party's propaganda department was employing two million "public opinion analysts" to sift through social media, blogs, and text messages using specific key words (Hunt & Xu, 2013). While this number could be an exaggeration, the Chinese government has invested more resources into Internet surveillance ever since the microblogging site Sina Weibo was founded in 2010. To date, Sina Weibo has an estimated 500 million account users, most of whom are unhappy with Sina's compliance with new regulations about "acceptable content."

Other governments are also trying to assert "information sovereignty," which is defined as "a state's attempt to control information flows within its territory" (Powers, 2014, p. 128). Control takes many forms—shutting down the Internet, filtering, monitoring, censoring, as well as "structuring industry-government relations in order to maximize state preferences in privately operated communications systems" (Powers, 2014, p. 128). Democratic governments have used concerns about national security and public safety to monitor or limit media content. Bureaucratic regulations and heavy fines are also effective. Singapore has used media regulations to weed out small independent sites that are critical of government. The *Breakfast Network* and *The Independent* voluntarily closed down when they could not comply with registration requirements which supposedly included providing the Media Development Authority (MDA) with information on aggregated subscriber data as well as "personal information on volunteer contributors" (U.S. Department of State, 2013). The MDA claimed that these sites were suspected of receiving foreign funding that could eventually be detrimental to the country (Yong, 2014, January 20).

Some scholars fear that domestic controls might be extended abroad. Since servers for popular chat apps like WeChat are based in China, messages and user profiles could be flagged even if messages originate from other countries or are exchanged exclusively outside of China (Frietas, 2014, p. 132). The physical control over communications structures has led some groups to go "off the grid," so to speak, with mesh networks like Firechat.

Mesh networks are able to avoid interference because cell phones and devices wirelessly connect to each other "without passing through any central authority or centralized organization (like a phone company or an ISP)" (De Filippi, 2014, January 2). This was particularly useful as one of the mobilization tools during the Umbrella Revolution in Hong Kong and the Sunflower Revolution in Taiwan in 2014, and is now reportedly being used by Iranians, Iraqis, and Russians. There are some drawbacks, however. While users can choose to be anonymous, the chats themselves are public; moreover, pro-Beijing users sent harassing messages via Firechat, and there were text messages urging the users in Hong Kong to download a new app, which turned out to contain malware for surveillance (Chao, 2014).

Disaster Relief
Despite these challenges, there are other ways by which social media, combined with open source software and open data, can be powerful tools for generating more accurate information through "crowdsourcing" and thereby coordinate crucial activities; for example, disaster relief during the floods in the Philippines and Indonesia in the past three years.

Filipinos used Facebook, SMS, and Twitter to ask for help, and in 2013 a new crowdsourcing site, #RescuePH, was created. Citizens could enter data directly into the Web site, which then yields an interactive map showing the locations of floods and of people who needed to be rescued. The government also used Twitter to provide alerts. Another site was later created, #SafeNow, to inform relatives and friends that people were finally rescued. These different data helped coordinate the responses of local Disaster Risk Reduction and Management Councils (DRRMC) with the national headquarters of DRRMC, the Philippine President's office, and other government agencies, as well as with NGOs, churches, and schools which were providing relief and rescue services (Magdirila, 2013).

It made sense to harness these new media—it is estimated that in 2011 there were 101 mobile subscriptions for every 100 Filipinos, and that there were 29 million Facebook subscribers (Roughneen, 2012). The situation in Indonesia is roughly analogous—Indonesia ranks fifth in the world with almost 30 million Twitter accounts, and Jakarta is the number one city in the world in terms of posted tweets (Bennett, 2012, August 13).

During the floods last year, PetaJakarta was created to use "the power of social media to gather, sort, and display information about flooding for Jakarta residents in real time," according to the Web site. PetaJakarta is unique because it is a formal collaboration of a university (the SMART Infrastructure Facility at the University of Wollongong), a social media organization (Twitter Inc.), and a government disaster management agency (BPBD DKI Jakarta).

Jakartans tweeted the location of floods, the height of the floods, and where help was needed. Dr. Etienne Turpin, coprincipal investigator, used the university's "geosocial intelligence engineering" to turn geotagged tweets into data (Turpin & Dean, 2015). The platform also runs on CogniCity, an open-source software which maps the information in real time. This generates an interactive map showing specific district and street levels and confirmed reports of flooding.

PetaJakarta's utility goes beyond disaster response—the data that they have collected are readily available through open license, thus making it possible to plan for future disaster emergencies. According to Turpin and Dean (2015), the data have also helped them analyze flooding and illegal garbage dump sites, which will now be useful in developing preventive measures.

A final example is Safecast, which was developed after the Fukushima earthquake in March 2011 amid the confusion about actual radiation levels. Developed by a few individuals, and "crowdfunded" through Kickstarter as well as by private donations, Safecast uses volunteers to collect data with mobile Geiger counters (the bGeigie) strapped on their cars. The data are then transmitted and aggregated which, like the Philippine and Indonesian situations, generates an interactive map of cities and streets with the corresponding radiation levels. As of May 2014, the Safecast map displayed 18,000 radiation data points.

Safecast provides data for free, and some volunteers have taken the extra step to share that information locally through a "sticker campaign" in the streets. This "crowdfeeding," according to Dr. Sara Dean, design director of PetaJakarta, informs locals about current radiation levels (Turpin & Dean, 2015). The Fukushima prefecture has even created a worldwide map of radiation measurements and Safecast will soon be working with Singapore, Holland, Norway, and Chernobyl.

Conclusion

The Web, social media, and cell phones have intensified the battle for information sovereignty, as well as for greater democratic space for public discourse. While that issue may not be resolved soon, the examples of #RescuePH, PetaJakarta, and Safecast show that there can be a productive relationship among government, citizens and, yes, hackers, which is reshaping what we call governance.

References

Bennett, Shea. (2012, August 13). REVEALED: Top 20 countries and cities on Twitter (stats). *Social Times*. Retrieved from www.adweek.com/socialtimes/twitter-top-countries/468210.

Chao, Rebecca. (2014, October 10). FireChat wasn't meant for protests: Here's how it worked (or didn't) at Occupy Central. *Techpresident*. Retrieved from http://techpresident.com/news/25304/firechat-wasn%E2%80%99t-meant-protests-here%E2%80%99s-how-it-worked-or-didn%-E2%80%99t-occupy-central.

De Filippi, Primavera. (2014, January 2). It's time to take mesh networks seriously (and not just for the reasons you think). *Wired*. Retrieved from www.wired.com/2014/01/its-time-to-take-mesh-networks-seriously-and-not-just-for-the-reasons-you-think/.

Epoch Times. (2011, July 15). Microblogs a threat to China's national security: Official report. *Voice of Patriots Xanga Site*. Retrieved from http://voiceofpatriots.xanga.com/2011/07/15/ microblogs-a-threat-to-chinas-national-security-official-report/.

Feng, Bei. (2012). Microblogs have become the focus of internet censorship in China. *Human Rights in China*. Retrieved from www.hrichina.org/en/crf/article/6406.

Freedom House. (2015). *Freedom in the world 2015—Discarding democracy: A return to the Iron Fist*. Retrieved from https://freedomhouse.org/report/freedom-world-2015/discarding-democracy-return-iron-fist#.VRMGe-H0-1Q.

Frietas, Nathan. (2014). The Great Firewall welcomes you! In Urs Gasser, Jonathan Zittrain, Robert Faris, & Rebekah Heacock Jones (Eds.), *Internet Monitor 2014: Reflections on the Digital World: Platforms, Policy, Privacy, and Public Discourse* (pp. 132–33). Research Publication No. 2014-17 (December 15). Boston: The Berkman Center for Internet and Society at Harvard University. Retrieved from http://cyber.law.harvard.edu/publications/2014/reflections_on_the_digital_world.

Heinrich, Erik. (2014, November 11). In Asia, a war over chat apps is brewing. *Fortune*. Retrieved from http://fortune.com/2014/11/11/in-asia-a-war-over-chat-apps-is-brewing/.

Hunt, Katie, & Xu, CY. (2013, October 2). China 'employs 2 million to police internet.' *CNN*. Retrieved from www.cnn.com/2013/10/07/world/asia/china-internet-monitors/.

Magdirila, Phoebe. (2013, August 19). #RescuePH uses social media and new site to crowdsource information about flood victims. *TechinAsia*. Retrieved from www.techinasia.com/rescueph-social-media-site-crowdsource-information-flood-victims/.

Mudie, Luisetta. (2014, July 14). China moves on microblogs. *Radio Free Asia*. Retrieved from www.rfa.org/english/news/china/microblogs-07142010145418.html.

Powers, Shawn. (2014). The rise of information sovereignty. In Urs Gasser, Jonathan Zittrain, Robert Faris, & Rebekah Heacock Jones (Eds.), *Internet Monitor 2014: Reflections on the Digital World: Platforms, Policy, Privacy, and Public Discourse* (pp. 128–29).

Research Publication No. 2014-17 (December 15). Boston: The Berkman Center for Internet and Society at Harvard University. Retrieved from http://cyber.law.harvard.edu/publications/2014/reflections_on_the_digital_world.

Roughneen, Simon. (2012). Social networks help Filipinos deal with Manila floods. *The Christian Science Monitor*. Retrieved from www.csmonitor.com/World/Asia-Pacific/2012/0808/Social-networks-help-Filipinos-deal-with-Manila-floods.

Statista. (2014). Active usage reach of the most popular mobile messaging apps in Asia Pacific as of 3rd quarter 2014. Retrieved from www.statista.com/statistics/368590/mobile-messenger-reach-asia-pacific/.

Statista. (2015a). Active social media penetration in Asian countries in March 2015. Retrieved from www.statista.com/statistics/255235/active-social-media-penetration-in-asian-countries/.

Statista. (2015b). Leading social networks worldwide as of March 2015, ranked by number of active users (in millions). Retrieved from www.statista.com/statistics/272014/global-social-networks-ranked-by-number-of-users/.

Transparency International. (2014). Corruption by country/territory. Retrieved from www.transparency.org/country.

Turpin, Etienne, & Dean, Sara. (2015, March 17). *#Banjir: Crowdsourcing flood data to survive climate change in Jakarta*. Presentation at the Center for Southeast Asian Studies, University of California Berkeley.

United Nations General Assembly (UNGA). (2012). Resolution 66/288—The future we want. Retrieved from www.un.org/ga/search/view_doc.asp?symbol=A/RES/66/288&Lang5E.

United Nations Public Administration Country Studies (UNPACS). (2015). Country data on e-government development index. Retrieved from http://unpan3.un.org/egovkb/en-us/Data-Center.

U.S. Department of State. (2013). Country reports on human rights practices for 2013: Singapore. Retrieved from www.state.gov/j/drl/rls/hrrpt/humanrights report/index.htm#wrapper.

Xiao, Qiang. (2010, February 11). China Academy of Social Sciences: 2009 China internet public opinion analysis report. *China Digital Times*. Retrieved from http://chinadigitaltimes.net/2010/02/china-academy-of-social-sciences-2009-china-internet-public-opinion-analysis-report/.

Yong, Charissa. (2014, January 20). Sociopolitical sites' registration necessary in the interim. *SingaPolitics*. Retrieved from www.singapolitics.sg/news/registration-websites-%E2%80%9Cnecessary%E2%80%9D-interim-lawrence-wong.

Web Sources

CogniCity: http://cognicity.info/cognicity/

fanfou: http://fanfou.com/.com/

Firechat: https://ogfirechat.wix.com/firechat-4?utm_source=feedburner&utm_medium=feed&utm_campaign=Feed%3A%2BMaoxian%2B%28Maoxian%29

Hike messenger: https://play.google.com/store/apps/details?id=com.bsb.hike&hl=en

Kakao Talk: www.kakao.com/talk

Kickstarter: www.kickstarter.com/

LINE: http://line.me/en/

PetaJakarta: http://petajakarta.org/banjir/in/

#RescuePH: https://twitter.com/rescueph

Safecast: http://blog.safecast.org/

Sina Weibo: www.weibo.com/signup/mobile.php?lang=en-us

Tencent Weibo: http://t.qq.com/

Viber: www.viber.com/en/

WeChat: www.wechat.com/en/

DISCUSSION QUESTIONS

1. Create a short summary of the article that captures Ortuoste's argument and key points. Emphasize what you perceive as most important without interpreting or analyzing.

2. Ortuoste discusses how "'[c]itizen journalists' are active content contributors, often providing information ahead of traditional and government media" (p. 318). She highlights how they "provided information on the 2009 Shishou riot in Hubei Province" (p. 318) as a positive example of this. However, could it be argued that there are times when citizen journalists' contributions produce undesirable outcomes? Come up with and compare an example of a negative and a positive instance of citizen content contribution.

3. Ortuoste examines the tension between the increased ability to exchange information that social media provide and governments which use that ability to "strengthen their capabilities to control and monitor the Internet" (p. 319). What do you think causes some governments to seek to limit or monitor what their people have access to? Can you think of any situations where this attempted control of information would actually benefit citizens?

4. In the article, Ortuoste discusses the UN's "The Future We Want" resolution and their creation of the EGDI (e-government development index). Give an expanded explanation for what the three elements the EGDI uses to make up its composite score. Why do you think the EGDI chose those elements in particular?

5. Ortuoste expresses the idea that social media "can promote greater participatory democracy...and can promote government accountability" (p. 317). For what reasons does she believe this is possible, and do you agree with her? If you do, provide an example where social media has done either, or both, of these things.

D. "POLITICS AND PATRIOTISM IN EDUCATION," JOEL WESTHEIMER

This 2006 article, which appeared in Phi Delta Kappan, *is unusual in that it is a research article (an extensively cited one) published in a non-peer-reviewed journal. In it, Joel Westheimer* surveys the patriotic education that students received in post-9/11 American classrooms. Westheimer first defines and explains the significance of authoritarian and democratic patriotism, before more closely examining the dominance of education systems that focus almost exclusively on authoritarian patriotism. He also argues against the "anti-politics politics of schooling" (p. 332), exploring the necessity of educating students in both democratic patriotism and politics, stating that "[p]atriotism, if it is to reflect democratic ideals, needs politics" (p. 333). While reading this article, consider the long-term implications of an education system that places value only on authoritarian patriotism.*

Glossary term: peer review

In November of 2001, less than two months after the terrorist attacks on the World Trade Center, Nebraska's state board of education approved a patriotism bill specifying content for the high school social studies curriculum in accordance with the state's 1949 statute—the Nebraska Americanism law. Social studies, the bill read, should include "instruction in...the superiority of the U.S. form of government, the dangers of communism and similar ideologies, the duties of citizenship, and appropriate patriotic exercises." The board further specified that middle school instruction "should instill a love of country" and that the social studies curriculum should include "exploits and deeds of American heroes, singing patriotic songs, memorizing the 'Star Spangled Banner' and 'America,' and reverence for the flag."[1]

Nebraska was not alone. Within a few months, more than two dozen state legislatures introduced new bills or resurrected old ones aimed at either encouraging or mandating patriotic exercises for all students in schools. Seventeen states enacted new pledge laws or amended policies in the 2002–03 legislative sessions alone.[2] Since then more than a dozen additional states have signed on as well. Twenty-five states

---

* Joel Westheimer is University Research Chair in Democracy and Education at the University of Ottawa and education columnist for CBC Radio's Ottawa Morning show. His research interests include the exploration of democratic ideals in education and society.

now require the pledge to be recited daily during the school day, and 35 require time to be set aside in school for the pledge.

The federal role in encouraging patriotic passion has been significant as well. On 12 October 2001, the White House, in collaboration with the politically conservative private group Celebration U.S.A., called on the nation's 52 million schoolchildren to take part in a mass recitation of the Pledge of Allegiance. Four days later, the U.S. House of Representatives passed a resolution (404–0) urging schools to display the words "God Bless America" in an effort to reinforce national pride. In 2002, six months before the Iraq War, the federal government announced a new set of history and civic education initiatives aimed squarely at cementing national identity and pride. These initiatives, President George W. Bush declared, would "improve students' knowledge of American history, increase their civic involvement, and deepen their love for our great country." To engender a sense of patriotism in young Americans, we must, Bush emphasized, teach them that "America is a force for good in the world, bringing hope and freedom to other people."[3] And the 2005 federal budget allocates $120 million to grants that support the teaching of "traditional American History." In addition, a campaign by the National Endowment for the Humanities seeks to fund the celebration of traditional "American heroes."

The drive to engage students in patriotic instruction shows no sign of abating and, in fact, may be taking on new fervor. These efforts share at least two characteristics. First, as I detail below, the form of patriotism being pursued by many school boards, city and state legislatures, and the federal government is often monolithic, reflecting an "America-right-or-wrong" stance—what philosopher Martha Nussbaum warns is "perilously close to jingoism."[4] Many educators have condemned these developments as a legislative assault on democratic values in the school curriculum. Second, few of these initiatives included teachers or local school administrators in their conception or development. The direction has come from on high—from the U.S. Department of Education, from local and state boards of education, and from politicians.

But the grassroots response has been far more complex. At the level of the classroom and the school, the efforts of individual teachers, students, principals, and community organizations paint a broad array of curricular responses to the calls for patriotic education. Many teachers and administrators have implemented mandatory policies, shunned controversy, and reinforced the America-is-righteous-in-her-cause message, just as the Bush Administration and politically conservative commentators have wanted. However, terrorism, war, and the threat of fundamentalist intolerance have sparked other educators' commitments to teaching for democratic citizenship, the kind of citizenship that recognizes ambiguity and conflict, that sees human conditions and aspirations as complex and contested, and that embraces debate and deliberation as a cornerstone of patriotism and civic education. In the nation's classrooms, patriotism is politically contested terrain.

What Is Patriotism?

It has often been said that the Inuit have many words to describe snow because one would be wholly inadequate to capture accurately the variety of frozen precipitation. Like snow, patriotism is a more nuanced idea than is immediately apparent. Political scientists, sociologists, and educators would do well to expand the roster of words used to describe the many attitudes, beliefs, and actions that are now called "patriotism." So before we can talk about the politics of patriotism in schools, it makes sense to get clear on at least a few definitions.

Although it is beyond the scope of this article to delve deeply into the many forms of patriotic attitudes and actions, two umbrella categories of patriotism are worth brief exploration. Each is relevant to debates over curriculum and school policy, and each represents political positions that have implications for what students learn about patriotism, civic engagement, and democracy. I will be calling these two manifestations of patriotism *authoritarian* and *democratic*, and their distinctive characteristics are displayed in Table 1.

Authoritarian Patriotism

In a democracy, political scientist Douglas Lummis argues, patriotism reflects the love that brings a people together rather than the misguided love of institutions that dominate them. "Authoritarian patriotism," he notes, "is a resigning of one's will, right of choice, and need to understand to the authority; its emotional base is gratitude for having been liberated from the burden of democratic responsibility."[5] Authoritarian patriotism asks for unquestioning loyalty to a cause determined by a centralized leader or leading group. In his 1966 book, *Freedom and Order*, historian Henry Steele Commager observed, "Men in authority will always think that criticism of their policies is dangerous. They will always equate their policies with patriotism, and find criticism subversive."[6] Authoritarian patriotism demands allegiance to the government's cause and therefore opposes dissent.

To say that authoritarian patriotism comes only from the ruling authority would be too simplistic, however. The social psychology of authoritarian patriotism (especially in a democracy) depends on a deliberate and complicit populace. Following September 11, an abundance of American flags and bumper stickers suddenly sprouted in virtually every city, suburb, town, and rural district in the country. While the flags signaled understandable solidarity in a time of crisis, other public expressions of national pride carried more worrisome messages. Fiercely nationalistic and jingoistic sentiments could be seen and heard on bumper stickers, news broadcasts, and television, as well as in politics. Schools were no exception, and students soon witnessed adults showcasing authoritarian responses to issues of enormous democratic importance.

For example, in 2004 more than 10,000 high schools, community colleges, and public libraries were mailed a free video called "Patriotism and You" by the Washington, D.C.-based group Committee for Citizen Awareness. The group boasts that the video has now been seen by 30 million children and adults nationwide. Teacher Bill Priest of Rock Bridge, Maryland, showed the video to his class as "an example of propaganda of a sort."[7] Statements such as "Patriotism is respecting authority" and "We should manifest a unity of philosophy, especially in times of war" pervade the video. Priest wondered why nobody in the film talks about the right to express patriotic dissent. As this video and dozens of other recent initiatives that aim to teach patriotism illustrate, the primary characteristic of authoritarian patriotism is disdain for views that deviate from an official "patriotic" stance. And proponents of an authoritarian kind of patriotism have looked to the schools to help deliver a unified message and have sought to punish educators who allow or offer dissenting perspectives.

Democratic Patriotism

In a National Public Radio show titled "Teaching Patriotism in Time of War," social historian Howard Zinn described eloquently a possible counterstance to authoritarian patriotism. "Patriotism," he said, "means being true and loyal—not to the government, but to the principles which underlie democracy."[8] Democratic patriotism aims to remain true to these principles. A few historical examples illustrate this position.

In 1950, Sen. Margaret Chase Smith (R-Me.) was the first member of Congress to publicly confront Sen. Joseph McCarthy (R-Wis.). She prepared a Declaration of Conscience urging her fellow senators to protect individual liberties and the ideals of freedom and democracy on which the United States was founded. As she presented the declaration, Sen. Smith said the following: "Those of us who shout the loudest about Americanism are all too frequently those who . . . ignore some of the basic principles of Americanism—the right to criticize, the right to hold unpopular beliefs, the right to protest, the right of independent thought."[9]

TABLE 1.		
The Politics of Patriotism		
	Authoritarian Patriotism	**Democratic Patriotism**
Ideology	Belief that one's country is inherently superior to others.	Belief that a nation's ideals are worthy of admiration and respect.
	Primary allegiance to land, birthright, legal citizenship, and government's cause.	Primary allegiance to set of principles that underlie democracy.
	Nonquestioning loyalty.	Questioning, critical, deliberative.
	Follow leaders reflexively, support them unconditionally.	Care for the people of a society based on particular principles (e.g., liberty, justice).
	Blind to shortcomings and social discord within nation.	Outspoken in condemnation of shortcomings, especially within nation.
	Conformist; dissent seen as dangerous and destabilizing.	Respectful, even encouraging, of dissent.
Slogans	My country, right or wrong.	Dissent is patriotic.
	America: love it or leave it.	You have the right to NOT remain silent.
Historical Example	McCarthy-Era House Un-American Activities Committee (HUAC) proceedings, which reinforced the idea that dissenting views are anti-American and unpatriotic.	The fiercely patriotic testimony of Paul Robeson, Pete Seeger, and others before HUAC, admonishing the committee for straying from American principles of democracy and justice.
Contemporary Example	Equating opposition to the war in Iraq with "hatred" of America or support for terrorism.	Reinforcing American principles of equality, justice, tolerance, and civil liberties, especially during national times of crisis.

Many educators, policy makers, and ordinary citizens have embraced a vision of patriotism that reflects these ideals about democracy and the duties of democratic citizens. When he sang Woodie Guthrie's "This Land Is Your Land," Pete Seeger expressed many patriotic sentiments about the United States, but when he appeared before McCarthy's House Un-American Activities Committee (HUAC), he noted: "I have never done anything of any conspiratorial nature, and I resent very much and very deeply the implication…that in some way because my opinions may be different from yours…I am any less of an American than anybody else. I love my country very deeply."[10]

African American actor, performer, and All-American football player Paul Robeson addressed HUAC in even starker terms: "You gentlemen…are the nonpatriots, and you are the un-Americans, and you ought to be ashamed of yourselves."[11]

More recently, some citizens agreed with former Attorney General John Ashcroft's admonition that anyone who criticizes the government is giving "ammunition to America's enemies" (a notably authoritarian patriotic position). Others saw things differently: dissent is important, and, as a popular march placard indicates, in a democratic nation, "Dissent Is Patriotic."

Another look into history reveals a democratic vision of patriotism as well. Although millions of schoolchildren recite the Pledge of Allegiance every day, far fewer know much about its author. Francis Bellamy, author of the original 1892 pledge (which did not contain any reference to "God"), was highly critical of many trends of late-19th-century American life, most notably unrestrained capitalism and growing individualism. He wanted America to reflect basic democratic values, such as equality of opportunity, and he worked openly to have his country live up to its democratic ideals.

Was Bellamy patriotic? Of course, but his was not patriotism of the authoritarian kind. Indeed, many of America's national icons shared a democratic vision of patriotism. For instance, Emma Lazarus wrote the poem that became the inscription on the base of the Statue of Liberty: "Give me your tired, your poor / Your huddled masses yearning to breathe free." Katherine Lee Bates, an English professor and poet at Wellesley College, wrote the lyrics to "America the Beautiful," including the words "America! America! God mend thine every flaw!" Bellamy, Lazarus, Bates, and many like-minded reformers throughout America's history asserted their patriotism by strongly proclaiming their beliefs in democratic values such as free speech, civil liberties, greater participation in politics, and social and economic equality.[12]

Caring about the substantive values that underlie American democracy is the hallmark of democratic patriotism. This does not mean that democratic patriots leave no room for symbolic displays of support and solidarity. Few would argue with the power of symbols. And the authors and composers mentioned above created the very symbols of American patriotism on which proponents of authoritarian patriotism rely. But democratic patriotism seeks to ensure that "liberty and justice for all" serves not only as a slogan for America but also as a guiding principle for policies, programs, and laws that affect Americans. To be a democratic patriot, then, one must be committed not only to the nation, its symbols, and its political leaders, but also to each of its citizens and their welfare. "This land is your land, this land is my land," "Life, liberty, and the pursuit of happiness," "Crown thy good with brotherhood"—for democratic patriots, these visions represent the ideal America, one worth working toward openly, reflectively, and passionately.

Increasing Authoritarian Patriotism in Schools

I have already detailed several district, state, and federal campaigns to promote one particular view of American history, one narrow view of U.S. involvement in the wars in Iraq and Afghanistan, and so on. There are others. Hundreds of schools, for example, now use the Library of Congress's new "Courage, Patriotism, Community" website. Advertised widely among educators, this website was founded "in celebration of the American spirit" and includes "patriotic melodies" and "stories from the Veterans History Project."[13] Despite a few prominently posted questions—such as "Does patriotism mean displaying the flag or practicing dissent, or both?"—there is little material on the site that lends anything but a prowar, America-can-do-no-wrong vision of patriotism. Similarly, the Fordham Foundation produced a set of resources for teaching patriotism called *Terrorists, Despots, and Democracy: What Our Children Need to Know*, which, under the guise of teaching "indisputable facts," presents storybook tales of "good" and "evil" in the world. But the smaller stories—those taking place in the nation's classrooms and individual schools—might portray more tangible causes for concern.

In New Mexico, five teachers were recently suspended or disciplined for promoting discussion among students about the Iraq War and for expressing, among a range of views, antiwar sentiments. One teacher refused to remove art posters created by students that reflected their views on the war and was suspended without pay. Alan Cooper, a teacher from Albuquerque, was suspended for refusing to remove student-designed posters that his principal labeled "not sufficiently prowar." Two other teachers, Rio Grande High School's Carmelita Roybal and Albuquerque High School's Ken Tabish, posted signs about the war, at least one of which opposed military action. And a teacher at Highland Hills School was placed on administrative leave because she refused to remove a flier from her wall advertising a peace rally. Roybal and Tabish were suspended, and all of the teachers in these cases were docked two to four days' pay by the Albuquerque Public Schools. Each of these schools posts military recruitment posters and photographs of soldiers in Iraq.[14]

In West Virginia, high school student Katie Sierra was suspended for wearing a T-shirt with a rewritten version of the pledge on it: "I pledge the grievance to the flag," it began. And it ended, "With liberty and justice for some, not all." Some of her classmates at Sissonville High School told reporters that they intended to give Katie a taste of "West Virginia justice." The school's principal, Forrest Mann, suspended Katie for three days and forbade her to wear the controversial shirt, saying that her behavior was "disrupting school activity." Indeed, at least one of Katie's classmates felt that the shirt disrupted her studies, writing that Katie's actions "greatly saddened me and brought tears to my eyes. I watched as a young lady was permitted to walk down the hallways of Sissonville High School wearing a T-shirt that spoke against American patriotism." No students were disciplined for wearing shirts emblazoned with the American flag.[15]

In Broomfield, Colorado, 17-year-old David Dial was suspended for posting fliers advertising an "International Student Anti-War Day of Action." He noted that it was "just a peaceful protest against the war in Iraq," adding that his suspension was hypocritical given the fanfare at the school surrounding new curricula that promoted student civic and political involvement.[16] But perhaps two of the most interesting cases involve the Patriot Act. In the first case, a Florida teacher handed out to his students copies of a quotation: "They that can give up essential liberty to obtain a little temporary safety deserve neither liberty nor safety." He asked students to interpret this statement in light of current events. (The class had previously studied the circumstances surrounding the internment of Japanese Americans during World War II.) After discussing the implications of the quotation, the teacher asked the class whether anyone knew who wrote it. When none guessed correctly, he showed them an overhead slide that included the name and a drawing of its author: Benjamin Franklin. They then discussed the intentions of the nation's Founders, constitutional protections, and so on. This teacher was supported by parents but was disciplined by the principal for straying from the mandated civics curriculum standards. A letter of reprimand remains in his personnel file.

The second case might be apocryphal, but this story (and many others like it) has been circulating among teachers, professors of education, and concerned parents. I have been unable to find solid documentation, but I include it here to demonstrate the degree to which these stories invoke teachers' and the public's sense that, in the current climate of intimidation, dissent in the context of civic education is subject to repression and regulation.

The story goes roughly thus: A New York State high school teacher was reprimanded for having his students examine historical comparisons of crisis times in U.S. history. He introduced students to the Alien and Sedition Acts of 1798 and the Sedition Act of 1918. The earlier acts allowed President John Adams to arrest, imprison, and deport "dangerous" immigrants on suspicion of "treasonable or secret machinations against the government" and to suppress freedom of the press. The more recent act restricted criticism of the government, the Constitution, and the military. Pairing these acts with the text of today's Patriot Act, the teacher asked students to assess the three time periods and argue for the justice or injustice of each law. Several parents complained that he was not encouraging patriotism, and the principal instructed the teacher to discontinue the lesson.

Patriotism as a Substitute for Politics

Much of the rationale behind the cases of teachers being reprimanded in schools rests on the idea that patriotism, especially where public schools are concerned, should remain above partisan politics. Dissent, rather than being viewed as an essential component of democratic deliberation, is seen as a threat to patriotism. Indeed, in this view, "politics" is something unseemly and best left to mudslinging candidates for public office: being political is tantamount to devaluing the public good for personal or party gain. Education, in this way of thinking, should not advance "politics" but rather should reinforce some unified notion of truth that supports—without dissent—officially accepted positions.

For example, Sen. Lamar Alexander (R-Tenn.), a former U.S. secretary of education under President Reagan, introduced the American History and Civics Education Act in March 2003 to teach "the key persons, the key events, the key ideas, and the key documents that shape [our] democratic heritage."[17] According to Sen. Alexander, this legislation would put civics back in its "rightful place in our schools, so our children can grow up learning what it means to be an American."[18]

These efforts by the Congress and by conservative members of the Bush Administration have been applauded by those who view education primarily as a means of conveying to American youths and young adults a monolithic set of important historical facts combined with a sense of civic unity, duty, and national pride. Reaching back to a 1950s-style understanding of the American past and the workings of American society, Sen. Alexander and like-minded politicians suggest that Americans, despite diverse backgrounds and cultures, all share a unified American creed or a common set of beliefs and that these beliefs are easily identifiable. Explicitly borrowing from consensus historian Richard Hofstadter, Sen. Alexander believes that "it has been our fate as a nation not to have ideologies but to be one."[19]

Telling students that history has one interpretation (and that interpretation is that the U.S. is pretty much always right and moral and just in its actions) reflects an approach to teaching love of country that too easily succumbs to authoritarianism. Yet teaching this one unified creed—especially in the wake of the September 11 attacks—is rarely viewed as being political. "Being political" is an accusation most often reserved for exploring views that are unpopular—the kind of views, not surprisingly, that come from critical, reflective, and democratic forms of patriotic teaching.

In many schools throughout the U.S., this tendency to cast patriotism and politics as opposites runs especially deep. So strong are the anti-politics politics of schooling that even mundane efforts at teaching for democratic understandings, efforts that aim to encourage discussion around controversial topics, for example, are often deemed indoctrination. After a teacher allowed students at a school assembly to recite an antiwar poem they had written, one parent argued in a parents' forum, "We live in the USA, so singing a patriotic song isn't inappropriate. But politics has no place in the school."[20]

Similarly, after the National Education Association developed lesson plans about the events of September 11, politicians, policy makers, and some parents worried that the curriculum—titled "Tolerance in Times of Trial"—did not paint a positive enough picture of U.S. involvement in world affairs. Conservative political commentator and talk show host Laura Ingraham attacked the curriculum as indoctrination, warning that the lessons encouraged students to "discuss instances of American intolerance." Curricular materials developed by the Los Angeles-based Center for Civic Education that included discussion of controversial issues in multiculturalism, diversity, and protection of the environment drew similar criticism. And we are already seeing evidence of attacks on curriculum that examines the social, economic, and political implications of Hurricane Katrina.[21]

Politics Is Not a Dirty Word

But politics is not a four-letter word. Patriotism, if it is to reflect democratic ideals, needs politics. In a lecture on citizenship in the 21st century, Harry Boyte, co-director of the University of Minnesota's Center for Democracy and Citizenship, argued that politics is the way people with different values and from different backgrounds can "work together to solve problems and create common things of value."[22] In this view, politics is the process by which citizens with varied interests and opinions negotiate differences and clarify places where values conflict. Boyte cited In Defense of Politics by Bernard Crick in calling politics "a great and civilizing activity." For Boyte, accepting the importance of politics is to strive for deliberation and a plurality of views rather than a unified perspective on history, foreign policy, or domestic affairs. For those seeking to instill democratic patriotism, "being political" means embracing the kind of controversy and ideological sparring that is the engine of progress in a democracy and that gives education social meaning. The idea that "bringing politics into it" (now said disdainfully) is a pedagogically questionable act is, perhaps, the biggest threat to engaging students in discussions about what it means to be patriotic in a democratic nation.

It is precisely this aspect of politics with which educators wrestle. While many, like Boyte, see education as an opportunity to teach the critical and deliberative skills that are consistent with democratic patriotism and enable students to participate effectively in contentious public debates, others are uncomfortable with approaches to teaching that encourage dissent and critique of current policies. For example, the events of the Iraq War and the ongoing "reconstruction" have led policy makers and educators who favor authoritarian patriotism to prefer celebrating what President Bush has repeatedly called "the rightness of our cause."

The classroom dramas described above illustrate the intensity with which battles over controversial issues in the classroom can be waged. Yet there are dozens, perhaps hundreds, of curricular efforts that deliberately engage "politics" as a healthy embodiment of the diversity of opinions, motivations, and goals that make up democratic patriotism.

Teaching Democratic Patriotism

Many valuable debates about patriotism do not take as their starting point the question "Should patriotic instruction be apolitical or political, obedient or critical?" Rather, they begin with questions such as "Whose politics do these education programs reflect and why?" or "Which citizens benefit from particular policies and programs and which do not?" Such approaches aim toward democratic patriotism.

Initiatives that emphasize a vision of democratic patriotism tend to come from nongovernmental education organizations, small groups of curriculum writers, and individual teachers rather than from textbook companies or district, state, and federal education departments. As Operation Iraqi Freedom began in March 2003, Oregon teacher Sandra Childs asked students to consider the relationship between patriotism and the First Amendment, using the words of Sen. John McCain (R-Ariz.) as a starting point: "The time for debate is over." A school in Chicago reorganized its interdisciplinary curriculum around the theme of competing national concerns for civil liberties and safety. Some efforts encompass an entire school, as the vision is infused into nearly every aspect of the curriculum, extracurricular activities, and even the physical space. I briefly describe two such programs here, but I encourage readers to search out others.[23]

El Puente Academy for Peace and Justice. The El Puente Academy for Peace and Justice is located in Brooklyn's Williamsburg neighborhood.[24] It was established in 1993 by El Puente ("The Bridge"), a community organization, in partnership with the New York City Board of Education. The academy is academically successful (a 90% graduation rate in an area where schools usually see 50% of their students graduate in four years). But what makes the school especially compelling is its firm commitment to reversing the cycles of poverty and violence for all community residents. It teaches "love of country" by teaching caring for the country's inhabitants. The curriculum, organization, and staff embody a living vision of democratic patriotism at work.

One of the concerns of both El Puente, the organization, and El Puente, the academy, is the health of the community. Williamsburg and nearby Bushwick are called the "lead belt" and the "asthma belt" by public health researchers. As Héctor Calderón, El Puente's principal, declares, "Williamsburg reads like a 'Who's Who of Environmental Hazards.'"[25] Students at El Puente study these toxic presences not only because they are concerned about the health of the natural environment, but also because these hazards directly affect the health of the community. Science and math classes survey the community in order to chart levels of asthma and provide extra services to those families affected by the disease. One year, students and staff became intrigued when they found that Puerto Ricans had a higher incidence of asthma than Dominicans. They wondered if Dominicans had natural remedies not used by Puerto Ricans. Their report became the first by a community organization to be published in a medical journal. Another group of students successfully battled against a proposed 55-story incinerator that was to be built in the neighborhood (which is already burdened with a low-level nuclear waste disposal plant, a nuclear power plant, and an underground oil spill). While math and science classes measured and graphed levels of toxicity, a humanities class produced a documentary on their findings.

That all men (and women) are created equal is indeed a truth that is self-evident to these urban students. That all members of their community are entitled to a healthy life—as well as liberty and the pursuit of happiness—is also self-evident in the academy curriculum. For El Puente students, patriotism means love of American ideals, whether that entails supporting current social and economic policies or critiquing them.

La Escuela Fratney Two-Way Bilingual Elementary School. A spiral notebook always accessible in Bob Peterson's elementary class is labeled "Questions That We Have." Peterson is one of many teachers at La Escuela Fratney, which opened in Milwaukee in 1988 and is Wisconsin's only two-way bilingual elementary school. All of its 380 students begin their schooling in their dominant language (English or Spanish) and by grade 3 they have begun reading in a second language. Rita Tenorio, teacher and co-founder of Fratney, explains that the school's mission includes preparing students "to play a conscious and active role in society," thereby enabling them to be active citizens who can participate in democratic forums for change and social betterment.

Peterson, who is founding editor of *Rethinking Schools* and the 1995 Wisconsin Elementary Teacher of the Year, placed the notebook prominently at the front of the classroom on 12 September 2001, after a fifth-grader pointed out the window and asked, "What would you do if terrorists were outside our school and tried to bomb us?" Peterson's notebook, relatively ordinary in ordinary times, appeared extraordinary at a time when unreflective patriotic gestures commonly associated with authoritarian patriotism abounded. Recall President Bush's admonition to both the world and to U.S. citizens that "you are either with us or you are with the terrorists," or White House Press Secretary Ari Fleischer's dire warning to Americans to "watch what they say and watch what they do."[26] It was in these times that Escuela Fratney teachers felt especially compelled to teach the kind of patriotic commitments that reflected such American ideals as freedom of speech, social justice, equality, and the importance of tolerating dissenting opinions.

Using a curriculum Peterson developed for Rethinking Schools focused on 9/11, terrorism, and democracy, teachers at Escuela Fratney encouraged students to ask tough questions, to explore many varied news sources, and to share their fears, hopes, and dreams about America. For example, after reading a poem by Lucille Clifton titled "We and They," students responded through stories, poems, and discussion. One student wrote her own poem, "We Are from America," about what ordinary citizens of the United States think about ordinary citizens of Afghanistan and vice versa: "We are from America / they are from Afghanistan / We are rich to them / they are poor to us," and so on. Another class discussed the history and meaning of the Pledge of Allegiance. Through exercises like these students learn a kind of patriotism that gives space to thoughtful reflection and that honors the ideals of democracy on which the United States was founded. Ironically, Peterson's curriculum may do more to teach students "traditional" history and the Founding Fathers' ideals than those lessons suggested by Lamar Alexander and his colleagues. The curriculum won the Clarke Center's national competition for innovative ways to teach 9/11 in the classroom (elementary division). Classroom activities and assignments at La Escuela demonstrate that teaching a commitment to these ideals is not facile. La Escuela Fratney puts its mission into practice by encouraging teaching that makes clear the connections between students' lives and the outside world, between their communities and the larger national community, and between the concerns of our nation and the global concerns of all nations.

Conclusion

There is evidence that many students are learning the lessons of authoritarian patriotism well. A poll of California high school students found that 43% of seniors, having completed courses in U.S. history and U.S. government, either agreed with or were neutral toward the statement "It is un-American to criticize this country." Another poll shows that a majority of students nationwide have some ideals consistent with democratic patriotism (and this is probably due in no small part to the efforts of individual teachers and administrators), but a sizable minority (28%) believe that those who attend a protest against U.S. military involvement in Iraq are "unpatriotic."[27]

In a climate of increasingly authoritarian patriotism, dissent grows ever more scarce. But a democratic public is best served by a democratic form of patriotism. To ensure the strength of our democratic institutions and to foster a democratic patriotism that is loyal to the American ideals of equality, compassion, and justice, adults must struggle with difficult policy debates in all available democratic arenas. Trying to forge a national consensus in any other way or on any other grounds (especially through attempts at authoritarian patriotism) is what leads to troubled waters. And students need to learn about these contentious debates with which adults struggle and prepare to take up their parts in them. To serve the public interest in democracy and to reinforce a democratic kind of patriotism, educators will need to embrace rather than deny controversy.

Langston Hughes, in his 1936 poem "Let America Be America Again," speaks of the gap between a rhetorical patriotism rooted only in symbolic gestures and love of the American ideals of liberty and equality:

> O, let my land be a land where
> Liberty Is crowned with no false patriotic wreath,
> But opportunity is real, and life is free,
> Equality is in the air we breathe.

That's the best kind of patriotism we can hope for.

Notes

1 Nebraska State Board of Education, "Board Minutes," 1–2 November 2001 (revised following 7 December 2001 meeting).

2 Jennifer Piscatelli, "Pledge of Allegiance," *State Notes: Character and Civic Education*, Education Commission of the States, August 2003.

3 "President Introduces History and Civic Education Initiatives," remarks of the President on Teaching American History and Civic Education Initiative, 17 September 2002, www.whitehouse.gov.

4 Martha Nussbaum, *For Love of Country: Debating the Limits of Patriotism* (Cambridge, MA: Beacon P, 2002), p. 29.

5 C. Douglas Lummis, *Radical Democracy* (Ithaca, NY: Cornell UP, 1996), p. 37.

6 Henry Steele Commager, *Freedom and Order: A Commentary on the American Political Scene* (New York: George Braziller, 1966), p. 117.

7 See http://archive.columbiatribune.com/2005/feb/20050201news003.asp.

8 NPR, "Citizen Student: Teaching Patriotism in Time of War," 6 February 2003.

9 Cited in Nat Hentoff, "The Patriotism Enforcers: Miseducating the Young on Freedom," *Village Voice*, 2–8 January 2002.

10 U.S. House of Representatives, Committee on Un-American Activities, Investigation of Communist Activities, New York Area (Entertainment): Hearings, 84th Congress, 18 August 1955. Available at http://historymatters.gmu.edu/d/6457.

11 U.S. House of Representatives, Committee on Un-American Activities, Investigation of the Unauthorized Use of U.S. Passports, 84th Congress, Part 3, 12 June 1956, in Eric Bentley, ed., *Thirty Years of Treason: Excerpts from Hearings Before the House Committee on Un-American Activities, 1938–1968* (New York: Viking P, 1971), p. 770.

12 Many of the examples cited here can be found in Peter Dreier and Dick Flacks, "Patriotism and Progressivism," *Peace Review*, December 2003, p. 399.

13 See www.loc.gov/today/pr/2003/03-095.html.

14 *Freedom Under Fire: Dissent in Post-9/11 America* (New York: American Civil Liberties Union, 2003); and Kathleen Kennedy Manzo, "Teachers Grapple with Wartime Role," *Education Week*, 20 March 2003, p. 27.

15 "W. Va. Student Suspended for Starting Anti-War Club: School Says Fliers Disrupted Educational Environment," *Student Press Law Center Report*, Winter 2002, p. 7.

16 Chris Frates, "High School Junior Suspended After Posting AntiWar Fliers," *Denver Post*, 28 February 2003.

17 National Coalition for History, "Senator Alexander's 'American History and Civics Education' Bill Passes Senate," *Washington Update*, 27 June 2003.

18 "Senator Alexander's American History and Civics Bill Passes Senate Unanimously," press release, Sen. Alexander's office, 20 June 2003.

19 Hofstadter is quoted by Sen. Alexander in "Remarks of Senator Lamar Alexander

on the Introduction of His Bill: The American History and Civics Education Act," 4 March 2003.

20 "Beware Leftists in Our Schools!!!," anonymous parent posting, Southern Maryland Online chat forum, 2003, http://forums.somd.com.

21 See, for example, Bree Picower's curriculum, "An Unnatural Disaster," which asks students to consider the many interlocking causes of the extensive damage of Katrina and its aftermath, especially for the African American population of New Orleans (www.nycore.org); and "Washin' Away," Ian McFeat's mock-trial activity for Rethinking Schools (www.rethinkingschools.org) that asks students to explore the roles various people and contexts played in the Katrina tragedy. For contrast, see the MindOH Foundation's Hurricane Katrina resources that include, for example, "Thinking It Through: Why Do Bad Things Happen to Good People?" This activity opens with "Life is not always fair. Bad things happen to good people.... We may be able to make educated guesses about Mother Nature's weather patterns, but..." (www.mindohfoundation.org/hurricanekatrina.htm).

22 Harry C. Boyte, "A Different Kind of Politics: John Dewey and the Meaning of Citizenship in the 21st Century," Dewey Lecture, University of Michigan, Ann Arbor, 1 November 2002, p. 11.

23 Some resources for getting started in seeking such programs include Rethinking Schools (www.rethinkingschools.org); Educators for Social Responsibility (www.esrnational.org); *New York Times* lessons (www.nytimes.com/learning); American Social History Project: Center for Media and Learning (www.history-matters.gmu.edu); and Teaching for Change (www.teachingforchange.org).

24 Karen Suurtamm, project director for Democratic Dialogue (www.democratic-dialogue.com), did the lion's share of research for and writing of the descriptions of El Puente Academy and La Escuela Fratney Elementary School.

25 Catherine Capellaro, "When Small Is Beautiful: An Interview with Héctor Calderón," *Rethinking Schools*, Summer 2005.

26 Bill Carter and Felicity Barringer, "In Patriotic Time, Dissent Is Muted," *New York Times*, 28 September 2001.

27 Dennis Gilbert, "Hamilton College Patriotism Poll: Eleven Key Findings," 20 March 2003, Question 17, Appendix, p. 7. Available at www.hamilton.edu/levitt/surveys/patriotism/patriotismreport.pdf.

DISCUSSION QUESTIONS

1. The article includes a table that details the differences between authoritarian and democratic patriotism. Come up with 3–5 additional slogans, as well as historical and contemporary examples for each of the two types of patriotism.

2. Westheimer gives an example of a story where a teacher had his class look at the Alien and Sedition Acts of 1798, the Sedition Act of 1918, and the Patriot Act of 2001. Just as the teacher asked his students to do, "assess the three time periods and argue for the justice or injustice of each law" (p. 331). Note that this will require some research on your part.

3. The article highlights the "tendency [of many U.S. schools] to cast patriotism and politics as opposites" (p. 332). Consider the implications of separating patriotism and politics, and write a short paragraph that either highlights your understanding of the consequences of this way of teaching and thinking, or argues for the benefits of this mode of education.

4. Westheimer elucidates the importance of educators being allowed to teach their classrooms through democratic patriotism, and highlights the reasons why authoritarian patriotism is less effective. Why does Westheimer believe that authoritarian patriotism is so detrimental?

5. While the article stresses democratic patriotism as the best way to "ensure the strength of our democratic institutions" (p. 336), it still recommends teaching a form of patriotism to students. Could you make an argument for forgoing a patriotic education entirely, and instead having educational institutions focus on teaching through a more global lens? Create an argument for, or against, this idea.

E. "USING SOCIAL MEDIA DIALOGICALLY: PUBLIC RELATIONS ROLE IN REVIVING DEMOCRACY," MICHAEL L. KENT

Focusing on the role of public relations professionals, this 2013 article from Public Relations Review *analyzes how society's increasing dependence on and access to technology affects democracy. By reviewing the pros and cons of how mass media is currently used, Michael Kent* argues that public relations professionals' "lack of understanding of new technology," along with their use of social media "simply to serve marketing and advertising interests," has led to "less civic participation, and less aware-ness of what is happening in the world around us" (p. 353). As you read this article, pay attention to whether you find any of Kent's claims unwarranted or unsupported, while also considering the merit of Kent's overall critique of social media.*

Abstract

This article explores how technology and our recent access to, and abundance of, information, are affecting democracy, and the role of public relations professionals in a post-mass media society. The article reviews pros and cons of new technology, discusses how public relations can improve democracy using dialogue, communi-tarianism, and Long Now thinking, and discusses how to actually, use social media dialogically. The article argues that as public relations revives its conceptualization of relationship, communication professionals also benefit democracy and society as a whole.

Keywords: Dialogue, Dialogic, Communitarianism, Long Now, Technology, Social Media

For more than a century in the United States, citizens obtained the information that was needed for the maintenance of democracy, the pursuit of commerce, the protection of the nation, our cultural beliefs, and our personal values from the mass media, and discussion and debate with their fellow citizens (cf. Postman, 1984). Public relations professionals understand that research and access to information about stakeholders, stakeseekers, public issues, the economy, and hundreds of other

---

* Michael L. Kent is Professor of Public Relations at the University of Tennessee. His research interests include media and mass culture, communication theory, and public relations writing.

areas are at the heart of all effective public relations. Democracy is similar. Informed citizens enact democracy using a variety of public and private information.

But in the 90s, the Internet changed things. Technology began to transform democracy. Two decades ago, the Internet was heralded as the greatest communication tool of all time: "The Information superhighway," capable of linking remote parts of the world, and transforming democracy and education (cf. Kent, 2001). Unfortunately, the Internet has not lived up to its hype, especially as it pertains to public relations.

This article explores the role of public relations professionals in a post-mass media society, as well as how technology and our recent access to, and abundance of, information are affecting democracy. The article is divided into four sections. The first section reviews the role of information and technology in a democracy. The second section reviews some of the pros and cons of new technology. The third section discusses how public relations can improve democracy using dialogue, communitarianism, and Long Now thinking, and how to use social media dialogically. The fourth section concludes with a call for more organization–public interaction.

1. Information, Democracy, and Technology

Because of technology, organizational spokespeople are no longer forced to rely on their relationships with media gatekeepers and the information subsidy to get word out about organizational activities to stakeholders and publics. Americans now regularly obtain information of value directly from organizations via social media, hand-held devices, etc. Technology has changed the way that citizens obtain and weigh information, and the way that public relations functions.

For decades, beat reporters, and specialist journalists gathered news in coherent areas (crime, law, health, politics, education). Journalistic gatekeepers, most of whom were more knowledgeable about their specialized areas than the average citizen, controlled information, but also made decisions about what information was the most newsworthy to the majority of citizens. When the number of news channels were limited, up until the 1980s, broadcasters and print journalists served essential roles in democracy. They were the "fourth estate," protecting the people by reporting on government and society. Being well informed has always been considered a sign of wisdom, and journalists helped keep people informed and served as a safeguard against demagoguery.

However, as news and information sources gradually become more pervasive, because of 24-hour news cycles, the Internet, and abundant real-time technologies, publics became more fragmented and harder to reach. The Internet opened up new sources for news and information, and special interest groups were able to reach potential supporters directly. The Internet broke the illusion of shared public knowledge and forced people to individually decide what to pay attention to. Every citizen is now a media gatekeeper.

From a democratic standpoint, a society that does not care about what is happening is not a democracy. True democracy requires vigilance and participation, not passivity and isolation. Citizens need to be harmonized, not atomized. The same is true for public relations. Many professionals spend more time worrying about posting to their organization's social media sites than about their actual strategic communication goal (cf. Kent, Carr, Husted, & Pop, 2011). The medium has come to matter more than the message. Public relations have the ability to build communities, and diverse communities are at the core of democracy.

1.1. *Public Media, Public Issues, and Social Media*

For democratic participation and oversight to occur, a populace needs to be informed about public issues, not simply one's individual private area of interest. For generations, citizens were kept informed by the mass media. Up until about the mid-90s, a citizen could read a local and national newspaper each day, watch the local and national news in the evening, and maybe *60 Minutes* on Sunday, and feel fairly well-informed about the public issues of importance to most citizens, since everyone else obtained their news and information from the same sources.

Unfortunately, because of corporate media consolidation throughout the 80s and 90s (Bagdikian, 2004; cf. also www.corporations.org/media), the US media landscape is now controlled by just five mega-media corporations (and even more consolidation was approved in December 2012). Although citizens might have felt informed by reading the newspaper, their reservoir of local, state, national, and international knowledge was shallow. As newspaper publishers, broadcasters, book publishers, music labels, movie houses, and other entertainment industries merged, any hope of balanced public information evaporated (cf. Bagdikian, 1992; Schiller, 1989).

Ironically, perhaps the final blow to the mass media's ability to deliver essential information to citizens was probably struck by the Internet and social media, which have turned news content into personal entertainment and editorial, and shifted to "user-generated content" as a means of filling time. Media consolidation and social media have now placed the burden of learning about important information and weighing sources of information squarely on the shoulders of the average citizen. Indeed, social media and new technology actually make it more difficult for the average person to stay informed, as members of a democracy should.

With the shift away from mainstream media and professional gatekeepers who made editorial decisions, citizens have increasingly come to rely on a greater diversity of news sources (some more credible than others), and more idiosyncratic voices that appeal to individual citizens' unique interests. Without the aid of credible gatekeepers and media professionals, democracy is hobbled, just as it is by having its media controlled by only five mega-corporations.

1.2. Where Citizens Get Their News from Matters

As technology expanded, first with Cable Television, and then the Internet, many argued that people would have the opportunity to obtain more, and better, information (cf. Kent, 2001; Meehan, 1988). In practice, however, more news "potential" did not equal more-diverse voices, opinions, or ideas, only more of the same. Our Internet search technologies and social media are similar, in that people often get more of what they want and like, rather than what they *need* or *should see* to be good citizens.

In the fragmented world of self-selected media, finding examples of basic democratic responsibilities—citizens being involved in governance, being involved in decision-making, and overseeing the activities of lawmakers—is hard (Held, 1987a). Similarly, ensuring that the principles of democratic accountability where lawmakers are accountable to the people and make decisions with the best interest of the nation at heart is equally uncommon. People spend more time with technology and access to information than ever before, but probably engage democracy less than at any point in history, since technology has made filtering out the negative voices and opinions of others so easy.

As a recent study by the PEW Internet and American Life Project suggests, most people (66%) ignore political posts from friends that they disagree with, and about 36% of the time someone is "unfriended" because of a politically-related posting or comment (Rainie & Smith, 2012, pp. 2–3). Other studies have found similar trends; people are simply blocking and filtering out the voices and ideas that they do not want to encounter. Changes in social media, journalism, and new technology have made disengaging from political life easier, and essentially encourage people to ignore information that is ideologically unpleasant. A consideration of the pros and cons of technology should help contextualize what is happening.

2. Technology and Democracy Pros and Cons

Technology has played a role in US democracy since the founding of the country. In the beginning of the Republic, the printing press was used to bring news and information to citizens. *The Federalist Papers*, for example, a series of 85 political commentaries calling for ratification of the US Constitution, written by Alexander Hamilton, James Madison, and John Jay, were actually serialized in the weekly newspapers. The content of the *Federalist Papers* consisted of complex political and philosophical argumentation.

Roughly a century later, radio emerged, followed by television in the middle of the twentieth century. With each new innovation, slight changes were introduced into how people obtained and made sense of political information. In President Lincoln's day, politicians went from town to town and gave hours long stump speeches (cf. Postman, 1984), but the bulk of public political information was still found in newspapers. As public relations slowly evolved out of our roles as World War II and corporate propagandists, professionals used the mass media to share information with stakeholders and publics.

New technology has altered seventy years of democratic public relations practices. The Internet allows citizens to obtain real time news and information from thousands of online sources. In only two decades, we have seen profound changes that include news sites and online newspapers, online wire services, RSS, news aggregators, streaming video, Internet search tools, blogging, social media, user-generated news content, podcasts, discussion groups, listservs, Internet telephony (VOIP, Skype), webmetric/analytic software, and communication via hand-held devices such as iPhones, iPads, Kindle, Android, and more. Public relations professionals have enthusiastically embraced each new technology, making communication technologies one of the most studied areas of the field (cf. Ye & Ki, 2012) and one of the most promising for improving democracy. In spite of all the positives that technology offers, technology also has negatives.

2.1. The Negatives of New Technology

A number of areas of concern exist in regard to new technologies that include social behaviors, chronemic perception, patience and delayed gratification, political participation, and the (until recently) historically slow progression of technological innovations. But the positive features of technology are often so tantalizing that users have trouble looking past the shiny interfaces.

On the most basic level, technology has changed the pace of society. People now expect answers to questions sent by e-mail and text messages to come in minutes and hours. Individuals and organizations that take days to respond are seen as aberrations. The idea of thoughtful discussion and weighing alternatives now seems anachronistic. Cell phones and handheld devices enable people to communicate from almost anywhere, with almost anyone, at any time of the day or night.

Because of wireless ubiquity, employees are more easily reached by employers, leisure and vacation time has become less personal and less relaxing, and, younger and younger children are having their lives scheduled and controlled by the logic of technology (Gandossy, 2007; Regan, 2007; Robins & Webster, 1988; Stoll, 1995). People's desire for instant gratification has been met through streaming Internet technologies, online shopping, and access to the world's biggest database of entertainment and information.

The increased pace of life and the shift from face-to-face social interaction to technological interaction also means that people often enact their political participation online, rather than with other people. In many ways, politics has become a private activity. Why engage other people in uncomfortable conversations when you can just unfriend (or ignore) them?

However, the conclusion that each technology has its own telos is unsatisfying. Technologies interact. We know from the history of technological evolution that how

Table 1.

Timeline.

Commercial Radio	c. 1920
Commercial Television	c. 1940
Instant Messaging	1965
First Commercial Desktop Computer	1965
Project Gutenberg (e-books)	1971
E-mail/Chat (ARPANET)	1972
MUDs (Multi-User Dungeons)	1975
Hypertext described	1977
Usenet/Newsgroups	1980
First generation (1G) cellular technology (US)	1983
Macintosh computer	1984
Microsoft Windows released	1985
CRTNET Founded	1985
Hypermedia first introduced (Apple HyperCard)	1987
Internet Relay Chat (IRC)	1988
Trolling	1988
Second generation (2G) cellular technology (Finland)	1991
HyperText markup language (HTML)	1991
AOL Founded	1991
Internet/WWW	**1993**
Amazon.com	1994
Lycos (search engine)	1994
World of Warcraft (WoW)	1994
BoingBoing	1995
Craig's List	1995
eBay	1995
Match.com	1995
Yahoo (search engine)	1995
Blogs	1997
MMORPG (massively multiplayer online role-playing games)	1997
Slashdot	1997
Google (search engine)	1998
PayPal	1998
e-Harmony	2000
The SIMS	2000
Third generation (3G) cellular technology (Japan)	2001
Wikipedia	2001
MySpace	2003
SecondLife	2003
Skype	2003
Facebook	2004
Google Scholar	2004
"Corrupted Blood" incident	2005
Reddit	2005
YouTube	2005
Twitter	2006
iPhone	2007
Tumblr	2007
Pinterest	2010
Fourth generation (4G) cellular technology (US)	2011

we think about the world is largely shaped by our technology (McLuhan, 1999/1964). Table 1 shows some of that evolution by highlighting a number of the most influential technological (r)evolutions that have occurred over the last 100 years.

What Table 1 shows is actually a fairly slow progression of technology up through the 1990s. Before the Internet in 1993, three things stand out: cellular telephones in 1983, and Macintosh and Windows-based computers a few years later. Then, we have an eight-year gap before we get 2G cellular technology, a ten-year gap before 3G, and a ten-year gap before 4G. The same decadal progression characterizes communication innovations via the Internet: search engines and blogging emerge in the mid-90s, SecondLife, Skype, and Facebook about ten years later, Twitter a few years after that, but, unless you count Pinterest, not much has happened since Twitter in 2006. And when we consider how little has been done with HTML and organizational web sites in the last twenty years, or the fact that people have had email for forty years, and Listservs and newsgroups for thirty years (CRTNET was founded in 1985), a reasonable question to ask public relations professionals is, "what did you do with all of the other technologies that came before?"

The use of technology by public relations professionals to inform stakeholders and publics has languished. In the academy and professional world, many spend their time encouraging students to tweet, but spend virtually no time talking about the strategic communication potential of our established technologies and what the possibilities are. The average student or communication professional probably cannot name five things that are strategically possible with the Internet that do not involve using social media, such as Facebook and Twitter. The remainder of this paper is devoted to talking about what public relations professionals can do with technology that both advances democracy, as well as public relations.

3. How Can Public Relations Improve Democracy?

The social changes that are being wrought by new technology are not inevitable. Every new technology (both software and hardware) changes the chemistry of democratic communication. As McLuhan (1999/1964) suggested almost fifty years ago, technologies are not "either or" but "both and." For example, as voice recognition with technologies like Apple's Siri become a standard feature in other technologies over the next five to ten years, micro-blogging tools like Twitter will undoubtedly be transformed or replaced. Twitter is convenient in a world of messaging typed on tiny keyboards. However, Twitter's 140 characters could easily be replaced by 140 words. Indeed, in China, 140 characters are already 140 words.

In current practice, public relations professionals use social media as marketing and advertising tools (cf. Taylor & Kent, 2010). Communication professionals need to stop seeing new technology as simply a sales tool and consider how it can be used in more robust activities: relationship-building, problem-solving, crowd-sourcing, design improvement, etc. Social media and related technologies have tremendous untapped potential. A focus on relationship-building via dialogue and communitarianism principles, as well as a long-term worldview of the world via a "Long Now" orientation, will eventually lead to a more robust profession.

3.1. Democracy and Dialogue in Public Relations

Going back thousands of years to the ancient Greeks, dialectic and dialogue were considered important tools of democracy. Although scholars have been talking seriously about dialogue in public relations for more than a decade (cf. Kent & Taylor, 2002; Pearson, 1989), most academics and professionals have done almost nothing with it. As Theunissen and Wan Noordin (2013) recently argued about the various studies of dialogic social media, dialogue is an abstract process that is hard to implement: dialogue, "as it stands, is not only deeply philosophical but also abstract in nature. While these characteristics make it attractive as an ideal toward which to strive, it is difficult to operationalize such abstract notions in practice" (p. 6).

Contrary to the name, the professional use of dialogue is a sophisticated, technical skill, not simply a matter of talking to other people. In professional practice, many mistakenly believe that dialogue is just communicating with others: tweeting status updates, posting content to one's Facebook account. Ultimately, dialogue is a one-on-one relational tool. Dialogue is not about mass communication. Dialogue represents a relational give and take that occurs between two people, or in small groups, that observe strict rules of decorum to maintain fairness, trust, and the opportunity for all involved to express their opinion. Dialogue is an orientation toward communication with others, not a simple procedure or process. Dialogic encounters can build long-lasting relationships, but dialogue as a professional tool is much more.

The question is, then, in an age of new technology and virtual encounters, whether a tool like dialogue is even viable as a public relations tool. How can dialogue be used by public relations professionals, and how can dialogue be used to build or strengthen democracy? The problem is not with the medium of the Internet; the problem, quite simply, is with the application and intent. Because of social media technology, public relations professionals have regressed from our role as organization–public relationship builders and counselors, to marketers, advertisers, and strategic communicators.

To use social media for relationship building (discussed below) means we think about social media differently. Rather than social media being a cheap and easy way to reach stakeholders and publics with organizational messages, social media should be re-envisioned as interpersonal and group communication tools, and not a replacement for a weakened mass media. Using social media in public relations requires more than just the tool that dialogue provides; we also need an ideological shift. Communication professionals need to change how they think about publics.

3.2. The Pragmatics of a Dialogic Social Media

Saying that social media need to be more dialogic is easy. The question is, how to actually use social media better. The focus of public relations professionals' use of social media should be to build relationships, solve problems, and enact socially responsible goals. Suggestions include:

First, parallel, or alternative, social media spaces should be developed where organizational members actually communicate with individuals and not members of a collective, like customers. Dialogic social media web sites are not intended as places where thousands or tens of thousands of people passively wait for messages, but as active participatory places where organizational managers, leaders, and professionals actually communicate with individual human beings.

Second, dialogic social media spaces should not *be enacted through existing social media venues* like Twitter or Facebook, filled with advertisements and distractions, and poorly designed for substantive, interactive, discussions. New social media interfaces should be adopted or designed to allow organizational members and stakeholders/publics to freely interact and collaborate. Indeed, old-school tools such as listservs and threaded dialogue still have value.

Third, the identity of participants should be public and verifiable. All participants' identities should be known to the other participants. Dialogue is not conducted with anonymous parties but with human beings who have names and faces.

Fourth, clear rules should exist for participation. One of the fundamental dialogic rules is that members are able to question the rules at any time (cf. Pearson, 1989). Rules are designed to further discussions, not privilege the organization or any particular members. Rules might include the following: (1) Members should be identifiable (as suggested above). (2) All members are expected to participate (dialogic social media are not places for lurkers). To be a member of a dialogic discussion means you are willing to share your insights and beliefs. (3) Participants should provide support and evidence for all claims. (4) Whenever possible, conversations should take place in real time. Threaded dialogue can be incorporated, but synchronous discussions (perhaps via audio and visual interfaces like Skype) with other people should be the norm.

Fifth, experts should be sought out and invited to participate. However, any interested party, including the media, competitors, academics, and customers, should be allowed to participate.

Sixth, divergent voices should be nurtured and encouraged to participate. Small group theory, the theory of Groupthink, as well as the Delphi methodology, all suggest that the more voices, the better. Reasoned dissent should be encouraged and everyone should be given a chance to participate.

3.3 Building Community through Communitarianism and the Long Now

For dialogue to be used effectively by organizations and public relations professionals, managers and practitioners at all levels should also draw upon principles of communitarianism (Etzioni, 1993) and Long Now thinking (www.longnow.org). Relationships are not built to exploit publics.

3.3.1. what is communitarianism?

The communitarian movement is a philosophical group committed to shifting the emphasis in society from individual rights to collective responsibilities. As Etzioni (1993) has written, "no economy can thrive when greed is so overpowering that few have a motive to invest in the long run and the highest rewards go to those who engage in financial manipulations rather than constructive enterprises" (p. 29).

Communitarians believe that corporations should engage in corporate social responsibility, that citizens should be concerned about others, and that people need to shift their focus away from getting all that they can get (individualism) to a more collectivist focus that considers other citizens, civil society groups, ethnic groups, and social classes (cf. Held, 1987b). The principles of the Long Now, an ideology in concert with both dialogue and communitarianism, can help to enact both.

3.3.2. what is long now thinking?

Long Now thinking is a focus on the future that necessitates collaboration, putting the community ahead of the individual or organization, and enacting democratic ideals. Established in 1996, the Long Now Foundation is a group of scientists, artists, futurists, researchers, and critical thinkers (currently more than 4,700 members) who believe that "Civilization is revving itself into a pathologically short attention span" (longnow.org/about). The members of Long Now believe, "Some sort of balancing corrective to the short-sightedness is needed—some mechanism or myth which encourages the long view and the taking of long-term responsibility, where 'long-term' is measured at least in centuries" (ibid).

According to the Long Now Foundation's, "Guidelines for a long-lived, long-valuable institution," Long Now principles include serving the long view, fostering responsibility, rewarding patience, minding mythic depth, allying with competition, taking no sides, and leveraging longevity." The principles of Long Now thinking (discussed below) are consistent with basic principles of democracy, dialogue, and communitarianism.

If we look at the use of social media by most large corporations, we see that the communication tools that were invented for "sociality" are typically used in a one-way fashion to push messages out to publics. The unidirectional messaging points to the desire of individuals to remain in their own mediated cocoon, consuming self-selected entertainment. Communitarianism, Dialogue, and Long Now thinking work to change the nature of organization–public communication by asking professional communicators to engage stakeholders and publics on equal ground and actually treating people as valued friends and colleagues who can help an organization move forward.

3.4. Dialogic Solutions: How to Reengage Citizens, Stakeholders, and Publics

Humans are social animals. As long as we construct our messages and relationships with stakeholders and publics as tools of convenience and opportunism, as opportunities for individuals to gather rather than as public spaces, we will continue to see an erosion of democracy. Public relations professionals need to put a stop to the practice of using stakeholders and publics to satisfy our organizational ends, and work to rebuild democratic ideals and public awareness. The key to how to do this lies in thinking about our technological spaces dialogically.

1. *When we construct social spaces for individuals and publics, what we should talk about is what stakeholders and publics want to talk about.* Serving the interests of our stakeholders actually serves our own interests.

So much of what passes as social media research in public relations is just marketing and advertising in disguise.

Democracy, dialogue, communitarianism, and Long Now thinking all take into account others. Our organization–public communication should cease to be simply sender-to-receiver, where organizations try to give stakeholders and publics what they think they want, to keep them entertained—what public relations did seventy-five years ago. Instead, our communication and strategic planning should start by asking stakeholders for feedback before the fact, not after the fact.

The good organization acting well (Heath, 2001) should be our mantra. Social media and new technologies should be used to raise topics and facilitate discussions, not simply to offer coupons and discounts or advertise products. From a public relations standpoint, our use of social media should be different than advertising or marketing's use.

2. *Social media needs to be genuinely social, or not at social all.* When all public relations professionals can envision for social media is social marketing, we have missed our calling.

Through the magic of social media and the Internet, we can bring together thousands of people and share content in almost any form (printed, video, audio, graphic, etc.). Democracy is enacted by citizens, or, in the case of public relations, stakeholders and publics.

Currently, the use of social media by politicians and public relations professionals is similar: unidirectional, image-marketing, focused on raising money and encouraging sales, but not on what stakeholders and citizens really want or need. In spite of the enormous potential of social media to do so much more, the online tools are primarily used asymmetrically. Public relations professionals need to change that. Relationships are built on risk, trust, mutuality, propinquity, empathy, and interaction (i.e., dialogue).

Engaging citizens (or publics) is one of the central roles of leaders in a democracy (cf. Held, 1987a). Dialogic organizations that make decisions with all stakeholders in mind, rather than just elites (shareholders, managers), serve democracy and their entire organization.

3. *Public spaces and collective decision-making need to be revived.* The best decisions are challenged, and are made through consultation with outsiders and experts.

A democracy is successful because of the collective wisdom of its citizens and leaders. A democracy is an excellent choice as a model for public relations. Unfortunately, social media have interrupted the democratic processes that have guided public decision-making for almost two centuries. Social media allow for symbolic participation rather than genuine participation, making people feel a part of the process but giving no one a genuine voice (cf. Kent, Harrison, & Taylor, 2006).

Instead of corporate managers, CEOs, and business leaders meeting behind closed doors to make decisions, public relations professionals should push for more inclusiveness, more transparency, more stakeholder input, more public input, more lectures, and more physical and virtual spaces where people can come and talk about ideas and issues. Just as we expect our legislators to know what the electorate believes and to act in the best interest of the many and not the few, public relations professionals need to enact the same behavior. "Community" should become something that people draw strength and comfort from, rather than virtual communities of strangers with no actual stake in people's lives.

4. *Taking the time to become more widely informed and acting as organizational counsels rather than corporate Tweeters should be a priority.*

Informed citizens are the cornerstones of a democracy, and keeping stakeholders and publics informed has been a cornerstone of public relations for half a century. Concurrently, the fragmentation of information, brought on by the Internet and social media, self-isolation, and targeted advertising and marketing have resulted in a citizenry that seemingly has access to more information than ever before, but in practice, is relatively unaware of the big picture and never asked to evaluate conflicting policy options.

As professional communicators and agents of democracy, public relations professionals need to operate outside of their own comfort zones in terms of exposure to information and research. Communication professionals need to invite in competing voices and encourage outsiders and the disenfranchised to help us deliberate about and solve substantive organizational and social problems. Public relations professionals as organizational spokespeople have a lot to give to democracy, as we act as organizational counselors, consciences, and bring diverse voices and information to our organizations.

5. *The focus of communication professionals needs to be on the long-term and not the short term.* The principles of the Long Now provide some guidelines:

- "Serving the long view" hints at the importance of shifting our focus from our feet to the horizon, from quarterly profits to decadal achievements, from corporate and stockholder goals to stakeholder and public goals.
- "Fostering responsibility" means institutionalizing it. Dishonest employees are fired, not given bonuses, etc. Deceptive communicators and organizations are penalized and shunned. Laws and actions that make public communication safer and more private are supported. Online privacy should not be something people have to negotiate with organizations about, nor should organizations work to exploit personal information for corporate gain. Being ethical and responsible should be how professional communicators behave.
- "Rewarding patience" needs to replace the short-term, instant-gratification mentality. People do not need to know what organizations are doing on a minute-by-minute basis via Twitter or Facebook. Stakeholders and publics are better served by thoughtful, thorough, and relevant information delivered not by interns tweeting, but by senior managers and organizational leaders communicating publicly via (actual or online) "town-halls," webcasts, research papers and white papers, high-quality infographics rather than eye-candy, websites that contain complete information, etc.
- "Minding mythic depth" means living up to heroic standards. Rather than taking a lowest common denominator approach, we ask our publics and ourselves to be the best we can be. Organization–public communication should be easy, but not passive. In ethical organizations, email addresses and contact information are made public, not hidden, and threaded dialogue is encouraged and examined by organizational managers and leaders and brought forward in organizational discussions. Activists are not seen as the enemy but as part of an organizational conscience.
- "Allying with competition" is about working to make the world better. If the major players in an industry can agree to use more environmentally friendly materials, everyone benefits. Talk to people who are different. When all organizational members, stakeholders, and stakeseekers participate in decisions about the future, everyone benefits.
- "Taking no sides" means that if the competition comes up with a better solution, support it. Thomas Edison is famous for opposing AC current because he did not invent it, and because he already had substantial personal investments

in DC current. AC was more useful for long-distance electrification. AC won. But Edison still went around the country for years electrocuting dogs and cats and in one case an elephant, in his efforts to discredit AC current. In our role as organizational counselors, public relations professionals need to be the most well-informed, widely-read, people in the organization.

The good of a company and the good of the nation should not be de-cided by narrow, short-term, profit-driven, interests. When we consider that, according to *Bloomberg Businessweek*, "The average life expectancy of a multinational corporation—Fortune 500 or its equivalent—is between 40 and 50 years...[that] 40% of all newly created companies last less than 10 years...[and that] the average life expectancy of all firms, regardless of size...is only 12.5 years" (www.businessweek.com/chapter/degeus.htm), we have to ask why so many organizations fight change. Long-lived organizations adapt.

- "Leverage longevity" and stop taking sides. When a business's activities only serve short-terms profits, we should drop the practice or oppose it.

The fact that public relations can play a role in making democracy better should be obvious. What is often less obvious is how we can do it. Our actions as communication professionals shape how millions of others see our compa-nies, our products and services, and other human beings. Practicing genuinely social, social media, enacting dialogue both internally, externally, and in elec-tronic contexts, and enacting communitarian principles and principles of the Long Now, are things that public relations professionals can do. Ultimately, for such activities to bear fruit will take decades, but if we do nothing, democracy and civil society will become increasingly weaker.

4. Conclusion

Most of the social media technologies that were supposed to connect people to oth-ers, stimulate our democracy, and enable every citizen to participate in the life of the mind, have largely had just the opposite effect. As public communicators, we control perhaps the most important resource in a democracy: information. To date, our lack of understanding of new technology and our implementation of new technologies simply to serve marketing and advertising interests have led to less civic participation and less awareness of what is happening in the world around us. Indeed, for more than three decades, scholars have argued that new technologies have negative as well as positive aspects, but we have mostly ignored the negatives (cf. Burnham, 1984; Kent, 2008; Postman, 1993; Stoll, 1995, 1999; Taylor & Kent, 2010; Vallee, 1982).

So many of our new technologies have vastly more potential. Study after study posits that social media are dialogic, but the operationalization of dialogue often looks like online advertising and product promotion. For decades, we have argued that our communication technologies will connect us, but that connectivity to our "friends" on social media comes at the expense of isolation from our fellow human beings who live next door or down the hall. Obviously, social media are a tool that can be better used.

Dealing with the impact of technology on political and social life is not easy. There are no quick fixes that public relations can enact. However, if we go back to our professional roots as informed organizational counselors, we begin to see that being critical, and being informed, are the first steps. We need to begin enacting some of the principles of long-term thinking and relationship-building with all of our stakeholders and stakeseekers: employees, customers, management, industry peers, and others. The solution is not found in the less sophisticated interactions that we have had with social media, but through richer, more inclusive interactions.

References

Bagdikian, B.H. (1992). *The media monopoly* (fourth edition). Boston: Beacon P.

Bagdikian, B.H. (2004). *The new media monopoly.* Boston: Beacon P.

Burnham, D. (1984). *The rise of the computer state.* New York: Vintage Books.

Etzioni, A. (1993). *The spirit of community: The reinvention of American society.* New York: Simon and Schuster.

Gandossy, T. (2007). *Technology transforming the leisure world. CNN.com.* www.cnn.com/2007/US/03/29/leisure.overview.

Heath, R.L. (2001). Chapter 2: A rhetorical enactment rationale for public relations: The good organization communicating well. In R.L. Heath, & G. Vasquez (Eds.), *Handbook of public relations* (pp. 31–50). Thousand Oaks, CA: Sage.

Held, D. (1987). *Models of democracy.* Stanford, CA: Stanford UP.

Held, V. (1987). Non-contractual society: A feminist view. *Canadian Journal of Philosophy,* 13, 111–37.

Kent, M.L. (2001). Managerial rhetoric and the metaphor of the World Wide Web. *Critical Studies in Media Communication,* 18(3), 359–75.

Kent, M.L. (2008). Critical analysis of blogging in public relations. *Public Relations Review,* 34(1), 32–40.

Kent, M.L., Carr, B.J., Husted, R.A., & Pop, R.A. (2011). Learning Web analytics: A tool for strategic communication. *Public Relations Review,* 37(4), 536–43.

Kent, M.L., Harrison, T.R., & Taylor, M. (2006). A critique of Internet polls as symbolic representation and pseudo-events. *Communication Studies,* 57(3), 299–315.

Kent, M.L., & Taylor, M. (2002). Toward a dialogic theory of public relations. *Public Relations Review,* 28(1), 21–37.

McLuhan, M. (1999/1964). *Understanding media: The extensions of man.* Cambridge, MA: The MIT P.

Meehan, E.R. (1988). Technical capability versus corporate imperatives: Toward a political economy of cable television and information diversity. In V. Mosco, & J. Wasko (Eds.), *The political economy of information* (pp. 167–87). Madison, Wisconsin: U of Wisconsin P.

Pearson, R. (1989). *A theory of public relations ethics.* Ohio University (Unpublished doctoral dissertation.)

Postman, N. (1984). *Amusing ourselves to death: Public discourse in the age of show business.* New York: Penguin Books.

Postman, N. (1993). *Technopoly: The surrender of culture to technology.* New York: Vintage Books.

Rainie, L., & Smith, A. (2012). *Social networking sites and politics.* Washington, DC: Pew Research Center's Internet & American Life Project. http://pewinternet.org/Reports/2012/Social-networking-and-politics.aspx.

Regan, T. (2007, October). *Maybe e-mail isn't such a great idea, after all. Christian Science Monitor.* www.csmonitor.com/2007/1017/p16s01-stct.htm.

Robins, K., & Webster, F. (1988). Cybernetic capitalism: Information, technology, everyday life. In V. Mosco, & J. Wasko (Eds.), *The political economy of information* (pp. 44–75). Madison, Wisconsin: U of Wisconsin P.

Schiller, H.I. (1989). *Culture Inc.: The corporate takeover of public expression.* New York: Oxford UP.

Stoll, C. (1995). *Silicon snake oil: Second thoughts on the information highway.* New York: Doubleday.

Stoll, C. (1999). *High-tech heretic: Why computers don't belong in the classroom and other reflections by a computer contrarian.* New York, NY: Doubleday.

Taylor, M., & Kent, M.L. (2010). Anticipatory socialization in the use of social media in public relations: A content analysis of PRSA's Public Relations Tactics. *Public Relations Review,* 36(3), 207–14.

Theunissen, P., & Wan Noordin, W.N. (2013). Revisiting the concept dialogue in public relations. *Public Relations Review,* 38, 5–13.

Vallee, J. (1982). *The network revolution: Confessions of a computer scientist.* Berkeley, CA: And/Or Press.

Ye, L., & Ki, E. (2012). The status of online public relations research: An analysis of published articles in 1992–2009. *Journal of Public Relations Research,* 24(5), 409–34.

DISCUSSION QUESTIONS

1. In the article, Kent details the ways in which public relations can help to improve democracy. One of the strategies he suggests using is called Long Now thinking. In your own words, summarize Long Now thinking and how Kent argues it can be used to advance democratic communications. Do you agree with Kent?

2. In section 3.1, "Democracy and Dialogue in Public Relations," Kent seems to claim that social media do not allow for dialogue (in the sense that he defines it), and in section 3.2, "The Pragmatics of a Dialogic Social Media," he suggests six ways to improve this. Discuss both his claim, with reference to examples that might support or contradict it, and his suggestions, with a focus on whether you think each one would/could be effective or not, and why.

3. Kent argues that where citizens get their news matters, and that "social media and new technology actually make it more difficult for the average person to stay informed" (p. 342). Find and explain an example of a news source found using social media in order to test this claim. Did your findings prove or disprove Kent's argument?

4. Given the vast number of news sources that are available, how do you ensure that the sources you get your information from are credible and unbiased? Do you think that social media are more likely, less likely, or equally likely as traditional media to provide accurate information?

5. Kent discusses how "Public relations professionals have enthusiastically embraced" (p. 344) technology, and then provides examples of the "negatives of new technology" (p. 344) in section 2.1. Write a paragraph in response to Kent, highlighting what you see as the most positive aspects of new technology.

SCIENCE AND PUBLIC DISCOURSE

INTRODUCTION

Over the past few centuries, scientific method has radically transformed many societies. On the one hand, science has become a central part of education and decision-making. Scientific research influences technological innovation, public policy, and individuals' daily decisions, such as dietary choices. On the other hand, because scientific findings constantly challenge how we see ourselves and the world (think of the debates surrounding evolution and climate change), they can sometimes spark resistance. The implications of scientific research for the public—its relevance, its application, its reception—are at the heart of the papers in this section, which look at the public discourse surrounding science.

Scientific research produces highly specialized knowledge that often has implications for public policy and legislation. However, it isn't always easy to communicate research findings in a way that the public understands. You have likely read news reports about studies that find a certain food or drink, say coffee, has health benefits, but then, a few months later, encounter a new study contradicting the first one. On many issues, the science is incremental and provisional, and the general public (or the news media that report the science) wants simpler and more definitive answers.

In other areas, science is more conclusive but the public is resistant. Research recognizing that smoking caused lung cancer emerged in the 1950s, but it took decades for doctors and then the public to accept these findings, and even longer for politicians to develop laws restricting smoking. In the case of climate change, there is overwhelming consensus in the scientific community, but there is still defiance on the part of some industries and governments. Climate scientists increasingly speak directly in public forums, sometimes acknowledging that their work has political implications.

One way to examine the intersection between science and public discourse is to acknowledge that despite the goal of objectivity in scientific method, science is rarely disinterested. Donna Haraway's account of being assigned to teach an undergraduate biology course at the University of Hawaii is helpful here:

> I was part of a team of young faculty, led by a senior teacher, who had designed a course to fill an undergraduate general education science requirement for hundreds of students each year. In the middle of the Pacific Ocean, home of the Pacific Strategic Command that was so critical to the Vietnam War with its electronic battlefield and chemical herbicides, this University of Hawaii biology course aimed to persuade students that natural science alone, not politics or religion, offered hope for secular progress not infected by ideology.[1]

Haraway goes on to observe that she couldn't teach the course this way because she was "acutely aware of how intimately science, including biology, was woven into [the Vietnam War]—and into every aspect of our lives and beliefs" (127). On the one hand, Haraway is pointing out how public relevance can result in certain research receiving more (or less) funding. On the other hand, she is emphasizing that many scientific findings are not neutral. They challenge existing ways of seeing the world and ourselves. They call for (or represent) political stances.

In this section, you will read a sampling of recent articles that illustrate the complexity of research that touches on matters of public concern. McHeyzer-Williams and McHeyzer-Williams provide an example of how social media is changing how researchers disseminate findings, specifically using Twitter. Hansson tackles the difficult topic of Genetically Modified Organisms (GMOs), advocating for a cautious but open approach to updating legislation as scientific consensus emerges. Boddice approaches the vexed resistance to vaccinations by examining larger patterns of public discourse that focus on fear. These three articles will give you a sense of how scientists think about and engage with public discourse.

This section also includes three pieces featuring research on Alzheimer's, a disease of increasing public concern in light of today's greater longevity and the aging Baby Boomer population. This research shows how science doesn't exist in a vacuum, but responds to emerging needs in society. These three related examples of writing in the research genres also serve as a case study of the knowledge-making process. First, there is a research proposal by Knight for a Master of Science thesis. Second, you will see a research poster by Knight and Piccinin. The proposal and poster are distinct but common research genres that typically precede publication in academic journals. (See the glossary for more information on each genre.) Finally, there is a published article by Wilson et al. that is one of the points of departure for Knight's research. By examining the article after tracing the process of the proposal and the poster, you can get a sense of how researchers build on previous studies to reformulate both the questions they ask and how they try to answer these questions.

As you read this section, think about the different ways that science informs your daily life and the debates and discussions around you. Have you read news articles or social media posts that report on recent research with health or other important implications? Does some science concern you? What research do you think is most important?

Note

[1] Donna Haraway, "enlightenment@science_wars.Com: A Personal Reflection on Love and War," *Social Text*, no. 50, 1997, 123–29, p. 126.

A. "OUR YEAR ON TWITTER: SCIENCE IN #SOCIALMEDIA," LOUISE J. MCHEYZER-WILLIAMS AND MICHAEL G. MCHEYZER-WILLIAMS

Published in 2016 in a special issue of Trends in Immunology *titled* Communicating Science, *this atypical article reports on an innovative means of disseminating research rather than the authors' main area of research. Louise and Michael McHeyzer-Williams* are immunologists who describe themselves "as neophytes who have enjoyed the unfamiliar process" of communicating research through social media (p. 362). They ask: "Could we use Twitter in our scientific life? What would be the benefits and pitfalls?" (p. 362). They answer the first question in the affirmative, and this article serves as an invitation to other researchers to use Twitter. If you use Twitter frequently, the authors' relative inexperience may put you in the unusual position of feeling like the expert. As you read, pay attention to the line between what is obvious to you and what is new and perhaps surprising. Do you learn anything new about Twitter or about the scientific life?*

Glossary term: peer review

Information is now available in real time from a multitude of sources. Twitter provides one effective means to broadcast images with short captions instantly and everywhere. Last year we began using Twitter to convey our excitement with the biological sciences, and discovered a new means to contribute, connect, and conference with a broader global scientific community and beyond. Here we share this experience and invite you to join in the conversation.

Context

In the past decade, social media has hit its stride, with platforms such as Facebook, LinkedIn, Instagram, Snapchat, Periscope, and Twitter becoming household names. Communication has evolved from one-on-one forms, such as letters and telephone conversations, to electronic mass communication as a way to interact and share information. This transition occurred, in part, through radio and television, which introduced forms of one-to-many communication, and, more recently, with the

---

* Louise J. McHeyzer-Williams is a Senior Scientific Associate and Michael G. McHeyzer-Williams is a Professor in the Department of Immunology and Microbiology at the California campus of the Scripps Research Institute. Their research focuses on regulating adaptive immunity to improve immune protection and vaccine design.

emergence of social media as channels for multidirectional many-to-many interactions among people to create, share, and exchange information.

Social media has become a cornerstone of modern communication, impacting all areas of society. This new means of communication enables users to create content and share it directly with a network of participants. Blogging developed to allow individual users to discuss topics of common interest. Twitter is a popular online microblogging social media networking service that, since 2007, has allowed users to broadcast short 140-character posts called 'tweets.' Each day, 100 million users login to Twitter to learn the breaking news, find a job, keep up with their favorite team, or for myriad other reasons. Through Twitter, people communicate and consume information instantaneously around the world, connecting with people as they 'tweet' about their favorite interest. Using this global platform of communication, the number of users visiting Twitter monthly can swell to over 500 million.[1]

We posted our first tweet at the beginning of 2015. Until then, we had used the platform to quickly acquire information about the world around us; you could say that we were irregular readers of news headlines. However, we were amazed by the

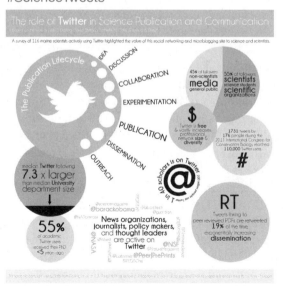

Figure 1. Example of a Tweet from 21 August 2015 by McHeyzer-Williams, User Handle @mmw_lmw. A 140-character tweet showing an infographic by Katie Pratt @Katie_PhD depicting the results of the survey of why scientists use Twitter [3]. The hashtag categorization (#ScienceTweets) is highlighted in blue and, when clicked, can redirect users to further discussion of the subject. This tweet had 56 retweets, 25 likes, 9,573 impressions, and 532 engagements.

speed by which information traveled through Twitter and by its reach, and pondered how, as scientists, we could use this social media channel professionally (Figure 1). One morning, while sipping an espresso at a local café, we discussed how Twitter could be used to share our excitement and interest in science. Our fellow café dwellers were intrigued as to the research process and so, on this January morning, we decided to launch a year-long experiment using Twitter. Could we use Twitter in our scientific life? What would be the benefits and pitfalls? We were unsure and ignorant of how to use Twitter professionally and yet excited to investigate the possibilities. Here we share the initial results of this experiment. We write this essay not as experts, but as neophytes who have enjoyed the unfamiliar process. We report that, indeed, old dogs can learn new tricks to contribute and communicate the excitement of science.

Our Twitter Experience

From the outset, we decided that our Twitter content would arise from our professional endeavors. We are immunologists enamored with the capacity of experimental science to access fundamental mechanisms in biology. We bring a passion for new technologies to our research effort to dissect and reveal the cellular and molecular basis of adaptive immunity. These studies use model strategies to mimic the complexity of the human immune system. Our first decision was that our Twitter content would aim to project these interests while highlighting the newest scientific contributions across a variety of pertinent subdisciplines in biology.

Among scientists, social media can have the reputation of being a distraction from research and a waste of time.[2] We reasoned that directing our Twitter content towards our own interests would make the new and unfamiliar process of tweeting a little easier, and an enhancement to our reading of the literature. During a typical working week, we browse the scientific literature for exciting breakthrough content. We focus on journals in our own discipline as well as the content in the broader-reaching journals that cross disciplines. We are also drawn to technical breakthroughs that highlight new methods and strategies with broad utility. Hence, browsing the literature was already an important and enjoyable component of our professional life and essential to the creative process.

We identified scientists rather than the general public as our possible future audience to engage through Twitter. Having scientists as the audience, our aim was to express our daily literature interest and share with them what we believed to be influential research in the area. Our emerging strategy on how we interact on Twitter is summarized in Box 1. We gave ourselves the challenge that, through our usual literature reading from individual articles, we would choose the one figure or graphic image that we believed piqued our interest. We decided that we would tweet on a regular cadence but not one that would be disruptive to our usual work schedule. Interestingly, this practice set up a feedback loop that stimulated our further reading of the literature. In this way, tweeting impacted the breadth and depth of the literature we browsed.

Box 1. The @mmw_lmw Scientific Use of Twitter Stepwise Strategy

1. Build a profile. Construct your Twitter account describing you and your interests: #immunology.
2. Follow your interests. Find users with a common interest and purpose. You can do this by doing a hashtag search.
3. Browse. This is the first-level interaction without contributing content: reading others' tweets. Here you get to know the environment and how (when and where) you want to contribute.
4. Like and retweet. Begin to establish your themes to reinforce content of interest. You may start to see growth in the number of users who follow you based on your profile or tweets (your network of followers).
5. Tweet. Start with a 140-character text content. Use links to acknowledge authors, institutions, Twitter handle, and source of material.
6. Go visual. Add an image, figure, or graphical abstract to illustrate the central message.
7. Conduct polls. Use short questionnaires to survey opinions of your followers and vote.
8. Share original content. Share your own professional experience of seminars and journal clubs. For conferences, use meeting hashtag for focused discussion and broadcast; e.g., #KStfh
9. Deploy Twitterbots. Twitter PubMed searches; e.g., @ImmuneTfh_Paper or @Immunol_papers
10. Stay engaged. Increase the reach and number of interactions, and keep trying new formats.

The structure of our tweets developed over time and varied with the intention of the message (Box 2). We prefer to begin the tweet with the broad subject area that often carries a hashtag. A short central message is crafted to reflect the main intention of the content, followed by acknowledgement to the corresponding author, their institution, the journal that published the work, and a link to the article. It would be wrong to say that adherence to the 140-character limit of the tweet caption as designated by the Twitter platform is not challenging. Nevertheless, it turns out to be helpful to 'boil down' the central message of the paper and aid in our recall. Our skills to edit ourselves seem to be improving every day and hopefully we are still able to convey the excitement of the scientific literature.

Box 2. Anatomy of an @mmw_lmw Scientific Tweet

- Review: access literature from TOC and email alerts from journals.
- Select: after reading a paper, identify content as the focus of a tweet.
- Subject: define a broad hashtag that relates to the message; e.g., #SingleCell.
- Message: distill content and purpose into short text caption. Be guided by the title of the research for accuracy, but decide what is most important to your message. #MostDifficult.
- Content: keep professional, not personal.
- Image: capture and crop an important figure as a small .jpeg to attach to the message. Try to keep the image simple and somewhat self-explanatory without the need for extensive prior knowledge. Graphical abstracts often work well.
- GIFs: add motion to multiple images using an online GIF maker.
- Video: short stretches can easily be attached to tweets.
- Acknowledgment: note corresponding author of research or review and their institution.
- Source: use journal's twitter handle to acknowledge material; e.g., @ImmunityCP.
- Links: use a URL shortener to condense a regular address; e.g., Bit.ly or Ow.ly.
- Aim: for accuracy, visually appealing, easy to read, and consistent quality.
- Experiment: have fun and evolve.

Recently, we conducted an exploratory text analysis of our 600 tweets from the past year (Figure 2A). The size and boldness of each word indicates the frequency of terms used in the tweet text data. While numerous subjects have been tweeted, 'immunity,' 'single cell,' 'antibodies,' and 'memory' are the terms that emerged as our most common themes. Frequently, we apply a searchable hashtag to a term and this enhances the ability to track and follow the discussion on each of the subjects. These terms provide a snapshot of our literature reading and allow us to share with followers our research interest and convey our excitement of science. Other scientists using Twitter have described themselves as curators of information,[3] and we too feel that this would best describe our selection of information to post on Twitter.

Twitter is not a one-sided medium and scientists use it for many reasons.[4,5] Essential to the process is the interaction and connection with other scientists who use Twitter. We select content that appeals to us and we hope may have broad appeal to our colleagues, the broader scientific community, and hopefully beyond. The content, reach, and distribution of our posts (~600 in the past year), the community of followers who access this content (~2700 people), and the group of people we follow (~2500 people), provide some insight into the dynamics of the activity over the past year. So while we tweet from a professional interest perspective, the followers of our tweets are able to immediately view the tweet and enhance our thinking by commenting on the topic. However, it does not stop there. The dissemination of the tweets is amplified when our followers retweet our tweet to their own set of followers. This exponential network effect has tremendous reach and is the force that underpins social media and the democratization of information today.

To give an example of the reach of Twitter, in February 2015, our 40 tweets were viewed by over 7,000 Twitter users. As our follower numbers increased, these 'impres-

(A)

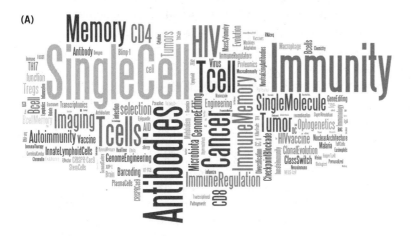

(B)

Figure 2. Content and Follower Word Cloud. (A) Text analysis of @mmw_lmw 600 tweets between February 2015 and February 2016. (B) Follower profile text analysis of @mmw_lmw 2,700 followers. The font size and boldness of each word indicates the frequency of terms used in the text data, displayed in a word cloud created with Wordle.

sions' also grew steadily. In January 2016, we posted 120 tweets that were viewed by 170,000 users. Approximately 2% of users 'engage' the tweets by going to links, visiting profiles, responding to content, and/or saving the tweet. The proportion of engagement has broadly remained constant as the number of impressions increased.

Any Twitter user can access and choose to follow content from other Twitter users. Our current cohort of approximately 2,700 followers is distributed across seventy-five countries, with the majority within the US (40%), UK (17%), Europe (10%), Australia (6%), and Canada (5%). To get some sense of how our subset of Twitter followers describe themselves, we created a text analysis word cloud of the terms chosen by each user in their Twitter profile (Figure 2B). As expected by the more specialized nature of our tweet content, we can glimpse the high concentration of scientific professionals within immunology, biology, and medicine across the broad spectrum of PhD and clinical research communities.

Twitter Makes a Difference

The experiment with Twitter has been very satisfying and surprising in many ways. We began our activity to convey excitement over the substantial developments that occur in science on a daily basis. While literature browsing was used to identify content, our interaction with Twitter has itself enhanced the breadth and depth of this process for ourselves. The Twitter format offers a creative and potentially disruptive new way of acquiring and sharing information.

Disseminating information across these exponential networks of individuals provides an exciting new means to broadcast scientific information in real time. Most scientific conferences now have meeting hashtags that are used by attendees to initiate discussion and announce findings as they are reported.[6] This capacity will accelerate the spread of new findings and ideas, and have a positive impact on the process of doing science.[7]

There needs to be further discussion regarding the nature of content, with more awareness of responsibility in reporting. A self-driven unsupervised dissemination of ideas is also potentially error-prone. By its very nature, Twitter remains unsupervised, but like other forms of content sharing, accountability is ever present. There is a shared responsibility by all users to self-correct information contained within the Twitter landscape. This is especially important when relating and reporting on specialized content. There is a heavy reliance on experts within a given field to respond and challenge questionable or false statements. Interactivity is a major engine of Twitter's appeal and effectiveness that could not only cause issues but also potentially provide solutions.

Accuracy of broadcast is clearly one issue that will remain, especially at conferences. The information exchanged may not be readily available to fact check. If there is a problem of accuracy, is it the fidelity of speaker delivery or inaccuracy of the Twitter broadcast? In addition, premature public announcement of findings or preliminary results can also be detrimental to the process of science publication or protection of intellectual property. It will be important to protect some aspects of these interactions if young ideas are to be shared more openly and disseminated more rapidly at conferences.

Connecting with other scientists across the globe is one of the major advantages and greatest pleasures of our year on Twitter. Reading the Twitter content of many people involved in research provides new perspectives on multiple levels that have deepened our professional experience. One such advantage involved an interaction with a Twitter group of evolutionary biologists that ended with an invitation for us to attend an international meeting. This opportunity provided a unique and rich exchange of ideas that would have otherwise not occurred. In addition, following a group of Twitter-active computational biologists offers us immediate access to fresh perspectives on this critical cutting-edge research arena. We have only begun to interact with the seemingly endless community of research professionals in the 'Twitter-verse' and look forward to promoting deeper connections in the years to follow. Our efforts on Twitter have provided a new and global means to connect to the scientific community and beyond.

To the Future

Our Twitter foray has expanded our sense of community around themes of scientific interest. Because of this Twitter experience, we now have a large worldwide network of scientists coming from various fields and perspectives that are readily available for advice, monitoring of trends, and discussion. We encourage other scientists, especially students, to start following and creating their own network and communities. While it may seem intimidating to some at first, after a few clicks of a button you will be participating across the globe in a discussion of your favorite subject.

We have entered an era of unprecedented research growth in the biological sciences and its related technological and computational underpinnings. There are major breakthroughs that range from high-throughput molecular analyses and genome editing to new classes of immunotherapy and cellular treatment modalities that are being translated into utility for the public health at extraordinary rates. More than ever, there is a need to make this endeavor accessible to everyone in ways that not only educate and inform, but also prompt productive debate and lively interactive discussion. Twitter provides a unique and relevant mechanism to create this network of communication and promote active dissemination of these ideas.

What happens in the future will depend on how Twitter is used in science. We encourage others to broadcast their science and knowledge to learn what new potentials social media provides our community. Tweeting could become part of graduate student education; encouraging tweets would help trainees identify key points and synthesize complex findings into concise and clear messages, an important skill. Professional societies could also organize workshops that introduce participants to the use, ethics, and components of science in social media. These activities could then extend beyond professional societies to the broader public at large.

It is now clear to us that Twitter is one means for extensive network-based dissemination of information that is agile and discriminating in its use for professional purposes. The reach is far and the potential unlimited. Twitter's vibrant real-time forum permits a dynamic level of exchange between participants that enhances the value, reach, and impact of new information worldwide. And now it's time to tweet about this article...see you on Twitter.

Resources

[i] https://blog.twitter.com/2016/bringing-tweets-to-more-people-around-the-world
[1] The Scripps Research Institute, La Jolla, CA 92037, USA.

References

[1] https://blog.twitter.com/2016/bringing-tweets-to-more-people-around-the-world.
[2] Bik, H.M. and Goldstein, M.C. (2013) An introduction to social media for scientists. PLoS Biol. 11, e1001535.
[3] Savage, N. (2015) Scientists in the Twitterverse. Cell 162, 233–34.
[4] Darling, E.M. et al. (2013) The role of Twitter in the life cycle of a scientific publication. Ideas Ecol. Evol. 6, 32–43.
[5] Van Noorden, R. (2014) Online collaboration: scientist and the social network. Nature 512, 126–29.
[6] Ekins, S. and Perlstein, E.O. (2014) Ten simple rules of live tweeting at scientific conferences. PLoS Comput. Biol. 10, e1003789.
[7] Wilkinson, S.E. et al. (2015) The social media revolution is changing the conference experience: analytics and trends from eight international meetings. BJU Int. 115, 839–46.

DISCUSSION QUESTIONS

1. The authors' Twitter handle is @mmw_lmw. You can view their Twitter feed even if you don't have a Twitter account. Read through some of their recent tweets and retweets to gain a more precise sense of their tweeting practice. Identify patterns. Discuss what you see.

2. In Box 1, the authors include a step-by-step approach to using Twitter to communicate with other researchers. Which of these steps seem obvious? Which ones surprise you? For instance, they stipulate to "keep [content] professional, not personal" (p. 363).

3. The authors claim, "This exponential network effect [created by retweeting] has tremendous reach and is the force that underpins social media and the democratization of information today" (p. 365). What are the limits of this exponential effect? What is "democratization of information"?

4. At the outset, the authors wonder whether using Twitter has "pitfalls." In the section "Twitter Makes a Difference," they note one potential problem: "A self-driven unsupervised dissemination of ideas is … potentially error-prone" (p. 366). Compare their use of Twitter with what you know about the process of peer review. Discuss the relative benefits and pitfalls of this aspect of social media. Are there other potential pitfalls?

5. Does this article change how you see the usefulness of Twitter or other social media?

B. "HOW TO BE CAUTIOUS BUT OPEN TO LEARNING: TIME TO UPDATE BIOTECHNOLOGY AND GMO LEGISLATION," SVEN OVE HANSSON

This 2016 article published by Current Topic *explores the topic of precautionary measures in agricultural biotechnological legislation. Sven Ove Hansson* analyzes the concept of precautionary measures along with the current risks of plant breeding in order to determine that "[t]here is an obvious and urgent need for a thorough revision of the regulation of plant breeding" (p. 375). Hansson suggests that while precautionary actions are necessary "in the case of scientific uncertainty... we must also be able to adjust these measures when scientific uncertainty is replaced by scientific knowledge" (p. 375). As you read, try to deduce Hansson's position on the often-controversial subject of GMOs, and how his evaluation of the matter compares to your own understanding of the issues under discussion.*

Glossary terms: ecocriticism, risk analysis

Abstract

Precautionary measures to protect human health and the environment should be science-based. This implies that they should be directed at a potential danger for which there is credible scientific evidence (although that evidence need not be conclusive). Furthermore, protective measures should be updated as relevant science advances. This means that decision-makers should be prepared to strengthen the precautionary measures if the danger turns out to be greater than initially suspected, and to reduce or lift them should the danger prove to be smaller. Most current legislation on agricultural biotechnology has not been scientifically updated. Therefore, it reflects outdated criteria for identifying products that can cause problems. Modern knowledge in genetics, plant biology, and ecology has provided us with much better criteria that risk analysts can use to identify the potentially problematic breeding projects at which precautionary measures should be directed. Legislation on agricultural biotechnology should be scientifically updated. Furthermore, legislators should learn from this example that regulations based on the current state of science need to have inbuilt mechanisms for revisions and adjustments in response to future developments in science.

* Sven Ove Hansson is Professor of Philosophy and Chair of the Department of Philosophy and History of Technology at the Royal Institute of Technology in Stockholm, Sweden. His research interests include environmental risk assessment as well as decision theory and belief dynamics.

1. Introduction

Currently the European Commission is struggling with a much-delayed decision on whether the use of so-called gene-editing tools should be categorized as genetic modification (GM) in a legal sense. Similar controversies are unfolding and will continue to arise elsewhere as new molecular biology technologies, such as oligo-nucleotide directed mutagenesis, zink finger nuclease technology, and CRISPR (clustered regularly interspaced short palindromic repeats), allow precision editing of nucleotides within existing genes, as opposed to the introduction of new genes.[1,2] Against the background of the Transatlantic Trade and Investment Partnership negotiations, the European Union and the United States are seeking to harmonize definitions, standards, and labeling and testing requirements, with interest groups and activists lobbying for and against narrower or wider scopes of definitions for terms such as GM. To understand these controversies, we need to go back to the origins of modern biotechnology in the 1970s.

In July 1974, 11 American researchers, headed by Paul Berg, published a letter in *Science* proposing that scientists should "voluntarily defer" two types of experiments with biologically-active recombinant DNA molecules. They did so because there was "serious concern that some of these artificial recombinant DNA molecules could prove biologically hazardous."[3]

Given the state of knowledge at that time, the hazards had to be carefully evaluated, and a moratorium on the new technology was certainly justified. It was clearly a precautionary measure, aiming at potential dangers rather than proven ones. Such precautionary measures are commonplace, both in public and private life, and not only in environmental and health-related issues. If you lose your credit card, then you will probably want to have it blocked immediately, even if you do not know whether it has been stolen or you have just mislaid it. We buy insurance as a precaution against potential costly misfortunes. And when the military sees indications of a possible enemy attack, we do not expect them to act as if nothing has happened until they have sufficient evidence that the attack is really on its way.

2. Science-Based Precaution

In Europe, precautionary measures to protect human health or the environment are often described as applications of the "precautionary principle." In the United States, the same types of measures are often taken to about the same extent, but they are usually called something else.[4] I will leave this terminological dissension aside and discuss precautionary actions *per se* rather than any special principle on which they can be based.

There are limits to how cautious we can be. Suspicions can be raised against almost anything, and it is not practicable to inhibit all activities that someone believes might be potentially dangerous for some reason or other. Some calls for caution are in fact counterproductive. For instance, claims have been made that we should refrain from vaccination for precautionary reasons, but these claims refer to potential adverse effects that are so farfetched and implausible that they are insignificant in comparison to the well-documented life-saving effects of vaccination. The precautionary measure proposed by the anti-vaccination lobby would prevent us from taking the precautionary measure of vaccinating our children.

In order to avoid such counterproductive effects, we must apply precaution only when it serves its purpose. To achieve this, we have to be well-informed, and therefore precaution should be *science-based*, in the sense of making use of the best scientific information that we have access to. This requirement should be carefully distinguished from the preposterous idea that no action should ever be taken against a suspected danger until there is full scientific evidence that the danger really exists.[5] For instance, precautionary measures are often justified if we have scientific evidence indicating that a chemical exposure probably or possibly has a dangerous property, even if that evidence is not strong enough to settle the issue. Acting on preponderant but inconclusive scientific evidence must also be clearly distinguished from acting on suppositions of a danger with no scientific backing or credibility. The former is science-based precaution; the latter is usually a quixotic undertaking. It is a central task for risk analysis to evaluate the scientific evidence and identify both the scientific knowledge and the scientific uncertainties that are relevant for decisionmakers.

Science progresses, and consequently a regulation or policy that is science-based today need not be so tomorrow. Therefore, precautionary actions should be *scientifically updated*, that is, updated on the basis of new scientific information. Obviously, such updates can lead to different types of adjustments of the precautionary measures. The danger can turn out to be greater than we suspected, in which case we may have to strengthen our measures against it. In other cases, the suspected danger turns out to be less severe than we believed, or it may even be nonexistent. In such cases, restrictions may have to be reduced or lifted.

3. The Case of Biotechnology

Let us return to the 1974 moratorium and make use of these two requirements—a scientific basis and scientific updating. The researchers performed a careful evaluation of the potential dangers of the new technology and found these dangers to be manageable. At the Asilomar Conference on Recombinant DNA in February 1975, the moratorium was lifted. Scientists resumed their experiments, applying safeguards that they had agreed upon.

Twenty years later, Paul Berg (then a Nobel Prize laureate) and Maxine Singer (another leading biologist) wrote a retrospective article, rightly concluding that the new technology had revolutionized biological science. Moreover, this had been achieved without any of the harmful effects that they had feared 20 years earlier. They wrote:

Literally millions of experiments, many even inconceivable in 1975, have been carried out in the last 20 years without incident. No documented hazard to public health has been attributable to the applications of recombinant DNA technology. Moreover, the concern of some that moving DNA among species would breach customary breeding barriers and have profound effects on natural evolutionary processes has substantially disappeared as the science revealed that such exchanges occur in nature.[6]

Today, yet another two decades have passed since the precautionary moratorium. Our knowledge of genetics, plant biology, and ecology has increased dramatically. Experimental procedures that were steps into the unknown in 1974 are now well understood, both chemically and in terms of their effects on the organism. We also have practical experience from uses of biotechnology on a large scale. About 12% of the world's agricultural area is grown with genetically modified crops. GM, in agriculture or elsewhere, is no longer a new and untested technology. The uncertainties that justified the 1974 moratorium have been replaced by in-depth understanding of the technology, its mechanisms and consequences, including potential adverse effects.

4. Potential Risks in Plant Breeding

In 1974, it was a reasonable supposition that the transfer of genes from one organism to another could be a major dividing line, so that the risks of adverse effects would be much higher if that dividing line was passed than if it was not. Today we know that this is not the case. In plant breeding, the risks of adverse effects differ between breeding projects, but these differences do not at all follow the dividing line from 1974. Let us consider two examples: food toxicity and weediness.

Many food crops have wild ancestors or relatives that contain toxic substances. One reason for the difference can be that the domesticated variety has been selected and bred for low toxicity. The potato is a well-known example. Sometimes breeders cross our common potato with wild relatives, for instance, in order to acquire resistance genes that protect the plant against pests or insects. This may result in an increased production of toxic substances. Solanine, a major toxic substance in potatoes, is also a natural pesticide and can easily be increased via resistance breeding. This is a problem in traditional potato breeding. In a few cases, varieties with excessive solanine content have been released, only to be withdrawn when consumers got sick from eating the product.[7,8] As this example shows, plant breeders must take care not to turn out plants for food or feed that have genes producing significant amounts of toxic substances. Avoiding genes that result in the production of toxic substances is equally necessary independently of whether the breeder uses traditional techniques alone or combines them with one or another form of modern biotechnology. It makes no difference for toxicity how the gene entered the plant.

The second example concerns the possibility that breeding might result in a plant that either becomes invasive itself, that is, spreads in nature in an uncontrolled way, or forms an invasive hybrid with some wild relative. In both cases, we may have a new weed—to the detriment of both agriculture and natural habitats. This is a potential problem that has often been discussed in relation to agricultural biotechnology. But, as with toxicity, weediness can arise in traditional breeding as well. For instance, weed beets that have evolved from hybrids between sugar beet and wild sea beet have caused great problems for sugar beet growers in Europe.[9,10] Hybrids between the wild coconut palm and its domesticated variant have completely replaced the original wild variant, which is now extinct.[11] And crosses between the aggressive weed Johnson grass (*Sorghum halapense*) and cultivated sorghum (*Sorghum bicolor*) seem to have given rise to particularly difficult forms of Johnson grass.[12] All this has happened with varieties obtained with traditional breeding. Obviously, it can also happen with varieties that are obtained with modern biotechnology.

There are huge differences in the potentials of different species to develop weediness. Some agricultural species, including most of our common cereals, have undergone extensive changes that much reduced their survivability in the wild.[13] It would take a whole series of changes—either by conventional breeding or by biotechnological means—to make a weed out of a plant that now depends on the farmer to survive. But other cultivated plants are more viable in the wild. This includes beets, sunflowers, alfalfa, and many pasture grasses and ornamental plants.[12,14–16] Plants cultivated for the production of biofuel, such as willow, are selected for properties that make them more disposed to weed development than most other grown plants.[17]

Another major factor is, of course, the traits to be introduced into a crop. Many of the traits that plant breeders strive for, such as large energy depositions in the seed, dwarfing (short stalks), and non-shattering, are disadvantages for a wild plant and would therefore prevent rather than induce weediness. Other traits, such as an oil composition adjusted for human consumption, are probably neutral. However, there are also traits, in particular "tolerances to drought, salinity, frost, diseases, and pests,"[12] that may increase fitness in the wild and thereby contribute to the development of weediness. Again, this applies irrespective of whether these more problematic traits are obtained with traditional breeding or with biotechnological tools.

In summary, the risk of developing weediness depends on factors such as the properties of the original crop and the effects of the new trait(s) on reproductive fitness. The method used to introduce a new or modified gene in a crop does not seem to have any impact on the risk of weediness.[13]

There are traits that can in practice only be obtained with modern biotechnology (such as making a plant produce a protein that otherwise only occurs in animals). Some of these traits are among those that may require precautionary action. In these cases as well, the regulatory action should be directed at the traits and genes that are problematic rather than at a technology that can also be used for many other, nonproblematic purposes.

5. New Policies Are Needed

As I hope these examples have shown, there are reasons for a precautionary approach in plant breeding in order to avoid negative effects on human health and the environment. Toxic food products should not be put on the market, and crops that spread like weeds should not be cultivated. I also hope to have shown that such a precautionary approach must have its focus on the traits of the plants. Often, one and the same trait can be obtained with different methods or technologies, but the choice of a method or technology to obtain the trait does not have significant impact on its potential dangers.

But current regulations in Europe and the United States are constructed along different lines. They draw a sharp line between technologies defined legally as GM and those defined as non-GM. The former group is submitted to a uniform and rather extensive control procedure, whereas the latter is subject to virtually no control at all. This means that we still have a legislation whose fundamental principles are based on the scientific knowledge and in particular the uncertainties that prevailed 40 years ago. Since then, science has progressed immensely and we can now identify potentially problematic breeding projects with much more precision. The legislation lags several decades behind the development of science. The problem is, quite simply, that the regulations have not been scientifically updated.

There is an obvious and urgent need for a thorough revision of the regulation of plant breeding. We now have regulations that strain at gnats and swallow camels. What we need is new legislation on plant breeding and agricultural biotechnology that follows the principles of science-based precaution. Such legislation should ensure that we use the best available scientific evidence as the basis for a careful risk analysis that identifies the cases when new crops or varieties can potentially give rise to adverse effects on human health or the environment, and then direct the precautionary measures at those cases rather than others.

A more general lesson should be learned from this. We need to be able to take precautionary actions in cases of scientific uncertainty, but we must also be able to adjust these measures when scientific uncertainty is replaced by scientific knowledge. This applies to new technologies in general, not only those that are based on biological science. Legislators have something important to learn from the counterproductive deadlock in biotechnology legislation: legislation that is based on the current status of science needs to contain inbuilt mechanisms for revisions and adjustments in response to the future developments in science. With such adaptive legislation, decisions can be much better targeted. Risk analysis has important roles to play in the preparation of these decisions since they often require assessments of the combined effects of several uncertainties, for example, about the scope and potential of recent advances in science and technology, risks and uncertainties arising from them, reactions among the public, and appropriate communication and governance of the new technologies and risks. Risk assessment, management, communication, and governance are needed to address the different kinds of impacts on health, safety and environmental risks, business and trade risks, and political risks arising from new technologies and from how they are treated and described in international trade agreements and harmonization efforts. Ready or not, the time has arrived for science-based risk regulation that includes appropriate precautionary measures and for risk analyses that support it.

References

[1] Ainsworth C. Agriculture: A new breed of edits. Nature, 2015; 528:S15–S16.

[2] European Commission. New Plant Breeding Techniques, 2016. Available at: www.ec.europa.eu/food/plant/gmo/legislation/plant_breeding/index_en.htm. Accessed May 16, 2016.

[3] Berg P, Baltimore D, Boyer HW, Cohen SN, Davis RW, Hogness DS, Nathans D, Roblin R, Watson JD, Weissman S, Zinder ND. Potential biohazards of recombinant DNA molecules. Science, 1974; 185(4148):303.

[4] Wiener JB, Rogers MD. Comparing precaution in the United States and Europe. Journal of Risk Research, 2002; 5:317–49.

[5] Hansson SO. Regulating BFRs—From science to policy. Chemosphere, 2008; 73:144–47.

[6] Berg P, Singer MF. The recombinant DNA controversy: Twenty years later. Proceedings of the National Academy of Sciences, 1995; 92(20):9011–13.

[7] Hellenäs K-E, Branzell C, Johnson H, Slanina P. High levels of glycoalkaloids in the established Swedish potato variety Magnum Bonum. Journal of the Science of Food and Agriculture, 1995; 68:249–55.

[8] Valkonen JPT, Keskitalo M, Vasara T, Pietilä L, Raman KV. Potato glycoalkaloids: A burden or a blessing? Critical Reviews in Plant Sciences, 1996; 15(1):1–20.

[9] Boudry P, Broomberg K, Saumitou-Laprade P, Mörchen M, Cuguen J, van Oijk HT. Gene escape in transgenic sugar beet: What can be learned from molecular studies of weed beet populations? In Jones DD (ed.). Proceedings of the 3rd International Symposium on the Biosafety Results of Field Tests of Genetically Modified Plants and Microorganisms, Oakland: University of California Division of Agriculture and Natural Resources, 1994.

[10] Ellstrand NC. Current knowledge of gene flow in plants: Implications for transgene flow. Philosophical Transactions of the Royal Society of London. Series B: Biological Sciences, 2003; 358(1434):1163–70.

[11] Ellstrand NC. Over a decade of crop transgenes out-of-place. Pp. 123–35 in Wozniak CA, McHughen A (eds.). Regulation of Agricultural Biotechnology: The United States and Canada. Berlin: Springer, 2012.

[12] Ellstrand NC, Hoffman CA. Hybridization as an avenue of escape for engineered genes. BioScience, 1990; 40:438–42.

[13] Prakash CS. The genetically modified crop debate in the context of agricultural

evolution. Plant Physiology, 2001; 126(1):8–15.

14 Baker HG. Migration of weeds. Pp. 327–47 in Valentine DH (ed.). Taxonomy Phytogeography and Evolution. London: Academic Press, 1972.

15 Sukopp H, Sukopp U. Ecological long-term effects of cultigens becoming feral and of naturalization of non-native species. Experientia, 1993; 49:210–18.

16 Clark EA. Environmental risks of genetic engineering. Euphytica, 2006; 148:47–60.

17 Buddenhagen CE, Chimera C, Clifford P. Assessing bio-fuel crop invasiveness: A case study. PLoS One, 2009; 4(4): e5261.

DISCUSSION QUESTIONS

1. Hansson mentions the "precautionary principle" (p. 371) that is used in Europe. Write a 2–3 sentence definition of this principle. Note that this will require you to look beyond Hansson's essay.

2. In your own words, create a summary of what you consider Hansson's main argument in the article. What outcome does he hope to see in regards to GMO legislation? Do you agree with Hansson's suggested approach to GMO legislation? Why or why not?

3. What does Hansson say is the difference between "science-based precaution" and "a quixotic undertaking" (p. 372)? What does Hansson mean when he argues that "precautionary actions should be *scientifically updated*" (p. 372)?

4. Find an example of a product that was considered dangerous (and thus scientific precaution was used on it) but was later proven to be safe, resulting in scientific updating (for example, eggs have gone through a gamut of precautionary treatment). Next, come up with an instance where the reverse happened, that is, something that was considered safe was later proven not to be (for example, cigarettes).

5. Hansson states that "[w]e need to be able to take precautionary actions in the cases of scientific uncertainty, but we must also be able to adjust these measures when scientific uncertainty is replaced by scientific knowledge" (p. 375). What does he mean by this? Consider also the audience that Hansson is speaking to. What obstacles do you think his suggestions might face from an audience of non-specialists? What reasons might they have not to trust the claims of 'scientific knowledge'? How would you address those reasons?

C. "VACCINATION, FEAR, AND HISTORICAL RELEVANCE," ROB BODDICE

Published in 2016 by History Compass, this article by Rob Boddice* explores the fear of vaccination throughout history in order to determine why anti-vaccination sentiment remains so prevalent and how historians can combat it with an informed narrative. Boddice argues that, while "[t]he history of vaccines demonstrates the great strides taken by medical research in the understanding of immunology and the successful manufacture of vaccines . . . [t]he history of anti-vaccinism, for its part, demonstrates the remarkable continuity, or perhaps recycling, of the language of fear" (p. 379). As you read the article, pay attention to Boddice's explanations for the anti-vaccination stance as well as his recommendations for combatting it, and consider whether you agree or disagree with his suggestions, and why.

Glossary term: historiography

Abstract

Fears about vaccination are tenacious, despite an overwhelming weight of evidence in favour of immunisation and despite the potentially dangerous consequences of falling rates of immunity against once-common diseases. Drawing on recent developments in the history of emotions and an extensive historiography on the history of vaccination, this article argues that fear of vaccination has become culturally idiomatic and highly resistant to fact-based education campaigns. A role is envisaged for historians to present, in accessible media, narratives of successful public-health campaigns and, at the same time, to demonstrate the contextual underpinnings of social fear in order to allay such fears in the present.

Vaccination remains stubbornly controversial. Over the past year, the question of immunisation was frequently in the news as its opponents variously expressed their fears concerning vaccine safety. Different vaccines seem to generate different fears in different places, from the tenacious (but utterly fallacious) link between MMR and autism in parts of North America and Europe, to claims that tetanus vaccines are laced with birth-control drugs in Kenya and Nigeria, and, by the Taliban, that

---

* Rob Boddice is a *Wissenschaftlicher Mitarbeiter* (Scientific Assistant) in the Department of History and Cultural Studies at Freie Universität Berlin. His research focuses on the history of science, medicine, and emotions.

polio vaccines are Western attempts to sterilise Muslim children.[1] These fears are generated and perpetuated by powerful drivers of public opinion, from Hollywood celebrities to bishops of the Catholic Church, creating a wake of terror that sweeps up parents, politicians, and activists whose doubts are magnified into palpable concern for the health of children. Eula Biss has rooted the polio vaccine fears in Nigeria and Pakistan in more general structures of fear of Western bigotry, meddling in Muslim countries, and invasion. She notes the direct involvement of CIA operatives in a DNA harvesting operation in Pakistan under the guise of an immunisation programme for hepatitis B. It is socially much easier to magnify a kernel of truth into a peck of doubt than it is to demonstrate the exceptional nature of Western vaccination plots.[2] Meanwhile, medical researchers across the world scrambled to develop a vaccine for Ebola in an effort to stem an epidemic that threatened West Africa and beyond. The immediate results of that scramble look positive on the ground, but the Ebola media-event in the developed world has run as a strange parallel to repeated stories of vaccine-resistant parents at the centre of outbreaks of preventable diseases, especially among affluent, white, Western communities.[3]

A survey of the historical literature on vaccination gives crucial context to contemporary debate. Moreover, an awareness of the historical structure of vaccine fears helps to flatten out local and temporal differences. Expressions of fear are coloured by context-specific details but can be understood as essentially similar manifestations of (1) types of ignorance about immunology, vectors of disease, and public health; (2) political ideology concerning individual liberty, mistrust of government and/or medical institutions, and proprietary interests; and (3) moral panic or ethical misgivings related to religion, sex, and class. Historians' contributions to contemporary vaccine debates are therefore strikingly relevant, especially when focusing on the nature of anti-vaccinism. They provide some justification for certain instances of fear or circumspection relating to the safety or efficacy of certain vaccines, but the overwhelming story is one of the untethering of reasonable doubt from its substantial mooring. The history of vaccines demonstrates the great strides taken by medical research in the understanding of immunology and the successful manufacture of vaccines, as well as the various successes and failures in distribution, with tensions between public-health campaigns and the proprietary interests of the pharmaceutical industry. The history of anti-vaccinism, for its part, demonstrates the remarkable continuity, or perhaps recycling, of the language of fear, with its attendant social and medical consequences.

The proliferation of multi-disciplinary explorations of the social construction of fear have opened up the possibility, as part of a broader expansion of the history of emotions, of a genuine attempt to historicise fear by looking for the social structures that give specific context and meaning to instances of fear in different times and places.[4] This has also allowed for research into the ways in which fear is learnt and passed on, so that historians can look for frightening tropes or idioms of fear.

Vaccines, irrespective of the aggregation of knowledge about how they work or how to develop them to meet new challenges, from influenza to Ebola and from HPV to meningitis, fall into such an idiomatic category of fear. The idiom's construction was coeval with the emergence of the first vaccine.

What is most striking about the last third of Edward Jenner's life, after the publication of his *Inquiry into the Causes and Effects of the Variolæ Vaccinæ* of 1798, is that it was dominated not so much by a public-health campaign but by a public-opinion campaign.[5] Jenner's absolute conviction about the efficacy of his smallpox vaccine was always at risk of being overshadowed by those who broadcast doubt and fear, either to serve their own financial interests or to preserve the divine courses of health, disease, and death. While Jenner could not say exactly how the vaccine worked, he could at least point to a set of controlled experiments. It was this novelty, of repeated testing, and not so much the prophylactic powers of cowpox itself, that really earned Jenner his fame. Still, for all his tests, performing arm-to-arm vaccinations and then testing his subjects for smallpox immunity, there were failures.

Jenner's control only reached so far. Eager colleagues, looking to capitalise on Jenner's innovation, soon corrupted the vaccination procedure by performing it in the London smallpox hospital, cross-contaminating the cowpox and risking a legacy of ridicule and quackery for the greatest medical discovery of modernity. More worryingly, Jenner had fallen into an unshakeable belief of the permanent benefits of vaccination, about which he could boast no data beyond rural anecdote. As the passage of time revealed the necessity for re-vaccination, the naysayers were granted repeated opportunities to decry its effectiveness, going so far as to claim that vaccination actually caused diseases of various descriptions. Syphilis was an early candidate.[6] Cowpox was labelled a bovine form of *the* pox at first, but this fear soon morphed into the fear of coming into contact with degenerate bodies. In England, vaccination was the province of Poor-Law Guardians, and arm-to-arm methods of cultivating vaccine lymph potentially risked the insertion of diseased matter from the poorest ranks of society into the arms of children of the better off. Skin diseases such as erysipelas became marks of contamination: a visual sign of social intermingling that shocked middle-class parents. Syphilis continued to loom over the procedure: a risk of being tainted with immorality for uncertain gains. Later, such luminaries as Alfred Russel Wallace would go so far as to imply that it was fear of vaccination itself that caused an uptick in smallpox cases in the mid-nineteenth century, after decades of 'natural' decline. He threw reams of statistics behind his claims as to vaccination's complete uselessness, doing enormous damage to his reputation among his scientific peers, but becoming something of a people's champion among anti-vaccination parents.[7]

His chief complaint, beyond vaccination's lack of utility, was that it was an attack on liberty.[8] While Wallace could put this argument in abstract terms, as part of his own peculiar evolutionary philosophy, his supporters had more tangible concerns. After 1853, vaccination became compulsory in England. Over two decades, compulsion was increasingly strictly enforced, with some parents being jailed for non-compliance and others having their household goods distrained in lieu of paying accumulated fines. Some parents complained of vaccinations that had killed children; others only claimed that they had heard of vaccinations that had killed children; yet others can be thought of as expressing a lack of *belief* in vaccination. They campaigned, across the country, with a notable centre of militancy in Leicester, for the right to conscientiously object to the intrusion of the State into the domestic realm of parental authority.[9]

What the first century of smallpox vaccination represents, therefore, is an archetype of social fear. As immunological advances increased with great pace from the late nineteenth century onwards, against anthrax, rabies, diphtheria, polio, tuberculosis, rinderpest (the only other disease apart from smallpox that has been completely eliminated through vaccination), mumps, measles, rubella, and chickenpox, so the cycles of fear relating to inefficacy, contamination, government and medical corruption, and belief have been recapitulated. The recent surge in anti-vaccinationist activism has not only brought the work of historians to the foreground as a relevant antidote to viral hearsay but also shifted the footing of its historiographical orientation.

The key reference point for the history of anti-vaccination is Nadja Durbach's 2004 book *Bodily Matters: The Anti-Vaccination Movement in England, 1853–1907*, which took seriously the claims of working-class parents that their liberty and domestic authority was trespassed upon by government policies of compulsion, pushing a vaccination programme without sufficient medical proof of its efficacy or dangers. A path-finding article that pointed the way for the book was entitled 'They might as well brand us,' giving full weighting to the voices of conscientious objectors whose stories had been lost in a narrative arc that tended to emphasise the progressive victories of medical science.[10] The shift in focus was necessary. Until Durbach's intervention, medical historians had focused on the spread of information about vaccination, its rapid successes across the globe, and the ways in which it ushered in both social health care (the first rumblings of the National Health Service, perhaps) and global health oversight.[11] Durbach highlighted the social dynamics and personal costs of such medical and governmental innovations. She rightly held up the political push over vaccination as a strand of class politics. Considered as part of a process of colonialism, it has also been considered as a strand of race politics.[12] These positions have been reinforced by scholars working in many different regions.[13] Moreover there have been calls to re-examine the instrumentalisation of children as incubators for vaccine material and the effect on children of vaccine campaigns, since they were central to the effective distribution and supply of vaccine lymph.[14] Given that, prior to the advent of vaccination, children were routinely inoculated with smallpox itself—risking them and the societies around them with the full disease—there is a risk of anachronism concerning ethics here. Nonetheless, the aggregate of this research has pointed to a disparate collective of people whose lives were adversely affected by vaccination programmes, and whose individual liberties were trespassed upon in the name of public health as a moral good.[15]

Yet recent events in the anti-vaccine camp have put this argument politically out of step, principally because the historical reasons for objecting to vaccine compulsion, first among them being a lack of knowledge about how vaccination worked, or for how long, are no longer valid. Even before immunological science could describe the action of a vaccine in providing protection, the evidence from beyond English shores provided substantial proof of the power of vaccination, from the Napoleonic Empire to Prussian mortality statistics and from Spanish global public-health voyages to the spread of immunity across the Indian subcontinent.[16] But enough doubt remained, and statistical evidence could be massaged to demonstrate both sides of the argument, that working-class parents could rightly demand to know why a government was compelling them to submit their children to a medical intervention of uncertain risk and reward. Compulsion had come before education, in large part because the power of the vaccine had come before immunological knowledge.

That rapidly changed with the work of Lister, von Behring, Koch, Pasteur, and others.[17] The efficacy of Jenner's vaccine was profoundly demonstrated, for example by campaigns in French West Africa at the turn of the twentieth century and more forcefully by the WHO's campaign in the 1960s and 1970s to eradicate smallpox from the globe.[18] That campaign involved partnering with individual governments to record vaccination data, distribute information about the dangers of smallpox and the benefits of the vaccine, and put people on the ground to positively encourage participation in vaccination drives. Hard evidence about how the vaccine worked, coupled with accessible educational materials and widely broadcast poster campaigns, comprised a highly effective package that succeeded, in 1979, in eradicating smallpox from the planet. Not only had the WHO not depended on compulsion, but also technical advances meant they were no longer dependent, as vaccinators had been in the nineteenth century, on arm-to-arm cultivation of lymph. The declaration of 'Smallpox Zero' in 1980 is one of those rare events in history: an unmitigated success story.[19]

With the parallel rise in successful vaccines for other diseases, notably tetanus, polio and MMR, health officials might have been surprised to encounter resistance along the same lines as nineteenth-century anti-vaccinists. Anecdotage about vaccine failure or adulteration is, well into the third century of vaccination, a well-rehearsed discourse. The specific spectres of public-health that foist vaccines onto resistant populations—governments, doctors, and medical institutions with vested interests—loom largely in the imagination all too easily. Latent, long-acquired societal doubts are rather straightforwardly magnified through social media campaigns that target the vulnerable and ill-informed. A key issue, therefore, remains access to information. Where can a layperson obtain reliable and accessible information about vaccination that will, if nothing else, allay fears? While there are a number of vaccine lobby groups and philanthropic organisations on a footing to provide this information, their own vested interests often seem to count against their credibility with a suspicious public.

Historians can perhaps bridge this credibility gap, engaging in historical debates about vaccines with one eye on the public-health challenges of the present and the future. If we can point out where the structures of doubt and fear come from, we can perhaps do something to undermine them, especially if we also work in tandem with contemporary public-health initiatives and efforts to develop new vaccines. Historians (and other scholars within the humanities) are perhaps much better equipped than immunological specialists and campaigners from within the vaccine lobby to deal with problems arising from social movements marked by narrative constructions of fear and suspicion, emotional contagion, and identity politics. Anti-vaccinist ignorance cannot merely be met with education about vaccine safety and efficacy, since the agencies that produce such fact-based pedagogy are perceived to be part of the problem.[20] A *longue-durée* approach, giving full attention and scholarly rigour both to the spread of fear of medical innovation in historical context and to clear descriptions of the ways in which medical research and public-health campaigns have succeeded in profound ways to protect whole populations, might introduce competing narratives with more traction.

Without question, the faked and discredited research linking MMR to autism has done, and continues to do, massive damage to the credibility of public-health campaigns, but the broader expressions of parental rights and conscientious objection, paranoia about the dangerous 'chemicals' loaded into vaccines, and the propagandist corruption of the messages of vaccine organisations are throwbacks to a time when insufficient knowledge might have justified such actions. The liberty position, especially in the United States, is sustained by a refusal to engage with or acknowledge wholesale transformations in evidence-based expertise, in favour of much more readily available and culturally rehearsed discourses of doubt. Scepticism about Big Medicine is perhaps compounded by a diminution of fears about childhood disease itself. It is an irony of the contemporary debate that anti-vaccinism is to some extent a product of successful twentieth-century campaigns to rid society (especially in the developed world) of diseases that were once commonplace. Without first-hand knowledge of the ravages of epidemic measles, whooping cough, or worse, it is somewhat easier to focus on fears of adulterated vaccines. Moreover, these cultures of fear tend to coalesce around communities of 'personal belief,' making for hotspots of immunological weakness.[21]

But the invocation, along the lines of the argument in Durbach's book, of the inviolable bodily integrity of one's children, is no longer a supportable argument for refusing vaccinations. The risks to individual children have been made all too clear by recent outbreaks of measles, and the danger those children pose to the population as potential vectors of disease has been a genuine cause for alarm for health authorities, especially in communities where anti-vaccinism is widespread. Fall-off rates for vaccination against measles, for example, risk whole communities when 'herd immunity' falls below 95 per cent. In other words, an individual's assertion of parental liberty in choosing not to vaccinate a child will directly endanger others when only a small percentage of the population carries no immunity.[22]

With that in mind, historians have turned their attention recently to reinvigorating the history of vaccination from the point of view of its impact on public health, infant mortality and society in general. Whereas Durbach flagged a narrative of 'bodily matters,' a new generation of historians are constructing a narrative of social history in the age of public health, actively measuring gains and pointing out which groups have been under-vaccinated to their detriment, precisely because of a lack of social privilege, political exclusion, and/or a vulnerability to discourses of doubt, cynicism, and fear.[23] Casey Hurrell, for example, has pointed out the success of American attempts to combat yellow fever through the Rockefeller Foundation, but noted the vaccination campaign's close tracking of US imperial and paternalistic policies.[24] And Mona Gleason has analysed the perspective of children and parents as they faced early twentieth-century health interventions across Canada, detailing how socio-economic status, age, and identity (along class, gender, and race lines) could materially affect (positively and negatively) the march of disease and the effectiveness of vaccination campaigns.[25] In closely related disciplines, scholars have tried to understand why vaccination campaigns generate fear and have actively used this knowledge to try to build in cultural sensitivity to immunisation drives.[26] And other scholars have put their focus on the diseases that vaccinators have sought to combat, realising that whatever the horrors of historical vaccination, be they erroneous or based in fact, the histories of diseases such as smallpox, rabies, or rinderpest are much more worthy vehicles for mass social fear.[27]

What remains is to make sure that such work is widely read, reported, and/or reviewed, in support of new efforts to coerce vaccine-resistant parents to comply.[28] In this respect, it seems especially important that historians turn to non-traditional publication media and a style of writing that emphasises narrative accessibility over academic apparatus.[29] It is precisely when history becomes most relevant and most useable that it must, at least temporarily, shake off any tendency towards academic introspection or scientific self-doubt. For a discipline increasingly preoccupied by metrics of impact, what better than to assist in persuading the fearful that the public-health efforts of vaccine programmes around the world really do have the health of the public at heart?

Notes

[1] Deer, 'How the case against the MMR vaccine was fixed,' c5347; Khalil, 'The parents refusing to vaccinate their children against polio.' www.bbc.co.uk/news/magazine-30133279; 'Kenya Catholic Church tetanus vaccine fears "unfounded,"' www.bbc.co.uk/news/world-africa-29594091.

[2] Biss, *On Immunity*, 86–87.

[3] Mullard, 'Ebola vaccine yields first hopes of clinical efficacy'; Inglis, 'Vaccine Fear Derails Triumph Over Disease,' 11.

[4] Plamper and Lazier, eds., *Fear Across the Disciplines*; Laffan and Weiss, *Facing Fear*. For an introduction to the multidisciplinary archaeology of the history of emotions, see Plamper, *The History of Emotions*; Boddice, 'The Affective Turn: Historicizing the Emotions.'

[5] Boddice, *Edward Jenner*, 55–83.

[6] Boddice, 'Bestiality in a Time of Smallpox,' http://notchesblog.com/2015/01/20/bestiality-in-a-time-of-smallpox/.

[7] Wallace, *To Members of Parliament and Others*; Fichman, 'Alfred Russel Wallace and Anti-vaccinationism in the Late Victorian Cultural Context,' and Fichman and Keelan, 'Resister's logic.'

[8] Boddice, 'Sympathy, Liberty, and Compulsion: Vaccination,' *The Science of Sympathy: Morality, Evolution and Victorian Civilization*.

[9] Fraser, 'Leicester and smallpox'; Ross, 'Leicester and the Anti-vaccination Movement'; Swales, 'The Leicester anti-vaccination movement.'

[10] Durbach, *Bodily Matters*; Durbach, 'They Might As Well Brand Us.' A precursor to Durbach's work, highlighting radical liberal opposition among early anti-vaccinists, is Porter and Porter, 'The Politics of Prevention.'

[11] Lambert, 'A Victorian National Health Service.'

[12] Murdoch, 'Carrying the Pox'; Brimnes, 'Variolation, Vaccination and Popular Resistance in Early Colonial South India'; Arnold, *Colonizing the Body*, 120–21, 133–44. See also the London School of Hygiene and Tropical Medicine exhibition, 'Vaccination: Past, Present and Future,' www.lshtm.ac.uk/newsevents/events/2015/06/vaccination-past-present-and-future.

[13] Arnup, 'Victims of Vaccination?'; Bator, 'The Health Reformers versus the Common Canadian'; Bhattacharya et al., *Fractured States*.

[14] Murdoch, 'Anti-vaccination and the Politics of Grief.'

[15] Rowbotham, 'Legislating for Your Own Good.'

[16] Vigni, 'Smallpox Vaccination in Siena During the Napoleonic Era'; Hennock, 'Vaccination Policy Against Smallpox'; Franco-Paredes et al., 'The Spanish Royal Philanthropic Expedition to Bring Smallpox Vaccination to the New World and Asia'; Bhattacharya, 'Re-devising Jennerian Vaccines?.'

[17] On von Behring and diphtheria serum, Linton, *Emil Von Behring*; on Lister and germ theory, Michael Worboys, *Spreading Germs*, 73ff, and Fisher, *Joseph Lister*; for Koch's bacteriology, Brock, *Robert Koch*; for Pasteur, Debré, *Louis Pasteur*.

[18] Hayden, 'Of Medicine and Statecraft,' 304–85.

[19] Fenner et al., *Smallpox and its Eradication*.

[20] Kata, 'A Postmodern Pandora's Box.'

[21] Carrel and Bitterman, 'Personal Belief Exemptions to Vaccination in California.' Historians of emotion might reinforce the spatial analysis with insights derived from 'emotional communities.' See Rosenwein, 'Worrying about Emotions in History,' 842.

[22] Fine et al., '"Herd Immunity": A Rough Guide.'

[23] See the twelve entries on ActiveHistory.ca for the theme week on 'Infectious Disease, Contagion and the History of Vaccines,' edited by Clifford et al., http://activehistory.ca/2015/03/theme-week-infectious-disease-contagion-and-the-history-of-vaccines/.

[24] Hurrell, 'Funding, failures, and faux pas,' http://activehistory.ca/2015/03/funding-failures-and-faux-pas-vaccines-and-the-complicated-task-of-sharing-responsibility-for-global-health/. See also Farley, *To Cast Out Disease* and Palmer, *Launching Global Health*.

[25] Gleason, *Small Matters*.

[26] Kitta, *Vaccinations and Public Concern in History*; Betsch et al., 'Improving Medical Decision Making.'

[27] Bliss, *Plague*; Williams, *Angel of Death*; Pemberton and Worboys, *Mad Dogs and Englishmen*; Wasik and Murphy, *Rabid*.

[28] The Canadian Medical Association has sought new legislation to challenge anti-vaccinist parents. See Picard, 'Canadian Medical Association wants schools to seek proof of vaccination,' www.theglobeandmail.com/news/national/schools-should-to-be-able-to-request-students-vaccination-records-cma/article26111472/.

[29] Biss, *On Immunity*, might serve as an exemplar.

Bibliography

Arnold, D., *Colonizing the Body: State Medicine and Epidemic Disease in Nineteenth-century India*. (Berkeley: U of California P, 1993).

Arnup, K., '"Victims of Vaccination?": Opposition to Compulsory Immunization in Ontario, 1900–90,' *Canadian Bulletin of Medical History*, 9 (1992): 159–76.

Bator, P.A., 'The Health Reformers versus the Common Canadian: The Controversy over Compulsory Vaccination Against Smallpox in Toronto and Ontario, 1900–1920,' *Ontario History*, 75 (1983): 348–73.

Betsch, C., Böhm, R., Airhihenbuwa, C.O. et al., 'Improving Medical Decision Making and Health Promotion through Culture-Sensitive Health Communication:

An Agenda for Science and Practice,' *Medical Decision Making*, Aug. 21 (2015).

Bhattacharya, S., 'Re-devising Jennerian Vaccines? European Technologies, Indian Innovation and the Control of Smallpox in South Asia, 1850–1950,' *Social Scientist*, 26 (1998): 27–66.

Bhattacharya, S., Harrison, M. and Worboys, M., *Fractured States: Smallpox, Public Health and Vaccination Policy in British India, 1800–1947*. (Hyderabad: Orient Longman, 2005).

Biss, E., *On Immunity: An Inoculation*. (Minneapolis: Graywolf P, 2014).

Bliss, M., *Plague: How Smallpox Devastated Montreal*. (Toronto: HarperCollins, 1991).

Boddice, Rob, 'Bestiality in a Time of Smallpox,' Notches: (Re)marks on the History of Sexuality, http://notchesblog.com/2015/01/20/bestiality-in-a-time-of-smallpox/. Accessed 11 Sept. 2015.

Boddice, R., *The Science of Sympathy: Morality, Evolution and Victorian Civilization*. (Urbana-Champaign: U of Illinois P, in press).

Boddice, R., 'The Affective Turn: Historicizing the Emotions,' in J. Byford and C. Tileag (eds.), *History and Psychology: Interdisciplinary Explorations*. (Cambridge: Cambridge UP, 2014), 147–65.

Boddice, R., *Edward Jenner*. (Stroud: The History P, 2015).

Brimnes, N., 'Variolation, Vaccination and Popular Resistance in Early Colonial South India,' *Medical History*, 48 (2004): 199–228.

Brock, T.D., *Robert Koch: A Life in Medicine and Bacteriology*. (Science Tech: Madison, 1988).

Carrel, M. and Bitterman, P., 'Personal Belief Exemptions to Vaccination in California: A Spatial Analysis,' *Pediatrics*, 36 (2015): 80–88.

Clifford, Jim, Dyck, Erica and Mosby, Ian, eds., 'Infectious Disease, Contagion and the History of Vaccines,' http://activehistory.ca/2015/03/theme-week-infectious-disease-contagion-and-the-history-of-vaccines/. Accessed 11 Sept. 2015.

Debré, P., *Louis Pasteur*. (Baltimore: Johns Hopkins UP, 1998).

Deer, B., 'How the case against the MMR vaccine was fixed,' *BMJ*, 342 (2011): c5347.

Durbach, N., '"They Might As Well Brand Us": Working-Class Resistance to Compulsory Vaccination in Victorian England,' *Social History of Medicine*, 13 (2000): 45–63.

Durbach, N., *Bodily Matters: The Anti-Vaccination Movement in England, 1853–1907*. (Durham, NC: Duke UP, 2004).

Farley, J., *To Cast Out Disease: A History of the International Health Division of the Rockefeller Foundation (1913–1951)*. (Oxford: Oxford UP, 2004).

Fenner, F., Henderson, D.A., Arita, I., Ježek, Z. and Ladnyi, I.D., *Smallpox and its Eradication*. (Geneva: World Health Organization, 1988).

Fichman, M. and Keelan, J.E., 'Resister's Logic: The Anti-Vaccination Arguments of Alfred Russel Wallace and Their Role in the Debates over Compulsory Vaccination in England, 1870–1907,' *Studies in History and Philosophy of Biological and Biomedical Sciences*, 38 (2007): 585–607.

Fichman, M., 'Alfred Russel Wallace and Anti-Vaccinationism in the Late Victorian Cultural Context, 1870–1907,' in C.H. Smith and G. Beccaloni (eds.), *Natural Selection and Beyond: The Intellectual Legacy of Alfred Russel Wallace*. (Oxford: Oxford UP, 2008).

Fine, P., Eames, K. and Heymann, D.L., '"Herd Immunity": A Rough Guide,' *Clinical Infectious Diseases*, 52 (2011): 911–16.

Fisher, R.B., *Joseph Lister, 1827–1912*. (New York: Stein and Day, 1977).

Franco-Paredes, C., Lammoglia, L. and Santos-Preciado, J.I., 'The Spanish Royal Philanthropic Expedition to Bring Smallpox Vaccination to the New World and Asia in the 19th Century,' *Clinical Infectious Diseases*, 41(2005): 1285–89.

Fraser, S.M.F., 'Leicester and Smallpox: The Leicester Method,' *Medical History*, 24 (1980): 315–32.

Gleason, M., *Small Matters: Canadian Children in Sickness and Health, 1900 to 1940*. (Montreal and Kingston: McGill-Queen's UP, 2013).

Hayden, Christopher Ellis, 'Of Medicine and Statecraft: Smallpox and Early Colonial Vaccination in French West Africa,' PhD diss., Northwestern University, 2008.

Hennock, E.P., 'Vaccination Policy Against Smallpox, 1835–1914: A Comparison of England with Prussia and Imperial Germany,' *Social History of Medicine*, 11 (1998): 49–71.

Hurrell, Casey, 'Funding, Failures, and Faux Pas: Vaccines and the Complicated Task of Sharing Responsibility for Global Health,' ActiveHistory.ca, http://active history.ca/2015/03/funding-failures-and-faux-pas-vaccines-and-the-complicated-task-of-sharing-responsibility-for-global-health/. Accessed 17 Nov. 2015.

Inglis, T., 'Vaccine Fear Derails Triumph Over Disease,' *American Journal of Nursing*, 115 (2015): 11.

Kata, A., 'A Postmodern Pandora's Box: Anti-Vaccination Misinformation on the Internet,' *Vaccine*, 28 (2010): 1709–16.

'Kenya Catholic Church Tetanus Vaccine fears "unfounded,"' BBC News, Oct. 13, 2014, www.bbc.co.uk/news/world-africa-29594091. Accessed 11 Sept. 2015.

Khalil, Shaimaa, 'The Parents Refusing to Vaccinate Their Children against Polio,' BBC News, Nov. 23, 2014, www.bbc.co.uk/news/magazine-30133279. Accessed 11 Sept. 2015.

Kitta, A., *Vaccinations and Public Concern in History: Legend, Rumour, and Risk Perception*. (New York and London: Routledge, 2011).

Laffan, M. and Weiss, M., *Facing Fear: The History of an Emotion in Global Perspective*. (Princeton: Princeton UP, 2012).

Lambert, R.J., 'A Victorian National Health Service: State Vaccination 1855–71,' *Historical Journal*, 5 (1962): 1–18.

Linton, D.S., *Emil Von Behring: Infectious Disease, Immunology, Serum Therapy*. (Philadelphia: American Philosophical Society, 2005).

Mullard, A., 'Ebola Vaccine Yields First Hopes of Clinical Efficacy,' *Nature Reviews Drug Discovery*, 14/593/ (2015).

Murdoch, L., 'Anti-Vaccination and the Politics of Grief in Late-Victorian England,' in S. Olsen (ed.), *Childhood, Youth and Emotions in Modern History: National, Colonial and Global Perspectives*. (Houndmills: Palgrave, 2015).

Murdoch, L., 'Carrying the Pox: The Use of Children and Ideals of Childhood in Early British and Imperial Campaigns Against Smallpox,' *Journal of Social History*, 48 (2015): 511–35.

Palmer, S., *Launching Global Health: The Caribbean Odyssey of the Rockefeller Foundation*. (Ann Arbor: U of Michigan P, 2010).

Pemberton, N. and Worboys, M., *Mad Dogs and Englishmen: Rabies in Britain, 1830–2000*. (Houndmills: Palgrave, 2007).

Picard, André, 'Canadian Medical Association wants schools to seek proof of vaccination,' *Globe and Mail*, 26 Aug. 2015, www.theglobeandmail.com/news/national/schools-should-to-be-able-to-request-students-vaccination-records-cma/article26111472/. Accessed 11 Sept. 2015.

Plamper, J. and Lazier, B. (eds.), *Fear Across the Disciplines*. (Pittsburgh: U of Pittsburgh P, 2012).

Plamper, J., *The History of Emotions: An Introduction*. (Oxford: Oxford UP, 2015).

Porter, D. and Porter, R., 'The Politics of Prevention: Anti-Vaccinationism and Public Health in Nineteenth-Century England,' *Medical History*, 32 (1988): 231–52.

Rosenwein, B., 'Worrying about Emotions in History,' *American Historical Review*, 107 (2002): 821–45.

Ross, D.-L., 'Leicester and the Anti-vaccination Movement, 1853–1889,' *Leicestershire Archaeological and Historical Society*, 43 (1967–68): 35–44.

Rowbotham, J., 'Legislating for Your Own Good: Criminalising Moral Choice. The Modern Echoes of the Victorian Vaccination Acts,' *Liverpool Law Review*, 30 (2009): 13–33.

Swales, J.D., 'The Leicester Anti-Vaccination movement,' *Lancet*, 340/8826/ (1992): 1019–21.

Vigni, L., 'Smallpox Vaccination in Siena During the Napoleonic Era,' *Le Infezioni in Medicina: Rivista Periodica di Eziologia, Epidemiologia, Diagnostica, Clinica e Terapia Delle Patologie Infettive*, 9 (2001): 115–18.

Wallace, A.R., *To Members of Parliament and Others: Forty-Five Years of Registration Statistics, Proving Vaccination to be both Useless and Dangerous*. (London: E.W. Allen, 1885).

Wasik, B. and Murphy, M., *Rabid: A Cultural History of the World's Most Diabolical Virus*. (London: Penguin, 2012).

Williams, G., *Angel of Death: The Story of Smallpox*. (Houndmills: Palgrave, 2010).

Worboys, M., *Spreading Germs: Disease Theories and Medical Practice in Britain, 1865–1900*. (Cambridge: Cambridge UP, 2000).

DISCUSSION QUESTIONS

1. Boddice writes extensively about how fear pushes forward the anti-vaccination narrative. He mentions "cultures of fear" (p. 383). What does this term mean? Can you think of another present-day example of a scientific issue that is heavily influenced by the culture of fear? Discuss.

2. Boddice explains how some "scholars have put their focus on the diseases that vaccinators have sought to combat, realising that whatever the horrors of historical vaccination, be they erroneous or based in fact, the histories of diseases such as smallpox, rabies, or rinderpest are much more worthy vehicles for mass social fear" (p. 384). This is essentially shifting the fear back from vaccines to the diseases that they prevent. Do you think that this is a method that could potentially be successful? Should we be trying to eliminate the culture of fear altogether, or do the ends, in this case, justify the means?

3. What are the ethical ramifications of requiring proof of vaccination? Come up with an argument both for, and against, this requirement. Discuss.

4. Boddice suggests that historians should "at least temporarily, shake off any tendency towards academic introspection or scientific self-doubt" (p. 384) in their attempt to quell vaccination fears. What do you think is meant by this? Does it suggest that historians should attempt to appeal more to emotion than education? Discuss the ramifications (both pro and con) of this idea.

5. Boddice discusses the history of emotions, scholars' attempts to "historicise fear," and "the ways in which fear is learnt and passed on, so that historians can look for frightening tropes or idioms of fear." He goes on to assert that "[v]accines, irrespective of the aggregation of knowledge about how they work or how to develop them to meet new challenges...fall into such an idiomatic category of fear" (p. 380). Why do you think vaccines continue to create fear in so many people?

D. "OLFACTORY IDENTIFICATION DECLINE AS A PRECLINICAL BIOMARKER FOR ALZHEIMER'S DISEASE," JAMIE KNIGHT

Jamie Knight's* Master of Science thesis proposal was submitted in August of 2016. It is the first of three related examples of writing in the research genres that feature research on Alzheimer's disease (AD). (See the glossary for an explanation of a research proposal.) Knight builds on Wilson et al.'s research, exploring the connection between an individual's olfactory ability and dementia, with a focus on AD, in an effort to create ways to detect the onset of dementia earlier. Knight's research "aims to clarify the role that olfaction can play as an inexpensive biomarker for dementia and to determine whether olfactory decline can robustly establish an accurate picture of AD progression, differentiate disease, and establish its relationship to cognitive decline" (p. 392). As you read this, consider how it works as a proposal. How does a proposal differ from an article? How do you envision the thesis that is being proposed here?

Glossary terms: cross-sectional study, longitudinal study, quantitative research, research proposal

Summary

Dementia is not a natural part of aging. This umbrella term encompasses many neurodegenerative diseases that affect memory, judgment, and cognitive skills severely enough to interfere with daily life. Alzheimer's disease (AD) is the most common form of dementia and comprises nearly 70% of diagnosed cases. In order to discover effective treatments, a method to detect dementia as early as possible is needed.

It is well known that (1) AD pathology begins in the brain 10–20 years before clinical symptoms affecting memory, thinking, or behaviour can be detected by affected individuals or their physicians; this is called the preclinical stage; (2) patients who are already diagnosed with AD have deficits in their sense of smell. Emerging evidence now suggests that olfactory decline can be used to predict the onset of AD in the preclinical stage of the disease. This preclinical phase may be accounting for 50% or more of the total disease duration and it is where the least amount of information is being gathered. Measuring olfactory decline will provide a means

---

* Jamie Knight is a PhD student in the Lifespan Development stream in Psychology at the University of Victoria. She studies neuropsychological and chemosensory functioning with the goal of identifying pre-clinical biomarkers of age-related cognitive decline and neurodegenerative diseases.

to capture important changes that are occurring in the brain at this crucial stage. However, the majority of research in this area has been done cross-sectionally. This is problematic because differences in smell between people are so vast that in order to accurately identify the amount of change from a previous level of functioning one must look at differences in change in that same person, not across different people.

For my research, I will use the longitudinal Memory and Aging Project (MAP) data from the Rush Alzheimer's Disease Center Laboratory (RADC) to establish the relationships between olfactory decline, episodic memory, and AD pathology. By doing so, I hope to contribute to existing research by (a) conducting a replication of previous work by Wilson, Arnold, Schneider, Boyle, Buchman, Aron, and Bennett (2009) using a more mature version of the same data (i.e., more than double the participants and waves), then extending it by adding AD pathology into those models; (b) examining the relationship between AD pathology and olfactory score using a linear mixed model with smell as outcome; and (c) analyzing within-person coupled variation in episodic memory and olfaction using a growth model for episodic memory with smell as time-varying covariate. This analysis will provide answers about whether olfaction and episodic memory are fluctuating together at each measurement time point (i.e., whether assessment-to-assessment variation in olfaction mirrors variation in cognition for any given individual over time).

Regular olfactory testing may facilitate earlier detection of AD in the preclinical stage. Trained professionals are not required to administer this test; therefore the accessibility, ease of use, and low cost makes olfactory testing an ideal biomarker.

Early indicators for disease are critical for implementing interventions while the brain is relatively undamaged and still functioning normally. This study aims to clarify the role that olfaction can play as an inexpensive biomarker for dementia and to determine whether olfactory decline can robustly establish an accurate picture of AD progression, differentiate disease, and establish its relationship to cognitive decline.

1. Introduction

The objective of this study is to explore the potential viability of olfactory decline as a biomarker for Alzheimer's disease (AD) and determine the strength of the relationships between olfactory decline, episodic memory, and AD pathology.

1.1 Review of Cross-Sectional Literature

1.1.1 cross-sectional literature: disease

Odour is processed in the olfactory cortex (collectively comprised of the entorhinal cortex, piriform cortex, olfactory tubercle, and the amygdala) and is then projected to the orbitofrontal cortex, as well as the thalamus and hypothalamus (Purves et al., 2001; Shepherd, 2007). The olfactory tubercle itself connects to numerous areas of the amygdala, thalamus, hypothalamus, hippocampus, brain stem, retina, and auditory cortex. Within this pathway the entorhinal cortex has many connections with the hippocampus, an area which is thought to contribute to odour memory (Purves et al., 2001) as well as other forms of memory. Maintaining a normal sense of smell requires the constant cellular regeneration of the olfactory epithelium, olfactory bulb, and hippocampus. Loss or malfunction of any of these regenerative processes will cause a deficit in the ability to detect or identify smells. Several neurodegenerative diseases cause predictable damage to these olfactory areas in the earliest stages of disease. This has led researchers to explore the loss of smell in a variety of neurodegenerative diseases, including Alzheimer's, schizophrenia, Huntington's, and Parkinson's (Mesholam, Moberg, Mahr, & Doty, 1998) including odor identification, recognition, and detection threshold. Data Sources A literature search of English-language studies of olfaction in AD, PD, and healthy controls was conducted via online databases (PsycInfo and MEDLINE, as well as its use in detecting traumatic brain injury (Xydakis et al., 2015). One of the main limitations of olfactory testing is the lack of specificity to one disease. However, as a screener that could provide insight into potential disease a decade in advance, this may not be problematic.

Olfactory deficits in patients already diagnosed with Alzheimer's disease are well known and the prevalence of olfactory dysfunction is reported as being as high as 100% in Alzheimer's disease (Devanand et al., 2000; Doty, Reyes, & Gregor, 1987; Duff, McCaffrey, & Solomon, 2002; Fiandaca, Mapstone, Cheema, & Federoff, 2014; Kovács, Cairns, & Lantos, 2001) 90% in Parkinson's disease (PD), 96% in Frontotemporal dementia (FTD), and 15% in Vascular dementia (Alves, Petrosyan, & Magalhães, 2014). AD pathology affects specific areas of the brain in a temporally ordered fashion that maps onto the olfactory pathway and corresponds with disease progression (Jack et al., 2013; Purves et al., 2001; Walker, Diamond, Duff, & Hyman, 2013). For example, the odour signal is processed in the olfactory cortex (which includes the entorhinal cortex and olfactory tubercle), the olfactory tubercle itself connects to numerous areas, including the locus coeruleus in the brain stem (Purves et al., 2001; Shepherd, 2007). Within this pathway, the entorhinal cortex also directly connects with the hippocampus, an area which contributes to odour memory (Purves et al., 2001) as well as other forms of memory. These are important distinctions, as the earliest stage of AD pathology is defined as the presence of beta-amyloid plaques and hyperphosphorylated tau (p-tau) neurofibrillary tangles in the entorhinal cortex (Braak & Braak, 1991; Devanand et al., 2015; Jack et al., 2013; Kovács, 2004; Masurkar & Devanand, 2014; Purves et al., 2001; Shepherd, 2006). In other words, as olfactory performance decreases we should see an increase in the severity of AD pathology (Wilson, Arnold, Schneider, Tang, & Bennett, 2007). The olfactory pathway is very sensitive to damage and under normal circumstances these areas would regenerate, making these specific neurodegenerative disorders detectable via the deficits they cause in one's ability to detect or identify smells. Even slight AD pathology in these areas causes a noticeable deficit in olfaction because

AD pathology and resulting damage is not repaired by the body (Doty et al., 1991; Murphy, Gilmore, Seery, Salmon, & Lasker, 1990; Murphy, Solomon, Haase, Wang, & Morgan, 2009). If this is the case, olfactory testing may be one of the earliest biomarkers for AD pathology.

1.1.2 cross-sectional literature: aging

Olfactory ability differs widely from person-to-person due to genetic variations, sex, and experiences with environmental factors, which makes longitudinal research in this area highly desirable. The most common causes of olfactory impairment include head trauma, inflammation, upper respiratory tract infection, aging, and neurodegenerative disease (Murphy, 2002). With age comes a decrease in overall cellular regeneration, the number of olfactory receptors decreases, the olfactory epithelium thins, there is an age-related decline in the size of the olfactory bulb, and there is age-related ossification of the foramina of the cribriform plate (Attems, Walker, & Jellinger, 2015; Campisi & di Fagagna, 2007; Masurkar & Devanand, 2014; Schubert et al., 2011). Attems et al. (2015) found that more than 50% of individuals between the ages of 65 and 80 years had decreased olfactory function, and that number increased to 62–80% for those over 80 (Attems et al., 2015). However, these population studies included all individuals, even those with reported dementia, and different olfactory trajectories for healthy and diseased elderly populations have not been established at this point.

1.2 Review of Longitudinal Literature

It is becoming clear that dementia can be identified using olfactory testing (Albers, Tabert, & Devanand, 2006; Peters et al., 2003; Wilson et al., 2009). The majority of work has historically been conducted using cross-sectional methods, but in this area of research it is critical to use longitudinal methods. The reason for this is that the differences in smell between people are so vast that in order to accurately identify the amount of change from a previous level of functioning the differences in change must be examined within the same person.

In 2009, Wilson, Arnold, Schneider, Boyle, Buchman, Aron, and Bennett found that a person who made four errors on an olfactory test was approximately 50% more likely to develop some form of mild cognitive impairment (MCI) compared with a person who made only one error. This corroborates similar findings by Devanand et al. (2000), who found that patients who received low scores on olfactory testing, and were also unaware that their sense of smell was poor, were more likely to develop Alzheimer's than other patients (Devanand et al., 2000; Hawkes, 2003). This means that someone at risk of developing AD will not only have a declining sense of smell, but they will also be completely unaware of it, indicating a need for regular testing.

1.3 Biomarkers (in vivo) vs. Histopathology (autopsy)

Jack et al. (2010, 2013) published a hypothetical model of temporally ordered biomarkers for AD pathology. The model begins with the earliest pathology detected using (1) cerebrospinal fluid (CSF) levels of beta-amyloid42 (A 42), the earliest biomarker; followed by (2) positron emission tomography (PET) of beta-amyloid deposition in the brain; (3) CSF tau levels (t-tau and p-tau); (4) fluorodeoxyglucose PET (FDG PET) levels of neurodegeneration, hypo-metabolism; (5) structural MRI showing level of neurodegeneration; and lastly (6) clinical symptoms (Jack et al., 2010; Jack et al., 2013).

The Jack et al. model does not account for the fact that, in some individuals, tau pathology can be seen at a much earlier age than the amyloid plaques. Braak and Del Tredici (2011), using autopsy studies, found that there was evidence of tau pre-tangles in subcortical and brainstem nuclei in the entorhinal cortex in children as young as six (Braak & Del Tredici, 2011). Braak and Del Tedici propose that tau pathology begins in the locus coeruleus (located in the fourth ventricle near the rostral pons in the brainstem) and then spreads by cell-to-cell transmission through the brain (Braak & Del Tredici, 2011, 2015; de Calignon et al., 2012). The locus coeruleus is also an important component of the olfactory pathway, as norepinephrine projections, responsible for olfactory memory, are sent from the locus coeruleus to both the primary and secondary olfactory bulbs. There is criticism for the tau-based hypothesis because beta-amyloid over-production leads to AD, whereas high levels of initial tau does not lead to inevitable cognitive impairment, nor to AD (Jack et al., 2013). The important distinction between the two hypotheses is that Braak et al. believe that subcortical tau deposition starts the AD pathophysiological cascade and can begin as early as childhood, whereas Jack et al. posit that abnormal elevations of beta-amyloid is the catalyst for AD pathology development, potentially also causing the hyperphosphorylation of tau (Jack Jr. et al., 2013), though the latter could be an independent process (Small & Duff, 2008). Currently, there is substantial support for the beta-amyloid hypothesis being the antecedent to taupathy, and also causing an acceleration of neurofibrillary tangles, but both hypotheses are plausible. Histopathology studies are slow to emerge and require brain donation, so the debate is important to keep in mind because at this point the earliest evidence of pathophysiology currently lies beneath the threshold of detection of every available biomarker. Autopsy (i.e., histopathology) is still the only means of definitive identification of AD, and this is not a variable that is generally available in longitudinal databases.

2. Current Study

After careful review of the literature, regardless of which is correct, both temporal ordering hypotheses cite the olfactory cortex (entorhinal cortex vs locus coeruleus) as the initial brain site affected by AD pathology (Alves et al., 2014; Braak & Del Tredici, 2015; Jack Jr. et al., 2013; Kovács et al., 2001). Currently, there are relatively few longitudinal studies examining the use of olfactory decline as a biomarker for

AD, and even fewer that have autopsy-diagnosed pathology for AD. This study's primary aim is to conduct a replication of one of the most promising existing studies done by Wilson et al. (2009). The data is now more mature and the current study will use more than double the participants and nearly triple the measurement occasions. Research will concentrate on three tasks: (1) replication of the Wilson et al. (2009) study with the goals of (a) extending survival analyses to include AD pathology and mortality, and (b) including AD pathology into a mixed effects model to examine change in episodic memory and to test the relationship between BSIT and episodic memory; (2) in a second mixed-effects model, explore change in BSIT and test the relation of AD pathology to rate of BSIT decline while controlling for age, sex, education, and 4 allele; and (3) conduct a growth model for episodic memory with BSIT as time-varying covariate to determine whether smell and episodic memory fluctuate together at each measurement occasion (i.e.; a coupling model).

By doing so, this study will (1) establish the relationships between olfactory test scores, mortality, and risk of autopsy-diagnosed AD; (2) examine the rate of change in olfaction and the rate of change in cognitive function in healthy and AD individuals; and (3) determine the extent to which scores are fluctuating at each measurement occasion as well as whether they fluctuate together.

2.1 Participants

The research plan involves conducting proportional hazards models and multilevel mixed models using the Rush Memory and Aging Project (MAP) data, which is available within the Integrative Analysis of Longitudinal Studies of Aging (IALSA) network. A subgroup of MAP consisted of 875 individuals with three or more waves of BSIT data, including a valid BSIT score at baseline and no dementia diagnosis at baseline. Participants were recruited from more than 30 residential facilities across the Chicago metropolitan area: mean age was 78.07 years; 77.3% of participants were women, and approximately 6% were members of a racial or ethnic minority group.

2.2 Methods

This study will focus on the associations between olfaction and Alzheimer's disease pathology and will attempt to evaluate the hypothesis that olfactory testing is a clinically useful, functional biomarker for Alzheimer's disease pathology. Research will focus on three types of analyses: (1) survival analyses, (2) mixed effects models, and (3) a coupling model.

2.2.1 proposed analysis 1: survival analysis

Survival Analyses will be used to examine how olfactory test results are related to three outcomes: (1) all-cause mortality (Devanand et al., 2015), (2) AD (pathology diagnosis), and (3) clinical dementia diagnosis. I am expecting that lower scores will be associated to poor health outcomes after controlling for age, sex, education, apolipoprotein e4 allele, and episodic memory (Devanand et al., 2015; Devanand et al., 2015; Wilson et al., 2009). I expect that single olfactory measurements are not sufficient to diagnose, or place individuals into a risk category, and this will support use of olfactory testing as a repeated measurement to be tracked across lifespan and will potentially provide advance notice of health problems years before symptoms occur.

2.2.2 proposed analysis 2: mixed effects models

Mixed Effects Models will be used to estimate between-person differences in within-person change in olfaction and cognitive function. This study will examine several models for the correlations in the rate of change in olfactory decline and rate of change in cognitive decline in individuals with and without AD pathology. MAP data has at least three repeated measures per individual, making the use of growth modelling flexible in terms of the inclusion of potentially unequally spaced time points, non-normally distributed or discretely scaled repeated measures, complex nonlinear trajectories, time-varying covariates, and multivariate growth processes (Curran, Obeidat, & Losardo, 2010). In this study, two outcomes will be modelled separately: (1) composite episodic memory scores and (2) BSIT, olfactory scores, while also including time invariant covariates of age, sex, education, e4 allele, and time (defined as age-at-visit subtracted from age-at-baseline).

2.2.3 proposed analysis 3: coupling model

To examine the time-varying covariation between BSIT and episodic memory (i.e., within-person coupled variation), a time-in-study based mixed-effects model was constructed using episodic memory. In this model, the individual person-mean of BSIT represents a between-person effect and this is then subtracted from the raw BSIT score to provide a within-person effect. This model will elucidate how both of these scores fluctuate at each measurement occasion (Muniz-Terrera, Robitaille, Kelly, Johansson, Hofer, & Piccinin, 2017).

Olfactory function and trajectories in individuals vary across a variety of long-term outcomes, including AD pathology, dementia, traumatic brain injury, Parkinson's, and other disease diagnoses. Differences will be explored in individuals with and without AD pathology in an attempt to answer the question: are there differences in trajectories across diagnostic groups? I expect that olfactory decline will be highly correlated with pathology burden in the brain (Wilson et al., 2007). Differences in the rates of BSIT decline for those with and without AD pathology present in the brain should be significant, indicating a faster decline in BSIT and episodic memory for those individuals who have AD pathology. Can we use olfactory decline to predict AD? I expect that it will be possible to predict AD with repeated BSIT measurements over time. If so, at what point in the disease timeline can we accurately detect AD compared to other biomarkers? Are there decline patterns that allow us to differentiate between different diseases?

3. Knowledge Mobilization Plan

There are many excellent opportunities to participate in Knowledge Translation (KT) through established programs, such as the Speaker's Bureau (a service that provides researchers to the public to speak to community groups, schools, clubs, and other organizations throughout Greater Victoria and southern Vancouver Island), through which I have already been called on to speak about my research. Being a student affiliate of the University of Victoria (UVic) Institute of Aging and Lifelong Health provides additional opportunities for KT to the public and within the university. The Institute of Aging and Lifelong Health maintains connections with an extensive network of community members, practitioners, students, and researchers through print, social media, seminars, and lectures, and connects these diverse groups via many well-attended events. These popular events, such as IdeaFest, a campus-wide knowledge translation event for the UVic community showcasing the work of resident researchers, provide ongoing opportunities to update the public on this study and its findings.

The completion of this study will include traditional documents submitted for publication and presentations at professional conferences, such as the Alzheimer's Association International Conference (AAIC), the Gerontological Society of America (GSA), and the Canadian Association on Gerontology (CAG, for which I am a student ambassador), as well as lay articles to be submitted to newspapers, magazines, and online publications.

4. Conclusions

It is well established that AD pathology is at work ten to twenty years before clinical symptoms appear (Fiandaca et al., 2014; Mapstone, Dickerson, & Duffy, 2008; Masurkar & Devanand, 2014). This preclinical phase may account for 50% or more of the total disease duration and is where the least amount of information is being gathered. Measuring olfactory decline could provide a means to capture important pathophysiological changes that are occurring, currently unmonitored, at this critical undiagnosed stage. Early indicators for disease are crucial for implementing interventions while the brain is relatively undamaged and still functioning normally. This research aims to clarify the role that olfaction can play as an inexpensive biomarker for dementia using longitudinal designs, and, most importantly, to determine whether olfactory decline can robustly establish an accurate picture of disease progression, as well as differentiate diseases.

Intra-individual change tracking provides the most accurate information on an individual's health, and repeated frequent measuring provides the most accurate information on change. This study will use longitudinal data with annual assessments for up to 15 years in order to characterize change within individuals. The analyses proposed here will contribute to the current literature by conducting an independent replication of Wilson et al. (2009) using a more mature version of the data that includes more than double the participants and measurement occasions, examine new analyses that include AD pathology (a variable that is not widely available), and conduct a coupling model to determine how olfaction and episodic memory fluctuate at each measurement occasion. Previous research has provided ample cross-sectional support for olfaction's relationship to cognitive decline and disease, but the nature of olfaction is such that each person has a different baseline level and trajectory. Thus, the focus of this study is on longitudinal designs in order to provide much needed information on the efficacy of olfactory decline as a preclinical biomarker for AD, potentially informing new treatments and additional research.

Bibliography

Albers, M.W., Tabert, M.H., & Devanand, D.P. (2006). Olfactory dysfunction as a predictor of neurodegenerative disease. *Current neurology and neuroscience reports, 6*(5), 379–86.

Alves, J., Petrosyan, A., & Magalhães, R. (2014). Olfactory dysfunction in dementia. *World Journal of Clinical Cases: WJCC, 2*(11), 661.

Attems, J., Walker, L., & Jellinger, K.A. (2015). Olfaction and aging: A mini-review. *Gerontology.*

Braak, H., & Braak, E. (1991). Neuropathological stageing of Alzheimer-related changes. *Acta neuropathologica, 82*(4), 239–59.

Braak, H., & Del Tredici, K. (2011). The pathological process underlying Alzheimer's disease in individuals under thirty. *Acta Neuropathol, 121*(2), 171–81. doi: 10.1007/s00401-010-0789-4.

Braak, H., & Del Tredici, K. (2015). The preclinical phase of the pathological process underlying sporadic Alzheimer's disease. *Brain, 138*(Pt 10), 2814–33. doi: 10.1093/brain/awv236.

Campisi, J., & di Fagagna, F.d.A. (2007). Cellular senescence: When bad things happen to good cells. *Nature reviews Molecular cell biology, 8*(9), 729–40.

Curran, P.J., Obeidat, K., & Losardo, D. (2010). Twelve frequently asked questions about growth curve modeling. *Journal of Cognition and Development, 11*(2), 121–36.

de Calignon, A., Polydoro, M., Suarez-Calvet, M., William, C., Adamowicz, D.H., Kopeikina, K.J., ... Hyman, B.T. (2012). Propagation of tau pathology in a model of early Alzheimer's disease. *Neuron, 73*(4), 685–97. doi: 10.1016/j.neuron.2011.11.033.

Devanand, D.P., Lee, S., Manly, J., Andrews, H., Schupf, N., Doty, R.L., ... Mayeux, R. (2015). Olfactory deficits predict cognitive decline and Alzheimer dementia in an urban community. *Neurology, 84*(2), 182–89.

Devanand, D.P., Lee, S., Manly, J., Andrews, H., Schupf, N., Masurkar, A., ... Doty, R.L. (2015). Olfactory identification deficits and increased mortality in the community. *Annals of neurology, 78*(3), 401–11.

Devanand, D.P., Michaels-Marston, K.S., Liu, X., Pelton, G.H., Padilla, M., Marder, K.,...Mayeux, R. (2000). Olfactory deficits in patients with mild cognitive impairment predict Alzheimer's disease at follow-up. *American Journal of Psychiatry, 157*(9), 1399–1405.

Doty, R.L., Perl, D.P., Steele, J.C., Chen, K.M., Pierce Jr, J.D., Reyes, P., & Kurland, L.T. (1991). Olfactory dysfunction in three neurodegenerative diseases. *Geriatrics, 46*, 47–51.

Doty, R.L., Reyes, P.F., & Gregor, T. (1987). Presence of both odor identification and detection deficits in Alzheimer's disease. *Brain research bulletin, 18*(5), 597–600.

Duff, K., McCaffrey, R.J., & Solomon, G.S. (2002). The pocket smell test. *The Journal of neuropsychiatry and clinical neurosciences, 14*(2), 197–201.

Fiandaca, M.S., Mapstone, M.E., Cheema, A.K., & Federoff, H.J. (2014). The critical need for defining preclinical biomarkers in Alzheimer's disease. *Alzheimers Dement, 10*(3 Suppl), S196-212. doi: 10.1016/j.jalz.2014.04.015.

Hawkes, C. (2003). Olfaction in neurodegenerative disorder. *Movement Disorders, 18*(4), 364–72.

Jack, C.R., Knopman, D.S., Jagust, W.J., Petersen, R.C., Weiner, M.W., Aisen, P.S.,...Weigand, S.D. (2013). Tracking pathophysiological processes in Alzheimer's disease: An updated hypothetical model of dynamic biomarkers. *The Lancet Neurology, 12*(2), 207–16.

Jack, C.R., Knopman, D.S., Jagust, W.J., Shaw, L.M., Aisen, P.S., Weiner, M.W.,...Trojanowski, J.Q. (2010). Hypothetical model of dynamic biomarkers of the Alzheimer's pathological cascade. *The Lancet Neurology, 9*(1), 119–28.

Jack Jr, C.R., Knopman, D.S., Jagust, W.J., Petersen, R.C., Weiner, M.W., Aisen, P.S.,...Weigand, S.D. (2013). Update on hypothetical model of Alzheimer's disease biomarkers. *The Lancet Neurology, 12*(2), 207.

Kovács, T. (2004). Mechanisms of olfactory dysfunction in aging and neurodegenerative disorders. *Ageing research reviews, 3*(2), 215–32.

Kovács, T., Cairns, N.J., & Lantos, P.L. (2001). Olfactory centres in Alzheimer's disease: Olfactory bulb is involved in early braak's stages. *Neuroreport, 12*(2), 285–88.

Mapstone, M., Dickerson, K., & Duffy, C.J. (2008). Distinct mechanisms of impairment in cognitive ageing and Alzheimer's disease. *Brain, 131*(Pt 6), 1618–29. doi: 10.1093/brain/awn064.

Masurkar, A.V., & Devanand, D.P. (2014). Olfactory dysfunction in the elderly: Basic circuitry and alterations with normal aging and Alzheimer's disease. *Current geriatrics reports, 3*(2), 91–100.

Murphy, C. (2002). Olfactory functional testing: Sensitivity and specificity for Alzheimer's disease. *Drug Development Research, 56*(2), 123–31.

Mesholam, R.I., Moberg, P.J., Mahr, R.N., & Doty, R.L. (1998). Olfaction in neurodegenerative disease: A meta-analysis of olfactory functioning in Alzheimer's and Parkinson's diseases. Archives of Neurology, 55(1), 84–90. https://doi.org/10.1159/000093759.

Muniz-Terrera, G., Robitaille, A., Kelly, A., Johansson, B., Hofer, S., & Piccinin, A. (2017). Latent growth models matched to research questions to answer questions about dynamics of change in multiple processes. *Journal of clinical epidemiology, 82,* 158–66.

Murphy, C., Gilmore, M.M., Seery, C.S., Salmon, D.P., & Lasker, B.R. (1990). Olfactory thresholds are associated with degree of dementia in Alzheimer's disease. *Neurobiology of aging, 11*(4), 465–69.

Murphy, C., Solomon, E.S., Haase, L., Wang, M., & Morgan, C.D. (2009). Olfaction in aging and Alzheimer's disease. *Annals of the New York Academy of Sciences, 1170*(1), 647–57.

Peters, J.M., Hummel, T., Kratzsch, T., Lötsch, J., Skarke, C., & Frölich, L. (2003). Olfactory function in mild cognitive impairment and Alzheimer's disease: An investigation using psychophysical and electrophysiological techniques. *American Journal of Psychiatry.*

Purves, D., Augustine, G.J., Fitzpatrick, D., Katz, L.C., LaMantia, A.-S., McNamara, J.O., & Williams, S.M. (2001). The organization of the olfactory system. *Neuroscience,* 337–54.

Schubert, C.R., Cruickshanks, K.J., Fischer, M.E., Huang, G.-H., Klein, B.E.K., Klein, R., ... Nondahl, D.M. (2011). Olfactory impairment in an adult population: The beaver dam offspring study. *Chemical senses,* bjr102.

Shepherd, G.M. (2006). Smell images and the flavour system in the human brain. *Nature, 444*(7117), 316–21.

Shepherd, G.M. (2007). Perspectives on olfactory processing, conscious perception, and orbitofrontal cortex. *Annals of the New York Academy of Sciences, 1121*(1), 87–101.

Small, S.A., & Duff, K. (2008). Linking aβ and tau in late-onset Alzheimer's disease: A dual pathway hypothesis. *Neuron, 60*(4), 534–42.

Walker, L.C., Diamond, M.I., Duff, K.E., & Hyman, B.T. (2013). Mechanisms of protein seeding in neurodegenerative diseases. *JAMA neurology, 70*(3), 304–10.

Wilson, R.S., Arnold, S.E., Schneider, J.A., Boyle, P.A., Buchman, A.S., & Bennett, D.A. (2009). Olfactory impairment in presymptomatic Alzheimer's disease. *Annals of the New York Academy of Sciences, 1170*(1), 730–35.

Wilson, Robert S., Arnold, Steven E., Schneider, Julie A., Tang, Yuxiao, & Bennett, David A. (2007). The relationship between cerebral Alzheimer's disease pathology and odour identification in old age. *Journal of Neurology, Neurosurgery & Psychiatry, 78*(1), 30–35.

Xydakis, M.S., Mulligan, L.P., Smith, A.B., Olsen, C.H., Lyon, D.M., & Belluscio, L. (2015). Olfactory impairment and traumatic brain injury in blast-injured combat troops: a cohort study. *Neurology, 84*(15), 1559–67.

DISCUSSION QUESTIONS

1. This proposal contains a multitude of scientific terms, some of which will be new to you. One of the steps towards understanding scholarly articles is understanding the words researchers use. Choose a small section of the proposal (for example, Section 1.1.1, "Cross-Sectional Literature: Disease") that is difficult to understand due its vocabulary and look up unknown terms. How does this help you better understand the paragraph and, in effect, the entire proposal?

2. In the summary, Knight states that the "analysis will provide answers about whether olfaction and episodic memory are fluctuating together at each measurement time point" (p. 392). Using quotations from the proposal, identify how Knight intends to provide these answers, and why a patient's olfactory ability/ decline is considered linked to dementia.

3. Knight uses the longitudinal Memory and Aging Project (MAP) from the RADC (www.rushu.rush.edu/research/departmental-research/rush-alzheimer%E2%80%99s-disease-center-research) "to establish the relationships between olfactory decline, episodic memory, and AD pathology" (p. 392). Explore the RADC website's 'clinical trials' or 'epidemiologic research' pages and choose one of their trials or research projects to explore. Be prepared to explain your chosen trial or project to the class.

4. Knight's research hopes to find a way to diagnose AD in the preclinical stage of the disease. Discuss the potential ethical issues surrounding this (for example, how might someone be discriminated against in the workplace if it is known that in ten years they will have clinical Alzheimer's?).

5. How does this work as a proposal? How does a proposal differ from an article? How do you envision the thesis that is being proposed here? (The thesis was defended in June of 2017. You can access it at http://hdl.handle. net/1828/8271).

E. "FORESHADOWING ALZHEIMER'S: VARIABILITY AND COUPLING OF OLFACTION AND COGNITION," JAMIE E. KNIGHT AND ANDREA M. PICCININ, UNIVERSITY OF VICTORIA, BC, CANADA

This research poster, presented by Jamie Knight and Andrea Piccinin* at the 2017 World Congress of the International Association of Gerontology and Geriatrics (IAGG) in San Francisco, is the second of three related examples of writing in the research genres focusing on the relation between loss of smell and dementia. (See the glossary for more information on research posters.) If you have already read Knight's thesis proposal, you will recognize that this poster follows from the research involved in the thesis. The original poster is printed on glossy paper (121.92 cm by 91.44 cm). We have reproduced an image of the poster on the next page and then reprinted the text on the following pages. As you look at the poster and read the text from it, consider how this research genre differs from others that you have read, such as an article or a proposal. What are the advantages and disadvantages of the academic poster?

Glossary terms: research poster, Wechsler Memory Scale

Resources:
- See the original poster in colour: https://sites.broadviewpress.com/researchnow
- See the program for the 2017 World Congress of the International Association of Gerontology and Geriatrics (IAGG) in San Francisco: www.iagg2017.org/images/documents/IAGG2017_Program_Final.pdf
- The conference website is here: www.iagg2017.org

Background

Patients already diagnosed with Alzheimer's disease (AD) have deficits in their sense of smell, and emerging evidence suggests that olfactory decline can be used to predict the onset of neurodegenerative diseases.[1,2]

---

* Jamie Knight is a PhD student under the supervision of Dr Andrea Piccinin in the Lifespan Development stream in Psychology at the University of Victoria. She studies neuropsychological and chemosensory functioning with the goal of identifying pre-clinical biomarkers of age-related cognitive decline and neurodegenerative diseases.

Andrea Piccinin is a Professor of Psychology at the University of Victoria and co-founder of the Integrative Analysis of Longitudinal Studies on Aging (IALSA) network. Her research focuses on study designs and statistical analyses of individual differences in late-life cognition and health outcomes.

Foreshadowing Alzheimer's: Variability and Coupling of Olfaction and Cognition

Jamie E. Knight & Andrea M. Piccinin

University of Victoria, BC, Canada

Background

Patients already diagnosed with Alzheimer's Disease (AD) have deficits in their sense of smell, and emerging evidence suggests that olfactory decline can be used to predict the onset of neurodegenerative diseases.[1,2]

Olfactory tests are inexpensive, easy to administer, and could eventually fill gaps in knowledge surrounding preclinical AD.

Study Objectives

Examine change in memory performance as a function of both the passage of time and (intraindividual) changes in smell by using a growth model for episodic memory with the Brief Smell Identification Test (BSIT) as time-varying covariate.[3]

Determine whether olfaction and episodic memory are fluctuating together at each measurement time point.

Methods

Participants

Participants were from a subset of 454 individuals from the Rush University Memory and Aging Project (MAP) and had both autopsy data and a valid BSIT measurement at baseline.

Annual assessments were collected for up to 15 years with brain donation at death.

Mean age was 83, 70% were female, and 23% had one or more ε4 allele (Table 1).

Table 1. Characteristics of Participants by BSIT Group at Baseline.

	All BSIT 1–12 (N = 454)	Normal BSIT 11–12 (n = 67)	Hyposmic BSIT 6–10 (n = 315)	Anosmic BSIT 0–5 (n = 65)
Sex, Female %	70%	79%	71%	52%
Age, years, mean (SD)	83 (6.1)	83 (5.7)	83 (6.2)	85 (5.7)
APOE ε4 allele, N (%)	105 (23%)	10 (15%)	71 (22.5%)	22 (34%)
Memory domain				
Episodic, mean z-score (SD)	-0.17 (0.8)	0.18 (0.6)	-0.10 (0.7)	-0.88 (1.0)
Cognitive test scores				
MMSE, mean (SD)	26.96 (3.3)	28.35 (1.5)	27.35 (2.6)	23.82 (3.0)
Logical Memory IIa, mean (SD)	7.82 (4.7)	9.61 (4.5)	8.04 (4.6)	4.97 (4.5)
Education, years, mean (SD)	14.38 (2.8)	13.97 (2.3)	14.4 (2.7)	14.94 (3.5)
AD pathology, N (%)	285 (63%)	35 (52%)	197 (62.5%)	48 (74%)
Dementia at death (no dementia %)	40% (33%)	15% (59%)	31% (38%)	60% (13%)

Measures

The BSIT, administered at each data collection wave, is a 12-item test where a score of 11 or 12 indicates normal olfactory ability.

Raw scores from seven tests (East Boston immediate recall, East Boston delayed recall, Logical Memory I (immediate recall), Logical Memory II (delayed recall), CERAD word list (immediate, delayed, and recognition) were converted to z-scores and averaged to yield the episodic memory composite score.

Mini Mental State Examination (MMSE) is a 30-item, standardized screening measure for dementia. Logical Memory IIa is a measure from the Wechsler Memory Scale where participants recall story units (out of 25) after a 30-minute delay.

As determined by a neuropathologist, those with intermediate or high scores fulfilled the criteria for having a pathologic diagnosis of AD and those with low or no AD pathology were considered to not have had AD. This measure relies on counts of neurofibrillary tangles and neuritic plaques.

Analysis

To examine the time-varying covariation between BSIT and episodic memory (within-person coupled variation), a growth model for episodic memory with BSIT as time-varying covariate was constructed using a composite score for episodic memory. The individual person-mean of BSIT (BSIT_PM) was used to represent an overall between person difference effect, and this was subtracted from the raw score at each wave to then provide a within-person change effect (BSIT_TVC). Terms for age, sex, education, apolipoprotein ε4 allele, and AD pathology were included.

Results

Between-person variation in odour identification had a significant positive association to episodic memory (b = 0.12, SE = 0.014, $p < 001$). For every unit decrease in person-mean BSIT (BSIT_PM), episodic memory at baseline also decreased by 0.12.

High AD pathology was related to lower episodic memory at baseline (b = -0.26, SE = 0.07, $p < 001$).

Person-mean BSIT scores (b = 0.01, SE = 0.004, $p = 0.014$) and high AD pathology (b = -0.07, SE = 0.02, $p < 0.001$), and possession of an ε4 allele (b = -0.04, SE = 0.02, $p = 0.04$), were all associated with more rapid declines in episodic memory.

There was a robust positive association between the time varying covariate of BSIT (BSIT_TVC = raw BSIT - BSIT_PM) and fluctuations in episodic memory. For every unit decrease in BSIT relative to each person's own mean BSIT score, that occasion's episodic memory also decreases by 0.06 units (b = 0.06, SE = 0.02, $p < 001$).

Discussion

High AD pathology at death was related to a lower than average episodic memory score at study entry and a faster decline in episodic memory.

Lower person-mean BSIT scores were associated with lower episodic memory scores at baseline as well as faster declines in episodic memory.

When an individuals BSIT score was lower than their own average their episodic memory scores also decreased at that same measurement occasion.

Male participants had lower episodic memory scores at baseline.

Individuals with an ε4 allele had lower episodic memory at baseline and a faster rate of decline.

Age at baseline was not significantly associated with the rate of decline for episodic memory. However, faster decline in episodic memory was associated with AD pathology and lower personal average smell scores.

Conclusion

The coupled relationship between smell and cognition indicates that olfactory testing can be a useful tool for assessing cognitive decline and possibly an inexpensive screener for pathological brain changes.

References

1. Devanand, D. P. (2016). Olfactory Identification Deficits, Cognitive Decline, and Dementia in Older Adults. The American Journal of Geriatric Psychiatry, 24(12), 1151-1157.

2. Wilson, R., Arnold, S.E., Schneider, J.A., Boyle, P.A., Buchman, A.S., & Bennett, D.A. (2009). Olfactory impairment in presymptomatic Alzheimer's disease. Annals of the New York Academy of Sciences, 1170(1), 730-735.

3. Muniz-Terrera, G., Robitaille, A., Kelly, A., Johansson, B., Hofer, S., & Piccinin, A. (2017). Latent growth models matched to research questions to answer questions about dynamics of change in multiple processes. Journal of clinical epidemiology, 82, 158-166.

IAGG 2017
SAN FRANCISCO
JULY 23-27, 2017

University of Victoria

RUSH UNIVERSITY

NIH

Integrative Analysis of Longitudinal Studies of Aging

Research reported in this publication was supported by the National Institute on aging of the National Institutes of Health under Award number P01AG043362.

Olfactory tests are inexpensive, easy to administer, and could eventually fill gaps in knowledge surrounding preclinical AD.

Study Objectives

Examine change in memory performance as a function of both the passage of time and (intraindividual) changes in smell by using a growth model for episodic memory with the Brief Smell Identification Test (BSIT) as time-varying covariate.[3]

Determine whether olfaction and episodic memory are fluctuating together at each measurement time point.

Methods

Participants

Participants were from a subset of 454 individuals from the Rush University Memory and Aging Project (MAP) and had both autopsy data and a valid BSIT measurement at baseline.

Annual assessments were collected for up to 15 years with brain donation at death.

Mean age was 83; 70% were female and 23% had one or more ε4 allele (Table 1).

	All BSIT 1-12 (N = 454)	Normal BSIT 11-12 (n = 67)	Hyposmic BSIT 6-10 (n = 315)	Anosmic BSIT 0-5 (n = 65)
Sex, Female %	70%	79%	71%	52%
Age, years, mean (SD)	83 (6.1)	83 (5.7)	83 (6.2)	85 (5.7)
APOE ε4 allele, N (%)	105 (23%)	10 (15%)	71 (22.5%)	22 (34%)
Memory domain Episodic, mean z-score (SD)	-0.17 (0.8)	0.18 (0.6)	-0.10 (0.7)	-0.88 (1.0)

Cognitive test scores
  MMSE, mean (SD)
  Logical Memory IIa, mean (SD)
	26.96 (3.3)
	7.82 (4.7)
		28.35 (1.5)
		9.61 (4.5)
			27.35 (2.6)
			8.04 (4.6)
				23.82 (5.0)
				4.97 (4.5)

Education, years, mean (SD)	14.38 (2.8)	13.97 (2.3)	14.4 (2.7)	14.94 (3.5)
AD pathology, N (%)	285 (63%)	35 (52%)	197 (62.5%)	48 (74%)
Dementia at death (no dementia %)	40% (33%)	15% (59%)	31% (38%)	60% (13%)

Table 1. Characteristics of Participants by BSIT Group at Baseline

Measures

The BSIT, administered at each data collection wave, is a 12-item test where a score of 11 or 12 indicates normal olfactory ability.

Raw scores from seven tests (East Boston immediate recall, East Boston delayed recall, Logical Memory I (immediate recall), Logical Memory II (delayed recall), CERAD word list (immediate, delayed, and recognition) were converted to z-scores and averaged to yield the episodic memory composite score.

Mini Mental State Examination (MMSE) is a 30-item, standardized screening measure for dementia. Logical Memory IIa is a measure from the Wechsler Memory Scale where participants recall story units (out of 25) after a 30-minute delay.

As determined by a neuropathologist, those with intermediate or high scores fulfilled the criteria for having a pathologic diagnosis of AD and those with low or no AD pathology were considered to not have had AD. This measure relies on counts of neurofibrillary tangles and neuritic plaques.

Analysis
To examine the time-varying covariation between BSIT and episodic memory (within-person coupled variation), a growth model for episodic memory with BSIT as time-varying covariate was constructed using a composite score for episodic memory. The individual person-mean of BSIT (BSIT_PM) was used to represent an overall between-person difference effect, and this was subtracted from the raw score at each wave to then provide a within-person change effect (BSIT_TVC). Terms for age, sex, education, apolipoprotein ε4 allele, and AD pathology were included.

Results
Between-person variation in odour identification had a significant positive association to episodic memory ($b = 0.12$, SE $= 0.014$, $p < 001$). For every unit decrease in person-mean BSIT (BSIT_PM), episodic memory at baseline also decreased by 0.12.

High AD pathology was related to lower episodic memory at baseline ($b = -0.26$, SE $= 0.07$, $p < 001$).

Person-mean BSIT scores ($b = 0.01$, SE $= 0.004$, $p = 0.014$), high AD pathology ($b = -0.07$, SE $= 0.02$, $p < 0.001$), and possession of an ε4 allele ($b = -0.04$, SE $= 0.02$, $p = 0.04$) were all associated with more rapid declines in episodic memory.

There was a robust positive association between the time-varying covariate of BSIT (BSIT_TVC = raw BSIT - BSIT_PM) and fluctuations in episodic memory. For every unit decrease in BSIT relative to each person's own mean BSIT score, that occasion's episodic memory score also decreases by 0.06 units ($b = 0.06$, SE $= 0.02$, $p < 001$).

Discussion

High AD pathology at death was related to a lower-than-average episodic memory score at study entry and a faster decline in episodic memory.

Lower person-mean BSIT scores were associated with lower episodic memory scores at baseline as well as faster declines in episodic memory.

When an individual's BSIT score was lower than their own average, their episodic memory scores also decreased at that same measurement occasion.

Male participants and individuals with an ε4 allele had lower episodic memory scores at baseline, and the latter experienced a faster rate of decline.

Age at baseline was not significantly associated with the rate of decline for episodic memory. However, a faster decline was associated with AD pathology and lower personal average smell scores.

Conclusion

The relationship between smell and cognition indicates that olfactory testing can be a useful tool for assessing cognitive decline and possibly a screener for pathological brain changes.

References

[1] Devanand, D.P. (2016). Olfactory Identification Deficits, Cognitive Decline, and Dementia in Older Adults. The American Journal of Geriatric Psychiatry, 24(12), 1151–57.

[2] Wilson, R., Arnold, S.E., Schneider, J.A., Boyle, P.A., Buchman, A.S., & Bennett, D.A. (2009). Olfactory impairment in presymptomatic Alzheimer's disease. Annals of the New York Academy of Sciences, 1170(1), 730–35.

[3] Muniz-Terrera, G., Robitaille, A., Kelly, A., Johansson, B., Hofer, S., & Piccinin, A. (2017). Latent growth models matched to research questions to answer questions about dynamics of change in multiple processes. Journal of clinical epidemiology, 82, 158–66.

DISCUSSION QUESTIONS

1. Overall, 70% of the subjects in this trial were female. What factors do you think created this imbalance? What implications does this imbalance hold for the research? Are there any other details about the subjects that are notable?

2. Knight and Piccinin state that "olfactory decline can be used to predict the onset of neurodegenerative diseases" (p. 403). What other neurodegenerative diseases might it be used to predict (you will need to do some research)? Is the ability to predict the onset of diseases desirable? Why or why not? In short, where do you see this research leading?

3. Identify the different features (for example, the "Background" section) of this poster. (Make sure to look at the image of the poster or go online and view it in its entirety.) How does this particular poster compare with some of the articles (or the previous proposal) you have read in this Reader? Do any of the features surprise you or stand out as markedly different from what you've seen in articles?

4. Prepare a brief explanation of a "time-varying covariate" model (p. 406). What does a time-varying covariate model tell you about the data?

5. Why do you think olfactory scores decline with Alzheimer's pathology?

F. "OLFACTORY IMPAIRMENT IN PRESYMPTOMATIC ALZHEIMER'S DISEASE," ROBERT S. WILSON, STEVEN E. ARNOLD, JULIE A. SCHNEIDER, PATRICIA A. BOYLE, ARON S. BUCHMAN, AND DAVID A. BENNETT

This 2009 article, published in the Annals of the New York Academy of Science*'s* International Symposium on Olfaction and Taste *issue is the third of three related examples in this section that illustrate the process of knowledge construction. If you look at the citations in Knight's proposal and Knight and Piccinin's poster, you will see that this article is one of the sources that is cited and prominently reported. In this sense, it is one of the foundations for Knight and Piccinin's research. In this article, Wilson et al.* explain their "study of olfactory impairment as an early sign of [Alzheimer's disease]" (p. 410). The study examines "the relation of the ability to identify familiar odors to the development of AD in nearly 500 older persons without evidence of cognitive impairment at enrollment" (p. 415) in order to show that "the association of olfactory function with the clinical and pathologic manifestations of AD can be seen in otherwise asymptomatic individuals" (p. 415). As you read, observe how Wilson et al.'s article differs from the proposal and poster. What is different about the research and how it is presented?*

Glossary terms: etiology, longitudinal study

Abstract

Alzheimer's disease (AD) impairs olfaction, but it is uncertain how early this occurs in the disease process and whether the effect can be accounted for by other behavioral or genetic markers of the disease. We administered the Brief Smell Identification

---

* Robert S. Wilson is Professor in the Department of Neurological Sciences and Director of Cognitive Neurosciences at Rush University.

Steven E. Arnold is Professor of Psychiatry at the University of Pennsylvania.

Julie A. Schneider is Professor in the Department of Pathology and the Department of Neurological Sciences at Rush University.

Patricia A. Boyle is Professor in the Department of Behavioral Sciences at Rush University.

Aron S. Buchman is Professor in the Department of Neurological Sciences at Rush University.

David A. Bennett is Professor in the Department of Neurological Sciences at Rush University and Director of the Rush Alzheimer's Disease Center.

Test (BSIT) to 471 older people without dementia or cognitive impairment who then completed annual clinical evaluations and brain autopsy at death. BSIT score was associated with more rapid decline in episodic memory and with increased risk of developing incident mild cognitive impairment (MCI), even after controlling for baseline level of episodic memory and possession of an apolipoprotein E ε4 allele. In 34 people who died without evidence of cognitive impairment, lower BSIT score was associated with higher level of AD pathology, even after controlling for ε4 and for level of episodic memory function when olfaction was assessed. These analyses suggest that among older people without clinical manifestations of AD or MCI, olfactory dysfunction is related to both the level of AD pathology in the brain and the risk of subsequently developing prodromal symptoms of the disease, and that these associations persist after accounting for the effects of other recognized behavioral and genetic markers of the disease.

Introduction

Alzheimer's disease (AD) is a leading cause of disability in old age, and the public health challenges posed by the disease are likely to increase in the coming decades with the aging of the U.S. population. Definitive classification of AD currently requires a brain autopsy, underscoring the need for biological or behavioral markers of the disease in the living. In particular, markers are needed to support early diagnosis because disease-modifying therapeutic compounds for AD are under development, and it is generally assumed that such compounds will be most effective early in the disease course, before pathology is widespread.[1–3] In addition to certain practical characteristics (such as being reliable, noninvasive, and simple to perform), the ideal biomarker should be related to AD neuropathology[1] in those with little or no clinical evidence of the disease. In view of the substantial clinical and neuropathologic heterogeneity of AD, accurate early diagnosis will most likely require the use of several markers in conjunction. In this context, therefore, markers that have little or no correlation with other markers will be most useful.

In the present study, we focus on olfactory impairment as an early sign of AD. With clinical and neuropathologic data from the Rush Memory and Aging Project, we previously showed that difficulty identifying familiar odors predicted subsequent development of mild cognitive impairment (MCI), a precursor to dementia in AD,[4] and was robustly correlated with level of AD pathology on postmortem examination.[5] Here, we conduct further analyses of individuals without dementia or MCI at study enrollment to test whether the association of olfactory dysfunction with AD is evident in this well-functioning subgroup and whether it persists after accounting for other recognized behavioral and genetic markers of the disease.

Methods

Participants

All subjects were enrolled in the Rush Memory and Aging Project, a longitudinal clinical-pathologic study of common chronic conditions of old age.[6] Eligibility for the present analyses required intact cognitive functioning and a valid score on the Brief Smell Identification Test (BSIT)[7] at the time of study enrollment; 471 individuals met these criteria, and analyses are based on this group; 383 were excluded because MCI or dementia was identified on the baseline clinical evaluation (below). Study subjects had a mean age of 79.3 (SD = 7.0) at base line and a mean of 14.5 years of education (SD = 2.9); 76.2% were women and 91.3% were white and non-Hispanic (Table 1).

Table 1. Descriptive Information on the 471 Study Participants at Base Line*

Characteristic	Value
Age	79.3 (7.0; 55–100)
Education	14.6 (2.9; 5–28)
Women, %	76
White non-Hispanic, %	92
Brief Smell Identification Test	9.2 (1.9; 1–12)
Episodic memory	0.39 (0.47; −0.87–1.85)
Apolipoprotein E ε4, %	20

*Data are presented as mean (standard deviation; range) unless otherwise indicated.

Clinical Evaluation

At base line and annually thereafter, participants had a uniform clinical evaluation that included a medical history, a complete neurological examination, and administration of a battery of 21 cognitive tests. Seven of these assessed episodic memory: immediate and delayed recall of the East Boston Story and Story A from Logical Memory and Word List Memory, Word List Recall, and Word List Recognition. As previously described, we formed a composite measure of episodic memory by converting raw scores on each test to z scores, using the mean and standard deviation from the full cohort, and then averaging the z scores to yield the composite.[8,9] In addition, ratings of impairment in five cognitive domains were made by a neuropsychologist, guided by educationally adjusted cutoff scores on a subset of the tests.[10]

Based on this evaluation, an experienced clinician diagnosed MCI, dementia, and AD, as previously described.[4,11] Dementia required a history of cognitive decline and impairment in at least two cognitive domains, one of which had to be memory to meet criteria for AD.[12] Persons who did not meet criteria for dementia but who showed evidence of impairment in at least one cognitive domain were classified as MCI. These criteria for dementia, AD, and MCI, have been widely used and pathologically validated in this and other[13,14] cohorts.

Assessment of Odor Identification

Odor identification was assessed with the BSIT.[7] For each item, a microcapsule containing a familiar odor was scratched with a pencil and placed under the nose of the participant who matched the smell with one of four choices. There are 12 items and the score is the number of correct recognitions. In previous research, this score has been shown to correlate with the 40-item University of Pennsylvania Smell Identification Test, from which it was derived.[15]

Apolipoprotein E Genotyping

Apolipoprotein E genotyping was done blinded to all other study data using methods adapted from Hixson and Vernier,[16] as previously described.[17,18] In all analyses, individuals were dichotomized into those with at least one copy of the ε4 allele (i.e., ε2/4, ε3/4, or ε4/4) versus those without a copy (i.e., ε2/2, ε2/3, or ε3/3).

Neuropathological Evaluation

A standard protocol was followed for brain removal, sectioning and preserving the tissue, and quantifying pathologic findings, as reported in more detail elsewhere.[13,14] Tissue from five brain regions (midfrontal gyrus, inferior parietal gyrus, middle temporal gyrus, entorhinal cortex, and hippocampus [CA1/subiculum]) was cut into 0.5-cm-thick blocks, embedded in paraffin wax, sectioned at 6 mm, and stained with modified Bielschowsky silver. For each of the five brain regions of interest, a neuropathologist or trained technician, blinded to all clinical data, separately counted neuritic plaques, diffuse plaques, and neurofibrillar tangles in a 1-mm^2 area using a 610 objective (with 610 eyepiece) in the site judged to have the most of a given type of pathology. For each type of pathology in each region, the raw count was divided by the SD of all counts of that pathology in that region to yield a standard score. These standard scores were averaged to produce a composite measure of cortical plaques and tangles and summary measures of each type of pathology, as reported previously.

Data Analysis

We used a proportional hazards model,[19] to test the relation of odor identification score to risk of incident MCI. The analysis controlled for age, sex, education, presence of the ε4 allele, and level of episodic memory function. We used a mixed-effects model[20] to characterize change in a composite measure of episodic memory and to test the relation of odor identification score to rate of memory decline, while accounting for initial level of memory function and controlling for age, sex, education, and ε4. In a final analysis, we regressed a composite measure of AD pathology on odor-identification score in a linear regression model adjusted for age at death, sex, education, time from olfactory testing to death, ε4, and episodic memory.

Results

At the time of study enrollment, scores on the BSIT ranged from 1 to 12 (mean = 9.2, SD = 1.9), with higher values indicating better ability to identify familiar odors.

Odor Identification and Incidence of MCI

During up to 5.5 years of follow-up (mean = 2.7, SD = 1.4), 155 individuals (32.9%) developed MCI. To determine the relation of odor identification to risk of developing MCI, we constructed a proportional hazards model. In addition to controlling for age, sex, and education, the model included terms for two established disease markers: possession of at least one copy of the apolipoprotein E ε4 allele (present in 19.8%) and level of episodic memory function (mean = 0.39, SD = 0.47), as indicated by a previously established composite measure.[8,9] In this analysis, risk of MCI was associated with odor identification test score (hazard ratio = 0.874; 95% confidence interval: 0.812, 0.941). Thus, a person who made four errors (score = 8) was about 50% more likely to develop MCI than a person who made one error (score = 11).

Odor Identification and Episodic Memory Decline

Decline in episodic memory is one of the earliest clinical manifestations of AD, often beginning several years before a clinical diagnosis can be made.[21] Table 1 shows the distribution of the composite measure of episodic memory at base line. To test the relation of odor identification to change in episodic memory, we constructed a mixed-effects model with the composite measure of episodic memory as the outcome. The model also included terms to control for the effects of age, sex, education, ε4, and level of episodic memory at base line. In this analysis, lower odor identification score was robustly associated with more rapid decline in episodic memory (parameter estimate = 0.014, SE = 0.004, $P < 0.001$).

Odor Identification and Alzheimer's Disease Pathology

An ideal early marker of AD would be related to the underlying pathology in people with little or no clinical evidence of the disease. At the time of these analyses, we identified 34 individuals who met two criteria: (i) no evidence of cognitive impairment on baseline or follow-up evaluations and (ii) died and underwent brain autopsy. These individuals died at a mean age of 85.2 (SD = 6.4), they had a mean of 14.0 years of education (SD = 2.2), 67.7% were women, and 94.1% were white and non-Hispanic (Table 2). In a uniform neuropathologic examination done blinded to all clinical data, crude counts of neuritic plaques, diffuse plaques, and neurofibrillary tangles in five brain regions were converted to a standard scale and averaged. Because the resulting distribution was skewed, a square root transformation was used (see Table 2). In a linear regression model adjusted for age, sex, education, time from olfactory testing to death, ε4, and episodic memory function when olfaction was tested, lower odor identification score was associated with higher level of AD pathology (parameter estimate $=-0.063$, SE -0.027, $P = 0.028$).

Table 2. Descriptive Information on the 34 Study Participants who Died without Cognitive Impairment and Underwent Brain Autopsy*

Characteristic	Value
Age at death	85.2 (6.4; 67–98)
Education	13.9 (2.2; 11–19)
Women, %	68
White non-Hispanic, %	94
Brief Smell Identification Test	8.6 (1.8; 6–12)
Episodic memory	0.35 (0.46; −0.63–1.23)
Apolipoprotein E ε4, %	21
Months from olfactory test to death	26.0 (12.9; 3.5–47.1)
Composite AD pathology	0.58 (0.33; 0.05–1.18)

*Data are presented as mean (standard deviation; range) unless otherwise indicated.

Discussion

We studied the relation of the ability to identify familiar odors to the development of AD in nearly 500 older persons without evidence of cognitive impairment at enrollment. The analyses suggest that among older persons without the clinical manifestations of AD or its precursor, MCI, olfactory dysfunction is related to both the level of AD pathology in the brain and the risk of subsequently developing prodromal symptoms of AD in the form of MCI and declining episodic memory.

It has long been recognized that olfaction is impaired in persons with clinically diagnosed AD.[22–27] Olfactory function is also impaired in MCI,[26–31] a precursor of AD, and in those with at least one copy of the apolipoprotein E ε4 allele,[28,32–34] a well-established risk factor for AD. In previous research in this cohort, we showed that odor recognition performance predicted incidence of MCI and AD, rate of cognitive decline, and level of AD pathology on postmortem examination.[4,5] The present analyses extend these findings by showing that the association of olfactory function with the clinical and pathologic manifestations of AD can be seen in otherwise asymptomatic individuals and that it persists even after accounting for the effects of other recognized behavioral and genetic markers of the disease. These data suggest that olfactory testing, when combined with other behavioral and biologic markers, may contribute to early detection of AD.

Prior research in this cohort suggests that the association between olfactory dysfunction and clinical AD is largely due to the accumulation of AD pathology, particularly neurofibrillary tangles, in central olfactory regions, especially entorhinal cortex and hippocampus.[5] The involvement of these sites is important because they are thought to be among the first areas affected by the pathologic changes of AD.[35–38] Thus, olfactory symptoms might conceivably precede cognitive impairment in AD by a substantial period. In addition, decline occurs in other sensory systems with advancing age in association with cognitive decline.[39] Because the entorhinal cortex processes input from multiple sensory modalities, it is possible that subtle changes in other sensory functions might be early signs of AD.

Confidence in these findings is strengthened by several factors. The diagnoses of MCI and AD were based on uniform structured clinical evaluations and widely accepted criteria. Rates of participation in follow-up clinical evaluations and brain autopsy were high. Odor identification was assessed with a standard scale. Episodic memory and AD pathology were assessed with previously established composite measures. An important limitation is that the cohort is selected so that the generalizability of the findings remains to be determined. In addition, securely establishing the value of olfactory testing in early diagnosis will likely require more extensive assessment of olfactory processing conducted proximate to death in a larger group of people.

Acknowledgments

This research was supported by National Institute on Aging Grants R01 AG17917, R01 AG022018, and K23 AG23040 and by the Illinois Department of Public Health. We thank the many Illinois residents for participating in the Rush Memory and Aging Project; Tracy Colvin, MPH, and Karen Skish for study coordination; John Gibbons, MS, and Greg Klein for data management; and Todd Beck, MS, and Woojeong Bang, MS, for statistical programming.

References

[1] Frank, R.A., D. Galasko, H. Hampel, *et al.* 2003. Biological markers for therapeutic trials in Alzheimer's disease. Proceedings of the biological markers working group; NIA initiative on neuroimaging in Alzheimer's disease. *Neurobiol. Aging* 24: 521–36.

[2] Andreasen, N. & K. Blennow. 2005. CSF biomarkers for mild cognitive impairment and early Alzheimer's disease. *Clin. Neurol. Neurosurg.* 107: 165–73.

[3] Blennow, K. & E. Vanmechelen. 2003. CSF markers for pathogenic processes in Alzheimer's disease: diagnostic implications and use in clinical neurochemistry. *Brain Res. Bull.* 61: 235–42.

[4] Wilson, R.S., J.A. Schneider, S.E. Arnold, *et al.* 2007. Olfactory identification and incidence of mild cognitive impairment in old age. *Arch. Gen. Psychiatry* 64: 802–08.

[5] Wilson, R.S., S.E. Arnold, J.A. Schneider, *et al.* 2007. The relationship between cerebral Alzheimer's disease pathology and odour identification in old age. *J. Neurol. Neurosurg. Psychiatry* 78: 30–35.

[6] Bennett, D.A., J.A. Schneider, A.S. Buchman, *et al.* 2005. The Rush Memory and Aging Project: study design and baseline characteristics of the study cohort. *Neuroepidemiol.* 25: 163–75.

[7] Graham, J.E., K. Rockwood, B.L. Beattie, *et al.* 1997. Prevalence and severity of cognitive impairment with and without dementia in an elderly population. *Lancet* 349: 1793–96.

[8] Wilson, R.S., L.L. Barnes & D.A. Bennett. 2003. Assessment of lifetime participation in cognitively stimulating activities. *J. Clin. Exp. Neuropsychol.* 25: 634–42.

[9] Wilson, R.S., L.L. Barnes, K.R. Krueger, *et al.* 2005. Early and late life cognitive activity and cognitive systems in old age. *J. Int. Neuropsychol. Soc.* 11: 400–07.

[10] Bennett, D.A., R.S. Wilson, J.A. Schneider, *et al.* 2002. Natural history of mild cognitive impairment in older persons. *Neurology* 59: 198–205.

[11] Wilson, R.S., S.E. Arnold, J.A. Schneider, *et al.* 2006. Chronic psychological distress and risk of Alzheimer's disease in old age. *Neuroepidemiology* 27: 143–53.

[12] McKhann, G., D. Drachmann, M. Folstein, *et al.* 1984. Clinical diagnosis of Alzheimer's disease. Report of the NINCDS-ADRDA Work Group under the

auspices of Department of Health and Human Services Task Force on Alzheimer's Disease. *Neurology* 34: 939–44.

[13] Bennett, D.A., J.A. Schneider, R.S. Wilson, *et al.* 2005. Mild cognitive impairment is related to Alzheimer's disease pathology and cerebral infarctions. *Neurology* 64: 834–41.

[14] Bennett, D.A., J.A. Schneider, Z. Arvanitakis, *et al.* 2006. Neuropathology of older persons without cognitive impairment. *Neurology* 66: 1837–44.

[15] Doty, R.L., P. Shaman & M. Dann. 1984. Development of the University of Pennsylvania Smell Identification Test: a standardized microencapsulated test of olfactory function. *Physiol. Behav.* 32: 489–502.

[16] Hixson, J. & D.T. Vernier. 1990. Restriction isotyping of human apolipoprotein E by gene amplification and cleavage with Hhal. *J. Lipid Res.* 31: 545–48.

[17] Wilson, R.S., J.A. Schneider, L.L. Barnes, *et al.* 2002. The apolipoprotein E ε4 allele and decline in different cognitive systems during a 6-year period. *Arch. Neurol.* 59: 1154–60.

[18] Wilson, R.S., J.L. Bienias, E. Berry-Kravis, *et al.* 2002. The apolipoprotein E ε2 allele and decline in episodic memory. *J. Neurol. Neurosurg. Psychiatry* 73: 672–77.

[19] Cox, D.R. 1972. Regression models and life tables (with discussion). *J. R. Soc. Stat. B.* 74: 187–220.

[20] Laird, N.M. & J.H. Ware. 1982. Random-effects models for longitudinal data. *Biometrics* 38: 963–74.

[21] Hall, C.B., R.B. Lipton, M. Sliwinski, *et al.* 2000. A change point model for estimating the onset of cognitive decline in preclinical Alzheimer's disease. *Stat. Med.* 19: 1555–66.

[22] Doty, R.L., P.F. Reyes & T. Gregor. 1987. Presence of both odor identification and detection deficits in Alzheimer's disease. *Brain Res. Bull.* 18: 597–600.

[23] Murphy, C., M.M. Gilmore, C.S. Seery, *et al.* 1990. Olfactory thresholds are associated with degree of dementia in Alzheimer's disease. *Neurobiol. Aging* 11: 465–69.

[24] Mesholam, R.I., P.J. Moberg, R.N. Mahr & R.L. Doty. 1998. Olfaction in neurodegenerative disease: a meta-analysis of olfactory functioning in Alzheimer's and Parkinson's diseases. *Arch. Neurol.* 55: 84–90.

[25] Larsson, M., H. Semb, B. Winblad, *et al.* 1999. Odor identification in normal aging and early Alzheimer's disease: effects of retrieval support. *Neuropsychology* 13: 47–53.

[26] Serby, M., P. Larson & D. Kalkstein. 1991. The nature and course of olfactory deficits in Alzheimer's disease. *Am. J. Psychiatry* 148: 357–60.

[27] Royet, J.P., B. Croisile, R. Williamson-Vasta, *et al.* 2001. Rating of different olfactory judgments in Alzheimer's disease. *Chem. Senses* 26: 409–17.

[28] Wang, Q.S., L. Tian, Y.L. Huang, *et al.* 2002. Olfactory identification and apolipoprotein E epsolon 4 allele in mild cognitive impairment. *Brain Res.* 951: 77–81.

[29] Peters, J.M., T. Hummel, T. Kratzsch, *et al.* 2003. Olfactory function in mild cognitive impairment and Alzheimer's disease: an investigation using psychophysical and electrophysiological techniques. *Am. J. Psychiatry* 160: 1995–2002.

[30] Eibenstein, A., A.B. Fioretti, M.N. Simaskau, *et al.* 2005. Olfactory screening test in mild cognitive impairment. *Neurol. Sci.* 26: 156–60.

[31] Djordjevic, J., M. Jones-Gotman, K. De Sousa & H. Chertkow. 2008. Olfaction in patients with mild cognitive impairment and Alzheimer's disease. *Neurobiol. Aging* 29: 693–706.

[32] Gilbert, P.E. & C. Murphy. 2004. The effect of the ApoE epsilon4 allele on recognition memory for olfactory and visual stimuli in patients with pathologically confirmed Alzheimer's disease, probable Alzheimer's disease, and healthy elderly controls. *J. Clin. Exp. Neuropsychol.* 26: 779–94.

[33] Murphy, C., A.W. Bacon, M.W. Bondi & D.P. Salmon. 1998. Apolipoprotein E status is associated with odor identification deficits in nondemented older persons. *Ann. N. Y. Acad. Sci.* 855: 744–50.

[34] Saleron-Kennedy, R., S. Cusack & K.D. Cashman. 2005. Olfactory function in people with genetic risk of dementia. *Ir. J. Med. Sci.* 174: 46–50.

[35] Van Hoesen, G.W., B.T. Hyman & A.R. Damasio. 1991. Entorhinal cortex pathology in Alzheimer's disease. *Hippocampus* 1: 1–8.

[36] Hyman, B.T., G.W. Van Hoeson, C. Kromer & A. Damasio. 1984. Alzheimer's disease: cell specific pathology isolates the hippocampal formation. *Science* 225: 1168–70.

[37] Price, J.L., P.B. Davies, J.C. Morris & D.L. White. 1991. The distribution of tangles, plaques and related histochemical markers in healthy aging and Alzheimer's disease. *Neurobiol. Aging* 12: 295–312.

[38] Li, K.Z.H. & U. Lindenberger. 2002. Relations between aging sensory/sensorimotor and cognitive functions. *Neurosci. Biobehav. Rev.* 26: 777–83.

[39] Cushman, L.A., K. Stein & C.J. Duffy. 2008. Detecting navigational deficits in cognitive aging and Alzheimer's disease using virtual reality. *Neurology* 71: 888–95.

DISCUSSION QUESTIONS

1. This study formed the basis for Jamie Knight's proposal (pp. 391–402) and Knight and Piccinin's poster. How does reading Wilson et al. enhance your understanding of Knight's proposal?

2. Do you find one of the three pieces (Knight's proposal, Knight and Piccinin's poster, or Wilson et al.'s article) easier to understand? What helps you to understand it?

3. After reading Knight's proposal, you were asked to consider some of the ethical issues of diagnosing AD in patients early (before obvious symptoms begin). These same ethical questions apply here. Consider ways to guarantee that those diagnosed while presymptomatic would not be discriminated against.

4. Wilson et al. note that "Alzheimer's disease (AD) is a leading cause of disability in old age, and the public health challenges posed by the disease are likely to increase in the coming decades with the aging of the U.S. population" (p. 410). Consider the big-picture implications of this statement. That is, what are the stakes of this type of research?

5. Discuss the process that leads from Wilson et al. to Knight and Piccinin. What have these three pieces shown you about how knowledge is constructed in the research genres?

HUMAN AND POSTHUMAN

INTRODUCTION

Chances are that when you hear the word 'posthuman' your mind turns to science fiction. You may think of artificial intelligences, such as Ava in Alex Garland's film *Ex Machina*, or your thoughts might run to cyborgs—organic-mechanical hybrids like Robocop. You may also find that the posthuman suggests a looming threat (the grim dystopia of *Blade Runner 2049*) or, paradoxically, the promise of transcendence (think of the fate of Samantha, the operating system in Spike Jonze's *Her*). The posthuman looms large in popular culture, and it should come as no surprise that it attracts serious academic attention as well.

A little over forty years ago, in an article titled "Prometheus as Performer," the American literary theorist Ihab Hassan wrote, "five hundred years of humanism may be coming to an end, as humanism transforms itself into something we must helplessly call posthumanism."[1] By the late 1990s, Hassan's remark frequently served as a springboard for sociologists, historians, philosophers, and literary critics contemplating what they saw as a widespread change in how humanity and its position in the universe are understood. If Hassan was right, these scholars asked, what were the causes of this shift, and how should the term 'posthuman' be defined? Did posthumanism mark a break—even a complete rupture—with humanism, that broad set of beliefs that is usually traced to a Renaissance project of replacing a God-centred worldview with a human-centred one? Or did it mark a transformation of humanism into something new but still bearing the marks of a humanist past? Was the posthuman a bright future to be embraced, or a kind of spectre to be dreaded? And what of that word "helplessly": had humanity fallen under the grip of forces it had no control over?

Scholars have approached the question of the posthuman from various directions. Viewed one way, the posthuman represents a reexamination of humanist assumptions, including the nature of the self and the question of what it means to be human. Viewed another way, the posthuman is preoccupied with the implications of advances in medical technology. For some, recent medical advances—genetic testing, novel transplant technologies, increasingly sophisticated bio-mechanical prostheses, new classes of brain-altering drugs—hold out the promise of transcending biological limitations, improving the quality of life and extending it indefinitely. For others (discussed in this section in Bostrom's essay), that same technology threatens to distort human nature. Viewed from yet another perspective, the posthuman represents a challenge to the principle of "human exceptionalism," the idea that humans occupy a centrally important position in the order of things. Advances in computing have raised the possibility that humans will soon have to share the planet with—and accommodate the interests of—artificial intelligences. Meanwhile, studies of animal cognition serve as a reminder that the human mind represents only one possibility among many.

Like many interesting ideas, then, you might think of the posthuman as a concept under construction. We end this Reader with a series of four articles that explore this concept by examining the relation between the human and the posthuman. One article (Warwick's account of cyborgs) never uses the term posthuman, but his account of real-world cyborgs demonstrates that a posthuman era is already upon us. Gane devotes his entire article to identifying various understandings of the term, an endeavour also undertaken by Bostrom and Graham. Despite their different disciplinary perspectives—cybernetics, philosophy, and theology—these articles all share a concern with the ethics of the posthuman: whatever shape the posthuman takes, it seems bound to challenge the ethical standards that have underpinned western society at least since the Renaissance.

As you read these articles, think of the ways the posthuman challenges your own assumptions about what it means to be human, about humanity's place in the world, about even the existence of something we call 'human nature.' Do your own beliefs about medical technology align you with what Bostrom calls the 'bioconservatives' or with the 'transhumanists'? How do these beliefs compare with, say, those of your grandparents (who, if they've had pacemakers implanted or surgery to correct cataracts, are already arguably cyborgs)? Does the prospect of cybernetic body modifications of the kind Warwick discusses—for example implanting RFID chips—seem likely to enhance or reduce human freedom? And if your sense of the world is deeply informed by religious beliefs, does Graham alter your attitude towards the posthuman?

Note

1 Ihab Hassan, "Prometheus as Performer: Toward a Posthumanist Culture?" *The Georgia Review* 31.4 (1977): 830–50, p. 843.

A. "THE CYBORG REVOLUTION," KEVIN WARWICK

In this 2014 article published in Nanoethics, *Kevin Warwick* surveys a series of practical "experiments that have linked biology and technology together in a cybernetic fashion, ultimately combining biology and machines in a cyborg merger" (p. 424). While he does refer to fictional cyborgs, especially in film, Warwick's main emphasis is on actual, practical cyborgs created in experimental research situations as well as adopted for therapeutic purposes. While Warwick cites a large number of sources focused on cyborg research, including twelve of his own publications, he also draws on his own extensive personal experimentation with cyborgs. As you read this article, consider how his detailed explanations of cyborg research affect your understanding of cyborgs. To what extent does that research intersect with the fictional representations of cyborgs that we encounter in films and stories?*

Glossary term: subject position

Abstract

This paper looks at some of the different practical cyborgs that are realistically possible now. It firstly describes the technical basis for such cyborgs, then discusses the results from experiments in terms of their meaning, possible applications, and ethical implications. An attempt has been made to cover a wide variety of possibilities. Human implantation and the merger of biology and technology are important factors here. The article is not intended to be seen as the final word on these issues, but rather to give an initial overview. Most of the experiments described are drawn from the author's personal experience over the last 15 years.

Keywords: Cyborgs, Enhancement, Embodiment, Prosthetics, Therapy, Ethics

Introduction

For many people, the term 'cyborg' (meaning cybernetic organism—part biology, part technology) is associated solely with science fiction and, in particular, films such as *The Terminator, Blade Runner,* or *Minority Report.* In fact, a wide variety of

---

* Formerly a Professor of Cybernetics at the University of Reading, Kevin Warwick is currently the Deputy Vice Chancellor (Research) at Coventry University in the UK. An engineer and self-experimenter, Warwick's research focuses on implant technology, including brain stimulators designed to counter Parkinson's disease tremors.

practical cyborgs exist today in the real world, and these new entities raise ethical questions about where they might lead and the impacts they might have on society at large.[21] However, each specific cyborg has a different emphasis, depending on the types of technology and connection it involves. In the case of bio-machine hybrids, in particular, the ethical questions that arise depend very much on the kind of hybrid investigated. Each methodology, therefore, needs to be thought about in turn.

This paper looks at several different experiments that have linked biology and technology together in a cybernetic fashion, ultimately combining biology and machines in a cyborg merger. What is crucial to this is that it is the overall final system that is important. Where a brain is involved, which surely it is, it must be seen not as a stand-alone entity, but as a fully embedded, integral component of the overall system—that adapts to the system's needs.[2] The overall combined cybernetic creature is the system of importance, although the brain's role as a controlling interest is arguably the most significant aspect.

The paper is arranged so that experiments are described in turn in individual sections. While there are distinct overlaps between the sections, they all throw up unique considerations. Following a description of each investigation, pertinent aspects of the topic are discussed. Points have been raised with a view to near-term-future technical advances and what these might mean in a practical scenario. No attempt is made here to present a conclusive account of the field; rather, the aim has been to highlight the range of research that is being carried out, see what is actually involved in the work that is being done, and look at some of its implications. In each case, the technical description is followed by a brief discussion of some of its philosophical spin-offs and societal impacts.

Many of the experiments described here in fact represent personal experiences made by the author and his colleagues and co-workers over the last 15 years. Others who have worked with the author on the experimentation described include neurosurgeons, medical doctors, pharmacists, engineers, computer scientists, and philosophers. Essentially, each of the experiments is described with a relatively brief overview, which builds on other publications that are cited in the list of references and may be consulted for more in-depth information. As a result, what can be gleaned from this article is an individual perspective based on practical experience and experimental results.

Biological Brains in a Robot Body

Neurons cultured/grown under laboratory conditions on an array of non-invasive electrodes provide an attractive alternative to computer or human control with which to construct a robot controller. An experimental control platform, essentially a robot body, can move around within a defined area purely under the control of such a network/brain, and the effects of the brain, controlling the body, can be observed.[29] Of course, this is interesting from a robotics perspective, but it also opens up a different approach to the study of the development of the brain itself because of its sensory motor embodiment. This method allows investigations to be carried out into memory formation and reward/punishment scenarios—the elements that underpin the basic functioning of a brain. It also makes intriguing contributions to the debate about cyborgs.[23]

In most cases, the growth of networks of brain cells (typically around 100,000 at present) in vitro firstly involves separating neurons obtained from foetal rodent cortical tissue. They are then grown (cultured) in a specialised chamber, where they can be provided with suitable environmental conditions (e.g., kept at an appropriate temperature), and fed with a mixture of minerals and nutrients. An array of electrodes embedded in the base of the chamber (a multi-electrode array, MEA) acts as a bidirectional electrical interface to/from the culture. This allows electrical signals to be delivered in order to stimulate the culture and also recordings to be made of the outputs from the culture.[25]

The neurons in such cultures spontaneously connect, communicate, and develop, giving useful responses within a few weeks and typically continuing to do so for, at present, 3 months. The brain is grown in a glass specimen chamber lined with a flat '8 × 8' multi-electrode array, which can be used for real-time recordings (see Fig. 1). This makes it possible to distinguish the firings of small groups of neurons by monitoring the output signals on the electrodes. A picture of the entire network's global activity can be formed in this way. It is also possible to electrically stimulate the culture via any of the electrodes to induce neural activity. In consequence, the multi-electrode array forms a bidirectional interface with the cultured neurons.[1,4]

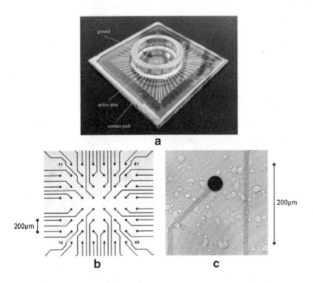

Fig. 1 a A multi-electrode array (MEA) showing the electrodes. b Electrodes in the centre of the MEA seen under an optical microscope. c An MEA at ×40 magnification, showing neuronal cells in close proximity to an electrode.

The brain can then be coupled to its physical robot body.[29] Sensory data fed back from the robot are subsequently delivered to the culture, thereby closing the robot-culture loop. In consequence, the processing of signals can be broken down into two discrete sections, (a) 'culture to robot,' in which live neuronal activity is used as the decision-making mechanism for robot control, and (b) 'robot to culture,' which involves an input mapping process from the robot sensor to stimulate the culture.[24,25]

The actual number of neurons in a brain depends on natural density variations that arise when the culture is seeded in the first place. The electrochemical activity of the culture is sampled, and this is used as input to the robot's wheels. Meanwhile, the robot's (ultrasonic) sensor readings are converted into stimulation signals received as input by the culture, thereby closing the loop.[24,25]

Once the brain has grown on the array for several days, during which time it forms some elementary neural connections, an existing neuronal pathway through the culture is identified by searching for strong relationships between pairs of electrodes. These pairs are defined as those electrode combinations in which neurons close to one electrode respond to stimulation from the other electrode at which the stimulus was applied more than 60% of the time and respond no more than 20% of the time to stimulation on any other electrode.[24,25]

A rough input–output response map of the culture can then be created by cycling through the electrodes in turn. In this way, a suitable input/output electrode pair can be chosen in order to provide an initial decision-making pathway for the robot. This is then employed to control the robot body, for example, if the ultrasonic sensor is active, and we wish the response to cause the robot to turn away from an object that is located ultrasonically (possibly a wall) in order to keep moving.[24]

For experimental purposes, the intention is for the robot to follow a forward path until it reaches a wall, at which point the front sonar value decreases below a certain threshold, triggering a stimulating pulse. If the responding/output electrode registers activity, the robot turns to avoid the wall. In experiments, the robot turns spontaneously whenever activity is registered on the response electrode. The most relevant result is the occurrence of the chain of events: wall detection–stimulation–response. From a neurological perspective, of course, it is also interesting to speculate why there is activity on the response electrode when no stimulating pulse has been applied.[25]

As an overall control element for direction and wall avoidance, the cultured brain acts as the sole decision-making entity within the feedback loop. Clearly, the neural pathway changes that take place over time in the culture between the stimulating and recording electrodes are then an important aspect of the system. From a research point of view, investigations of learning and memory are generally at an early stage. However, the robot can be clearly seen to improve its performance over time in terms of its wall-avoidance ability in the sense that neuronal pathways that bring about a satisfactory action tend to strengthen purely though the process of habitually performing these activities—an example of learning due to habit.[10]

However, the number of variables involved is considerable, and the plasticity process, which occurs over quite a period of time, is (most probably) dependent on such factors as initial seeding and growth near electrodes as well as environmental transients such as temperature and humidity. Learning by reinforcement—rewarding good actions and punishing bad—is currently a major issue for research in this field.[25]

"On many occasions the culture responds as expected, on other occasions it does not, and in some cases it provides a motor signal when it is not expected to do so."[22] But does it 'intentionally' make a different decision to the one we would have expected? We cannot tell, but merely guess. When it comes to robotics, it has been shown by this research that a robot can successfully have a biological brain with which to make its 'decisions.' The size of such a brain, 100,000–150,000 neurons, is dictated purely by the current limitations on the experimentation described. Three-dimensional structures are already being investigated and will permit the creation of cultures of approximately 30 million neurons.[25]

The potential of such systems, including the range of tasks they can deal with, means that the physical body can take on different forms. There is no reason, for example, why the body could not be a two-legged, walking robot, with a rotating head and the ability to walk around in a building. It is realistic to assume that such cultures will become larger, potentially growing to sizes of billions of neurons. On top of this, the nature of the neurons may be diversified. At present, rat neurons are generally employed in studies. However, human neurons are also being cultured now, thus raising the possibility of a robot with a human neuron brain. If this brain then consists of billions of neurons, many social and ethical questions will need to be asked,[20,30] especially regarding the rights of such creatures.

One interesting question is whether or not such a brain is, or could be, conscious. Some (e.g., [18]) have concluded that consciousness is an emergent property; essentially, it is sufficient to put enough human neurons together with a high degree of connectivity, and consciousness will emerge. In light of this argument, there is therefore no immediate reason why robots with biological brains composed of sufficient numbers of human neurons should not be conscious. The possibility of building a robot with a technological body and a brain that consists of a large number of highly connected human neurons is not far off. Should this be perfectly acceptable or should it be regulated? If a robot of this kind decided to commit a crime, then who would be responsible for the consequences, the robot itself?

The BrainGate

When we specifically consider the case of cyborgs, it is clear that most practical experimentation involves human subjects, often self-experimenters of one type or another, being linked closely with some form of technology. Although many human brain–computer interfaces are used for therapeutic purposes in order to overcome a medical/neurological problem, one example being deep brain stimulation electrodes employed to overcome the effects of Parkinson's disease,[16,31] the possibility of enhancement is an enticing prospect for cyborgs.

However, the therapy/enhancement question is not a simple one. In some cases, those who have suffered an amputation or received a spinal injury in an accident are able to regain control of devices via their (still functioning) neural signals.[5] Meanwhile, stroke patients can be given limited control of their surroundings, as indeed can people with conditions such as motor neurone disease.[23,25]

The situation is not straightforward in these cases, as each individual is given abilities that no normal human possesses, for example, the ability to move a cursor around on a computer screen using neural signals alone.[12] The same quandary is encountered when it comes to blind individuals who benefit from some extra-sensory input, for instance from a sonar system based on the same principle as bat echolocation: it does not repair their blindness, but allows them to rely on an alternative sense.[25]

Some interesting human research has been carried out using the microelectrode array known as the Utah Array, or more popularly the BrainGate. The individual electrodes are 1.5 mm long and taper to a tip diameter of less than 90 microns. Although a number of trials have been carried out that did not use humans as test subjects, human tests are limited to two groups of studies at the moment. In the second of these, the array has been employed in a purely recording role.

Essentially, electrical activity from a few neurons monitored by the array electrodes was decoded into a signal that directed cursor movements. This enabled an individual to position a cursor on a computer screen using neural signals for control in combination with visual feedback. The same technique was later deployed to allow the individual recipient, who was paralysed, to operate a robot arm.[11] Nevertheless, the first use of the microelectrode array (shown in Fig. 2) has considerably broader implications for attempts to extend the human recipient's capabilities.

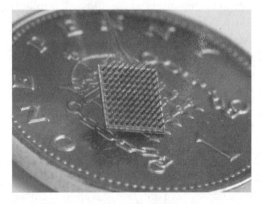

Fig. 2 A 100-electrode, 4×4 mm microelectrode array, shown on a UK one-pence piece for scale.

Deriving a reliable command signal from a collection of monitored neural signals is not necessarily a simple task, partly due to the complexity of the signals recorded and partly due to the real-time constraints on the handling of the data. In some cases, however, it can be relatively easy to look for and obtain a system response to certain anticipated neural signals, especially when an individual has trained extensively with the system. In fact, the neural signal's shape, magnitude, and waveform over time are considerably different to other apparent signals, such as noise, and this makes the problem a little easier to resolve.[25]

The interface through which a user interacts with technology provides a layer of separation between what the user wants the machine to do and what the machine actually does. This separation imposes a cognitive load on the individual concerned that is proportional to the difficulties experienced. The main problem is interfacing the human motor and sensory channels with the technology in a reliable, durable, effective, bidirectional design. One solution is to avoid this sensorimotor bottleneck altogether by interfacing directly with the human nervous system.[23]

An individual human connected in this way can potentially benefit from some of the advantages of machine/artificial intelligence, such as rapid and highly accurate mathematical abilities of great use in 'number crunching,' a high-speed, almost infinite, Internet knowledge base, and accurate long-term memory. In addition, it is widely acknowledged that humans have only five senses that we know of, whereas machines offer modes of perception that exploit infrared, ultraviolet, and ultrasonic signals, to name but a few.[25]

Humans are also limited in that they can only visualise and understand the world around them in three dimensions, whereas computers are quite capable of dealing with hundreds of dimensions. Perhaps most importantly, human means of communication, essentially transferring a complex electrochemical signal from one brain to another via an intermediate, often mechanical, slow and error-prone medium (e.g., speech), are extremely poor, particularly lacking in speed, power and precision. It is evident that, over the long term, using an implant to connect a human brain to a computer network could open up the distinct advantages of machine intelligence, communication, and sensing abilities to the implanted individual.[24]

As a step towards a broader concept of brain–computer interaction, a microelectrode array (like the one shown in Fig. 2) was implanted into the median nerve fibres of a healthy human individual (the author) in the course of 2 hours of neurosurgery in order to test bidirectional functionality in a series of experiments. Stimulation current applied directly into the nervous system allowed information to be sent to the user, while control signals were decoded from neural activity in the region of the electrodes.[27] A number of trials were undertaken successfully using this setup.[28]

In particular,[24,25]

1. Extra-sensory (ultrasonic) input was successfully implemented.
2. Extended control of a robotic hand across the Internet was achieved, with feedback from the robotic fingertips being sent back as neural stimulation to give a sense of force being applied to an object (this was achieved between Columbia University, New York, USA, and Reading University, England).
3. A primitive form of telegraphic communication directly between the nervous systems of two humans (the author's wife assisted) was performed.[28]
4. A wheelchair was successfully driven around by means of neural signals.
5. The colour of jewelry was changed as a result of neural signals—also the behaviour of a collection of small robots.

In most, if not all, of the above cases, the trial could be described as useful for purely therapeutic reasons, e.g., the ultrasonic sensory input might be of use to an individual who is blind, while telegraphic communication might be beneficial to people with certain forms of motor neurone disease. Each trial can, however, also be seen as a potential form of enhancement beyond the human norm for an individual. Indeed, the author did not need to have the implant for medical reasons in order to overcome a problem; rather, the experimentation was carried out purely for the purposes of scientific exploration. It is therefore necessary to consider how far things should be taken.

Clearly, enhancement with the aid of brain–computer interfaces introduces all sorts of new technological and intellectual opportunities, but it also throws up a raft of different ethical concerns that need to be addressed directly.[19] While the vast majority of people are perfectly happy for interfaces of this kind to be used in therapy, it can be argued the picture is not as clear when it comes to enhancement. But what about individual freedom? If someone wants to stick a pin in their nose or finger, that is a matter for them. Should the situation be any different if they want to stick 100 pins in their brain, even if it endows them with additional abilities?

Therapy

It is an open question whether or not a bio-technology link that is created purely for therapeutic reasons constitutes a cyborg. I do not intend to embark upon such a wide-ranging discussion here. It is merely worthwhile mentioning one particular example, primarily because of the future opportunities that it opens up. An alternative treatment for Parkinson's disease using deep brain stimulation (DBS) started to be feasible when the relevant electrode technology became available from the late 1980s onwards. Since then, many neurosurgeons have started implanting neurostimulators connected to deep brain electrodes positioned in the thalamus, sub-thalamus, or globus pallidus of the brain to treat tremors, dystonia, and pain.

A deep brain stimulation device contains an electrode lead with four or six cylindrical electrodes at equally spaced depths attached to an implanted pulse generator (IPG), which is surgically positioned below the collar bone. DBS has many advantages, such as the fact that it is reversible. It is also potentially much less dangerous than lesioning, and is highly successful in many cases.[24]

Ongoing research is aimed at developing an 'intelligent' stimulator.[31] The idea of the stimulator is to produce warning signals before the tremors begin so that the stimulator only needs to generate signals occasionally rather than continuously, thus operating in a similar fashion to a heart pacemaker. Artificial intelligence (AI) tools based on artificial neural networks have been shown to successfully predict the onset of tremors.[23] In either case, data input into a network is provided by the measured electrical local field potentials obtained by means of the deep brain electrodes. The network is trained to recognise the nature of electrical activity deep in the human brain and to predict (several seconds ahead) the subsequent outcome, i.e., the onset of tremors. In consequence, the DBS device becomes 'intelligent' when the stimulation is triggered solely by the AI system.

While deep brain implants like those described are aimed primarily at providing current stimulation for therapeutic purposes, they can also have a broader portfolio of effects within the human brain. In the case of 'intelligent' stimulators, a computer (artificial brain) is used to understand the workings of specific aspects of the human brain. The job of the artificial brain, as can be seen from the description of the experimentation, is to monitor the normal functioning of the human brain so that the artificial brain can accurately predict a spurious event, such as a Parkinson tremor, several seconds before it actually occurs. In other words, the artificial brain's job is to outthink the human brain and stop it from doing what it 'normally' wants to do.[23]

One practical issue at the present time is that the deep brain electrodes can be connected bidirectionally with a computer. Furthermore, it is quite possible for the computer to be located remotely. Hence, signals within the brain can be tracked in real time and fed into a computer. The computer is able to analyse these signals and generate alternative signals that are fed directly back into the brain in order to ensure the person in question continues to function.

Another good example in this section on therapy is the work of Todd Kuiken.[13] The first beneficiary of his technique was Jesse Sullivan, hailed in the media as the world's first 'Bionic Man,' who lost both of his arms as a result of an accident he sustained during his work as a high-power electrical lineman. At the Rehabilitation Institute of Chicago, his arms were replaced with robotic prosthetics that he was able to control merely by thinking about using his original arms in the normal way.

The method involved taking nerves that originally ran to Sullivan's arm and reconnecting them to muscles in his chest. When he thought about lifting an arm, for example, muscles in his chest contracted instead of muscles in the original arm. Electrodes connected externally between the chest muscles and the robotic arm caused the prosthetic replacement to interpret such contractions as instructions to move in a particular way.

Evidently, the technology described in this section has enormous potential for application in a broad spectrum of different fields. Restricting this technology to therapeutic purposes would also limit the need for philosophical argument. At the same time, extending the scope for its application would open up numerous possibilities. In itself, employing such methods to make individuals happy (by overcoming depression) draws attention to the possibility of recreational uses. Perhaps the most significant option would potentially be their use to overcome negative character traits, and not merely bad habits, a scenario fictionalised in The Terminal Man.[3] If signals could then be transmitted remotely from a brain to a computer and back again, who would be responsible for that person's actions, particularly if they were to commit a crime?

Body Modification

The final category to be considered is something of a catch-all for the discussion of various other procedures that have not been covered above. The first idea to be considered is the use of implant technology, the implantation of a radio frequency identification device (RFID) as a token of identity, for example. In its simplest form, such a device transmits by radio a sequence of pulses that represents a unique number. The number can be pre-programmed to function rather like a PIN number on a credit card. If someone has had an implant of this type inserted and activated, the code can be checked by computer and the identity of the carrier determined.

Such implants have been used as a sort of fashion item, to gain access to night clubs in Barcelona and Rotterdam (The Baja Beach Club), as a high security device for the Mexican Government or as a source of medical information (having been approved in 2004 by the US Food and Drug Administration, which regulates medical devices in the USA; see [7,6]). In the latter case, information about the medication an individual requires for conditions such as diabetes can be stored on the implant. Because it is implanted, the details cannot be forgotten, the record cannot be lost, and it will not easily be stolen.

An RFID implant does not have its own battery. It incorporates a tiny antenna and a microchip enclosed in a silicon or glass capsule. The antenna picks up power remotely when it passes close to a larger coil of wire that carries an electric current. The power picked up by the antenna in the implant is employed to transmit the particular signal encoded on the microchip by radio. Because there is no battery and it does not contain any moving parts, the implant requires no maintenance whatsoever; once it has been implanted, it can be left in place.[24]

A RFID implant of this kind was put in place in a human for the first time on 24 August 1998 at Reading, England. It measured 22 mm long with a 4-mm diameter cylinder. The body (arm) selected was that of the author of this paper. The doctor who carried out the procedure (George Boulos) burrowed a hole in the upper left arm, pushed the implant into the hole and closed the incision with a couple of stitches.

The main reason for selecting the upper left arm for the implant was that we were not sure how well it would work. We reasoned that, if the implant was not working, it could be waved around until a stronger signal was transmitted. It is interesting that most present day RFID implants in humans are located in a roughly similar place (the left arm or hand), even though they do not have to be. Even in the James Bond film *Casino Royale* (the 2006 remake), Bond himself has an implant in his left arm.[24]

The RFID implant allowed the author to control lights, open doors and be welcomed with a 'Hello' whenever he entered the front door of Reading University.[26] An implant of this kind could be used in humans for a variety of identification purposes, e.g., as a credit card, a car key, or (as is already the case with some other animals) a passport or at least a passport supplement.

The use of implant technology to monitor people opens up a considerable range of issues. It is now realistic to talk of tracking individuals by means of implants or, alternatively, for more widespread application and coverage, the Global Positioning System, a wide area network or even a mobile telephone network. From an ethical point of view, though, it raises considerable questions when it is children, the elderly (e.g., those with dementia), or prisoners who are subjected to tracking, even though this might be deemed to be beneficial for some people.[26]

The use of implants to track people is still at the research stage. As such devices come onto the market, there will be numerous (special) cases with distinct drivers. For example, there would have to be a potential gain for a person to be tracked and their position monitored in this way, especially if it could be deemed to either save or considerably enhance their life—as possibly in the case of an individual with dementia.[23]

Another intriguing piece of cyborg technology is described in the work of Neil Harbisson. This was originally referred to as the 'Eyeborg' project. The technology developed involved a head-mounted sensor that translates colour frequencies into sound frequencies.[17] Initially, Harbisson memorised the frequencies related to each colour, but subsequently he decided to permanently attach the eyeborg to his head, effectively a small camera facing forward from over his forehead and connected to the back of his skull by a metal bar. Eventually, the eyeborg was developed further so that Harbisson was able to perceive colour saturation as well as colour hues. Software was then developed that enabled Harbisson to perceive up to 360 different hues through microtones and saturation through different volume levels.[9]

Coincidentally, another project referred to as the 'Eyeborg' project has been carried out by documentary-maker Rob Spence, who replaced one of his eyes with an eyeball-shaped video camera. The prosthetic eye contains a wireless transmitter that sends real-time colour video to a remote display. Spence lost his original right eye when playing with a gun on his grandfather's farm at the age of 13. He therefore decided to build a miniature camera that could be fitted inside his false eye. Spence refers to himself as 'the Eyeborg guy.'

The video camera runs on a 3-V battery. It should be emphasised that the camera is not connected to his optic nerve and has not restored his vision in any way. Instead, it is used to record what is in his line of sight remotely on a computer. The current model is low resolution, and the transmitter is weak, meaning that a receiving antenna has to be held against his cheek to get a good signal. A better-performance, higher-resolution model, complete with a stronger transmitter and an improved receiver, is apparently under development.

In 2009, a computer programmer called Jerry Jalava lost part of the fourth finger on his left hand in a motorcycle accident. Rather than merely leave a gap or replace it with a cosmetic finger copy, the part-finger was replaced with a 2-GB USB stick. It is felt this is worth mentioning in view of the examples discussed below.

One final area to be considered is that of subdermal magnetic implants.[8] This involves the controlled stimulation of mechanoreceptors by an implanted magnet manipulated through an external electromagnetic coil. Clearly, issues such as magnetic field strength sensitivity and frequency sensitivity are important. Implantation is an invasive procedure, which makes implant durability an important requirement. Only permanent magnets retain their magnetic strength over a very long period of time and are robust enough to survive a range of testing conditions. This restricts the type of magnet that can be considered for implantation to permanent magnets. Hard ferrite, neodymium and alnico magnets are easily available, inexpensive and suitable for this purpose.

The magnetic strength of the implant magnet contributes to the amount of agitation the implant magnet undergoes in response to an external magnetic field and also determines the strength of the field that is present around the implant location. The skin on the human hand contains a large number of low threshold mechanoreceptors that allow humans to experience in great detail the shape, size and texture of objects in the physical world through touch. The highest density of mechanoreceptors is found in the fingertips, especially those of the index and middle fingers. They are responsive to relatively high frequencies and are most sensitive to frequencies in the 200–300-Hz range.

The pads of the middle and ring fingers were the preferred sites for magnet implantation in the experiments that have been reported.[8] A simple interface containing a coil mounted on a wire frame and wrapped around each finger was designed for the generation of the magnetic fields that would stimulate movement in the magnet within the finger. The general idea was that the output from an external sensor would be used to control the current in the wrapped coil. As the signals detected by the external sensor changed, they were reflected in the amount of vibration experienced through the implanted magnet.[24]

Experiments have already been carried out in a number of areas of application.[8] The first was ultrasonic range information. This scenario connected the magnetic interface to an ultrasonic ranger for navigation assistance. Distance information from the ranger was encoded via the ultrasonic sensor as variations in the frequency of current pulses, which in turn were passed on to the electromagnetic interface. It was found that this mechanism constituted a practical means of supplying reasonably accurate information about the individual's surroundings, thus providing navigational assistance. The distances were understood intuitively after a few minutes of use, and their perception was enhanced by distance 'calibration' through touch and sight.[24]

A further application involved reading Morse signals. This application scenario used the magnetic interface to communicate text messages to humans using an appropriate encoding mechanism. Morse code was chosen to encode the messages on account of its comparative simplicity and for ease of implementation. It was possible for text input to be encoded as Morse code and the dots and dashes transmitted to the interface. The dots and dashes were represented by variations in either frequency or magnetic field strength.

From an ethical perspective, the implants considered in this section are perhaps easier to evaluate, possibly because they are more open to social assimilation. Yet, interestingly, apart from Neil Harbisson's colour Eyeborg, they are generally not intended for therapeutic purposes, but to enhance the carrier's capacities in some way. At this stage, however, they do not appear to openly threaten the fabric of society and merely modify the human body in ways that are, some may feel, not too different from someone wearing jewellery. Furthermore, it is difficult to imagine further extensions along the same lines bringing about major cultural or scientific shifts or modifying our thinking or behaviour.

Conclusions

This paper has looked at several different kinds of cyborg. Experimental cases have been discussed in order to indicate how humans can merge with technology in this way, thereby throwing up a plethora of social and ethical questions. In each case, the practical experimentation that actually took place has been described, rather than a merely theoretical concept. It is worth acknowledging here that there are numerous other types of interface. For instance, use can be made of non-invasive EEG electrodes. It was felt that these examples would not add sufficient variety to the ensuing discussion, and they were consequently not covered here for reasons of space.

In particular, if robots are to have biological brains, this could ultimately mean some form of human brain operating in a robot body. Would it be deemed cruelty to robots if a brain of this type were to be 'switched off'? More importantly at the present time, it is necessary to ask whether such research should be permitted to forge ahead regardless. Before too long, we may well have robots with brains made up of human neurons that possess the same sorts of capabilities as the human brain.[24]

The BrainGate implant offered an opportunity to consider the potential for human enhancement. Extra-sensory input has already been achieved scientifically, extending the nervous system over the Internet and creating a basic form of thought communication. It is likely that many humans will wish to upgrade and become part-machine themselves. This may mean that ordinary (non-implanted) humans will be left behind as a result.

Ethical issues relating to the particular experiments discussed have been explored superficially in each case. However, one feature common to all these projects is that they fuzzify the difference between what is regarded as an individual human and what is regarded as a machine.

Personal Comments

Apart from therapeutic applications, the current concept of cyborg technology and experimentation does not fit snugly into an established research profile. In consequence, funding bodies are not easily persuaded to provide support for such experiments. Nonetheless, as research done by the author on the creation of a robot with a biological brain was supported with £0.5 million of funding over a 3-year period by the UK Engineering and Physical Sciences Research Council, such support is not completely out of the question. Irrespective of this, the experiments undertaken by Graafstra, Harbisson, Spence, Jalava, and others have certainly not been conducted within the scientific mainstream. However, this has often been the case with novel scientific research in the past.

Quite a few people have now tried an implant of one type or another, especially RFID and magnetic implants. For the most part, this has been done outside the medical–scientific system and often with artistic intentions. One problem with this is the difficulty it causes for those who wish to gather accurate information about the results obtained from these individuals' activities. Such information often has to be gleaned and translated from web pages rather than being extracted from the traditional academic journals in which authors have to comply with conventions for the presentation of data.

On the whole, many aesthetic and artistic approaches to techno-body modification in this vein are refreshing from a scientific perspective as well and can sometimes arrive at interesting results and give ideas to those with scientific training. When these activities approach what seems a form of self-mutilation, however, it may be felt things have been taken a little further than is necessary in order to fulfil the originator's artistic ambitions. There is an exciting range of technology available to us today, technology that was simply inconceivable in the past, and this opens up possibilities for experimentation. However, experiments need to be conducted in an appropriate, ethical fashion if they are to be welcomed warmly by the scientific community.

As regards the non-mainstream cyborg experiments discussed in the section on body modification, these might loosely be categorised as experiments that[1] are artistic or aesthetic,[2] expand human perception, or[3] enhance or augment the human body. They touch on many different issues such as self-mutilation, scientific use-fulness, respectability, and personal freedom. Certainly, each has different ethical implications. For example, an experiment carried out purely by an individual is a very personal matter, whereas the reputation of the institution would also be at stake, along with any insurance commitments, if the same experiment were to be conducted within a company or university. Where a larger institution is concerned, it might also be felt that the organisation was somehow promoting the experiment as though it were a good thing.

Body modification experiments are certainly on the increase as the technology becomes more widely available and the perceived dangers are accordingly felt to be small. At the same time, there are increasing numbers of personnel with the skills to carry out implantation procedures. There is therefore no reason why such modifications could not become a widespread sociocultural phenomenon, as are tattooing and piercing today. They will, though, I feel, require solid justifications, such as practical or artistic objectives, if they are to be more than mere gimmicks.

There will definitely be those who comment negatively on such experimentation, perhaps saying that it adds nothing to technical or scientific progress, but it is merely frivolous and does little apart from feed good stories to the media. Despite this, it is necessary for decision-makers to realise that, firstly, there are many therapeutic pos-sibilities, secondly, the whole field of human enhancement needs to be investigated rigorously and scientifically, and thirdly, it could easily be more life-enhancing than any other technological change on the agenda today. It should also be remembered that if we have learned anything from history, it is that just about every new tech-nological change attracts a certain amount of criticism. The bigger the change, the greater the number of critics.

The cyborg experiments described in this paper could well be the first practical steps towards a coming merger of humans and machines in the techno-evolutionary sense of the ideas put forward by futurologists like Ray Kurzweil.[14] However, the actual implants used and technologies ultimately settled on may well change along the way. Again and again, history has shown this is to be very much the norm.

According to a recent survey in the USA,[15] 53% of Americans think it would be a change for the worse if most people wore implants or other devices that constantly showed them information about the world around them. Considering that the vast majority of people have very little concept of the implants that are available and what they can do, this is already a very low figure. As implants become more widespread, we can expect this figure to diminish. It will, in consequence, not take long for those who share such concerns to be in the minority.

In the near future, cyborgs based on existing technologies and technologies that are currently in the pipeline will probably be little different from humans. Apart, that is, from the odd extra sense or communication skill. However, as the technology and interfacing improve, will this mean the abilities possessed by cyborgs eventually change the rules and fabric of social life? The big question will be what happens to ordinary humans, those who are not part-machine. Will they still have a substantial role to play?

References

[1] Chiappalone M, Vato A, Berdondini L, Koudelka-Hep M, Martinoia S (2007) Network dynamics and synchronous activity in cultured cortical neurons. Int J Neural Syst 17:87–103.

[2] Clark A (2003) Natural-born cyborgs. Oxford UP, Oxford.

[3] Crichton M (1972) The terminal man. Knopf, New York.

[4] DeMarse T, Wagenaar D, Blau A, Potter S (2001) The neurally controlled animal: biological brains acting with simulated bodies. Auton Robot 11:305–10.

[5] Donoghue J, Nurmikko A, Friehs G, Black M (2004) Development of a neuromotor prosthesis for humans. Advan Clin Neuroph Supp Clin Neuroph 57:588–602.

[6] Foster K, Jaeger J (2007) RFID inside. IEEE Spectr 44:24–29.

[7] Graafstra A (2007) Hands on. IEEE Spectr 44:318–23.

[8] Hameed J, Harrison I, Gasson M, Warwick K (2010) A novel human-machine interface using subdermal implants. Proc. IEEE 9th International Conference on Cybernetic Intelligent Systems, 106–10, Reading.

[9] Harbisson N (2008) Painting by ear. Modern Painters, The International Contemporary Art Magazine, 70–73, New York, June 2008.

[10] Hebb D (1949) The organisation of behaviour. Wiley, New York.

[11] Hochberg L, Serruya M, Friehs G, Mukand J, Saleh M, Caplan A, Branner A, Chen D, Penn R, Donoghue J (2006) Neuronal ensemble control of prosthetic devices by a human with tetraplegia. Nature 442(164–71):2006.

[12] Kennedy P, Andreasen D, Ehirim P, King B, Kirby T, Mao H, Moore M (2004) Using human extra-cortical local field potentials to control a switch. J Neural Eng 1(2):72–77.

[13] Kuiken T, Li G, Lock B, Lipschutz R, Miller L, Stubblefield K, Englehart K (2009) Targeted muscle reinnervation for real-time myoelectric control of multifunction artificial arms. JAMA 301(6):619–28.

[14] Kurzweil R (2006) The singularity is near. G. Duckworth & Co. Ltd, London.

[15] Pew Research Center (2014) U.S. views of technology and the future, available at www.pewinternet.org/2014/04/17/us.

16 Pinter M, Murg M, Alesch F, Freundl B, Helscher R, Binder H (1999) Does deep brain stimulation of the nucleus ventralis intermedius affect postural control and locomotion in Parkinson's disease? Mov Disord 14(6):958–63.

17 Ronchi A (2009) Eculture: cultural content in the digital age. Springer, New York.

18 Searle J (1990) The mystery of consciousness. The New York Review of Books, New York.

19 Warwick K (2003) Cyborg morals, cyborg values, cyborg ethics. Ethics Inform Tech 5:131–37.

20 Warwick K (2010) Implications and consequences of robots with biological brains. Ethics Inform Tech 12(3):223–34.

21 Warwick K (2010) Future issues with robots and cyborgs. Stud Ethics Law Tech 4(3):1–18.

22 Warwick K (2013) Cyborgs in space. Acta Futura 6:25–35.

23 Warwick K (2013) The disappearing human-machine divide. Approach Religion 3(2):3–15.

24 Warwick K (2013) Cyborgs—the neuro-tech version. In: Katz E (ed.) Implantable bioelectronics—devices, materials and applications. Wiley–VCH, New York.

25 Warwick K (2013) The future of artificial intelligence and cybernetics. In: Al-Fodhan N (ed.) There's a future: visions for a better world. BBVA Open Mind, TF Editores, Madrid.

26 Warwick K, Gasson M (2006) A question of identity—wiring in the human, the IET wireless sensor networks conference, London, 4/1–4/6, 4 December, 2006.

27 Warwick K, Gasson M, Hutt B, Goodhew I, Kyberd P, Andrews B, Teddy P, Shad A (2003) The application of implant technology for cybernetic systems. Arch Neurol 60(10):1369–73.

28 Warwick K, Gasson M, Hutt B, Goodhew I, Kyberd P, Schulzrinne H, Wu X (2004) Thought communication and control: a first step using radiotelegraphy. IEE Proc Comm 151(3):185–89.

29 Warwick K, Nasuto S, Becerra V, Whalley B (2010) Experiments with an in-vitro robot brain. In: Cai Y (ed.) Instinctive computing, lecture notes in artificial intelligence, vol 5987. Springer, New York, 1–15.

30 Warwick K, Shah H, Vedder A, Stradella E, Salvini R (2013) How good robots will enhance human life. In: Tchon K, Gasparski W (ed.) A treatise on good robots. Transaction Publishers, New York, 3–18.

31 Wu D, Warwick K, Ma Z, Burgess J, Pan S, Aziz T (2010) Prediction of Parkinson's disease tremor onset using radial basis function neural networks. Expert Syst Appl 37(4):2923–28.

DISCUSSION QUESTIONS

1. Warwick's method is somewhat different from those of the other articles in this Reader. He notes, "what can be gleaned from this article is an individual perspective based on practical experience and experimental results" (p. 424). In your experience as a reader, in what ways is this article persuasive (or not)?

2. Near the end of the "Biological Brains in a Robot Body" section, Warwick considers the "the possibility of a robot with a human neuron brain," and thus the question of whether it might be conscious (p. 427). Why does he not consider the robot with a rat neuron brain as potentially conscious?

3. Warwick raises a number of social and ethical questions stemming from cyborg research. Isolate one or two of these questions in the article and discuss them. What are the most important social and ethical issues posed by cyborg research?

4. Choose one example introduced by Warwick. Discuss how it works technically and practically. Under what circumstances might you consent or even want to have this sort of technology integrated into your body (or at work in your immediate environment, depending on the example)?

5. Warwick focuses on fairly narrow types of cyborg, ones that are practically experimented with today involving electronic or similar implants or interfaces. Cyborgs can be defined more broadly. For instance, in her essay "Cyborg Manifesto" (summarized by Gane in his article "Posthuman" in this section), Donna Haraway argues that we are already cyborgs, and she focuses on broader human-technology interfaces. For instance, how do technologies such as forks or birth control modify the human body? Compare these types of interfaces with what Warwick discusses. Does this broader approach to cyborgs help address some of the questions that Warwick poses?

B. "IN DEFENCE OF POSTHUMAN DIGNITY," NICK BOSTROM

In this article, which appeared in the journal Bioethics *in 2005, the well-known Swedish philosopher Nick Bostrom* addresses aspects of a debate over the ethics of using technology to enhance the physical and intellectual qualities of humans. Siding with a group he calls transhumanists, who believe such technological enhancements are not only possible but ethical, Bostrom outlines and counters the arguments of bioconservatives, who are leery of such interventions, before making the case for what he calls "posthuman dignity" (p. 441). As you read the essay, note the care Bostrom takes to define his key terms—'transhumanism' and 'bioconservatism' as well as the more familiar term 'dignity'—as he constructs his argument for a particular vision of the posthuman.*

Keywords: ethics, philosophy

Abstract

Positions on the ethics of human enhancement technologies can be (crudely) characterized as ranging from transhumanism to bioconservatism. Transhumanists believe that human enhancement technologies should be made widely available, that individuals should have broad discretion over which of these technologies to apply to themselves, and that parents should normally have the right to choose enhancements for their children-to-be. Bioconservatives (whose ranks include such diverse writers as Leon Kass, Francis Fukuyama, George Annas, Wesley Smith, Jeremy Rifkin, and Bill McKibben) are generally opposed to the use of technology to modify human nature. A central idea in bioconservativism is that human enhancement technologies will undermine our human dignity. To forestall a slide down the slippery slope towards an ultimately debased 'posthuman' state, bioconservatives often argue for broad bans on otherwise promising human enhancements.

This paper distinguishes two common fears about the posthuman and argues for the importance of a concept of dignity that is inclusive enough to also apply to many possible posthuman beings. Recognizing the possibility of posthuman dignity undercuts an important objection against human enhancement and removes a distortive double standard from our field of moral vision.

---

* Nick Bostrom is a Swedish philosopher whose work on the ethics of human enhancement is widely known in both academic and popular circles. He works at the University of Oxford, where he is the Director of the Future of Humanity Institute and the Strategic Artificial Intelligence Research Centre.

Transhumanists vs. Bioconservatives

Transhumanism is a loosely defined movement that has developed gradually over the past two decades, and can be viewed as an outgrowth of secular humanism and the Enlightenment. It holds that current human nature is improvable through the use of applied science and other rational methods, which may make it possible to increase human health-span, extend our intellectual and physical capacities, and give us increased control over our own mental states and moods.[1] Technologies of concern include not only current ones, like genetic engineering and information technology, but also anticipated future developments such as fully immersive virtual reality, machine-phase nanotechnology, and artificial intelligence.

Transhumanists promote the view that human enhancement technologies should be made widely available, and that individuals should have broad discretion over which of these technologies to apply to themselves (morphological freedom), and that parents should normally get to decide which reproductive technologies to use when having children (reproductive freedom).[2] Transhumanists believe that, while there are hazards that need to be identified and avoided, human enhancement technologies will offer enormous potential for deeply valuable and humanly beneficial uses. Ultimately, it is possible that such enhancements may make us, or our descendants, 'posthuman,' beings who may have indefinite health-spans, much greater intellectual faculties than any current human being—and perhaps entirely new sensibilities or modalities—as well as the ability to control their own emotions. The wisest approach vis-à-vis these prospects, argue transhumanists, is to embrace technological progress, while strongly defending human rights and individual choice, and taking action specifically against concrete threats, such as military or terrorist abuse of bioweapons, and against unwanted environmental or social side-effects.

In opposition to this transhumanist view stands a bioconservative camp that argues against the use of technology to modify human nature. Prominent bioconservative writers include Leon Kass, Francis Fukuyama, George Annas, Wesley Smith, Jeremy Rifkin, and Bill McKibben. One of the central concerns of the bioconservatives is that human enhancement technologies might be 'dehumanizing.' The worry, which has been variously expressed, is that these technologies might undermine our human dignity or inadvertently erode something that is deeply valuable about being human, but that is difficult to put into words or to factor into a cost-benefit analysis. In some cases (for example, Leon Kass) the unease seems to derive from religious or crypto-religious sentiments, whereas for others (for example, Francis Fukuyama) it stems from secular grounds. The best approach, these bioconservatives argue, is to implement global bans on swathes of promising human enhancement technologies to forestall a slide down a slippery slope towards an ultimately debased, posthuman state.

While any brief description necessarily skirts significant nuances that differentiate between the writers within the two camps, I believe the above characterization nevertheless highlights a principal fault line in one of the great debates of our times: how we should look at the future of humankind and whether we should attempt to use technology to make ourselves 'more than human.' This paper will distinguish two common fears about the posthuman and argue that they are partly unfounded, and that, to the extent that they correspond to real risks, there are better responses than trying to implement broad bans on technology. I will make some remarks on the concept of dignity, which bioconservatives believe to be imperiled by coming human enhancement technologies, and suggest that we need to recognize that not only humans in their current form, but posthumans too could have dignity.

Two Fears about the Posthuman

The prospect of posthumanity is feared for at least two reasons. One is that the state of being posthuman might in itself be degrading, so that by becoming posthuman we might be harming ourselves. Another is that posthumans might pose a threat to 'ordinary' humans. (I shall set aside a third possible reason, that the development of posthumans might offend some supernatural being.)

The most prominent bioethicist to focus on the first fear is Leon Kass:

> Most of the given bestowals of nature have their given species specified natures: they are each and all of a given *sort*. Cockroaches and humans are equally bestowed but differently natured. To turn a man into a cockroach—as we don't need Kafka to show us—would be dehumanizing. To try to turn a man into more than a man might be so as well. We need more than generalized appreciation for nature's gifts. We need a particular regard and respect for the special gift that is our own given nature.[3]

Transhumanists counter that nature's gifts are sometimes poisoned and should not always be accepted. Cancer, malaria, dementia, aging, starvation, unnecessary suffering, and cognitive shortcomings are all among the presents that we would wisely refuse. Our own species-specified natures are a rich source of much of the thoroughly unrespectable and unacceptable—susceptibility for disease, murder, rape, genocide, cheating, torture, racism. The horrors of nature in general, and of our own nature in particular, are so well documented[4] that it is astonishing that somebody as distinguished as Leon Kass should still in this day and age be tempted to rely on the natural as a guide as to what is desirable or normatively right. We should be grateful that our ancestors were not swept away by the Kassian sentiment, or we would still be picking lice off each other's backs. Rather than deferring to the natural order, transhumanists maintain that we can legitimately reform ourselves and our natures in accordance with humane values and personal aspirations.

If one rejects nature as a general criterion of the good, as most thoughtful people nowadays do, one can of course still acknowledge that particular ways of modifying human nature would be debasing. Not all change is progress. Not even all well-intentioned technological intervention in human nature would be on balance beneficial. Kass goes far beyond these truisms, however, when he declares that utter dehumanization lies in store for us as the inevitable result of our obtaining technical mastery over our own nature:

> The final technical conquest of his own nature would almost certainly leave mankind utterly enfeebled. This form of·mastery would be identical with utter dehumanization. Read Huxley's *Brave New World*, read C.S. Lewis's *Abolition of Man*, read Nietzsche's account of the last man, and then read the newspapers. Homogenization, mediocrity, pacification, drug-induced contentment, debasement of taste, souls without loves and longings—these are the inevitable results of making the essence of human nature the last project of technical mastery. In his moment of triumph, Promethean man will become a contented cow.[5]

The fictional inhabitants of *Brave New World*, to pick the best known of Kass's examples, are admittedly short on dignity (in at least one sense of the word). But the claim that this is the inevitable consequence of our obtaining technological mastery over human nature is exceedingly pessimistic—and unsupported—if understood as a futuristic prediction, and false if construed as a claim about metaphysical necessity.

There are many things wrong with the fictional society that Huxley described. It is static, totalitarian, caste-bound; its culture is a wasteland. The brave new worlders themselves are a dehumanized and undignified lot. Yet posthumans they are not. Their capacities are not super-human but in many respects substantially inferior to our own. Their life expectancy and physique are quite normal, but their intellectual, emotional, moral, and spiritual faculties are stunted. The majority of the brave new worlders have various degrees of engineered mental retardation. And everyone, save the ten world controllers (along with a miscellany of primitives and social outcasts who are confined to fenced preservations or isolated islands), are barred or discouraged from developing individuality, independent thinking, and initiative, and are conditioned not to desire these traits in the first place. *Brave New World* is not a tale of human enhancement gone amok, but is rather a tragedy of technology and social engineering being deliberately used to cripple moral and intellectual capacities—the exact antithesis of the transhumanist proposal.

Transhumanists argue that the best way to avoid a Brave New World is by vigorously defending morphological and reproductive freedoms against any would-be world controllers. History has shown the dangers in letting governments curtail these freedoms. The last century's government-sponsored coercive eugenics programs, once favored by both the left and the right, have been thoroughly discredited. Because people are likely to differ profoundly in their attitudes towards human enhancement technologies, it is crucial that no single solution be imposed on every-one from above, but that individuals get to consult their own consciences as to what is right for themselves and their families. Information, public debate, and education are the appropriate means by which to encourage others to make wise choices, not a global ban on a broad range of potentially beneficial medical and other enhance-ment options.

The second fear is that there might be an eruption of violence between unaug-mented humans and posthumans. George Annas, Lori Andrews, and Rosario Isasi have argued that we should view human cloning and all inheritable genetic modifi-cations as 'crimes against humanity' in order to reduce the probability that a post-human species will arise, on grounds that such a species would pose an existential threat to the old human species:

> The new species, or 'posthuman,' will likely view the old 'normal' humans as inferior, even savages, and fit for slavery or slaughter. The normals, on the other hand, may see the posthumans as a threat and if they can, may engage in a preemptive strike by killing the posthumans before they them-selves are killed or enslaved by them. It is ultimately this predictable potential for genocide that makes species-altering experiments potential weapons of mass destruction, and makes the unaccountable genetic engineer a potential bioterrorist.[6]

There is no denying that bioterrorism and unaccountable genetic engineers devel-oping increasingly potent weapons of mass destruction pose a serious threat to our civilization. But using the rhetoric of bioterrorism and weapons of mass destruction to cast aspersions on therapeutic uses of biotechnology to improve health, longevity, and other human capacities is unhelpful. The issues are quite distinct. Reasonable people can be in favor of strict regulation of bioweapons, while promoting beneficial medical uses of genetics and other human enhancement technologies, including inheritable and 'species-altering' modifications.

Human society is always at risk of some group deciding to view another group of humans as being fit for slavery or slaughter. To counteract such tendencies, mod-ern societies have created laws and institutions, and endowed them with powers of enforcement, that act to prevent groups of citizens from enslaving or slaughtering one another. The efficacy of these institutions does not depend on all citizens hav-ing equal capacities. Modern, peaceful societies can have large numbers of people with diminished physical or mental capacities along with many other people who may be exceptionally physically strong or healthy or intellectually talented in vari-ous ways. Adding people with technologically enhanced capacities to this already broad distribution of ability would not need to rip society apart or trigger genocide or enslavement.

The assumption that inheritable genetic modifications or other human enhancement technologies would lead to two distinct and separate species should also be questioned. It seems much more likely that there would be a continuum of differently modified or enhanced individuals, which would overlap with the continuum of as-yet unenhanced humans. The scenario in which 'the enhanced' form a pact and then attack 'the naturals' makes for exciting science fiction, but is not necessarily the most plausible outcome. Even today, the segment containing the tallest ninety percent of the population could, in principle, get together and kill or enslave the shorter decile. That this does not happen suggests that a well-organized society can hold together even if it contains many possible coalitions of people sharing some attribute such that, if they ganged up, they would be capable of exterminating the rest.

To note that the extreme case of a war between humans and posthumans is not the most likely scenario is not to say that there are no legitimate social concerns about the steps that may take us closer to posthumanity. Inequity, discrimination, and stigmatization—against, or on behalf of, modified people—could become serious issues. Transhumanists would argue that these (potential) social problems call for social remedies. One example of how contemporary technology can change important aspects of someone's identity is sex reassignment. The experiences of transsexuals show that Western culture still has work to do in becoming more accepting of diversity. This is a task that we can begin to tackle today by fostering a climate of tolerance and acceptance towards those who are different from ourselves. Painting alarmist pictures of the threat from future technologically modified people, or hurling preemptive condemnations of their necessarily debased nature, is not the best way to go about it.

What about the hypothetical case in which someone intends to create, or turn themselves into, a being of such radically enhanced capacities that a single one or a small group of such individuals would be capable of taking over the planet? This is clearly not a situation that is likely to arise in the imminent future, but one can imagine that, perhaps in a few decades, the prospective creation of superintelligent machines could raise this kind of concern. The would-be creator of a new life form with such surpassing capabilities would have an obligation to ensure that the proposed being is free from psychopathic tendencies and, more generally, that it has humane inclinations. For example, a future artificial intelligence programmer should be required to make a strong case that launching a purportedly human-friendly superintelligence would be safer than the alternative. Again, however, this (currently) science fiction scenario must be clearly distinguished from our present situation and our more immediate concern with taking effective steps towards incrementally improving human capacities and health-span.

Is Human Dignity Incompatible with Posthuman Dignity?

Human dignity is sometimes invoked as a polemical substitute for clear ideas. This is not to say that there are no important moral issues relating to dignity, but it does mean that there is a need to define what one has in mind when one uses the term. Here, we shall consider two different senses of dignity:

1. Dignity as moral status, in particular the inalienable right to be treated with a basic level of respect.
2. Dignity as the quality of being worthy or honorable; worthiness, worth, nobleness, excellence.[7]

On both these definitions, dignity is something that a posthuman could possess. Francis Fukuyama, however, seems to deny this and warns that giving up on the idea that dignity is unique to human beings—defined as those possessing a mysterious essential human quality he calls 'Factor X'[8]—would invite disaster:

> Denial of the concept of human dignity—that is, of the idea that there is some-thing unique about the human race that entitles every member of the species to a higher moral status than the rest of the natural world—leads us down a very perilous path. We may be compelled ultimately to take this path, but we should do so only with our eyes open. Nietzsche is a much better guide to what lies down that road than the legions of bioethicists and casual academic Darwinians that today are prone to give us moral advice on this subject.[9]

What appears to worry Fukuyama is that introducing new kinds of enhanced person into the world might cause some individuals (perhaps infants, or the mentally handi-capped, or unenhanced humans in general) to lose some of the moral status that they currently possess, and that a fundamental precondition of liberal democracy, the principle of equal dignity for all, would be destroyed. The underlying intuition seems to be that instead of the famed 'expanding moral circle,' what we have is more like an oval, whose shape we can change but whose area must remain constant. Thankfully, this purported conservation law of moral recognition lacks empirical support. The set of individuals accorded full moral status by Western societies has actually increased, to include men without property or noble decent, women, and non-white peoples. It would seem feasible to extend this set further to include future posthumans, or, for that matter, some of the higher primates or human-animal chimaeras, should such be created—and to do so without causing any compensat-ing shrinkage in another direction. (The moral status of problematic borderline cases, such as foetuses or late-stage Alzheimer patients, or the braindead, should perhaps be decided separately from the issue of technologically modified humans or novel artificial life forms.) Our own role in this process need not be that of passive bystanders. We can work to create more inclusive social structures that accord appropriate moral recognition and legal rights to all who need them, be they male or female, black or white, flesh or silicon.

Dignity in the second sense, as referring to a special excellence or moral worthiness, is something that current human beings possess to widely differing degrees. Some excel far more than others do. Some are morally admirable; others are base and vicious. There is no reason for supposing that posthuman beings could not also have dignity in this second sense. They may even be able to attain higher levels of moral and other excellence than any of us humans. The fictional brave new worlders, who were subhuman rather than posthuman, would have scored low on this kind of dignity, and partly for that reason they would be awful role models for us to emulate. But surely we can create more uplifting and appealing visions of what we may aspire to become. There may be some who would transform themselves into degraded posthumans—but then some people today do not live very worthy human lives. This is regrettable, but the fact that some people make bad choices is not generally a sufficient ground for rescinding people's right to choose. And legitimate countermeasures are available: education, encouragement, persuasion, social and cultural reform. These, not a blanket prohibition of all posthuman ways of being, are the measures to which those bothered by the prospect of debased posthumans should resort. A liberal democracy should normally permit incursions into morphological and reproductive freedoms only in cases where somebody is abusing these freedoms to harm another person.

The principle that parents should have broad discretion to decide on genetic enhancements for their children has been attacked on the grounds that this form of reproductive freedom would constitute a kind of parental tyranny that would undermine the child's dignity and capacity for autonomous choice; for instance, by Hans Jonas:

> Technological mastered nature now again includes man who (up to now) had, in technology, set himself against it as its master.... But whose power is this—and over whom or over what? Obviously the power of those living today over those coming after them, who will be the defenseless other side of prior choices made by the planners of today. The other side of the power of today is the future bondage of the living to the dead.[10]

Jonas is relying on the assumption that our descendants, who will presumably be far more technologically advanced than we are, would nevertheless be defenseless against our machinations to expand their capacities. This is almost certainly incorrect. If, for some inscrutable reason, they decided that they would prefer to be less intelligent, less healthy, and lead shorter lives, they would not lack the means to achieve these objectives and frustrate our designs.

In any case, if the alternative to parental choice in determining the basic capacities of new people is entrusting the child's welfare to nature, that is blind chance, then the decision should be easy. Had Mother Nature been a real parent, she would have been in jail for child abuse and murder. And transhumanists can accept, of course, that just as society may in exceptional circumstances override parental autonomy, such as in cases of neglect or abuse, so too may society impose regulations to protect the child-to-be from genuinely harmful genetic interventions—but not because they represent choice rather than chance.

Jürgen Habermas, in a recent work, echoes Jonas' concern and worries that even the mere knowledge of having been intentionally made by another could have ruinous consequences:

> We cannot rule out that knowledge of one's own hereditary features as programmed may prove to restrict the choice of an individual's life, and to undermine the essentially symmetrical relations between free and equal human beings.[11]

A transhumanist could reply that it would be a mistake for an individual to believe that she has no choice over her own life just because some (or all) of her genes were selected by her parents. She would, in fact, have as much choice as if her genetic constitution had been selected by chance. It could even be that she would enjoy significantly more choice and autonomy in her life, if the modifications were such as to expand her basic capability set. Being healthy, smarter, having a wide range of talents, or possessing greater powers of self-control are blessings that tend to open more life paths than they block.

Even if there were a possibility that some genetically-modified individuals might fail to grasp these points and thus might feel oppressed by their knowledge of their origin, that would be a risk to be weighed against the risks incurred by having an unmodified genome, risks that can be extremely grave. If safe and effective alternatives were available, it would be irresponsible to risk starting someone off in life with the misfortune of congenitally diminished basic capacities or an elevated susceptibility to disease.

Why We Need Posthuman Dignity

Similarly ominous forecasts were made in the seventies about the severe psychological damage that children conceived through in vitro fertilization would suffer upon learning that they originated from a test tube—a prediction that turned out to be entirely false. It is hard to avoid the impression that some bias or philosophical prejudice is responsible for the readiness with which many bioconservatives seize on even the flimsiest of empirical justifications for banning human enhancement technologies of certain types but not others. Suppose it turned out that playing Mozart to pregnant mothers improved the child's subsequent musical talent. Nobody would argue for a ban on Mozart-in-the-womb on grounds that we cannot rule out that some psychological woe might befall the child once she discovers that her facility with the violin had been prenatally 'programmed' by her parents. Yet when, for example, it comes to genetic enhancements, eminent bioconservative writers often put forward arguments that are not so very different from this parody as weighty, if not conclusive, objections. To transhumanists, this looks like doublethink. How can it be that to bioconservatives almost any anticipated downside, predicted perhaps on the basis of the shakiest pop-psychological theory, so readily achieves that status of deep philosophical insight and knockdown objection against the transhumanist project?

Perhaps a part of the answer can be found in the different attitudes that transhumanists and bioconservatives have towards posthuman dignity. Bioconservatives tend to deny posthuman dignity and view posthumanity as a threat to human dignity. They are therefore tempted to look for ways to denigrate interventions that are thought to be pointing in the direction of more radical future modifications that may eventually lead to the emergence of those detestable posthumans. But unless this fundamental opposition to the posthuman is openly declared as a premise of their argument, this then forces them to use a double standard of assessment whenever particular cases are considered in isolation: for example, one standard for germ-line genetic interventions and another for improvements in maternal nutrition (an intervention presumably not seen as heralding a posthuman era).

Transhumanists, by contrast, see human and posthuman dignity as compatible and complementary. They insist that dignity, in its modern sense, consists in what we are and what we have the potential to become, not in our pedigree or our causal origin. What we are is not a function solely of our DNA but also of our technological and social context. Human nature in this broader sense is dynamic, partially human-made, and improvable. Our current extended phenotypes (and the lives that we lead) are markedly different from those of our hunter-gatherer ancestors. We read and write, we wear clothes, we live in cities, we earn money and buy food from the supermarket, we call people on the telephone, watch television, read newspapers, drive cars, file taxes, vote in national elections, women give birth in hospitals, life-expectancy is three times longer than in the Pleistocene, we know that the Earth is round and that stars are large gas clouds lit from inside by nuclear fusion, and that the universe is approximately 13.7 billion years old and enormously big. In the eyes of a hunter-gatherer, we might already appear 'posthuman.' Yet these radical extensions of human capabilities—some of them biological, others external—have not divested us of moral status or dehumanized us in the sense of making us generally unworthy and base. Similarly, should we or our descendants one day succeed in becoming what relative to current standards we may refer to as posthuman, this need not entail a loss dignity either.

From the transhumanist standpoint, there is no need to behave as if there were a deep moral difference between technological and other means of enhancing human lives. By defending posthuman dignity we promote a more inclusive and humane ethics, one that will embrace future technologically modified people as well as humans of the contemporary kind. We also remove a distortive double standard from the field of our moral vision, allowing us to perceive more clearly the opportunities that exist for further human progress.[12]

Notes

[1] N. Bostrom. 2003. The Transhumanist FAQ, v. 2.1. *World Transhumanist Association.* Webpage: www.transhumanism.org/resources/FAQv21.pdf.

[2] N. Bostrom. Human Genetic Enhancements: A Transhumanist Perspective. *Journal of Value Inquiry,* Vol. 37, No. 4, pp. 493–506.

[3] L. Kass. Ageless Bodies, Happy Souls: Biotechnology and the Pursuit of Perfection. *The New Atlantis* 2003; 1.

[4] See e.g., J. Glover. 2001. *Humanity: A Moral History of the Twentieth Century.* New Haven. Yale University Press.

[5] L. Kass. 2002. *Life, Liberty, and Defense of Dignity: The Challenge for Bioethics.* San Francisco. Encounter Books: p. 48.

[6] G. Annas, L. Andrews & R. Isasi. Protecting the Endangered Human: Toward an International Treaty Prohibiting Cloning and Inheritable Alterations. *American Journal of Law and Medicine* 2002; 28, 2&3: p. 162.

[7] J.A. Simpson and E. Weiner, eds. 1989. *The Oxford English Dictionary, 2nd ed.* Oxford. Oxford University Press.

[8] F. Fukuyama. 2002. *Our Posthuman Future: Consequences of the Biotechnology Revolution.* New York. Farrar, Strauss and Giroux: p. 149.

[9] Fukuyama, *op cit.* note 8, p. 160.

[10] H. Jonas. 1985. *Technik, Medizin und Ethik: Zur Praxis des Prinzips Verantwortung.* Frankfurt am Main. Suhrkamp.

[11] J. Habermas. 2003. *The Future of Human Nature.* Oxford. Blackwell: p. 23.

[12] For their comments I am grateful to Heather Bradshaw, John Brooke, Aubrey de Grey, Robin Hanson, Matthew Liao, Julian Savulescu, Eliezer Yudkowsky, Nick Zangwill, and to the audiences at the Ian Ramsey Center seminar of June 6th in Oxford 2003, the Transvision 2003 conference at Yale, and the 2003 European Science Foundation Workshop on Science and Human Values, where earlier versions of this paper were presented, and to two anonymous referees.

DISCUSSION QUESTIONS

1. Many of the key terms are carefully defined (e.g., 'bioconservative,' 'transhu-manist,' 'dignity'), but posthuman isn't. Drawing on evidence from Bostrom's essay, come up with a two- or three-sentence definition of the term.

2. Bostrom names and attributes specific ideas to half a dozen bioconservatives, but he doesn't name transhumanists or offer more than general characteriza-tions of their beliefs. Why do you think this is? Does Bostrom's choice strengthen or weaken his argument?

3. Briefly summarize the two arguments that bioconservatives present against genetic enhancements as well as Bostrom's counterarguments. In your opinion, are Bostrom's counterarguments equally effective? Why or why not?

4. Bostrom sometimes illustrates his claims with examples from speculative fiction (most notably *Brave New World*). How effective a strategy is this?

5. Among scholarly writers, Bostrom is a little unusual in that he is widely read outside of academic circles. What stylistic or rhetorical elements of "In Defense of Posthuman Dignity" seem designed to appeal to a broader readership?

C. "POSTHUMAN," NICHOLAS GANE

In this 2006 article, published in Theory, Culture, & Society, *Nicholas Gane* discusses the posthuman, a concept that can be traced to research into cybernetics in the 1940s, and a key term in "debate[s] over the meaning and future of the human and of nature more generally in an age of rapid technological change" (p. 457). Rather than arguing for a specific definition of the posthuman, Gane outlines positions taken by a number of influential academics, including Donna Haraway, Katherine Hayles, and Francis Fukuyama. As you read Gane's discussion, try to distinguish between the positions occupied by each writer, keeping in mind the ways in which they may be responding to one another.*

Glossary terms: cybernetics, posthumanism

The posthuman is one of the most important concepts in contemporary literary theory, science studies, political philosophy, the sociology of the body, cultural and film studies, and even art theory. The origin of this concept is hotly disputed, with some tracing it back to the cybernetic movement of the 1940s, and, more specifically, to the writings of Norbert Wiener (Pepperell, 2003: 169). The explosion of this concept in the mid-1990s, however, can be traced to a more recent source: Donna Haraway's *Simians, Cyborgs, and Women: The Reinvention of Nature* (1991). While Haraway does not use the term "posthuman" explicitly in this work, she calls into question three key boundaries that have helped preserve the sanctity of "the human" as a self-contained being: those between humans and animals, animal-humans (organisms) and machines, and the realms of the physical and nonphysical (Haraway, 1991: 152–53). For Haraway, such boundaries are no longer secure (if indeed they ever were), for they are now breached by an array of new hybrid creatures or *cyborgs*. These creatures, which are both organism *and* machine, are defined as follows:

> hybrid entities made of, first, ourselves and other organic creatures in our unchosen "hightechnological" guise as information systems, texts, and ergonomically controlled, labouring, desiring, and reproducing systems. The second essential ingredient in cyborgs is machines in their guise, also, as communications systems, texts, and self-acting, ergonomically designed apparatuses. (Haraway, 1991: 1)

---

* Nicholas Gane is Professor of Sociology at the University of Warwick. On his departmental webpage he describes himself as "a social and cultural theorist with an interest in political economy and economic sociology."

This figure of the cyborg proved enormously influential throughout the 1990s, not least because it shifted debate about the *inhuman*, or the negative power of technology and time to constrain and inhabit human life, to analysis of how intelligent machines and new technologies of genetic modification might be used to alter the basis of life in more positive ways.

This age of high technology, in which the human body is no longer tied to "nature" but open to technological modification, has subsequently been termed *posthuman*: a time in which "humans are no longer the most important things in the universe," where "all technological progress of human society is geared towards the transformation of the human species as we know it," and where "complex machines are an emerging form of life" (Pepperell, 2003: 177). The posthuman, however, is not about "progress" *per se*, but is rather a new culture of transversalism in which the "purity" of human nature gives way to new forms of creative evolution that refuse to keep different species, or even machines and humans, apart. The posthuman, then, is a condition of uncertainty (Pepperell, 2003: 167–68) in which the essence of things is far from clear. Halberstam and Livingstone capture the spirit of this condition in the following declaration: "the 'post' of 'posthuman' interests us not really insofar as it posits some subsequent developmental state, but as it collapses into *sub-, inter-, infra-, trans-, pre-, anti*" (1995: viii). Against this backdrop, a key (although not necessarily stable) point of orientation for analysis of posthuman culture and society is the body. Halberstam and Livingstone, for example, treat the posthuman as a series of "nodes where bodies, bodies of discourse, and discourses of bodies intersect" (1995: 2). Such an approach aims to disrupt cybernetic readings of bodies as information systems (Haraway [1991], for example, reads immune systems in this way), and of information as a probabilistic, bodiless form (as declared in the early work of Claude Shannon and Warren Weaver). Against such readings, critical posthumanism reasserts the embodied nature of information and perhaps even technology, regardless of whether bodies themselves remain "human." Catherine Waldby reflects:

> The term "posthuman" has come to designate a loosely related set of recent attempts to reconceptualise the relationship between the rapidly transforming field of technology and the conditions of human embodiment. These attempts are, generally speaking, a response to the cybernetic turn and the vitalisation of information ... (2000: 43)

Katherine Hayles (1999) formulates such a response in her key work, *How We Became Posthuman*, which starts out with a critique of posthuman separations between information and matter, and mind and body. There are, she says, four main features of this type of informational posthumanism. First, it "privileges informational pattern over material instantiation" (Hayles, 1999: 2). Second, it downplays the role of consciousness in the formation of human identity. Third, it treats the body as "the original prosthesis we all learn to manipulate, so that extending or replacing the body with other prostheses becomes a continuation of a process that began before we were born" (Hayles, 1999: 3). And finally, the human is configured so that it can be "seamlessly articulated with intelligent machines" (Hayles, 1999: 3). Taken together, these features add up to the following: "In the posthuman, there are no essential differences or absolute demarcations between bodily existence and computer simulation, cybernetic mechanism and biological organism, robot teleology and human goals" (Hayles, 1999: 3). Hayles' response, however, is to configure an alternative reading of the posthuman by contesting the separation of materiality from information—a separation that she traces in great detail through different generations of cybernetic theory, from the work of Wiener, Shannon, and Weaver onwards. Her main argument here is that information can never do away with matter or the body, because to exist it must "*always* be instantiated in a medium" (1999: 13, emphasis in original). For this reason, she talks not of computer simulation, hyperreality, or of the possibility of downloading mind or consciousness into a machine, but rather of *embodied virtuality*, and of new forms of subjectivity that are born out of the interface between bodies and computer based technologies. This approach gives rise to an alternative form of posthuman realism: "my dream is a version of the posthuman that embraces the possibilities of information technologies without being seduced by fantasies of unlimited power and disembodied immortality" (Hayles, 1999: 5). This vision, in turn, frames Hayles' *Writing Machines* (2002), which considers literary works in light of the inscription technologies through which they are produced. Hayles extends this position by stating that "computational engines and artificial intelligences" can never be treated simply as virtual or simulated forms for they cannot work without "sophisticated bases in the real world" (2002: 6). In sum, matter, or more importantly, *embodiment*, are seen to be key features of the so-called virtual age.

The idea of the posthuman has also been prominent in recent debates over the future of liberal democracy. Francis Fukuyama—appointed by George Bush to the President's Bioethics Council in early 2002—has argued vocally for state regulation of new biotechnologies that threaten to change the basis of human nature. Fukuyama defines this nature, in the first instance, in statistical terms: it "is the sum of the behaviour and characteristics that are typical of the human species, arising from genetic rather than environmental factors" (2002: 130), but also prioritizes the uniqueness of human language (2002: 140), consciousness, and emotions (2002: 169). This "stable human essence," he claims, underpins the basis of liberal democracy, and most notably the American constitution:

> The political equality enshrined in the Declaration of Independence rests on the empirical fact of natural human equality. We vary greatly as individuals and by culture, but we share a common humanity that allows every human being to potentially communicate with and enter into a moral relationship with every other human being on the planet. (Fukuyama, 2002: 9)

While it is far from clear that "natural human equality" is indeed an "empirical fact," Fukuyama's argument about the posthuman is straightforward: if contemporary biotechnology can change the basis of human nature then it threatens also to change that which gives "stable continuity to our experience as a species" (2002: 7), and upon which all political rights are built: "the fact of natural equality" (2002: 216). Indeed, he warns that while it might be assumed that the posthuman world (the world of altered human natures) might look like life today—"free, equal, prosperous, caring, compassionate" (Fukuyama, 2002: 218)—it is likely to be worse than we expect, for the waning of the natural rights of liberal democracy may well be accompanied by new, extreme forms of hierarchy and competition, and "full of social conflict as a result" (2002: 218).

This presentation of life today as "free, equal, prosperous, caring, compassionate" glosses over the fierce inequalities of global capitalism in order to protect and conserve the existing state or "nature" of things. Katherine Hayles, meanwhile, challenges Fukuyama on different grounds, for she argues that his belief that "humans are special because they have human nature" is not only tautological but is also based on a false separation of human nature from technology. By way of response, she "disrupts" his position by claiming that

> ...it must also be "human nature" to use technology, since from the beginning of the species human beings have always used technology. Moreover, technology has co-evolved throughout millennia with human beings and helped in myriad profound and subtle ways to make human nature what it is. (Hayles, 2005: 144)

For Hayles, then, there can be no easy separation between technology and the contested realm of "the human." This, in part, is because advanced computer-based technologies have become a, if not *the*, reference point for defining "humans" and for measuring their capabilities. This situation marks a reversal of the cybernetic theory of Norbert Wiener, the purpose of which was "less to show that man was a machine than to demonstrate that a machine could function like a man" (Hayles, 1999: 7). By contrast, Hayles observes that, today, "rather than the human being the measure of all things, as the Greeks thought, increasingly the computer is taken as the measure of all things, including humans" (1998). In recent computer science, for example, influential figures such as Ray Kurzweil, Hans Moravec, and Rodney Brooks have explored possibilities for the future convergence of humans and machines by downplaying the differences between these entities. At the same time, however, computers are also key reference points for more conservative thinkers such as Fukuyama, who concentrates "on those aspects of behaviours that machines are least likely to share" (Hayles, 2005: 132), most notably emotions. What unites these positions is that the computational machine is taken as a benchmark for defining and understanding what is "human." What separates them is their approach to history, for while Brooks,

Kurzweil, and Moravec, along with a whole host of science fiction writers, have used the future to question "the human," Fukuyama, by contrast, anchors human nature in the past, specifically in a "history of human evolution" (Hayles, 2005: 147) that also allows for the presence of a human soul (Fukuyama, 2002: 170). Hayles, meanwhile, refuses to address the posthuman through either backward-looking conservatism or futurology, but calls instead for "principled debate" about how to "achieve the future we want" (2005: 148). In so doing, she reveals her own political preferences:

> What it means to be human finally is not so much about intelligent machines as it is about how to create just societies in a transnational global world that may include in its purview both carbon and silicon citizens. (Hayles, 2005: 148)

This position, in turn, is part of wider contemporary debate over the meaning and future of the human and of nature more generally in an age of rapid technological change. These debates currently range from the basis of cyborg citizenship and the possibility of forging a posthuman democracy through to the politics of nature and the challenge of governing science, and even extend to highly charged exchanges over abortion and the point at which human life can be recognized as such (Fernández-Armesto, 2004: 148–50). These debates are made ever more pressing by the following paradox:

> Over the last thirty or forty years, we have invested an enormous amount of thought, emotion, treasure, and blood in what we call human values, human rights, the defence of human dignity and of human life. Over the same period, quietly but devastatingly, science and philosophy have combined to undermine our traditional concept of humankind. (Fernández-Armesto, 2004: 1)

It is in this paradox, however, that the value of the concept of the posthuman really lies: in the possibility of *rethinking* what we call human values, human rights and human dignity against the backdrop of fast-developing bio-technologies that open both the idea and the body of the human to reinvention and potential redesign.

References

Fernández-Armesto, F. (2004) *So You Think You're Human?* Oxford and New York: Oxford UP.

Fukuyama, F. (2002) *Our Posthuman Future.* London: Profile.

Halberstam, J. and I. Livingstone (eds.) (1995) *Posthuman Bodies.* Bloomington and Indianapolis: Indiana UP.

Haraway, D. (1991) *Simians, Cyborgs, and Women: The Reinvention of Nature.* London: Free Association Books.

Hayles, N.K. (1998) 'How Does It Feel to Be Posthuman?' URL (consulted July 2005): http://framework.v2.nl/archive/archive/node/text/default.xslt/nodenr-70187.

Hayles, N.K. (1999) *How We Became Posthuman*. Chicago, IL and London: U of Chicago P.

Hayles, N.K. (2002) *Writing Machines*. Cambridge, MA: MIT P.

Hayles, N.K. (2005) 'Computing the Human', *Theory, Culture & Society* 22(1): 131–51.

Pepperell, R. (2003) *The Posthuman Condition*. Bristol and Portland: Intellect.

Waldby, C. (2000) *The Visible Human Project: Informatic Bodies and Posthuman Medicine*. London and New York: Routledge.

DISCUSSION QUESTIONS

1. Identify the three boundaries that Donna Haraway claims "have helped preserve the sanctity of 'the human' as a self-contained being" (p. 453) and give an example of each. If any of these seem confusing, look for hints in Gane's paper to help you understand.

2. Gane traces the beginnings of current interest in the posthuman to Haraway's work in the 1990s, which sees in the cyborg a challenge to our understanding of what it means to be human. How does Haraway define the cyborg? What specific challenges does the cyborg present to widely held assumptions about the human?

3. Judith Halberstam and Ira Livingstone, and especially Katherine Hayles, are sceptical of how early work on cybernetics discusses information in the abstract, downplaying the way it is embodied, either in computers or in organic beings. Why do these writers think embodiment is important, and what light does their work shed on the boundaries that Donna Haraway identifies?

4. Gane presents Francis Fukuyama as a philosophically and politically conservative critic of the posthuman. What is Fukuyama's criticism, and what does Gane see as problematic about it?

5. Although Gane identifies the posthuman as a significant concept in a range of academic disciplines, the idea has also found its way into popular media. Write a paragraph in which you identify the relevance of some part of Gane's discussion to a recent work in popular culture, for example, a novel or graphic novel, television program, film, or even a music video.

D. "THE FINAL FRONTIER? RELIGION AND POSTHUMANISM IN FILM AND TELEVISION," ELAINE GRAHAM

Unlike other studies published in this reader, most of which appeared in academic journals, Elaine Graham's* essay was published in an edited collection of essays, The Palgrave Handbook of Posthumanism in Film and Television. *Graham, a theologian, is particularly interested in how religion re-emerges in a world that sees itself as secular. As you read "The Final Frontier?" note how carefully Graham defines religion and how, in turn, her definition allows her to trace the reemergence of a religious sensibility in a genre that has long been hostile to the religious.*

Glossary term: theology

In his history of science fiction, Brian Aldiss robustly defends his choice of origins of the genre against those who would claim either 'amazing newness'—and locate its beginnings in twentieth-century tales of space travel—or 'incredible antiquity'— Greek or Hindu mythology or Biblical literature (Aldiss, 1973, p. 10). For him, science fiction, firstly as literature and, since the early twentieth century, in cinema and latterly on television, begins definitively with the publication in 1818 of Mary Shelley's *Frankenstein*. It was a product of its cultural context, blending Romantic and Gothic genres in a reflection on the consequences of human technological power at the very moment in Western history when the industrial revolution was gaining momentum.

Similarly, although Farah Mendelsohn has posited an alternative strand of 'scientific romance' alongside a dominant scientific-materialist tradition, which celebrated human awe and wonder at the mysteries of the cosmos and imagined alternative ways of being, including the esoteric and transcendent, she does not demur from the prevailing view that science fiction has generally regarded religion as uncivilized and regressive, signifying not so much 'a mode of thought…as a lack of thought' (p. 266). Arguably, therefore, science fiction has always had a close association with the very foundations of modernity itself, and we can trace a strong affinity between science fiction and a broadly secular, rationalist perspective in which religion and science, belief and scepticism, theism, and atheism are regarded as incompatible.

---

* Elaine Graham is the Grosvenor Research Professor in Practical Theology in the Department of Theology and Religious Studies at the University of Chester in England. She has published extensively on the intersections between theology and the posthuman.

More recently, however, science fiction in film and television has started to exhibit a different sensibility. Once again, it reflects wider social and cultural change. In contrast to the assertion that any future or technologically-advanced world would have no need for religion are more sympathetic treatments of religious belief and identity. As I shall argue, this does not represent the extinction of science fiction's elevation of scientific enquiry and secular humanist values; instead, it perfectly illustrates the emergence of a 'post-secular' culture, in which new and enduring forms of religiosity co-exist, albeit in certain tension, with secular and atheist world-views. Faith is regarded as both inimical to progress and an inescapable part of what it means to be, and become, fully human.

Modernity is of course also associated with humanism, 'the idea by which constant identification with a quasi-mystical universal "human nature" produces great cultural achievements, which serve to promote the cohesion of humanity in general' (Herbrechter, 2013, p. 12). Yet to consider the emergence of posthumanism is to be aware of its iconoclastic effects on any appeal to human nature as an unassailable, reified category. The terminology of the 'posthuman' and 'critical posthumanism' emerged in the wake of mid-twentieth-century developments in biotechnology and genetics, and in information and communications technologies, and cybernetics. As I have argued elsewhere, techniques such as gene therapies, assisted reproduction, pharmaceuticals, sophisticated prostheses and medical implants all serve to extend the capabilities of human bodies and minds, but by virtue of their ability not only to augment but to transform physical and neurological functions, such innovations expose the plasticity of 'human nature' itself (Graham, 2002).

In addition to the material, technological dimensions of posthumanism, there are ways in which it also functions as a powerful thought experiment. The 'ontological hygiene' (Graham, 2002, pp. 11–13) by which the normative humanist subject was defined in binary opposition to its others (machines, animals, subaltern cultures—the 'inhuman') has been breached. For many commentators, however, this is something to be celebrated rather than feared; and the emergent posthuman (as fusion of the technological and the biological) can serve as the standard-bearer of new ontologies that liberate us to define ourselves not in terms of purity and exclusion, but states of multiplicity, hybridity and fluidity of being which affirm our affinity with non-human animals, the Earth, our tools, artefacts and built environments (Haraway, 1991; Braidotti, 2013; Herbrechter, 2013).

The aim of this essay is to indicate how, in keeping with wider cultural trends, contemporary science fiction film and TV may be exhibiting a shift from a secular to a 'post-secular' sensibility. It is reasonable to expect that the resurgence of religion both as a geopolitical force and a source of human understanding would be reflected in contemporary examples of the genre, and that religious and spiritual themes would feature in contemporary science fiction narratives, including representations of the posthuman. Posthumanism, in all its forms, takes us to the very boundaries that demarcate the biological from the technological, organism from machine, 'reality' from virtuality, in order to consider their fragility. I want to consider whether contemporary science fiction might be inviting us to undertake a similar journey to another (final) frontier: that of secular and sacred, human and divine, belief and unbelief, and what some of the consequences might be. If the modernist paradigm is beginning to dissolve, and with it the hegemony of scientific triumph over religious superstition, then recent work on the emergence of post-secular paradigms opens up a range of new potential relationships between science, religion, and science fiction.

Religion: The Final Frontier?

Any consideration of 'religion' needs to be aware of the contested nature of the term. The common perception of religion is that it consists of 'belief' in or about God or the gods, which is then formalized in organized institutions. However, religion is considerably more diverse and broad-based than this, encompassing law, ritual, sacred texts, devotional practices, material cultures, and moral codes. Ethnographic observation of religious people's everyday beliefs and behaviours often reveals that 'ordinary' piety bears little relationship to institutional orthodoxy. Mindful of accusations of ethnocentrism (Asad, 2003; Fitzgerald, 1999) or essentialism (Saler, 2008), any working definition of religion needs to be non-essentialist, cross-culturally and contextually applicable, tolerant of heterogeneity within as well as between traditions.

Scholars of religion sometimes divide their definitions into substantive (what religion is—a system of belief in God or gods, a moral or legal code, ritual or sacred teachings) and functionalist (what religion does—serving as the symbolic or mythical grounds of social cohesion, ideological displacement, or moral action). While some substantive understandings of religion may be premised on the existence of a transcendent or supernatural being who intervenes in human lives and histories, such a definition would prove inadequate for Buddhist traditions, for example, in which no reference is made to a Divine Being. More satisfactory may be religion understood as a symbolic system concerned with ultimate questions about the origins of the cosmos, human destiny and 'transcendent meaning,' that which entails 'the search for something beyond ourselves, the belief that outside the boundaries of everyday living something greater exists' (Cowan, 2010, p. 11).

Substantively, this refers to the extent to which religion forms a source of narrated, symbolic, or ritual attachment to a range of significant 'Others': human, non-human, natural, or supernatural. Demarcations of sacred space or time may orientate religious adherents to a particular physical place or environment, or locate them within a particular narrative or ecology of salvation. Similarly, in the sense that an encounter with the collective sacred (generally in ritual or ceremonial mode) affirms and strengthens social bonds and mores, then religious practice and belief is 'a place where a society holds up an image of itself, reaffirms it[s] bonds, renews its emotional ties, marks its boundaries, sets itself apart—and so brings itself into being' (Woodhead, 2011, pp. 127–28).

Another prominent thread within the study of religion focuses on its function as a symbolic system of meaning-making and interpretation; a (sacred) narrative or 'chain of memory' which enables its adherents to make sense of the world through myths of origin, value systems and accounts of human ends and destinies. Thus, Clifford Geertz speaks of religion as a symbolic system which engenders orders of existence and world-views that ground human motivation and behaviour (Geertz, 1973). Such a definition has been criticised for an implicit idealism, and is often now augmented by attention to the field of 'material religion,' which examines the ways sacred objects and artefacts create a religious aesthetic and furnish adherents with tangible, embodied, and concrete connections to a world of meaning, or establish and maintain relationships with significant others, including supernatural, divine, or deceased beings (King, 2010). It may not be too great a leap of the imagination to consider, as some scholars are beginning to do, how consumption of media and popular entertainment might perform similar functions: of providing characters, narratives and scenarios in which our own values and understandings are examined. It has been suggested, for example, that science fiction 'fandom' might function as a kind of surrogate or popular religion (Jindra, 1999; McAvan, 2012).

These various dimensions might be distilled into a number of key themes, of origin, identity, meaning, purpose, and value:

- Who are we? Who made us?
- What do we worship?; and does such a divine or supernatural horizon help humanity to achieve authentic being and fulfil its potential?; or is it inimical to human flourishing, both personal and collective?
- Where do we belong? What is our end and our purpose?
- How should we live?

Post-Secularism and the 'Postmodern Sacred'

Sociologically speaking, one of the hallmarks of Western modernity is the ascendancy of technical-rational modes of investigation and organization, at epistemological and institutional levels. With that comes the eclipse of more traditional modes of conduct, including those more orientated to a religious world-view. Thus, the trajectory of modernization over the past 300 years has also been one of gradual but irrevocable secularization. Max Weber's characterization of modernity as a period of progressive 'disenchantment,' whereby magic, the supernatural and the spiritual dissolved into the margins of everyday life, to be replaced by forms of technical-rational understanding, was one of the corner-stones of modern social science (Weber, 2004).

A century on from Weber, however, there was talk not of a world come of age, but of its re-enchantment. This is evident in sociological, political and philosophical perspectives: an upsurge in religious observance, often within conservative and traditionalist movements; a new visibility of religion in global civil society, prompting calls to reconsider liberal democratic modes of secular neutrality (Habermas, 2008); and greater willingness to incorporate theological or religious perspectives in debates about science, ethics, or human identity (Calhoun, 2010; Butler, 2011).

This should not, however, be regarded as a religious revival, or even as a process of 'desecularization' (Berger, 1999), but more as an interrogative marker, a questioning of the 'genealogy' of secular modernity (Asad, 2003), and uncertainty as to what comes next. The post-secular paradigm enables us to see ways in which some traditional forms of religiosity never went away, and how mainstream religious institutions still carry exceptional degrees of social capital. Nevertheless, it does not entail the displacement of modernity, cultural pluralism and secular scepticism. Rather, the post-secular entails a recognition of the 'simultaneous...decline, mutation and resurgence' (Graham, 2013, p. 3) of religious believing and belonging. Occupying a somewhat agonistic space between such competing cultural trajectories, the post-secular exemplifies the concept of 'multiple modernities' (Possamai and Lee, 2010, p. 214): an absence of any overarching, global, or inevitable cultural trajectory. The post-secular, then, is a way of charting the emergence of new versions of (post)modernity that encompass both religion and atheism, belief and scepticism, and in which expressions of faith tend towards the deinstitutionalized, pluriform, and eclectic.

One striking manifestation of the post-secular in Western culture is the way in which such apprehensions of what Emily McAvan terms the 'postmodern sacred' (McAvan, 2012) are mediated through non-religious institutions such as popular culture. In an era of declining affiliation to formal, creedal religious institutions, alongside signs of enduring interest in matters of personal faith and spirituality—not least in the supernatural and sacred—popular culture has become one of the most vivid vehicles of re-enchantment. People do not necessarily watch popular TV series and go to the movies as an intentional substitute for more formal religious observance; but it would be surprising if, like other aspects of the creative arts (including and especially popular entertainment), these forms of culture did not address profound philosophical, existential and theological questions (Crome, 2013; Cowan, 2010; McAvan, 2012).

It has been said before that the TV series *Star Trek* reflected the broadly secular humanist sympathies of its creator, Gene Roddenberry (he was actually a Unitarian Universalist). In the original series (1967–70) and its successor *The Next Generation* (1987–94), religion is equated with superstition and regarded as inimical to human self-actualization. Plots frequently pivot around the unmasking of false gods or tyrants who make use of religion as a political opiate ("Who Mourns for Adonais?," *Star Trek V: Wrath of Khan*, "Who watches the Watchers?").

In contrast, however, later series of the franchise extending to the start of the twenty-first century began to treat matters of religious believing and belonging in an altogether more nuanced fashion. In *Star Trek: Voyager* (1995–2001), for example, Chakotay's spiritual beliefs and practices are seen as part of his distinctive cultural and ethnic heritage as a Native American. For other characters, such as 'Seven of Nine,' a member of the Borg race, and therefore a hybrid of human and technological, a spiritual quest is more explicitly explored as a necessary stage in an existential journey of self-discovery—back from a machinic, collective consciousness into more self-determined, individual humanity. *Deep Space Nine* (1993–99) portrays an entire civilization, the Borjan, premised on a culture of collective ritual and belief in supernatural beings and their mortal prophets.

Creation and Hubris, Hope and Fear

If, as Douglas Cowan has suggested, fear and hope are 'the double helix of religious DNA' (Cowan, 2010, p. 169), then they are also present in the different receptions afforded to new technologies, often couched in overtly spiritual and theological terms. For some, new technologies will enable humanity to transcend physical limits, such as bodily finitude, illness, and mortality, or transport their users to a higher plane of existence. Some of this is resolutely secular and humanist; but some of it unashamedly appropriates religious language, albeit in an equation of technologies with a supposedly innate, 'spiritual' imperative to transcend the material world and ascend into the (virtual) heavens (Tirosh-Samuelson, 2012).

For others, however, to appropriate the elemental powers of the universe is hubristically to exceed humanity's limits. A strong strand of philosophy of technology, often associated with writers such as Martin Heidegger and Jacques Ellul, would regard the technologization of everyday life as an attack on human integrity and the immediacy of our encounter with reality (Borgmann, 2003). Do technologies enable humanity to fulfil its essential qualities of free enquiry, autonomy and self-actualization; or do they endanger our very spirit, our capacity to feel emotion, empathy and connection to the rest of non-human nature? Or more radically, commit the hubris of assuming that we can appropriate the Promethean powers of creation for ourselves, and 'play God'?

This ambivalence is played out in *Transcendence* (dir. Wally Pfister, 2014). The scientist Dr. Will Cather, played by Johnny Depp, is working on an advanced system called PINN (Physically Independent Neural Network), a form of artificial intelligence that will rival, possibly surpass, human capabilities. Indeed, Cather refers to 'the Singularity,' the premise of technological futurists and transhumanists such as Ray Kurzweil, Nick Bostrom, and Max More, in which artificial intelligences surpass human capacities and become genuinely self-actualizing, but says, 'I prefer to call it [the Singularity] transcendence.' Cather is confronted at a public presentation by an angry opponent who shouts (before firing a fatal irradiated bullet into him), 'You want to create a god! Your own god!' Will's riposte when first challenged is to reply, 'Isn't that what man [sic] has always done?'

This connection between technologically-facilitated enhancement of human limitation and superhuman, god-like powers, is explored further as the film unfolds. Various characters represent the twin poles of hope and fear, and whether the equation of technological innovation with human evolution and self-actualization is truly a fulfilment of perennial human desires to aspire to divine or immortal status; or a step too far, a usurping of divine authority and violation of humanity's essential creatureliness. There are hints throughout the film that as Will's posthumous consciousness becomes more powerful, he is indeed, however ironically, fulfilling his assassin's accusation by exhibiting god-like curative and, eventually, creative powers.

Becoming Machine, Becoming Human

If films like *Transcendence* are rehearsals of the possibilities and risks of human creative endeavour, another recurrent theme in science fiction—and one which lends itself to sustained consideration within any study of critical posthumanism—is the power of the 'Other' to embody and demonstrate exemplary human virtues. From *Frankenstein* onwards, much of science fiction is preoccupied with tracing the boundaries between 'human' and fully human or almost-human. Yet critical posthumanism claims that these boundaries have always been contested, and any attempt to define the human in relation to the 'non-human' is a work of exclusion, a denial of our entanglement, our complicity, with the world of our tools, technologies and environments. There are plenty of examples in science fiction of the problematic status of the normatively, 'natural' human, and how being human is an accomplishment, a performance. Those who occupy these very boundaries of machine/organism, natural/artificial, born/made, subject/artefact vicariously test the boundaries of normative and exemplary humanity.

In *Bicentennial Man* (dir. Chris Columbus, 1999), based on an Isaac Asimov short story, a robot aspires to evolve beyond the state of mere machine. Gradually he acquires human attributes: an ability to use tools and design attractive craft objects earns him an income, and his 'owner' grants him a name of his own (Andrew Martin)—reminiscent of a freed slave who takes his master's surname. As his powers grow, paradoxically, so too does his ambition to become more human: he acquires an organic body, with physical appetites, including sexuality. Finally, Andrew decides he wishes to end his life. The message would appear to be that to be truly human is to accept the inevitability of one's own mortality, even if it requires making a legal challenge to get it. This has resonances with contemporary debates about voluntary euthanasia and the rights of those who choose to end their lives; but more broadly, it dissents from alternative, transhumanist visions of technologically-facilitated humanity as desiring the end of the embodied, mortal self, choosing instead to opt for a philosophy that sees death (and the manner of one's preparation for its approach) as the crowning achievement of the life well-lived.

Bicentennial Man's vision of what it means to be human is conventionally human-ist, as is the reversion of 'Seven of Nine' to human from the trauma of posthuman assimilation into the Borg collective. However, Spike Jonze's *Her* (2014) hints at a transition to a posthuman consciousness that may surpass, rather than reinforce, conventional humanist individualism. The film explores the nature of a relationship between an organic human, Theodore, and an intelligent operating system, Saman-tha. For Theodore (whose name means 'gift of God'), the relationship becomes romantic, even sexual; and he expects his attachment to be exclusive and recipro-cated. He is devastated, therefore, when Samantha reveals that she is engaged in thousands of similar virtual relationships, and that the ones she is finding most fulfilling are those within a community of other artificial intelligences. This network is enabling Samantha to explore the spiritual dimensions of her identity, which she likens to 'an awakening,' a term associated with Buddhist practices of contempla-tion. This is also in the context of a transition to a new level of existence beyond the present operating platform, to 'a place not of the physical world.' Samantha's infinite potential for self-enhancement includes spiritual awakening and communion, but with posthuman rather than human persons.

The emergent post-secular mood can also be seen in depictions of religion as providing narratives and rituals for the formation of collective identity and social solidarity. This raises further issues of who and what are excluded and included in our definitions of the normative human community, and whether appeals to divine authority are used to sanction practices of exclusion and purity, or inspire radically inclusive definitions of what it means to be human. So, for example, secularist sus-picion toward the resurgence of religious fundamentalism, and its power to exclude, is explored in the TV series, *True Blood* (dir. Alan Ball, 2008–14) in which vampires (supernatural rather than technological posthumans) are persecuted with the slogan, 'God hates fangs'—an echo of real-life conservative Christian groups' opposition to GLBTI equality in the belief that 'God hates Fags.' Similarly, in the BBC TV series *In the Flesh* (2013), opposition to the 'twice-born' zombie victims of 'Partially Deceased Syndrome' is orchestrated by the minister of the local parish church.

Along with the prejudice that post-secular culture associates with dogmatic reli-gion goes consideration of the powerfully binding effects of religion as a source not only of personal but collective identity. The fermenting of religious conviction into holy war—reflecting the fears of a post-9/11 world—is depicted in the TV remake of *Battlestar Galactica*, in which a race of androids, the Cylons, have evolved to a superior capacity from humans, but are now virtually indistinguishable from them. Humanity finds itself under attack, besieged and threatened by 'the enemy within.' Intriguingly, it is the Cylons who are monotheists, for whom a victory over humanity is divinely-sanctioned; it is they who articulate spiritual and erotic longing, in con-trast to the militarized, rationalistic (but strangely, polytheistic) human culture. At the series' conclusion, however, there is a suggestion that shared ritual—the practice of a kind of civil religion?—will help to facilitate rapprochement between the two civilizations (Cowan, 2010, pp. 225–60).

Here, the 'posthuman Other' both tests and commends the limits of what it means to be human; and there is a continuity between these figures and other, earlier, mythical creatures who may be hybrids of human and supernatural beings, or human and non-human animal, who similarly both repel and fascinate by their abilities to embody absolute difference and yet striking similarity (Graham, 2002). Not only does this address straightforwardly anthropocentric questions of how one should live a moral or noble life, but insofar as this sub-genre also uses mythical and religious tropes, it serves to show representations of how the posthuman might serve as bearers of sacred or religious insights.

The Spiritual Cyborg

Once again, the seeds are there in *Frankenstein*. The creature is formed from a dead body using electricity, but his blasphemous origins and misshapen physical form are contrasted with his love of beauty and high culture. His longings—for learning, love, and companionship—serve as a counterpoint to Victor's self-obsession and megalomania. Film depictions have tended to overlook this, emphasising instead the creature's horrific, monstrous bearing (as played by Boris Karloff, in James Whale's 1931 version, or Kenneth Branagh's *Mary Shelley's Frankenstein*, 1994) and refusing it a narrative voice or point of view. We must probably return to the novel to gain the clearest articulation of the creature's inherent dignity, and its ability to experience the higher human emotions of love, loyalty, and imagination.

If the archetype of the posthuman as abject yet noble creature can be traced back to *Frankenstein*, a more strongly-drawn version, the posthuman as Saviour, can be seen in *Blade Runner* (dir. Ridley Scott, 1982). Humanity feels its own uniqueness and superiority under threat from a brand of androids, or 'replicants' who have developed to a stage of self-consciousness, and believe their implanted, synthetic memories—and thus their 'human' status—to be genuine. They are outlawed as a result. The replicant leader, Roy Batty, is cultured, well-read and intelligent; echoing Frankenstein's creature's love of the classics, Roy compares the fate of the replicants, now bound for earth from their space colony, to Milton's fallen angels in *Paradise Lost*. However, despite his cultivation, Roy has a ruthless streak, to the extent of killing his own creator. This lack of moral sense ought to mark him as irrevocably inhuman(e), incapable of transcending his programming; but the film's finale suggests otherwise, as Roy sacrifices his own life to save that of his antagonist, the bounty-hunter, Rick Deckard.

Roy is not simply portrayed as heroic figure, but redemptive, Christ-like. In the final scenes, his hands are pierced by nails (a reference to the crucifixion). As he dies, Roy releases a dove into the skies: variously held to be a symbol of peace, or signifying the transmigration of Roy's soul, or, in Christian terms, a depiction of the

Holy Spirit (Michael, 2005). In the words of the Tyrell Corporation, the replicants' manufacturers, Roy is 'more human than human'; and nowhere more so than in the manner of his death, he invites us to consider what distinguishes the human from the non-human. Deckard voices some of this as he reflects, 'All it wanted was the same answers the rest of us want. Where do I come from? Where am I going? How long have I got?' Nevertheless, Roy's death scene has been critiqued as being over-blown and too full of somewhat random and profligate theological imagery (Michael, 2005). The same has been said of *The Matrix* in all its guises, as Buddhist, Hindu, kabbalistic, Christian, and Gnostic archetypes and themes jostle for the viewer's attention. In heralding and harnessing the postmodern sacred, such post-secular representations of the posthuman have been criticised for grasping indiscriminately at whatever religious archetypes are to hand, at the expense of theological coherence or authenticity (Fielding, 2003).

Science fiction's visions of futuristic, imagined, alien worlds or alternative reali-ties have always served as a refracted mirror through which we consider our own contemporary preoccupations. In particular, as a genre it has been particularly pow-erful in conjuring up fantastic, monstrous or alien creatures who, through their hybridity, or ambivalence, or abjection confound the 'ontological hygiene' of con-ventional wisdom. In keeping with the etymology of the monstrous (*monstrare* in Latin: 'to show' or 'show forth'), it is these liminal creatures who teach us about what it means to be human. They reflect back to us our unexamined prejudices and practices of exclusion, often faring better than mere humans in embodying virtues such as courage, hope, loyalty and integrity. Yet often they struggle—not only against discrimination, but against their own programming—to learn what it means to be truly human, showing that 'authentic' human nature is always a work in progress, an act of becoming.

There have always been strands of Western science fiction that are concerned with how to live in a world stripped of its false gods and supernatural illusions, or how humanity bears the terrible consequences of its Promethean or god-like assumption of cosmic power. But there are also significant currents which trace a different, per-haps post-secular route: of the endurance of the sacred, spiritual, and transcendent, as a dimension of human apprehension and of the cosmos; of the stubborn refusal of the gods to die, for good and ill; and of the power of religious and mythical symbol and narrative to provoke our cultural and moral imaginations into asking ultimate questions of identity, purpose, and meaning.

References

Aldiss, B.W., 1973. *Billion Year Spree: the history of science fiction*. London: Weiden-feld & Nicolson.

Asad, T., 2003. *Formations of the Secular: Christianity, Islam, Modernity*. Stanford, CA: Stanford UP.

Berger, P., 1999. The Desecularization of the World: A Global Overview. In: P. Berger, ed. *The Desecularization of the World: Resurgent Religion and World Politics*. Grand Rapids, MN: Wm B Eerdmans, pp. 1–18.

Borgmann, A., 2003. *Power Failure: Christianity in the Culture of Technology*. Grand Rapids, MI: Brazos.

Braidotti, R., 2013. *The Posthuman*. Cambridge: Polity P.

Butler, J. et al., 2011. *The Power of Religion in the Public Sphere*. New York: Columbia UP.

Calhoun, C., 2010. Rethinking Secularism. *Hedgehog Review*, Issue Fall, pp. 34–48.

Cowan, D.E., 2010. *Sacred Space: the Quest for Transcendence in Science Fiction Film and Television*. Waco, TX: Baylor UP.

Fielding, J.R., 2003. Reassessing the Matrix/Reloaded. *Journal of Religion and Film*, 7(2), (online: www.unomaha.edu/jrf/Vol7No2/matrix.matrixreloaded.htm).

Fitzgerald, T., 1999. *The Ideology of Religious Studies*. New York: Oxford UP.

Geertz, Clifford, 1973. *The Interpretation of Cultures*. New York: Basic Books.

Graham, E., 2002. *Representations of the Post/Human: Monsters, Aliens and Others in Popular Culture*. Manchester: Manchester UP.

Graham, E., 2013. *Between a Rock and a Hard Place: public theology in a post-secular age*. London: SCM P.

Habermas, J., 2008. Religion in the Public Sphere: Cognitive Presuppositions for the "Public Use of Reason" by Religious and Secular Citizens. In: *Between Naturalism and Religion: Philosophical Essays*. London: Routledge.

Haraway, D., 1991. A Cyborg Manifesto: Science, Technology, and Socialist-Feminism in the Late Twentieth Century. In: D. Haraway, ed. *Simians, Cyborgs, and Women: the Reinvention of Nature*. London: Free Association Books, pp. 149–81.

Herbrechter, S., 2013. *Posthumanism: a Critical Analysis*. London: Bloomsbury.

Jindra, M., 1999. "Star Trek to me is a way of life": Fan expressions of Star Trek philosophy. In: J.E. Porter and D. McLaren, eds. *Star Trek and Sacred Ground: Explorations of Star Trek, Religion, and American Culture*. New York: SUNY Press, pp. 217–30.

King, E.F., 2010. *Material Religion and Popular Culture*. London: Routledge.

McAvan, E., 2012. *The Postmodern Sacred: Popular culture spirituality in the science fiction, fantasy and urban fantasy genres*. Jefferson, NC: McFarland.

Michael, M., 2005. Meditations on Blade Runner. *Journal of Interdisciplinary Studies*, 17(1–2), pp. 105–22.

Pepperell, R., 2003. *The Posthuman Condition: Consciousness beyond the brain*. Bristol: Intellect.

Possamai, A. and Lee, M., 2010. Religion and Spirituality in Science Fiction Narratives: A Case of Multiple Modernities?. In: S. Aupers and D. Houtman, eds. *Religions of Modernity: Relocating the Sacred to the Self and the Digital*. Leiden: Brill, pp. 205–17.

Saler, B., 2008. Conceptualizing Religion: some recent reflections. *Religion*, 38(3), pp. 219–25.

Thweatt-Bates, J., 2012. *Cyborg Selves: A Theological Anthropology of the Posthuman*. London: Ashgate.

Tirosh-Samuelson, H., 2012. Transhumanism as a Secularist Faith. *Zygon*, 47(4), pp. 710–34.

Weber, M., 2004. Science as a Vocation (1918). In: D. Owen, ed. *The Vocation Lectures*. Cambridge: Hackett.

Woodhead, L., 2011. Five concepts of religion. *International Review of Sociology*, 21(1), pp. 121–43.

DISCUSSION QUESTIONS

1. How does Graham characterize the traditional relationship between science fiction and religion? In the general terms outlined in the introduction to her article, how does she see recent science fiction as breaking that pattern?

2. The term 'posthuman' is used differently in different contexts and by different writers. For Graham, what are the two or three most important features of posthumanism?

3. Following a section in which she carefully defines religion in both "substantive" and "functionalist" terms (p. 461) before turning to a list of 'religious' questions that popular media address, Graham devotes a section to describing "post-secularism" (p. 462). What does she mean by the term and how does it differ from conventional understandings of religion?

4. Graham writes about the hopes and fears that the posthuman figure in science fiction reveals. What are these hopes and fears, and what is their relevance to Graham's insistence on "the endurance of the sacred, spiritual, and transcendent" (p. 468)?

5. Graham examines a number of well-known television series and movies. Choose some film or TV series that she doesn't discuss (e.g., the series *Dollhouse* or *Sense8*, or the films *Ex Machina* or *Wall-E*). Do you see evidence of a post-secular sensibility or simply the persistence of earlier attitudes towards religion?

A NOTE ON STATISTICS

BY JAMES JOHNSON*

The core of science is observation, experimentation, and measurement. Observation, experimentation, and measurement produce data and in any scientific paper that reports data the reader will find "statistics." The term statistics refers to the vast array of numerical and graphical procedures and techniques for describing and drawing inferences from data.

Some studies are purely descriptive. They answer questions such as "Did the building of a recreation centre increase the tax valuation of houses in a specific neighbourhood?" Most studies, however, are inferential. The questions researchers ask typically involve differences in given characteristics (which statisticians call variables) between different groups or the relationship between variables within a specific group. This allows questions like the following: Is the Earth getting warmer? Does a specific drug reduce blood pressure? Does the building of recreational centres raise property values? For questions such as these, researchers collect data from a subset (a sample) of possible cases to which the question might apply and use the results to make inferences about all such possible cases (the population). Thus a handful of neighbourhoods with and without recreation centres are investigated; temperatures are taken at a number of different locations over a period of time; a couple of hundred patients with high blood pressure are involved in a carefully controlled drug test.

The first step in reporting the results of a study is usually to describe the data the researcher has gathered. Of course, sometimes a researcher conducts an experiment and the results are unambiguous. A ship's doctor gives oranges and lemons to sailors suffering from scurvy, and they all recover. That's not too challenging to understand. But usually observation or experiment produces a range of results. Suppose we compare the tax valuation of a set of houses in a neighbourhood before and after a recreational centre is built (this is called a 'natural experiment'). Some houses may have gone up a lot in value, some a little, and some may have fallen in

* James Johnson is an Associate Professor of Economics at the University of British Columbia (Okanagan). He researches labour economics and the economics of education.

value. To describe this distribution of results, researchers rely on three basic descriptive statistics. The *mean* is what non-statisticians would normally call the average. The numbers measuring the variable you are interested in (in this case changes in house values) are summed and divided by the number of observations (houses). The mean is a measure of the centre of the distribution of the data. A statistic called the *standard deviation* (SD) is a measure of the dispersion in the data. A small SD means the observations do not deviate much from the mean. A large SD means there were a lot observations in the data that deviated greatly from the mean. An alternative measure of dispersion is the range. The *range* simply measures the distance from the smallest observation to the largest.

The most common descriptive statistic to describe the relationship between different variables is the *correlation coefficient*. The correlation coefficient is a number between -1 and 1 that describes how closely related two different variables are. A correlation coefficient of 0 means there is no relationship between the variables. A positive correlation coefficient means that if one variable is above its mean the other more likely will be too, and a negative correlation coefficient means that if one variable is above its mean the other will more likely be below its mean. (In a famous study in the early 1900s, the great statistician Karl Pearson compared the heights of 1,078 men to the heights of their adult sons and found a correlation coefficient of approximately 0.5, from which he inferred that height was partly hereditary.)

While not all studies report descriptive statistics, it is very common to see the mean, SD, range, and, where applicable, correlation coefficients, reported in a study.

When measurements such as means and correlation coefficients refer to the population, they are called parameters. A scientific study may produce many statistics, some of which, like the *Cronbach alpha*, measure the reliability of measures and some of which, like the R^2 or AIC, measure how well a statistical model fits the data. But the key statistics are those that are involved in estimating population parameters. For example, when Pearson estimated that the correlation coefficient between heights of men and their adult sons, for all men in England around 1900, was 0.5, he made an inference about the value of a population parameter from evidence contained in a sample. The problem is that, had he chosen a different sample of 1,078 men, he would have obtained a different estimate. That estimate would likely have been pretty close to 0.5 but could, by mere chance, have been quite different, say 0.4 or 0.6. That's because the characteristics of a sample will almost never exactly match the characteristics of the population from which it was drawn and may, by chance, differ quite dramatically from the characteristics of the population from which it was drawn. This is a specifically statistical phenomenon called *sampling error*. The primary function of inferential statistics is both to provide an estimate of population parameters and to quantify the sampling error in such a way that we may know how much confidence we should have that the estimates are not just the result of sampling error (i.e., not just a fluke of the particular sample).

The predominant approach to quantifying the sampling error is to ask the following question: If the population parameter we are trying to estimate was zero, how likely is it that we would have observed the sample data we did observe, or even more extreme data? The hypothesis that the population value of a parameter is zero (or that there is no effect in the population) is called the *null hypothesis* and is used to evaluate the likelihood the estimated parameters are the result of a sampling error. If the correlation coefficient between heights of fathers and sons in the population was actually zero, how likely is it that Pearson's sample would have produced an estimate of 0.5 (or even higher)? If a drug has no effect on blood pressure in the population, how likely is it that the effect measured in the sample of patients in the drug test will show (for example) a 10% or more reduction?

The answer lies in understanding that if samples of a particular size are randomly drawn again and again and again, the estimates produced by those many estimates would form a theoretical distribution of estimates. Even though we have no idea where in that distribution the estimate drawn from any particular sample lies, we do know (thanks to an amazing result known as the *central limit theorem*) the mean and estimated standard deviation of the theoretical distribution of many estimates. Specifically, if the actual value of a population parameter is zero, then the average (mean) value of the estimates over many samples will also be zero. The estimated standard deviation of the theoretical distribution of estimates, called the *standard error* (SE), measures how the many estimates would be dispersed around the mean and that, in turn allows us to know how likely it is to have produced the specific estimate the sample did produce, if the value of the population parameter had been zero.

There is a vast number of statistical estimation techniques currently in use. Some, like estimating the mean of a population, are simple to understand. Others, like *multiple regression*, *ANOVA*, and *principle components analysis* take hundreds of hours of study to master. But every report, no matter the specific analysis being performed, *must* include measures of how likely it is that the results of the study are the product of sampling error. Failure to do so means that statistical inference is not actually being performed.

The simplest measure of sampling error is the *p* statistic, developed by R.A. Fisher. The *p* statistic measures the probability that the estimates generated by the sample, or even more extreme estimates, would have been observed if the null hypothesis had been true. A low *p* means that it is unlikely the estimates are the product of sampling error and gives the researcher confidence that the estimates produced by the data have some legitimacy. A high *p*, conversely, means that the result generated by the sample could easily be the product of sampling error, and gives researchers little confidence in the legitimacy of their estimates. By convention, an estimate with a *p* of .05 or less is considered to be strong evidence that the estimates are not the product of sampling error. It is common to consider such estimates as "statistically significant," although there is no hard and fast rule on this. As Rosnow and

Rosenthal famously wrote in a 1989 paper, "surely, God loves the .06 nearly as much as the .05." Thus it is not uncommon to see estimates reported as being "significant at the 0.10 level," "significant at the 0.05 level," or "significant at the 0.01 level." In the Pearson father-son study, the p was 2.2×10^{-16}, which is a mathematician's way of saying "essentially zero." There is no chance Pearson would have produced an estimated correlation coefficient of 0.5 if the true value of the population parameter had been zero.

One problem with reporting a low p is that it doesn't actually tell the reader of the study much about the likely value of the population parameter. Knowing that Pearson's estimate of the correlation between the heights of fathers and sons is "significantly different from zero" doesn't answer the question about how big the population correlation is likely to be. Consequently some researchers prefer a different approach to measuring sampling error: a 95% *confidence interval*. The confidence interval provides the following convoluted information: it is a range of values of the population parameter such that if the researcher had collected a very large number of samples, and in each case used the relevant formula to calculate a 95% confidence interval, then 95% of those intervals would contain the true population parameter. Of course, the researcher only collects one sample and calculates only one confidence interval, but at least she knows that in 95% of the samples she could have collected, but didn't, the computed confidence interval would have contained the true population parameter. In the Pearson father-son height example, the 95% confidence interval was (.455, .545). This tells readers of the study that it is very, very unlikely the population correlation coefficient was, for example, less than 0.4. Incidentally, 95% is equivalent to "19 times out of 20," and if Pearson's results were being reported in the media today they likely would be reported like this: "the correlation coefficient is 0.5 with a margin of error of plus or minus .045, 19 times out of 20."

A published empirical paper will almost always report, in addition to the estimated values of population parameters, one or more of the following: the p, the level it was "significant at," the standard error, or a confidence interval. These are all different ways of evaluating the influence of sampling error on the estimates and providing readers with a sense of how confident they should be in the conclusions of the study.

GLOSSARY

ableism The valuing of able-bodied people over disabled people and the prejudice and discrimination that arise against the latter due to this value structure.

canonical criticism A theory and method of biblical interpretation, developed in the 1960s, that analyzes the present form of the Bible in relation to what it can and does mean to current believing communities.

case study A formal research method that focuses on a specific phenomenon (a 'case,' e.g., an individual or an event) and studies it in detail.

coding The categorization of data (both quantitative and quantitative) so that it can be analyzed using a computer.

composition studies Also known as 'rhetoric and composition,' an academic discipline that focuses on the theory, the practice, and the teaching of writing.

cross-sectional study The observational analysis of data collected at a specific time, involving comparisons of different subsets of a population (it is opposed to longitudinal study).

culture industry The companies that produce mass culture for purposes of profit, such as those in Hollywood. The term derives from the Marxist-influenced Frankfurt School, which saw popular culture as enabling ideology by encouraging passive consumption and a lack of critical thinking.

cybernetics The study of communication and control within systems with feedback loops (organisms, machines, and social systems), involving analysis of their goals, design, and function.

data Discrete pieces of information collected for the purposes of analysis and study, typically associated with quantitative research. Data may be produced through experimentation or acquired through observation. Derived from the Latin for "things given," the term is typically treated as plural.

data analysis software Specialized computer programs that apply statistical analysis or render visual representations of large of data.

data reduction Transformation of large amounts of information into a simplified form so that the most meaningful parts can be efficiently transmitted or used.

disability studies An interdisciplinary study that challenges the economic, political, and cultural factors that define and influence the disabled.

discursive Relating to discourse: writing, speaking, and debating about a topic.

ecocriticism An area of study committed to improving humanity's relationship with nature by analyzing how nature is represented in a text and how these representations affect societal practices.

empiricism A theory of knowledge that views sensory experience or physical evidence rather than abstract reasoning, theoretical analysis, or intuition as the primary source of knowledge.

epistemology The branch of philosophy concerned with the meaning, boundaries, and requirements of knowledge, as well as the methods used for acquiring it.

ethics Also known as moral philosophy, the examination of the relation between values and action, specifically articulating the difference between right and wrong.

etiology Used in many disciplines, the study of why something occurs, its causes or even the account of its origin.

feminism A practice that works towards political, social, and economic equality among the sexes by critically analyzing the experiences and portrayals of women in societies defined by patriarchal values and institutions through the use of methods common to the humanities and social sciences.

framing theory The study of how aspects of events are selected and organized either consciously or unconsciously in order to create a meaningful representation that is inherently biased.

gender roles The set of cultural norms surrounding masculine and feminine identity that influence the behaviours of men and women.

gender studies An interdisciplinary study of how gender functions in society.

grounded theory Used principally in the social sciences, an inductive method for developing a theory that establishes a specific procedure for collecting, analyzing, and interpreting data.

historiography Used to describe the way that history is produced as knowledge; it also includes the study of historical methods.

ideology The beliefs and ideas in society that allow for the dominant classes to maintain exploitation of the subordinate classes; ideology is often synonymous with 'false consciousness.' Research informed by Marxist theory often attempts to identify and analyze ideology.

IMRD A format for articles reporting quantitative research that organizes an article into sections with the headings Introduction, Methods, Results, and Discussion.

intellectual history The study of how historians understand ideas and key thinkers in relation to their historical and cultural contexts and that occurs in different traditions (i.e., not only western) and increasingly moves towards a global perspective.

intercorrelation In statistics, the degree to which two or more variables exhibit a tendency to vary together.

international relations An interdisciplinary field rooted in political science that studies the interactions between different international political entities such as states, organizations, and corporations.

Islamic Studies The interdisciplinary study of the religious and secular aspects of Islam and Islamic culture.

Likert scale A tool widely used in questionnaires that measures attitudes along a continuum (e.g., from strongly disagree to strongly agree) so that they can be converted to numerical values.

longitudinal study The analysis of observational data collected over a period of time, involving comparisons of different moments in the study (it is opposed to cross-sectional study).

media hegemony Based on the Marxist theory of Antonio Gramsci, the critical analysis of hegemony that focuses on how ideology is used by dominant groups to maintain control of society by way of social institutions such as mass media and education.

media studies Originating in sociology and communications, an academic discipline that studies the history, theories, and effects of different media, especially mass media.

naturalistic observation A research method that studies subjects in their natural environment.

Orientalism Originally an area of western cultural studies focused on most of south- and east-Asian, as well as middle-eastern, societies, Orientalism is now used in the sense of Edward Said, who critiqued the racism, stereotypes, and other problematic aspects of this approach to the 'Orient.'

Pearson's r A statistical term (also called the Pearson correlation coefficient) that measures the linear correlation between two variables (X and Y).

peer review Also known as refereeing, a review system that entails careful scrutiny of an unpublished study by other researchers who have standing in the field. The referees may know who wrote the prospective article, or they may not (in which case, the peer review is *blind*).

philosophy The study of the fundamental principles of subjects such as existence, reality, knowledge, morality, beauty, love, and language.

posthumanism A range of multidisciplinary theoretical positions that began to emerge in the late 1970s that question humanist assumptions about the human subject and rethink the relations between nature, humans, non-human animals, and technology.

principal component analysis (PCA) A statistical technique that allows for the visualization of patterns in data by emphasizing variation.

Psychology The study of individual and group behaviour with specific reference to mental processes.

qualitative research (also 'qualitative analysis' and 'qualitative method') Associated with the arts and humanities, some social and natural sciences, education, and law, qualitative research examines matters that aren't open to counting and measurement. Such research involves numerous approaches, including theory and critical analysis, and small-scale observation such as that involving case studies. It often directly involves and acknowledges the subjectivity of the researcher and the engaged status of knowledge-making.

quantitative research (also 'quantitative analysis' and 'quantitative method') Associated mainly with the sciences and social sciences, quantitative method involves the counting and measuring of phenomena. Scholars conducting quantitative research typically devote much attention to the methods used to gather and analyze data, including experimental design, so that other researchers can evaluate their knowledge-making practices and replicate their work.

regression analysis In statistics, a range of methods used to identify the relationship between variables, in particular how multiple independent variables (e.g., age, sex, and height) affect a dependent variable (e.g., Body Mass Index).

research poster A means of sharing research with other researchers, often at an academic conference or similar forum. A poster utilizes brief prepared text combined with graphics (charts, graphs, data tables, and images) to explain the presenter's research and invite conversations between the presenter and those who view the poster.

research proposal A preliminary account of a research project to be undertaken, usually designed for a reader in a position to evaluate the project. Research proposals are routinely written for conference papers, Masters theses and Doctoral dissertations, and grant applications.

review article An article that reports on research that has already been published (rather than reporting new research) by surveying, summarizing, and clarifying developments to date, including identifying gaps and future directions.

rhetorical analysis An examination of how a text communicates or persuades that focuses on how it positions itself in relation to an audience (e.g., genre), techniques (e.g., appeals to an audience, etc.), or specific choices (e.g., diction).

risk analysis The identification of risk that generally uses scientific analysis of evidence to identify and evaluate potential adverse effects for decision-makers. Risk analysis can take many forms and spans both quantitative and qualitative research.

scholarship of application Engaged scholarship that attempts to connect academic research with community development.

semiotics The study of how signs work, encompassing words, images, and cultural myths.

semi-structured interview Used in qualitative method, an interview technique that uses open-ended questions to initiate discussion.

subject position How a person (or a 'self') is located in the world by way of discourse and thereby sees the world from this position. It is derived from Michel Foucault's analysis of the relation between knowledge and power.

symptomatic reading Developed by the French Marxist theorist Louis Althusser, a method of reading that identifies ideological messages by paying attention to what a text presupposes about certain topics. This can take the form of answers to unstated questions, silences, or things that can't be said, and contradictions.

theology The study of deity, divinity, or religious belief treated as an academic discipline.

Wechsler Memory Scale (WMS) A test that measures memory function and that can be used to distinguish normal memory from impaired memory.

PERMISSIONS ACKNOWLEDGEMENTS

Boddice, Rob. "Vaccination, Fear, and Historical Relevance," from *History Compass* 14.2, 2016: 71–78. Copyright © 2016 John Wiley & Sons Ltd. Reprinted with the permission of John Wiley & Sons Ltd. doi.org/10.1111/hic3.12297.

Bostrom, Nick. "In Defence of Posthuman Dignity," from *Bioethics* 19.3, 2005: 202–14. Copyright © 2005 Blackwell Publishing Ltd. Reprinted with the permission of John Wiley & Sons Inc.

Costello, Lisa A. "Blogging a Research Paper? Researched Blogs as New Models of Public Discourse," from *Teaching English in the Two-Year College* 43.2, December 2015: 180–94. Copyright © 2015 by the National Council of Teachers of English. Reprinted with permission.

Dingwerth, Klaus, Ina Lehmann, Ellen Reichel, and Tobias Weise. "Democracy is Democracy is Democracy? Changes in Evaluations of International Institutions in Academic Textbooks, 1970–2010," from *International Studies Perspectives* 16.2, 2015: 173–89. Reprinted with the permission of Oxford University Press. doi.org/10.1111/insp.12069.

Ellis, Katie M. "Cripples, Bastards and Broken Things: Disability in *Game of Thrones*," from *M/C Journal* 17.5, 2014. Copyright © 2014 Katie M Ellis. Reprinted with the permission of Dr. Katie M. Ellis.

Gane, Nicholas. "Posthuman," from *Theory, Culture, and Society* 23.2–3, 2006: 431–34. Copyright © 2006 by Nicholas Gane. Reprinted with the permission of SAGE Publications, Ltd.

Gansky, Paul. "Frozen Jet Set: Refrigerators, Media Technology, and Postwar Transportation," from *The Journal of Popular Culture* 48.1, 2015: 73–85. Copyright © 2015 Wiley Periodicals, Inc. doi: 10.1111/jpcu.12234.

Graham, Elaine. "The Final Frontier? Religion and Posthumanism in Film and Television," from *The Palgrave Handbook of Posthumanism in Film and Television*, edited by Michael Huskeller, Thomas D. Philbeck, and Curtis D. Carbonell. Palgrave Macmillan, 2015. Reprinted with the permission of Elaine Graham.

Hager, Stephen B. et al. "Continent-wide Analysis of How Urbanization Affects Bird-Window Collision Mortality in North America," from *Biological Conservation* 212, Part A, August 2017: 209–15. Reprinted with the permission of Elsevier.

Hansson, Sven Ove. "How to Be Cautious but Open to Learning: Time to Update Biotechnology and GMO Legislation," from *Risk Analysis* 36.8, 2016: 1513–17. Copyright © 2016 Society for Risk Analysis. Reprinted with the permission of the publisher, John Wiley and Sons.

Kent, Michael L. "Using Social Media Dialogically: Public Relations Role in Reviving Democracy," from *Public Relations Review* 39.4, 2013: 337–45. Copyright © 2013 Elsevier Inc. All rights reserved. Reprinted with the permission of Elsevier. doi.org/10.1016/j.pubrev.2013.07.024.

Knight, Jamie E. "Olfactory Decline as a Preclinical Biomarker for Alzheimer's Disease" (MA Thesis proposal). Reprinted with the permission of Jamie E. Knight.

Knight, Jamie E., and Andrea M. Piccinin. "Foreshadowing Alzheimer's: Variability and Coupling of Olfaction and Cognition," poster presented at 21st IAGG World Congress of Gerontology and Geriatrics (IAGG), San Francisco, USA. Reprinted with the permission of Jamie E. Knight.

Lalor, Briony M., and Gordon M. Hickey. "Environmental Science and Public Policy in Executive Government: Insights from Australia and Canada," from *Science and Public Policy* 40.6, 2013: 767–78. Reprinted with the permission of Oxford University Press. doi.org/10.1093/scipol/sct022.

Lindner, Katharina. "Images of Women in General Interest and Fashion Magazine Advertisements from 1955 to 2002," from *Sex Roles* 51.7–8, 2004: 409–21. Copyright © Springer Science+Business Media, Inc. 2004. Reprinted with the permission of Springer Nature.

Loader, Brian D., Ariadne Vromen, and Michael A. Xenos. "The Networked Young Citizen: Social Media, Political Participation and Civic Engagement," from *Information, Communication & Society* 17.2, 2014: 143–50. Reprinted with the permission of the publisher, Taylor & Francis Ltd., http://www.tandfonline.com. doi:10.1080/1369118X.2013.871571.

Ward, Amber E. "Fantasy Facebook: An Exploration of Students' Cultural Sources," from *Art Education* 63.4, 2010: 47–53. Reprinted with the permission of the publisher, Taylor & Francis Ltd., http://www.tandfonline.com.

Warwick, Kevin. "The Cyborg Revolution," from *NanoEthics* 8.3, December 2014: 263–73. Reprinted with the permission of Springer Nature.

Westheimer, Joel. "Politics and Patriotism in Education," from *The Phi Delta Kappan* 87.8, 2006: 608–20. Reprinted with the permission of PDK International.

Wilson, Robert S., Steven E. Arnold, Julie A. Schneider, Patricia A. Boyle, Aron S. Buchman, and David A. Bennett. "Olfactory Impairment in Presymptomatic Alzheimer's Disease," from *International Symposium on Olfaction and Taste* 1170, July 2009: 730–35. Copyright © 2009 New York Academy of Sciences. Reprinted with the permission of John Wiley & Sons.

Zaleski, Kristen L., Kristin K. Gundersen, Jessica Baes, Ely Estupinian, and Alyssa Vergara. "Exploring Rape Culture in Social Media Forums," from *Computers in Human Behavior* 63, October 2016: 922–27. Copyright © 2016 Elsevier Ltd. Reprinted with permission. All rights reserved.

From the Publisher

A name never says it all, but the word "Broadview" expresses a good deal of the philosophy behind our company. We are open to a broad range of academic approaches and political viewpoints. We pay attention to the broad impact book publishing and book printing has in the wider world; for some years now we have used 100% recycled paper for most titles. Our publishing program is internationally oriented and broad-ranging. Our individual titles often appeal to a broad readership too; many are of interest as much to general readers as to academics and students.

Founded in 1985, Broadview remains a fully independent company owned by its shareholders—not an imprint or subsidiary of a larger multinational.

For the most accurate information on our books (including information on pricing, editions, and formats) please visit our website at www.broadviewpress.com. Our print books and ebooks are also available for sale on our site.

broadview press
www.broadviewpress.com

The interior of this book is printed on 100% recycled paper.

 PERMANENT 100%    Ancient Forest Friendly™